Elmira Prison Camp Roster

Volume I

Elmira Prison Camp Roster

Volume I, A-F

By

Richard H. Triebe

ISBN—13: 978-0-9798965-7-6

ISBN—10: 0-9798965-7-6

Cover photograph: This photograph shows 5,000 prisoners who were living in tents lined up for morning roll call. The photograph was taken in November or early December of 1864 as evidenced by the lack of leaves on the tree in the foreground. Note the hills, which had been heavily forested before the war, are now nearly devoid of trees. *Photograph courtesy of the North Carolina Museum of History.*

All photographs in this book are from the author's collection unless otherwise noted.

Other books by this author:

Confederate Fort Fisher, ISBN 1484032497

Elmira Prisoner of War Camp ISBN 1539496791

Fort Fisher to Elmira, ISBN 1530023238

On A Rising Tide, ISBN 1-4208-7849-2

Point Lookout Prison Camp and Hospital, ISBN 1495310140

Port Royal, ISBN 0-9798-9650-9

Printed in the United States of America
This book is printed on acid-free paper.

Coastal Books

Acknowledgements

I owe a debt of gratitude to these people and institutions. I wish to thank Tom Fagart for his help in furnishing important Elmira Prison documents. Also, I want to thank Joe Beasley for helping me with the Excel Spreadsheet regarding the prisoners. I also wish to commend the Federal Army for its meticulous record keeping. Without the prisoners records this book would not have been possible. I also owe a debt of gratitude to the National Archives for storing these records in such an organized manner.

Table of Contents

Additional Volumes in This Series:

Elmira Prison Camp Roster, Volume II includes:

Roster of prisoner's Surnames which begin with G-N

Elmira Prison Camp Roster, Volume III includes:

Roster of prisoner's Surnames which begin with O-Z

Deadly Civil War Diseases

Civil War Medical Terminology

Elmira Monthly Returns to the Commissary General of Prisoners

Confederate Prisoners Not Found In Archival Regimental Records

Confederate Prisoners Who Have No Grave in Woodlawn National Cemetery

Confederate Prisoners Who Died During Exchange

Monthly Graph of Number of Prisoners Who Died At Elmira Prison Camp

Monthly Graph of Deaths of Prisoners Who Were Sick

Introduction

A Roster of the Confederate Soldiers
Sent to Elmira Prison Camp

I had always wanted to write a comprehensive roster of all the Confederate soldiers who had been captured and sent to Elmira Prisoner of War Camp. I did not think this was likely since I had only seen lists of the men who had died in that prison. I had searched online for the entire roster of Confederate soldiers who were sent to Elmira prison camp, but to no avail. However, the wonderful thing about doing research involving the Civil War Union Army is almost everything had been written down. The reason for this is the Commissary General of Prisoners required all Union prisons to make meticulous daily and monthly records of the men in their prisons. These records included a complete register of all the men who entered the prison. They also involved all the transfers that came into and out of the prison camp and the Morning Reports. These daily reports contained vital information about the prison camp such as how many prisoners were present for duty, how many were sick, and the number of men that joined the camp. It

The prisoner's names on the left of this page from the "Roll of Prisoners of War" is so light it is unreadable.

also contained information on how many prisoners were transferred to other prisons, died, escaped, took the oath of allegiance, or were exchanged. All this information was gathered and put into a monthly report to show the Commissary General the condition of that prison. I also knew that registers containing other essential information such as a complete roster of all the prisoners, transfers into the camp and the death ledger were also available.

The Archival Records contain regimental records that include the soldier's name, age, place of enlistment, regiment, and other information regarding a prisoner's exchange or death. Some of the records may indicate the man died of disease shortly after his exchange. Many times, these records indicated the nature of the wound a soldier received, often specifying whether it was caused by a rifle bullet or a shell fragment.

The information in this roster came from a variety of sources. One of the main research tools was the National Archives where I found the "Elmira Prison Register". This supplied most of the names, regiments, places captured and outcome of a prisoner's incarceration. Other sources were the prison transfer records and the Daily Morning Reports of each prison.[1] Also, Fold3, an internet military database, was used to get further information such as a soldier's regimental records.

When I examined these records, I discovered they were handwritten. Most of the pages were legible, but parts of them were either too light or dark to read or had deteriorated to such a degree they had just fallen apart, and pieces of the page were missing. Even though the writing was usually readable some of the names could not be determined. They were either hastily written, misspelled, or the men had the wrong regiment or state entered. All of this aside, approximately 90% of these names on the roster could be deciphered.

Generally, Elmira prison camp confined prisoners captured in the 1864-65 battles in Virginia, Maryland, and North Carolina. I decided that some of the missing names could be found by seeing what regiments had some of their men captured and sent to Elmira prison camp. These regiments were more likely to have additional men taken prisoner who were not reported. I discovered Elmira's prisoners came from thousands of different regiments. This meant searching one to two thousand soldier's records from each of those regiments. This is a slow process and does not guarantee that all the men will be found, but it is the best plan I have. This is where the readers can become involved in my search. If you know of a soldier who was captured and sent to Elmira prison camp and is not mentioned in my book, please write me, and tell me his name, age, rank, date of enlistment, his company, regiment, and what state his regiment was from. The soldier's service records will be examined and if they show that he was sent to Elmira prison camp, my book will be amended to reflect that information. My address is:

Richard Triebe
1014 Hunting Ridge Road
Wilmington, NC 28412

Email: richtriebe@aol.com

Why Make a Roster of Confederate Soldiers at Elmira Prison Camp?

There are several reasons why this roster needed to be made. One of the most important things to come out of this study was possibly learning the identities of the seven unknown soldiers buried at Woodlawn National Cemetery in Elmira, New York. While the exact graves could not be determined, it was discovered twenty-six prisoners died and had no grave at Woodlawn. These men need to be recognized for their sacrifice just as their fellow prisoners were. The unknown graves came about when the original wooden headboards that contained the men's names, company, regiment, and state had deteriorated to such a degree that seven of the graves lost their information. In 1907 the Federal government authorized the wooden grave markers to be replaced with marble headstones and so the graves without identifying marks were subsequently listed as unknown. This led me to wonder why there were more dead men were than graves to fill them. I originally thought maybe this discrepancy could be explained by a relative's removal of the prisoner's bodies from the graveyard. Unfortunately, I was unable to locate the names of the prisoners removed from the cemetery. I was told by the sexton at Elmira National Cemetery that once the solder's body had been disinterred the headstone was destroyed. My research showed that Clay W. Holmes, author of *"The Elmira Prison Camp"*, wrote that the US Army's Quartermaster's office reported on September 23, 1874, that twenty prisoners' bodies were removed by relatives, but their empty graves remained at Woodlawn Cemetery.[1]

I also wanted to find out what were the deadliest diseases that the prisoners faced. After accumulating all the data regarding prisoners cause of death, it was discovered that chronic diarrhea was the leading killer followed by pneumonia, then smallpox, and typhoid fever. There were many other diseases that prisoners succumbed to, but to a smaller degree.

Another purpose was to determine how many Confederate soldiers died in the infamous prisoner exchange on October 11, 1864. The Commissary General of prisoners ordered Colonel Benjamin Tracy, the commandant of Elmira prison camp, to prepare all invalid prisoners for the prisoner exchange to take place on October 11, 1864. Colonel William Hoffman stipulated that these men had to be ill enough, so that they would be unable to join the Confederate Army for at least sixty days. Tracy was also instructed to have these prisoners examined by his medical staff to determine if they could survive the journey to be exchanged.[2] According to historians five prisoners died after a two-day train trip to Baltimore, Maryland. Another sixty men were unable to continue their journey and were hospitalized, but unfortunately, the public was never told what became of them. My research has uncovered 31 prisoners died in all. The rest of the prisoners took several steamers to Point Lookout prison camp where many more also died from disease. When I finished compiling the roster, I had discovered 89 of these men died before they were ever exchanged. This is shocking when you consider only 1,264 Confederate prisoners were involved in the exchange. It is difficult to believe that surgeons, who dedicated their lives to ease the suffering of mankind, could turn a blind eye to the severity of the diseases the prisoners had and let them be exchanged.

There were several questions that came to light during my investigation. One that I did not anticipate was finding a substantial difference in the prison death rate of soldiers who were from the Eastern Theater versus the Western Theater of war. What was the cause of this? I can only attribute it to the fact that during the last year of the war the Confederate army in Virginia did more campaigning, fighting and had less food than the soldiers in the Western Theater.

Another thing that I discovered was men who were in the cavalry died less frequently in prison than the men in the infantry. I suppose this indicates that a cavalry man's life is less stressful on the body than an infantry man's life.

Equally important was to assist people who are researching their relatives from the American Civil War. Many people today are certain their great-great grandfather or uncle went to prison, but they are not sure which prison he went to. If they went to Elmira Prisoner of War Camp it should be easy to find them in this book.

Elmira Prisoner of War Camp

When Major General Ulysses S. Grant ended the prisoner exchange in March 1864 this created an unexpected problem.[1] If the North continued to capture prisoners and could not release any, where would the new prisoners be kept? A suitable camp was located just a few miles north of the Pennsylvania border in western New York State. In 1861 four large training camps were built to answer President Lincoln's call for 75,000 volunteers to help put down the Southern rebellion. These were officially designated as the Arnot Barracks, Post Barracks, Camp Rathbun and Camp Robinson.

Arnot barracks was located about one mile north of Elmira, New York. It was constructed on a 300 by 300-yard square plot with ten barracks designed to house 100 men each. Two hundred feet to the rear of the barracks were the officer's quarters. Across from this was a large building with six rooms for the field and staff officers. To the west stood a guard house and a mess hall with a kitchen capable of feeding 1,000 men. The camp was supplied with water from a stream of fresh water and by two wells with good, limestone water.[2]

The next training facility was the Post Barracks. This was located about one mile west of Elmira on a plot of land not easily drained and considerably lower than the surrounding country. The 400 by 200-yard area contained twenty barracks designed to house 100 men each. To the southeast stood the officer's quarters

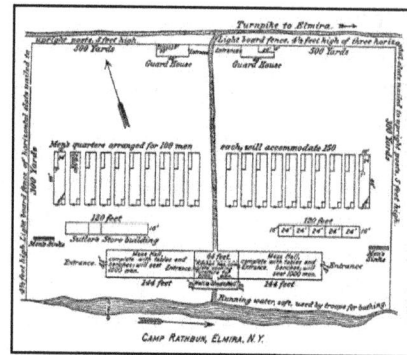

Camp Rathbun would be renamed Elmira prison of war camp in 1864.

composed of six rooms. In front of the enlisted men's barracks were two guard houses, and a mess hall and a kitchen under one roof. The water from the wells and from the junction of canal south of it was unfit for use and water needed to be brought in to supply the garrison.[3]

Camp Rathbun, which later became Elmira prisoner of war camp, was built along Water Street about a mile west of downtown Elmira. The 300 by 500-yard plot of land slopes toward Foster's Pond on the south side. The camp was as high as the surrounding country on firm, gravelly soil which did not become soft even during violent storms. Twenty barracks, 88 by 18 feet, were constructed under the specifications by Jervis Langdon, and had two rows of wooden bunks running down the sides. Each building was designed for 100 men and contained a small room for noncommissioned officers. To the rear of the enlisted men's barracks were the officer's quarters and sutler store. Behind these buildings were two mess halls and a kitchen under one roof. The two 144 by 41-foot mess halls occupied the two ends of the building and the kitchen the middle portion. The camp was provided with limestone water from two wells.[4]

Camp Robinson was a 400 by 360-yard area a mile and a half southwest of downtown Elmira. This camp supported 2,000 troops in twenty barracks and had two wells with abundant, pure water. To the left and rear of men's quarters was a building of 100 by 20 feet with six rooms which composed the officer's quarters. In the rear of this building were two guard houses, and two mess halls with a kitchen under one roof. The two 144 by 41-foot mess halls occupied the two ends of the building and the kitchen the middle portion.[5]

In the spring of 1864 Colonel William Hoffman, the Commissary General of Prisoners, was troubled by the quickly growing prison population since the end of the prisoner exchange. Union prisons were filled to overflowing and opening new prison camps needed to be considered. Also, he knew that General Grant had begun his all-out offensive against Robert E. Lee's army and the bloody fighting in Virginia had already captured thousands of Confederate soldiers. Most of these men were sent to the already crowded Point Lookout prison camp in Maryland or the Old Capital prison in Washington, DC.

On May 14th Hoffman received a telegram from General E. D. Townsend saying, "Sir: I am informed that there are quite a number of barracks at Elmira, N. Y., which are not occupied, and are fit to hold Rebel prisoners. Quite a large number of those lately captured could be accommodated at this place."[6]

General Townsend had aroused Hoffman's interest because the camp near Elmira possessed everything a prison would need. It had excellent railroad connections to transfer large numbers of prisoners, a thriving lumber business to supply wood for extra barracks and fuel for the fires that were necessary to fight the harsh northern winters. It was also located in a fertile valley that produced ample fruits and vegetables and had abundant fresh water from the Chemung River. The addition of fruits and vegetables into a prisoner's diet was vital for the prevention of scurvy. Camp Rathbun already possessed twenty barracks, a large mess hall, and with some construction could be converted into an excellent prison camp at a minimal cost. This was important to Hoffman who throughout his military career demonstrated an aptitude for thrift. Another factor to be considered was the fact that the camp was close to the seat of war in Virginia and prisoners could be transported easily.

Five days later, Colonel Hoffman sent a letter to Colonel Seth Eastman, Camp Rathbun's commanding officer, giving him instructions to "set apart the barracks on the Chemung River at Elmira as a depot for prisoners" because as many as 10,000 prisoners would be transferred there from other Northern compounds. Hoffman further ordered Eastman to construct a twelve-foot-high fence, framed on the outside with a sentries' walk four feet below the top, and built at a safe distance from the barracks in order "that prisoners may not approach it unseen."[7]

Commissary General of Prisoners Colonel William Hoffman

Colonel Eastman replied to Hoffman's order on May 23rd and said the camp's barracks could comfortably house 3,000 men without crowding, but he added that it could also accommodate 4,000 prisoners. Eastman further stated that there was enough room where tents could be pitched to quarter 1,000 more. He stated that the mess hall was sufficiently large enough to accommodate 1,500 men and the kitchen could cook 5,000 meals daily. There was an excellent bakery that could make 6,000 rations daily. Eastman cautiously pointed out that since there was no hospital, hospital tents would need to be erected.[8]

We know now that most of the deaths at Elmira prison camp was caused by overcrowding. So why was Colonel Hoffman so insistent about Elmira prison camp holding 10,000 prisoners even after Eastman told him Camp Rathbun's barracks could only accommodate 4,000 prisoners with crowding and another 1,000 could be housed in tents?[9] If Hoffman had any doubt about this figure he need only remember what Eastman told him that the mess hall was large enough to seat 1,200 to 1,500.[10] Yet on June 22nd Hoffman stubbornly told Eastman, "In establishing the fence it is advisable to enclose ground enough to accommodate in barracks and tents 10,000 prisoners."[11] So why was he refusing to believe this man who had an intimate knowledge of the camp? If we examine the official records, I believe we can find the answer. On May 19th Hoffman wrote to Secretary of War Stanton and said, "I am informed there are barracks available which have, by crowding, can receive 12,000 volunteers. By fencing them in at a cost of about $2,000 they may be relied on to receive 8,000 or possibly 10,000 prisoners."[12] So, as early as May 19th Hoffman told Stanton, his superior, that Elmira could receive 10,000 prisoners. Hoffman then in turn related this information to Colonel Eastman. When Eastman protested by saying the camp could only quarter 4,000 prisoners and another 1,000 and tents, Hoffman would not listen. As far as Hoffman was concerned, he was Eastman's superior; the prison commandant had his orders and according to military protocol it was his job was to make it happen.

Camp Rathbun officially became Elmira Prisoner of War Camp in June of 1864. The thirty-two-acre site lay along the banks of the Chemung River. A one-acre lagoon, called Foster's Pond, stood within the walls of the stockade. Prison buildings were located on the high northern bank of the lagoon. The lower southern level, known to flood easily, later became a hospital area for thousands of smallpox and diarrhea victims. The entire prison was surrounded by a twelve-foot-high fence which contained a wooden walkway for the guards. This walkway was eight feet off the ground with forty-seven sentry boxes set at intervals where the guards could retreat in case of inclement weather. The sentry boxes were four feet in length, open at the sides and had a diamond-shaped window so nearly the entire prison yard could be seen.

On June 30, 1864, Colonel Eastman sent a telegram to General Lorenzo Thomas that Elmira was ready to receive prisoners. A more unhealthy site could not have been selected. A one-acre body of water, a stagnant backwash from the Chemung River, stood within the stockade and would be the cause of several epidemics because prisoners used the pond as a convenient latrine and garbage dump. The first person to call attention to this was the prison's commandant, Colonel Seth Eastman, who reported to Hoffman, "Colonel: I have the honor to report to you that the pond inside of the prisoners' camp at Barracks, No. 3, (Elmira prison) has become very offensive, and may occasion sickness unless the evil is remedied very shortly."[13]

This was later verified by Chief Surgeon Eugene Sanger who wrote, "(Foster's Pond's) trouble does not seem to arise altogether from the decayed matter which has been thrown in, but from the daily accumulation. The drainage of the camp is into this pond or pool of standing water, and one large sink (outdoor latrine) used by the prisoners stands directly over the pond which receives its fecal matter hourly. Seven thousand men will pass 2,600 gallons of urine daily, which is highly loaded with nitrogenous material. A portion is absorbed by the earth, still a large amount decomposes on the top of the earth or runs into the pond to purify."[14]

Lt. Colonel Seth Eastman was Elmira prison camp's first commandant.

Sanger later amended his initial assessment of Foster's Pond. In a November 1, 1864 letter to Surgeon General of the U. S. Army, General Joseph K. Barnes, Sanger reported, "I have the honor to forward the monthly report of sick and wounded at prisoners' hospital, Elmira, N. Y., for the month of October. The ratio of disease and deaths has been fearfully and unprecedentedly large and requires an explanation from me to free the medical department from censure. . . . (Foster's) pond received the contents of the sinks and garbage of the camp until it became so offensive that vaults were dug on the banks of the pond for sinks and the whole left a festering mass of corruption, impregnating the entire atmosphere of the camp with its pestilential odors, night and day. . . .The pond remains green with putrescence, filling the air with its messengers of disease and death, the vaults give out their sickly odors, and the hospitals are crowded with victims for the grave."[15]

On July 1, 1864 Federal authorities announced that newly constructed Elmira prison camp, also known as Barracks No. 3, was ready to receive thousands of captured Confederate soldiers from overcrowded Northern prisons.[16] It is difficult to understand how the prison was allowed to open when it did not have a hospital or medical staff available. Such things were essential to any civil war prison. In the meantime, an assistant surgeon from the U. S. Army hospital in town visited the prison each day.

Surgeon C. T. Alexander, Medical Inspector for the U. S. Army, conducted an inspection of Elmira prison camp on the 11th of July. His report to Colonel William Hoffman pointed out several potentially hazardous conditions that needed immediate attention. Alexander reported the sinks, or outdoor latrines, were constructed on a slough. The Merriam-Webster dictionary defines slough as: "a place of deep mud or mire". To correct this situation Surgeon Alexander recommended either bringing water from the city of Elmira and construct new sinks with suitable drainage or cause the Chemung River to increase the water flow to Foster's Pond so it would create a running stream through the camp. Alexander described Foster's pond as "a stagnant body of water which may soon become offensive and a source of disease."

Another factor affecting the water quality was the number of people in the camp. Camp Chemung was built to house 2,000 men. When it was converted into Elmira Prison Camp over a thousand tents were added, increasing the capacity of the camp. Until the new barracks were built, which took place from January through March, 5,190 men camped outdoors in tents while 3,873 were housed in barracks. The camp designed to accommodate 4,000 men now had over 9,000 going into the harsh northern winter.

Inspector Alexander also pointed out there was no "proper hospital organization". He said that "a surgeon from the hospital for troops in Elmira visits the prison camp daily. One of these men was an assistant surgeon who was a former medical cadet and was not a suitable person to organize or control a hospital." Alexander stated in his report, "Your attention is called to the immediate necessity of a competent surgeon to take charge." He found that the sick men did not have adequate shelter, their diets were not suitable, and some prisoners did not have bedsacks or blankets. In closing his report, Alexander summed up the condition of the sick prisoners as "bad".[17]

On July 27th the *Elmira Daily Advertiser* announced construction of a hospital for the camp using prison labor. Unfortunately, only four of the proposed seven hospital wards were completed by September 1st. It would be another month until the hospital would be fully operational. On August 6th, a full month after the prison opened its gates, Chief Surgeon Major Eugene Sanger reported for duty at Elmira. Why it took so long to get a competent doctor was never explained. Critics who consider Elmira to be a camp for retaliation say that the endless army red tape in selecting doctors can be traced to Secretary of War Stanton. Bureaucratic delays were a favorite tactic used successfully by Stanton in the months to come when he did not want anything to aid the prisoners. Although this does sound like something Stanton might dream up the author has no evidence to

Point Lookout prisoner-of-war camp transferred over nine thousand prisoners to Elmira prison camp between July and September 1864.

support such a claim. However, it was because of Stanton's order that the prison was allowed to open. The fact that Elmira prison camp did not have a hospital or medical staff should have been brought to his attention. This shows probable retaliation through careless regard for the prisoner's safety.

The typical Northern Prisoner of War Camp averaged an 11.7 percent death rate. Elmira had a 24.4 percent death toll making it by far the worst prison in the north. In comparison, the notorious Andersonville Prison in Georgia had a death rate of 28.7 percent. While Andersonville's mortality rate was unquestionably the highest during the war, it was closely rivaled by Elmira. Many of these Northern deaths can be attributed to an effective Union Naval blockade which reduced to a trickle vital food, medicine and clothing which might have aided the Federal prisoners. Sherman's march tore up Southern railroads and pursued a scorched earth policy that burned buildings and crops during the last six months of the war. It is difficult to understand why Elmira, a prison camp located in the heart of a lush Northern valley, had such a high mortality rate. What could have possibly made it so unhealthy that a quarter of its prisoners died from disease?

Point Lookout prison camp, Maryland, and Old Capital Prison in Washington, DC, sent the bulk of captured Confederate soldiers to the new prison camp at Elmira, New York. By June of 1864 Point Lookout's prison population had swelled to 15,500 men due to the North halting the prisoner exchange. From July through August Point Lookout sent 9,606 prisoners to the camp at Elmira—approximately three fourths of the final total of 12,123 imprisoned.[18] Because the prison camp at Point Lookout sent so many prisoners to Elmira it is important to understand what dramatic events were happening at the time that led to the North building a new prison camp. Too many prisoners were a dangerous situation since the limited well water at Point Lookout was unable to support so many people. Barrels of freshwater had to be brought in by ship at least once a week to meet the ever increasing demand. Also increasing the demand was the fact that Hammond General Military Hospital was located outside the prison gates. What made this a dangerous situation was the hospital's water consumption would increase dramatically after a large battle.

On June 30th Colonel Hoffman sent a letter to Colonel Alonzo G. Draper, Commandant of Point Lookout prison camp, informing him to start 2,000 of his prisoners for the new prison camp at Elmira, New York. The men were to be divided into groups of 400, with 100 guards assigned to each party.[19] Draper was relieved to hear that some of the men at his prison camp were being sent to Elmira but was also concerned that Hoffman did not intend to send a larger group. In the weeks and months to come Point Lookout Prison would send a total of a little over 8,000 prisoners to Elmira Prison Camp.

Moving Confederate prisoners from Point Lookout, Maryland, to Elmira was an arduous three-and-a-half-day journey which involved transporting the men by steamer up the Atlantic Coast, to Jersey City, New Jersey. There they boarded the Erie Railroad prison train for an all-day all-night 273-mile trip from northern New Jersey through Pennsylvania along the upper Delaware and Susquehanna Rivers, then into New York where they continued to the Elmira Railroad station. What made this process so difficult and time consuming was that each mode of transportation that was used made it necessary to conduct a roll call to see if everyone was present or accounted for. If a prisoner remained hidden aboard, the guards needed to search for the

Prisoner transport USS California

man until he was found. The prisoner-of-war trains made frequent stops to load firewood and take on water but were also delayed by switching tracks to let higher priority trains through.

Prisoner Walter D. Addison remembered being loaded aboard a steamship at Point Lookout. "(We) were crowded upon this old tub between decks with only the hatches open, and there (the prisoners) remained crowded together like sheep for many days. The site of these holds was sickening in the extreme and the condition and the sufferings of the prisoners therein was indeed horrible."[20]

Anthony Keiley wrote, "The man who first invented going to sea was an infidel and a fool. Nature has implanted in every human stomach and instinctive and vigorous protest against this practice. We were packed like sheep on a cattle-train, in the hold of a villainous tub, in the middle of July, with no ventilation except what was afforded by two narrow hatchways."[21]

Most of the men were already sick when they left the prison and the steamship's lack of ventilation and the constant motion of the ocean waves made them more ill. There was no room for them to sit down, so they continued to stand or collapsed and vomited on the floor. With the foul, stale air below decks when someone threw up it was not long before other prisoners became ill also. The prisoners were overjoyed when the ship docked at Jersey City so they could be on dry land once again.

Six o'clock on the morning of July 6, 1864, a locomotive bearing two red prison flags chugged into the Elmira railroad station amid clouds of hissing steam and the clangor of the locomotive's bell. This was the first of many trains to carry prisoners-of-war from Point Lookout prison camp. Three hundred ninety-nine prisoners hopped out of the boxcars under the watchful gaze of the guards. They were quickly formed into ranks and a sergeant stepped forward to take roll call. It was then determined that one of the original 400 captured Confederates managed to escape en route. A search was immediately conducted but nothing of the prisoner was found.

Hundreds of Elmira citizens gathered near the railroad station in anticipation of seeing the notorious Confederate soldiers who had given their army so much trouble. Imagine their surprise when they saw four columns of weary, dirty soldiers wearing tattered gray and butternut, marching down the street instead of the formidable army they expected. A sobering thought occurred to the crowd as they watched this ragamuffin body of men march by. If these men represented the often victorious Confederate army; what does that say about their soldier's ability to win the war.

South Carolina's Sergeant Berry Benson recollected his introduction to Elmira citizens, "As we marched through the streets of Elmira, two by two, ragged dirty faces pinched with hunger, the people came out on the sidewalks to see Lee's soldiers going to prison. Had I seen any of the men, I know I would've hated them, but I had only eyes for the pretty girls."[22]

In describing the prisoner's march to the stockade, reporter Charles Fairman for the Elmira Daily Advisor noted:

The 'rebs,' who arrived yesterday, wore all sorts of nondescript uniforms, besides the regular dark, dirty gray. Some had nothing on but drawers and shirts. . . . They were a fine body of men physically, taller than average, for the most part, made up of two classes, the old and the young, the middle-age having a small representation. They did not exhibit a high degree of intelligence but looked to be men that would go where they are told, let what might happen: although lean and lanky, yet evidently possessing the vigor and litheness to go through thick and thin. Of course, they were black, sunburnt and dirty;[23]

The prisoners were marched to Water Street, then turned west and went about a mile farther until they entered the tall, stockade gates. Once inside the prison the gates swung shut and the men were again formed into ranks. After roll call was taken the prisoners were separated into companies of one hundred men and assigned to a barracks. An officer was given charge of each company and an enlisted man was made the Orderly Sergeant. A ward sergeant was selected from the group of prisoners. His task was to supervise the

Prisoners marching from the train station to Elmira prison camp. Drawing is from *Frank Leslie's Illustrated Newspaper*, October 8, 1864.

company, assign men to police the barracks and grounds. He was also responsible to form the men into two columns and march them to the mess hall twice a day.

The Shohola Train Wreck

One of the most tragic chapters in Elmira's history was set into motion on the evening of July 12th as 833 prisoners, 125 guards and 3 officers of the 11th and 20th Veterans Reserve Corps prepared to leave Point Lookout prison camp. The men boarded the transport steamer *Crescent* and reached New York harbor by 3 PM the following day. Early the next morning they climbed into cars of the Erie Railway in Jersey City. Whenever prisoners switched modes of transportation a head count was conducted to see if everyone was present or accounted for. At this point it was discovered that three men were missing and likely remained hidden aboard the steamer. A search was immediately conducted of the ship

The prisoner-of-war train which wrecked near Shohola was pulled by a wood burning steam locomotive like the one in the photograph.

and the men were found an hour later. However, during this delay a drawbridge was allowed to open and then took two hours to close. The delays set the train's departure behind almost four hours. To make up the time lost, Engineer William Ingram increased the steam locomotive's speed from 15 to 20 miles an hour.

The prisoner-of-war train containing three boxcars and twelve coaches proceeded through the Upper Delaware Valley and crossed the Delaware River into a mountainous area of Pennsylvania. The landscape was composed of steep ledges and woods of the Poconos as the passengers gazed from their windows at the twisting river below. Trying to keep on schedule the engineer Ingram pushed the locomotive's speed to 25 miles an hour until they reached the town of Shohola, Pennsylvania. Here the dual track merged into a single track to pass a particularly steep mountainous area. At 2:35 PM the stationmaster at Shohola signaled the train that all was clear to the end of the single-track section at Lackawaxen Junction. Douglas Kent, the telegraph operator at the next station, had been heavily drinking the night before and was sleepy. He had not heard the Shohola operator's message telling him that the prisoner-of-war train was given sole procession of the rails and the order not to let any eastbound trains through. Thinking the lone track was not in use, Kent gave the all clear signal to a heavily laden coal train of fifty cars not realizing that he had set the two trains on a deadly collision course.

By mid-afternoon on July 15th the Elmira bound train was chugging around a tricky curved section of track that reduced visibility to fifty feet. Suddenly a locomotive loomed ahead blowing an urgent warning with its whistle as it bore down on the other train. Ingram frantically reversed his engine while the engineer of the other train leaped out of the oncoming locomotive. The combined speed of both trains was 50 miles an hour. In an instant there was a tremendous boom, twisting and tearing of metal, screeching, and breaking of wood as the cars collapsed into one another. Upon impact, the troop train's wood tender jolted forward and buckled upright, throwing its load of firewood into the engine cab killing fireman Tuttle instantly. In a minute all was silent except for the rushing sound of escaping steam and the heartrending cries and groans of injured and dying passengers.

The fronts of the two locomotives were raised in the air, appearing like two great beasts trying to crawl onto the top of the other. The wooden coaches either telescoped into one another, split open, or overturned in a sea of crushed wood, glass, and large iron train wheels. One of the cars closest to the engine was reduced from its former length of 40 feet and compressed into barely 6 feet. The soldiers and many of the prisoners near the front of the train suffered the worst. The first boxcar contained 38 prisoners and only one survivor. Hideously mangled bodies, some missing arms, legs, and heads, were strewn about the wreckage. Ingram was pinned against the split boiler plate and the wreckage of the cab amid a cloud of scalding steam. He was barely conscious and warned the rescuers to stay back from the boiler because it was ready to explode. His voice became fainter as he was roasted alive.

Two miles away the village of Shohola heard the terrible collision and dozens of people rushed down the lone track to find the source. As the searchers neared the wreck, bodies and parts of bodies appeared on or alongside the track. Some corpses were so severely disfigured that they were unrecognizable. Captain Morris H. Church of the 11th Regiment Veteran Reserve Corps quickly organized a ring of guards around the site to prevent any prisoners from escaping. Rescuers, soldiers, and prisoners helped remove the dead and injured from the wreckage until well into the night. A relief train from the nearby town of Port Jervis brought doctors and railway employees to help with the injured. Over several hundred injured Union soldiers and

Sketch of train wreck from Frank Leslie's Illustrated Weekly.

Confederate prisoners were being treated at the scene and in the town of Shohola. Within days three more guards and eight more prisoners would die. Captain Church would later put in his report that the dead "were so disfigured that it was impossible to recognize them, and five escaping whose names are unknown, I am unable to give a correct list of killed."[1] At least 51 Confederate prisoners, 17 Union guards and 3 railroad employees died in the wreck.

Railroad employees and prisoners dug a seventy-six-foot-long trench between the railroad track and the Delaware River to bury the bodies. Men were identified if possible and put into hastily made coffins. Most of the prisoners were buried four to a coffin on one side of the trench and seventeen Union guards were placed in separate coffins on the other. The bodies rested there until 1911 when they were exhumed and reinterred at Woodlawn Cemetery in Elmira, NY.

Elmira's Saturday morning newspaper alerted the city's population to the deadly prison train wreck near Shohola, Pennsylvania. The July 16, 1864, *Elmira Daily Advertiser* reported that a 50-car coal train had collided with a train bearing a large number of prisoners and guards destined for the prison camp outside the city. The paper went on to report that 48 prisoners and 17 guards were killed, and 100 prisoners and 18 guards were injured and required immediate medical attention.[2]

When the officers at the prison camp heard the news they sprang into action, busily deciding how to handle the arrival of the injured. Surgeon William C. Wey enlisted all the help he could get, but the scarcity of lint and bandages crippled them in their work. The supply on hand was adequate for normal conditions but would not be enough for a large emergency such as this. Since almost all of Elmira's doctors were at the front assisting in the war effort, Surgeon Wey was aided by nurses and medical students.

The suddenness of the tragedy and the scarcity of medical staff and supplies made it impossible to properly care for such a great number of victims. Surgeon Wey did not have time to submit an official requisition to satisfy this need; instead, he notified all the cities pastors to appeal to the ladies at the Sunday service for lint and bandages. The same request was also published in the Monday morning newspaper. Not only did the ladies of Elmira respond to this tremendous crisis, but donations from adjoining cities came in as well. The Ladies Hospital Aid Association responded with dressings that they had earmarked for the soldiers at the front and instead diverted these to the prison camp.

On July 22nd Captain M. H. Church of the 11th Veteran Reserve Corps was sent to Shohola with a train of twenty cars to assist the transfer of the injured to Elmira. When he returned to the city Saturday evening the train was met at the station by Colonel Seth Eastman and Surgeon Wey with a dozen hay-lined wagons to carry the injured men as comfortable as possible to the prison camp. One of the barracks had been emptied so the injured could all be placed together under the care of Surgeon Wey and the nurses. The doctor and his staff worked tirelessly from 9:30 Saturday evening until daylight the next morning cleaning and dressing wounds. Despite Wey's best efforts six more men eventually succumbed to their injuries.[3]

Several days after the train wreck one newspaper reporter described the macabre scene "the fearful groans and heart-rending cries of the injured and expiring will never be forgotten. Some of the corpses were shockingly mutilated, heads completely crushed, bodies transfixed, impaled on timbers or iron rods, or smashed between the colliding beams, while one man was discovered dead, sitting on the top of the upturned tender, in grotesque and ghastly mockery of the scene around him."[4]

A week later a jury convened in Lackawaxen to investigate the cause of the Shohola train wreck and to determine a verdict in the case. Engineer Hoitt and his conductor, John Martin, from the coal train both testified that telegraph operator Douglas Kent had made a fatal mistake by telling them the track was clear that morning. When the coal train left the Hawley Branch and went on the Erie Railroad's main line, conductor Martin testified that he descended from his post in the caboose and entered Lackawaxen Station asking if the track was clear to Shohola. His question was answered by telegraph operator Kent, indicating that the track was clear for him to proceed. Engineer Hoitt then sent G. M. Boyden, the brake man, ahead to open the main switch so the train could go on to Shohola.

The Shohola monument at Elmira's national Cemetery marks graves of Confederate prisoners of war who died in a train accident on July 15, 1864, near Shohola, Pennsylvania.

During the investigation it was discovered Douglas Kent had gone to a dance the evening before at nearby town of Hawley and had consumed a fair amount of alcohol. Even though the jury had enough evidence against Kent, they determined the accident was unavoidable. The public outcry was so great at the finding that another investigation was ordered. Although the second jury found Kent guilty, nothing could be done since he had disappeared the day after the wreck along with the incriminating evidence of his station log.

Elmira's Observatories

Making a profit on someone else's misfortune seemed to be the motivation behind a man building an observation tower across the street from Elmira Prisoner of War Camp. Near the end of July, Mr. Nichols purchased the northeast corner next to the prison and built a two-story observation platform. Then he erected a sign reading, "an observation tower from which to view the prisoners—admission 15¢, refreshments served below." The New York Evening Post of August 17, 1864, stated that "a man of genius" "who sought his opportunity and was equal to the occasion, suddenly appeared at the camp, and apparently determined that the rebels should make his fortune."[1]

The *Elmira Daily Advertiser* reported that it was "often crowded with sightseers and must prove a paying institution." Most people had never seen the enemy before and flocked to the observatory to get a glimpse of the rebel prisoners. The first level was advantageous because it had a roof over it to shelter the crowd from inclement weather, but the upper level offered a superior view. One business partner said the tower paid for itself in two weeks. *The Rochester Daily Union* reported that the proprietor of the observatory "intends to keep in this tower a powerful glass, by the aid of which visitors can see the vermin which are said to be so plenty upon the bodies of the prisoners."[2] Body lice called "graybacks" infested every part of Elmira and made their homes in the men's clothing. James Huffman remembered, "Some fellows did not wash their clothes nor themselves and you could see the gray-backs crawling over their clothes on the outside."[3]

This observatory was so successful that several weeks later another tower was built down the street from the original. W. W. Mears made their observatory twenty feet higher and charged their customers five cents less. This new tower boasted three decks instead of two and promised "a fine view of the rebel prisoners."[4] Wooden stands sprang up where hungry visitors could buy ginger cakes, crackers and peanuts or refresh themselves with a cool lemonade, beer, or liquor. A writer would recall three decades later, "(These establishments) took on the look of a long row of rude wooden booths like those at a fair, or more like those that spring up in a night along a street that is the route to the grounds where a circus tent is to be spread."[5] After observing the prisoners one

The three-story Mears brothers' observatory can be seen to the right of this photograph. Northern entrepreneurs built these towers to profit from the prisoners' misery. *Photograph courtesy of the Chemung County Historical Society.*

man claimed they, "have a rough appearance, wearing as they do, clothing of as many hues as the rainbow but none so brilliant. The men are generally of good size, and what would be called fair specimens of the race, if they were not Rebels."[6]

A Tennessee sergeant, George W. D. Porter, recalled how "hundreds would crowd daily to get a view of the prisoners—many to gloat, perhaps, on their sufferings; some to gaze in wonder and awe upon the ragged, bob-tailed crew who had on many fields conquered their best armies; and some, no doubt, to sigh for an exchange of these men for fathers, sons, and brothers who were suffering kindred miseries at Libby, Salisbury and Andersonville."[7] James Huffman remembered there was "a constant stream of people winding their way to the top of these observatories to get a glimpse of the Rebs, as they supposed us to be like some kind of curious, monkey-shaped animals."[8]

The diary of Ausburn Towner was discovered thirty years after the war and described his visit to one of the observatories:

"It was like looking down into an immense beehive. There was a constant motion on all sides, but without noise or confusion that could be heard. Groups were standing here and there, formed one minute, broken up the next; some men had built a fire underneath a tree and were baking cornmeal cakes; someone was coming or going every instant to or from every building whose entrance was in sight, and many were seated in the shadow of the trees whittling or fashioning some object, the character of which the distance forbade making out. In the space between the buildings and the fence nearest sat a small circle of men, with one on his feet who seemed to be speaking and making the most violent gestures. When he finished, he seated himself in his place in the ring and another rose to go through similar exercises in his turn. A few feet from these men were five men playing cards. In the corner close at hand was a large tent that had a lonesome look. Into it, during the half hour of our visit, came two men five times, bearing each time on a stretcher the dead body of a man covered over with a piece of canvas." Towner did confess that he and his friends all "speedily grew melancholy over the spectacle and cut our visit to the top of the tower very short."[9]

Both observatories and the refreshment stands did a thriving business through September. The *Elmira Daily Gazette* proudly proclaimed: "Upper Observatory (the original observation tower) should be visited by all strangers and citizens. The pictures taken from there will always be remembered with delightful interest. Photograph views of the rebel camp, and surroundings . . . have been taken and can be obtained by the public in a few days."[10]

On September 19th the lucrative observatory business came to an end. The Elmira officials were concerned that the towers could be used for communication between rebel spies on the outside and the prisoners. It was also possible, they theorized, that the towers might be used to organize an escape. The commissary general of prisoners ordered Captain John Elwell, Elmira's assistant quartermaster, to seize the ground occupied by the two observatories. The Confederates were relieved that these observatories were no longer in use. "I am surprised that Barnum has not taken the prisoners off the hands of Abe, divided them into companies, and carried them in caravans through the country," wrote prisoner Anthony M. Keiley after the war had ended.[11]

Ration Reduction

Colonel William Hoffman, who was known for being tight-fisted, found a way to save the United States government thousands of dollars. His plan not only saved money, but also supported his idea of retaliation. Hoffman theorized since the prisoners were sedentary and not actively fighting or marching in the field that they could get along with less food. The rations saved could then be sold back to the commissary and the money would be put in a Prison Fund. This was like a slush fund that could be used to cover the cost of making improvements to the prison and the prisoner diet. Secretary of War Edwin Stanton liked the idea and authorized Hoffman to implement the reduction of rations on April 20, 1862.[1]

This order made no sense. If Hoffman's only motive was to save the government money, wouldn't it make sense to let the prisoners have more food, so they don't become sick and fill the hospital? Sick prisoners require a doctor's care, medicine, and a special diet. All of this would drive up the cost of prisoner care. If Hoffman's sole reason for the reduction of food was to save the government money, then he was doing a poor job. It is far more likely Hoffman's only motive was to seek retaliation. However, Secretary of War Stanton's absolute control of the Northern prison system should not be underestimated. Stanton's vindictive nature toward Confederate prisoners was well known by his officers. Colonel William Hoffman frequently communicated with the Secretary and should be considered within Stanton's sphere of influence.

Ration reduction at Union prison camps caused many prisoners to waste away and eventually become victims of disease and death.

With the winter season coming Colonel Hoffman made sure the prisoners were not too comfortable by issuing the following order on November 12, 1863:

"You will issue no clothing of any kind except in cases of utmost necessity. So long as a prisoner has clothing upon him, however much torn, you must issue nothing to him, nor must you allow him to receive clothing from any but members of his immediate family, and only when they are in absolute want."[2]

Still not satisfied with the prisoners food, Colonel Hoffman advised his prison commandants on November 9, 1863, "I do not think it well to permit (the prisoners) to receive boxes of eatables from friends," "and I suggest you have them informed that such articles will not hereafter be delivered."[3] Why did Hoffman object to the prisoners having extra food? The only answer that seems to fit is that this would be interfering with the reduced rations he prescribed. Hoffman had explained earlier how reducing the prisoner's rations would be saving the government money, but now he was turning away free food being mailed to the prisoners. This fact is very telling as it exposed his true motivation was vengeance against the Confederate prisoners entrusted to his care. Secretary of War Stanton's lack of response to this order may have been an indication that Hoffman had the Secretary's tacit approval in reducing the prisoner's food once more.

The next year Colonel Hoffman noticed that the prisoners were not adversely affected by the reduction of rations and thought their food could be decrease further. He notified the Secretary of War that the prisoner's food could once again be reduced without adversely affecting the men's health.

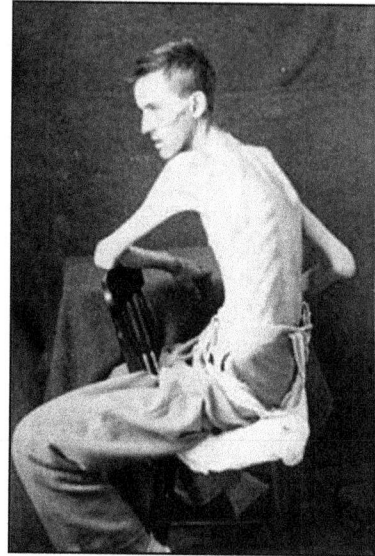

22

Stanton happily agreed and ordered a 20 percent reduction in rations effective June 1, 1864.[4] It must be remembered that this order was in addition to the initial reduction of rations. A conservative estimate would place the total reduction of rations at least one-third of a full ration or possibly more.

"These orders put the prisoners on half rations," complained prisoner James F. Crocker about the ration reduction. "The result of these orders was that the prisoners were kept in a state of hunger—I will say in a state of sharp hunger—all the time."[5]

Constant hunger can influence a prisoner's everyday life through long-term depression. All prisoners have depression to a degree, but as the conditions become worse the greater the effect they will have. Prisoner exchanges had been halted so there was little hope that anyone would be allowed to leave prison anytime soon. Seeing so many of their friends die from disease, prisoners began to wonder with mounting concern if they would survive long enough to go home. Studies have been done and show there is a strong link between depression and illness.[6] If a prisoner has no hope of freedom, it is likely his resistance will go down and he is liable to catch one of the deadly diseases he had been so worried about. Many prisoners at Elmira never got the chance to go home and their remains can be found at Woodlawn Cemetery.

This is Private William E. Crawford's drinking cup made from a steer's horn. Crawford made this cup at Elmira when the prison ran out of tableware. Crawford was in Company G, 25th South Carolina when he was captured at Fort Fisher on January 15, 1865. Private Crawford died of pneumonia and is buried at Woodlawn Cemetery near Elmira, New York. *Photograph courtesy of Mike McCarley*

Former Elmira prisoner John R. King remembered how the men died at prison. "The poor fellows died rapidly, despondent, homesick, hungry and wretched. I have stood day after day watching the wagons carry the dead outside to be buried and each day for several weeks 16 dead men were taken through the gate."[7]

Former prisoner George M. Neese recalled the dark cloud of gloom which had settled over him in prison. "The true aspects, experiences, and characteristics of prison life in general can never be described, even by the most impressive writer, so that he who has never experienced its realities cannot form the faintest conception of the melancholy gloom that settles down like eternal night on the spirit of the man and crushes hope to the dark recesses of its lowest stage, so that life itself becomes a burden that may be dragged, but too wearisome to bear. No painter's palette ever held the color black enough to truthfully delineate the shadows that constantly hang around a prisoner of war in these United States."[8]

Some prisoners resorted to disgusting behavior even by lax prison standards because of the food reduction order. Prisoner Erastus Palmer remembered seeing a comrade returning from the hospital and stopped to chat. During the conversation, he noticed that the man picked up a discarded mush poultice and began scraping off the side used for treating lesions. Palmer watched him carefully remove the sickening gunk from the dirty poultice while nonchalantly mentioning that he was preparing to eat it, to which Palmer wrote, "I did not stay to see him do it."[9]

Under these new orders the Elmira prisoners were limited to two meals a day and ate in shifts that ran from 6 to 9 AM and from 3 to 6 PM. With well drilled efficiency only the army could instill, the Confederate Ward Sergeants gathered the men together in the barracks to go to the mess hall for breakfast. Every morning the men fall in between 6 and 9 AM while he called the roll. If any man was sick and unable to go, it was the Ward Sergeant's duty to bring these men their meals. The ration was four ounces of bread and a thin piece of salt pork. Dinner had the same amount of bread, but the meat was replaced by a soup or broth so clear you could see the bottom of the cup.

Starvation, manifested in stages, would become visibly evident inside the prison camp. Weight loss, headache, fatigue, irritability, insomnia, and depression were the prevailing signs that became apparent to anyone who had access to the stockade. "I have seen groups of battle-worn, homesick

Confederates," Union Lieutenant Frank Wilkeson, an officer in charge of a guard detail inside Elmira prison camp, would recollect nearly a quarter-century later, "their thin blankets drawn tightly around their shoulders, stand in the lee of a barracks for an hour without speaking to one another. They stood motionless and gazed into one another's eyes. There was no need to talk, as all topics of conversation had long since been exhausted."[10]

In the beginning, when the number of men was fewer, the prisoners sat on benches and had eating utensils consisting of a tin plate, fork, and spoon. As Elmira prison camp became more crowded the benches were removed to make room for more tables. With the seats gone the 41 x 396 x 8-foot dining hall could accommodate more men. When the eating utensils ran out many men brought their own tableware to eat with. Former prisoner Anthony M. Keiley lamented, "gone were the tin plates; gone the knives and forks; gone the seats at all the tables; gone the encouragement to cry out for more (food)."[11]

Former prisoner John A. Wyeth provided an example of this when he wrote, "I know from personal observation that many of my comrades died from starvation. Day after day it was easy to observe the progress of emaciation until they became so weak that when attacked with an illness which a well-nourished man would easily have resisted and recovered from, they rapidly succumbed."[12]

As the harsh winter winds of December tightened its icy grip on Elmira's prisoners the men started to show signs of malnutrition and starvation. Prisoner James Huffman recalled that many inmates "moped about, pining away for want of sufficient food to eat, losing their humanity, eating almost anything a brute would eat—as rats, gangrene poultices and the like." Huffman remembered the prisoners at Elmira "were known by their pallid color and lifeless movements. Most of them died there, not from disease but pining away for lack of more food, some even sending word to their friends at home that they were being starved to death. These poor men grew so lean that they seemed to have no flesh at all, before their spirits left their bodies."[13]

Elmira's prisoners line up for morning roll call. Men were required to stand in line regardless of the weather was bad or they were sick. *Photograph courtesy of the Chemung County Historical Society.*

An outbreak of scurvy became so acute in August and September that it soon reached epidemic proportions and prompted Post Surgeon Eugene Sanger to ask Colonel Hoffman to increase the supply of vegetables. Colonel Hoffman, who had previously forbidden the sutler from selling fruit and vegetables, complied with the request and permitted him to resume selling these items to the prisoners. Still the question remains why Surgeon Sanger, who knew that the lack vitamin D would cause disease, did not say anything until there was a serious outbreak of scurvy? It appears that this disease was a real threat since Elmira's records indicate that over forty prisoners died from the disease.

The disease caused assorted spots and irritations on the body, but John R. King noted that it also "attacked the mouth and gums, becoming so spongy and sore that portions could be removed with the fingers."[14] In addition to losing their teeth, victims frequently saw their hair fall out and felt their stomachs cramp, leaving some men too weak to walk.

If this were not bad enough, the beef rations were reduced on October 3rd by Special Order No. 336 issued by post commandant Colonel Benjamin Tracy. The order reads, "Whereas the fresh beef now being furnished at this post is in the opinion of the Colonel commanding unfit for issue, and inferior in quality to that required by contract. Therefore: Colonel S. Moore and Major Henry V. Colt are hereby designated to hold a survey upon said beef and to reject such parts or the whole of the said beef as to them appears to be unfit for issue, or of a quality inferior to that contracted for."[15] The daily meat inspection frequently resulted in large amounts of beef being rejected. The supposedly inferior beef was then sold to local meat markets while the prisoners simply had to do without meat.

In 1878 the flawed nature of Special Order 336 was revealed by Brigadier General Alexander S. Diven when he wrote a letter which stated that he accompanied Colonel Tracy to the slaughter yard where the beef was inspected. He recalled Tracy rejected "beef, which, though it was such as I would often be glad to have for myself and my command."[16] General Diven's observation that he would have been glad to receive the unwanted beef brings into question the reason Colonel Tracy had for rejecting it. It appears he could have

Confederate prisoners sold rats at five cents apiece. This became a thriving business in the camp. *Photograph courtesy of the Chemung County Historical Society.*

been seeking his own brand of revenge against the Confederates or perhaps more accurately his superiors' demand for retaliation. No doubt the starving prisoners would have loved to have had some of the beef rejected by the uncaring Colonel Benjamin Tracy.

"The meat ration," prisoner Anthony M. Keiley wrote, "was invariably scanty; and I learned, on inquiry, that the fresh beef sent to the prison usually fell short from 1000 to 1200 pounds in each consignment." Keiley added that "when this happened, many had to lose a large portion of their allowance; and sometimes it happened that the same man got bones only for several successive days. The (things) resorted to by the men to supply the want for animal food was disgusting. Many found an acceptable substitute in rats, which the place abounded."[17] Keiley bitterly added that "in a nation, whose boast is that the people of the United States do not feel the war, and supplies of all sorts are wonderfully abundant, it is simply infamous to starve the sick as they did there [Elmira]."[18]

If the meat was substandard, as Colonel Tracy claimed, why was it good enough to be sold to Elmira's citizens? Many historians agree that Secretary Stanton's approval of this controversial order was intended to force a bread-and-water diet on the prisoners without actually going on record as ordering it. It can be argued that a systematic reduction of rations was intentionally ordered to lower the prisoner's resistance to more deadly diseases. If one considers Elmira's 25% death rate, which was more than twice as high as the rate for the other Northern prisons, the numbers seem to support such a claim.

The New Prison Meat: Rats

Thousands of rats migrated into the prison camp attracted by the foul stench from tons of garbage rotting outside the cookhouses. These rodents grew to alarming size and hid under buildings and burrowed in deep holes alongside the pond. Encouraged by the gathering darkness of evening, the rats became bold and would venture out to make forages on the trash heaps.

Former prisoner Berry Benson recalled, "Another item of fare which was not on the list furnished by the government was—rats! The prison swarmed with them—big rusty fellows which lived about the 'cook house' as the kitchen was always called, and also under the house used as quarters. The floors of these houses were close to the ground, and the sides came down all the way. The rats burrowed holes underneath to go in and out, sometimes as large as a man's leg."[19]

One evening a prisoner was arrested for prowling around the camp during the night. The next morning, he was taken to headquarters and questioned by Major Colt, who asked, "What were you doing?" The prisoner answered, "Huntin', sir." Colt wondered what type of animal would be in his prison camp at night and asked, "What are you hunting?" The man replied, "Rats!". Toward dusk, prisoners armed with rocks and clubs waited for the rats to gather. One prisoner remarked, "[when a rat was seen] such a hurrah and such a chase and such a volley of stones! You would have thought it was our Battalion of Sharpshooters in charge."[20]

After the rats were killed and cleaned they were either grilled or fried. Marcus Toney remembered men catching and then eating the rats. "I am glad that I did not have to go on this diet; but I have tasted a piece of rat, and it is much like squirrel."[21] Everything on a rat was used. No part of the rodent was wasted. After a prisoner got every bit of nourishment from the animal possible, he would sew several hides together to make gloves for the winter months.[22]

Walter D. Addison wrote, "Rats, dogs, cats nor any other animals wouldn't long exist amongst that hungry throng of prisoners. Catching rats and selling them for food became quite a business, and they pursued the avocation with quite a profit, the demand being steady."[23]

Former prisoner James B. Stamp remembered that in December 1864 the "insufficiency of food increased, and in many instances, prisoners were reduced to absolute suffering. All the rats that could be captured were eaten, and on one occasion a small dog that had followed a wood hauler into camp was caught and prepared for food."[24]

Killed and dressed rats were an important commodity in the prison camp and sold anywhere from four to twenty-five cents apiece. Former Elmira prisoner of war R. B. Ewan recalled, "Our mart of trade was about in the center of the ground, and at 10 o'clock every day dressed rats on boards and tin plates, and sick prisoners' rations were offered for five cents and sometimes more."[25]

Disease Becomes Epidemic

Captured Confederate soldiers were the first to experience "Hard War" in May of 1863 when the prisoner exchanges were halted. Secretary of War Edwin M. Stanton had always contended that general exchanges of prisoners who were healthy enough to return to their regiments should not be allowed. Now he was able to make it a reality. This is not to say all prisoner exchanges were halted. If a sick prisoner wanted to be exchanged, he needed to be examined by a surgeon to guarantee he was unfit to return to duty for sixty days. If the prisoner did so, he would be permitted to be released in a special exchange. An exception to this rule was made at Vicksburg, Mississippi. Over 30,000 Confederates had been captured July 4, 1863, and then paroled four days later. These men were paroled because an additional 5,400 prisoners had been captured at Gettysburg and Northern prisons did not have enough space to incarcerate such a large number of men. The government also thought caring for so many men would place a heavy financial burden on the North.

Confederate soldier drinking water. Photograph courtesy Pamplin Historical Park, Virginia.

At this point in the war many government and military officials felt retaliation was called for because of rumored abuse of Northern soldiers in Southern prisons.[1] With prisoners no longer being exchanged Secretary of War Edwin M. Stanton was free to advance his policy of vengeance against Confederate prisoners. In the next year and a half many unreasonable restrictions were placed on items that were essential to the men's survival. Among the things reduced were rations, clothing, safe drinking water, shelter, hospital care and medicine. At best it can be said that these restrictions were placed on the prisoners to hobble the Confederate army by only releasing weakened soldiers who were unfit for military duty. At worst it can be argued that halting the prisoner exchange and introducing severe reductions of food, medicine and clothing was deliberately designed to create a death camp like atmosphere.

Ration reduction was the biggest factor effecting prisoner's health. Prisoner rations were reduced on multiple occasions at the suggestion of Colonel William Hoffman, the Commissary Genral of Prisoners. The rations, which were scanty to begin with, were systematically reduced to half the normal ration. Although prisoners have been known to exaggerate their hardships, it is difficult to not believe the numerous prisoner's journals and diaries that consistently complain about the meals containing only half a ration. Without enough food the men's bodies no longer had the strength required to fight disease.[2]

Another problem created by halting the prisoner exchange was the overcrowding of the prisons which in turn placed great stress on their water supply. Typically, a prison had only so much freshwater available for a specific number of people. In the case of Elmira Prison camp, New York, the prisoner's supply of water became quickly polluted and spread deadly disease. Unfortunately, the scientific study of germs did not exist during the Civil War. If thirsty men could see water, they will drink it. If prisoners became sick from drinking water from a certain source, then the others knew to avoid it. This method worked fine for water

Title page of The Medical and Surgical History of the War of the Rebellion, Part III, Volume I.

that is heavily contaminated and the effects are observed right away. However, germs can be insidious creatures that do not necessarily make a person ill right away. It may be weeks or sometimes months for germs from polluted water to make their presence known. A prisoner in reasonable health is usually able to withstand and shake off an illness. He may only get some diarrhea as a result. Nevertheless, even this if continued long enough can become deadly. Now add to that equation the fact that the same man's quality of health is lowered by an insufficient diet. The bout with chronic diarrhea now robs him of any nutrients provided by his already scanty rations. Introduce a waterborne illness and the way is now open for a more lethal disease to be introduced to his already weakened system. String a few hundred of these sick men in close proximity and you have an epidemic in the making.

Overcrowding of the prison camps was a very serious problem for several reasons. Once a disease is introduced to a densely populated prison environment it can spread like wildfire. The first sign of an epidemic is when an overcrowded hospital does not have enough beds for sick prisoners. This problem is greatly magnified because these men are then forced to remain in their barracks where they could possibly infect other prisoners.

Other problems with overcrowding of the prison include blankets, clothing, shelter, and medicine. Every month the prison commandants would submit a requisition for thet supplies were needed the following month for the prison. With more men coming in every month and none being exchanged these requisition numbers were always far behind the actual numbers. Therefore, there was never enough clothing, shelter, and medicine to go around. Add to this the fact that Secretary of War Stanton and Colonel William Hoffman did their best to deprive prisoners of the supplies they needed by issuing orders that further reduced the prisoner rations.

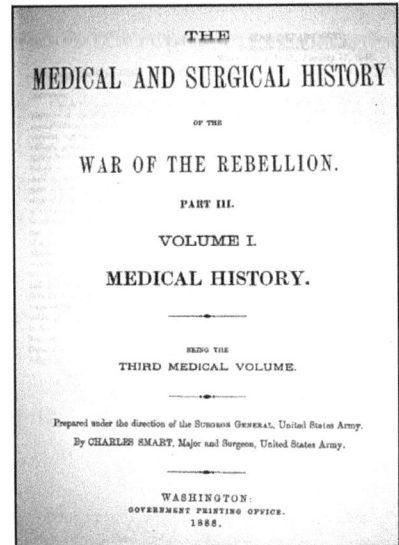

There has been a school of thought that believes Elmira prison camp was built as a retaliatory prison because of the alleged abuses suffered by Northern prisoners of war. These claims have always been denied by the Federal government. However, there is now growing evidence to support this accusation of retaliation. The evidence I speak of was discovered while I was studying *The Medical and Surgical History of the War of the Rebellion, (1861-65).* This is a series of medical books that were assembled by Joseph K. Barnes, Surgeon General of the United States Army. There is a table in Volume I, part 3 that contains troubling statistics regarding the death by disease at Elmira prison camp. Table XVIII lists data regarding eleven different types of disease from the nine largest prison camps in the North.[3] I wanted to find out what type of medical care the prisoners were receiving. I compared the results to the data from Elmira. After evaluating the figures, I found the prison camp at Elmira had the worst death record for every disease on that table. Six of the eleven diseases had such an alarming difference from the other Northern prisons that I was compelled to write about them. For instance, a prisoner suffering from bronchitis at Elmira was 6.4 times more likely to die from that disease than men at other Northern prisons. The grouping of "other diseases" indicated the men at Elmira were dying five times more often as at other prisons. This medical volume does not specify what these diseases were. I then checked the statistics for diarrhea and dysentery and found the men at Elmira prison camp were over four times more likely to die than at any other Northern prison. This is troubling, but there is more. The list

Elmira's Chief Surgeon Major Eugene F. Sanger

of lethal diseases goes on. "Malarial fevers" found the prisoners at Elmira four times more likely to die. The diseases of scurvy and rheumatism found the men at Elmira dying three times more often than those as in other prisons. The gap is so great in all six of these diseases that the abnormalities do not appear to be a random occurrence. It is becoming increasingly difficult to believe these events were merely a result of the incompetence of Elmira's medical staff. If anyone bears responsibility for the conduct at Elmira's prison camp hospital it was the Chief Surgeon, Major Eugene F. Sanger.

Evidence has come to light that casts Major Sanger in an incriminating position for possible criminal activity. In the hopes of obtaining a transfer from his duties at Elmira, Major Sanger sent letters requesting a position in another part of the country. One of those letters was sent to Brigadier General John L. Hodson in which Sanger inquired about a recruiting position in Augusta, Maine. In his letter Sanger not only explained the duties of his current job as chief surgeon at the prison, but also bragged about the number of prisoner deaths under his care. This is what he wrote, "I now have charge of 10,000 Rebels a very worthy occupation for a patriot . . . but I think I have done my duty having relieved 386 of them of all earthly sorrow in one month." Did Sanger indicate that he had deliberately contributed to the deaths of hundreds of patients in his care? Sanger's last sentence suggests that this was a willful act.[4]

Former Elmira prisoner Anthony M. Keiley worked for Major Sanger as a hospital clerk and had the opportunity to see many things regarding the hospital patients in the course of his duties. Keiley claimed that Sanger refused to sign any report that listed a prisoner's cause of death as being related to malaria. This would also include intermittent and remittent fever. The reason according to Keiley was that "in the medical department in a Yankee prison-camp . . . (there are) opportunities of plunder . . . Vast quantities of quinine were prescribed that were never taken, the price (eight dollars an ounce) tempting the cupidity of the physicians beyond all resistance." Keiley suggested that Major Sanger was selling the medicine and attributing the resulting death to another disease. Elmira had over four times as many deaths for diarrhea as other Northern prisons. This is an unbelievably high number. Were some of these deaths caused by other diseases because there was no medicine left to treat the patients? According to Keiley's statement they were.[5]

<u>Introduction of Smallpox at Elmira Prison Camp</u>

The first incidents of variola, more commonly known as smallpox, occurred at Elmira Prison camp when infected prisoners from Fort Morgan, Alabama, were captured on the Gulf Coast. These prisoners were held in New Orleans, Louisiana, then sent to Ship Island, near Gulfport, Mississippi, sent briefly to Fort Columbus in New York Harbor and finally transferred to Elmira Prison Camp.

A few of the prisoners from Fort Morgan, Alabama, developed symptoms of smallpox in October. By December 12th two of these men became the first smallpox related deaths at the prison. These were Privates Alcide Carmonche, Company K, 2nd Louisiana Cavalry and Oscar Davidson, Company G, 37th Texas Cavalry. Both men were captured near Morganza, Louisiana, and sent to a temporary prison in New Orleans, then on October 4th they were transferred to Ship Island, Mississippi. The men were again transferred November 16th to Fort Columbus, New York Harbor, and then to Elmira Prison Camp. It is important to track where the men had been to see if we can determine the source of the dreaded disease. They probably weren't exposed to the virus in Morganza since the two were captured a month apart. The first incidence of them travelling together is when they were sent to Ship Island, Mississippi, on the same boat. From then on, the men traveled along with the other prisoners. It is not known if the men shared the same tent once they reached Elmira. When these prisoners developed symptoms of the disease in October the prison did not have a hospital that could handle cases of smallpox.

On December 23rd Major Anthony E. Stocker replaced Eugene Sanger as chief surgeon and immediately had his hands full with an out-of-control smallpox epidemic. On Christmas morning Captain William Jordon reported that the virus had been transmitted to sixty-three more men and two more deaths had occurred that week.[1] With the epidemic increasing Colonel Benjamin Tracy was advised on January 5th by General Wilson T. Hartz that if the disease spreads further he should isolate the carriers by building a hospital some distance away from the prison population. A mere three days later there was more bad news when an inspecting officer reported that there were now 126 cases of smallpox along with 10 deaths.

Shortly after this Tracy ordered a "Smallpox Hospital" be erected in a remote corner of the prison on a strip of land that existed between the Chemung River and Foster's Pond. This hospital, if it could be called that, consisted of several rows of A-frame tents which house three patients and a wood burning stove. Another inspection January 24th reported a total of 397 smallpox cases proving that the disease was on the rise.[2]

Despite several attempts to halt the spread of smallpox everything proved futile except for the moderating spring temperatures of 1865. Smallpox during the Civil War was considered a seasonal disease. Doctors noticed that during the warm months of the year the rate of smallpox cases was considerably below average and during cold months increased to well above normal. The season for this disease typically lasts from October through April with its peak being in March.[3]

One of the precautions taken to halt the spread of smallpox was when a patient recovered from a case of the disease, he was required to take a bath and put on new clothes. In the meantime, his old clothes and blankets were burned to destroy the smallpox virus. Surgeon Stocker and his staff busily administered 5,600 vaccinations in January, but they had some terrible side effects. Many of the prisoners developed an ulcer on their arm and a few even had to undergo amputation which sometimes resulted in death.

Former prisoner Walter D. Addison wrote about the horrors of 19th century vaccinations. "The courageous manner in which men were vaccinated excelled anything I have ever witnessed even surpassing the acts of savages. The modus operandi was to assemble the men in long lines with coats off and arms bared; then the butchering began by illiterate and irresponsible men. They would take hold of a thick piece of flesh, dip a lancet into the diluted virus, and then thrust it entirely through the pinched-up flesh. The spurious virus soon produced such fearfully disastrous results that it became necessary to construct gangrene hospitals, from which arose a dreadful stench. Scores died from the effects; others losing arms. I have seen the sickening effects of their villainous vaccinations. There are many who can verify the above."[4]

Medical Director Charles S. Tripler presented an interesting report on the large number of prisoners who had developed bad ulcers from smallpox vaccinations. The Medical Department suspected that the vaccine purveyors had provided tainted serum. The ulcers on the patient's arm were described as occurring on the third day with a cyst which filled with pus. This speedily became an irritable sore, from 1 to 4 inches in length, and finally degenerated into an ulcer that was extremely slow to heal. At the time of his report Surgeon Tripler cited 1,580 cases of ulcers. Of these 668 had healed while 912 remained obstinately open wounds.

Tripler noticed that the same vaccine was used on Federal troops as the prisoners, and they suffered very little occurrence of ulcers from the vaccinations. Tripler said that the only difference between these men was their diet. He therefore concluded, "The prison diet in this department (prison system) is sufficient in quantity, but it lacks those component parts which are essential to health. Aside from soft bread the only vegetable issued is 30 pounds of potatoes to 100 men per day. This is not sufficient to ward off scurvy, and as long as it is continued a mortality not credible to our government may be expected among our prisoners of war."[5]

Private Adam Cunningham died of syphilis after recieving the smallpox vaccine.

According to prisoner Marcus Toney the medical staff largely ignored the men in the smallpox hospital. On January 25th Toney was experiencing "a severe chill, with pains in my spine and back of head." He also said his bunkmates were worried because he had been delirious for two days. Being the Ward Sergeant Toney goes on to say, "When I came to, I was out calling the roll of the ward. I noticed that my hands were badly pimpled, but as we did not have a mirror, I could not see my face. Before I finished the roll call along came Doctor Burchard, one of the prison surgeons. The doctor looked at me and said: 'Toney, you have the smallpox.'"

Toney then went to the smallpox hospital where he spent a total of four days. He goes on to say, "It was way below zero, and the hospital was across a little lake inside the prison walls, and the patients were in A tent, tents shaped as the letter A, and having a capacity of three patients each. I walked across the lake on the ice and commenced my search at the head of the row of tents, trying to find some bedfellows that had a light attack as myself. Nearly all the tents were filled with patients who had the confluent type, but finally I found a tent with two patients—one very bad and the other lighter—and I crawled in.

We did not see a doctor while there, but once a day a waiter brought us some tea and bread. As the hospital was some distance from the cookhouse and the weather was below zero, the tea was cold when it reached us. My bedfellows could not eat or drink anything, and I had all the rations, yet I could not get enough. The second night one of our bedfellows died, and all the vermin came to us, and we had plenty of company. The vermin will leave a body as soon as it gets cold. We had about eight blankets but could not keep warm; and to make the situation worse, the men who died were dragged out and left in front of the tents, and in whatever position a man was when death overtook him in that position he froze. Some with arms and legs extended presented a horrible sight."[6]

If Tony's account is to be believed, where were the doctors? Apparently, the smallpox victims were ignored by the medical staff and left to fend for themselves.

Here's an intriguing fact that I think you should be aware of. *The Medical and Surgical History of the War of the Rebellion, (1861-65),* volume I, part III, presented an interesting fact when it reported "No case of smallpox or varioloid was reported among the 49,394 men of the Confederate Army during the nine months, July 1861-March 1862, while 380 cases occurred during this period in the United States Army. Smallpox may, therefore, be considered as having invaded the South during the progress of the war."

As you recall Elmira received over 9,000 prisoners from Point Lookout from July through August 1864. It has been confirmed that Point Lookout prison had 466 cases and 212 deaths from smallpox that began as early as November 1863.[7] Isn't it conceivable that the virus had already been at Elmira when the Fort Morgan prisoners arrived? Since smallpox has a two to three-week incubation period this would place fullblown smallpox at Elmira prison camp in September. It had been reported that the first cases of variola appeared in October. This is not to say the disease was carried to Elmira in this way, but this information is given as an alternative scenario that could have taken place.

Trades Flourished in Elmira Prison Camp

Like all forms of society, people with money fare better than those without. So, it was the same with the prisoners of Elmira. A few prisoners were fortunate enough to have friends and relatives send them money to make life easier in prison. Yet ninety percent of the men either did not receive any money or very little and had to rely on what the United States government furnished them. Sadly, this was never enough. Many prisoners' immune systems were weakened by a lack of food and disease was the inevitable result.

Prisoners sought to supplement their inadequate diet and clothing through profitable activities. Men with some education or skill were able to increase their chances of survival by making goods to sell to other prisoners. Others practiced a trade or learned a new one. The benefits of having a trade were many. First, it kept the inmate occupied and made the time go by faster. Second, he earned a wage which allowed him to purchase items that would make life in prison more comfortable. Food and clothing were the most sought-after things because it was nearly impossible to live on what the government issued the prisoners.

Prisoner carved bone necklace. *Photograph courtesy of the Chemung County Historical Society.*

All that was needed for creative prisoners to setup shop was to hang the appropriate sign outside his tent and display his wares on a cracker-box table. These items could range from artwork, coffee, fans, rats, rings, watch fobs, and many others. Some men performed a service such as barbers, tailors, shoemakers, and laundry men. There was practically no end to the possibilities if a prisoner had the desire to succeed and set his mind to it. Private David Holt remembers many men sold a service to other prisoners. "In our tent we had a barber. Every man who had a trade or profession was trying to follow his calling. As I had neither, I followed my nose and roamed around like a roaring lion."[1]

Men gathered at the prison market place, buying and selling various goods they had made. A fiddler entertained the men by playing an instrument he designed from a cracker box and string. Prisoners traded cups of coffee, slices of bread, and meat rations for tobacco. Many used old wooden crates as makeshift stands, so they could display their wares. In his book Berry Benson wrote about the trades that flourished at Elmira. "It was a curious sight to see, different trades being plied, such as cobbling, perhaps some kind of small carpenters work."[2] It should be explained here that the extra meat rations sold generally came from prisoners who were in the hospital and either had no appetite or passed away. Other times the extra rations had been stolen or flanked by other prisoners. One example was 11th Mississippi infantryman James M. Gilmore who worked as a waiter in the mess hall. Gilmore admitted stealing twenty-five to thirty rations during his daily shift. "After eating all I wanted, I sold the remainder. We aggregated the amount to be something like 10,000 (rations), so you can see we cared little about how the government issued rations." Unfortunately, activity like this did not come without a price as other prisoners were deprived of a meal.

John R. King wrote, "The prisoners passed the time making trinkets. Capt. Munger and Capt. Peck, secured the material and after the articles were completed, they sold them in the city for the best price possible, always remitting the money. In passing through the prison one would see a boisterous lot playing cards or some other game, numbers making rings out of Gutta-percha buttons and riveting sets on to them of real silver which the captains had purchased, others were making pretty trinkets out of bone, such as tooth picks and seals for watch chains, with birds, squirrels and other figures designed on them. Some made watch chains out of horsehair with single links, with two links interlocked and others with three links interlocked making a round chain. This was done with horsehairs and two common needles. Others in our pen made fans out of white pine wood, the board was cut in the shape of a paddle with a fancy handle, then the part which formed the paddle was notched and cut into thin slices with a very sharp knife. The wood was softened with warm water and then the slices bended like a fan. Different colored ribbons were worked through the notches and the ends tied in a bow around the handle. They were very pretty, but frail. One man made a small parasol on the same plan."[3]

Prisoner carved bone thimble. *Photograph courtesy of the Chemung County Historical Society.*

Prison Letters and Packages

One of the most enjoyable pastimes for prisoners was reading letters from loved ones. These letters from home were extremely important for the men's morale and they provided a brief respite from the woes of prison life. When a prisoner was writing a letter to his family it could only be a single page and not mention anything critical of the camp or their treatment. The envelope remained unsealed, so it could be examined by a censor. If a letter contained anything forbidden, it was not mailed.

Packages were especially looked forward to. Many times, the prisoners would receive money or clothing which was intercepted by the prison censors. When mail for a prisoner was received the sensor would open it and see if it contained anything that was contraband. All Federal uniform clothing, boots, or equipment of any kind for military service, weapons of all kinds and intoxicating liquors, were among the contraband articles. All money prisoners received was taken by the Provost Marshall, and he gave the prisoner a receipt for it. These funds were recorded in a ledger by the camp sutler, and the prisoners were given credit for any purchases made at the sutler's store. When prisoners were paroled, their money was returned to them.

Former prisoner Anthony M. Keiley recalled there were ways to send a letter longer than one page. "One had to acquire a telegraphic habit of writing or be content to say very little. Some geniuses were in the habit of writing their letters in the usual long length, then sending them by detail (separate envelopes). Others cultivated a microscopic penmanship."[1]

Somehow Elmira prisoner John Brusnan got a letter past the military censors to his sister in Maryland.

"I will give you some idea of my situation," Brusnan wrote. *"I would have never written to you for money, but I am almost starved to death. I only get two meals a day, breakfast, and supper. For breakfast I get one-third a pound of bread and a small piece of meat; for supper the same quantity of bread and not any meat, but a small plate of warm water called soup. When I came here this prison contained 10,000 prisoners, and they have all died except for about 5,000. They are now dying at the rate of twenty-five a day."*[2]

On January 10, 1865, Lieutenant P. E. O'Conner sent a copy of Brusnan's letter to his sister to the War Department where it caused quite a stir. O'Conner pointed out that the letter had somehow gotten past the censors at Elmira. Colonel Benjamin F. Tracy, Elmira prison camp's commandant, was informed of this letter and asked for his comment. Tracy examined the letter and wrote back, "it is almost unnecessary for me to say that the statements made by the prisoner Brusnan are outrageously false. The daily ration for each prisoner is uniformly as follows: For breakfast, 8 ounces bread, 8 ounces meat; for supper, 8 ounces bread, 1 pint and a half soup of excellent quality, made from the meat, potatoes, onions, and beans." Tracy also stated, "as regards to letters prisoners of war secret out of camp, I have the honor to state that about January 1st we discovered that letters were mailed which did not pass through the hands of the examiner. We have intercepted some hundreds of such letters and discovered the parties engaged in this business. One commissioned officer, one acting assistant surgeon, and two enlisted men have been arrested and charges preferred against them. We

Prisoners' letters sent from Elmira had to be left open, so censors could inspect the letter for anything forbidden. This letter passed inspection and bears a "Prisoner's Letter Examined, Elmira, N. Y." stamp from the censor.

have adopted such measures for the future for the detection of parties attempting to secret letters out of camp and it will be very difficult, if not impossible, for them to escape discovery."[3]

Tracy's letter is very enlightening, but what Union Lieutenant Frank Wilkerson says about the prisoner rations can shed more light on the meals. It is important to note that Wilkerson was a guard at Elmira and had no ax to grind regarding the prisoners. In a book he had written after the war, he said, "The prisoners, it was alleged, were allowed the same rations, excepting coffee and sugar, that their guards received. They did not get it. I repeatedly saw the Confederate prisoners draw their provisions, and they never got more than 2/3's of a ration."[4]

So, who do you believe? Apparently, the full ration Colonel Benjamin Tracy spoke of was only on paper. It has already been shown that because of the two ration reductions the full ration had shrunk by at least 25%. By the time the prisoner's food was issued by the commissary, the ration was pilfered by men in the handling and preparation of the prisoner's food. So, on one end of the spectrum, you have Colonel Tracy saying the prisoners were issued a full (reduced) ration. On the other end of the spectrum, there are hundreds of prisoners who say they received 4 ounces of meat and an inch-thick slice of bread. In the middle is Lieutenant Wilkeson who says he never saw the prisoner receive more than 2/3 of a (reduced) ration. Historians have always cautioned readers not to believe everything a prisoner says because his words may be influenced by his hatred for his captors or a bitter memory of his time while he was in prison. While I can't discount so many accounts from prisoners, I also can't believe Colonel Tracy saying that the prisoners received a full (reduced) ration. I believe the truth lies somewhere between, probably closer to Lieutenant Wilkeson's 2/3's ration. Wilkeson's testimony has several things going for it. The first thing is the time element. Due to the reductions and availability of certain foods, rations would vary in size and content. The time he had written about was the winter of 1864-65. Brusnan's letter was written on December 30, 1864. This would be about the same time that

Lieutenant Wilkeson made his observation of the 2/3's ration being issued to the prisoners. Another thing his account has going for it is that he was merely reporting what he saw day after day. As stated before, he was not being partial to either side. If Colonel Tracy said a full ration was 8 ounces of bread and 8 ounces of meat, two/thirds of the same ration would be 5.3 ounces. This amount seems far more likely to be close to the actual amount the prisoners received.

Since Lieutenant Wilkeson did not comment on the soup it is difficult to determine if it was of excellent quality as Colonel Tracy said it was. I will note that virtually all the prisoners complained about the soup not having any meat in it and three or four beans.

Prisoner Marcus B. Toney had charge of the Ward—a duty that required his calling the roll once a day, and submitting a report of the sick men who went to the hospital. "In the cookhouse," Toney stated in the Civil War memoir, "were a large number of iron kettles or cauldrons in which the meat and beans were boiled. I suppose these cauldrons would hold 50 gallons. The salt pork was shipped in barrels and rolled up to the cauldrons, and with a pitchfork tossed in, then the beans—I have heard the boys say four beans to a gallon of water. Now when this is boiled down it gets very salty, and after three weeks of a diet of this kind the prisoner will commence to get sick." [5]

Under Colonel Hoffman the prison fund was growing by leaps and bounds. Not only did the fund save money by selling rations back to the commissary, but it also collected money belonging to deceased prisoners and a 3½ cent sales tax on any money made by the sutler. The money from this fund could be used to purchase materials for the prison camps that were not provided by the War Department. Although Elmira existed only a year, the prison camp fund amounted to $239,857. Fifty-eight thousand dollars remained unspent at the end of the war and was returned to the Federal Government. The prisoners of Elmira could have certainly used this money to stave off death by buying extra food and clothing. If Northern officials were doing all they could to prevent prison deaths, why wasn't this money used to

A straw watch chain made by prisoners and sold at the prison market. *Photograph courtesy of the Chemung County Historical Society.*

help these prisoners? To carry this idea a step further, $1,845,126 remained in the collective Prison Fund from all the Northern prisons at the end of the war. [6] Why on earth was this money unspent? Who knows how many prisoner's lives could have been spared by releasing the money in the prison fund. It was after all, their money not the governments. The main reason this money was not spent to aid the prisoners is because Colonel Hoffman tightly held the purse strings. Was Hoffman's motivation to show the government what an excellent job he was doing by returning a large portion of the money, or was his cost-cutting measures really designed to further his retaliation against the Confederates?

In a November 14, 1864, report Medical Inspector Surgeon William Sloan said when he asked the quartermaster about the lack of insulation for the prisoner's barracks at Elmira he was told, "I was informed that everything being referred to the Commissary General of Prisoners, (Colonel William Hoffman) the requisition of lining (insulation) the buildings to make them comfortable for the winter was disapproved and the stopping of cracks and open places ordered." Was this another case of Hoffman's being frugal or was it really retaliation in disguise by stopping up the cracks? Inspector Sloan goes on to say this was imperative because the barracks were "hastily erected of green lumber, which is cracking, splitting, and warping in every direction. An inside lining would prevent the access of cold winds, snow, and rain." Sloan pointed out that the barracks at Elmira needed this insulation as it was currently being ravaged by pneumonia and scurvy. [7]

Escapes From Elmira Prison Camp

All soldiers know that one of their first duties as prisoners of war is to try and escape.[1] Since this knowledge is so well known it is remarkable that only seventeen men managed to breakout of Elmira prisoner of war camp during the twelve months of its existence. The lack of successful escapes wasn't for a lack of trying. Many captive soldiers attempted this feat, but few succeeded. The reason for this can be attributed to several factors. The first of these is that these men were on half rations and many of them were too sick or in the hospital to try and escape. These prisoners needed to conserve their energy just to survive the harsh day-to-day existence that prison life entails. They could not dig hundred-foot escape tunnels because they did not possess the physical stamina for such a demanding task. Another reason for the lack of escape attempts was the fact that five months out of the year, Elmira prison camp has the coldest weather of all northern prisons and digging in the frozen ground was impossible. An added component was the vigilance of the guards. Elmira had a famous spy by the name of Sergeant Melvin M. Conklin whose chief employment was that of secret police or detective. However, Conklin was aided by a network of spies known as Confederate "oath takers" who in hopes of being released early reported their fellow prisoners for digging tunnels. Conklin went about the camp in all sorts of disguise, often pretending to be a Confederate prisoner to find out any plans to escape. This man was so successful at ferreting out tunnels that he discovered every single one except for the big one on October 7th which allowed ten prisoners to escape.

Union spy Lieutenant Melvin Conklin *Photograph courtesy of the Chemung County Historical Society.*

After the war Conklin was interviewed by author Clay Homes in 1912 when he was writing his famous book titled, *The Elmira Prison Camp*. "The first tunnel I found was started under Hospital No. 1," Conklin recalled. "The men worked nights. In the daytime they covered up the hole with boards and put sod on top. I found it and reported it. My orders were to let the men dig." Conklin checked the hole every day and dropped into the tunnel to see how it was progressing.[2] When it was near completion extra guards were assigned to watch the area where it was expected to come out. "The night they chose for escape happened to be a bright moonlit night. When they broke through and the first "Johnnie" stuck his head up he discovered, much to his surprise, that he was right in the midst of the guard camp, with a dozen guards looking right at him." The prisoner disappeared down the hole, but before he could get back to the entrance with his companions, Conklin and the guards were waiting for them.[3]

Sergeant Conklin remembered that some of the prisoners were quite ingenious in their tunnels. He recalled that, "The occupants of one tent built the chimney at the rear of the tent and tunneled down from inside the chimney. This one was directed northward and would have come out very near where Ed Warner's grocery now stands near Hoffman Creek. There were two started in the tents on the flat near the fence, next to the river, and two started in the barracks next to the east fence, about halfway between Water Street and the pond. There were twenty-eight in all. Most of the tunneling was on the east side of the camp, and someone was digging nearly all the time during the fall of 1864. All being discovered, they finally became discouraged, and none were attempted after November."[4]

The first escape occurred shortly after Elmira prison camp opened its gates. The initial group of prisoners to arrive at Elmira on July 6th tested their new home the next day by planning an escape.

Privates Charles D. Slack and Edwin James of Company G, 7th Louisiana Infantry, escaped on the night of July 8th by successfully scaling a fence. Slack was recaptured in Newport, PA, and taken back to the stockade in chains. James eluded his pursuers and made his way back to Dixie.[5]

The next prison break was October 7th and involved ten men tunneling out of the prison. This escape is perhaps the single most remarkable story of Elmira prison camp. Fortunately, six of the men who participated in the escape left written accounts of their harrowing exploits. Sergeant Berry Benson of the 1st South Carolina infantry and Private John Fox Maull of the Jeff Davis Artillery, have written accounts so fascinating that they seem to take the reader along with them as they dig the tunnel. Their efforts become so real that you practically cringe when the men are nearly discovered, and you want to cheer when they reach the fence and finally make their escape to freedom![6]

Their story begins when Private John F. Maull is transferred to Elmira from Point Lookout on August 15, 1864. As luck would have it Maull was assigned to occupy an A-frame tent near the prison's fence. He quickly explained his plan to escape to his tent mates, but only J. P. Putegnat liked his idea and thought it had a chance to succeed. Since the rest of his tent mates were not on board with his plan, the

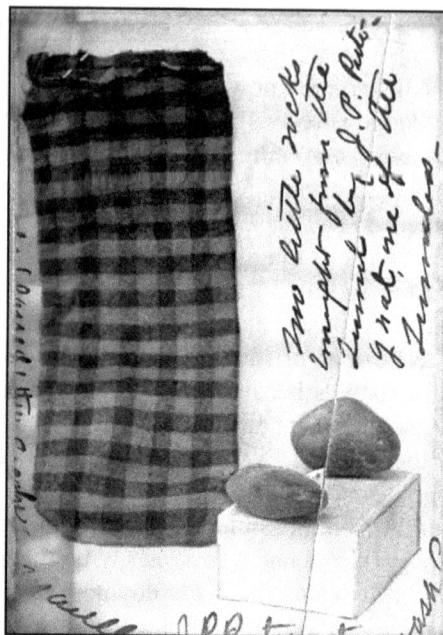

Elmira prisoner Putegnat made some bags to carry dirt from an extra shirt. *Photograph courtesy of the Chemung County Historical Society.*

two men needed to move to a vacant tent. However, they had to get the Ward Sergeant to agree to remove them both from the tent, so they pretended to have a fight with the others and then moved angrily out. At this time Private Washington B. Traweek of South Carolina joined the two men. Traweek was a valuable addition since he was a daring man who never seemed to tire no matter how much work he did. With their hands on a bible the men took a solemn oath pledging their "sacred honor that if betrayed we would follow the betrayer and knife him, that if caught at work by any of the prisoners, the discoverer must join us or die."[7]

On August 24th the men stole a spade from a contractor that was constructing trenches for the prison camp's streets and began digging their tunnel at nine o'clock that evening. "We were all young and ambitious," Maull would write later, "and we thought we could dig our way out in four or five days, but soon discovered it was no easy task."[8] They dug a round hole three feet in diameter, carefully removed the sod, and dug down until the hole would hide the digger's head when sitting down. Another man laid planks across the hole and sat on the wood until the dirt needed to be taken from the digger below. A candle was used to illuminate the tunnel where the men were working. They discovered the shovel made too much noise when it scraped against rocks, so the prisoners chose to dig with a knife. This pocketknife was later exchanged for a stronger 12-inch knife made from a file. The next problem was how to hide the dirt. This was solved when J. P. Putegnat donated his extra shirt to make bags to haul away the dirt.

While the others were in the tunnel, a man wearing a special jacket and cape carried the bags of dirt outside. His coat had a slit on either side where two or three-pint sized bags could be hidden in the pockets. The bags were then emptied of their contents in the street. Imagine the men's horror the next morning when it was discovered the fresh dirt was a different color than that in the street! Fortunately, no one noticed and future bags were emptied in Foster's pond.[9]

One day as Traweek was emptying rocks from his pocket, a fellow prisoner came up to him and said, "You'd better take care of yourself."

Surprised, Traweek asked him what he meant.

"I saw you put the stones in the water." Sergeant Berry Benson replied.

Traweek shrugged his shoulders and told him, "Well, there's no harm in that, is there?"

Benson shook his head, and said, "No if you were not digging a tunnel. No man would take such pains if you were not digging a tunnel. Here, I'll stand between you and the crowd. Empty your pockets."

Without another word, he got rid of all his stones; then rising Traweek said, "Walk with me a little way."[10]

Traweek finally admitted, "We're all bound by an oath not to tell it nor hint of it to the dearest friend, but you've found it out without my telling it, and now, if you want to join us, I've no doubt the boys will all be willing enough to take you in."[11] The man, Sergeant Berry Benson of the first Regiment South Carolina infantry, said that he would. Benson proved to be one of the best men in the group. He was always ready to work and had excellent ideas to improve the men's efforts in digging the tunnel. "One of his first suggestions was there was too much crawling to get out a little dirt, which could be saved by getting a box with a cord in each end, so it could be pulled into the digger, and pulled back when full. We got the box, attached two long cords to it, and put it to use. It was a great success, saving much time and crawling back-and-forth."[12]

Berry Benson recalled that he had a unique way to get rid of stones. "A favorite place to deposit stones was in rat holes. I would sit by a rat hole and drop the stones in until I could see the top of his stones, then move to another hole. The next day it could be filled again, for during the night the rats would move all the stones away in order to get in and out of their holes."[13]

One would think the best time to dig would be at night, but this was not the case. The best time was between dusk

The only successful tunnel escape from Elmira Prison camp was accomplished by Sharpshooter Sergeant Berry Benson and six other prisoners. *Photograph courtesy of the Chemung County Historical Society.*

and eight o'clock. This was when men were walking about, and activity was at its peak. A silence would settle over the prison after lights out and any little sound could be easily detected. Another good time to dig was during the day because everybody was up and creating noise that would drown out any sounds coming from the tunnel. To keep their clothing from getting covered with fresh dirt and attracting attention, the men turned their clothes inside out and worked in them that way. When a man was finished for the day, he reversed the process and exposed the clean side.[14]

In his book, Sergeant Berry Benson eloquently described what it was like working in the tunnel. "After the blankets and dried grass were removed and the planks taken up, you got into the vertical section of the shaft. Then on hands and knees you crawled into the tunnel and lay flat. Beyond the first body length, the tunnel decreased in size until it was only large enough to admit the body, and in some places, it was a squeeze at that. Thus, only the toes and the points of the elbows were used in propelling yourself forward. Having got to the end of the tunnel, your body blocking the way behind and leaving the least bit of air in front to breathe, you began to dig with a butcher knife. In less than a minute you were panting like a dog for air. A minute was enough to give you the most violent, racking headache, and you knew perfectly well in entering the tunnel that you had this to expect."[15]

The longer the tunnel became the more difficult it was to breath because of the lack of proper ventilation. The digger then crawled forward and resumed digging, meanwhile fighting against suffocation. After an hour of this, the man, his hand sore from scrapping with the knife and his head groggy from breathing "poisoned air", would call over his shoulder, "Back out!" The two men would crawl backward until they reached the entrance, stood and exited the shaft, gasping for air. After the exhausted men left the hole, a fresh team dropped down the shaft and crawled out of sight.[16]

About this time John F. Maull got sick from lack of air in the tunnel which became so fouled every day that a candle would not burn. "It was torture to all, and used me up completely, so that I could do no work inside. The dust created in digging, and the lack of air so affected my lungs, but I was useless for inside work, and I suggested taking in two fresh men from our artillery company, George Jackson, and William Templin, both good and tried men. They accepted and took the oath. From this time, I did little but carry away dirt and rocks."[17]

The men had been excavating the tunnel for nearly a month now and found the work was much harder than anticipated. So much so, they decided to take on another member. J. P. Putegnat suggested S. Cecrops Malone, one of his friends from the 9th Alabama. Everyone agreed so he took the oath and was added to the group.

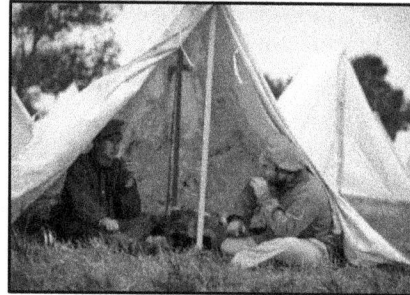

One day a surprise inspection was announced. The men were terrified because they had two men in the tunnel digging at that moment. They quickly placed the planks in the hole, back filled it with dirt, placed sod on top along with a layer of dried grass, and finally covered it with a blanket that would serve as a bed. Agonizing minutes turned into hours as the men waited for the guards to search their tent. While standing at attention in front of their tent, Maull and Putegnat would glance nervously behind them, praying the two men in the tunnel would remain quiet and not try to come out of the hole. Finally, a guard entered their tent and began moving things around and stamping on the ground to see if there was a weakness in the sod that might reveal a hidden

Prisoners seeking a bit of shade from the hot sun.

tunnel. Finding nothing, the guard left and continued to the next tent. A shaken Maull remembered, "We were badly frightened by this sudden (inspection) and decided it would be safer if we had our Orderly Sergeant on our side to keep us posted. He was a good man, from South Carolina named Brawley. He did us good service by keeping us advised about everything, but he did not work on the tunnel on account of a sore arm, through a bad vaccination."[18]

As work on the tunnel progressed the men grew weary from the demanding excavation and the progress slowed. It was then decided that the men doing the hardest work needed more food. The problem was solved by taking in J. P. Scruggs, who was a "sick sergeant". Scruggs routinely ordered and delivered food to the men of his company who were too ill to walk to the mess hall. He would go to kitchen and claimed he was getting food for sick prisoners in their tents. "He brought us two water buckets full of soup and plenty of fresh bread every day, which gave us renewed strength and put us in fine shape for hard work."[19]

The length of the tunnel was measured with a string and compared with the estimated distance of sixty-eight feet to the camp's northern fence. It was found that the tunnel should be within three feet of the fence. But the men who worked at the end of the tunnel could hear the footsteps of the guards making their rounds just inside the fence. The guards did not appear to pass overhead but some distance away. To find where the end of the tunnel was, Benson suggested that someone should stand where he thinks the end of the tunnel is and make some noise. This way the man in the tunnel could tell if he was left or right of where the noise was. It was decided to get a piece of tin and strike it with a rock on the pretext of making a spoon. Prisoners were hammering on pieces of tin all the time trying to make trinkets and fashioning tableware for the messhall, so it was thought this would not arouse the guard's suspicions.[20]

Four men went outside and walked over to where they thought the tunnel should end. They took turns banging on the piece of tin, using a stone as a hammer. Pretty soon word came to them from the man in the tunnel that they were to move six feet to the right. He'd move to the spot indicated and start banging on the tin again. After several more adjustments, the man banging on the spoon stood over the end of the tunnel. Word came to him that he was to halt right there and mark that location with a several stones.[21]

To the men's surprise the tunnel veered to the right about fifteen feet from where it should have been. At first the men were perplexed by this, but then Benson suggested that since the men were all right-handed, this could've caused the tunnel to shift its course to the right. From then on, the men had a rifle ramrod in the excavation and every so often they would poke it through the ceiling. Other men would be watching for it. When they saw the ramrod poke up through the grass they would hurry over and step on it, marking that spot with a distinctive stone. The word was then passed to the man in the tunnel if he needed to go right or left to go in the direction of the fence.

Benson suggested they enlarge the ramrod hole to let more air into the tunnel. This was done, and it was widened to a width of three fingers. An enlarged chamber was also dug out where a man could sit up and catch his breath before continuing. This part of the tunnel was called the ventilator and was very important because the longer the tunnel became the more difficult it was to breathe.[22]

Major Colt arrested Washington Traweek for digging a tunnel. *Photograph courtesy of the Chemung County Historical Society.*

One day an order came from Major Colt for Traweek to report to headquarters. Supposing that he had gotten a letter containing money or a box from home, he went to retrieve it. When Traweek didn't return to the tent the other men became worried. Finally, the Orderly Sergeant went to inquire. He came back with the news that Traweek was not only in the guard house but locked up in a cell under close confinement! The rest of the men were sure their plot had been discovered and that they would all be arrested and thrown in jail. They figured that Traweek was a good man and had given his solemn oath not to tell on the others, but who knew what cruel ways the Yankees would use to make him talk. Meanwhile Traweek wondered who had betrayed him. It was then he remembered talking with some friends and unwisely bragging about his part in digging tunnels. A prisoner, who volunteered to take the Oath of Allegiance to the Union, overheard his remarks and reported him.

"Well, lad," Major Colt said, "you are a tunneller I suppose." Traweek replied that he did not know what the major meant that he was a tunneller. Major Colt told him that he had ways to make him talk. The major then asked Traweek again who his partners were.

"When I answered that I did not know, he ordered me placed in a straight jacket. I was bound down and the pressure applied. For possibly a minute the breath was squeezed nearly out of my body, and the agony was fierce. I was released in a few minutes and again asked to tell names. "I said, "Major Colt, you are a coward and no soldier, and I will see you in hell before I will tell you a thing."[23]

About that time an officer standing near the room walked forward and said to Major Colt, "You let this boy come with me and I am sure he will tell me everything he knows." The officer, Captain Bennett Munger, questioned Traweek about the tunnel. As they spoke, Traweek learned that Munger taught Sunday school at the same church that he went to. This made for a pleasant conversation until the captain asked Traweek to tell him about the tunnel and who his friends were. Traweek finally persuaded Bennett that he did not know the names of the others because it was dark, and he couldn't see anyone distinctly. The only name that he was aware of was a man named Jim. This of course was a figment of Traweek's imagination as he would never reveal anything about the others.[24]

Captain Munger went back to Major Colt with the story, and Traweek was ordered to be held in close confinement in the guardhouse. During the Civil War "close confinement" is described as being in solitary confinement on bread and water.

Three weeks after his arrest Major Colt sent word that he would release Traweek if he would give his honor not to try to escape from prison again. Traweek sent back word and thanked him, but he could not in justice to himself make such a promise, for if an opportunity to escape should present itself, he would feel bound to take advantage of it. To this the Major replied, "Oh, very well! There is no other tunnel going on that I'm aware of, and it's hardly probable that you'll break down the fence."[25]

The longer the tunnel became the more men were required; one man was needed to dig, one man rested in the ventilator catching his breath, one in the shaft and one to stand at the door and keep anybody from coming into the tent. At least one other man was required to dispose of bags of dirt and stones.

Two days before the escape the prisoners knew they were near the fence because they could hear the guards walking their post. The men worked steadily and planned their escape for 10 o'clock on the night of the sixth.

On the day of their escape, the men gathered everything they would need to take with them. For Benson this was two pocketknives, half a mess kit to cook in, a few matches, a pencil map that he had drawn of the area, a pocket compass, and a strong cord to serve as a bridle on the chance he could steal a horse.

It was soon discovered that a little more work in the tunnel needed to be done than expected. By 10 o'clock the men had still not reached the fence. In the tunnel Benson was hastily digging with his knife and the box with the dirt slid back and forth. It was decided to leave the dirt in the tent that night because it didn't need to be hidden anymore. Benson could stand the suffocation no longer, making it necessary for both him and Traweek to back out of the tunnel and change places.

The next section I am quoting directly from Benson's book because I want to convey the unbelievable tension that he experienced. "In the tent I was eagerly listening to the faint sounds from the tunnel, low whispers, a grasp on a fellow's arm to any sound from without. In all hearts were hope, fear, and anxiety, as long as the box slid back-and-forth and the knife pegged away."

"Fighting suffocation all the while, I became wretchedly sick, with a violent headache and nausea, and so did Traweek. Once as I crawled back to the ventilator, the roof of the tunnel broke in, quantities of dirt and stone falling on my legs. I called quietly to the shaft-man, who came and removed the dirt. This consumed so much time. It was now past midnight."

"Once as I occupied the ventilator, I worked my hand up and widened the hole a little, to admit more air. This could do no harm now, it being the last night. Traweek called, 'Benson, let's change; I can't stand it any longer.'"

"This time, instead of inching slowly backward the length of the tunnel, I squeezed my back against one side of the ventilator, saying, 'Traweek, see if we can't pass one another here.' Down he came slowly, first his feet in my face, then further and further, while I jammed myself against the side of the tunnel. Now we were face-to-face. I tried to move forward but could not. He tried to move down, and he could not. We couldn't move either way—we were wedged! We had begun to think we had made an end of it, when a desperate effort set us free, and I went to digging, he to the ventilator."

"And now as I plied my knife, my head seemed on the point of bursting. My mouth wide open, tongue protruding, panting like a dog, I felt the lack of breath not in my lungs only, in my whole body. With every beat of my heart, great throbs of pain coursed through me. Having stood it as long as I could, I was relieved by Traweek, we were passing one another more easily at the ventilator this time."

"During his turn at digging, Traweek called softly, "Benson, I've struck a fence post!"

"Good!' I whispered back, for this meant that our digging was near an end. Taking my turn, I worked to the right around the post, until I knew the end of the tunnel was outside the fence. Feeling that I was dying for air, I reached out my hand and worked it through the pebbly soil, which came raining down in my face—my eyes shut, for of what use are eyes in the tunnel? I felt cold air on my fingers, and withdrew my arm, the cold stream following. I lay on my back, enjoying that feast of air, that luxury of breath. Then I crawled back and sent Traweek up to get his share of it."

"Pretty soon we had hollowed out all but a thin shell on top, and our last work was to dig a hole under that for the dirt to drop into when the break was made. Then Traweek and I went out and announced the tunnel was ready, and the boys began gathering up what they needed to take with them."
26

It was agreed that everyone should leave in the order that they had joined the group. The men could not go all at once because of the lack of air in the tunnel, so it was decided that they would go in groups of two. The first couple of men, Washington B. Traweek and James W. Crawford, eagerly climbed into the hole and disappeared down the shaft. The others were required to wait for ten minutes to allow the first group time to exit the tunnel. Next John F. Maull and J. P. Scruggs lowered themselves into the tunnel. Ten minutes later they were followed by S. Cecrops Malone and J. P. Putegnat. Webster was too sick to leave with the others, Sergeant Brawley, with his bad arm from his vaccination, thought he stood a good chance of exchange, so he decided to stay.

Prisoners's Tunnel Entrance.

While all of this was going on Benson, still groggy and lightheaded from lack of air, could no longer stand on his feet and lowered himself to the ground. "I lay down, to get some ease for my head, which almost crazed me. Directly I fell into sort of a doze, only half conscious of what was going on in the tent. I was suffering such pain in my head that I didn't care whether I went or stayed."

Waking up a few minutes later Benson found all the others had gone before him except for Glenn Shelton and his partner. Shelton was convinced he could still hear the others in the tunnel, and they had not left yet. Benson told him that was impossible, and he would prove it by going first and calling back to him that the way was clear. Shelton agreed and Benson crawled into the tunnel. After several minutes Benson found he was all alone in the tunnel and called back to Shelton and his partner that the way was clear for them to escape.[27]

Benson raised his head through the tunnel's opening and looked around. Across the street were three sentinels with rifles sitting around a fire. He crawled out and went along close to the fence. From the platform above Benson could hear the sentinels tramping above his head and got down on his hands and knees so he could move more quickly. As he neared the street, Benson rose to his feet and walked away rapidly, "I felt every moment that I would hear a shot and feel a bullet pierce my back. But there was no shot and no challenge."

Reaching the other side of the street, Benson walked down the pavement and then jumped into a yard and ran behind the house where a dog barked and growled at him. He quickly jumped the back fence and fled towards the mountains.[28]

Nine of the ten men made their way back South.

The October tunnel escape is perhaps the single most remarkable story of Elmira prison camp. The men's escape from prison is even more miraculous when it is considered that ten prisoners needed to work in absolute secrecy for seven weeks in an overcrowded environment. Not only that, but they had to overcome terrific obstacles in digging the tunnel such as cave-ins, lack of air and choking dust. Each time the men encountered a seemingly insurmountable problem they did not give up but worked to solve it and continue toward their ultimate goal of freedom!

One of the more humorous escapes occurred in November 1864, and involved a prisoner named Jimmie Jones. Jones earned the nickname buttons because he wore so many shiny brass buttons on his bluecoat that he appeared to glow in the dark. Jones convinced the prison doctors that he was infected with smallpox and was immediately transferred to the hospital for that disease far away from the other prisoner's barracks. This was also near the dead house where his friend and fellow prisoner F. S. Wade worked. Jones snuck unobserved to the dead house, wrapped himself in a blanket and climbed into one of the coffins. His friend later discovered him, and Jones revealed his plan along with a bribe. Buttons handed him a small package of flour and told him, "Sprinkle my face and hands with flour, then fasten the coffin lid slightly down, and when the dead wagon comes around, be sure to put my coffin on top of the other dead."

Sometime later the dead wagon came by for another load of bodies to take to the cemetery. Wade carefully loaded it as instructed and sent the wagon on its way. Jones waited inside the casket, listening until the creaking wagon was far enough from the prison before attempting to surprise the driver. Wanting to play the part of a dead body coming to life, Jones began knocking on the coffin lid. When this failed to draw the driver attention, he opened the lid and sat up, calling in a scary voice, "Come to judgment." The startled Negro driver turned around and saw the ghostly white, cadaver sitting up in his casket. This was more than the wide-eyed black man could take. He threw down the reins and leapt from the moving wagon, yelling, "Ghosties! Ghosties!" With shaking arms raised to the heavens, he ran to the safety of the nearest woods.[29]

The Fort Fisher Prisoners

One of the most tragic events in the history of Elmira was set in motion when 1,128 Confederate prisoners arrived in late January from Fort Fisher, North Carolina. These men had endured great suffering during two battles barely three weeks apart. These Confederate soldiers withstood a tremendous bombardment by the largest federal fleet to sail until D-Day in World War II. This fleet contained 58 Warships mounting 644 cannons, unleashing more than 30,000 shot and shell in three days. These guns ranged in size from 6" Dahlgren's and Brookes rifles to monstrous 15" smooth bore Dahlgrens cannon on five ironclad-monitors.[1]

The reason I am mentioning the Fort Fisher prisoners here is to dispute something that was

Harper's Weekly drawing of Federal Infantry assaulting Fort Fisher, North Carolina.

written in *The Medical and Surgical History of the War of the Rebellion, (1861-65)*. The statement I am referring to was made by an inspector who was trying to explain the large loss of life at Elmira Prison Camp. This inspector wrote, "This is due to the broken-down condition of the prisoners on their arrival."[2] Let's examine the statement he made. In the instance of the Fort Fisher prisoners, I am sure that these men were not "broken-down." I speak from authority because I have written a book titled *Fort Fisher to Elmira*. This book not only describes the battle, but the prisoner's experience at Elmira Prison Camp. During my research for this book, I had examined the Fort Fisher soldiers under the discerning eye of a writer. The soldiers at Fort Fisher, North Carolina, were garrison troops. Yes, they received the standard Confederate rations like everybody else. However, the fort was surrounded on three sides by water. Two of these bodies of water were the Atlantic Ocean and the third was the Cape Fear River. This being the case, the soldiers at the fort were able to supplement their diet with fresh fish and oysters. Colonel Lamb regularly detailed men who had had previously worked as fishermen to go out in boats and catch fish for the garrison. The fort also had its own vegetable garden tended by the soldiers. As a result, these men were extremely well fed for Confederate troops. As for being rundown, these men slept in wooden barracks every night. They were not marching hundreds of miles in a campaign and eating meager rations. These soldiers were in the best of health up until the moment they became prisoners.

Now let's examine how these men fared at Elmira and Point Lookout Prison Camps. During January and February 1,128 Fort Fisher prisoners were sent to the prison at Elmira and 643 prisoners entered Point Lookout, Maryland. Of the soldiers who went to Elmira 528 men died from disease within five months of captivity. Of the 643 soldiers who went to Point Lookout only 58 died.[3] Both groups of men had the same diet and experience before being captured. What made this huge difference?

Obviously, it was the men's prison environment and diet. A clear majority of the men who died at Elmira succumbed to chronic diarrhea. This was due to overcrowding of the prison which led to water pollution. The second deadliest disease for the Fort Fisher soldiers was pneumonia. These men went north to prison the last week in January. This is the coldest month of the year in upstate New York. "The condition of the patients is pitiable," a federal inspector wrote. "The diseases are nearly all of the typhoid type, and much of the sickness is justly attributable to crowd-poisoning. In addition to this the clothing during the winter was insufficient." The inspector goes on to say, "The Fort Fisher prisoners, especially, arrived in cold weather very much depressed, poorly clad, and great numbers were soon taken sick with pneumonia and diarrhea, rapidly assuming a typhoid character."[4]

It is a known fact that the Union prison system reduced rations several times during the war. When the Fort Fisher prisoners arrived in January 1865, the men were eating approximately one half the original ration and their meager diet often lacked vegetables. It is known that chronic diarrhea depletes the men's bodies of vital nutrients and electrolytes needed to maintain a normal heartbeat and blood pressure. Unfortunately, this severe diet did nothing to relieve their suffering and made it worse. Is it any wonder why the prisoners died at such a terrific rate?

A sea of tents housing 5,000 Elmira prisoners dominates this photo but also shows the hills surrounding the camp were practically barren of trees and thus facilitated the prison camp's flooding. This clear-cutting of timber was a result of the prison needing lumber to build more barracks and provided firewood for the camp's stoves. When the 2 ½ feet of winter snow melted in March 1865 the lack of vegetation allowed the spring thaw to cause the Chemung River to overflow its banks and flood the prison. *Photograph courtesy of the Chemung County Historical Society.*

Elmira Prison Camp Flood

The extreme weather for the years 1864-65 made headlines in the newspapers of New York State. The area suffered under a severe summertime drought that wilted fruits and vegetables and affected the cattle that were sold to Elmira prison camp. Scurvy patients at the prison hospital suffered the most because the dry weather also made it difficult to obtain fresh onions, potatoes, etc. Farmers did not have enough grass to fatten their cattle and found it necessary to sell their stock before they became too weakened and died from lack of food. Elmira farmer Roswell R. Moss said, "In the summer of 1864 there was a severe drought; hay and grain crops were almost nothing, and pastures dried up. Because there was no feed, father sold a number of young cattle that otherwise he would have kept for a year or two longer."[1]

Captain Benjamin Munger's inspection report of December 4, 1864, confirmed this by saying, "The beef is very lean. Cows milked through the summer and too poor for a respectable farmer to winter are slaughtered and the beef issued to the prisoners."[2]

Colonel Tracy issued controversial Special Order No. 336 on October 3rd because he thought that the government was being cheated because the prison's shipments of beef were consistently underweight. This order declared the prison camp's beef would be inspected by Colonel S. Moore and Major Henry Colt and if it did not meet the government contract specifications it would be rejected as being inferior.[82] The consequence of this order was that the prisoners did not receive any meat for three or four days. String enough of these rejected shipments of beef together and the prisoners would be forced to subsist on a bread and water diet. Certainly, this matter could have been resolved without making the prisoners suffer unnecessarily. Any amount of beef in a prisoner's diet would have been preferable to having none.

The next big weather event happened October 10th when an Arctic blast of cold air brought four inches of snow to the Chemung Valley. Heavy snow fell throughout the winter and temperatures plunged to 18 degrees below zero. It was so cold that from January 1st through the first week of March that the thermometer seldom got far above zero.[3]

Frigid winter winds gave way to warmer temperatures on the 14th of March, melting the two-and-a-half-foot blanket of snow in New York. Freshets of water ran down the hills around Elmira and drained into the Chemung River, turning the normally slow body of water into a raging torrent that threatened to overflow its banks. Normally this was not a problem because these hills were heavily forested, and the dense canopy of trees held in the cooler temperatures, which kept the snow from melting too quickly. The water that gathered would be held in place and consumed by the rich vegetation. On arriving at Elmira prisoner Anthony M. Keiley wrote, "The whole site is a basin surrounded by hills which rise several hundred feet and are covered richly and thickly with the luxurious foliage of the hemlock, ash, poplar, and pine." However, this was not a typical winter because these hills were largely denuded of trees to provide lumber to build the prison camp. What trees had not been cut down during the summer months were harvested that autumn to provide fuel for the stoves of Elmira prison camp to combat the frigid winter weather. Thus, there were no trees to keep the snow from melting and very little vegetation to provide a barrier against the water draining down from the hills.[4] Many consider this terrible flood to be an act of nature, but man helped it to become the epic disaster that it was by removing the only natural obstacle to flowing water there was.

On the morning of March 15th, the river reached flood stage and began to overflow its banks; the muddy water continued to get higher, reaching the edge of the stockade. Being worried about the rising water, Colonel Tracy held an emergency meeting with the other prison officers at 9 PM that evening. The smallpox hospital was located on lower ground close to the river, so it was decided to evacuate the 300 sick prisoners to land farthest away from the rising water. A dozen men under Major Norton were assigned to build several large rafts from two-inch planks to ferry the sick men from the hospital. The construction of the flat boats was finished by morning and the process of rescuing the prisoners got underway.[5]

It was soon discovered that the large, unwieldy rafts became unmanageable in the strong current. The men secured two ropes and tied one to the front and the other to the rear of the rafts. Teams of prisoners worked in relays allowing the raft to drift toward the hospital, where it was loaded with prisoners, and then pulled it back again. It was reported the men became so exhausted from their labors that as soon they accomplished their task each one was given a cup of whiskey.[6]

A few hours after the smallpox hospital was evacuated, the water continued to rise until it reached every building in the prison. Former prisoner John R. King remembered, "We were surrounded by a wilderness of water. A great part of the prison wall was gone, and we could see about half of the cookhouse extending above the water."[7] The water not only covered the prison camp, but had crossed Water Street, flooding the camp of the 19th Veteran Reserve Corps.[8]

The prison barracks were built on stilts several feet off the ground to discourage the prisoners from digging tunnels to escape. Now the water had submerged the stilts, entered the barracks, and covered the lower bunks, forcing the men to climb up to the second or third tier of bunks. The near freezing water crested at four feet above the barrack floor. The men remained in the upper bunks for two days and were visited by soldiers in rowboats several times a day to bring them something to eat. King remarked, "Men came into our wards through doors in rowboats, passing near where we were roosting. They gave us something to eat. My, but it tasted good!"[9]

The flood's high-water mark was reached when it overflowed the river's 20-foot slope, engulfing the prison camp and invading the appropriately named Water Street. The morning of the 17th the muddy waters began to recede, revealing what damage had been done to the prison camp. Twenty-seven-hundred feet of the stockade's fence had been washed away requiring the guards to stand watch until it could be repaired. Several of the older barracks were so badly damaged by the flood that they were no longer safe to occupy and needed to be destroyed. Other buildings had stairs ripped off, boards loosened or swept away completely. All the buildings were coated with several inches of foul-smelling mud and dead fish and eels were scattered everywhere.

The Elmira Daily Advertiser urged its readers to use caution when looking for firewood and items from the flood ravaged prison. Some of the objects had been contaminated by the smallpox virus which remained viable for up to eighteen months. "Several tents and the flooring of the board barracks occupied last winter, for the rebels having smallpox, passed down the river yesterday, and everybody therefore along the river looking after flood wood and refuse should handle these articles gingerly."[10]

Camp Douglas barracks on stilts were similar to the ones built at Elmira. Barracks on stilts allowed guards to observe any escape tunnels being dug and greatly helped to eliminate them.

There is some confusion as to the loss of life due to the flood. In his March 21, 1865, report to General William Hoffman, Colonel Tracy says his command responded to the flood and "accomplished (their task) with great promptness; with no escape of prisoners, and what is still more remarkable with but slightly increased loss of life."[11] Tracy statement concerning loss of life is rather vague because it never gave exact numbers. You would think that four days after the tragedy that Tracy would've conducted a roll call to see who was still among the prisoners. When Prisoner John R. King waded out to the pump near the dead house to get some water, he made a gruesome discovery. "On the way to the pump I noticed several old blankets near my feet. Looking closer I discovered a number of dead men concealed under them. The high water had prevented the people from taking them to the graveyard."[12] It is assumed these men were washed out from the dead house, but they could have also been victims of the flood. Prisoner James Huffman recalled, "The sick were taken out in boats and a great many died before they returned."[13] However, Lieutenant James R. Reid conducted an inspection of the prison camp and noted that the flood caused but "slight increase of mortality among patients."[14] One prison guard is reported to have said "effects of the flood were plainly visible upon the health of the men for some time"[15] Certainly moving so many deathly ill prisoners had a consequence. We know from the Official Records that the March death total was the highest month in Elmira's history with 491 deaths.[16] However, we will never know how many of these deaths were caused by the flood.

Prisoner Exchanges Resume

At the end of January 1865 Robert Ould, agent of exchange for the Confederate Government, contacted Lieutenant General Ulysses S. Grant and proposed a resumption of the prisoner exchange. Ould pointed out that Union prisoners were suffering greatly because of the inability of the Confederacy to care for so many men. Grant, knowing the end of the war was in sight, agreed to the exchange of prisoners beginning in February.[1] General Grant then informed Colonel Benjamin Tracy, the Elmira Prison commandant, to prepare 3000 prisoners of war to be exchanged in early February.[2]

After the tragedy of October 11, 1864, Tracy warned General William Hoffman against using the Northern Central Railroad. He reminded him about the ill-fated transfer of prisoners that fall where the transportation was provided by the Northern Central Railroad. The journey to Baltimore took 40 hours and resulted in five deaths with more than sixty men being hospitalized. Tracy suggested that it would be desirable to send the prisoners on the Erie Railroad to New York City and then on to Baltimore by either railroad or steamer. Tracy remarked that the Erie Railroad would have taken only fifteen hours and was the preferred method of travel.[3]

The next day the *Elmira Daily Advertiser* gave a vivid account of prisoners at the railway station.

The sick and disabled were removed in a long line of baggage wagons and stowed away in the cars comfortably as could be arranged for them. A few so ill to be unable to sit up were tenderly cared for by the hospital ambulance, in which they were carried to the train. There were many stout, healthy looking ones among the entire number, but as a general thing the sick and complaining who were able to be moved or travel were those selected for the first 500 exchanged. They looked hopeful even through the diseases under which many of them labored or were recovering from. The glad prospect of home once more, even in its devastation and desolation, seemed to light up the countenances of all, and the sick and weary took a fresh cling to life, that they might have strength to greet loved ones once more. The sight, if a sad one, best illustrated the effects and terrible results of a most unrighteous and unjust rebellion which they were the suffering victims. They were living testimonies of the suffering and losses for which the Southern leaders have made themselves accountable.[4]

On February 25th Colonel Tracy informed the Commissary General of Prisoners of a report on the transportation prisoners to Baltimore.

Headquarters Depot Prisoners of War, Elmira, N. Y., February 25, 1865. Respectfully returned to Commissary General of Prisoners with the following extracts from the report of Colonel Trotter, in charge of the detachment, as to transportation:

"The train left Elmira at 5 PM February 13th and reached Baltimore, via Northern Central Railroad at 10 AM February 15th, after many delays. During the night of February 14th neither water nor lights were provided for any car upon the train, as required by the terms of the contract, and three of the prisoners died from the continued exposure. The train consisted of seventeen cars, with only one brakeman for the entire number, to which ten or more cattle cars were added when the train left Williamsport. * * * I would beg leave to call attention to the indifference of the officials of the Northern Central Railroad, who paid not the least attention to repeated applications for lights for the cars, which I was finally compelled to purchase myself. Neither did they supply any water or fuel after the train left Elmira."[5]

Despite the warning from Colonel Tracy, Commissary General of Prisoners William Hoffman continued to use the Northern Central Railroad for the rest of the exchanges. The author found eighty-nine prisoners that died while being exchanged. Could some of these deaths have been prevented by using a more humane way to transport these men?

After the exchanges were completed in March the remaining prisoners would be released after taking the Oath of Allegiance. The last large release of over 2,500 men occurred June 30, 1865. The only prisoners that remained at Elmira Prison Camp were in the post hospital until they either recovered or died.

Woodlawn Cemetery Sextant John W. Jones

One of the men who profited from Elmira's war-time economic boom was the sextant of Woodlawn Cemetery. John W. Jones had been a slave in Leesburg, Virginia, and escaped along the Underground Railroad to Elmira, New York. Some might think that Jones was born under a lucky star, but it appears he made his own good fortune. Immediately after his arrival, this industrious man not only found himself a job, but enrolled in a school where he received an education. This helped him advance in his current position to that of sextant at Woodlawn Cemetery. The only part luck played in his story is the timing of Elmira prison opening its gates in June of 1864.

At the end of that month Commissary General of Prisoners Colonel William Hoffman approved spending $300 from the Prisoner Fund to purchase a half acre of land to bury deceased Confederate prisoners. Hoffman also authorize the purchase of a wagon to help the sextant transport the bodies for burial. Prison carpenters fashioned the pine coffins to have straight sides so six caskets could be loaded on the wagon at one time. Every morning the wagon would pick up the dead bodies from the prison morgue and deliver them to the cemetery. The government paid Jones $2.50 per burial for his services instead of the accepted rate of $40 per month. This proved to be greatly in his favor.

Former slave and Woodlawn Cemetery Sextant John W. Jones. *Photograph courtesy of the Chemung County Historical Society.*

To help Jones, twenty-eight Confederate prisoners were employed by the government to dig graves for the deceased. Jones services included directing where the graves were to be dug, collecting pertinent information such as—name, state, regiment, and date of death and transcribing this information inside the coffin's lid. He also wrote this information on a piece of paper, placed it in a bottle and tucked it under the arm of the deceased to be buried with him. Jones job wasn't through after the burial, however. He needed to make sure the headboards were straightly aligned, contained the correct information and were on the proper graves. This attention to detail caused former prisoner Marcus Toney to comment sarcastically, "(This) admirable system took care of the dead better than that bestowed on the living."[1]

The Confederate prisoners began to die so rapidly that Colonel Hoffman leased another 1/2 acre of land on January 1, 1865. Several years after the war had ended sextant Jones would comment, "The first day that I was called in my capacity of sextant to bury a prisoner who had died, I thought nothing of it. . . . Directly there were more dead. One day I had seven to bury. After that they began to die very fast." The most burials performed by Jones was forty-three in one day. The highest month of deaths occurred in March of 1865 where 491 men died from disease in prison.

During the year Elmira prison camp remained open, thirty-six trenches were dug containing 2,973 Confederate soldiers who had died at the prison in Elmira. At $2.50 per burial this amounted to $7,432.50 for Jones making him the wealthiest black man in the state.[2]

The Proclamation of Amnesty and Reconstruction

BY THE PRESIDENT OF THE UNITED STATES OF AMERICA:

A PROCLAMATION.

WHEREAS, in and by the Constitution of the United States, it is provided that the President "shall have power to grant reprieves and pardons for offences against the United States, except in cases of impeachment;" and

Whereas, a rebellion now exists whereby the loyal state governments of several states have for a long time been subverted, and many persons have committed, and are now guilty of, treason against the United States; and

Whereas, with reference to said rebellion and treason, laws have been enacted by congress, declaring forfeitures and confiscation of property and liberation of slaves, all upon terms and conditions therein stated, and **also declaring that the President was thereby authorized at any time thereafter, by proclamation, to extend to persons who may have participated in the existing rebellion, in any state or part thereof, pardon and amnesty, with such exceptions and at such times and on such conditions as he may deem expedient for the public welfare;** and

Whereas, the congressional declaration for limited and conditional pardon accords with well-established judicial exposition of the pardoning power; and

Whereas, with reference to said rebellion, the President of the United States has issued several proclamations, with provisions in regard to the liberation of slaves; and

Whereas, it is now desired by some persons heretofore engaged in said rebellion to resume their allegiance to the United States, and to reinaugurate loyal state governments within and for their respective states: Therefore–

I, ABRAHAM LINCOLN, President of the United States, do proclaim, declare, and make known to all persons who have, directly or by implication, participated in the existing rebellion, except as hereinafter excepted, that a full pardon is hereby granted to them and each of them, with restoration of all rights of property, except as to slaves, and in property cases where rights of third parties shall have intervened, and upon the condition that every such person shall take and subscribe an oath, and thenceforward keep and maintain said oath inviolate; and which oath shall be registered for permanent preservation, and shall be of the tenor and effect following, to wit:–

"I, ____ ____, do solemnly swear, in presence of Almighty God, that I will henceforth faithfully support, protect, and defend the Constitution of the United States and the Union of the States thereunder; and that I will, in like manner, abide by and faithfully support all acts of congress passed during the existing rebellion with reference to slaves, so long and so far as not repealed, modified, or held void by congress, or by decision of the supreme court; and that I will, in like manner, abide by and faithfully support all proclamations of the President made during the existing rebellion having reference to slaves, so long and so far as not modified or declared void by decision of the supreme court. So help me God."

The persons excepted from the benefits of the foregoing provisions are all who are, or shall have been, civil or diplomatic officers or agents of the so-called Confederate government; all who have left judicial stations under the United States to aid the rebellion; all who are, or shall have been, military or naval officers of said so-called Confederate government above the rank of colonel in the army or of lieutenant in the navy; all who left seats in the United States congress to aid the rebellion; all who resigned commissions in the army or navy of the United States and afterwards aided the rebellion; and all who have engaged in any way in treating colored persons, or white persons in charge of such, otherwise than lawfully as prisoners of war, and which persons may have been found in the United States service as soldiers, seamen, or in any other capacity.

And I do further proclaim, declare, and make known that whenever, in any of the States of Arkansas, Texas, Louisiana, Mississippi, Tennessee, Alabama, Georgia, Florida, South Carolina, and North Carolina, a number of persons, not less than one tenth in number of the votes cast in such state at the presidential election of the year of our Lord one thousand eight hundred and sixty, each having taken the oath aforesaid, and not having since violated it, and being a qualified voter by the election law of the state existing immediately before the so-called act of secession, and excluding all others, shall reëstablish a state government which shall be republican, and in nowise contravening said oath, such shall be recognized as the true government of the state, and the state shall receive thereunder the benefits of the constitutional provision which declares that "the United States shall guaranty to every state in this Union a republican form of government, and shall protect each of them against invasion; and on application of the legislature, or the executive, (when the legislature cannot be convened,) against domestic violence."

And I do further proclaim, declare, and make known that any provision which may be adopted by such state government in relation to the freed people of such state, which shall recognize and declare their permanent freedom, provide for their education, and which may yet be consistent as a temporary arrangement with their present condition as a laboring, landless, and homeless class, will not be objected to by the National Executive.

And it is suggested as not improper that, in constructing a loyal state government in any state, the name of the state, the boundary, the subdivisions, the constitution, and the general code of laws, as before the rebellion, be maintained, subject only to the modifications made necessary by the conditions hereinbefore stated, and such others, if any, not contravening said conditions, and which may be deemed expedient by those framing the new state government.

To avoid misunderstanding, it may be proper to say that this proclamation, so far as it relates to state governments, has no reference to states wherein loyal state governments have all the while been maintained. And, for the same reason, it may be proper to further say, that whether members sent to congress from any state shall be admitted to seats constitutionally rests exclusively with the respective houses, and not to any extent with the Executive. And still further, that this proclamation is intended to present the people of the states wherein the national authority has been suspended, and loyal state governments have been subverted, a mode in and by which the national authority and loyal state governments may be reëstablished within said states, or in any of them; and while the mode presented is the best the Executive can suggest, with his present impressions, it must not be understood that no other possible mode would be acceptable.

Given under my hand at the city of Washington the eighth day of December, A.D. one thousand eight hundred and sixty-three, and of the Independence of the United States of America the eighty-eighth.

ABRAHAM LINCOLN.

By the President:
WILLIAM H. SEWARD, *Secretary of State.*

Roster of Prisoners Volume I, A-F
July 6, 1864-July 5, 1865

All prisoners who died are buried in Woodlawn National Cemetery, Elmira, New York, unless otherwise noted.

Name & Rank	Age	Enlisted	Regiment and State	Where Captured	Prison	Remarks
Abbot, W. Private	Unk	September 22, 1862, Waynesville, Georgia	Co. G, 7th Georgia Cavalry	June 11, 1864, Trevilian Station, Louisa Court House, Virginia	Point Lookout, Maryland, transferred to Elmira Prison, NY July 25, 1864	Oath of Allegiance May 29, 1865
Abel, Charles T. Private	Unk	February 15, 1863, Fauquier, Virginia	Co. H, 4th Virginia Cavalry	September 14, 1863, Near Culpepper, Virginia	Point Lookout, Maryland, transferred to Elmira Prison, NY August 18, 1864	Died November 5, 1864 of Chronic Diarrhea, Grave No. 836
Abel, Jacob Private	Unk	September 26, 1862, Transferred from Wheat's Battalion, Louisiana	Co. G, 6th Louisiana Infantry	May 5, 1864, Wilderness, Virginia	Point Lookout, Maryland, transferred to Elmira Prison, NY August 17, 1864	Exchanged March 10, 1865 at Boulware's Wharf on the James River, Virginia
Abernathy, F. D. Private	Unk	February 10, 1864, Millford Station, Virginia	Co. B, 2nd North Carolina Cavalry	May 27, 1864, Hanover Junction, Virginia	Point Lookout, Maryland, transferred to Elmira Prison, NY July 9, 1864	Died August 6, 1864 of Chronic Diarrhea, Grave No. 141
Ables, James Private	Unk	June 2, 1864, Cold Harbor, Virginia	Co. K, 23rd Virginia Infantry	July 15, 1864, Leesburg, Virginia	Old Capital Prison, Washington, D. C. Transferred to Elmira Prison, NY August 12, 1864	Oath of Allegiance February 13, 1865. Early Release per Lincoln's Proclamation, 12/8/1863.
Abraham, I. Private	23	January 1, 1862, Darlington District, South Carolina	Co. B, 21st South Carolina Infantry	June 24, 1864, Near Petersburg, Virginia	Point Lookout, Maryland, transferred to Elmira Prison, NY August 18, 1864	Transferred For Exchange October 11, 1864 to Point Lookout Prison Camp, MD. Nothing Further.

Name & Rank	Age	Enlisted	Regiment and State	Where Captured	Prison	Remarks
Abston, John Private	Unk	September 3, 1862, Choctaw County, Alabama	Co. E, Rodney's Escort, 1st Alabama Artillery	August 23, 1864, Fort Morgan, Alabama	New Orleans, Louisiana transferred to Elmira December 4, 1864.	Oath of Allegiance July 7, 1865
Acord, James F. Private	Unk	March 15, 1862, Augusta, Virginia	Co. F, 5th Virginia Infantry	May 12, 1864, Spotsylvania Court House, Virginia	Point Lookout, Maryland, transferred to Elmira Prison, NY July 25, 1864	Oath of Allegiance May 15, 1865
Acree, George W. Private	18	July 1, 1863, Knoxville, Tennessee	Co. E, 63rd Tennessee Infantry	May 16, 1864, Near Drury's Bluff, Virginia	Point Lookout, Maryland, transferred to Elmira Prison, NY August 17, 1864	Exchanged March 10, 1865 at Boulware's Wharf on the James River, Virginia
Acrey, Daniel H. Corporal	Unk	April 27, 1861, Tuskegee, Alabama	Co. C, 3rd Alabama Infantry	May 12, 1864, Spotsylvania Court House, Virginia	Point Lookout, Maryland, transferred to Elmira Prison, NY August 12, 1864	Oath of Allegiance June 16, 1865
Adair, George W. Private	18	August 16, 1861, Luka, Mississippi	Co. G, 26th Mississippi Infantry	May 5, 1864, Wilderness, Virginia	Point Lookout, Maryland, transferred to Elmira Prison, NY August 14, 1864	Oath of Allegiance June 14, 1865
Adair, H. W. Private	Unk	May 7, 1862, Talladega, Alabama	Co. E, 10th Alabama Infantry	May 6, 1864, Wilderness, Virginia	Point Lookout, Maryland, transferred to Elmira Prison, NY August 17, 1864	Died May 19, 1865 of Pneumonia, Grave No. 2946. Name W. H. Adair on Headstone.
Adams, A. Private	Unk	May 4, 1862, Charleston, South Carolina	Co. H. 25th South Carolina Infantry	January 15, 1865, Fort Fisher, North Carolina	Elmira Prison Camp January 30, 1865	Died February 17, 1865 of Chronic Diarrhea, Grave No. 2219
Adams, Charles Private	20	April 5, 1862, Wilkesboro, North Carolina	Co. F, 52nd North Carolina Infantry	May 12, 1864, Spotsylvania Court House, Virginia	Point Lookout, Maryland, transferred to Elmira Prison, NY August 12, 1864	Oath of Allegiance June 12, 1865

Name & Rank	Age	Enlisted	Regiment and State	Where Captured	Prison	Remarks
Adams, Conly E. Private	Unk	July 17, 1861, Wytheville, Virginia	Co. B, 50th Virginia Infantry	May 12, 1864, Spotsylvania Court House, Virginia	Point Lookout, Maryland, transferred to Elmira Prison, NY August 2, 1864	Died February 11, 1865 of Variola (Smallpox), Grave No. 2083
Adams, Franklin Robert Private	Unk	June 15, 1861, Buena Vista, Georgia	Co. K, 12th Georgia Infantry	May 12, 1864, Spotsylvania Court House, Virginia	Point Lookout, Maryland, transferred to Elmira Prison, NY July 25, 1864	Oath of Allegiance July 14, 1865
Adams, H. Private	Unk	Unknown	Co. J, 15th Virginia Cavalry	June 4, 1864, Gaines Farm, Cold Harbor, Virginia	Point Lookout, Maryland, transferred to Elmira Prison, NY July 17,1864	Exchanged March 2, 1865 at Akins Landing on the James River, Virginia
Adams, Harry Private	Unk	May 12, 1863, Tappahannock Virginia	Co. J, 14th Virginia Cavalry	June 1, 1864, Penola Station, Virginia	Point Lookout, Maryland, transferred to Elmira Prison, NY July 17,1864	Exchanged March 2, 1865 at Akins Landing on the James River, Virginia
Adams, Hugh K. Private	Unk	March 10, 1864, Orange County Court House, Virginia	Co. E, 5th North Carolina Infantry	May 10, 1864, Spotsylvania Court House, Virginia	Point Lookout, Maryland, transferred to Elmira Prison, NY August 6, 1864	Exchanged October 29, 1864, at Venus Point, Savannah River, GA.
Adams, J. Private	Unk	Unknown	Co. D, 14th Virginia Infantry	May 24, 1864, Hanover, Virginia	Point Lookout, Maryland, transferred to Elmira Prison, NY July 17,1864	Exchanged February 13, 1865 at Boulware's wharf on the James River, Virginia
Adams, J. O. Private	Unk	Unknown	Co. G, 7th Carolina Cavalry	May 6, 1864, Wakefield, Virginia	Point Lookout, Maryland, transferred to Elmira Prison, NY August 17, 1864	Transferred For Exchange October 11, 1864 to Point Lookout Prison Camp, MD. Nothing Further.
Adams, Jacob T. Corporal	21	July 16, 1862, Camp Holmes, Raleigh, North Carolina	Co. D, 24th North Carolina Infantry	June 17, 1864, Petersburg, Virginia	Point Lookout, Maryland, transferred to Elmira Prison, NY July 30, 1864	Oath of Allegiance June 27, 1865

Name & Rank	Age	Enlisted	Regiment and State	Where Captured	Prison	Remarks
Adams, James Private	Unk	March 28, 1861, Wetumpka, Alabama	Co. E, 1st Battalion Alabama Artillery	August 23, 1864, Fort Morgan, Alabama	Point Lookout, Maryland, transferred to Elmira Prison, NY August 27, 1864	Died December 19, 1864 of Variola (smallpox), Grave No. 1734
Adams, James W. Private	Unk	August 24, 1861, White County, Georgia	Co. C, 24th Georgia Infantry	June 1, 1864, Cold Harbor, Virginia	Point Lookout, Maryland, transferred to Elmira Prison, NY, July 17,1864	Died March 20, 1865 of Variola (smallpox), Grave No. 1599
Adams, John Private	Unk	October 13, 1861, Mobile, Alabama	Co. A, 21st Alabama Infantry	August 23, 1864, Fort Morgan, Alabama	Steam Press No. 4, New Orleans, Louisiana transferred to Elmira Prison, October 8, 1864.	Died November 21, 1864 of Pneumonia Grave No. 942
Adams, John A. Private	Unk	October 15, 1862, Camp Bunker Hill, Georgia	Co. A, 38th Georgia Infantry	May 20, 1864, Spotsylvania Court House, Virginia	Point Lookout, Maryland, transferred to Elmira Prison, NY July 3, 1864	Died October 10, 1864, Pneumonia, Grave No. 687
Adams, John A. Private	Unk	July 15, 1862, Raleigh, North Carolina	Co. G, 3rd North Carolina Infantry	May 12, 1864, Near Spotsylvania Court House, Virginia	Point Lookout, Maryland, transferred to Elmira Prison, NY August 12, 1864	Died October 6, 1864 of Chronic Diarrhea, Grave No. 591
Adams, John Q. Private	Unk	May 31, 1861, Yellow Branch, Virginia	Co. D, 42nd Virginia Infantry	May 12, 1864, Spotsylvania Court House, Virginia	Point Lookout, Maryland, transferred to Elmira Prison, NY August 6, 1864	Oath of Allegiance June 30, 1865
Adams, Joseph Private	Unk	May 25, 1863, Camp Holmes, North Carolina	Co. A, 51st North Carolina Infantry	June 1, 1864, Cold Harbor, Virginia	Transferred From Point Lookout Prison, MD, July 12, 1864. Train Never Arrived at Elmira Prison Camp, NY.	Died July 15, 1864 in Train Accident at Shohola, Pennsylvania.
Adams, Joseph A. Private	Unk	February 16, 1863, Atlanta, Georgia	Co. A, 64th Georgia Infantry	August 16, 1864, New Market, Virginia	Old Capital Prison, Washington, DC transferred to Elmira Prison, NY August 29, 1864	Oath of Allegiance May 15, 1865

Name & Rank	Age	Enlisted	Regiment and State	Where Captured	Prison	Remarks
Adams, Joshua J. Private	19	March 27, 1862, Surrey County, North Carolina	Co. J, 53rd North Carolina Infantry	July 13, 1864, Near Washington, DC,	Old Capital Prison, Washington, DC, transferred to Elmira Prison, NY, July 23, 1864	Transferred for Exchange 10/11/64. Died 10/26/64 of Chronic Diarrhea at Point Lookout, MD.
Adams, L. H. Private	Unk	July 17, 1864, Center Hill, Georgia	Co. B, 16th Georgia Infantry	August 16, 1864, Front Royal, Virginia	Point Lookout, Maryland, transferred to Elmira Prison, NY August 29, 1864	Died February 20, 1865 of Variola (Smallpox), Grave No. 2312
Adams, Leander Corporal	19	February 3, 1864, Bristol, Tennessee	Co. E, 63rd Tennessee Infantry	June 17, 1864, Near Petersburg, Virginia	Point Lookout, Maryland, transferred to Elmira Prison, NY July 30, 1864	Exchanged February 13, 1865 at Boulware's wharf on the James River, Virginia
Adams, M. T. Private	Unk	July 17, 1864, Center Hill, Georgia	Co. B, 16th Georgia Infantry	August 16, 1864, Front Royal, Virginia	Point Lookout, Maryland, transferred to Elmira Prison, NY August 29, 1864	Oath of Allegiance June 14, 1865
Adams, Nathan Private	18	July 6, 1861, Wilmington, North Carolina	Co. C, 7th North Carolina Infantry	May 6, 1864, Wilderness, Virginia	Point Lookout, Maryland, transferred to Elmira Prison, NY August 14, 1864	Oath of Allegiance June 19, 1865
Adams, Nathanial Corporal	24	June 11, 1861, Henderson, North Carolina	Co. K, 23rd North Carolina Infantry	May 12, 1864, Near Spotsylvania Court House, Virginia	Point Lookout, Maryland, transferred to Elmira Prison, NY August 14, 1864	Oath of Allegiance June 16, 1865
Adams, Robert Corporal	31	July 6, 1862, McPherson-ville, South Carolina	Co. K, 4th South Carolina Cavalry	May 30, 1864, Old Church, Virginia	Old Capital Prison, Washington, DC, transferred to Elmira Prison, NY, July 25, 1864	Exchanged February 13, 1865 at Boulware's wharf on the James River, Virginia
Adams, Robert W. Private	Unk	July 5, 1862, Grahamville, South Carolina	Co. B, 4th South Carolina Cavalry	May 28, 1864, Hall's Shop, Virginia	Point Lookout, Maryland, transferred to Elmira Prison, NY July 17, 1864	Died January 3, 1865 of Pneumonia, Grave No. 1267

Name & Rank	Age	Enlisted	Regiment and State	Where Captured	Prison	Remarks
Adams, Samuel Private	Unk	Unknown	Co. B, 5th Louisiana Infantry	September 21, 1864, Baton Rouge, Louisiana	New Orleans, Louisiana, Transferred to Elmira Prison, NY November 19, 1864	Died February 28, 1865 of Chronic Diarrhea, Grave No. 942
Adams, Samuel Private	Unk	Unknown	Co. Unknown, 18th Battalion Louisiana Cavalry	September 21, 1864, East Baton Rouge, Louisiana	New Orleans, Louisiana. Transferred to Elmira Prison Camp, NY, November 20, 1864	Died February 28, 1865 of Diarrhea, Grave No. 2135
Adams, Thomas H. Private	28	May 14, 1861, Cumberland Court House, Virginia	Co. G, 3rd Virginia Cavalry	May 9, 1864, Spotsylvania Court House, Virginia	Point Lookout, Maryland, transferred to Elmira Prison, NY August 17, 1864	Exchanged March 14, 1865 at Boulware's Wharf on the James River, Virginia
Adams, Thomas J. Private	Unk	March 4, 1862, McDonough, Georgia	Co. B, 44th Georgia Infantry	July 8, 1864 Harper's Ferry, Virginia	Old Capital Prison, Washington, DC, transferred to Elmira Prison, NY, July 23, 1864	Exchanged October 29, 1864, at Venus Point, Savannah River, GA.
Adams, William Private	Unk	Unknown	Co. E, 1st Battalion Alabama Artillery	August 23, 1864, Fort Morgan, Alabama	New Orleans, Louisiana transferred to Elmira December 4, 1864.	Died December 27, 1864 of Variola (Smallpox), Grave No. 1293
Adams, William Private	35	May 18, 1863, Raleigh, North Carolina	Co. K, 30th North Carolina Infantry	May 19, 1864, Spotsylvania Court House, Virginia	Point Lookout, Maryland, transferred to Elmira Prison, NY July 17, 1864	Died September 18, 1864 of Chronic Diarrhea, Grave No. 514
Adams, William B. Private	Unk	Unknown	Co. D, 44th Virginia Infantry	May 12, 1864, Spotsylvania, Virginia	Point Lookout Prison Camp, Maryland. Transferred to Elmira Prison, August 2, 1864	Died March 13, 1865 of Pneumonia, Grave No. 1816
Adams, William F. Private	Unk	September 19, 1861, Dalton, Georgia	Co. B, 60th Georgia Infantry	June 2, 1864, Old Church, Virginia	Point Lookout, Maryland, transferred to Elmira Prison, NY July 17, 1864	Exchanged October 29, 1864, at Venus Point, Savannah River, GA.

Name & Rank	Age	Enlisted	Regiment and State	Where Captured	Prison	Remarks
Adams, William H. Sergeant	Unk	October 15, 1861, Haley's Store, Georgia	Co. F, 38th Georgia Infantry	May 6, 1864, Wilderness, Virginia	Point Lookout, Maryland, transferred to Elmira Prison, NY August 14, 1864	Oath of Allegiance June 14, 1865
Adams, William J. Private	18	July 5, 1861, Halifax County, North Carolina	Co. I, 8th North Carolina Infantry	May 31, 1864, Cold Harbor, Virginia	Point Lookout, Maryland, transferred to Elmira Prison, NY July 17,1864	Exchanged March 2, 1865 at Akins Landing on the James River, Virginia
Adams, William L. Private	24	December 29, 1861, Springfield, Missouri	Co. F, 1st Missouri Cavalry	May 17, 1863, Big Black Bridge, Champion Hill, Mississippi	Point Lookout, Maryland, transferred to Elmira Prison, NY August 18, 1864	Exchanged February 13, 1865 at Boulware's wharf on the James River, Virginia
Adams, William M. Private	Unk	March 11, 1863, Hartwell, Georgia	Co. C, 16th Georgia Infantry	June 1, 1864, Gaines Farm, Cold Harbor, Virginia	Point Lookout, Maryland, transferred to Elmira Prison, NY July 17,1864	Exchanged March 10, 1865 at Boulware's wharf on the James River, Virginia
Adams, William M. Sergeant	23	June 7, 1861, Statesville, North Carolina	Co. C, 4th North Carolina Infantry	May 8, 1864, Wilderness, Virginia	Point Lookout, Maryland, transferred to Elmira Prison, NY August 14, 1864	Oath of Allegiance June 21, 1865
Adamson, William S. Private	Unk	February 12, 1863, Fort Morgan, Louisiana	Co. E, 1st Battalion Alabama Artillery	August 23, 1864, Fort Morgan, Louisiana	Point Lookout, Maryland, transferred to Elmira Prison, NY August 27, 1864	Died December 27, 1864 of Variola (smallpox), Grave No. 1293
Adcock, Green B. Private	24	July 30, 1861, Livingston, Tennessee	Co. G, 25th Tennessee Infantry	May 16, 1864, Near Drury's Bluff, Virginia	Point Lookout, Maryland, transferred to Elmira Prison, NY August 17, 1864	Died October 8, 1864 of Chronic Diarrhea, Grave No. 652
Addeston, W. S. Private	Unk	Unknown	Co. I, 17th North Carolina Infantry	May 18, 1864, Spotsylvania Court House, Virginia	Point Lookout, Maryland, transferred to Elmira Prison, NY July 17,1864	Transferred for Exchange October 11, 1864. Nothing Further.

Name & Rank	Age	Enlisted	Regiment and State	Where Captured	Prison	Remarks
Addison, Berry A. Private	25	June 27, 1861, Polk County, Georgia	Co. D, 21st Georgia Infantry	May 30, 1864 Mechanicsville, Virginia	Point Lookout, Maryland, transferred to Elmira Prison, NY July 17,1864	Oath of Allegiance June 14, 1865
Adkins, Harvey Private	Unk	September 3, 1862, Choctaw County, Alabama	Co. E, Rodney's Escort, 1st Alabama Artillery	August 23, 1864, Fort Morgan, Alabama	New Orleans, Louisiana transferred to Elmira December 4, 1864.	Oath of Allegiance July 7, 1865
Adkins, Robert J. Private	21	October 9, 1861, Enfield, North Carolina	Co. F, 36th Regiment, 2nd North Carolina Artillery	January 15, 1865, Fort Fisher, North Carolina	February 1, 1865, Elmira Prison Camp, New York	Oath of Allegiance July 7, 1865
Adkins, Wiley Private	20	July 15, 1862, Raleigh, North Carolina	Co. D, 1st North Carolina Infantry	May 12, 1864, Spotsylvania Court House, Virginia	Point Lookout, Maryland, transferred to Elmira Prison, NY August 6, 1864	Died January 6, 1865 of Variola (Smallpox), Grave No. 1246. Name Atkins on Headstone.
Adkins, William H. Private	18	September 13, 1861, Mecklenburg County, North Carolina	Co. K, 30th North Carolina Infantry	May 17, 1864, Spotsylvania Court House, Virginia	Point Lookout, Maryland, transferred to Elmira Prison, NY July 6, 1864	Died January 15, 1865 of Chronic Diarrhea, Grave No. 1450
Agee, Charles L. Private	Unk	May 22, 1861, Spoon Creek, Virginia	Co. H, 42nd Virginia Infantry	May 12, 1864, Near Spotsylvania Court House, Virginia	Point Lookout, Maryland, transferred to Elmira Prison, NY August 6, 1864	Died February 19, 1865 of Chronic Diarrhea, Grave No. 2325
Agerton, John W. Private	Unk	April 16, 1862, Grahamville, Georgia	Co. D, 48th Georgia Infantry	July 3, 1863, Gettysburg, Pennsylvania	Point Lookout, Maryland, transferred to Elmira Prison, NY July 17,1864	Died December 11, 1864 of Pneumonia Grave No. 1058
Aiken, Malachan A. Private	Unk	December 18, 1863, Calhoun, Georgia	Co. C, 23rd Georgia Infantry	August 19, 1864, Weldon Railroad, North Carolina	DeCamp US Army Hospital, David's Island, NY Harbor. Transferred to Elmira Prison, NY Date Unknown.	Died April 5, 1865 of Pneumonia, Grave No. 2626

Name & Rank	Age	Enlisted	Regiment and State	Where Captured	Prison	Remarks
Aikin, David Corporal	Unk	August 15, 1861, Livingston, Alabama	Co. G, 5th Alabama Infantry	May 5, 1864, Wilderness, Virginia	Point Lookout, Maryland, transferred to Elmira Prison, NY August 17, 1864	Oath of Allegiance May 13, 1865
Airheart, George P. Sergeant	25	June 4, 1861, Salem, Virginia	Co. E, 42nd Virginia Infantry	May 12, 1864, Near Spotsylvania Court House, Virginia	Point Lookout, Maryland, transferred to Elmira Prison, NY August 6, 1864	Exchanged March 14, 1865 at Boulware's Wharf on the James River, Virginia
Akens, Malachan Private	Unk	December 18, 1863, Calhoun, Georgia	Co. C, 23rd Georgia Infantry	August 19, 1864, Weldon Railroad, Near Petersburg, Virginia. Gunshot Wound Leg.	DeCamp General Hospital, David's Island New York Harbor.	Died April 8, 1865 of Pneumonia, Grave No. 2626
Akers, P. R. Private	Unk	March 12, 1862, Petersburg, Virginia	Co. E, 13th Virginia Cavalry	July 24, 1863, Front Royal, Virginia	Point Lookout, Maryland, transferred to Elmira Prison, NY August 18, 1864	Oath of Allegiance June 22, 1865
Akins, David W. Private	32	June 10, 1862, Savannah, Georgia	Co. K, 7th Georgia Cavalry	June 11, 1864, Trevilian Station, Louisa Court House, Virginia	Point Lookout, Maryland, transferred to Elmira Prison, NY July 25, 1864	Died September 17, 1864 of Chronic Diarrhea, Grave No. 170. Name Akens on Headstone.
Akres, E. A. Private	Unk	February 1, 1864, Lynchburg, Virginia	Co. B, 2nd Virginia Cavalry	May 11, 1864, Yellow Tavern, Hanover County, Virginia	Point Lookout, Maryland, transferred to Elmira Prison, NY August 17, 1864	No Addional Information.
Albright, Jacob Corporal	Unk	March 1, 1864, Orange County Court House, North Carolina	Co. H, 1st North Carolina Infantry	May 12, 1864, Spotsylvania, Virginia	Point Lookout, Maryland, transferred to Elmira Prison, NY August 6, 1864	Died October 1, 1864 of Chronic Diarrhea, Grave No. 403. Name John Allbright on Headstone.
Alcott, James Private	Unk	Unknown	Co. J, 13th Tennessee Infantry	May 6, 1864, Near Martinsburg, Virginia	Old Capital Prison, Washington, D. C. Transferred to Elmira Prison, NY July 25, 1864	Oath of Allegiance May 19, 1865

Name & Rank	Age	Enlisted	Regiment and State	Where Captured	Prison	Remarks
Alderman, Andrew C. Corporal	Unk	May 18, 1861, Huntersville, Virginia	Co. I, 25th Virginia Infantry	May 12, 1864, Spotsylvania Court House, Virginia	Point Lookout, Maryland, transferred to Elmira Prison, NY August 12, 1864	Died November 27, 1864 of Scorbutus (Scurvy), Grave No. 901
Alderman, Daniel Private	Unk	July 12, 1862, Sampson County, North Carolina	Co. C, 5th North Carolina Cavalry	July 12, 1863, Ashby Gap, Virginia	Point Lookout, Maryland, transferred to Elmira Prison, NY August 18, 1864	Exchanged March 10, 1865 at Boulware's Wharf on the James River, Virginia
Alderman, E. Private	Unk	November 9, 1863, Camp Jackson, Georgia	Co. D, 20th Battalion Georgia Cavalry	May 31, 1864, Cold Harbor, Virginia	Point Lookout, Maryland, transferred to Elmira Prison, NY July 17,1864	Oath of Allegiance June 19, 1865
Alderman, Eli M. Private	Unk	June 1, 1861, Hillsville, Virginia	Co. D, 29th Virginia Infantry	May 31, 1864, Cold Harbor, Virginia	Point Lookout, Maryland, transferred to Elmira Prison, NY August 17, 1864	Oath of Allegiance June 19, 1865
Alderman, Henry Sergeant	Unk	September 7, 1861, Quitman County, Georgia	Co. C, 61st Georgia Infantry	May 12, 1864, Spotsylvania Court House, Virginia	Point Lookout, Maryland, transferred to Elmira Prison, NY July 30, 1864	Exchanged October 29, 1864, at Venus Point, Savannah River, GA.
Alderman, Isaac E. Private	Unk	September 7, 1861, Quitman, Georgia	Co. C, 61st Georgia Infantry	May 12, 1864, Spotsylvania Court House, Virginia	Point Lookout, Maryland, transferred to Elmira Prison, NY July 25, 1864	Died December 20, 1864 of Pneumonia, Grave No. 1074
Aldman, Archibald Private	23	March 15, 1862, Salisbury, North Carolina	Co. D, 42nd North Carolina Infantry	June 2, 1864, Cold Harbor, Virginia	Point Lookout, Maryland, transferred to Elmira Prison, NY July 17, 1864	Oath of Allegiance July 3, 1865
Aldridge, Ransom Private	30	July 17, 1862, Randolph County, North Carolina	Co. H, 3rd North Carolina Infantry	May 12, 1864, Spotsylvania Court House, Virginia	Point Lookout, Maryland, transferred to Elmira Prison, NY August 14, 1864	Died March 3, 1865 of Variola (smallpox), Grave No. 2013
Aldridge, Thomas D. Private	20	March 10, 1862, Camp Anderson, Florida	Co. K, 5th Florida Infantry	May 12, 1864, Spotsylvania Court House, Virginia	Point Lookout, Maryland, transferred to Elmira Prison, NY July 30, 1864	Oath of Allegiance June 14, 1865

Name & Rank	Age	Enlisted	Regiment and State	Where Captured	Prison	Remarks
Aleshire, George W. Private	28	June 2, 1861, Luray, Virginia	Co. K, 10th Virginia Infantry	July 8, 1864 Harper's Ferry, Virginia	Old Capital Prison, Washington, DC, transferred to Elmira Prison, NY, July 23, 1864	Exchanged March 2, 1865 at Akins Landing on the James River, Virginia
Alexander, Daniel L. Sergeant	22	July 20, 1861, Rocky River, North Carolina	Co. H, 7th North Carolina Infantry	July 28, 1864, Deep Bottom, Virginia. Gunshot Wound of Left Leg.	Old Capital Prison, Washington, DC, transferred to Elmira Prison, NY, December 17, 1864	Exchanged March 14, 1865 at Boulware's Wharf on the James River, Virginia
Alexander, David Sergeant	24	October 4, 1861, Portsmouth, Virginia	Co. A, 32nd North Carolina Infantry	May 10, 1864, Spotsylvania, Virginia	Point Lookout, Maryland, transferred to Elmira Prison, NY August 6, 1864	Oath of Allegiance June 23, 1865
Alexander, E. C. Private	Unk	October 1, 1861, Santa Fe, Tennessee	Co. B, Jackson's 1st Regiment, Tennessee Heavy Artillery	August 23, 1864, Fort Morgan, Alabama	New Orleans, Louisiana transferred to Elmira December 4, 1864.	Exchanged March 10, 1865 at Boulware's Wharf on the James River, Virginia
Alexander, J. W. Private	19	April 14, 1862, Richmond, Virginia	Co. G, 5th Virginia Cavalry	May 11, 1864, Yellow Tavern, Hanover County, Virginia	Point Lookout, Maryland, transferred to Elmira Prison, NY August 17, 1864	Oath of Allegiance June 23, 1865
Alexander, Jesse T. Sergeant	29	May 31, 1861, Raleigh, North Carolina	Co. B, 1st North Carolina Infantry	May 12, 1864, Spotsylvania Court House, Virginia	Point Lookout, Maryland, transferred to Elmira Prison, NY August 6, 1864	Exchanged March 14, 1865 at Boulware's Wharf on the James River, Virginia
Alexander, John Private	Unk	Unknown	Co. H, 3rd Tennessee Cavalry	August 6, 1864, Smoketown, Maryland	Point Lookout, Maryland, transferred to Elmira Prison, NY August 18, 1864	Oath of Allegiance May 13, 1865
Alexander, John Private	Unk	May 27, 1861, Staunton, Virginia	Co. D, 25th Virginia Infantry	May 12, 1864, Spotsylvania Court House, Virginia	Point Lookout, Maryland, transferred to Elmira Prison, NY August 2, 1864	Died November 18, 1864 of Chronic Diarrhea, Grave No. 966

Name & Rank	Age	Enlisted	Regiment and State	Where Captured	Prison	Remarks
Alexander, John W. Private	23	August 10, 1861, Lightwood Knott Springs, South Carolina	Co. A, 14th South Carolina Infantry	July 21, 1864, Pickett's Farm, Cunles Neck, Virginia	Point Lookout, Maryland, transferred to Elmira Prison, NY August 18, 1864	Exchanged March 14, 1865 at Boulware's Wharf on the James River, Virginia
Alexander, Laird H. Private	25	April 19, 1861, Concord, North Carolina	Co. A, 20th North Carolina Infantry	May 12, 1864, Near Spotsylvania Court House, Virginia	Point Lookout Prison, Maryland. Transferred to Elmira Prison Camp New York August 14, 1864.	Exchanged March 2, 1865 at Akins Landing on the James River, Virginia
Alexander, Newton Private	18	April 13, 1863, Camp Holmes, North Carolina	Co. E, 32nd North Carolina Infantry	May 10, 1864, Wilderness, Virginia	Point Lookout, Maryland, transferred to Elmira Prison, NY August 6, 1864	Died September 20, 1864 of Chronic Diarrhea, Grave No. 333. Name W. H. Alexander on Headstone.
Alexander, T. R. Civilian	Unk	Unknown	Citizen of Prince William County, Virginia	November 30, 1863, Prince William County, Virginia	Point Lookout, Maryland, transferred to Elmira Prison, NY July 25, 1864	Exchanged October 11, 1864. Nothing Further.
Alexander, Thomas A. Private	31	August 15, 1862, Statesville, North Carolina	Co. E, 37th North Carolina Infantry	May 12, 1864, Spotsylvania Court House, Virginia	Point Lookout, Maryland, transferred to Elmira Prison, NY July 25, 1864. Ward No. 32	Died August 11, 1864 of Chronic Diarrhea, Grave No. 134
Alexander, Thomas B. Sergeant	Unk	October 1, 1861, Santa Fe, Tennessee	Co. B, Jackson's 1st Regiment, Tennessee Heavy Artillery	August 23, 1864, Fort Morgan, Alabama	New Orleans, Louisiana transferred to Elmira December 4, 1864.	Exchanged March 10, 1865 at Boulware's Wharf on the James River, Virginia
Alexander, Tzavella Sergeant	Unk	April 23, 1861, Brownsburg, Virginia	Co. H, 25th Virginia Infantry	May 5, 1864, Wilderness, Virginia	Point Lookout, Maryland, transferred to Elmira Prison, NY August 2, 1864	Oath of Allegiance June 21, 1865
Alexander, William A. Private	Unk	May 11, 1861, New Orleans, Louisiana	Co. K, 2nd Louisiana Infantry	May 12, 1864, Spotsylvania, Virginia	Point Lookout, Maryland, transferred to Elmira Prison, NY August 14, 1864	Oath of Allegiance June 19, 1865

Name & Rank	Age	Enlisted	Regiment and State	Where Captured	Prison	Remarks
Alford, Daniel J. Private	20	July 1, 1861, Selma, Alabama	Jeff Davis Alabama Artillery	May 5, 1864, Wilderness, Virginia	Point Lookout, Maryland, transferred to Elmira Prison, NY August 17, 1864	Exchanged March 14, 1865 at Boulware's Wharf on the James River, Virginia
Alford, John Private	Unk	June 5, 1861, Asheboro, North Carolina	Co. L, 22nd North Carolina Infantry	May 6, 1864, Wilderness, Virginia	Point Lookout, Maryland, transferred to Elmira Prison, NY August 14, 1864	Oath of Allegiance June 19, 1865
Alford, Josiah Private	20	January 27, 1862, Rolesville, North Carolina	Co. I, 1st North Carolina Infantry	May 12, 1864, Spotsylvania, Virginia	Point Lookout Prison Camp, Maryland. Transferred to Elmira Prison Camp August 6, 1864	Died October 24, 1864 of Chronic Diarrhea, Grave No. 861
Alford, Miles A. Private	Unk	September 4, 1862, Coffee County, Alabama	Co. K, 5th Alabama Infantry	May 5, 1864, Wilderness, Virginia	Point Lookout, Maryland, transferred to Elmira Prison, NY August 17, 1864	Exchanged February 13, 1865 at Boulware's wharf on the James River, Virginia
Algers, Isaac H. Corporal	Unk	March 12, 1861, Newton, Alabama	Co. F, 1st Battalion Alabama Artillery	August 23, 1864, Fort Morgan, Alabama	Steam Press No. 4, New Orleans, Louisiana transferred to Elmira Prison, October 8, 1864.	Died April 11, 1865 of Chronic Diarrhea, Grave No. 2697
Alison, R. H. Corporal	Unk	April 20, 1861, Belle Roi., Virginia	Co. A, 26th Virginia Infantry	June 15, 1864, Near Petersburg, Virginia	Point Lookout, Maryland, transferred to Elmira Prison, NY July 17,1864	Transferred to Post Hospital July 13, 1865. Nothing Further.
All, William Private	Unk	September 29, 1863 Macon, Georgia	Co. D, 44th Georgia Infantry	July 13, 1864, Near Washington, DC,	Old Capital Prison, Washington, DC, transferred to Elmira Prison, NY, July 23, 1864	Died January 3, 1865 of Chronic Diarrhea, Grave No. 1266
Allan, John Private	Unk	October 29, 1861, Camp Letcher, Bullsford, Virginia	Field & Staff 6th Virginia Cavalry	May 11, 1864, Yellow Tavern, Hanover County, Virginia	Point Lookout, Maryland, transferred to Elmira Prison, NY August 17, 1864	Died September 27, 1864 of Chronic Diarrhea, Grave No. 388

Name & Rank	Age	Enlisted	Regiment and State	Where Captured	Prison	Remarks
Allan, William O. Sergeant Major	19	July 16, 1861, Forestville, North Carolina	Field & Staff, 1st North Carolina Infantry	May 12, 1864, Spotsylvania Court House, Virginia	Point Lookout, Maryland, transferred to Elmira Prison, NY August 6, 1864	Exchanged March 10, 1865 at Boulware's Wharf on the James River, Virginia
Allcock, George W. Private	Unk	July 15, 1864, Lynchburg, Virginia	Co. D, 42nd Virginia Infantry	May 12, 1864, Near Spotsylvania Court House, Virginia	Point Lookout, Maryland, transferred to Elmira Prison, NY August 6, 1864	Oath of Allegiance June 19, 1865
Allen, Alexander T. Private	Unk	June 22, 1861, High Point, North Carolina	Co. F, 2nd North Carolina Cavalry	June 5, 1864, Petersburg, Virginia	Old Capital Prison, Washington, DC, transferred to Elmira Prison, NY, July 23, 1864	Died February 1, 1865 of Variola (Smallpox), Grave No. 1762
Allen, Alphonso S. Private	Unk	December 21, 1861, Nashville, Tennessee	Co. J, 44th Tennessee Infantry	June 17, 1864, Petersburg, Virginia	Point Lookout, Maryland, transferred to Elmira Prison, NY July 30, 1864	Oath of Allegiance May 12, 1865
Allen, Arthur Private	Unk	Unknown	Co. J, 53rd North Carolina Infantry	May 5, 1864, Wilderness, Virginia	Old Capital Prison, Washington, DC, transferred to Elmira Prison, NY, July 23, 1864	Exchanged October 29, 1864, at Venus Point, Savannah River, GA.
Allen, Arthur F. Sergeant	Unk	May 21, 1861, Tappahannock, Virginia	Co. A, 55th Virginia Infantry	July 14, 1863, Falling Waters, Maryland	Point Lookout, Maryland, transferred to Elmira Prison, NY August 18, 1864	Exchanged March 10, 1865 at Boulware's Wharf on the James River, Virginia
Allen, Barton H. Private	Unk	May 27, 1861, Staunton, Virginia	Co. D, 25th Virginia Infantry	May 12, 1864, Spotsylvania Court House, Virginia	Point Lookout, Maryland, transferred to Elmira Prison, NY August 2, 1864	Died October 16, 1864 of Diphtheria, Grave No. 559
Allen, Britton Private	25	March 14, 1862, Jasper, Florida	Co. B, 5th Florida Infantry	May 12, 1864, Spotsylvania Court House, Virginia	Point Lookout, Maryland, transferred to Elmira Prison, NY July 30, 1864	Oath of Allegiance June 16, 1865

Name & Rank	Age	Enlisted	Regiment and State	Where Captured	Prison	Remarks
Allen, Charles Private	Unk	Unknown	Co. C, Richardson's Battery Light Artillery, CSA	September 18, 1863, Leesburg, Virginia	Point Lookout, Maryland, transferred to Elmira Prison, NY August 18, 1864	Exchanged February 13, 1865 at Boulware's wharf on the James River, Virginia
Allen, Daniel J. Private	18	February 24, 1864, Fort Holmes, Near Raleigh, North Carolina	Co. K, 40th Regiment, 3rd North Carolina Artillery	January 15, 1865, Fort Fisher, North Carolina	February 1, 1865, Elmira Prison Camp, New York	Oath of Allegiance August 7, 1865
Allen, David J. Private	17	Unknown	Co. D, Ogden's Louisiana Cavalry	August 20, 1864, Morganza, Louisiana	Point Lookout, Maryland, transferred to Elmira Prison, NY November 19, 1864	Died December 22, 1864 of Chronic Diarrhea, Grave No. 1089
Allen, Drury A. Private	37	April 12, 1862, Battery Island, South Carolina	Co. E, 25th South Carolina Infantry	January 15, 1865, Fort Fisher, North Carolina	Elmira Prison Camp, NY, January 30, 1865	Died February 20, 1865 of Pneumonia, Grave No. 2308
Allen, Edwin Private	Unk	October 13, 1861, Mobile, Alabama	Co. A, 21st Alabama Infantry	August 23, 1864, Fort Morgan, Alabama	Steam Press No. 4, New Orleans, Louisiana transferred to Elmira Prison, October 8, 1864.	Oath of Allegiance June 14, 1865
Allen, Erasmus H. Private	Unk	April 1, 1863, Rappahannock, Virginia	Co. J, 25th Virginia Infantry	May 5, 1864, Wilderness, Virginia	Point Lookout, Maryland, transferred to Elmira Prison, NY August 17, 1864	Exchanged 2/20/65. Died 3/8/65 of Chronic Diarrhea and Phthisis Pulmonalis, at Chimborrazo Hospital, Richmond, VA
Allen, G. W. Private	Unk	Unknown	Co. B, 45th Georgia Infantry	May 6, 1864, Wilderness, Virginia	Point Lookout, Maryland, transferred to Elmira Prison, NY August 14, 1864	Oath of Allegiance June 16, 1865
Allen, George Frank Private	20	May 6, 1862, Elizabethtown, North Carolina	Co. K, 40th Regiment, 3rd North Carolina Artillery	January 15, 1865, Fort Fisher, North Carolina	February 1, 1865, Elmira Prison Camp, New York	Exchanged March 2, 1865 at Akins Landing on the James River, Virginia

Name & Rank	Age	Enlisted	Regiment and State	Where Captured	Prison	Remarks
Allen, George W. Private	37	September 19, 1862, Calhoun, Georgia	Co. D, 13th Georgia Infantry	May 20, 1864, Spotsylvania Court House, Virginia	Point Lookout, Maryland, transferred to Elmira Prison, NY July 3, 1864	Exchanged March 10, 1865 at Boulware's Wharf on the James River, Virginia
Allen, Harrison Private	Unk	February 28, 1862, Walton County, Georgia	Co. G, 35th Georgia Infantry	May 6, 1864, Wilderness, Virginia	Point Lookout, Maryland, transferred to Elmira Prison, NY August 17, 1864	Oath of Allegiance June 14, 1865
Allen, Ivey Private	34	July 15, 1862, Raleigh, North Carolina	Co. D, 3rd North Carolina Infantry	May 12, 1864, Near Spotsylvania Court House, Virginia	Point Lookout Prison, Maryland. Transferred to Elmira Prison Camp New York August 14, 1864.	Exchanged February 13, 1865 at Boulware's wharf on the James River, Virginia
Allen, J. D. Corporal	21	July 16, 1861, Forestville, North Carolina	Co. I, 1st North Carolina Infantry	May 12, 1864, Spotsylvania Court House, Virginia	Point Lookout, Maryland, transferred to Elmira Prison, NY August 6, 1864	Oath of Allegiance June 12, 1865
Allen, J. R. Private	Unk	September 26, 1863, Morgan County, Georgia	Co. J, 7th Georgia Cavalry	June 11, 1864, Trevilian Station, Louisa Court House, Virginia	Point Lookout, Maryland, transferred to Elmira Prison, NY July 25, 1864	Exchanged October 29, 1864, at Venus Point, Savannah River, GA.
Allen, J. R. Private	Unk	June 20, 1861, Camp McDonald, Georgia	Co. A, 3rd Battalion Georgia Sharp shooters	August 16, 1864, Front Royal, Virginia	Point Lookout, Maryland, transferred to Elmira Prison, NY August 29, 1864	Oath of Allegiance July 11, 1865
Allen, J. W. Private	Unk	Unable to Locate Soldier's Records	Co. A, 1st Alabama Artillery	August 23, 1864, Fort Morgan, Alabama	New Orleans, Louisiana transferred to Elmira December 4, 1864.	Oath of Allegiance June 14, 1865
Allen, John A. Private	Unk	July 3, 1861, White Sulfur Springs, Virginia	Co. G, 22nd Virginia Infantry	June 3, 1864, Gaines Mill, Cold Harbor, Virginia	Point Lookout, Maryland, transferred to Elmira Prison, NY July 17,1864	Transferred for Exchange October 11, 1864. Died October 17, 1864 of Unknown Disease at US Army Hospital, Baltimore, MD.

Name & Rank	Age	Enlisted	Regiment and State	Where Captured	Prison	Remarks
Allen, John E. Private	32	October 13, 1861, Hall's Mill, Alabama	Co. J, 21st Alabama Infantry	August 23, 1864, Fort Morgan, Alabama	Steam Press No. 4, New Orleans, Louisiana transferred to Elmira Prison, October 8, 1864.	Exchanged February 13, 1865 at Boulware's wharf on the James River, Virginia
Allen, John R. B. Private	Unk	March 2, 1861, Tallapoosa, Alabama	Co. C, 1st Battalion Alabama Artillery	August 23, 1864, Fort Morgan, Alabama	New Orleans, Louisiana transferred to Elmira December 4, 1864.	Died April 19, 1865 of Pneumonia, Grave No. 1368
Allen, Joseph B. Private	27	May 6, 1862, Elizabethtown, North Carolina	Co. K, 40th Regiment, 3rd North Carolina Artillery	January 15, 1865, Fort Fisher, North Carolina	February 1, 1865, Elmira Prison Camp, New York	Oath of Allegiance June 12, 1865
Allen, Joseph J. Private	19	May 30, 1861 Webster, North Carolina	Co. B, 25th North Carolina Infantry	June 17, 1864, Petersburg, Virginia	Point Lookout, Maryland, transferred to Elmira Prison, NY July 30, 1864	Exchanged March 14, 1865. Died March 28th of Debilitas at Jackson Hospital, Richmond, VA
Allen, Miles Private	18	July 3, 1863, Fort Caswell, North Carolina	Co. D, 36th, 2nd North Carolina Artillery	January 15, 1865, Fort Fisher, North Carolina	February 1, 1865, Elmira Prison Camp, New York	Exchanged March 14, 1865 at Boulware's Wharf on the James River, Virginia
Allen, Perry W. Private	Unk	October 13, 1861, Hall's Mill, Alabama	Co. J, 21st Alabama Infantry	August 23, 1864, Fort Morgan, Alabama	Steam Press No. 4, New Orleans, Louisiana transferred to Elmira Prison, October 8, 1864.	Oath of Allegiance May 17, 1865
Allen, Peter W. Sergeant	Unk	June 20, 1861, Richmond, Virginia	Co. H, 44th Virginia Infantry	May 12, 1864, Spotsylvania Court House, Virginia	Point Lookout, Maryland, transferred to Elmira Prison, NY August 2, 1864	Exchanged October 29, 1864, at Venus Point, Savannah River, GA.
Allen, Richard B. Private	Unk	Unknown	Co. K, 59th Alabama Infantry	June 17, 1864, Near Petersburg, Virginia	Point Lookout, Maryland, transferred to Elmira Prison, NY July 30, 1864	Died December 13, 1864 of Pneumonia, Grave No. 1122

Name & Rank	Age	Enlisted	Regiment and State	Where Captured	Prison	Remarks
Allen, Rufus Private	20	May 6, 1862, Elizabethtown, North Carolina	Co. K, 40th Regiment, 3rd North Carolina Artillery	January 15, 1865, Fort Fisher, North Carolina	February 1, 1865, Elmira Prison, New York	Exchanged February 20, 1865 on the James River, Virginia
Allen, Thomas Private	Unk	March 21, 1861, Tallapoosa, Alabama	Co. E, 1st Battalion Alabama Artillery	August 23, 1864, Fort Morgan, Alabama	New Orleans, Louisiana transferred to Elmira Prison December 4, 1864.	Died February 8, 1865 of Chronic Diarrhea, Grave No. 1934
Allen, Thomas C. Private	Unk	Unknown	Co. C, 1st Battalion Alabama Artillery	August 23, 1864, Fort Morgan, Alabama	New Orleans, Louisiana transferred to Elmira December 4, 1864.	Died February 10, 1865 of Chronic Diarrhea, Grave No. 2092
Allen, Thomas F. Private	27	January 29, 1862, Newbern, North Carolina	Co. F, 36th Regiment, 2nd North Carolina Artillery	January 15, 1865, Fort Fisher, North Carolina	February 1, 1865, Elmira Prison Camp, New York	Died February 19, 1865 of Pneumonia, Grave No. 2327
Allen, Thomas V. Private	Unk	February 1, 1862, Lawrenceville, Gwinnette County, Georgia	Co. B, 35th Georgia Infantry	May 5, 1864, Wilderness, Virginia	Point Lookout, Maryland, transferred to Elmira Prison, NY July 30, 1864	Exchanged October 29, 1864 at Venus Point, Savannah River, GA.
Allen, W. J. Private	Unk	Unknown	Co. C, 26th Virginia Infantry	June 15, 1864, Petersburg, Virginia	Point Lookout, Maryland, transferred to Elmira Prison, NY July 17, 1864	Oath of Allegiance June 21, 1865
Allen, W. S. Private	Unk	May 20, 1861, Louisburg, North Carolina	Co. K, 32nd North Carolina Infantry	May 10, 1864, Spotsylvania, Virginia	Point Lookout, Maryland, transferred to Elmira Prison, NY August 6, 1864	Oath of Allegiance June 16, 1865
Allen, William A. Private	Unk	October 13, 1861, Mobile, Alabama	Co. A, 1st Alabama Artillery	August 23, 1864, Fort Morgan, Alabama	New Orleans, Louisiana transferred to Elmira December 4, 1864.	Oath of Allegiance May 19, 1865

Name & Rank	Age	Enlisted	Regiment and State	Where Captured	Prison	Remarks
Allen, William B. Private	Unk	January 13, 1862, Fort Gaines, Alabama	Co. A, 21st Alabama Infantry	August 23, 1864, Fort Morgan, Alabama	Steam Press No. 4, New Orleans, Louisiana transferred to Elmira Prison, October 8, 1864.	Oath of Allegiance June 14, 1865
Allen, William Rufus Private	Unk	Unknown	Co. K, 40th Regiment, 3rd North Carolina Artillery	January 15, 1865, Fort Fisher, North Carolina	February 1, 1865, Elmira Prison Camp, New York	Exchanged February 20, 1865 at Boulware's or Cox Wharf on the James River, Virginia
Alley, John Private	Unk	August 12, 1864, Marianna, Florida	Co. C, 1st Reserve Florida Infantry	September 27, 1864, Marianna, Florida	Point Lookout, Maryland, transferred to Elmira Prison, NY November 19, 1864	Died February 22, 1865 of Chronic Diarrhea, Grave No. 2298
Alley, Thomas K. Private	47	October 15, 1863, Elyton, Alabama	Captain Griffin's Battery, 1st Virginia Light Artillery	July 3, 1864, Allen's Farm, Virginia. Deserted to the US Gunboat Hunchback on the James River, Virginia	Point Lookout, Maryland, transferred to Elmira Prison, NY July 23, 1864	Died September 19, 1864 of Chronic Diarrhea, Grave No. 320
Alley, William R. Private	Unk	May 17, 1861, Nashville, Tennessee	Co. D, 3rd Tennessee Infantry	May 12, 1863, Raymond, Mississippi	Point Lookout, Maryland, transferred to Elmira Prison, NY August 18, 1864	Exchanged February 13, 1865 at Boulware's wharf on the James River, Virginia
Allingsworth, James J. Private	29	October 12, 1861, King George Court House, Virginia	Co. J, 9th Virginia Cavalry	September 14, 1863, Near Culpepper, Virginia	Point Lookout, Maryland, transferred to Elmira Prison, NY August 18, 1864	Oath of Allegiance June 19, 1865
Allison, David S. Corporal	18	April 18, 1861, Marion, Virginia	Co. D, 4th Virginia Infantry	May 12, 1864 Spotsylvania Court House, Virginia	Point Lookout, Maryland, transferred to Elmira Prison, NY August 2, 1864	Oath of Allegiance June 16, 1865
Allison, Humphrey T. Sergeant	18	March 8, 1862, Lake City, Florida	Co. B, 5th Florida Infantry	May 6, 1864, Wilderness, Virginia	Point Lookout, Maryland, transferred to Elmira Prison, NY July 12, 1864	Died October 28, 1864 of Typhoid-Pneumonia, Grave No. 719

Name & Rank	Age	Enlisted	Regiment and State	Where Captured	Prison	Remarks
Allison, James Private	Unk	January 20, 1864, Greenville, South Carolina	Co. E, Hampton Legion, South Carolina Infantry	June 13, 1864, Malvern Hill, Virginia	Point Lookout, Maryland, transferred to Elmira Prison, NY July 30, 1864	Died January 8, 1865 of Variola (Smallpox), Grave No. 1503. Name Ellison on Headstone.
Allison, Lemuel R. Corporal	Unk	August 24, 1861, White County, Georgia	Co. G, 24th Georgia Infantry	August 16, 1864, Front Royal, Virginia	Point Lookout, Maryland, transferred to Elmira Prison, NY August 18, 1864	Exchanged February 20, 1865 at Boulware's or Cox Wharf on the James River, Virginia
Allison, William M. Private	Unk	Unknown	Co. A, Mosby's Virginia Cavalry	May 6, 1863, Aldie, Virginia	Point Lookout, Maryland, transferred to Elmira Prison, NY August 18, 1864	Exchanged March 10, 1865 at Boulware's wharf on the James River, Virginia
Allred, Daniel F. Private	18	June 18, 1861, Randolph County, North Carolina	Co. L, 22nd North Carolina Infantry	May 6, 1864, Wilderness, Virginia	Point Lookout, Maryland, transferred to Elmira Prison, NY August 14, 1864	Exchanged March 2, 1865 at Akins Landing on the James River, Virginia
Alman, Gideon Private	44	September 22, 1863, Cabarrus County, North Carolina	Co. A, 30th North Carolina Infantry	May 12, 1864, Near Spotsylvania Court House, Virginia	Point Lookout, Maryland, transferred to Elmira Prison, NY August 14, 1864	Oath of Allegiance June 12, 1865
Almand, James M. Private	Unk	July 29, 1861, Madison, Georgia	Co. D, 3rd Battalion Georgia Sharp shooters	August 16, 1864, Front Royal, Virginia	Point Lookout, Maryland, transferred to Elmira Prison, NY August 29, 1864	Died May 19, 1865 of Chronic Diarrhea, Grave No. 2952. Headstone has J. W. Almond.
Almand, John B. Private	Unk	September 21, 1861, Conyers, Georgia	Co. B, 35th Georgia Infantry	May 7, 1864, Wilderness, Virginia	Point Lookout, Maryland, transferred to Elmira Prison, NY July 30, 1864	Oath of Allegiance May 16, 1865
Almandinger, George E. Private	27	April 25, 1861, New Orleans, Louisiana	Co. A, 1st Louisiana Infantry	May 5, 1864, Wilderness, Virginia	Point Lookout, Maryland, transferred to Elmira Prison, NY August 17, 1864	Exchanged February 25, 1865 at Boulware's or Cox Wharf on the James River, Virginia

Name & Rank	Age	Enlisted	Regiment and State	Where Captured	Prison	Remarks
Almond, James M. Private	Unk	July 29, 1861, Madison, Georgia	Co. D, 3rd Battalion Georgia Sharp Shooters	August 16, 1864, Front Royal, Virginia	Old Capitol Prison, Washington, D. C., transferred to Elmira October 28, 1864	Died May 18, 1865 of Chronic Diarrhea, Grave No. 2952
Alphin, Calvin M. Private	20	August 6, 1861, Weldon, North Carolina	Co. B, 24th North Carolina Infantry	June 17, 1864, Petersburg, Virginia	Point Lookout, Maryland, transferred to Elmira Prison, NY July 30, 1864	Oath of Allegiance June 19, 1865
Alsom, Floyd Private	Unk	Unknown	Co. K, 2nd Virginia Cavalry	Unknown	Unknown	Died December 20, 1864 of Unknown Causes, Grave No. 932
Alsop, Richard B. Private	Unk	June 17, 1861, King's Mill, Virginia	Co. B, 15th Virginia Infantry	April 6, 1865, Sailor's Creek, Virginia	Old Capital Prison, Washington D. C. Transferred to Elmira Prison, NY May 2, 1865.	Oath of Allegiance June 23, 1865
Alston, Arthur L. Sergeant	33	May 15, 1862, Halifax County, North Carolina	Co. D, 24th North Carolina Infantry	June 17, 1864, Petersburg, Virginia	Point Lookout, Maryland, transferred to Elmira Prison, NY July 30, 1864	Oath of Allegiance June 21, 1865
Alston, Gideon Private	Unk	July 16, 1862, Camp Holmes, Raleigh, North Carolina	Co. D, 24th North Carolina Infantry	June 17, 1864, Petersburg, Virginia	Point Lookout, Maryland, transferred to Elmira Prison, NY July 30, 1864	Exchanged March 2, 1865 at Akins Landing on the James River, Virginia
Alston, Willis E. Corporal	32	March 12, 1862, Fort Pillow, Tennessee	Co. A, 1st Tennessee Heavy Artillery	August 23, 1864, Fort Morgan, Alabama	Fort Columbus, New York Harbor. Transferred February 4, 1865 Elmira, Prison Camp, NY	Oath of Allegiance July 7, 1865
Altman, James A. Civilian	Unk	Unknown	Citizen of Virginia	Unknown	Unknown	Died August 3, 1864 of Unknown Causes, Grave No. 5

Name & Rank	Age	Enlisted	Regiment and State	Where Captured	Prison	Remarks
Altman, James P. Private	27	January 1, 1862, Camp Harlee Britton's Neck, South Carolina	Co. A, 21st South Carolina Infantry	June 16, 1864, Petersburg, Virginia	Point Lookout, Maryland, transferred to Elmira Prison, NY July 12, 1864	Died March 29, 1865 of Chronic Diarrhea, Grave No. 2536
Altman, John J. Private	Unk	March 15, 1864, Marion, South Carolina	Co. J, 21st South Carolina Infantry	January 15, 1865, Fort Fisher, North Carolina	Elmira Prison Camp January 30, 1865	Exchanged March 10, 1865 at Boulware's Wharf on the James River, Virginia
Altman, Nathan T. Private	18	July 23, 1863, Wilmington, North Carolina	Co. G, 40th Regiment, 3rd North Carolina Artillery	January 15, 1865, Fort Fisher, North Carolina	Elmira Prison Camp, New York, January 30, 1865	Died April 18, 1865 of Chronic Diarrhea, Grave No. 1361
Altman, Owen Private	21	July 15, 1861, Whippy Swamp, South Carolina	Co. D, 11th South Carolina Infantry	January 15, 1865, Fort Fisher, North Carolina	February 1, 1865, Elmira Prison Camp, New York	Exchanged March 14, 1865 at Boulware's Wharf on the James River, Virginia
Altmore, Sitgreaves Private	Unk	March 6, 1864, Camp Holmes, North Carolina	Co. K, 1st North Carolina Artillery	January 15, 1865, Fort Fisher, North Carolina	Elmira Prison Camp January 30, 1865	Exchanged February 20, 1865 at Boulware's or Cox Wharf on the James River, Virginia
Ames, Abel Civilian	Unk	Unknown	Citizen of Chesterfield County Virginia	May 14, 1864, Chesterfield County Court House, Virginia	Point Lookout, Maryland, transferred to Elmira Prison, NY July 25, 1864	Died August 3, 1864 of Chronic Diarrhea. Grave No. 5
Amieson, William Private	Unk	December 30, 1861, Nashville, Tennessee	Co. I, 44th Tennessee Infantry	June 17, 1864, Petersburg, Virginia	Point Lookout, Maryland, transferred to Elmira Prison, NY July 30, 1864	Exchanged March 10, 1865 at Boulware's Wharf on the James River, Virginia
Ammons, Thomas Private	Unk	January 13, 1862, Skidaway, Georgia	Co. G, 60th Georgia Infantry	May 25, 1864, Hanover Junction, Virginia	Point Lookout, Maryland, transferred to Elmira Prison, NY July 11, 1864	Oath of Allegiance May 19, 1865
Amole, James P. Private	23	June 2, 1861, Lexington, Virginia	Co. J, 4th Virginia Infantry	May 12, 1864, Near Spotsylvania Court House, Virginia	Point Lookout, Maryland, transferred to Elmira Prison, NY August 6, 1864	Oath of Allegiance June 16, 1865

Name & Rank	Age	Enlisted	Regiment and State	Where Captured	Prison	Remarks
Amos, David Private	22	March 16, 1864, Atlanta, Georgia	Co. B, Jackson's 1st Regiment, Tennessee Heavy Artillery	August 23, 1864, Fort Morgan, Alabama	New Orleans, Louisiana transferred to Elmira December 4, 1864.	Had orders for Elmira, New York. Died December 10, 1864 of Variola (Smallpox) at Fort Columbus NY Harbor.
Amos, James P. Private	Unk	June 8, 1861, Isbell's Store, Virginia	Co. D, 44th Virginia Infantry	May 12, 1864, Spotsylvania Court House, Virginia	Point Lookout, Maryland, transferred to Elmira Prison, NY August 2, 1864	Oath of Allegiance June 16, 1865
Amos, Pinkney M. Private	24	March 11, 1862, Spring Garden, North Carolina	Co. D, 45th North Carolina Infantry	July 13, 1864, Near Washington, DC	Old Capital Prison, Washington, DC, transferred to Elmira Prison, NY, December 17, 1864	Exchanged February 13, 1865 at Boulware's Wharf on the James River, Virginia
Amoss, W. Private	Unk	September 12, 1861, Darien, Georgia	Co. B, 26th Georgia Infantry	May 6, 1864, Wilderness, Virginia	Point Lookout, Maryland, transferred to Elmira Prison, NY August 14, 1864	Oath of Allegiance June 16, 1865
Anders, Burras Private	Unk	May 3, 1862, Gap Civil, Allegheny County, North Carolina	Co. J, 61st North Carolina Infantry	June 16, 1864, Petersburg, Virginia	Point Lookout, Maryland, transferred to Elmira Prison, NY July 25, 1864	Oath of Allegiance June 21, 1865
Anders, John G. Private	17	July 23, 1861, Camp Johnson, Democrat, North Carolina	Co. B, 25th North Carolina Infantry	June 17, 1864, Petersburg, Virginia	Point Lookout, Maryland, transferred to Elmira Prison, NY July 30, 1864	Exchanged February 20, 1865 at Boulware's or Cox Wharf on the James River, Virginia
Anderson, Charles R. Private	25	January 1, 1863, Mississippi	Co. H, 1st Missouri Cavalry	May 17, 1863, Big Black Bridge, Champion Hill, Mississippi	Point Lookout, Maryland, transferred to Elmira Prison, NY August 18, 1864	Exchanged February 13, 1865 at Boulware's wharf on the James River, Virginia
Anderson, David B. 1st Sergeant	Unk	November 1, 1862, Lebanon, Tennessee	Co. A, Jackson's 1st Regiment, Tennessee Heavy Artillery	August 23, 1864, Fort Morgan, Alabama	New Orleans, Louisiana transferred to Elmira December 4, 1864.	Exchanged March 10, 1865 at Boulware's Wharf on the James River, Virginia

Name & Rank	Age	Enlisted	Regiment and State	Where Captured	Prison	Remarks
Anderson, Francis M. Private	Unk	October 15, 1861, Bowling Green, Kentucky	Co. G, 23rd Tennessee Infantry	June 17, 1864, Petersburg, Virginia	Point Lookout, Maryland, transferred to Elmira Prison, NY July 30, 1864	Exchanged February 13, 1865 at Boulware's wharf on the James River, Virginia
Anderson, G. W. Sergeant	Unk	July 24, 1861, Clarksville, Georgia	Co. E, 16th Georgia Infantry	August 16, 1864, Front Royal, Virginia	Point Lookout, Maryland, transferred to Elmira Prison, NY August 18, 1864	Oath of Allegiance June 21, 1865
Anderson, George Private	40	September 14, 1861, Camp Macon, Pitt County, North Carolina	Co. G, 8th North Carolina Infantry	June 1, 1864, Cold Harbor, Virginia	Point Lookout, Maryland, transferred to Elmira Prison, NY July 17, 1864	Died September 18, 1864 of Pneumonia, Grave No. 152
Anderson, George H. Private	45	October 5, 1863, Fort Caswell, Brunswick County, North Carolina	Co. D, 36th, 2nd North Carolina Artillery	January 15, 1865, Fort Fisher, North Carolina	February 1, 1865, Elmira Prison Camp, New York	Died April 10, 1865 of Chronic Diarrhea, Grave No. 2674
Anderson, George W. Private	Unk	January 1, 1864, Monroe County Draft, Virginia	Co. D, 26th Battalion Virginia Infantry	June 3, 1864, Gaines Farm, Cold Harbor, Virginia	Point Lookout, Maryland, transferred to Elmira Prison, NY July 17,1864	Died January 13, 1865 of Pneumonia, Grave No. 1476
Anderson, George W. Private	Unk	Unknown	Co. H, 4th Virginia Cavalry	October 23, 1864, Chester's Gap, Virginia	Old Capital Prison, Washington, DC, transferred to Elmira Prison, NY, December 17, 1864	Exchanged March 10, 1865 at Boulware's Wharf on the James River, Virginia
Anderson, George W. Sergeant	24	September 14, 1861, Smyth County, Virginia	Co. E, 23rd Battalion Virginia Infantry	July 15, 1864, Rockville, Virginia	Old Capital Prison, Washington, DC, transferred to Elmira Prison, NY, July 23, 1864	Died October 9, 1864 of Chronic Diarrhea, Grave No. 673
Anderson, Henry Private	Unk	May 10, 1864, Wayne County, North Carolina	Co. D, 40th Regiment, 3rd North Carolina Artillery	January 15, 1865, Fort Fisher, North Carolina	February 1, 1865, Elmira Prison Camp, New York	Oath of Allegiance July 19, 1865

Name & Rank	Age	Enlisted	Regiment and State	Where Captured	Prison	Remarks
Anderson, J. B. Private	Unk	Unknown	Tanner's Battery State Unknown	July 27, 1864, Petersburg, Virginia	Point Lookout, Maryland, transferred to Elmira Prison, NY August 12, 1864	Oath of Allegiance May 13, 1865
Anderson, J. W. Private	Unk	February 1, 1864, Halifax County, Virginia	Co. C, 3rd Virginia Cavalry	August 21, 1864, Front Royal, Virginia	Old Capitol Prison, Washington, D. C., transferred to Elmira October 28, 1864	Died October 19, 1864 of Chronic Diarrhea, Grave No. 537
Anderson, James P. Private	Unk	April 30, 1862, Macon, Georgia	Co. J, 61st Georgia Infantry	May 12, 1864, Spotsylvania Court House, Virginia	Point Lookout, Maryland, transferred to Elmira Prison, NY July 25, 1864	Died February 12, 1865 of Pneumonia, Grave No. 2043
Anderson, James S. Private	34	July 15, 1862, Forsyth County, North Carolina	Co. G, 33rd North Carolina Infantry	May 12, 1864, Spotsylvania Court House, Virginia	Point Lookout, Maryland, transferred to Elmira Prison, NY August 12, 1864	Oath of Allegiance May 19, 1865
Anderson, John Corporal	Unk	June 11, 1864, Marianna, Florida	Co. A, 1st Reserves Florida Infantry	September 27, 1864, Marianna, Florida	New Orleans, Louisiana transferred to Elmira November 19, 1864.	Exchanged February 13, 1865 at Boulware's Wharf on the James River, Virginia
Anderson, John M. Corporal	21	August 1, 1861, Athens, Clark County, Georgia	Co. C, Cobb's Legion Georgia	May 31, 1864, Hanover Court House, Virginia	Point Lookout, Maryland, transferred to Elmira Prison, NY July 17, 1864	Died October 7, 1864 of Remittent Fever, Grave No. 586
Anderson, Julius C. Private	18	August 1, 1861, Covington, Newton County, Georgia	Co. A, Cobb's Legion Georgia	August 16, 1864, Front Royal, Virginia	Old Capitol Prison, Washington, D. C., transferred to Elmira August 28, 1864	Exchanged March 14, 1865 at Boulware's Wharf on the James River, Virginia
Anderson, Richard Private	25	May 17, 1863, Camp Holmes, North Carolina	Co. D, 7th North Carolina Infantry	May 6, 1864, Wilderness, Virginia	Point Lookout, Maryland, transferred to Elmira Prison, NY July 23, 1864	Died January 26, 1865 of Chronic Diarrhea, Grave No. 1630

Name & Rank	Age	Enlisted	Regiment and State	Where Captured	Prison	Remarks
Anderson, Robert Private		June 15, 1861, Lynchburg, Virginia	Co. A, 42nd Virginia Infantry	May 12, 1864, Spotsylvania Court House, Virginia	Point Lookout, Maryland, transferred to Elmira Prison, NY August 2, 1864	Died January 16, 1865 of Chronic Diarrhea, Grave No. 1439
Anderson, S. Private	Unk	May 26, 1861, Grafton, Virginia	Co. H, 25th Virginia Infantry	May 5, 1864, Wilderness, Virginia	Point Lookout, Maryland, transferred to Elmira Prison, NY August 2, 1864	Oath of Allegiance June 27, 1865
Anderson, Samuel B. Private	Unk	February 5, 1862, Amelia Springs, Virginia	Co. G, 22nd Battalion Virginia Infantry	May 5, 1864, Wilderness, Virginia	Point Lookout, Maryland, transferred to Elmira Prison, NY August 14, 1864	Exchanged March 10, 1865 at Boulware's Wharf on the James River, Virginia
Anderson, Thomas Private	Unk	Unknown	Co. B, Hood's Battalion, Virginia Reserves	June 15, 1864, Petersburg, Virginia	Point Lookout, Maryland, transferred to Elmira Prison, NY July 30, 1864	Oath of Allegiance August 7, 1865 at US Army Hospital, Elmira, NY
Anderson, William Sergeant	25	June 3, 1861, New Orleans, Louisiana	Co. B, 14th Louisiana Infantry	May 12, 1864, Spotsylvania Court House, Virginia	Point Lookout, Maryland, transferred to Elmira Prison, NY July 25, 1864	Oath of Allegiance May 13, 1865
Anderson, William J. Private	24	October 16, 1861, Duplin County, North Carolina	Co. G, 40th Regiment, 3rd North Carolina Artillery	January 15, 1865, Fort Fisher, North Carolina	February 1, 1865, Elmira Prison Camp, New York	Exchanged February 20, 1865 at Boulware's or Cox Wharf on the James River, Virginia
Anderson, William W. Private	Unk	June 29, 1861, Wytheville, Virginia	Co. B, 50th Virginia Infantry	May 12, 1864, Spotsylvania, Virginia	Point Lookout, Maryland, transferred to Elmira Prison, NY July 23, 1864	Oath of Allegiance May 29, 1865
Andrew, Frank C. Private	Unk	March 6, 1863, Vienna, Louisiana	Co. M, 12th Louisiana Infantry	May 16, 1863, Baker's Creek, Champion Hill, Mississippi	Point Lookout, Maryland, transferred to Elmira Prison, NY August 18, 1864	Exchanged February 13, 1865 at Boulware's wharf on the James River, Virginia

Name & Rank	Age	Enlisted	Regiment and State	Where Captured	Prison	Remarks
Andrew, Rufus Private	18	July 8, 1862, Greensboro, North Carolina	Co. H, 1st North Carolina Infantry	May 12, 1864, Spotsylvania Court House, Virginia	Point Lookout, Maryland, transferred to Elmira Prison, NY August 6, 1864	Oath of Allegiance June 12, 1865
Andrews, B. T. Corporal	Unk	October 1, 1861, Nashville, Tennessee	Co. B, Jackson's 1st Regiment, Tennessee Heavy Artillery	August 23, 1864, Fort Morgan, Alabama	New Orleans, Louisiana transferred to Elmira December 4, 1864.	Exchanged March 10, 1865 at Boulware's Wharf on the James River, Virginia
Andrews, Charles Private	30	April 15, 1861, Wilmington, North Carolina	Co. E, 8th North Carolina Infantry	May 31, 1864, Cold Harbor, Virginia	Point Lookout, Maryland, transferred to Elmira Prison, NY July 11, 1864	Oath of Allegiance May 29, 1865
Andrews, George Private	Unk	Unknown	Co. A, 10th Tennessee Infantry	October 4, 1864, Fairfax County, Virginia	Old Capital Prison, Washington, DC transferred to Elmira Prison, NY August 27, 1864	Oath of Allegiance May 19, 1865
Andrews, John J. D. Sergeant	22	October 8, 1861, Hamilton, Martin County, North Carolina	Co. F, 31st North Carolina Infantry	May 31, 1864, Gaines Farm, Cold Harbor, Virginia	Point Lookout, Maryland, transferred to Elmira Prison, NY July 17, 1864	Died April 10, 1865 of Chronic Diarrhea, Grave No. 2662
Andrews, John W. Private	Unk	Unknown	Co. A, 21st Virginia Cavalry	May 8, 1864, Wilderness, Virginia	Point Lookout, Maryland, transferred to Elmira Prison, NY July 12, 1864	Died September 19, 1864 of Unknown Causes, Grave No. 322
Andrews, John W. Private	26	July 1, 1861, Camp Carolina, North Carolina	Co. P, 12th North Carolina Infantry	May 17, 1864, Spotsylvania Court House, Virginia	Point Lookout, Maryland, transferred to Elmira Prison, NY July 6, 1864	Exchanged February 13, 1865 at Boulware's wharf on the James River, Virginia
Andrews, Robert A. Private	36	March 16, 1863, Wilmington, North Carolina	Co. G, 40th Regiment, 3rd North Carolina Artillery	January 15, 1865, Fort Fisher, North Carolina	February 1, 1865, Elmira Prison Camp, New York	Oath of Allegiance June 12, 1865

Name & Rank	Age	Enlisted	Regiment and State	Where Captured	Prison	Remarks
Andrews, Samuel Private	37	September 6, 1862, Drury's Bluff, Virginia	Co. G, 45th North Carolina Infantry	May 10, 1864, Spotsylvania Court House, Virginia	Point Lookout, Maryland, transferred to Elmira Prison, NY August 6, 1864	Oath of Allegiance May 13, 1865
Andrews, T. F. Private	20	July 15, 1862, Chatham County, North Carolina	Co. D, 61st North Carolina Infantry	August 27, 1863, Battery Wagner, Morris Island, South Carolina	Point Lookout, Maryland, transferred to Elmira Prison, NY August 18, 1864	Exchanged October 29, 1864, at Venus Point, Savannah River, GA.
Andrews, Thomas J. Private	Unk	May 9, 1861, Camp Walker, New Orleans, Louisiana	Co. F, 2nd Louisiana Infantry	May 12, 1864, Spotsylvania Court House, Virginia	Point Lookout, Maryland, transferred to Elmira Prison, NY August 14, 1864	Exchanged March 10, 1865 at Boulware's wharf on the James River, Virginia
Andrews, Thomas W. Private	19	April 26, 1861, Townsville, North Carolina	Co. D, 12th North Carolina Infantry	May 18, 1864, Spotsylvania Court House, Virginia	Point Lookout, Maryland, transferred to Elmira Prison, NY July 6, 1864	Exchanged March 10, 1865 at Boulware's Wharf on the James River, Virginia
Andrews, Vincent T. Private	Unk	July 15, 1861, Richmond, Virginia	Co. E, 44th Virginia Infantry	May 12, 1864, Spotsylvania Court House, Virginia	Point Lookout, Maryland, transferred to Elmira Prison, NY August 12, 1864	Oath of Allegiance May 15, 1865
Andrews, W. L. Private	Unk	December 1, 1862, Grahamville, South Carolina	Co. G, 27th South Carolina Infantry	June 24, 1864, Near Petersburg, Virginia	Point Lookout, Maryland, transferred to Elmira Prison, NY August 17, 1864	Oath of Allegiance June 14, 1865
Andrews, William O. Corporal	20	May 18, 1861, Lumberton, North Carolina	Co. D, 18th North Carolina Infantry	May 12, 1864, Spotsylvania Court House, Virginia	Point Lookout, Maryland, transferred to Elmira Prison, NY August 6, 1864	Died November 21, 1864 of Chronic Diarrhea, Grave No. 974
Andrews, William W. Private	Unk	July 19, 1861, Montgomery, Alabama	Co. I, 13th Alabama Infantry	May 12, 1864, Spotsylvania Court House, Virginia	Point Lookout, Maryland, transferred to Elmira Prison, NY August 12, 1864	Died December 26, 1864 of Chronic Diarrhea, Grave No. 1288
Andrews, William W. Private	21	October 8, 1861, Hamilton, Martin County, North Carolina	Co. F, 31st North Carolina Infantry	June 1, 1864, Gaines Farm, Cold Harbor, Virginia	Point Lookout, Maryland, transferred to Elmira Prison, NY July 17, 1864	Exchanged October 29, 1864 at Venus Point, Savannah River, GA.

Name & Rank	Age	Enlisted	Regiment and State	Where Captured	Prison	Remarks
Angel, Marcus L. Corporal	21	March 1, 1862, Newton, North Carolina	Co. F, 23rd North Carolina Infantry	May 12, 1864, Near Spotsylvania Court House, Virginia	Point Lookout, Maryland, transferred to Elmira Prison, NY August 14, 1864	Exchanged October 29, 1864, at Venus Point, Savannah River, GA.
Angle, James Private	16	May 3, 1862, Macon, Georgia	Captain Slayton's Battery, Macon Light Artillery, Georgia Artillery	June 17, 1864, Near Petersburg, Virginia	Point Lookout, Maryland, transferred to Elmira Prison, NY July 30, 1864	Exchanged March 2, 1865 at Akins Landing on the James River, Virginia
Anglin, John G. Private	31	April 24, 1862, Randolph County, Alabama	Co. F, 59th Alabama Infantry	March 25, 1865, Hatchers Run, Virginia. Gunshot Wound Jaw and Right and left Cheek.	Old Capital Prison, Washington D. C. Transferred to Elmira Prison, NY May 2, 1865.	Oath of Allegiance July 19, 1865
Ankers, James E. Private	Unk	October 1, 1862, Snickersville, Virginia	Co. K, 6th Virginia Cavalry	January 8, 1865, Loudoun County, Virginia	Old Capital Prison, Washington D. C. Transferred to Elmira Prison, NY March 27, 1865.	Oath of Allegiance July 11, 1865
Anthony, Anderson Private	Unk	November 13, 1862, Tullahoma, Tennessee	Co. B, 17th Tennessee Infantry	June 17, 1864, Petersburg, Virginia	Point Lookout, Maryland, transferred to Elmira Prison, NY July 30, 1864	Exchanged February 13, 1865 at Boulware's wharf on the James River, Virginia
Anthony, David B. Private	Unk	Unknown	Co. G, 18th North Carolina Infantry	July 14, 1864, Near Washington, DC,	Old Capital Prison, Washington, DC, transferred to Elmira Prison, NY, July 23, 1864	Oath of Allegiance May 13, 1865
Anthony, John A. Private	Unk	May 22, 1862, Lincolnton, North Carolina	Co. D, 1st North Carolina Infantry	May 12, 1864, Spotsylvania Court House, Virginia	Point Lookout, Maryland, transferred to Elmira Prison, NY August 6, 1864	Died October 26, 1864 of Typhoid Fever, Grave No. 715

Name & Rank	Age	Enlisted	Regiment and State	Where Captured	Prison	Remarks
Anthony, Miskel Private	Unk	June 4, 1861, Warsaw, Virginia	Co. D, 40th Virginia Infantry	May 5, 1864, Wilderness, Virginia	Point Lookout, Maryland, transferred to Elmira Prison, NY August 14, 1864	Died December 13, 1864 of Pneumonia, Grave No. 1129
Antley, M. Furman Private	Unk	April 11, 1862, Coles Island, South Carolina	Co. G. 25th South Carolina Infantry	January 15, 1865, Fort Fisher, North Carolina	Elmira Prison Camp January 30, 1865	Oath of Allegiance June 27, 1865
Anton, J. G. Private	Unk	Unknown	Co. D, 5th North Carolina Infantry	Unknown	Unknown	Died March 19, 1865 of Unknown Disease, Grave No. 1727
Apel, T. Private	Unk	May 8, 1862, Augusta, Georgia	Co. A, 7th Georgia Cavalry	June 11, 1864, Trevilian Station, Louisa Court House, Virginia	Point Lookout, Maryland, transferred to Elmira Prison, NY July 25, 1864	Oath of Allegiance June 21, 1865
Apple, Andrew F. Private	17	March 20, 1862, Greensboro, North Carolina	Co. B, 5th North Carolina Infantry	May 12, 1864, Spotsylvania Court House, Virginia	Point Lookout, Maryland, transferred to Elmira Prison, NY August 6, 1864	Oath of Allegiance June 27, 1865
Applewhite, Thomas J. Private	21	May 13, 1862, Goldsboro, North Carolina	Co. A, 3rd Virginia Infantry	May 12, 1864, Near Spotsylvania County Court House, Virginia	Point Lookout, Maryland, transferred to Elmira Prison, NY August 14, 1864	Oath of Allegiance June 19, 1865
Archer, B. T. Private	Unk	Unknown	Co. C, Archer Battalion, Virginia	June 9, 1864, Petersburg, Virginia	Unknown	Transferred for Exchange October 11, 1864. Nothing Further.
Archer, F. M. Private	Unk	August 1, 1861, Louina, Alabama	Co. K, 14th Alabama Infantry	May 31, 1864, Mechanicsville, Virginia	Point Lookout, Maryland, transferred to Elmira Prison, NY July 8, 1864	Oath of Allegiance July 11, 1865
Archer, John M. Private	Unk	July 20, 1861, Jefferson, Georgia	Co. E, 3rd Battalion Georgia Sharp shooters	August 16, 1864, Front Royal, Virginia	Point Lookout, Maryland, transferred to Elmira Prison, NY August 29, 1864	Oath of Allegiance June 14, 1865

Name & Rank	Age	Enlisted	Regiment and State	Where Captured	Prison	Remarks
Archer, Robert C. Private	Unk	March 10, 1862, Wytheville, Virginia	Co. A, 4th Virginia Infantry	May 12, 1864, Spotsylvania Court House, Virginia	Point Lookout, Maryland, transferred to Elmira Prison, NY August 2, 1864	Oath of Allegiance June 21, 1865
Archibald, James Private	Unk	July 10, 1861, Grand Junction, Tennessee	Co. A, Jackson's 1st Regiment, Tennessee Heavy Artillery	August 23, 1864, Fort Morgan, Alabama	New Orleans, Louisiana transferred to Elmira December 4, 1864.	Oath of Allegiance May 17, 1865
Ard, Benjamin R. Corporal	18	January 27, 1862, Williamsburg, South Carolina	Co. K, 25th South Carolina Infantry	January 15, 1865, Fort Fisher, North Carolina	January 30, 1865, Elmira Prison Camp, NY	Died June 1, 1865 of Pneumonia, Grave No. 2904
Ard, E. G. Private	23	April 12, 1862, Battery Island, South Carolina	Co. C. 25th South Carolina Infantry	January 15, 1865, Fort Fisher, North Carolina	Elmira Prison Camp January 30, 1865	Oath of Allegiance July 26, 1865
Ard, Emanuel H. Private	Unk	January 1, 1862, Georgetown, South Carolina	Co. K, 21st South Carolina Infantry	May 16, 1864, Near Drury's Bluff, Virginia	Point Lookout, Maryland, transferred to Elmira Prison, NY August 17, 1864	Died September 20, 1864 of Chronic Diarrhea, Grave No. 340
Ard, S. R. Private	Unk	April 12, 1862, Battery Island, South Carolina	Co. C. 25th South Carolina Infantry	January 15, 1865, Fort Fisher, North Carolina	Elmira Prison Camp January 30, 1865	Oath of Allegiance July 26, 1865
Armand, E. R. Private	Unk	May 9, 1861, Camp Walker, New Orleans, Louisiana	Co. E, 2nd Louisiana Infantry	May 13, 1864, Spotsylvania Court House, Virginia	Point Lookout, Maryland, transferred to Elmira Prison, NY August 17, 1864	Died March 28, 1865 of Variola (Smallpox), Grave No. 2496
Armentrout, Charles A. Private	Unk	April 16, 1862, Rudes Hill, Virginia	Co. D, 2nd Virginia Infantry	May 12, 1864, Spotsylvania Court House, Virginia	Point Lookout, Maryland, transferred to Elmira Prison, NY August 6, 1864	Oath of Allegiance June 27, 1865
Armstrong, Alfred Corporal	Unk	March 30, 1862, Camp Allegheny, Virginia	Co. F, 25th Virginia Infantry	May 5, 1864, Wilderness, Virginia	Point Lookout, Maryland, transferred to Elmira Prison, NY August 14, 1864	Oath of Allegiance June 23, 1865

Name & Rank	Age	Enlisted	Regiment and State	Where Captured	Prison	Remarks
Armstrong, Henry A. Private	27	May 16, 1861, Columbia, North Carolina	Co. A, 32nd North Carolina Infantry	July 13, 1864, Near Washington, DC,	Old Capital Prison, Washington, DC, transferred to Elmira Prison, NY, July 23, 1864	Oath of Allegiance July 3, 1865
Armstrong, Henry W. Private	35	July 26, 1861, Edgecombe County, North Carolina	Co. C, 8th North Carolina Infantry	June 1, 1864, Cold Harbor, Virginia	Point Lookout, Maryland, transferred to Elmira Prison, NY July 17, 1864	Died December 7, 1864 of Chronic Diarrhea, Grave No. 1176
Armstrong, Hudson Private	Unk	March 30, 1862, Camp Allegheny, Virginia	Co. F, 25th Virginia Infantry	May 12, 1864, Spotsylvania Court House, Virginia	Point Lookout, Maryland, transferred to Elmira Prison, NY August 12, 1864	Exchanged March 14, 1865 at Boulware's Wharf on the James River, Virginia
Armstrong, J. J. Private	Unk	November 1, 1863, Talladega, Alabama	Co. C, 13th Alabama Infantry	May 12, 1864, Spotsylvania Court House, Virginia	Point Lookout, Maryland, transferred to Elmira Prison, NY July 30, 1864	Exchanged October 29, 1864 at Venus Point, Savannah River, GA.
Armstrong, Joseph H. Private	Unk	March 7, 1862, Abbeville, Alabama	Co. B, 6th Alabama Infantry	May 20, 1864, Spotsylvania Court House, Virginia	Point Lookout Prison Camp, Maryland. Transferred to Elmira Prison Camp, NY, July 6, 1864	Oath of Allegiance June 23, 1865
Armstrong, Josiah Private	Unk	March 30, 1862, Camp Allegheny, Virginia	Co. F, 25th Virginia Infantry	May 5, 1864, Wilderness, Virginia	Point Lookout, Maryland, transferred to Elmira Prison, NY August 14, 1864	Died September 14, 1864 of Chronic Diarrhea, Grave No. 273. Joseph on Headstone.
Armstrong, Price O. T. Private	Unk	June 8, 1862, Isabel's Store, Virginia	Co. D, 44th Virginia Infantry	May 12, 1864, Spotsylvania Court House, Virginia	Point Lookout, Maryland, transferred to Elmira Prison, NY August 2, 1864	Died August 24, 1864 of Chronic Diarrhea, Grave No. 40
Armstrong, R. C. Private	32	July 17, 1861, Navarrow County, Texas	Co. J, 4th Texas Infantry	May 10, 1864, Spotsylvania Court House, Virginia	Point Lookout, Maryland, transferred to Elmira Prison, NY August 17, 1864	Died January 28, 1865 of Pneumonia, Grave No. 1811

Name & Rank	Age	Enlisted	Regiment and State	Where Captured	Prison	Remarks
Armstrong, S. Private	Unk	Unknown	Co. P, 6th Alabama Infantry	May 16, 1864, Spotsylvania Court House, Virginia	Point Lookout, Maryland, transferred to Elmira Prison, NY July 23, 1864	Oath of Allegiance June 13, 1865
Armstrong, Stephen P. Private	Unk	June 8, 1861, Isbell's Store, Virginia	Co. D, 44th Virginia Infantry	May 12, 1864, Spotsylvania Court House, Virginia	Point Lookout, Maryland, transferred to Elmira Prison, NY August 2,1864	Oath of Allegiance June 16, 1865
Armstrong, William Private	Unk	June 18, 1861, Camp Trousdale, Tennessee	Co. C, 17th Tennessee Infantry	June 17, 1864, Petersburg, Virginia	Point Lookout, Maryland, transferred to Elmira Prison, NY July 30, 1864	Exchanged February 13, 1865 at Boulware's wharf on the James River, Virginia
Armstrong, William F. Private	24	April 9, 1862, Charleston, South Carolina	Co. G, 18th South Carolina Infantry	July 30, 1864, Petersburg, Virginia	Point Lookout, Maryland, transferred to Elmira Prison, NY August 12, 1864	Exchanged October 29, 1864 at Venus Point, Savannah River, GA.
Armstrong, William H. Sergeant	Unk	June 12, 1861, Union, Tennessee	Co. B, 13th Alabama Infantry	May 5, 1864, Wilderness, Virginia	Point Lookout, Maryland, transferred to Elmira Prison, NY July 30, 1864	Exchanged October 29, 1864 at Venus Point, Savannah River, GA.
Arnett, Neill H. Private	21	February 19, 1862, Fayetteville, North Carolina	Co. C, 3rd North Carolina Infantry	May 12, 1864, Near Spotsylvania Court House, Virginia	Point Lookout, Maryland, transferred to Elmira Prison, NY August 12, 1864	Oath of Allegiance June 27, 1865
Arnold, J. G. Sergeant	18	August 23, 1861, Camp Trousdale, Tennessee	Co. H, 23rd Tennessee Infantry	June 17, 1864, Petersburg, Virginia	Point Lookout, Maryland, transferred to Elmira Prison, NY July 30, 1864	Oath of Allegiance May 15, 1865
Arnold, James Private	Unk	Unknown	Co. B, 50th Virginia Infantry	July 18, 1864, Snickers Gap, Virginia	Old Capital Prison, Washington, D. C. Transferred to Elmira Prison, NY August 12, 1864	Oath of Allegiance June 14, 1865

Name & Rank	Age	Enlisted	Regiment and State	Where Captured	Prison	Remarks
Arnold, James J. Private	23	November 23, 1861, Franklin, North Carolina	Co. K, 1st North Carolina Cavalry	May 27, 1864, Hanover Junction, Virginia	Point Lookout, Maryland, transferred to Elmira Prison, NY July 17, 1864	Exchanged October 29, 1864, at Venus Point, Savannah River, GA.
Arnold, John N. Private	21	November 23, 1861, Franklin, North Carolina	Co. K, 1st North Carolina Infantry	September 13, 1863, Culpepper, Virginia	Point Lookout, Maryland, transferred to Elmira Prison, NY August 18, 1864	Exchanged March 10, 1865 at Boulware's wharf on the James River, Virginia
Arnold, John N. Private	21	November 3, 1861, Franklin, North Carolina	Co. K, 1st North Carolina Cavalry	September 23, 1863, Near Culpepper Court House, Virginia	Point Lookout, Maryland, transferred to Elmira Prison, NY August 16, 1864	Exchanged March 10, 1865 at Boulware's Wharf on the James River, Virginia
Arnold, John. W. Private	Unk	October 1, 1861, Macon, Georgia	Co. I, 61st Georgia, Infantry	May 17, 1864, Spotsylvania Court House, Virginia	Point Lookout, Maryland, transferred to Elmira Prison, NY July 6, 1864	Oath of Allegiance June 16, 1865
Arnold, Needham Corporal	Unk	May 6, 1862, Savannah, Georgia	Co. K, 26th Georgia Infantry	May 20, 1864, Spotsylvania Court House, Virginia	Point Lookout, Maryland, transferred to Elmira Prison, NY July 3, 1864	Oath of Allegiance July 11, 1865
Arnold, Parris D. Private	27	March 8, 1862, Camp Leon, Madison, Florida	Co. D, 5th Florida Infantry	May 12, 1864, Spotsylvania Court House, Virginia	Point Lookout, Maryland, transferred to Elmira Prison, NY July 30, 1864	Oath of Allegiance June 16, 1865
Arnold, R. A. Corporal	21	July 13, 1861, Jacksonville, Florida	Co. L, 2nd Florida Infantry	May 12, 1864, Spotsylvania Court House, Virginia	Point Lookout, Maryland, transferred to Elmira Prison, NY August 12, 1864	Exchanged October 29, 1864 at Venus Point, Savannah River, GA.
Arnold, Thomas Private	Unk	July 3, 1861, Lynchburg, Virginia	Co. G, 42nd Virginia Infantry	May 12, 1864, Near Spotsylvania Court House, Virginia	Point Lookout, Maryland, transferred to Elmira Prison, NY August 2, 1864	Oath of Allegiance June 27, 1865
Arnold, William J. Private	Unk	December 28, 1861, Camp Hampton, South Carolina	Co. F, Holcombe Legion, South Carolina	May 8, 1864, Jarrett's Depot, Virginia	Point Lookout, Maryland, transferred to Elmira Prison, NY August 17, 1864	Exchanged October 29, 1864 at Venus Point, Savannah River, GA.

Name & Rank	Age	Enlisted	Regiment and State	Where Captured	Prison	Remarks
Aron, Henry Private	Unk	July 7, 1862, Rowan County, North Carolina	Co. K, 57th North Carolina Infantry	August 22, 1864, Charlestown, Virginia	Point Lookout, Maryland, transferred to Elmira Prison, NY August 29, 1864	Oath of Allegiance July 19, 1865
Arrington, James L. Private	33	August 16, 1861, Warren County, North Carolina	Co. B, 30th North Carolina Infantry	May 20, 1864, Spotsylvania Court House, Virginia	Point Lookout, Maryland, transferred to Elmira Prison, NY July 23, 1864	Died February 7, 1865 of Variola (smallpox), Grave No. 1925
Arrington, James L. Private	25	February 4, 1862, Newbern, North Carolina	Co. F, 36th, 2nd North Carolina Artillery	January 15, 1865, Fort Fisher, North Carolina	February 1, 1865, Elmira Prison Camp, New York	Exchanged March 2, 1865 at Akins Landing on the James River, Virginia
Arrington, Robert E. Private	Unk	July 24, 1861, John Pasley's, Franklin County Virginia	Co. E, 58th Virginia Infantry	May 20, 1864, Spotsylvania Court House, Virginia	Point Lookout, Maryland, transferred to Elmira Prison, NY July 6, 1864	Oath of Allegiance June 16, 1865
Arrington, T. H. Private	18	June 11, 1863, Raleigh, North Carolina	Co. H, 32nd North Carolina Infantry	May 10, 1864, Spotsylvania, Virginia	Point Lookout, Maryland, transferred to Elmira Prison, NY August 6, 1864	Oath of Allegiance June 23, 1865
Arrowood, David Private	Unk	March 23, 1863, Moore County, North Carolina	Co. D, 13th Battalion North Carolina Light Artillery	January 15, 1865, Fort Fisher, North Carolina	February 1, 1865, Elmira Prison Camp, New York	Died March 14, 1865 of Diarrhea, Grave No. 1815. Headstone has David Arwood.
Arther, Charles E. Private	Unk	May 31, 1861, Yellow Branch, Virginia	Co. D, 42nd Virginia Infantry	May 12, 1864, Near Spotsylvania Court House, Virginia	Point Lookout, Maryland, transferred to Elmira Prison, NY August 6, 1864	Oath of Allegiance June 19, 1865
Arthur, William Sergeant	19	April 18, 1861, Halltown, Virginia	Co. B, 2nd Virginia Infantry	May 12, 1864, Near Spotsylvania Court House, Virginia	Point Lookout, Maryland, transferred to Elmira Prison, NY August 6, 1864	Exchanged March 14, 1865 at Boulware's Wharf on the James River, Virginia

Name & Rank	Age	Enlisted	Regiment and State	Where Captured	Prison	Remarks
Ary, Richard T. Private	Unk	September 3, 1862, Statesville, North Carolina	Co. F, 23rd North Carolina Infantry	May 12, 1864, Near Spotsylvania Court House, Virginia	Point Lookout, Maryland, transferred to Elmira Prison, NY August 14, 1864	Died February 17, 1865 of Variola (Smallpox), Grave No. 2220. Name Ayre on Headstone.
Asbury, Sidney M. Private	18	August 12, 1863, Newton, North Carolina	Co. C, 28th North Carolina Infantry	May 12, 1864, Spotsylvania Court House, Virginia	Point Lookout, Maryland, transferred to Elmira Prison, NY August 12, 1864	Oath of Allegiance June 19, 1865
Asbury, William H. Private	Unk	March 5, 1864, Charlotte, North Carolina	Co. C, 28th North Carolina Infantry	May 12, 1864, Spotsylvania Court House, Virginia	Point Lookout, Maryland, transferred to Elmira Prison, NY August 12, 1864	Oath of Allegiance June 27, 1865
Ash, F. J. Sergeant	Unk	Unknown	Co. A, 26th Virginia Infantry	June 15, 1864, Near Petersburg, Virginia	Point Lookout, Maryland, transferred to Elmira Prison, NY July 30, 1864	Oath of Allegiance July 3, 1865
Ash, George C. Private	26	March 14, 1862, Jasper, Florida	Co. B, 5th Florida Infantry	May 12, 1864, Spotsylvania Court House, Virginia	Point Lookout, Maryland, transferred to Elmira Prison, NY July 30, 1864	Oath of Allegiance June 19, 1865
Ashbaugh, Joseph H. Private	Unk	March 10, 1862, Winchester, Virginia	Co. A, 2nd Virginia Infantry	May 12, 1864, Near Spotsylvania Court House, Virginia	Point Lookout, Maryland, transferred to Elmira Prison, NY August 6, 1864	Exchanged February 13, 1865 at Boulware's wharf on the James River, Virginia
Ashby, Benjamin A. Private	Unk	Unknown	Co. I, 2nd Virginia Infantry	October 31, 1864, Front Royal, Virginia	November 11, 1864, Old Capital Prison, Washington, DC. February 15, 1865 Elmira, Prison Camp, NY.	Oath of Allegiance May 17, 1865
Ashby, Charles L. Private	26	April 18, 1861, Berryville, Virginia	Co. J, 2nd Virginia Infantry	May 12, 1864, Near Spotsylvania Court House, Virginia	Point Lookout, Maryland, transferred to Elmira Prison, NY August 2, 1864	Exchanged March 10, 1865 at Boulware's wharf on the James River, Virginia

Name & Rank	Age	Enlisted	Regiment and State	Where Captured	Prison	Remarks
Ashcraft, Stephen H. Private	27	August 23, 1862, Union County, North Carolina	Co. A, 48th North Carolina Infantry	May 12, 1864, Spotsylvania Court House, Virginia	Point Lookout, Maryland, transferred to Elmira Prison, NY August 12, 1864	Died September 9, 1864 of Chronic Diarrhea, Grave No. 208. Headstone has State as VA.
Ashford, Robert A. Private	Unk	February 4, 1864, Augusta, Georgia	Co. F, 12th Battalion Georgia Light Artillery	July 16, 1864, Poolesville, Maryland	Old Capital Prison, Washington, DC, transferred to Elmira Prison, NY, July 25, 1864	Exchanged February 20, 1865 at Boulware's or Cox Wharf on the James River, Virginia
Ashley, Cary Private	Unk	February 12, 1864, Jefferson, North Carolina	Co. A, 26th North Carolina Infantry	May 12, 1864, Spotsylvania Court House, Virginia	Point Lookout, Maryland, transferred to Elmira Prison, NY July 30, 1864	Oath of Allegiance June 12, 1865
Ashley, William Private	29	May 14, 1862, Saltillo, Mississippi	Co. K, 42nd Mississippi Infantry	May 5, 1864, Wilderness, Virginia	Point Lookout, Maryland, transferred to Elmira Prison, NY August 14, 1864	Exchanged February 20, 1865 at Boulware's or Cox Wharf on the James River, Virginia
Ashton, Gurden C. Sergeant	37	March 8, 1862, Norfolk County, Virginia	Co. D, 61st Virginia Infantry	June 10, 1864, Cold Harbor, Virginia	Point Lookout, Maryland, transferred to Elmira Prison, NY July 23, 1864	Oath of Allegiance 12/21/1864. Early Release per Lincoln's Proclamation, 12/8/1863.
Ashton, Lawrence Private	Unk	April 25, 1861, Warrenton, Virginia	Co. H, 4th Virginia Cavalry	May 12, 1864, Spotsylvania Court House, Virginia	Point Lookout, Maryland, transferred to Elmira Prison, NY August 12, 1864	Exchanged October 29, 1864 at Venus Point, Savannah River, GA.
Askew, Thomas Corporal	18	September 11, 1862, Richmond, Virginia	Co. H, 1st North Carolina Infantry	May 12, 1864, Spotsylvania Court House, Virginia	Point Lookout, Maryland, transferred to Elmira Prison, NY August 6, 1864	Died December 13, 1864 of Pneumonia, Grave No. 1132
Aston, Leander Private	Unk	May 28, 1863, North Carolina	Co. A, 51st North Carolina Infantry	June 15, 1864, Petersburg, Virginia	Point Lookout, Maryland, transferred to Elmira Prison, NY July 12, 1864	Died December 3, 1864 of Pneumonia, Grave No. 880

Name & Rank	Age	Enlisted	Regiment and State	Where Captured	Prison	Remarks
Atkins, Thomas Private	Unk	Unknown	Co. J, 26th North Carolina Infantry	June 17, 1864, Near Petersburg, Virginia	Point Lookout, Maryland, transferred to Elmira Prison, NY July 30, 1864	Oath of Allegiance June 19, 1865
Atkins, W. N. Private	Unk	May 30, 1862, Richmond, Virginia	Co. D, 5th Virginia Cavalry	May 14, 1864, Hanover County, Virginia	Point Lookout, Maryland, transferred to Elmira Prison, NY August 17, 1864	Oath of Allegiance June 16, 1865
Atkinson, Henry A. Private	19	March 1, 1864, Richmond, Virginia	Co. F, 3rd Virginia Cavalry	May 8, 1864, Spotsylvania Court House, Virginia	Old Capital Prison, Washington, DC, transferred to Elmira Prison, NY, July 23, 1864	Exchanged February 25, 1865 at Boulware's or Cox Wharf on the James River, Virginia
Atkinson, Hinton C. Private	Unk	May 22, 1864, Fort Morgan, Alabama	Co. E, 1st Battalion Alabama Artillery	August 23, 1864, Fort Morgan, Alabama	Steam Press No. 4, New Orleans, Louisiana transferred to Elmira Prison, October 8, 1864.	Exchanged February 13, 1865 at Boulware's wharf on the James River, Virginia
Atkinson, J. W. Private	30	Date Unknown, Wade County, North Carolina	Co. D, 10th Regiment, 1st North Carolina Artillery	January 15, 1865, Fort Fisher, North Carolina	February 1, 1865, Elmira Prison Camp, New York	Oath of Allegiance June 30, 1865
Atkinson, John T. Private	Unk	May 1, 1862, South Mills, North Carolina	Co. D, 32nd North Carolina Infantry	May 10, 1864, Spotsylvania, Virginia	Point Lookout, Maryland, transferred to Elmira Prison, NY August 6, 1864	Oath of Allegiance August 7, 1865
Atkinson, M. W. Corporal	Unk	May 20, 1862, Summit Station, Virginia	Co. I, 59th Virginia Infantry	May 8, 1864, Nottaway Bridge, Virginia	Point Lookout, Maryland, transferred to Elmira Prison, NY August 17, 1864	Died May 1, 1865 of Chronic Diarrhea, Grave No. 2110
Atkinson, Thomas W. Private	Unk	May 1, 1862, Camp Simmons, South Carolina	Co. G, 21st South Carolina Infantry	January 15, 1865, Fort Fisher, North Carolina	Elmira Prison Camp January 30, 1865	Died April 6, 1865 of Chronic Diarrhea, Grave No. 2631
Atkinson, William E. Private	Unk	March 20, 1864, Richmond, Virginia	Co. F, 3rd Virginia Cavalry	August 16, 1864, Front Royal, Virginia	Point Lookout, Maryland, transferred to Elmira Prison, NY August 29, 1864	Exchanged October 29, 1864, at Venus Point, Savannah River, GA.

Name & Rank	Age	Enlisted	Regiment and State	Where Captured	Prison	Remarks
Atterberry, Charles Private	23	Unknown	Co. C, 2nd Texas Cavalry	April 18, 1864, Chickipage, Louisiana	New Orleans, Louisiana transferred to Elmira November 19, 1864.	Orders for Elmira Prison Camp but Died in Transit November 25, 1864 at General Hospital Fort Columbus, NY.
Attmore, Sitgreaves Private	Unk	March 6, 1864, Camp Holmes, North Carolina	Co. K, 10th Regiment, 1st North Carolina Artillery	January 15, 1865, Fort Fisher, North Carolina	Elmira Prison Camp January 30, 1865	Exchanged February 28, 1865 at Boulware's Wharf on the James River, Virginia
Aucoin, Franklin Private	Unk	October 5, 1861, Camp Moore, Louisiana	Co. G, Consolidated 18th Louisiana Infantry	September 16, 1864, Lafouche Parish, Louisiana	New Orleans, Louisiana transferred to Elmira November 19, 1864.	Oath of Allegiance June 19, 1865
Aumand, Fletcher H. Private	23	October 10, 1862, Raleigh, North Carolina	Co. B, 52nd North Carolina Infantry	May 6, 1864, Wilderness, Virginia	Point Lookout, Maryland, transferred to Elmira Prison, NY July 23, 1864	Oath of Allegiance May 29, 1865
Ausbon, John H. Private	18	May 1, 1862, Williamston, Martin County, North Carolina	Co. J, 1st North Carolina Infantry	May 12, 1864, Near Spotsylvania Court House, Virginia	Point Lookout Prison, Maryland. Transferred to Elmira Prison Camp New York August 6, 1864.	Oath of Allegiance June 21, 1865
Ausley, Albert Private	31	July 21, 1862, Pittsboro, North Carolina	Co. D, 61st North Carolina Infantry	August 27, 1863, Battery Wagner, Morris Island, South Carolina	Point Lookout, Maryland, transferred to Elmira Prison, NY August 18, 1864	Exchanged March 10, 1865 at Boulware's Wharf on the James River, Virginia
Austin, Floyd B. Private	Unk	March 20, 1862, Elk Creek, Virginia	Co. F, 4th Virginia Infantry	May 12, 1864 Spotsylvania Court House, Virginia	Point Lookout, Maryland, transferred to Elmira Prison, NY August 2, 1864	Exchanged March 14, 1865 at Boulware's Wharf on the James River, Virginia
Austin, J. E. Private	Unk	July 16, 1862, Raleigh, North Carolina	Co. D, 5th North Carolina Infantry	May 18, 1864 Spotsylvania Court House, Virginia	Point Lookout, Maryland, transferred to Elmira Prison, NY July 6, 1864	Died March 19, 1865 of Variola (Smallpox). No Grave in Woodlawn National Cemetery.

Name & Rank	Age	Enlisted	Regiment and State	Where Captured	Prison	Remarks
Austin, J. Wesley Private	27	November 1, 1862, Camp Holmes, North Carolina	Co. F, 32nd North Carolina Infantry	May 10, 1864, Wilderness, Virginia	Point Lookout, Maryland, transferred to Elmira Prison, NY August 6, 1864	September 3, 1864 of Chronic Diarrhea, Grave No. 60
Austin, John W. Private	Unk	September 14, 1861, Marion, Virginia	Co. F, 23rd Battalion Virginia Infantry	July 14, 1864, Near Washington, DC,	Old Capital Prison, Washington, DC, transferred to Elmira Prison, NY, July 23, 1864	Oath of Allegiance May 13, 1865
Austin, Richard Private	Unk	July 20, 1864, St. Johns, North Carolina	Co. C, 3rd Battalion North Carolina Light Artillery	January 15, 1865, Fort Fisher, North Carolina	February 1, 1865, Elmira Prison Camp, New York	Died June 11, 1865 of Chronic Diarrhea, Grave No. 2886
Austin, Robert G. Private	17	July 6, 1861, Corinth, Mississippi	Co. B, 20th Mississippi Infantry	May 14, 1862, Raymond, Mississippi	Point Lookout, Maryland, transferred to Elmira Prison, NY August 18, 1864	Exchanged March 10, 1865 at Boulware's wharf on the James River, Virginia
Austin, Samuel D. Private	28	September 7, 1861, Albemarle, North Carolina	Co. K, 28th North Carolina Infantry	May 12, 1864, Spotsylvania Court House, Virginia	Point Lookout, Maryland, transferred to Elmira Prison, NY August 12, 1864	Died December 11, 1864 of Pneumonia, Grave No. 1148
Austin, T. J. Private	Unk	February 1, 1863, Choctaw Bluff, Alabama	Co. A, 21st Alabama Infantry	August 23, 1864, Fort Morgan, Alabama	Steam Press No. 4, New Orleans, Louisiana transferred to Elmira Prison, October 8, 1864.	Died July 7, 1865 of Chronic Diarrhea, Grave No. 2839
Austin, Thomas J. Private	18	January 4, 1864, Greenville, Alabama	Co. C, 1st Battalion Alabama Artillery	August 23, 1864, Fort Morgan, Alabama	New Orleans, Louisiana transferred to Elmira December 4, 1864.	Exchanged March 14, 1865 at Boulware's Wharf on the James River, Virginia
Autry, Isaac Blackman Private	18	April 1, 1863, Kinston, North Carolina	Co. F, 24th North Carolina Infantry	April 1, 1865, Southside Railroad, Virginia	Old Capital Prison, Washington, DC. Transferred to Elmira Prison Camp, NY, May 23, 1865.	Died May 23, 1865 of Pneumonia, Grave No. 2931

Name & Rank	Age	Enlisted	Regiment and State	Where Captured	Prison	Remarks
Autry, James C. Private	28	August 14, 1862, Camp Holmes, Sampson County North Carolina	Co. F, 32th North Carolina Infantry	May 10, 1864, Wilderness, Virginia	Point Lookout, Maryland, transferred to Elmira Prison, NY August 6, 1864	Died November 15, 1864, Chronic Diarrhea, Grave No. 802
Autry, Micajah Private	33	February 9, 1863, Clinton, North Carolina	Co. E, 36th Regiment, 2nd North Carolina Artillery	January 15, 1865, Fort Fisher, North Carolina	February 1, 1865, Elmira Prison Camp, New York	Died April 9, 1865 of Chronic Diarrhea, Grave No. 2621
Autry, Miles C. Private	23	June 1, 1861, Lock's Creek, Fayetteville, North Carolina	Co. F, 24th North Carolina Infantry	June 17, 1864, Near Petersburg, Virginia	Point Lookout, Maryland, transferred to Elmira Prison, NY July 30, 1864	Died October 24, 1864 of Diphtheria, Grave No. 859
Autry, William B. Private	24	June 10, 1861, Fayetteville, North Carolina	Co. A, 5th North Carolina Infantry	May 12, 1864, Spotsylvania Court House, Virginia	Point Lookout, Maryland, transferred to Elmira Prison, NY August 6, 1864	Oath of Allegiance May 17, 1865
Avant, James H. Private	Unk	April 11, 1862, Coles Island, South Carolina	Co. G. 25th South Carolina Infantry	January 15, 1865, Fort Fisher, North Carolina	Elmira Prison Camp January 30, 1865	Exchanged March 2, 1865 at Boulware's Wharf on the James River, Virginia
Avant, O. R. Private	23	December 20, 1861, Camp Harley, Britton's Neck, South Carolina	Co. G, 21st South Carolina Infantry	January 15, 1865, Fort Fisher, North Carolina	Elmira Prison Camp January 30, 1865	Oath of Allegiance July 11, 1865
Avant, Samuel Sergeant	Unk	December 20, 1861, Georgetown, South Carolina	Co. A, 21st South Carolina Infantry	June 24, 1864, Near Petersburg, Virginia	Point Lookout, Maryland, transferred to Elmira Prison, NY August 18, 1864	Died September 26, 1864 of Chronic Diarrhea, Grave No. 447. Headstone has 27th SC.
Avar, L. Private	Unk	Unknown	Co. C, 10th Alabama Infantry	May 7, 1864, Wilderness, Virginia	Point Lookout, Maryland, transferred to Elmira Prison, NY August 17, 1864	Oath of Allegiance June 14, 1865
Avend, John Engineer	Unk	Unknown	Unassigned	May 7, 1864, Homan's Mills, Virginia	Point Lookout, Maryland, transferred to Elmira Prison, NY August 17, 1864	Died December 12, 1864 of Diphtheria, Grave No. 1146

Name & Rank	Age	Enlisted	Regiment and State	Where Captured	Prison	Remarks
Averitt, John Private	36	June 1, 1861, Lock's Creek, Fayetteville, North Carolina	Co. F, 24th North Carolina Infantry	May 16, 1864, Near Drury's Bluff, Virginia	Point Lookout, Maryland, transferred to Elmira Prison, NY July 23, 1864	Exchanged October 29, 1864 at Venus Point, Savannah River, GA.
Averitt, Jonathan H. Private	23	June 1, 1861, Lock's Creek, Fayetteville, North Carolina	Co. F, 24th North Carolina Infantry	June 17, 1864, Petersburg, Virginia	Point Lookout, Maryland, transferred to Elmira Prison, NY July 30, 1864	Exchanged October 29, 1864 at Venus Point, Savannah River, GA.
Averitt, Jordan Private	24	September 3, 1861, Pitt County, North Carolina	Co. G, 8th North Carolina Infantry	May 31, 1864, Cold Harbor, Virginia	Point Lookout, Maryland, transferred to Elmira Prison, NY July 11, 1864	Died January 13, 1865 of Smallpox, Grave No. 1455. Headstone has Jordan Everett.
Averitt, Shepard S. Sergeant	27	May 17, 1861, Lower Black River District, North Carolina	Co. G, 1st North Carolina Infantry	May 12, 1864, Spotsylvania Court House, Virginia	Point Lookout, Maryland, transferred to Elmira Prison, NY August 6, 1864	Exchanged March 14, 1865 at Boulware's Wharf on the James River, Virginia
Averitt, Wiley D. Private	19	June 1, 1861, Lock's Creek, Fayetteville, North Carolina	Co. F, 24th North Carolina Infantry	June 17, 1864, Petersburg, Virginia	Point Lookout, Maryland, transferred to Elmira Prison, NY July 30, 1864	Oath of Allegiance July 26, 1864
Avinger, Alexander P. Sergeant	24	April 11, 1862, Coles Island, South Carolina	Co. F. 25th South Carolina Infantry	January 15, 1865, Fort Fisher, North Carolina	Elmira Prison Camp January 30, 1865	Oath of Allegiance July 7, 1865
Awtry, W. Private	Unk	Unknown	Co. B, 45th Georgia Infantry	May 6, 1864, Wilderness, Virginia	Point Lookout, Maryland, transferred to Elmira Prison, NY August 14, 1864	Oath of Allegiance June 16, 1865
Aymes, O. Private	Unk	September 10, 1862, Baton Rouge, Louisiana	Co. A, Ogden's Regiment Louisiana Cavalry	September 12, 1864, East Baton Rouge, Louisiana	New Orleans, Louisiana transferred to Elmira November 19, 1864.	Exchanged February 13, 1865 at Boulware's wharf on the James River, Virginia

Name & Rank	Age	Enlisted	Regiment and State	Where Captured	Prison	Remarks
Babson, George W. Private	19	April 24, 1861, Columbus County, North Carolina	Co K, 20th North Carolina Infantry	May 12, 1864, Near Spotsylvania Court House, Virginia	Point Lookout, Maryland, transferred to Elmira Prison, NY August 14, 1864	Oath of Allegiance June 14, 1865
Bachemire, A. Civilian	Unk	Registered Enemy	Citizen of Louisiana	July 26, 1864, New Orleans, Louisiana	New Orleans, Louisiana transferred to Elmira November 19, 1864.	Oath of Allegiance June 20, 1865
Bacon, Alfred E. Corporal	Unk	May 9, 1862, Reidsville, Georgia	Co. H, 61st Georgia Infantry	May 12, 1864, Spotsylvania Court House, Virginia	Point Lookout, Maryland, transferred to Elmira Prison, NY July 25, 1864	Exchanged February 20, 1865 at Boulware's or Cox Wharf on the James River, Virginia
Badeaux, Pierre Private	Unk	April 1, 1862, New Orleans, Louisiana	Co. C, 15th Louisiana Infantry	May 20, 1864, Spotsylvania Court House, Virginia	Old Capital Prison, Washington, DC, transferred to Elmira Prison, NY, July 23, 1864	Exchanged February 13, 1865 at Boulware's wharf on the James River, Virginia
Bagby, Josiah W. Sergeant	Unk	June 6, 1861, New Canton, Virginia	Co. C, 44th Virginia Infantry	May 12, 1864, Spotsylvania Court House, Virginia	Point Lookout, Maryland, transferred to Elmira Prison, NY August 2, 1864	Oath of Allegiance June 14, 1865
Bagerly, Tiglman F. Private	31	August 8, 1862, Raleigh, North Carolina	Co. I, 5th North Carolina Infantry	May 12, 1864, Spotsylvania Court House, Virginia	Point Lookout, Maryland, transferred to Elmira Prison, NY August 6, 1864	Oath of Allegiance May 19, 1865
Baggett, James T. Private	18	January 13, 1862, Jackson, North Carolina	Co. F, 1st North Carolina Infantry	May 12, 1864, Spotsylvania Court House, Virginia	Point Lookout, Maryland, transferred to Elmira Prison, NY August 6, 1864	Oath of Allegiance May 29, 1865
Bagnal, Isaac J. M. Private	18	January 1, 1862, Camp Harley, Georgetown, South Carolina	Co. J, 25th South Carolina Infantry	January 15, 1865, Fort Fisher, North Carolina	Elmira Prison Camp January 30, 1865	Oath of Allegiance June 27, 1865
Bail, William F. Private	Unk	March 17, 1862, Charleston, South Carolina	Co. J, 27th South Carolina Infantry	June 24, 1864, Near Petersburg, Virginia	Point Lookout, Maryland, transferred to Elmira Prison, NY August 17, 1864	Oath of Allegiance July 3, 1865

Name & Rank	Age	Enlisted	Regiment and State	Where Captured	Prison	Remarks
Bailey, Alexander T. Private	Unk	October 17, 1861, Hyde County, North Carolina	Co. H, 33rd North Carolina Infantry	July 29, 1864, Petersburg, Virginia	Point Lookout, Maryland, transferred to Elmira Prison, NY August 12, 1864	Oath of Allegiance July 3, 1865
Bailey, Benjamin A. Engineer	Unk	Unknown	Unassigned	May 8, 1864, Jarrett's Depot, Virginia	Point Lookout, Maryland, transferred to Elmira Prison, NY August 17, 1864	Transferred For Exchange October 11, 1864 to Point Lookout Prison Camp, MD. Nothing Further.
Bailey, Charles M. Private	Unk	April 11, 1862, Coles Island, South Carolina	Co. G, 25th South Carolina Infantry	January 15, 1865, Fort Fisher, North Carolina	Elmira Prison Camp January 30, 1865	Died April 19, 1865 of Typhoid Fever, Grave No. 1377
Bailey, Daniel P. Sergeant	22	April 29, 1862, White Sulfur Springs, Virginia	Co. C, 26th Battalion Virginia Infantry	June 3, 1864, Cold Harbor, Virginia. Gunshot Wound Head. Bayonet in Back Penetrating Chest Cavity.	Old Capital Prison, Washington, DC, transferred to Elmira Prison, NY, July 23, 1864	Exchanged March 14, 1865 at Boulware's Wharf on the James River, Virginia
Bailey, David B. Private	Unk	March 12, 1862, Camp Guerin, South Carolina	Co. K, 18th South Carolina Infantry	July 30, 1864, Petersburg, Virginia	Point Lookout, Maryland, transferred to Elmira Prison, NY August 12, 1864	Oath of Allegiance June 14, 1865
Bailey, Elias D. Private	21	September 17, 1862, Raleigh, North Carolina	Co. K, 30th North Carolina Infantry	July 8, 1864, Near Harper's Ferry, Virginia	Old Capital Prison, Washington, DC, transferred to Elmira Prison, NY, July 23, 1864	Died February 19, 1865 of Chronic Diarrhea, Grave No. 2353
Bailey, George T. Private	Unk	February 10, 1863, Choctaw Bluff, Alabama	Co. A, 21st Alabama Infantry	August 23, 1864, Fort Morgan, Alabama	Steam Press No. 4, New Orleans, Louisiana transferred to Elmira Prison, October 8, 1864.	Exchanged February 13, 1865 at Boulware's wharf on the James River, Virginia
Bailey, H. M. Private	Unk	September 5, 1861, Hartwell, Georgia	Co. C, 16th Georgia Infantry	June 1, 1864, Gaines Farm, Cold Harbor, Virginia	Point Lookout, Maryland, transferred to Elmira Prison, NY July 17, 1864	Died February 13, 1865 of Variola (Smallpox), Grave No. 2039

Name & Rank	Age	Enlisted	Regiment and State	Where Captured	Prison	Remarks
Bailey, Henry L. Private	Unk	April 14, 1862, Orangeburg, South Carolina	Co. G, 25th South Carolina Infantry	January 15, 1865, Fort Fisher, North Carolina	Elmira Prison Camp, NY	Died March 13, 1865 of Chronic Diarrhea, Grave No. 2426
Bailey, J. C. Private	Unk	Unknown	Co. C, 45th Georgia Infantry	May 6, 1864, Wilderness, Virginia	Point Lookout, Maryland, transferred to Elmira Prison, NY August 14, 1864	Oath of Allegiance June 16, 1865
Bailey, James D. T. Private	Unk	May 10, 1863, Bulltown, Virginia	Co. E, 20th Virginia Cavalry	July 10, 1864, Near Frederick, Maryland	Old Capital Prison, Washington, DC, transferred to Elmira Prison, NY, July 23, 1864	Died December 9, 1864 of Pneumonia, Grave No. 1163
Bailey, James H. Private	Unk	June 15, 1861, Charlottesville, Virginia	Co. D, 46th Virginia Infantry	June 17, 1864, Petersburg, Virginia	Point Lookout, Maryland, transferred to Elmira Prison, NY July 30, 1864	Oath of Allegiance June 21, 1865
Bailey, James M. Private	Unk	April 16, 1862, Rudes Hill, Virginia	Co. E, 2nd Virginia Infantry	June 10, 1864, Spotsylvania, Virginia	Point Lookout, Maryland, transferred to Elmira Prison, NY July 25, 1864	Oath of Allegiance June 10, 1865
Bailey, John A. Private	Unk	May 16, 1864, Camp 38, Georgia	Co. F, 38th Georgia Infantry	June 1, 1864, Cold Harbor, Virginia	Point Lookout, Maryland, transferred to Elmira Prison, NY July 17, 1864	Oath of Allegiance July 11, 1865
Bailey, John A. Private	Unk	Unknown	Co. E, 66th North Carolina Infantry	August 31, 1863, Big Black, Mississippi	Point Lookout, Maryland, transferred to Elmira Prison, NY August 18, 1864	Exchanged March 10, 1865 at Boulware's wharf on the James River, Virginia
Bailey, John B. Private	Unk	March 14, 1862, Walterboro, South Carolina	Co. I, 11th South Carolina Infantry	May 16, 1864, Near Drury's Bluff, Virginia	Point Lookout, Maryland, transferred to Elmira Prison, NY August 17, 1864	Died March 19, 1865 of Chronic Diarrhea, Grave No. 1726
Bailey, John W. Private	Unk	June 21, 1863, Fetterman, Virginia	Co. A, 25th Virginia Infantry	May 12, 1864, Spotsylvania Court House, Virginia	Point Lookout, Maryland, transferred to Elmira Prison, NY August 2, 1864	Oath of Allegiance June 30, 1865

Name & Rank	Age	Enlisted	Regiment and State	Where Captured	Prison	Remarks
Bailey, Joseph B. Private	Unk	November 1, 1862, Raleigh Court House, Virginia	Co. A, 22nd Virginia Infantry	July 16, 1864, Poolesville, Maryland	Old Capital Prison, Washington, DC, transferred to Elmira Prison, NY, July 23, 1864	Oath of Allegiance May 15. 1865
Bailey, Livingston Sergeant	Unk	May 1, 1861, Talladega, Alabama	Co. E, 5th Alabama Infantry	May 31, 1864, Cold Harbor, Virginia	Point Lookout, Maryland, transferred to Elmira Prison, NY July 11, 1864	Oath of Allegiance June 23, 1865
Bailey, Pleasant Private	Unk	May 1, 1862 White Sulfur Springs, Virginia	Co. C, 22nd Virginia Infantry	July 13, 1864, Near Washington, DC,	Old Capital Prison, Washington, DC, transferred to Elmira Prison, NY, July 23, 1864	Oath of Allegiance May 15, 1865
Bailey, Robert Private	31	May 23, 1861, Richmond, Virginia	Co. C, Captain Young's Company, Halifax Light Artillery Virginia	April 2, 1865, Petersburg, Virginia. Gunshot Wound Hand.	Old Capital Prison, Washington D. C. Transferred to Elmira Prison, NY May 12, 1865.	Oath of Allegiance July 7, 1865
Bailey, William A. Private	19	July 16, 1861, Forestville, North Carolina	Co. I, 1st North Carolina Infantry	May 12, 1864, Spotsylvania Court House, Virginia	Point Lookout, Maryland, transferred to Elmira Prison, NY August 6, 1864	Exchanged February 20, 1865 at Boulware's or Cox Wharf on the James River, Virginia
Bain, Angus Private	27	June 1, 1861, Lock's Creek, Fayetteville, North Carolina	Co. F, 24th North Carolina Infantry	June 17, 1864, Petersburg, Virginia	Point Lookout, Maryland, transferred to Elmira Prison, NY July 30, 1864	Oath of Allegiance July 3, 1865
Bain, Daniel B. Sergeant	23	June 1, 1861, Lock's Creek, Fayetteville, North Carolina	Co. F, 24th North Carolina Infantry	June 17, 1864, Petersburg, Virginia	Point Lookout, Maryland, transferred to Elmira Prison, NY July 30, 1864	Died October 27, 1864 of Pneumonia, Grave No. 714
Baird, James H. Private	31	August 20, 1862, Camp Hill, North Carolina	Co. C, 18th North Carolina Infantry	May 12, 1864, Spotsylvania, Virginia	Point Lookout, Maryland, transferred to Elmira Prison, NY July 23, 1864	Died August 28, 1864 Chronic Diarrhea, Grave No. 50

Name & Rank	Age	Enlisted	Regiment and State	Where Captured	Prison	Remarks
Baird, Lucian B. Private	Unk	July 27, 1863, Culpepper County Court House, Virginia	Co. C, 5th Virginia Cavalry	June 10, 1864, Cold Harbor, Virginia	Point Lookout, Maryland, transferred to Elmira Prison, NY July 30, 1864	Exchanged March 2, 1865 at Akins Landing on the James River, Virginia
Baity, James D. Private	31	August 13, 1862, Camp Hill, North Carolina	Co. G, 5th North Carolina Infantry	May 12, 1864, Spotsylvania Court House, Virginia	Point Lookout, Maryland, transferred to Elmira Prison, NY August 6, 1864	Oath of Allegiance June 30, 1865
Baker, Charles Private	35	June 7, 1861, Camp Moore, Louisiana	Co. B, 7th Louisiana Infantry	May 11, 1864, Near Spotsylvania Court House, Virginia	Point Lookout, Maryland, transferred to Elmira Prison, NY August 17, 1864	Exchanged March 10, 1865 at Boulware's wharf on the James River, Virginia
Baker, Daniel Private	31	March 17, 1862, Wilson, North Carolina	Co. G, 5th North Carolina Infantry	May 12, 1864, Spotsylvania Court House, Virginia	Point Lookout, Maryland, transferred to Elmira Prison, NY August 6, 1864	Oath of Allegiance June 21, 1865
Baker, George Private	Unk	October 4, 1861, Santa Rosa County, Florida	Co. J, 15th Confederate Cavalry	September 27, 1864, Marianna, Florida	New Orleans, Louisiana transferred to Elmira November 19, 1864.	Exchanged February 13, 1865 at Boulware's Wharf on the James River, Virginia
Baker, George H. Corporal	37	October 31, 1861, Catawba County, North Carolina	Co. B, 38th North Carolina Infantry	May 6, 1864, Wilderness, Virginia	Point Lookout, Maryland, transferred to Elmira Prison, NY August 14, 1864	Exchanged February 13, 1865 at Boulware's Wharf on the James River, Virginia
Baker, George S. Corporal	27	February 28, 1862, Coles Island, South Carolina	Co. A, 25th South Carolina Infantry	January 15, 1865, Fort Fisher, North Carolina	Elmira Prison Camp January 30, 1865	Exchanged February 13, 1865 at Boulware's Wharf on the James River, Virginia
Baker, Harrison Private	Unk	August 1, 1862, Tallapoosa County, Alabama	Co. B, 5th Alabama Infantry	May 5, 1864, Wilderness, Virginia	Point Lookout, Maryland, transferred to Elmira Prison, NY August 17, 1864	Transferred for Exchange October 11, 1864. Died Cause and Date Unknown, at Fort Monroe, VA

Name & Rank	Age	Enlisted	Regiment and State	Where Captured	Prison	Remarks
Baker, Ira D. Private	34	March 1, 1862, Chalk Level, North Carolina Cumberland County, North Carolina	Co. C, 36th Regiment 2nd North Carolina Artillery	January 15, 1865, Fort Fisher, North Carolina	Elmira Prison Camp, New York, January 30, 1865	Died April 18, 1865 of Chronic Diarrhea, Grave No. 1361
Baker, James Anderson Private	34	February 26, 1862, Chalk Level, North Carolina	Co. C, 36th Regiment, 2nd North Carolina Artillery	January 15, 1865, Fort Fisher, North Carolina. Wounded.	February 1, 1865, Elmira Prison Camp, New York	Died March 14, 1865, Variola (Smallpox), Grave No. 1666
Baker, Jesse E. Private	Unk	May 1, 1862, Nichol's Depot, South Carolina	Co. F, 51st North Carolina Infantry	June 1, 1864, Cold Harbor, Virginia	Transferred From Point Lookout Prison, MD, July 12, 1864. Train Never Arrived at Elmira Prison Camp, NY.	Died July 15, 1864 in Train Wreck at Shohola, Pennsylvania.
Baker, John H. Private	Unk	June 13, 1863, Lewisburg, Virginia	Co. A, 26th Battalion Virginia Infantry	May 31, 1864, Chickahominy, Cold Harbor, Virginia	Point Lookout, Maryland, transferred to Elmira Prison, NY July 11, 1864	Oath of Allegiance June 30, 1865
Baker, John W. Private	Unk	March 13, 1864, Petersburg, Virginia	Co. G, 31st North Carolina Infantry	June 1, 1864, Cold Harbor, Virginia	Point Lookout, Maryland, transferred to Elmira Prison, NY July 17,1864	Oath of Allegiance July 11, 1865
Baker, John W. Private	20	May 5, 1861, Corinth, Mississippi	Co. H, 12th Mississippi Infantry	June 6, 1864, Cold Harbor, Virginia	Point Lookout, Maryland, transferred to Elmira Prison, NY July 23, 1864	Oath of Allegiance May 29, 1865
Baker, Joseph A. Private	Unk	August 23, 1862, Camp Muddy Creek, Virginia	Co. E, 26th Virginia Infantry	June 3, 1864, Gaines Farm, Cold Harbor, Virginia	Point Lookout, Maryland, transferred to Elmira Prison, NY July 17,1864	Died May 4, 1865 of Pneumonia, Grave No. 2757
Baker, Lemuel S. Private	Unk	July 8, 1861, Griffin, Georgia	Co. D, 13th Georgia Infantry	July 13, 1864, Near Washington, DC,	Old Capital Prison, Washington, DC, transferred to Elmira Prison, NY, July 23, 1864	Exchanged October 29, 1864 at Venus Point, Savannah River, GA.

Name & Rank	Age	Enlisted	Regiment and State	Where Captured	Prison	Remarks
Baker, M. R. D. Corporal	17	April 12, 1862, Battery Island, South Carolina	Co. A, 25th South Carolina Infantry	January 15, 1865, Fort Fisher, North Carolina	Elmira Prison Camp January 30, 1865	Died March 31, 1865 of Diarrhea, Grave No. 2601
Baker, Marsalis C. Private	Unk	May 20, 1861, Louisburg, North Carolina	Co. K, 32nd North Carolina Infantry	May 10, 1864, Spotsylvania, Virginia	Point Lookout, Maryland, transferred to Elmira Prison, NY August 6, 1864	Oath of Allegiance June 30, 1865
Baker, Michael Private	30	October 16, 1862, Raleigh, North Carolina	Co. H, 55th North Carolina Infantry	May 5, 1864, Wilderness, Virginia. Gunshot Wound Right Shoulder and Right to Heel.	Old Capital Prison, Washington, DC, transferred to Elmira Prison, NY, December 17, 1864	Exchanged March 2, 1865 at Akins Landing on the James River, Virginia.
Baker, Noah Private	18	June 16, 1861, Camp Shops, North Carolina	Co. A, 7th North Carolina Infantry	May 6, 1864, Wilderness, Virginia	Point Lookout, Maryland, transferred to Elmira Prison, NY August 14, 1864	Oath of Allegiance June 12, 1865
Baker, Vardrey E. Corporal	19	June 18, 1861, Lincoln Factory, North Carolina	Co. D, 1st North Carolina Infantry	May 12, 1864, Spotsylvania Court House, Virginia	Point Lookout, Maryland, transferred to Elmira Prison, NY August 6, 1864	Oath of Allegiance June 19, 1865
Baker, W. D. Private	Unk	April 7, 1863, Warrenton, Alabama	Co. B, 48th Alabama Infantry	July 14, 1863, Falling Waters, Maryland	Point Lookout, Maryland, transferred to Elmira Prison, NY August 18, 1864	Exchanged October 29, 1864 at Venus Point, Savannah River, GA.
Baker, W. D. Private	Unk	December 10, 1862, McMinnville, Tennessee	Co. E, 25th Tennessee Infantry	May 16, 1864, Near Drury's Bluff, Virginia	Point Lookout, Maryland, transferred to Elmira Prison, NY August 17, 1864	Exchanged February 13, 1865 at Boulware's wharf on the James River, Virginia
Baker, William C. Private	Unk	June 13, 1863, Lewisburg, Virginia	Co. A, 26th Virginia Infantry	May 31, 1864, Chickahominy, Cold Harbor, Virginia	Point Lookout, Maryland, transferred to Elmira Prison, NY July 11, 1864	Exchanged March 2, 1865 at Akins Landing on the James River, Virginia

Name & Rank	Age	Enlisted	Regiment and State	Where Captured	Prison	Remarks
Baldwin, Albert M. Private	18	April 15, 1863, Fort Fisher, North Carolina	Co. K, 40th Regiment, 3rd North Carolina Heavy Artillery	January 15, 1865, Fort Fisher, North Carolina	February 1, 1865, Elmira Prison Camp, New York	Oath of Allegiance June 12, 1865
Baldwin, David S. Private	Unk	July 23, 1861, Arkansas	Co. H, 22nd Virginia Infantry	June 3, 1864, Gaines Farm, Cold Harbor, Virginia	Point Lookout, Maryland, transferred to Elmira Prison, NY July 17,1864	Exchanged March 10, 1865 at Boulware's wharf on the James River, Virginia
Baldwin, R. W. Private	28	May 16, 1862, Charleston, Tennessee	Co. H, 63rd Tennessee Infantry	June 17, 1864, Petersburg, Virginia	Point Lookout, Maryland, transferred to Elmira Prison, NY July 30, 1864	Died December 10, 1864 of Pneumonia, Grave No. 1054
Baldwin, William Corporal	19	February 18, 1862, Wilmington, North Carolina	Co. D, 36th Regiment, 2nd North Carolina Artillery	January 15, 1865, Fort Fisher, North Carolina. Wounded.	February 1, 1865, Elmira Prison Camp, New York	Oath of Allegiance July 11, 1865
Ball, Adam Private	Unk	Unknown	Co. F, 8th North Carolina Infantry	June 1, 1864, Cold Harbor, Virginia	Point Lookout, Maryland, transferred to Elmira Prison, NY July 17,1864	Exchanged March 10, 1865 at Boulware's wharf on the James River, Virginia
Ball, Adam Private	Unk	Unknown	Co. F, 2nd South Carolina Infantry	June 1, 1864, Cold Harbor, Virginia	Point Lookout, Maryland, transferred to Elmira Prison, NY July 17,1864	Exchanged March 10, 1865 at Boulware's wharf on the James River, Virginia
Ball, George D. Private	32	June 19, 1861, New Orleans, Louisiana	Co. F, 14th Louisiana Infantry	May 20, 1864, Spotsylvania Court House, Virginia	Point Lookout, Maryland, transferred to Elmira Prison, NY July 3, 1864	Exchanged February 13, 1865 at Boulware's wharf on the James River, Virginia
Ball, George M. Private	22	June 11, 1861, Henderson County, North Carolina	Co. G, 23rd North Carolina Infantry	May 20, 1864, Spotsylvania Court House, Virginia	Point Lookout, Maryland, transferred to Elmira Prison, NY July 6, 1864	Oath of Allegiance June 19, 1865

Name & Rank	Age	Enlisted	Regiment and State	Where Captured	Prison	Remarks
Ball, John O. Private	19	June 4, 1861, Duplin County, North Carolina	Co. B, 3rd North Carolina Infantry	May 12, 1864, Near Spotsylvania, Virginia	Point Lookout, Maryland, transferred to Elmira Prison, NY August 14, 1864	Exchanged February 20, 1865 at Boulware's or Cox Wharf on the James River, Virginia
Ball, Levi Private	18	November 13, 1862, Camp French, North Carolina	Co. H, 44th North Carolina Infantry	May 24, 1864, Gurne Station, Virginia	Point Lookout, Maryland, transferred to Elmira Prison, NY July 8, 1864	Died March 18, 1865 of Pneumonia, Grave No. 1720
Ball, Thomas M. Landsman	Unk	Unknown	Confederate States Navy	May 5, 1864, Albemarle Sound on Steamer CSS Bombshell	Point Lookout, Maryland, transferred to Elmira Prison, NY August 17, 1864	Oath of Allegiance June 19, 1865
Ball, William Sergeant	Unk	April 22, 1861, Leesburg, Virginia	Co. K, 6th Virginia Cavalry	September 27, 1864, Leesburg, Virginia	Old Capital Prison, Washington, DC transferred to Elmira Prison, NY August 27, 1864	Exchanged February 25, 1865 at Boulware's or Cox Wharf on the James River, Virginia
Ballance, Holloway Private	Unk	September 20, 1863, Hyde County, North Carolina	Co. H, 33rd North Carolina Infantry	July 31, 1864, Petersburg, Virginia	Point Lookout, Maryland, transferred to Elmira Prison, NY August 12, 1864	Died November 7, 1864 of Pneumonia, Grave No. 772
Ballance, James W. Private	19	August 1, 1861, Coinjock, Currituck County, North Carolina	Co. B, 8th North Carolina Infantry	May 31, 1864, Cold Harbor, Virginia	Point Lookout, Maryland, transferred to Elmira Prison, NY July 12, 1864	Exchanged March 10, 1865 at Boulware's Wharf on the James River, Virginia
Ballance, Robert Private	20	August 1, 1861, Coinjock, Currituck County, North Carolina	Co. B, 8th North Carolina Infantry	May 31, 1864, Cold Harbor, Virginia	Point Lookout, Maryland, transferred to Elmira Prison, NY July 12, 1864	Exchanged October 29, 1864 at Venus Point, Savannah River, GA.
Ballentine, Brobstone Sergeant	28	September 27, 1861, Wilmington, North Carolina	Co. B, 36th Regiment North Carolina, 2nd Artillery	January 15, 1865, Fort Fisher, North Carolina	February 1, 1865, Elmira Prison Camp, New York	Exchanged March 20, 1865 at Boulware's Wharf on the James River, Virginia

Name & Rank	Age	Enlisted	Regiment and State	Where Captured	Prison	Remarks
Ballard, Archibald Sergeant	Unk	June 12, 1861, Red Sulfur Springs, Virginia	Co. F, 26th Battalion Virginia Infantry	June 3, 1864, Gaines Farm, Cold Harbor, Virginia	Point Lookout, Maryland, transferred to Elmira Prison, NY July 17, 1864	Died January 6, 1865 of Variola (Smallpox), Grave No. 1504
Ballentine, Brobstone C. Sergeant	28	September 27, 1861, Bladen County, North Carolina	Co. B, 36th Regiment, 2nd North Carolina Artillery	January 15, 1865, Fort Fisher, North Carolina	February 1, 1865, Elmira Prison Camp, New York	Exchanged February 20, 1865 at Boulware's or Cox Wharf on the James River, Virginia
Ballentine, Calvin R. Private	Unk	October 24, 1863, Camp Ransom, Virginia	Co. F, 26th Battalion Virginia Infantry	June 3, 1864, Gaines Mill, Cold Harbor, Virginia	Point Lookout, Maryland, transferred to Elmira Prison, NY July 17,1864	Exchanged October 29, 1864 at Venus Point, Savannah River, GA.
Ballinger, Jabez B. Private	Unk	January 14, 1862, Camp Walsh, South Carolina	Co. J, Holcombe Legion, South Carolina Infantry	May 7, 1864, Stony Creek, Virginia	Point Lookout, Maryland, transferred to Elmira Prison, NY August 17, 1864	Oath of Allegiance June 19, 1865
Balthtrope, Jeremiah A. Private	Unk	April 24, 1861, Salem, Fauquier County, Virginia	Co. H, 6th Virginia Cavalry	January 14, 1865, Recktown, Virginia	November 11, 1864, Old Capital Prison, Washington, DC. February 4, 1865 Elmira, Prison Camp, NY.	Oath of Allegiance July 7, 1865
Bandy, Allen Private	Unk	September 14, 1862, Bryan County, Georgia	Co. H, 7th Georgia Cavalry	June 11, 1864, Trevilian Station, Louisa Court House, Virginia	Point Lookout, Maryland, transferred to Elmira Prison, NY July 25, 1864	Exchanged October 29, 1864 at Venus Point, Savannah River, GA.
Bandy, George D. Private	Unk	April 6, 1863, Fredericksburg, Virginia	Co. B, 58th Virginia Infantry	May 30, 1864 Mechanics-ville, Virginia	Point Lookout, Maryland, transferred to Elmira Prison, NY July 11, 1864	Oath of Allegiance June 30, 1865
Banks, Albert A. Private	Unk	January 28, 1863, Craig County, Virginia	Co. K, 60th Virginia Infantry	July 20, 1864, Berryville, Virginia	Old Capital Prison, Washington, D.C. Transferred to Elmira Prison, NY August 12, 1864	Oath of Allegiance May 13, 1865

Name & Rank	Age	Enlisted	Regiment and State	Where Captured	Prison	Remarks
Banks, Amos Private	Unk	April 3, 1862, Bryan County, Georgia	Co. H, 7th Georgia Cavalry	June 11, 1864, Trevilian Station, Louisa Court House, Virginia	Point Lookout, Maryland, transferred to Elmira Prison, NY July 25, 1864	Died February 12, 1865 of Chronic Diarrhea. Grave No. 2077
Banks, C. F. Private	Unk	April 3, 1862, Bryan County, Georgia	Co. H, 7th Georgia Cavalry	June 11, 1864, Trevilian Station, Louisa Court House, Virginia	Point Lookout, Maryland, transferred to Elmira Prison, NY July 25, 1864	Exchanged October 29, 1864 at Venus Point, Savannah River, GA.
Banks, Ezekiel Private	20	June 6, 1861, Campbellton, Georgia	Co. A, 21st Georgia Infantry	July 13, 1864, Near Washington, DC,	Old Capital Prison, Washington, DC, transferred to Elmira Prison, NY, July 23, 1864	Oath of Allegiance June 16, 1865
Banks, George W. Private	26	November 27, 1863, Charlottesville, Virginia	Co. D, 9th Virginia Infantry	February 4, 1864, Newbern, North Carolina	Point Lookout, Maryland, transferred to Elmira Prison, NY July 25, 1864	Died August 2, 1864 of Chronic Diarrhea, Grave No. 146
Banks, John A. Private	18	May 4, 1861, Pasquotank County, North Carolina	Co. B, 8th North Carolina Infantry	June 1, 1864, Cold Harbor, Virginia	Point Lookout, Maryland, transferred to Elmira Prison, NY July 17, 1864	Died January 14, 1865 of Pneumonia, Grave No. 1462
Banks, Robert R. Private	21	March 20, 1862, Selma, Alabama	Co. C, 4th Alabama Infantry	July 29, 1864, Petersburg, Virginia	Point Lookout, Maryland, transferred to Elmira Prison, NY August 12, 1864	Died October 17, 1864 of Congestion of the Brain, Grave No. 541
Banks, William H. Private	20	June 7, 1861, Camp Moore, Louisiana	Co. B, 7th Louisiana Infantry	May 11, 1864, Near Spotsylvania Court House, Virginia	Point Lookout, Maryland, transferred to Elmira Prison, NY August 17, 1864	Exchanged February 25, 1865 at Boulware's or Cox Wharf on the James River, Virginia
Bankston, John E. Private	35	April 28, 1862, Fayetteville, Georgia	Co. A, 53rd Georgia Infantry	June 1, 1864, Gaines Mill, Cold Harbor, Virginia	Point Lookout, Maryland, transferred to Elmira Prison, NY July 17, 1864	Oath of Allegiance June 16, 1865

Name & Rank	Age	Enlisted	Regiment and State	Where Captured	Prison	Remarks
Bankston, Joseph C. Corporal	Unk	April 27, 1861, Wetumpka, Alabama	Co. I, 3rd Alabama Infantry	May 12, 1864, Spotsylvania Court House, Virginia	Point Lookout, Maryland, transferred to Elmira Prison, NY August 12, 1864	Died November 24, 1864 of Pleurisy Pneumonia, Grave No. 919
Banton, Samuel R. Private	Unk	August 18, 1863, Lynchburg, Virginia	Co. C, 34th Virginia Infantry	May 15, 1864 Near Petersburg, Virginia	Point Lookout, Maryland, transferred to Elmira Prison, NY July 12, 1864	Oath of Allegiance June 16, 1865
Banty, Newbern J. Private	19	January 20, 1862, Meharrin, Virginia	Co. G, 61st Virginia Infantry	May 30, 1864, Cold Harbor, Virginia	Point Lookout, Maryland, transferred to Elmira Prison, NY August 29, 1864	Exchanged October 29, 1864, at Venus Point, Savannah River, GA.
Barbar, William R. Private	26	July 15, 1862, Raleigh, North Carolina	Co. E, 3rd North Carolina Infantry	May 12, 1864, Spotsylvania Court House, Virginia	Point Lookout, Maryland, transferred to Elmira Prison, NY August 14, 1864	Died March 29, 1865 of Chronic Diarrhea, Grave No. 2539
Barbee, James J. Sergeant	21	May 1, 1861, Nashville, North Carolina	Co. H, 12th North Carolina Infantry	May 12, 1864, Near Spotsylvania Court House, Virginia	Point Lookout, Maryland, transferred to Elmira Prison, NY August 14, 1864	Died November 18, 1864 of Pneumonia, Grave No. 971. Name J. J. Barber on Headstone.
Barber, George D. Private	Unk	April 11, 1862, Coles Island, South Carolina	Co. K, 25th South Carolina Infantry	January 15, 1865, Fort Fisher, North Carolina	January 30, 1865, Elmira Prison Camp, NY	Died June 26, 1865 of Chronic Diarrhea, Grave No. 2823
Barber, J. Sergeant	Unk	July 12, 1861, Atlanta, Georgia	Co. J, 14th Georgia Infantry	May 12, 1864, Spotsylvania Court House, Virginia	Point Lookout, Maryland, transferred to Elmira Prison, NY August 6, 1864	Died May 12, 1865 of Pneumonia, Grave No. 2798
Barber, Joseph W. Sergeant	Unk	July 12, 1861, Jackson, Georgia	Co. J, 14th Georgia Infantry	May 6, 1864, Chancellors-ville, Virginia	Point Lookout, Maryland, transferred to Elmira Prison, NY July 28, 1864	Oath of Allegiance May 13, 1865
Barber, William T. Private	Unk	May 13, 1862, Corrine, Mississippi	Co. F, 3rd Battalion Missouri Cavalry	May 17, 1863, Big Black River, Mississippi	Point Lookout, Maryland, transferred to Elmira Prison, NY August 18, 1864	Exchanged February 13, 1865 at Boulware's or Cox Wharf on the James River, Virginia

Name & Rank	Age	Enlisted	Regiment and State	Where Captured	Prison	Remarks
Barbie, Josiah Private	27	August 8, 1862, Raleigh, North Carolina	Co. B, 5th North Carolina Infantry	May 12, 1864, Spotsylvania Court House, Virginia	Old Capital Prison, Washington, DC transferred to Elmira Prison, NY August 27, 1864	Exchanged February 20, 1865 at Boulware's or Cox Wharf on the James River, Virginia
Barbor, William R. Private	26	July 15, 1862, Wayne County, North Carolina	Co. E, 3rd North Carolina Infantry	May 12, 1864, Near Spotsylvania Court House, Virginia	Point Lookout Prison, Maryland. Transferred to Elmira Prison Camp New York August 14, 1864.	Died March 29, 1865 of Chronic Diarrhea, Grave No. 2539
Barbour, J. R. Private	27	November 28, 1861, Troy, Tennessee	Co. A, 1st Tennessee Heavy Artillery	August 23, 1864, Fort Morgan, Alabama. Shell Wound of Head and Right Side.	Steam Press No. 4, New Orleans, Louisiana transferred to Elmira Prison, October 8, 1864.	Exchanged March 10, 1865 at Boulware's Wharf on the James River, Virginia
Barco, Willoughby Private	22	August 1, 1861, Plymouth, North Carolina	Co. B, 8th North Carolina Infantry	May 31, 1864, Cold Harbor, Virginia	Point Lookout, Maryland, transferred to Elmira Prison, NY July 11, 1864	Died January 13, 1865 of Pneumonia, Grave No. 1489
Bardwell, David A. Corporal	Unk	May 12, 1862, West Point, Mississippi	Co. L, 48th Mississippi Infantry	July 10, 1864, Petersburg, Virginia	Old Capital Prison, Washington, DC, transferred to Elmira Prison, NY, July 23, 1864	Oath of Allegiance June 16, 1865
Barefoot, David M. Corporal	18	April 23, 1861, Whiteville, North Carolina	Co. H, 37th North Carolina Infantry	July 29, 1864, Petersburg, Virginia	Point Lookout, Maryland, transferred to Elmira Prison, NY August 12, 1864	Exchanged October 29, 1864 at Venus Point, Savannah River, GA.
Barger, George A. Private	17	September 15, 1862, Salisbury, North Carolina	Co. K, 8th North Carolina Infantry	June 1, 1864, Gaines Farm, Cold Harbor, Virginia	Point Lookout, Maryland, transferred to Elmira Prison, NY July 17, 1864	Exchanged March 14, 1865 at Boulware's Wharf on the James River, Virginia
Barger, Jacob Private	21	August 23, 1861, Salisbury, North Carolina	Co. K, 8th North Carolina Infantry	May 31, 1864, Cold Harbor, Virginia	Point Lookout, Maryland, transferred to Elmira Prison, NY July 11,1864	Oath of Allegiance June 12, 1865

Name & Rank	Age	Enlisted	Regiment and State	Where Captured	Prison	Remarks
Barham, Benjamin F. Private	Unk	March 19, 1862, Luray, Virginia	Co. K, 10th Virginia Infantry	May 12, 1864, Spotsylvania Court House, Virginia	Point Lookout, Maryland, transferred to Elmira Prison, NY August 2, 1864	Oath of Allegiance June 27, 1865
Barham, George S. Private	34	June 18, 1863, Raleigh, North Carolina	Co. I, 1st North Carolina Infantry	May 12, 1864, Spotsylvania Court House, Virginia	Point Lookout, Maryland, transferred to Elmira Prison, NY August 6, 1864	Exchanged February 20, 1865 at Boulware's or Cox Wharf on the James River, Virginia
Barham, Samuel P. Private	Unk	March 20, 1864, Goldsboro, North Carolina	Co. F, 1st North Carolina Artillery	January 15, 1865, Fort Fisher, North Carolina	Elmira Prison Camp January 30, 1865	Died February 24, 1865 of Chronic Diarrhea, Grave No. 2258
Barker, John Private	Unk	August 17, 1863, Americus, Georgia	Co. H, 64th Georgia Infantry	June 17, 1864, Petersburg, Virginia	Point Lookout, Maryland, transferred to Elmira Prison, NY July 30, 1864	Exchanged February 20, 1865 at Boulware's or Cox Wharf on the James River, Virginia
Barker, John D. Private	21	December 5, 1861, Sac River, St. Clair County, Missouri	Co. K, 1st Missouri Cavalry	May 17, 1863, Big Black Bridge, Champion Hill, Mississippi	Point Lookout, Maryland, transferred to Elmira Prison, NY August 18, 1864	Exchanged October 29, 1864 at Venus Point, Savannah River, GA.
Barker, Joshua Private	40	March 20, 1862, Pickens Court House, South Carolina	Co. A, 1st South Carolina Infantry	May 12, 1864, Spotsylvania Court House, Virginia	Point Lookout, Maryland, transferred to Elmira Prison, NY August 29, 1864	Died February 9, 1865 of Pneumonia, Grave No. 1949
Barker, Quinton Private	24	July 15, 1862, Raleigh, North Carolina	Co. G, 1st North Carolina Infantry	May 12, 1864, Spotsylvania Court House, Virginia	Point Lookout, Maryland, transferred to Elmira Prison, NY August 6, 1864	Died February 16, 1865 of Chronic Diarrhea, Grave No. 2212
Barker, William D. Private	20	October 1, 1861, Nashville, Tennessee	Co. L, 1st Jackson's Tennessee Heavy Artillery	August 23, 1864, Fort Morgan, Alabama.	New Orleans, Louisiana transferred to Elmira December 4, 1864.	Oath of Allegiance July 7, 1865

Name & Rank	Age	Enlisted	Regiment and State	Where Captured	Prison	Remarks
Barkley, Henry S. Private	18	September 1, 1863, Mecklenburg County, North Carolina	Co. H, 35th North Carolina Infantry	June 17, 1864, Petersburg, Virginia	Point Lookout, Maryland, transferred to Elmira Prison, NY July 30, 1864	Exchanged February 20, 1865 at Boulware's or Cox Wharf on the James River, Virginia
Barlow, Jesse F. Private	Unk	October 9, 1863, Camden, Alabama	Co. E, 1st Battalion Alabama Artillery	August 23, 1864, Fort Morgan, Alabama	New Orleans, Louisiana transferred to Elmira December 4, 1864.	Died May 15, 1865 of Chronic Diarrhea, Grave No. 2807
Barlow, Joseph J. Sergeant	28	July 1, 1861, Selma, Alabama	Jeff Davis Alabama Artillery	May 5, 1864, Wilderness, Virginia	Point Lookout, Maryland, transferred to Elmira Prison, NY August 17, 1864	Oath of Allegiance June 14, 1865
Barlow, Joseph S. Private	19	September 20, 1862, Charleston, Virginia	Co. A, 26th Virginia Infantry	May 31, 1864, Cold Harbor, Virginia	Point Lookout, Maryland, transferred to Elmira Prison, NY July 11, 1864	Oath of Allegiance May 29, 1865
Barlow, Mason Private	Unk	November 6, 1863, Mobile, Alabama	Co. E, 1st Battalion Alabama Artillery	August 23, 1864, Fort Morgan, Alabama	New Orleans, Louisiana transferred to Elmira December 4, 1864.	Oath of Allegiance July 7, 1865
Barlow, T. W. Private	Unk	August 18, 1863, Pleasant Hill, Alabama	Jeff Davis Alabama Artillery	May 5, 1864, Wilderness, Virginia	Point Lookout, Maryland, transferred to Elmira Prison, NY August 17, 1864	Exchanged October 29, 1864, at Venus Point, Savannah River, GA.
Barlow, William R. Private	32	August 21, 1862, Statesville, North Carolina	Co. B, 18th North Carolina Infantry	May 12, 1864, Spotsylvania, Virginia	Point Lookout, Maryland, transferred to Elmira Prison, NY August 6, 1864	Died of Pneumonia January 31, 1865, Grave No. 1787
Barmer, William J. Private	17	May 12, 1862, Richmond County, North Carolina	Co. E, 52nd North Carolina Infantry	July 14, 1863, Falling Waters, Maryland	Point Lookout, Maryland, transferred to Elmira Prison, NY August 18, 1864	Exchanged March 10, 1865 at Boulware's Wharf on the James River, Virginia

Name & Rank	Age	Enlisted	Regiment and State	Where Captured	Prison	Remarks
Barnard, J. Private	Unk	Unknown	Co. H, 50th Virginia Infantry	May 12, 1864, Spotsylvania Court House, Virginia	Point Lookout, Maryland, transferred to Elmira Prison, NY August 2, 1864	Oath of Allegiance June 27, 1865
Barnard, James W. Private	Unk	Unknown	Co. E, 50th Virginia Infantry	May 12, 1864, Near Spotsylvania Court House, Virginia	Point Lookout, Maryland, transferred to Elmira Prison, NY August 2, 1864	Exchanged October 29, 1864 at Venus Point, Savannah River, GA.
Barnard, Richard J. Private	Unk	Unknown	Co. K, 50th Virginia Infantry	May 5, 1864, Wilderness, Virginia	Point Lookout, Maryland, transferred to Elmira Prison, NY August 14, 1864	Died September 22, 1864 of Typhoid Fever, Grave No. 487
Barnes, Alfred A. Private	Unk	May 1, 1862, Camp Holmes, New Hanover, North Carolina	Co. E, 51st North Carolina Infantry	June 1, 1864, Cold Harbor, Virginia	Point Lookout, Maryland, transferred to Elmira Prison, NY July 17,1864	Died October 4, 1864 of Pneumonia, Grave No. 640
Barnes, C. M. Private	Unk	Unknown	Co. B, 45th Georgia Infantry	May 6, 1864, Wilderness, Virginia	Point Lookout, Maryland, transferred to Elmira Prison, NY August 14, 1864	Died February 17, 1865 of Variola (Smallpox), Grave No. 2197
Barnes, Christopher Private	18	January 11, 1864, New Hanover County, North Carolina	Co. B, 40th North Carolina Artillery	January 15, 1865, Fort Fisher, North Carolina	Elmira Prison Camp, NY	Died April 23, 1865 of Unknown Disease, Grave No. 1400
Barnes, Clark Private	30	June 20, 1861, Lumberton, North Carolina	Co. D, 18th North Carolina Infantry	May 12, 1864, Spotsylvania Court House, Virginia	Point Lookout, Maryland, transferred to Elmira Prison, NY August 6, 1864	Oath of Allegiance June 30, 1865
Barnes, D. E. Private	Unk	November 1, 1862, Shelbyville, Tennessee	Co. G, 17th Tennessee Infantry	June 17, 1864, Petersburg, Virginia	Point Lookout, Maryland, transferred to Elmira Prison, NY July 30, 1864	Exchanged February 25, 1865 at Boulware's or Cox Wharf on the James River, Virginia

Name & Rank	Age	Enlisted	Regiment and State	Where Captured	Prison	Remarks
Barnes, David T. Private	21	May 1, 1862, South Mills, North Carolina	Co. D, 32nd North Carolina Infantry	May 10, 1864, Spotsylvania, Virginia	Point Lookout, Maryland, transferred to Elmira Prison, NY August 6, 1864	Died December 5, 1864 of Pneumonia, Grave No. 1016. Name Barnes, D. F. 22nd NC on Headstone.
Barnes, F. H. Private	Unk	February 23, 1863, Manning, South Carolina	Co. J, 25th South Carolina Infantry	January 15, 1865, Fort Fisher, North Carolina	Elmira Prison Camp January 30, 1865	Died April 1, 1865 of Diarrhea, Grave No. 2587
Barnes, Francis Private	Unk	May 1, 1862, Mills, North Carolina	Co. A, 32nd North Carolina Infantry	May 10, 1864, Spotsylvania, Virginia	Point Lookout, Maryland, transferred to Elmira Prison, NY August 16, 1864	Died October 5, 1864 of Chronic Diarrhea, Grave No. 642
Barnes, James H. Private	19	July 1, 1862, Raleigh, North Carolina	Co. A, 33rd North Carolina Infantry	May 6, 1864, Wilderness, Virginia	Point Lookout, Maryland, transferred to Elmira Prison, NY August 14, 1864	Oath of Allegiance June 23, 1865
Barnes, John S. Private	16	September 15, 1862, Camp Mangum, Raleigh, North Carolina	Co. B, 31st North Carolina Infantry	May 31, 1864, Cold Harbor, Virginia	Point Lookout, Maryland, transferred to Elmira Prison, NY July 17, 1864	Oath of Allegiance July 7, 1865
Barnes, Levi Private	Unk	September 13, 1862, Kinston, North Carolina	Co. H, 5th North Carolina Cavalry	May 31, 1864, The Woods Near Hanover Court House, Virginia	Point Lookout, Maryland, transferred to Elmira Prison, NY July 17, 1864	Oath of Allegiance May 29, 1865
Barnes, Samuel M. Private	Unk	October 20, 1863, Dallas, Alabama	Co. F, 1st Battalion Alabama Artillery	August 23, 1864, Fort Morgan, Alabama	Steam Press No. 4, New Orleans, Louisiana transferred to Elmira Prison, October 8, 1864.	Died March 7, 1865 of Remittent Fever, Grave No. 1958
Barnes, W. J. Private	52	July 12, 1862, Mocksville, North Carolina	Co. H, 5th North Carolina Cavalry	September 22, 1863, Near Madison Court House, Virginia	Point Lookout, Maryland, transferred to Elmira Prison, NY August 18, 1864	Exchanged October 29, 1864 at Venus Point, Savannah River, GA.

Name & Rank	Age	Enlisted	Regiment and State	Where Captured	Prison	Remarks
Barnes, William T. Private	27	August 13, 1862, Camp Hill, North Carolina	Co. G, 5th North Carolina Infantry	May 20, 1864, Spotsylvania Court House, Virginia	Point Lookout Prison. Transferred to Elmira Prison, New York, July 6, 1864.	Oath of Allegiance June 30, 1865
Barnes, William W. Private	Unk	August 24, 1861, Atlanta, Georgia	Co. B, 3rd Battalion Georgia Sharp shooters	August 16, 1864, Front Royal, Virginia	Point Lookout, Maryland, transferred to Elmira Prison, NY August 29, 1864	Exchanged February 20, 1865 at Boulware's or Cox Wharf on the James River, Virginia
Barnett, Alonzo M. Private	Unk	August 22, 1861, Union Court House, South Carolina	Co. B, 15th South Carolina Infantry	July 27, 1864, Petersburg, Virginia	Point Lookout, Maryland, transferred to Elmira Prison, NY August 12, 1864	Oath of Allegiance July 7, 1865
Barnett, Henry H. Private	44	March 4, 1861, Selma, Alabama	Co. C, 1st Alabama Artillery	August 23, 1864, Fort Morgan, Alabama	Fort Columbus, NY Harbor. Transferred to Elmira Prison Camp, NY, February 21, 1865.	Died March 12, 1865 of Pneumonia, Grave No. 1831
Barnett, J. P. Private	Unk	September 22, 1862, Calhoun, Georgia	Co. I, 16th Georgia Infantry	June 1, 1864, Gaines Farm, Cold Harbor, Virginia	Point Lookout, Maryland, transferred to Elmira Prison, NY July 17,1864	Oath of Allegiance July 7, 1865
Barnett, James Private	18	January 15, 1863, Lenoir County, North Carolina	Co. E, 61st North Carolina Infantry	August 27, 1863, Battery Wagner, Morris Island, South Carolina	Point Lookout, Maryland, transferred to Elmira Prison, NY August 18, 1864	Exchanged March 10, 1865 at Boulware's Wharf on the James River, Virginia
Barnett, John S. Private	Unk	October 17, 1863, Charleston, South Carolina	Co. B, 27th South Carolina Infantry	June 24, 1864, Near Petersburg, Virginia	Point Lookout, Maryland, transferred to Elmira Prison, NY August 18,1864	Exchanged October 29, 1864 at Venus Point, Savannah River, GA.
Barnett, Malon Private	17	July 1, 1861, Scott Creek, Scott County, Virginia	Co. A, 48th Virginia Infantry	May 12, 1864 Spotsylvania Court House, Virginia	Point Lookout, Maryland, transferred to Elmira Prison, NY August 2, 1864	Exchanged October 29, 1864 at Venus Point, Savannah River, GA.

Name & Rank	Age	Enlisted	Regiment and State	Where Captured	Prison	Remarks
Barnett, William S. Sergeant	29	May 10, 1861, Washington, North Carolina	Co. I, 3rd North Carolina Infantry	May 12, 1864, Near Spotsylvania Court House, Virginia	Point Lookout, Maryland, transferred to Elmira Prison, NY August 12, 1864	Oath of Allegiance June 27, 1865
Barney, J. C. Private	Unk	Unknown	Co. K, 40th Regiment, 3rd North Carolina Heavy Artillery	January 15, 1865, Fort Fisher, North Carolina	February 1, 1865, Elmira Prison Camp, New York	Died April 23, 1865 of Chronic Diarrhea, Grave No. 1400. Headstone has C. C. Barnes.
Barney, Samuel Private	26	July 2, 1861, New Orleans, Louisiana	Co. K, 15th Louisiana Infantry	May 5, 1864, Wilderness, Virginia	Point Lookout, Maryland, transferred to Elmira Prison, NY July 25, 1864	Exchanged February 13, 1865 at Boulware's wharf on the James River, Virginia
Barnhart, Benjamin Private		May 1, 1862, White Sulphur Springs, Virginia	Co. F, 22nd Virginia Infantry	May 31, 1864, Cold Harbor, Virginia	Point Lookout, Maryland, transferred to Elmira Prison, NY July 11, 1864	Died May 31, 1865, of Smallpox, Grave No. 2906
Barnhart, John H. Private	21	May 10, 1861, Camp Moore, Louisiana	Co. B, 5th Louisiana Infantry	May 12, 1864, Spotsylvania Court House, Virginia	Point Lookout, Maryland, transferred to Elmira Prison, NY August 17, 1864	Exchanged October 29, 1864 at Venus Point, Savannah River, GA..
Barnhill, Duncan R. Private	25	March 9, 1862, Wilmington, North Carolina	Co. H, 36th Regiment, 2nd North Carolina Artillery	January 15, 1865, Fort Fisher, North Carolina. Wounded.	February 1, 1865, Elmira Prison Camp, New York	Died March 9, 1865, Variola (Smallpox), Grave No. 1878
Barnhill, J. H. Private	Unk	Unknown	Co. H, 20th North Carolina Infantry	May 20, 1864, Spotsylvania Court House, Virginia	Point Lookout, Maryland, transferred to Elmira Prison, NY July 6, 1864	Oath of Allegiance June 19, 1865
Barnhill, William H. Private	19	May 17, 1861, Lower Black River District, North Carolina	Co. E, 18th North Carolina Infantry	May 12, 1864, Spotsylvania Court House, Virginia	Point Lookout, Maryland, transferred to Elmira Prison, NY August 6, 1864	Oath of Allegiance June 19, 1865

Name & Rank	Age	Enlisted	Regiment and State	Where Captured	Prison	Remarks
Barr, Martin L. Private	20	April 18, 1861, Berryville, Virginia	Co. J, 2nd Virginia Infantry	November 27, 1864, Clarkson, Virginia	Old Capital Prison, Washington, DC, transferred to Elmira Prison, NY, December 17, 1864	Exchanged March 14, 1865 at Boulware's Wharf on the James River, Virginia
Barr, William T. Sergeant	Unk	May 9, 1861, New Orleans, Louisiana	Co. F, 2nd Louisiana Infantry	May 12, 1864, Spotsylvania Court House, Virginia	Point Lookout, Maryland, transferred to Elmira Prison, NY August 17, 1864	Oath of Allegiance June 30, 1865
Barrentine, Evander Private	17	February 25, 1863, Fort Caswell, North Carolina	Co. E, 40th Regiment, 3rd North Carolina Heavy Artillery	January 15, 1865, Fort Fisher, North Carolina	February 1, 1865, Elmira Prison Camp, New York	Died March 24, 1865 of Diarrhea, Grave No. 2453. Headstone has Lander Barrington.
Barrer, B. F. Private	Unk	Unknown	Co. F, 42nd Virginia Infantry	May 12, 1864, Near Spotsylvania Court House, Virginia	Point Lookout, Maryland, transferred to Elmira Prison, NY August 6, 1864	Exchanged October 29, 1864 at Venus Point, Savannah River, GA.
Barrett, A. J. Sergeant	18	July 3, 1861, Atlanta, Georgia	Co. A, 11th Georgia Infantry	June 24, 1864, Hanover Junction, Virginia	Point Lookout, Maryland, transferred to Elmira Prison, NY July 8, 1864	Oath of Allegiance May 19, 1865
Barrett, Benjamin J. Private	Unk	May 1, 1862, Mount Tabour, North Carolina	Co. C, 3rd Battalion North Carolina Light Artillery	January 15, 1865, Fort Fisher, North Carolina	February 1, 1865, Elmira Prison Camp, New York	Exchanged March 14, 1865 at Boulware's Wharf on the James River, Virginia
Barrett, Charles W. Private	Unk	Unknown	Co. A, 12th Virginia Cavalry	July 31, 1864, Upperville, Virginia	Old Capital Prison, Washington, D. C. Transferred to Elmira Prison, NY August 12, 1864	Exchanged February 20, 1865 at Boulware's or Cox Wharf on the James River, Virginia
Barrett, Franklin Private	22	April 27, 1861, Cleveland County, North Carolina	Co. C, 15th North Carolina Infantry	June 2, 1864, Near Talapatomoy Creek, Cold Harbor, Virginia	Point Lookout, Maryland, transferred to Elmira Prison, NY July 17, 1864	Exchanged March 14, 1865 at Boulware's Wharf on the James River, Virginia.

Name & Rank	Age	Enlisted	Regiment and State	Where Captured	Prison	Remarks
Barrett, George B. Private	Unk	March 4, 1862, Perry, Georgia	Co. H, 45th Georgia Infantry	May 6, 1864, Wilderness, Virginia	Point Lookout, Maryland, transferred to Elmira Prison, NY August 14, 1864	Exchanged March 10, 1865 at Boulware's Wharf on the James River, Virginia
Barrett, James B. Private	Unk	July 1, 1864, Roxobel, North Carolina	Co. C, 3rd Battalion North Carolina Light Artillery	January 15, 1865, Fort Fisher, North Carolina	February 1, 1865, Elmira Prison Camp, New York	Exchanged March 14, 1865 at Boulware's Wharf on the James River, Virginia
Barrett, James E. Corporal	32	March 1, 1861, Nashville, North Carolina	Co. H, 32nd North Carolina Infantry	May 10, 1864, Spotsylvania, Virginia	Point Lookout, Maryland, transferred to Elmira Prison, NY August 6, 1864	Exchanged October 29, 1864 at Venus Point, Savannah River, GA.
Barrett, James G. Private	20	June 18, 1861, Salisbury, North Carolina	Co. E, 5th North Carolina Infantry	May 12, 1864, Spotsylvania Court House, Virginia	Point Lookout, Maryland, transferred to Elmira Prison, NY August 6, 1864	Oath of Allegiance June 30, 1865
Barrett, James T. Private	Unk	May 10, 1861, New Orleans, Louisiana	Co. A, 5th Louisiana Infantry	May 12, 1864, Spotsylvania Court House, Virginia	Point Lookout, Maryland, transferred to Elmira Prison, NY August 17, 1864	Exchanged February 13, 1865 at Boulware's Wharf on the James River, Virginia
Barrett, Laban Private	Unk	July 9, 1861, Cartersville, Georgia	Co. K, 14th Georgia Infantry	May 12, 1864, Spotsylvania Court House, Virginia	Point Lookout, Maryland, transferred to Elmira Prison, NY July 30, 1864	Died July 14, 1864 of Pneumonia, Grave No. 288
Barrett, Milton Corporal	Unk	June 13, 1861, Camp McDonald, Georgia	Co. E, 3rd Battalion Georgia Sharp shooters	August 16, 1864, Front Royal, Virginia	Point Lookout, Maryland, transferred to Elmira Prison, NY August 29, 1864	Died February 12, 1865 of Variola (Smallpox), Grave No. 2031. Headstone has Barrick.
Barrett, William R. Private	32	January 27, 1863, Carthage, North Carolina	Co. D, 49th North Carolina Infantry	June 2, 1864, Bermuda Hundred, Virginia	Point Lookout, Maryland, transferred to Elmira Prison, NY July 12, 1864	Exchanged October 29, 1864 at Venus Point, Savannah River, GA.

Name & Rank	Age	Enlisted	Regiment and State	Where Captured	Prison	Remarks
Barrier, L. C. Private	19	August 11, 1862, Mount Pleasant, North Carolina	Co. H, 8th North Carolina Infantry	June 1, 1864, Gaines Mill, Cold Harbor, Virginia	Point Lookout, Maryland, transferred to Elmira Prison, NY July 17,1864	Exchanged October 29, 1864 at Venus Point, Savannah River, GA.
Barrier, Tobias A. Private	29	August 6, 1861, Mount Pleasant, North Carolina	Co. H, 8th North Carolina Infantry	May 31, 1864, Cold Harbor, Virginia	Point Lookout, Maryland, transferred to Elmira Prison, NY July 8, 1864	Died March 23, 1865 of Pneumonia, Grave No. 1509, L. C. Barrier on Headstone.
Barrineau, Ebenezer M. Private	16	April 12, 1862, Battery Island, South Carolina	Co. C, 25th South Carolina Infantry	January 15, 1865, Fort Fisher, North Carolina	Elmira Prison Camp January 30, 1865	Oath of Allegiance July 11, 1865
Barrineau, R. H. Private	30	April 12, 1862, Battery Island, South Carolina	Co. C, 25th South Carolina Infantry	January 15, 1865, Fort Fisher, North Carolina	Elmira Prison Camp January 30, 1865	Exchanged March 2, 1865 at Boulware's Wharf on the James River, Virginia
Barringer, A. L. Private	21	August 8, 1862, Stanley County, North Carolina	Co. F, 5th North Carolina Infantry	May 20, 1864, Spotsylvania Court House, Virginia	Point Lookout, Maryland, transferred to Elmira Prison, NY July 6, 1864	Died February 15, 1864 of Variola (Smallpox), Grave No. 2193
Barringer, C. D. Private	18	March 3, 1863, Mount Pleasant, North Carolina	Co. H, 8th North Carolina Infantry	June 3, 1864, Gaines Mill, Cold Harbor, Virginia	Point Lookout, Maryland, transferred to Elmira Prison, NY July 17,1864	Exchanged March 2, 1865 at Akins Landing on the James River, Virginia
Barringer, Caleb E. Corporal	21	August 6, 1861, Mount Pleasant, North Carolina	Co. H, 8th North Carolina Infantry	June 3, 1864, Gaines Mill, Cold Harbor, Virginia	Point Lookout, Maryland, transferred to Elmira Prison, NY July 17,1864	Exchanged March 2, 1865 at Akins Landing on the James River, Virginia
Barringer, Mathias Private	34	August 8, 1862, Raleigh, North Carolina	Co. B, 5th North Carolina Infantry	May 12, 1864, Spotsylvania Court House, Virginia	Point Lookout, Maryland, transferred to Elmira Prison, NY August 6, 1864	Died September 21, 1864 of Chronic Diarrhea, Grave No. 336, Name Banninger on Headstone.

Name & Rank	Age	Enlisted	Regiment and State	Where Captured	Prison	Remarks
Barrington, W. T. Private	17	March 1, 1863, Craven County, North Carolina	Co. D, 36th Regiment, 2nd North Carolina Artillery	January 15, 1865, Fort Fisher, North Carolina. Wounded.	February 1, 1865, Elmira Prison Camp, New York	Exchanged February 20, 1865 at Boulware's or Cox Wharf on the James River, Virginia
Barron, Albert B. Sergeant	26	May 7, 1862, Clarksville, Georgia	Co. K, 24th Georgia Infantry	June 1, 1864, Cold Harbor, Virginia. Gunshot wound Ankle & Calf.	DeCamp General Hospital, David's Island New York Harbor.	Oath of Allegiance June 21, 1865
Barron, Ben Pressley Private	Unk	November 5, 1863, Pocotaligo, South Carolina	Co. J, 4th South Carolina Cavalry	June 11, 1864, Trevilian Station, Louisa Court House, Virginia	Point Lookout, Maryland, transferred to Elmira Prison, NY July 25, 1864	Exchanged February 20, 1865 at Boulware's or Cox Wharf on the James River, Virginia
Barron, William M. Sergeant	Unk	July 19, 1861, Montgomery, Alabama	Co. B, 13th Alabama Infantry	May 6, 1864, Wilderness, Virginia	Point Lookout, Maryland, transferred to Elmira Prison, NY August 14, 1864	Oath of Allegiance June 16, 1865
Barrow, James Private	43	August 18, 1863, Wilson County, North Carolina	Co. K, 40th Regiment, 3rd North Carolina Artillery	January 15, 1865, Fort Fisher, North Carolina	Elmira Prison Camp, New York, February 1, 1865	Died the May 2, 1865 of Chronic Diarrhea, Grave No. 2746
Barrow, John A. Private	Unk	May 24, 1864, Christiansburg, Virginia	Co. K, 36th Virginia Infantry	July 8, 1864, Near Harper's Ferry, Virginia	Old Capital Prison, Washington, DC, transferred to Elmira Prison, NY, July 23, 1864	Oath of Allegiance July 11, 1865
Barrow, Joseph W. Private	16	Unknown	Co. G, 40th Regiment, 3rd North Carolina Artillery	January 15, 1865, Fort Fisher, North Carolina	February 1, 1865, Elmira Prison Camp, New York	Exchanged March 14, 1865 at Boulware's Wharf on the James River, Virginia
Barrow, William H. Sergeant	Unk	March 23, 1862, Bowden, Georgia	Co. B, Cobb's Legion, Georgia	June 2, 1864, Gaines Mill, Cold Harbor, Virginia	Point Lookout, Maryland, transferred to Elmira Prison, NY July 17, 1864	Exchanged October 29, 1864 at Venus Point, Savannah River, GA.

Name & Rank	Age	Enlisted	Regiment and State	Where Captured	Prison	Remarks
Barry, Charles Private	Unk	September 23, 1863, Chattanooga, Tennessee	Co. A, Cobb's Legion Georgia	August 16, 1864, Front Royal, Virginia	Point Lookout, Maryland, transferred to Elmira Prison, NY August 29, 1864	Oath of Allegiance July 7, 1865
Barry, James A. Private	31	May 7, 1862, Orange County, North Carolina	Co. D, 56th North Carolina Infantry	March 25, 1865, Fort Steadman, Petersburg, Virginia. Shell Wound Right Elbow.	Old Capital Prison, Washington D. C. Transferred to Elmira Prison, NY May 2, 1865.	Oath of Allegiance July 7, 1865
Barry, John R. Private	22	September 15, 1862, Camp Mangum, Raleigh, North Carolina	Co. E, 31st North Carolina Infantry	May 30, 1864, Cold Harbor, Virginia. Gunshot Wound in Right Shoulder and Hand.	Point Lookout, Maryland, transferred to Elmira Prison, NY August 29, 1864	Oath of Allegiance June 23, 1865
Barry, Ned Private	32	April 15, 1861, Pittsboro, North Carolina	Co. I, 32nd North Carolina Infantry	May 10, 1864, Wilderness, Virginia	Point Lookout, Maryland, transferred to Elmira Prison, NY August 6, 1864	Exchanged March 10, 1865 at Boulware's wharf on the James River, Virginia
Barthel, Ferdinand Private	19	July 22, 1861, Camp Moore, Louisiana	Co. F, 10th Louisiana Infantry	July 8, 1864, Near Harper's Ferry, Virginia	Old Capital Prison, Washington, DC, transferred to Elmira Prison, NY, July 23, 1864	Died October 2, 1864 of Pneumonia, Grave No. 624
Bartholomew Joel W. Private	26	March 24, 1862, Davis Crossroads, North Carolina	Co. K, 12th North Carolina Infantry	May 12, 1864, Near Spotsylvania County Court House, Virginia	Point Lookout, Maryland, transferred to Elmira Prison, NY August 14, 1864	Died September 3, 1864 of Typhoid Fever, Grave No. 225. Name I. W. Bartholomew on Headstone.
Bartlett, Nathan H. Private	Unk	February 16, 1863, Atlanta, Georgia	Co. A, 64th Georgia Infantry	August 16, 1864, New Market, Virginia	Point Lookout, Maryland, transferred to Elmira Prison, NY August 29, 1864	Exchanged October 29, 1864, at Venus Point, Savannah River, GA.
Bartlett, Richard Private	22	July 15, 1861, Statesburg, Sumter District, South Carolina	Co. G, Hampton Legion, South Carolina Infantry	July 29, 1864, Petersburg, Virginia	Point Lookout, Maryland, transferred to Elmira Prison, NY August 12, 1864	Exchanged March 14, 1865 at Boulware's Wharf on the James River, Virginia

Name & Rank	Age	Enlisted	Regiment and State	Where Captured	Prison	Remarks
Bartley, Thomas Private	Unk	June 4, 1861, Camp Moore, Louisiana	Co. K, 6th Louisiana Infantry	May 5, 1864, Wilderness, Virginia	Point Lookout, Maryland, transferred to Elmira Prison, NY August 17, 1864	Exchanged February 25, 1865 at Boulware's or Cox Wharf on the James River, Virginia
Barto, Henry Private	Unk	June 7, 1861, Camp Moore, Louisiana	Co. K, 7th Louisiana Infantry	July 9, 1864, Near Harper's Ferry, Virginia	Old Capital Prison, Washington, DC, transferred to Elmira Prison, NY, July 23, 1864	Oath of Allegiance May 15, 1865
Barton, Alexander Private	Unk	June 4, 1861, Camp Moore, New Orleans, Louisiana	Co. C, 6th Louisiana Infantry	May 5, 1864, Wilderness, Virginia	Point Lookout, Maryland, transferred to Elmira Prison, NY August 18, 1864	Exchanged February 25, 1865 at Boulware's or Cox Wharf on the James River, Virginia
Barton, Harry H. Private	Unk	June 12, 1861, Red Sulfur Springs, Virginia	Co. F, 26th Battalion, Virginia Infantry	June 3, 1864, Gaines Farm, Cold Harbor, Virginia	Point Lookout, Maryland, transferred to Elmira Prison, NY July 12, 1864	Exchanged March 14, 1865 at Boulware's Wharf on the James River, Virginia
Barton, John J. Private	Unk	May 3, 1862, Bainbridge, Georgia	Co. D, 17th Georgia Infantry	June 1, 1864, Gaines Mill, Cold Harbor, Virginia	Point Lookout, Maryland, transferred to Elmira Prison, NY July 17, 1864	Oath of Allegiance June 16, 1865
Barton, John T. Private	Unk	August 27, 1861, Camp Stephens, Georgia	Co. A, 61st Georgia Infantry	May 18, 1864, Spotsylvania Court House, Virginia	Point Lookout, Maryland, transferred to Elmira Prison, NY July 6, 1864	Exchanged February 18, 1865 on the James River, Virginia
Barwick, George W. Private	Unk	May 18, 1862, Charleston, South Carolina	Co. J, 25th South Carolina Infantry	January 15, 1865, Fort Fisher, North Carolina	Elmira Prison Camp January 30, 1865	Exchanged February 20, 1865. Died March 10, 1865 of Debility and Frostbite at Howard's Grove Hospital, Richmond, VA.

Name & Rank	Age	Enlisted	Regiment and State	Where Captured	Prison	Remarks
Barwick, John Private	Unk	May 23, 1865, Macon, Georgia	Co. F, 64th Georgia Infantry	August 16, 1864, New Market, Virginia	Old Capital Prison, Washington, DC transferred to Elmira Prison, NY August 27, 1864	Died January 13, 1865 of Pneumonia, Grave No. 1477
Barwick, John Private	Unk	August 17, 1861, Light Wood Knot Springs, North Carolina	Co. G, 14th South Carolina Infantry	July 28, 1864, Malvern Hill, Virginia. Gunshot Wound Arm, Fracture.	Old Capital Prison, Washington, DC transferred to Elmira Prison, NY August 27, 1864	Exchanged February 20, 1865 at Boulware's or Cox Wharf on the James River, Virginia
Barwick, Richard M. Musician Private	Unk	November 7, 1862, Lenoir County, North Carolina	Co. G, 36th Regiment, 2nd North Carolina Artillery	January 15, 1865, Fort Fisher, North Carolina. Wounded.	February 1, 1865, Elmira Prison Camp, New York	Exchanged February 20, 1865 at Boulware's or Cox Wharf on the James River, Virginia
Barwick, William Private	Unk	July 17, 1863, Fort Branch, Martin County, North Carolina	Co. G, 36th Regiment, 2nd North Carolina Artillery	January 15, 1865, Fort Fisher, North Carolina. Wounded.	February 1, 1865, Elmira Prison Camp, New York	Exchanged March 14, 1865 at Boulware's Wharf on the James River, Virginia
Basden, Jackson Private	Unk	June 15, 1863, Goldsboro, North Carolina	Co. C, 66th North Carolina Infantry	June 3, 1864, Gaines Farm, Cold Harbor, Virginia	Point Lookout, Maryland, transferred to Elmira Prison, NY July 17, 1864	Died September 27, 1864 of Chronic Diarrhea, Grave No. 386
Basdon, Kinion H. Private	18	June 25, 1862, Johnston County, North Carolina	Co. K, 51st North Carolina Infantry	May 16, 1864, Near Drury's Bluff, Virginia	Point Lookout, Maryland, transferred to Elmira Prison, NY August 17, 1864	Died April 5, 1865 of Chronic Diarrhea, Grave No. 2551. Headstone has Baisden.
Basham, John L. Private	Unk	September 20, 1863, Monroe County, Virginia	Co. F, 26th Battalion, Virginia Infantry	June 3, 1864, Gaines Farm, Cold Harbor, Virginia	Point Lookout, Maryland, transferred to Elmira Prison, NY July 17,1864	Exchanged October 29, 1864 at Venus Point, Savannah River, GA.
Bashlor, W. D. Private	Unk	December 9, 1862, Bryan County, Georgia	Co. H, 7th Georgia Cavalry	June 11, 1864, Trevilian Station, Louisa Court House, Virginia	Point Lookout, Maryland, transferred to Elmira Prison, NY July 25, 1864	Oath of Allegiance June 14, 1865

Name & Rank	Age	Enlisted	Regiment and State	Where Captured	Prison	Remarks
Basinger, Andrew Corporal	Unk	July 27, 1861, Salisbury, North Carolina	Co. H, 8th North Carolina Infantry	May 31, 1864, Cold Harbor, Virginia	Point Lookout, Maryland, transferred to Elmira Prison, NY July 11,1864	Died May 1, 1865 of Chronic Diarrhea, Grave No. 2739
Bass, Aaron Private	Unk	March 12, 1864, Wilson, North Carolina	Co. C, 43rd North Carolina Infantry	June 25, 1864, Hanover Junction, Virginia	Point Lookout, Maryland, transferred to Elmira Prison, NY July 8, 1864	Oath of Allegiance June 14, 1865
Bass, Andrew J. Private	28	April 15, 1862, Union County, North Carolina	Co. I, 53rd North Carolina Infantry	May 20, 1864, Spotsylvania Court House, Virginia	Point Lookout, Maryland, transferred to Elmira Prison, NY July 6, 1864	Exchanged February 20, 1865 at Boulware's or Cox Wharf on the James River, Virginia
Bass, Benjamin F. Private	22	March 4, 1862, Perry, Georgia	Co. H, 45th Georgia Infantry	May 6, 1864, Wilderness, Virginia	Point Lookout, Maryland, transferred to Elmira Prison, NY August 14, 1864	Died January 17, 1865 of Variola (Smallpox), Grave No. 1443
Bass, Benjamin F. Private	24	March 1, 1862, Nashville, North Carolina	Co. H, 32nd North Carolina Infantry	May 10, 1864, Wilderness, Virginia	Point Lookout, Maryland, transferred to Elmira Prison, NY August 6, 1864	Oath of Allegiance June 30, 1865
Bass, Cornelius Private	21	October 14, 1861, Red Banks, North Carolina	Co. E, 40th Regiment, 3rd North Carolina Artillery	January 15, 1865, Fort Fisher, North Carolina	February 1, 1865, Elmira Prison Camp, New York	Died May 24, 1865 of Chronic Diarrhea Grave No. 2924
Bass, George P. Private	Unk	June 14, 1861, Valdosta, Georgia	Co. J, 12th Georgia Infantry	May 10, 1864, Spotsylvania Court House, Virginia	Point Lookout, Maryland, transferred to Elmira Prison, NY July 25, 1864	Oath of Allegiance June 27, 1865
Bass, George W. Private	38	March 1, 1862, Nashville, North Carolina	Co. H, 32nd North Carolina Infantry	May 10, 1864, Wilderness, Virginia	Point Lookout, Maryland, transferred to Elmira Prison, NY August 6, 1864	Died March 24, 1865 of Pneumonia, Grave No. 1508
Bass, J. B. Private	Unk	Unknown	Co. A, Phillips Legion, Georgia	June 1, 1864, Gaines Farm, Cold Harbor, Virginia	Point Lookout, Maryland, transferred to Elmira Prison, NY July 17,1864	Exchanged October 29, 1864 at Venus Point, Savannah River, GA.

Name & Rank	Age	Enlisted	Regiment and State	Where Captured	Prison	Remarks
Bass, John Private	18	March 18, 1862, Laurens Court House, South Carolina	Co. A, 3rd South Carolina Infantry	July 28, 1864, Malvern Hill, Virginia. Gunshot Wound Right Thigh. Amputated Right Leg.	November 11, 1864, Old Capital Prison, Washington, DC. February 4, 1865 Elmira, Prison Camp, NY	Exchanged February 13, 1865 at Boulware's wharf on the James River, Virginia
Bass, John N. Private	18	March 18, 1862, Laurens Court House, Virginia	3rd South Carolina Infantry	July 28, 1864, Malvern Hill, Virginia	November 11, 1864, Old Capital Prison, Washington, DC. February 4, 1865 Elmira, Prison Camp, NY.	Exchanged February 13, 1865 at Boulware's wharf on the James River, Virginia
Bass, Joseph J. Private	24	July 15, 1862, Raleigh, North Carolina	Co. C, 1st North Carolina Infantry	May 12, 1864, Spotsylvania Court House, Virginia	Point Lookout, Maryland, transferred to Elmira Prison, NY August 6, 1864	Oath of Allegiance June 27, 1865
Bass, William E. Corporal	Unk	April 20, 1861, Sampson County, North Carolina	Co. A, 30th North Carolina Infantry	May 8, 1864, Wilderness, Virginia	Point Lookout, Maryland, transferred to Elmira Prison, NY August 14, 1864	Oath of Allegiance May 29, 1865
Bass, William M. Private	21	July 15, 1861, Whippy Swamp, South Carolina	Co. D, 11th South Carolina Infantry	January 15, 1865, Fort Fisher, North Carolina	February 1, 1865, Elmira Prison Camp, New York	Exchanged March 2, 1865 at Akins Landing on the James River, Virginia
Bassell, Joseph H. Private	Unk	May 27, 1861, Buckhannon, Virginia	Co. B, 25th Virginia Infantry	May 12, 1864, Spotsylvania Court House, Virginia	Point Lookout, Maryland, transferred to Elmira Prison, NY August 12, 1864	Oath of Allegiance June 21, 1865
Bassham, William H. Private	Unk	April 29, 1862, White Sulfur Springs, Virginia	Co. F, 26th Battalion, Virginia Infantry	June 3, 1864, Gaines Farm, Cold Harbor, Virginia	Point Lookout, Maryland, transferred to Elmira Prison, NY July 17, 1864	Died October 16, 1864 of Scorbutus (Scurvy), Grave No. 556
Batchelor, Earley Private	Unk	April 2, 1862, Eatonton, Georgia	Co. G, 12th Georgia Infantry	May 10, 1864, Spotsylvania Court House, Virginia	Point Lookout, Maryland, transferred to Elmira Prison, NY July 25, 1864	Oath of Allegiance July 26, 1865

Name & Rank	Age	Enlisted	Regiment and State	Where Captured	Prison	Remarks
Batchelor, Richard Private	Unk	April 2, 1862, Eatonton, Georgia	Co. G, 12th Georgia Infantry	May 10, 1864, Spotsylvania Court House, Virginia	Point Lookout, Maryland, transferred to Elmira Prison, NY July 25, 1864	Oath of Allegiance June 19, 1865
Batchelor, Robert H. Private	22	July 15, 1862, Alamance County, North Carolina	Co. B, 1st North Carolina Infantry	May 12, 1864, Spotsylvania Court House, Virginia	Point Lookout, Maryland, transferred to Elmira Prison, NY August 6, 1864	Oath of Allegiance June 27 1865
Bateman, D. O. Private	Unk	March 18, 1862, Wadmalaw Island, South Carolina	Co. C, 1st South Carolina Infantry	September 22, 1863, Near Madison Court House, Virginia	Point Lookout, Maryland, transferred to Elmira Prison, NY August 18, 1864	Exchanged March 10, 1865 at Boulware's wharf on the James River, Virginia
Bateman, Daniel L. Private	23	May 11, 1861, Wytheville, Virginia	Co. A, 4th Virginia Infantry	May 12, 1864, Spotsylvania Court House, Virginia	Point Lookout, Maryland, transferred to Elmira Prison, NY July 25, 1864	Oath of Allegiance June 27, 1865
Bates, Francis M. Private	18	February 25, 1862, Jefferson, Georgia	Co. C, 18th Georgia Infantry	June 1, 1864, Cold Harbor, Virginia	Point Lookout, Maryland, transferred to Elmira Prison, NY July 17, 1864	Exchanged October 29, 1864 at Venus Point, Savannah River, GA.
Bates, George W. Private	Unk	January 1, 1862, Georgetown, South Carolina	Co. K, 21st South Carolina Infantry	July 10, 1863, Morris Island, South Carolina	Point Lookout, Maryland, transferred to Elmira Prison, NY August 18, 1864	Exchanged March 10, 1865 at Boulware's Wharf on the James River, Virginia
Bates, James H. Private	Unk	April 12, 1864, Atlanta, Georgia	Co. E, Phillips Legion, Georgia	June 2, 1864, Gaines Farm, Cold Harbor, Virginia	Point Lookout, Maryland, transferred to Elmira Prison, NY July 17, 1864	Oath of Allegiance July 7, 1865
Bates, Newton G. Private	20	July 9, 1861, Camp McDonald, Cobb County, Georgia	Co. E, Phillips Legion, Georgia	June 2, 1864, Gaines Farm, Cold Harbor, Virginia	Point Lookout, Maryland, transferred to Elmira Prison, NY July 17, 1864	Oath of Allegiance July 7, 1865
Bates, William T. Private	Unk	September 8, 1862, Lowndes County, Alabama	Co. E, 1st Battalion Alabama Artillery	August 23, 1864, Fort Morgan, Alabama	New Orleans, Louisiana transferred to Elmira December 4, 1864.	Oath of Allegiance July 26, 1865

Name & Rank	Age	Enlisted	Regiment and State	Where Captured	Prison	Remarks
Bath, Hyman Private	Unk	June 4, 1861, Camp Moore, Louisiana	Co. A, 6th Louisiana Infantry	May 5, 1864, Wilderness, Virginia	Point Lookout, Maryland, transferred to Elmira Prison, NY August 17, 1864	Exchanged February 20, 1865 at Boulware's or Cox Wharf on the James River, Virginia
Battan, Abram Corporal	36	July 15, 1862, Raleigh, North Carolina	Co. C, 1st North Carolina Infantry	May 12, 1864, Spotsylvania Court House, Virginia	Point Lookout, Maryland, transferred to Elmira Prison, NY August 6, 1864	Oath of Allegiance June 30, 1865
Battle, John B. Private	22	Unknown	Co. A, Jackson's 1st Regiment, Tennessee Heavy Artillery	August 23, 1864, Fort Morgan, Alabama	New Orleans, Louisiana transferred to Elmira December 4, 1864.	Exchanged February 13, 1865 at Boulware's wharf on the James River, Virginia
Battle, William D. Private	17	December 28, 1861, Alexandria, Louisiana	Co. H, 32nd North Carolina Infantry	May 10, 1864, Spotsylvania, Virginia	Point Lookout, Maryland, transferred to Elmira Prison, NY August 6, 1864	Exchanged March 10, 1865 at Boulware's wharf on the James River, Virginia
Baucum, Thomas Private	Unk	July 1, 1862, Anson, North Carolina	Co. E, 33rd North Carolina Infantry	May 6, 1864, Wilderness, Virginia	Point Lookout, Maryland, transferred to Elmira Prison, NY August 14, 1864	Died December 1, 1864 of Chronic Diarrhea, Grave No. 1012
Baugh, Leonidas Private	Unk	October 26, 1861, Cleveland, Tennessee	Co. H, 63rd Tennessee Infantry	June 17, 1864, Petersburg, Virginia	Point Lookout, Maryland, transferred to Elmira Prison, NY July 30, 1864	Exchanged 2/13/65. Died 3/19/65 of Chronic Diarrhea at Chimborazo Hopital, No. 2, Richmond, VA.
Baugh, P. Private	Unk	September 29, 1864, Edgefield District, South Carolina	Co. H, 25th South Carolina Infantry	January 15, 1865, Fort Fisher, North Carolina	Elmira Prison Camp January 30, 1865	Oath of Allegiance July 11, 1865
Baugher, Isaac A. Private	Unk	March 4, 1862, Winchester, Virginia	Co. G, 7th Virginia Cavalry	July 5, 1863, Gettysburg, Pennsylvania	Point Lookout, Maryland, transferred to Elmira Prison, NY July 23, 1864	Oath of Allegiance May 13, 1865

Name & Rank	Age	Enlisted	Regiment and State	Where Captured	Prison	Remarks
Bauserman, George W, Private	35	April 18, 1861, McGaheysville, Virginia	Co. E, 10th Virginia Infantry	May 12, 1864, Spotsylvania Court House, Virginia	Point Lookout, Maryland, transferred to Elmira Prison, NY August 2, 1864	Exchanged February 13, 1865 at Boulware's wharf on the James River, Virginia
Bauserman, John W. Private	Unk	September 24, 1862, Berryville, Virginia	Co. G, 18th Virginia Cavalry	October 28, 1864, Fishers Hill, Strasburg, Virginia	Old Capital Prison, Washington, DC, transferred to Elmira Prison, NY, December 17, 1864	Oath of Allegiance July 7, 1865
Baxley, Henry L. Private	21	March 10, 1862, Lumberton, North Carolina	Co. F, 51st North Carolina Infantry	June 15, 1864, Bottoms Church, Near Petersburg, Near Bermuda Hundred, Virginia	Point Lookout, Maryland, transferred to Elmira Prison, NY July 12, 1864	Oath of Allegiance July 11, 1865
Baxley, John W. Private	Unk	March 11, 1863, Charleston, South Carolina	Co. E, 31st North Carolina Infantry	June 1, 1864, Gaines Farm, Cold Harbor, Virginia	Transferred From Point Lookout Prison, MD, July 12, 1864. Train Never Arrived at Elmira Prison Camp, NY.	Died July 15, 1864 in Train Wreck at Shohola, Pennsylvania.
Baxley, Joseph C. Private	Unk	April 21, 1864, Charlottesville, Virginia	Co. H, 11th Georgia Infantry	May 6, 1864, Wilderness, Virginia	Point Lookout, Maryland, transferred to Elmira Prison, NY August 14, 1864	Died January 29, 1865 of Pneumonia, Grave No. 1804
Baxley, Simeon B. Private	Unk	October 28, 1861, Fayetteville, North Carolina	Co. G, 33rd North Carolina Infantry	May 6, 1864, Wilderness, Virginia	Old Capital Prison, Washington D. C. Transferred to Elmira Prison, NY July 14, 1864	Exchanged October 29, 1864 at Venus Point, Savannah River, GA.
Baxter, George H. Sergeant	Unk	May 18, 1861, Sutton, Virginia	Co. C, 25th Virginia Infantry	May 5, 1864, Wilderness, Virginia	Point Lookout, Maryland, transferred to Elmira Prison, NY August 14, 1864	Died January 9, 1865 of Pleuro-Pneumonia, Grave No. 1222

Name & Rank	Age	Enlisted	Regiment and State	Where Captured	Prison	Remarks
Baxter, William F, Private	21	June 1, 1863, Culpeper, Virginia	Co. A, 35th Battalion Virginia Cavalry	May 7, 1864, Dranesville, Loudoun County, Virginia	Old Capital Prison, Washington, DC, transferred to Elmira Prison, NY, July 23, 1864	Exchanged October 29, 1864 at Venus Point, Savannah River, GA.
Bayles, Andrew J. Private	45	September 28, 1862, Jefferson County, Alabama	Co. A, 21st Alabama Infantry	August 23, 1864, Fort Morgan, Alabama	Steam Press No. 4, New Orleans, Louisiana transferred to Elmira Prison, October 8, 1864.	Died October 21, 1864 of Pneumonia, Grave No. 527. Headstone has Bayless.
Bayles, H. B. Private	Unk	Unknown	Co. H, 26th Mississippi Infantry	May 16, 1863, Baker's Creek, Champion Hill, Mississippi	Point Lookout, Maryland, transferred to Elmira Prison, NY August 18, 1864	Transferred For Exchange October 11, 1864 to Point Lookout Prison Camp, MD. No Additional Information.
Bayley, Thomas A. Private	Unk	June 10, 1861, Camp Anderson, North Carolina	Co. A, 4th North Carolina Infantry	May 20, 1864, Spotsylvania Court House, Virginia	Point Lookout, Maryland, transferred to Elmira Prison, NY July 6, 1864	Oath of Allegiance June 27, 1865
Bayne, Edmond G. Private	36	September 1, 1862, Richmond, Virginia	Co. D, 59th North Carolina Infantry	June 17, 1864, Petersburg, Virginia	Point Lookout, Maryland, transferred to Elmira Prison, NY July 30, 1864	Died April 3, 1865 of Chronic Diarrhea, Grave No. 2568. Name Edmund Barnes on Headstone.
Bayne, H. V. Private	28	September 26, 1861, Decatur, Georgia	Co. K, 38th Georgia Infantry	May 6, 1864, Wilderness, Virginia	Point Lookout, Maryland, transferred to Elmira Prison, NY August 14, 1864	Oath of Allegiance June 19, 1865
Beach, Rizon Newman Private	21	Unknown	Co. A, 49th Virginia Infantry	May 15, 1864, Fairfax County, Virginia	November 11, 1864, Old Capital Prison, Washington, DC. February 4, 1865 Elmira, Prison Camp, NY.	Died March 4, 1865 of Pneumonia, Grave No. 1982

Name & Rank	Age	Enlisted	Regiment and State	Where Captured	Prison	Remarks
Beachum, James A. Private	Unk	March 15, 1863 Wadesboro, North Carolina	Co. K, 43rd North Carolina Infantry	June 25, 1864, Hanover Junction, Virginia	Point Lookout, Maryland, transferred to Elmira Prison, NY July 8, 1864	Died February 13, 1865 of Chronic Diarrhea, Grave No. 2069
Beachum, Joseph J. Private	18	May 15, 1862, Camp Davis, North Carolina	Co. K, 43rd North Carolina Infantry	May 10, 1864, Spotsylvania Court House, Virginia	Point Lookout, Maryland, transferred to Elmira Prison, NY August 14, 1864	Died January 25, 1865 of Chronic Diarrhea, Grave No. 1616
Beagle, William T. Sergeant	Unk	December 31, 1861, Springfield, Missouri	Co. H, 1st Missouri Cavalry	May 17, 1863, Big Black Bridge, Champion Hill, Mississippi	Point Lookout, Maryland, transferred to Elmira Prison, NY August 18, 1864	Exchanged February 13, 1865 at Boulware's wharf on the James River, Virginia
Beal, Henry S. Private	Unk	May 8, 1862, Augusta, Georgia	Co. A, 7th Georgia Cavalry	June 11, 1864, Trevilian Station, Louisa Court House, Virginia	Point Lookout, Maryland, transferred to Elmira Prison, NY July 25, 1864	Oath of Allegiance June 21, 1865
Beal, John W. Private	Unk	June 1, 1861, Cartersville, North Carolina	Co. E, 26th North Carolina Infantry	May 12, 1864, Spotsylvania Court House, Virginia	Point Lookout, Maryland, transferred to Elmira Prison, NY July 30, 1864	Oath of Allegiance June 23, 1865
Beale, Robert A. Private	Unk	May 25, 1861, Hagne, Virginia	Co. K, 40th Virginia Infantry	May 5, 1864, Wilderness, Virginia	Point Lookout, Maryland, transferred to Elmira Prison, NY August 14, 1864	Oath of Allegiance June 21, 1865
Beale, Zebedee Private	42	Unknown	Co. B, Hood's Battalion, Virginia Reserves	June 15, 1864, Petersburg, Virginia	Point Lookout, Maryland, transferred to Elmira Prison, NY July 30, 1864	Oath of Allegiance January 14, 1865. Early Release per Lincoln's Proclamation, 12/8/1863.
Beall, Albert B. Private	41	July 24, 1863, Montgomery, Alabama	Co. B, 12th Georgia Infantry	May 10, 1864, Spotsylvania Court House, Virginia	Point Lookout, Maryland, transferred to Elmira Prison, NY July 25, 1864	Died February 20, 1865 of Pneumonia, Grave No. 2311

Name & Rank	Age	Enlisted	Regiment and State	Where Captured	Prison	Remarks
Beall, Egbert Sergeant	Unk	August 17, 1863, Macon, Georgia	Co. B, 12th Georgia Infantry	August 22, 1864, Charlestown, Virginia	Old Capital Prison, Washington, DC transferred to Elmira Prison, NY August 29, 1864	Oath of Allegiance July 7, 1865
Beals, Amos Private	32	March 10, 1864, Green County, Tennessee	Co. D, 7th Tennessee Infantry	May 6, 1864, Wilderness, Virginia	Point Lookout, Maryland, transferred to Elmira Prison, NY July 23, 1864. Ward No. 7	Died August 13, 1864 of Chronic Diarrhea, Grave No. 17
Bean, Alexander Private	Unk	November 25, 1863, Richmond, Virginia	Co. K, 5th North Carolina Infantry	May 12, 1864, Spotsylvania Court House, Virginia	Point Lookout, Maryland, transferred to Elmira Prison, NY August 6, 1864	Died January 5, 1865 of Chronic Diarrhea, Grave No. 1237
Bean, Andrew J. Private	Unk	Unknown	Co. A, 2nd Virginia Cavalry	July 25, 1864, Adamstown, Virginia	Old Capital Prison, Washington D. C. Transferred to Elmira Prison, NY August 12, 1864	Oath of Allegiance May 13, 1865
Bean, Berry F. Private	21	July 15, 1862, Asheboro, North Carolina	Co. I, 5th North Carolina Infantry	May 12, 1864, Spotsylvania Court House, Virginia	Point Lookout, Maryland, transferred to Elmira Prison, NY August 6, 1864	Died December 7, 1864 of Chronic Diarrhea, Grave No. 1178
Bean, William M. Private	Unk	May 1, 1862 White Sulfur Springs, Virginia	Co. C, 22nd Virginia Infantry	July 13, 1864, Hagerstown, Virginia	Old Capital Prison, Washington, DC, transferred to Elmira Prison, NY, July 23, 1864	Oath of Allegiance November 18, 1864. Joined US Army and Deserted.
Beans, Aaron H. Private	32	October 1, 1862, Purcellsville, Virginia	Co. K, 6th Virginia Cavalry	September 14, 1863, near Rapidan Station, Virginia	Point Lookout, Maryland, transferred to Elmira Prison, NY August 18, 1864	Exchanged March 10, 1865 at Boulware's wharf on the James River, Virginia
Beard, Isaac C. Private	25	July 30, 1862, Weldon, North Carolina	Co. F, 24th North Carolina Infantry	June 17, 1864, Petersburg, Virginia	Point Lookout, Maryland, transferred to Elmira Prison, NY July 30, 1864	Oath of Allegiance July 3, 1865

Name & Rank	Age	Enlisted	Regiment and State	Where Captured	Prison	Remarks
Bearden, A. H. Private	Unk	July 18, 1861, Camp Trousdale, Tennessee	Co. A, 17th Tennessee Infantry	June 17, 1864, Petersburg, Virginia	Point Lookout, Maryland, transferred to Elmira Prison, NY July 30, 1864	Exchanged February 25, 1865 at Boulware's or Cox Wharf on the James River, Virginia
Beasley, Alexander Private	Unk	March 7, 1862, Roxboro, North Carolina	Co. A, 24th North Carolina Infantry	June 17, 1864, Near Petersburg, Virginia	Point Lookout, Maryland, transferred to Elmira Prison, NY July 30, 1864	Exchanged March 14, 1865 at Boulware's Wharf on the James River, Virginia
Beasley, Ashley Private	Unk	July 16, 1862, Raleigh, North Carolina	Co. B, 61st North Carolina Infantry	June 16, 1864, Bermuda Hundred, Virginia	Point Lookout, Maryland, transferred to Elmira Prison, NY July 12, 1864	Exchanged March 2, 1865 at Akins Landing on the James River, Virginia
Beasley, Richard Private	Unk	July 17, 1862, Camp Narrows of New River, Virginia	Co. K, 50th Virginia Infantry	May 12, 1864, Spotsylvania Court House, Virginia	Point Lookout, Maryland, transferred to Elmira Prison, NY August 2, 1864	Transferred for Exchange 10/11/1864. Died 10/20/64 of Chronic Diarrhea at US Army Hospital, Baltimore, MD.
Beasley, Richard R. Private	Unk	March 14, 1861, Skipperville, Alabama	Co. F, 1st Battalion Alabama Artillery	August 23, 1864, Fort Morgan, Alabama	Steam Press No. 4, New Orleans, Louisiana transferred to Elmira Prison, October 8, 1864.	Oath of Allegiance July 7, 1865
Beason, J. T. Private	25	January 1, 1862, Oxford, Alabama	Co. F, 1st Battalion Alabama Artillery	August 23, 1864, Fort Morgan, Alabama	Steam Press No. 4, New Orleans, Louisiana transferred to Elmira Prison, October 8, 1864.	Died May 20, 1865 of Chronic Diarrhea, Grave No. 2943
Beaston, George M. Private	44	July 1, 1863, Richmond, Virginia	Co. F, 1st Maryland Cavalry	May 27, 1864, Hanover Junction, Virginia	Point Lookout, Maryland, transferred to Elmira Prison, NY July 8, 1864	Oath of Allegiance May 13, 1865
Beaty, Alexander Private	Unk	May 11, 1863, Secessionville, South Carolina	Co. D, 17th South Carolina Infantry	July 30, 1864, Petersburg, Virginia	Point Lookout, Maryland, transferred to Elmira Prison, NY August 12, 1864	Exchanged October 29, 1864 at Venus Point, Savannah River, GA.

Name & Rank	Age	Enlisted	Regiment and State	Where Captured	Prison	Remarks
Beatty, Cephus B. Private	Unk	August 14, 1861, Catawba, North Carolina	Co. A, 18th North Carolina Infantry	May 12, 1864, Spotsylvania Court House, Virginia	Point Lookout, Maryland, transferred to Elmira Prison, NY August 6, 1864	Died February 24, 1865 of Chronic Diarrhea, Grave No. 2255
Beatty, Jonathan P. Private	Unk	September 4, 1863, Raleigh, North Carolina	Co. B, 28th North Carolina Infantry	May 12, 1864, Spotsylvania Court House, Virginia	Point Lookout, Maryland, transferred to Elmira Prison, NY August 12, 1864	Died November 26, 1864 of Scorbutus (Scurvy), Grave No. 907
Beauchamp, James S. Private	Unk	Unknown	Co. E, 6th Louisiana Cavalry	September 26, 1864, Bullets Bayou, Louisiana	Fort Columbus, Washington DC, transferred to Elmira Prison, NY November 19, 1864	Died February 10, 1865 of Chronic Diarrhea, Grave No. 2089
Beauchamp, Jasper C. Private	31	August 1, 1861, Decatur, Georgia	Co. D, 3rd Battalion Georgia Sharp shooters	August 16, 1864, Front Royal, Virginia	Point Lookout, Maryland, transferred to Elmira Prison, NY August 29, 1864	Oath of Allegiance June 23, 1865
Beauchamp, John E. Private	23	May 27, 1861, Lauderdale County, Alabama	Co. D, 9th Alabama Infantry	July 29, 1864, Petersburg, Virginia	Point Lookout, Maryland, transferred to Elmira Prison, NY August 12, 1864	Oath of Allegiance May 29, 1865
Beauchampe, James T. Private	19	December 25, 1863, Camp Moore, Louisiana	Co. E, 6th Louisiana Cavalry	August 26, 1864, Bullets Bayou, Concordia Parish, Louisiana	New Orleans, Louisiana transferred to Elmira November 19, 1864.	Died February 10, 1865 of Chronic Diarrhea, Grave No. 2089
Beaver, E. M. Private	Unk	August 8, 1863, Statesville, North Carolina	Co. K, 5th North Carolina Infantry	May 20, 1864, Spotsylvania Court House, Virginia	Point Lookout, MD, transferred to Elmira Prison, NY July 3, 1864	Died March 28, 1865, Chronic Diarrhea, Grave No. 2504
Beaver, Levi A. Private	Unk	August 8, 1862, Statesville, North Carolina	Co. K, 5th North Carolina Infantry	May 12, 1864, Near Spotsylvania County Court House, Virginia	Point Lookout, Maryland, transferred to Elmira Prison, NY August 14, 1864	Oath of Allegiance June 12, 1865
Beaver, Michael M. Private	22	July 6, 1861, China Grove, North Carolina	Co. B, 4th North Carolina Infantry	May 30, 1864, Mechanics-ville, Virginia	Point Lookout, MD, transferred to Elmira Prison, NY July 12, 1864	Oath of Allegiance June 12, 1865

Name & Rank	Age	Enlisted	Regiment and State	Where Captured	Prison	Remarks
Beavers, Lucius Private	Unk	Unknown	Co. H, 15th Virginia Cavalry	August 31, 1863, Dumphries, Virginia	Point Lookout, Maryland, transferred to Elmira Prison, NY August 18, 1864	Exchanged March 2, 1865 at Akins Landing on the James River, Virginia
Beazley, Cornelius J. Private	Unk	March 3, 1862 Fort Marks, Florida	Co. G, 5th Florida Infantry	May 12, 1864, Spotsylvania Court House, Virginia	Point Lookout, Maryland, transferred to Elmira Prison, NY July 30, 1864	Oath of Allegiance June 19, 1865
Beck, Calvin Private	Unk	August 27, 1862, Raleigh, North Carolina	Co. C, 61st North Carolina Infantry	June 16, 1864, Petersburg, Virginia	Point Lookout, Maryland, transferred to Elmira Prison, NY July 25, 1864	Exchanged October 29, 1864 at Venus Point, Savannah River, GA.
Beck, Jeffrey Private	Unk	August 24, 1861, Clarksville, Georgia	Co. K, 24th Georgia Infantry	June 1, 1864, Cold Harbor, Virginia	Point Lookout, Maryland, transferred to Elmira Prison, NY July 17,1864	Exchanged March 10, 1865 at Boulware's wharf on the James River, Virginia
Beck, Jesse Private	Unk	August 24, 1861, Clarksville, Habersham County, Georgia	Co. K, 24th Georgia Infantry	August 16, 1864, Front Royal, Virginia	Point Lookout, Maryland, transferred to Elmira Prison, NY August 29, 1864	Oath of Allegiance June 21, 1865
Beck, William S. Private	23	June 17, 1862, Macon, Georgia	Co. K, 59th Georgia Infantry	May 6, 1864, Wilderness, Virginia	Point Lookout, Maryland, transferred to Elmira Prison, NY August 14, 1864	Died October 12, 1864 of Chronic Diarrhea, Grave No. 567
Beckem, William N. Private	Unk	Unknown	Co. D, 44th Virginia Infantry	May 12, 1864, Spotsylvania Court House, Virginia	Point Lookout, Maryland, transferred to Elmira Prison, NY August 2,1864	Oath of Allegiance June 30, 1865
Beckerdite, P. F. Civilian	18	Unknown	Citizen of Randolph County, North Carolina	April 21, 1864, Near Wilmington, North Carolina	Point Lookout, Maryland, transferred to Elmira Prison, NY July 25, 1864	Died October 4, 1864 of Chronic Diarrhea, Grave No. 613

Name & Rank	Age	Enlisted	Regiment and State	Where Captured	Prison	Remarks
Beckham, William J. Private	Unk	August 15, 1862, Statesville, North Carolina	Co. B, 37th North Carolina Infantry	April 2, 1865, Petersburg, Virginia. Gunshot Wound Scalp.	Old Capital Prison, Washington D. C. Transferred to Elmira Prison, NY May 12, 1865.	Oath of Allegiance July 7, 1865
Beckholt, J. T. Private	21	Unknown	Co. E, 16th Mississippi Infantry	July 11, 1864 Rockville, Maryland	Old Capital Prison, Washington, DC, transferred to Elmira Prison, NY, July 23, 1864	Oath of Allegiance May 14, 1865
Beckley, Charles W. Private	Unk	August 6, 1861, Camp Pulaski, Louisiana	Co. G, 15th Louisiana Infantry	May 12, 1864, Spotsylvania Court House, Virginia. Gunshot Wound Right Breast.	Old Capital Prison, Washington, D. C. Transferred to Elmira Prison, NY August 12, 1864	Exchanged October 29, 1864 at Venus Point, Savannah River, GA.
Beckner, S. B. Private	36	April 10, 1863, Fincastle, Virginia	Co. L, 26th Battalion, Virginia Infantry	June 3, 1864, Gaines Farm, Cold Harbor, Virginia	Point Lookout, Maryland, transferred to Elmira Prison, NY July 17,1864	Died August 2, 1864 of Chronic Diarrhea, Grave No. 4
Beddingfield, Thomas W. Private	Unk	June 17, 1861, Lewisburg, North Carolina	Co. K, 24th North Carolina Infantry	June 17, 1864, Near Petersburg, Virginia	Point Lookout, Maryland, transferred to Elmira Prison, NY July 30, 1864	Oath of Allegiance May 17, 1865
Bedeaux, Pierre Private	Unk	April 1, 1862, Plaguemim, Louisiana	Co. C, 15th Louisiana Infantry	May 20, 1864, Spotsylvania Court House, Virginia	Point Lookout, Maryland, transferred to Elmira Prison, NY July 6, 1864	Exchanged February 18, 1865 on the James River, Virginia
Bedgood, Henry Private	Unk	March 1, 1861, Nashville, North Carolina	Co. H, 32nd North Carolina Infantry	May 10, 1864, Spotsylvania, Virginia	Point Lookout, Maryland, transferred to Elmira Prison, NY August 6, 1864	Exchanged February 20, 1865 at Boulware's or Cox Wharf on the James River, Virginia

Name & Rank	Age	Enlisted	Regiment and State	Where Captured	Prison	Remarks
Bedsaul, Alexander Sergeant	Unk	April 3, 1862, Saltville, Virginia	Co. F, 29th Virginia Infantry	June 3, 1864, Gaines Farm, Cold Harbor, Virginia	Point Lookout, Maryland, transferred to Elmira Prison, NY July 17,1864	Exchanged February 13, 1865 at Boulware's wharf on the James River, Virginia
Bedsaul, Byron Sergeant	Unk	April 3, 1862, Saltville, Virginia	Co. F, 29th Virginia Infantry	June 1, 1864, Gaines Farm, Cold Harbor, Virginia	Point Lookout, Maryland, transferred to Elmira Prison, NY July 17,1864	Oath of Allegiance June 19, 1865
Beemer, John W. Private	Unk	November 1, 1862, Opequon, Virginia	Co. F, 2nd Virginia Infantry	May 12, 1864, Spotsylvania Court House, Virginia	Point Lookout, Maryland, transferred to Elmira Prison, NY August 6, 1864	Died March 8, 1865 of Pneumonia, Grave No. 2383
Beene, A. Hiram Private	Unk	February 26, 1862, Columbia County, Arkansas	Co. B, 19th Arkansas Infantry	May 16, 1863, Big Black River, Mississippi	Point Lookout, Maryland, transferred to Elmira Prison, NY August 18, 1864	Exchanged February 13, 1865 at Boulware's or Cox Wharf on the James River, Virginia
Beheler, J. Private	25	Unknown	Co. F, 17th South Carolina Infantry	Unknown	Point Lookout, Maryland, transferred to Elmira Prison, NY July 17,1864	Died August 1, 1864 of Unknown Disease, Grave No. 77
Beilly, John Private	Unk	Unknown	Co. D, Hampton Legion, South Carolina	July 28, 1864, Petersburg, Virginia	Point Lookout, Maryland, transferred to Elmira Prison, NY August 12, 1864	Oath of Allegiance June 21, 1865
Beir, Frank Civilian	Unk	Unknown	Citizen of Louisiana	June 21, 1864, Came into Lines at New Orleans, Louisiana	Point Lookout, Maryland, transferred to Elmira Prison, NY July 23, 1864	Oath of Allegiance June 20, 1865
Belch, Joseph T. Sergeant	Unk	May 1, 1862, South Mills, North Carolina	Co. L, 32nd North Carolina Infantry	May 10, 1864, Spotsylvania, Virginia	Point Lookout, Maryland, transferred to Elmira Prison, NY August 6, 1864	Oath of Allegiance June 27, 1865

Name & Rank	Age	Enlisted	Regiment and State	Where Captured	Prison	Remarks
Belcher, John F. Private	Unk	May 1, 1863, Danville, Virginia	Co. D, 39th Battalion Virginia Cavalry	May 9, 1864, Caroline County, Virginia	Point Lookout, Maryland, transferred to Elmira Prison, NY August 17, 1864	Oath of Allegiance June 23, 1865
Belcher, William Private	Unk	June 13, 1862, Savannah, Georgia	Co. B, 7th Georgia Cavalry	June 11, 1864, Louisa Court House, Trevilian Station, Virginia	Point Lookout, Maryland, transferred to Elmira Prison, NY July 25, 1864	Died November 28, 1864 of Pneumonia, Grave No. 983
Belk, H. C. Private	Unk	June 11, 1861, Camp McDonald, Georgia	Co. A, 3rd Battalion Georgia Sharp shooters	August 16, 1864, Front Royal, Virginia	Point Lookout, Maryland, transferred to Elmira Prison, NY August 29, 1864	Oath of Allegiance July 7, 1865
Bell, C. J. Private	Unk	February 4, 1864, Camp Lay, South Carolina	Co. B, 4th South Carolina Cavalry	June 11, 1864, Louisa Court House, Trevilian Station, Virginia	Point Lookout, Maryland, transferred to Elmira Prison, NY July 25, 1864	Exchanged March 14, 1865 at Boulware's Wharf on the James River, Virginia
Bell, Charles E. Private	Unk	March 6, 1862, Winchester, Virginia	Co. F, 2nd Virginia Infantry	May 12, 1864, Near Spotsylvania Court House, Virginia	Point Lookout, Maryland, transferred to Elmira Prison, NY August 6, 1864	Oath of Allegiance June 21, 1865
Bell, F. C. Sergeant	Unk	May 13, 1862, Savannah, Georgia	Co. E, 7th Georgia Cavalry	June 11, 1864, Louisa Court House, Trevilian Station, Virginia	Point Lookout, Maryland, transferred to Elmira Prison, NY July 25, 1864	Died October 24, 1864 of Typhoid-Pneumonia, Grave No. 852
Bell, J. Private	Unk	Unknown	Co. E, 41st Georgia Infantry	May 31, 1864, Cold Harbor, Virginia	Point Lookout, Maryland, transferred to Elmira Prison, NY July 17, 1864	Oath of Allegiance June 30, 1865
Bell, J. E. Civilian	Unk	Registered Enemy	Citizen of Louisiana	July 27, 1864, New Orleans, Louisiana	New Orleans, Louisiana transferred to Elmira November 19, 1864.	Oath of Allegiance June 20, 1865
Bell, J. H. Jr. Private	Unk	November 1, 1862, Savannah, Georgia	Co. A, 7th Georgia Cavalry	June 11, 1864, Louisa Court House, Trevilian Station, Virginia	Point Lookout, Maryland, transferred to Elmira Prison, NY July 30, 1864	Oath of Allegiance June 21, 1865

Name & Rank	Age	Enlisted	Regiment and State	Where Captured	Prison	Remarks
Bell, James M. Private	30	April 16, 1862, Rudes Hill, Virginia	Co. B, 2nd Virginia Infantry	May 12, 1864, Near Spotsylvania Court House, Virginia	Point Lookout, Maryland, transferred to Elmira Prison, NY August 6, 1864	Oath of Allegiance June 27, 1865
Bell, John Private	Unk	May 20, 1862, Columbus, Florida	Co. H, 8th Florida Infantry	July 29, 1864, Petersburg, Virginia	Point Lookout, Maryland, transferred to Elmira Prison, NY August 12, 1864	Died May 3, 1865 of Pneumonia, Grave No. 2751
Bell, John Private	Unk	February 20, 1863, Camp Radford, Montgomery County, Virginia	Co. I, 8th Virginia Cavalry	July 16, 1864, Loudoun County, Virginia	Old Capital Prison, Washington, DC, transferred to Elmira Prison, NY, July 23, 1864	Oath of Allegiance June 26, 1865
Bell, John E. Private	Unk	April 22, 1862, Lee's Farm, Virginia	Co. E, 10th Louisiana Infantry	May 12, 1864, Spotsylvania Court House, Virginia	Point Lookout, Maryland, transferred to Elmira Prison, NY July 25, 1864	Exchanged February 25, 1865 at Boulware's or Cox Wharf on the James River, Virginia
Bell, John S. Corporal	16	June 25, 1861, Wytheville, Virginia	Co. I, 50th Virginia Infantry	May 12, 1864, Spotsylvania Court House, Virginia	Point Lookout, Maryland, transferred to Elmira Prison, NY August 2, 1864	Died October 17, 1864 of Chronic Diarrhea, Grave No. 551
Bell, Joseph T. Private	37	May 4, 1863, Quitman, Georgia	Co. H, 64th Georgia Infantry	June 17, 1864, Petersburg, Virginia	Point Lookout, Maryland, transferred to Elmira Prison, NY July 30, 1864	Oath of Allegiance June 14, 1865
Bell, Josephus Private	Unk	Unknown	Home Guard, North Carolina	May 9, 1864, Near Swansboro, North Carolina	Point Lookout, Maryland, transferred to Elmira Prison, NY August 17, 1864	Exchanged March 10, 1865 at Boulware's Wharf on the James River, Virginia
Bell, Manning A. Private	Unk	January 1, 1862, Camp Harley, Georgetown, South Carolina	Co. J, 25th South Carolina Infantry	January 15, 1865, Fort Fisher, North Carolina	Elmira Prison Camp January 30, 1865	Oath of Allegiance July 3, 1865

Name & Rank	Age	Enlisted	Regiment and State	Where Captured	Prison	Remarks
Bell, Robert Private	Unk	July 28, 1863, Camp Holmes, North Carolina	Co. A, 23rd North Carolina Infantry	May 12, 1864, Spotsylvania Court House, Virginia	Point Lookout, Maryland, transferred to Elmira Prison, NY August 14, 1864	Exchanged October 29, 1864, at Venus Point, Savannah River, GA.
Bell, Thomas J. Private	25	July 2, 1861, Camp Trousdale, Tennessee	Co. H, 17th Tennessee Infantry	June 17, 1864, Petersburg, Virginia	Point Lookout, Maryland, transferred to Elmira Prison, NY July 30, 1864	Exchanged February 13, 1865 at Boulware's wharf on the James River, Virginia
Bell, W. B. Private	Unk	December 28, 1861, Camp Hampton Legion, South Carolina	Co. F, Holcombe Legion, South Carolina	May 8, 1864, Jarrett's Depot, Virginia	Point Lookout, Maryland, transferred to Elmira Prison, NY August 17, 1864	Oath of Allegiance June 19, 1865
Bell, William A. Private	Unk	June 4, 1861, Montevallo, Alabama	Co. K, 10th Alabama Infantry	May 6, 1864, Wilderness, Virginia	Point Lookout, Maryland, transferred to Elmira Prison, NY August 17, 1864	Exchanged October 29, 1864, at Venus Point, Savannah River, GA.
Bell, William L. Private	Unk	March 25, 1862, Grahamville, South Carolina	Co. K, 4th South Carolina Cavalry	May 30, 1864, Old Church, Virginia. Gunshot Wound Buttocks.	Old Capital Prison, Washington, D.C. Transferred to Elmira Prison, NY August 12, 1864	Exchanged October 29, 1864 at Venus Point, Savannah River, GA.
Bellamy, Richard C. Private	17	February 13, 1862, Monticello, Florida	Co. A, 5th Florida Infantry	May 12, 1864, Spotsylvania Court House, Virginia	Point Lookout, Maryland, transferred to Elmira Prison, NY August 12, 1864	Died November 27, 1864 of Pneumonia, Grave No. 903
Bellflower, Henry M. Private	34	July 17, 1863, Camp Leon, Virginia	Co. G, 64th Georgia Infantry	June 17, 1864, Petersburg, Virginia	Point Lookout, Maryland, transferred to Elmira Prison, NY July 30, 1864	Exchanged October 29, 1864 at Venus Point, Savannah River, GA.
Bellington, William H. Private	32	Unknown	Co. I, 42nd Virginia Infantry	May 12, 1864, Spotsylvania Court House, Virginia	Point Lookout, Maryland, transferred to Elmira Prison, NY August 2, 1864	Transferred for Exchange 10/11/64. Died 10/15/64 of Unknown Causes at US Army Hospital, Baltimore, MD.

Name & Rank	Age	Enlisted	Regiment and State	Where Captured	Prison	Remarks
Bellotte, John David Private	32	February 22, 1863, Pendleton, South Carolina	Co. C, 4th South Carolina Cavalry	May 28, 1864, Hanover County, Virginia. Gunshot Wound Right Chest.	Old Capital Prison, Washington, DC, transferred to Elmira Prison, NY, December 17, 1864	Died March 16, 1865 of Chronic Diarrhea, Grave No. 1700
Belton, James R. Private	Unk	May 4, 1861, Dobson, North Carolina	Co. A, 28th North Carolina Infantry	May 12, 1864, Spotsylvania Court House, Virginia	Point Lookout, Maryland, transferred to Elmira Prison, NY August 12, 1864	Died March 11, 1865 of Pleurisy, Grave No. 1869
Belton, Thornton Private	33	March 11, 1862, Elm Grove, Rockingham County, North Carolina	Co. F, 45th North Carolina Infantry	May 10, 1864, Spotsylvania Court House, Virginia	Point Lookout, Maryland, transferred to Elmira Prison, NY August 6, 1864	Died February 6, 1865 of Chronic Diarrhea, Grave No. 1911
Belvins, Robert Private	Unk	August 15, 1862, Statesville, North Carolina	Co. B, 37th North Carolina Infantry	May 12, 1864, Spotsylvania Court House, Virginia	Point Lookout, Maryland, transferred to Elmira Prison, NY August 12, 1864	Oath of Allegiance June 16, 1865
Bender, Philemon Sergeant	29	May 15, 1862, Trenton, North Carolina	Co. F, 66th North Carolina Infantry	June 3, 1864, Gaines Mill, Cold Harbor, Virginia	Point Lookout, Maryland, transferred to Elmira Prison, NY July 17,1864	Exchanged October 29, 1864 at Venus Point, Savannah River, GA.
Bendick, B. B. Private	Unk	May 1, 1862, Augusta, Georgia	Co. D, 12th Battalion Georgia Light Artillery	August 10, 1864, Berryville, Virginia	Point Lookout, Maryland, transferred to Elmira Prison, NY August 29, 1864	Exchanged March 2, 1865. Died August 20, 1865 of Phthisis Pulmonalis at Stanton General Hospital, Washington, DC.
Benefield, David Private	34	August 1, 1862, Coffee County, Alabama	Co. F, 1st Battalion Alabama Artillery	August 23, 1864, Fort Morgan, Alabama	Steam Press No. 4, New Orleans, Louisiana transferred to Elmira Prison, October 8, 1864.	Died February 20, 1865 of Pneumonia, Grave No. 2309

Name & Rank	Age	Enlisted	Regiment and State	Where Captured	Prison	Remarks
Benfield, Balis E. Sergeant	18	September 3, 1861, Mecklenburg County, North Carolina	Co. H, 35th North Carolina Infantry	June 17, 1864, Petersburg, Virginia	Point Lookout, Maryland, transferred to Elmira Prison, NY July 30, 1864	Oath of Allegiance June 19, 1865
Benfield, Riley A. Private	Unk	February 29, 1864, Camp Holmes, North Carolina	Co. F, 32nd North Carolina Infantry	May 10, 1864, Wilderness, Virginia	Point Lookout, Maryland, transferred to Elmira Prison, NY August 6, 1864	Died February 26, 1865 of Variola (Smallpox), Grave No. 2284
Benfield, William M. Private	18	August 20, 1862, Camp Hill, in North Carolina	Co. C, 18th North Carolina Infantry	May 10, 1864, Spotsylvania Court House, Virginia	Point Lookout, Maryland, transferred to Elmira Prison, NY August 6, 1864	Exchanged February 13, 1865 at Boulware's wharf on the James River, Virginia
Benge, Nathan Private	Unk	August 13, 1861, Yadkinville, North Carolina	Co. I, 28th North Carolina Infantry	May 12, 1864, Spotsylvania Court House, Virginia	Point Lookout, Maryland, transferred to Elmira Prison, NY August 12, 1864	Exchanged October 29, 1864 at Venus Point, Savannah River, GA.
Benn, William Private	23	June 18, 1861, Front Royal, Virginia	Co. E, 7th Virginia Cavalry	October 31, 1864, Warren County Virginia	Old Capital Prison, Washington, DC. Transferred to Elmira Prison, New York December 17, 1864	Died April 21, 1865 of Pneumonia, Grave No. 1389
Bennett, Aaron B. Private	31	February 28, 1863, Fort Caswell, North Carolina	Co. K, 36th Regiment, 2nd North Carolina Artillery	January 15, 1865, Fort Fisher, North Carolina. Wounded.	February 1, 1865, Elmira Prison Camp, New York	Oath of Allegiance May 15, 1865
Bennett, Albert A. Private	Unk	January 31, 1862, Pocahontas County, Virginia	Co. B, 12th Georgia Infantry	May 10, 1864, Spotsylvania, Virginia	Old Capital Prison, Washington, DC, transferred to Elmira Prison, NY, December 17, 1864	Died February 13, 1865 of Variola (Smallpox), Grave No. 2037
Bennett, Andrew J. Private	Unk	November 27, 1862, Drury's Bluff, Virginia	Co. E, 45th North Carolina Infantry	May 10, 1864, Spotsylvania Court House, Virginia	Point Lookout, Maryland, transferred to Elmira Prison, NY August 6, 1864	Died January 25, 1865 of Typhoid Fever, Grave No. 1626

Name & Rank	Age	Enlisted	Regiment and State	Where Captured	Prison	Remarks
Bennett, Asa B. Private	Unk	May 5, 1862, Fort St. Philip, North Carolina	Co. G, 36th Regiment, 2nd North Carolina Artillery	January 15, 1865, Fort Fisher, North Carolina. Wounded.	February 1, 1865, Elmira Prison Camp, New York	Died March 9, 1865 of Chronic Diarrhea, Grave No. 2371. Headstone has Barnett.
Bennett, C. Private	Unk	April 28, 1862, White Sulfur Springs, Virginia	Co. H, 22nd Virginia Infantry	June 3, 1864, Gaines Farm, Cold Harbor, Virginia	Point Lookout, Maryland, transferred to Elmira Prison, NY July 17,1864	Oath of Allegiance July 3, 1865
Bennett, Christian G. Private	Unk	Unknown	Co. B, 20th Georgia Infantry	May 31, 1864, Cold Harbor, Virginia	Point Lookout, Maryland, transferred to Elmira Prison, NY July 8, 1864	Died September 28, 1864, Chronic Diarrhea, Grave No. 356
Bennett, Eli Private	18	May 18, 1861, Franklin, Virginia	Co. K, 25th Virginia Infantry	May 5, 1864, Wilderness, Virginia	Point Lookout, Maryland, transferred to Elmira Prison, NY August 14, 1864	Oath of Allegiance June 27, 1865
Bennett, George M. Private	Unk	April 1, 1862, Camp Leon, Madison, Florida	Co. D, 5th Florida Infantry	May 12, 1864, Spotsylvania Court House, Virginia	Point Lookout, Maryland, transferred to Elmira Prison, NY July 30, 1864	Oath of Allegiance June 16, 1865
Bennett, James P. Private	Unk	March 21, 1864, Henry County, Virginia	Co. F, 42nd Virginia Infantry	May 12, 1864, Near Spotsylvania Court House, Virginia	Point Lookout, Maryland, transferred to Elmira Prison, NY August 6, 1864	Died July 30, 1865 of Unknown Causes, Grave No. 2862. All information on headstone is wrong except last name.
Bennett, John Private	Unk	March 15, 1862, Gaston County, North Carolina	Co. K, 49th North Carolina Infantry	July 19, 1864, Petersburg, Virginia	Old Capital Prison, Washington, DC, transferred to Elmira Prison, NY, July 23, 1864	Oath of Allegiance May 15, 1865

Name & Rank	Age	Enlisted	Regiment and State	Where Captured	Prison	Remarks
Bennett, John H. Private	Unk	March 30, 1864, Kinston, North Carolina	Co. F, 21st North Carolina Infantry	July 10, 1864, Middleton, Maryland	Old Capital Prison, Washington, DC, transferred to Elmira Prison, NY, December 17, 1864	Died June 1, 1865 of Chronic Diarrhea, Grave No. 2905
Bennett, Sebastian Private	Unk	August 23, 1861, Brunswick, Georgia	Co. F, 26th Georgia Infantry	May 20, 1864, Spotsylvania Court House, Virginia	Point Lookout, Maryland, transferred to Elmira Prison, NY July 3, 1864	Exchanged February 20, 1865 at Boulware's or Cox Wharf on the James River, Virginia
Bennett, U. M. Private	Unk	October 13, 1863, Bryan County, Georgia	Co. H, 7th Georgia Cavalry	June 11, 1864, Trevilian Station, Louisa Court House, Virginia	Point Lookout, Maryland, transferred to Elmira Prison, NY July 25, 1864	Exchanged October 29, 1864 at Venus Point, Savannah River, GA.
Bennett, W. W. Private	Unk	Unknown	Co. B, Jalmon's Artillery, State Unknown	September 14, 1863, Falling Waters, Maryland	Point Lookout, Maryland, transferred to Elmira Prison, NY August 18, 1864	Exchanged March 10, 1865 at Boulware's wharf on the James River, Virginia
Bennett, William A. 1st Sergeant	Unk	July 19, 1861, Montgomery, Alabama	Co. G, 13th Alabama Infantry	May 12, 1864, Spotsylvania Court House, Virginia	Point Lookout, Maryland, transferred to Elmira Prison, NY July 30, 1864	Oath of Allegiance June 23, 1865
Bennezette, Clinton L. Private	27	April 20, 1861, Alexandria, Virginia	Co. F, 6th Virginia Cavalry	September 14, 1863, Near Culpepper, Virginia	Point Lookout, Maryland, transferred to Elmira Prison, NY August 18, 1864	Exchanged March 10, 1865 at Boulware's wharf on the James River, Virginia
Bennington, Mathew Private	Unk	July 23, 1861, Mount Airy, Wythe County, Virginia	Co. B, 29th Virginia Infantry	May 14, 1864, Bermuda Hundred, Virginia. Deserted to Union Lines.	Point Lookout, Maryland, transferred to Elmira Prison, NY July 12, 1864	Oath of Allegiance February 7, 1865
Benson, Berry G. Sergeant	Unk	August 2, 1861, Hamburgh, South Carolina	Co. H, 1st South Carolina Infantry	May 17, 1864, Spotsylvania, Virginia	Old Capital Prison, Washington, DC, transferred to Elmira Prison, NY, July 23, 1864	Escaped October 7, 1864 by Tunneling Under Fence.

Name & Rank	Age	Enlisted	Regiment and State	Where Captured	Prison	Remarks
Benson, Daniel J. Private	Unk	July 23, 1862, Fort St. Philip, North Carolina	Co. G, 36th Regiment, 2nd North Carolina Artillery	January 15, 1865, Fort Fisher, North Carolina. Wounded.	February 1, 1865, Elmira Prison Camp, New York	Oath of Allegiance June 23, 1865
Benson, Jacob Sergeant	Unk	August 1, 1861, Staunton, Virginia	Co. H, 25th Virginia Infantry	May 5, 1864, Wilderness, Virginia	Point Lookout, Maryland, transferred to Elmira Prison, NY August 17, 1864	Exchanged February 13, 1865 at Boulware's wharf on the James River, Virginia
Benson, James S. Private	30	March 1, 1864, Ashland, Virginia	Co. G, 4th Virginia Cavalry	August 16, 1864, Front Royal, Virginia	Point Lookout, Maryland, transferred to Elmira Prison, NY August 29, 1864	Exchanged February 25, 1865 at Boulware's or Cox Wharf on the James River, Virginia
Benson, John M. Sergeant	Unk	1113 1861, Wilmington, North Carolina	Co. B, 36th Regiment, 2nd North Carolina Artillery	January 15, 1865, Fort Fisher, North Carolina. Wounded	February 1, 1865, Elmira Prison Camp, New York	Oath of Allegiance July 7, 1865
Benson, Oscar Sergeant	Unk	August 11, 1861, Gwinnett, Georgia	Co. E, 3rd Battalion Georgia Sharp shooters	August 16, 1864, Front Royal, Virginia	Point Lookout, Maryland, transferred to Elmira Prison, NY August 29, 1864	Exchanged March 14, 1865 at Boulware's Wharf on the James River, Virginia
Benton, Joshua Private	Unk	January 4, 1862, Waterboro, South Carolina	Co. J, 11th South Carolina Infantry	June 24, 1864, Petersburg, Virginia	Point Lookout, Maryland, transferred to Elmira Prison, NY August 18, 1864	Died October 1, 1864 of Chronic Diarrhea, Grave No. 419
Benton, S. J. Private	Unk	August 8, 1862, Monticello, Florida	Co. K, 10th Florida Infantry	July 29, 1864, Petersburg, Virginia	Point Lookout, Maryland, transferred to Elmira Prison, NY August 12, 1864	Oath of Allegiance May 29, 1865
Benton, Thomas Private	Unk	September 5, 1862, Baton Rouge Barracks, Louisiana	Co. B, 1st Louisiana Cavalry	September 24, 1864, East Baton Rouge, Louisiana	New Orleans, Louisiana transferred to Elmira November 19, 1864.	Died December 10, 1864 of Chronic Diarrhea, Grave No. 1158

Name & Rank	Age	Enlisted	Regiment and State	Where Captured	Prison	Remarks
Berger, Charles L. Private	Unk	August 30, 1862, Camp Randolph, Georgia	Co. C, 44th Georgia Infantry	July 13, 1864, Near Washington, DC,	Old Capital Prison, Washington, DC, transferred to Elmira Prison, NY, July 23, 1864	Oath of Allegiance June 19, 1865
Bergmann, Ambrose Private	30	February 25, 1864, Charleston, South Carolina	Co. I, 1st South Carolina Infantry	July 29, 1864, Petersburg, Virginia	Point Lookout, Maryland, transferred to Elmira Prison, NY August 12, 1864	Oath of Allegiance May 15, 1865
Berkley, James A. Private	Unk	December 31, 1861, Charlotte, Virginia	Co. B, 22nd Battalion Virginia Infantry	July 14, 1863, Falling Waters, Maryland	Point Lookout, Maryland, transferred to Elmira Prison, NY August 18, 1864	Exchanged March 2, 1865 at Akins Landing on the James River, Virginia
Berkshire, Joseph J. Private	Unk	June 30, 1862, Clarksville, Georgia	Co. K, 16th Georgia Infantry	August 16, 1864, Front Royal, Virginia	Point Lookout, Maryland, transferred to Elmira Prison, NY August 29, 1864	Oath of Allegiance July 7, 1865
Berlin, A. Jackson Private	30	June 22, 1861, Harper's Ferry, Virginia	Co. C, 2nd Virginia Infantry	May 12, 1864, Near Spotsylvania Court House, Virginia	Point Lookout, Maryland, transferred to Elmira Prison, NY August 6, 1864	Oath of Allegiance June 23, 1865
Berlin, Sanford W. Private	Unk	March 13, 1862, Fredericksburg, Virginia	Co. K, 55th Virginia Infantry	May 5, 1864, Wilderness, Virginia	Point Lookout, Maryland, transferred to Elmira Prison, NY August 14, 1864	Oath of Allegiance June 23, 1865
Berrong, Leander J. Sergeant	Unk	August 24, 1861, Hiawassee, Georgia	Co. D, 24th Georgia Infantry	June 1, 1864, Cold Harbor, Virginia	Point Lookout, Maryland, transferred to Elmira Prison, NY July 17,1864	Oath of Allegiance July 7, 1865
Berry, Andrew F. Private	Unk	April 24, 1862, Centerville, Florida	Co. K, 5th Florida Infantry	May 12, 1864, Spotsylvania Court House, Virginia	Point Lookout, Maryland, transferred to Elmira Prison, NY July 30, 1864	Oath of Allegiance June 16, 1865

Name & Rank	Age	Enlisted	Regiment and State	Where Captured	Prison	Remarks
Berry, Benjamin B. Private	Unk	January 22, 1864, Bristol, Tennessee	Co. I, 14th Tennessee Infantry	May 5, 1864, Wilderness, Virginia	Point Lookout, Maryland, transferred to Elmira Prison, NY July 23, 1864	Died November 27, 1864 of Pneumonia, Grave No. 898
Berry, Charles W. Private	Unk	August 18, 1862, Mill Point, Virginia	Co. G, 25th Virginia Infantry	May 5, 1864, Wilderness, Virginia	Point Lookout, Maryland, transferred to Elmira Prison, NY August 14, 1864	Died July 8, 1865 of Chronic Diarrhea, Grave No. 2841
Berry, Granville S. Sergeant	Unk	June 24, 1861, Beverly, Virginia	Co. G, 25th Virginia Infantry	May 5, 1864, Wilderness, Virginia	Point Lookout, Maryland, transferred to Elmira Prison, NY August 14, 1864	Oath of Allegiance June 23, 1865
Berry, Isaac S. Sergeant	Unk	December 21, 1861, Nashville, Tennessee	Co. J, 44th Tennessee Infantry	June 17, 1864, Petersburg, Virginia	Point Lookout, Maryland, transferred to Elmira Prison, NY July 30, 1864	Exchanged February 25, 1865 at Boulware's or Cox Wharf on the James River, Virginia
Berry, J. H. Corporal	Unk	April 21, 1861, Memphis, Tennessee	Co. A, Jackson's 1st Regiment, Tennessee Heavy Artillery	August 23, 1864, Fort Morgan, Alabama	New Orleans, Louisiana transferred to Elmira December 4, 1864.	Exchanged February 25, 1865 at Boulware's or Cox Wharf on the James River, Virginia
Berry, James W. Private	Unk	August 18, 1862, Mill Point, Virginia	Co. G, 25th Virginia Infantry	May 5, 1864, Wilderness, Virginia	Point Lookout, Maryland, transferred to Elmira Prison, NY August 14, 1864	Oath of Allegiance June 23, 1865
Berry, John Private	Unk	March 12, 1862, Norfolk County, Virginia	Co. F, 15th Virginia Cavalry	May 12, 1864, Mechanics-ville, Virginia	Point Lookout, Maryland, transferred to Elmira Prison, NY August 17, 1864	Died September 25, 1864 of Meningitis, Grave No. 367
Berry, John Private	Unk	May 20, 181, Keysville, Virginia	Co. K, 23rd Virginia Infantry	May 20, 1864, Spotsylvania Court House, Virginia	Point Lookout, Maryland, transferred to Elmira Prison, NY July 6, 1864	Oath of Allegiance May 29, 1865

Name & Rank	Age	Enlisted	Regiment and State	Where Captured	Prison	Remarks
Berry, John T. Private	Unk	July 3, 1861, Glennville, Alabama	Co. H, 15th Alabama Intantry	May 6, 1864, Wilderness, Virginia	Point Lookout, Maryland, transferred to Elmira Prison, NY August 17, 1864	Oath of Allegiance June 14, 1865
Berry, Silas Private	18	May 1, 1862, Morganton, Burke County, North Carolina	Co. K, 35th North Carolina Infantry	June 17, 1864, Petersburg, Virginia	Point Lookout, Maryland, transferred to Elmira Prison, NY July 30, 1864	Oath of Allegiance June 12, 1865
Berry, Sylvester A. Private	Unk	May 12, 1864, Petersburg, Virginia	Co. D, 59th Virginia Infantry	June 17, 1864, Petersburg, Virginia	Point Lookout, Maryland, transferred to Elmira Prison, NY July 30, 1864	Exchanged February 13, 1865 at Boulware's wharf on the James River, Virginia
Berry, William Private	Unk	Unknown	Co. G, 62nd Georgia Infantry	July 16, 1864, Loudoun County, Virginia	Old Capital Prison, Washington, DC, transferred to Elmira Prison, NY, July 23, 1864	Exchanged October 29, 1864 at Venus Point, Savannah River, GA.
Berry, William S. Private	Unk	February 25, 1864, Rappahannock, Virginia	Co. B, 41st Virginia Infantry	June 24, 1864, Petersburg, Virginia	Point Lookout, Maryland, transferred to Elmira Prison, NY July 25, 1864	Oath of Allegiance May 13, 1865
Berryhill, Alfred Private	Unk	November 20, 1863, Montgomery, Alabama	Co. E, 1st Battalion Alabama Artillery	August 23, 1864, Fort Morgan, Alabama	New Orleans, Louisiana transferred to Elmira December 4, 1864.	Died February 10, 1865 of Typhoid-Pneumonia, Grave No. 2095
Berryhill, Pinkney Private	23	March 15, 1862, Gaston County, North Carolina	Co. K, 49th North Carolina Infantry	July 17, 1864, Petersburg, Virginia	Old Capital Prison, Washington, DC, transferred to Elmira Prison, NY, July 23, 1864	Oath of Allegiance May 29, 1865
Berryman, John N. Private	Unk	February 28, 1862, Camp Pryor, Virginia	Co. G, 13th Virginia Cavalry	September 14, 1863, Near Culpepper, Virginia	Point Lookout, Maryland, transferred to Elmira Prison, NY August 18,1864	Exchanged at Venus Point, Savannah River, GA, 11/15/1864.

Name & Rank	Age	Enlisted	Regiment and State	Where Captured	Prison	Remarks
Bersch, Benjamin H. Private	Unk	March 5, 1863, Camp Lee, Pamplin's, Virginia	Co. D, 18th Virginia Infantry	June 1, 1864, Gaines Mill, Cold Harbor, Virginia	Point Lookout, Maryland, transferred to Elmira Prison, NY July 17, 1864	Exchanged October 29, 1864, at Venus Point, Savannah River, GA.
Bertrand, Alcee Private	21	March 3, 1862, St. Landry, Louisiana	Co. C, 6th Louisiana Infantry	May 5, 1864, Wilderness, Virginia	Point Lookout, Maryland, transferred to Elmira Prison, NY August 17, 1864	Exchanged February 25, 1865 at Boulware's or Cox Wharf on the James River, Virginia
Bess, John F. Private	18	August 31, 1861, Lincolnton, North Carolina	Co. E, 34th North Carolina Infantry	May 6, 1864, Wilderness, Virginia	Point Lookout, Maryland, transferred to Elmira Prison, NY August 14, 1864	Exchanged February 20, 1865 at Boulware's or Cox Wharf on the James River, Virginia
Bess, Lemuel B. Corporal	33	May 16, 1861, Columbia, North Carolina	Co. A, 32nd North Carolina Infantry	May 10, 1864, Spotsylvania, Virginia	Point Lookout, Maryland, transferred to Elmira Prison, NY August 6, 1864	Oath of Allegiance June 27, 1865
Bessaul, Samuel Private	Unk	Unknown	Co. F, 62nd Georgia Infantry	July 16, 1864, Loudoun County, Virginia	Old Capital Prison, Washington, DC, transferred to Elmira Prison, NY, July 23, 1864	Exchanged February 13, 1865 at Boulware's wharf on the James River, Virginia
Bessent, James H. Corporal	Unk	March 9, 1863, James Island, South Carolina	Co. G, 51st North Carolina Infantry	June 3, 1864, Gaines Mill, Cold Harbor, Virginia	Transferred From Point Lookout Prison, MD, July 12, 1864. Train Never Arrived at Elmira Prison Camp, NY.	Died July 15, 1864 in Train Wreck at Shohola, Pennsylvania
Best, Archibald Private	Unk	March 23, 1863, Marianna, Florida	Co. H, 11th Florida Infantry	July 29, 1864, Petersburg, Virginia	Point Lookout, Maryland, transferred to Elmira Prison, NY August 12, 1864	Died September 11, 1864 of Pleuritis, Grave No. 258
Best, James P. Private	Unk	January 20, 1862, Darlington District, South Carolina	Co. H, 21st South Carolina Infantry	July 10, 1863, Morris Island, South Carolina	Point Lookout, Maryland, transferred to Elmira Prison, NY August 18, 1864	Exchanged February 20, 1865 at Boulware's or Cox Wharf on the James River, Virginia

Name & Rank	Age	Enlisted	Regiment and State	Where Captured	Prison	Remarks
Best, Matthew J. Private	36	February 6, 1863, Whiteville, North Carolina	Co. E, 36th Regiment, 2nd North Carolina Artillery	January 15, 1865, Fort Fisher, North Carolina. Wounded.	February 1, 1865, Elmira Prison Camp, New York	Oath of Allegiance July 7, 1865
Best, William Corporal	18	June 24, 1861, Williamston, North Carolina	Co. H, 1st North Carolina Infantry	May 12, 1864, Spotsylvania Court House, Virginia	Point Lookout, Maryland, transferred to Elmira Prison, NY August 6, 1864	Transferred for Exchange 10/11/64. Died 11/12/64 at Port Royal, South Carolina.
Betts, J. H. Sergeant	Unk	July 16, 1861, Lawrenceville, Georgia	Co. I, 16th Georgia Infantry	June 1, 1864, Gaines Farm, Cold Harbor, Virginia	Point Lookout, Maryland, transferred to Elmira Prison, NY July 17, 1864	Died January 27, 1865 of Variola (Smallpox), Grave No. 1651
Bever, Daniel F. Private	25	July 15, 1862, Raleigh, North Carolina	Co. E, 15th North Carolina Infantry	April 2, 1865, Hatchers Run, Virginia. Gunshot Wound Head.	Old Capital Prison, Washington D. C. Transferred to Elmira Prison, NY May 12, 1865.	Oath of Allegiance July 7, 1865
Beverage, John Private	23	March 31, 1862, Allegheny, Virginia	Co. E, 31st Virginia Infantry	June 10, 1864, Spotsylvania Court House, Virginia	Point Lookout, Maryland, transferred to Elmira Prison, NY July 23, 1864	Exchanged March 2, 1865 at Akins Landing on the James River, Virginia
Beverly, John Private	Unk	April 20, 1862, Marion, South Carolina	Co. D, 25th South Carolina Infantry	January 15, 1865, Fort Fisher, North Carolina	January 30, 1865, Elmira Prison Camp, NY	Died February 27, 1865 of Variola (Smallpox), Grave No. 2123
Bezanson, Joseph Private	22	June 10, 1861, Mt. Meridian, Virginia	Co. B, 10th Virginia Infantry	May 12, 1864, Spotsylvania Court House, Virginia	Point Lookout, Maryland, transferred to Elmira Prison, NY August 2, 1864	Oath of Allegiance May 19, 1865
Bibb, Doddridge L. Private	Unk	July 2, 1861, Bethel Am., Virginia	Co. F, 50th Virginia Infantry	May 12, 1864, Spotsylvania Court House, Virginia	Point Lookout, Maryland, transferred to Elmira Prison, NY August 2, 1864	Died September 24, 1864 of Chronic Diarrhea, Grave No. 472

Name & Rank	Age	Enlisted	Regiment and State	Where Captured	Prison	Remarks
Bible, Adam W. Corporal	Unk	May 18, 1861, Franklin, Virginia	Co. E, 25th Virginia Infantry	May 5, 1864, Wilderness, Virginia	Point Lookout, Maryland, transferred to Elmira Prison, NY August 14, 1864	Oath of Allegiance June 23, 1865
Bickham, J. T. Private	Unk	May 9, 1861, Camp Walker, New Orleans, Louisiana	Co. H, 2nd Louisiana Infantry	May 12, 1864, Spotsylvania Court House, Virginia	Point Lookout, Maryland, transferred to Elmira Prison, NY August 17, 1864	Exchanged February 25, 1865 at Boulware's or Cox Wharf on the James River, Virginia
Biggs, George W. Private	Unk	June 15, 1861, Macon County, Georgia	Co. C, 12th Georgia Infantry	May 10, 1864, Spotsylvania Court House, Virginia	Point Lookout, Maryland, transferred to Elmira Prison, NY July 25, 1864	Oath of Allegiance June 30, 1865
Biggs, Hector Private	20	June 4, 1861, St. Paul's, Floral, North Carolina	Co. G, 24th North Carolina Infantry	June 17, 1864, Near Petersburg, Virginia	Point Lookout, Maryland, transferred to Elmira Prison, NY July 30, 1864	Oath of Allegiance July 7, 1865
Biggs, Jefferson Private	18	July 23, 1862, Fort St. Philip, Brunwick County, North Carolina	Co. G, 36th Regiment, 2nd North Carolina Artillery	January 15, 1865, Fort Fisher, North Carolina. Wounded.	February 1, 1865, Elmira Prison Camp, New York	Died March 30, 1865 of Hospital Gangrene, Grave No. 2590
Biggs, Moses Private	Unk	Unknown	Co. F, 36th Regiment, 2nd North Carolina Artillery	January 15, 1865, Fort Fisher, North Carolina. Wounded.	February 1, 1865, Elmira Prison Camp, New York	Oath of Allegiance June 23, 1865
Biggs, Resden Private	23	September 6, 1861, Lumberton, North Carolina	Co. A, 31st North Carolina Infantry	June 1, 1864, Gaines Farm, Cold Harbor, Virginia	Transferred From Point Lookout Prison, MD, July 12, 1864. Train Never Arrived at Elmira Prison Camp, NY.	Died July 15, 1864 in Train Wreck at Shohola, Pennsylvania.
Bilbro, Henry M. Private	Unk	March 20, 1864, Orange County, Virginia	Co. C, 42nd Virginia Infantry	May 12, 1864, Spotsylvania Court House, Virginia	Point Lookout, Maryland, transferred to Elmira Prison, NY August 2,1864	Exchanged February 20, 1865 at Boulware's or Cox Wharf on the James River, Virginia

Name & Rank	Age	Enlisted	Regiment and State	Where Captured	Prison	Remarks
Biles, John W. Private	32	May 10, 1862, Wadesboro, North Carolina	Co. A, 4th North Carolina Cavalry	July 12, 1863, Ashby Gap, Virginia	Point Lookout, Maryland, transferred to Elmira Prison, NY August 18, 1864	Exchanged October 29, 1864, at Venus Point, Savannah River, GA.
Billings, Affee Private	Unk	Unknown	Co. H, Unknown Regiment, South Carolina Infantry	Unknown	Unknown	Died September 2, 1864 of Unknown Disease, Grave No. 75
Billings, Samuel Private	21	May 3, 1862, Gap Civil, Allegheny County, North Carolina	Co. J, 61st North Carolina Infantry	June 16, 1864, Petersburg, Virginia	Point Lookout, Maryland, transferred to Elmira Prison, NY July 25, 1864	Oath of Allegiance June 19, 1865
Bilton, Jacob J. Private	31	February 22, 1862, Charleston, South Carolina	Co. E, 25th South Carolina Infantry	January 15, 1865, Fort Fisher, North Carolina	Elmira Prison Camp, New York, January 30, 1865	Oath of Allegiance May 17, 1865
Bilton, William H. Private	30	March 1, 1864, Columbia, South Carolina	Co. E, 25th South Carolina Infantry	January 15, 1865, Fort Fisher, North Carolina	Elmira Prison Camp January 30, 1865	Oath of Allegiance May 17, 1865
Bingham, James C. Private	Unk	July 25, 1861, Columbia County, Georgia	Co. K, 16th Georgia Infantry	August 16, 1864, Front Royal, Virginia	Point Lookout, Maryland, transferred to Elmira Prison, NY August 29, 1864	Oath of Allegiance July 11, 1865
Bingham, William Private	Unk	June 20, 1861, Woodville, Alabama	Co. G, 12th Alabama Infantry	May 7, 1864, Wilderness, Virginia	Point Lookout, Maryland, transferred to Elmira Prison, NY August 17, 1864	Oath of Allegiance June 14, 1865
Birchett, Isaac Private	16	June 5, 1861, Oxford, North Carolina	Co. E, 23rd North Carolina Infantry	July 8, 1864, Near Harper's Ferry, Virginia	Old Capital Prison, Washington, DC, transferred to Elmira Prison, NY, July 23, 1864	Oath of Allegiance June 12, 1865
Birchum, Iradel Private	Unk	July 2, 1861, Wytheville, Virginia	Co. C, 50th Virginia Infantry	May 12, 1864, Spotsylvania Court House, Virginia	Point Lookout, Maryland, transferred to Elmira Prison, NY August 2, 1864	Died March 2, 1865 of Pneumonia, Grave No. 2096. Name Jodel Burchum on Headstone.

Name & Rank	Age	Enlisted	Regiment and State	Where Captured	Prison	Remarks
Bird, Benjamin Private	Unk	October 12, 1863, Camp Belton, Florida	Co. L, 11th Florida Infantry	July 29, 1864, Petersburg, Virginia	Point Lookout, Maryland, transferred to Elmira Prison, NY August 12, 1864	Died December 21, 1864 of Chronic Diarrhea, Grave No. 936.
Bird, Benjamin O. Private	Unk	August 22, 1862, Mercer County, Virginia	Co. D, 17th Virginia Cavalry	July 16, 1864, Loudoun County, Virginia	Old Capital Prison, Washington, DC, transferred to Elmira Prison, NY, July 23, 1864	Died February 17, 1865 of Variola (Smallpox), Grave No. 2225
Bird, Jackson G. Private	31	April 26, 1862, Albemarle, North Carolina	Co. J, 52nd North Carolina Infantry	May 12, 1864, Spotsylvania Court House, Virginia	Point Lookout, Maryland, transferred to Elmira Prison, NY August 12, 1864	Exchanged February 20, 1865 at Boulware's or Cox Wharf on the James River, Virginia.
Bird, John S. Private	Unk	November 25, 1862, Floyd Court House, Virginia	Co. I, 26th Battalion Virginia Infantry	June 3, 1864, Gaines Farm, Cold Harbor, Virginia	Transferred From Point Lookout Prison, MD, July 12, 1864. Train Never Arrived at Elmira Prison Camp, NY.	Died July 15, 1864 in Train Wreck at Shohola, Pennsylvania.
Bird, William H. Corporal	Unk	July 19, 1861, Montgomery, Alabama	Co. G, 13th Alabama Infantry	May 5, 1864, Wilderness, Virginia	Point Lookout, Maryland, transferred to Elmira Prison, NY July 30, 1864	Exchanged October 29, 1864 at Venus Point, Savannah River, GA.
Birkenson, Robert Corporal	Unk	Unknown	Co. B, Hood's Battalion, Virginia Reserve Infantry	June 15, 1864, Petersburg, Virginia	Point Lookout, Maryland, transferred to Elmira Prison, NY July 30, 1864	Transferred for Exchange October 11, 1864. Nothing Further.
Birkhead, Francis M. Sergeant	21	June 18, 1861, Randolph County, North Carolina	Co. L, 22nd North Carolina Infantry	May 6, 1864, Near Fredericksburg Virginia	Point Lookout, Maryland, transferred to Elmira Prison, NY August 6, 1864	Oath of Allegiance June 30, 1865
Birt, W. B. Private	Unk	December 9, 1861, Camp Hampton, South Carolina	Co. H, 17th South Carolina Infantry	July 30, 1864, Petersburg, Virginia	Point Lookout, Maryland, transferred to Elmira Prison, NY August 12, 1864	Died August 30, 1864 of Typhoid Fever, Grave No. 56

Name & Rank	Age	Enlisted	Regiment and State	Where Captured	Prison	Remarks
Bishop, Andrew E. Private	18	May 6, 1861, Knoxville, Tennessee	Co. A, 3rd Tennessee, Lillard's Mounted Infantry	May 17, 1863, Big Black, Mississippi	Point Lookout, Maryland, transferred to Elmira Prison, NY August 18, 1864	Exchanged February 13, 1865 at Boulware's wharf on the James River, Virginia
Bishop, Francis M. Private	Unk	August 25, 1862, Camp Randolph, Georgia	Co. F, 13th Georgia Infantry	May 20, 1864, Spotsylvania Court House, Virginia	Point Lookout, Maryland, transferred to Elmira Prison, NY July 6, 1864	Oath of Allegiance June 16, 1865
Bishop, George W. Private	Unk	May 9, 1861, Camp Walker, New Orleans, Louisiana	Co. C, 2nd Louisiana Infantry	May 12, 1864, Spotsylvania Court House, Virginia	Point Lookout, Maryland, transferred to Elmira Prison, NY August 17, 1864	Exchanged 2/20/65. Died 3/14/65 of Unknown Causes at Howard Grove Hospital, VA.
Bishop, George W. Private	Unk	January 14, 1862, Camp Walsh, South Carolina	Co. J, Holcombe Legion, South Carolina Infantry	May 7, 1864, Stony Creek, Virginia	Point Lookout, Maryland, transferred to Elmira Prison, NY August 17, 1864	Oath of Allegiance June 23, 1865
Bishop, Ira T. Private	19	May 10, 1861, Washington, North Carolina	Co. I, 3rd North Carolina Infantry	May 12, 1864, Near Spotsylvania Court House, Virginia	Point Lookout, Maryland, transferred to Elmira Prison, NY August 12, 1864	Oath of Allegiance June 19, 1865
Bishop, Isaac T. Private	19	June 17, 1861, Duplin County, North Carolina	Co. B, 3rd North Carolina Infantry	May 12, 1864, Near Spotsylvania, Virginia	Point Lookout, Maryland, transferred to Elmira Prison, NY August 14, 1864	Oath of Allegiance June 30, 1865
Bishop, J. W. Private	Unk	April 30, 1864, Raleigh, North Carolina	Co. B, 32nd North Carolina Infantry	July 13, 1864, Near Washington, DC,	Old Capital Prison, Washington, DC, transferred to Elmira Prison, NY, July 23, 1864	Died December 13, 1864 of Typhoid-Pneumonia, Grave No. 1126
Bishop, James Private	Unk	January 25, 1864, Chester Court House, South Carolina	Co. D, 17th South Carolina Infantry	July 30, 1864, Petersburg, Virginia	Point Lookout, Maryland, transferred to Elmira Prison, NY August 12, 1864	Died November 9, 1864 of Chronic Diarrhea, Grave No. 784

Name & Rank	Age	Enlisted	Regiment and State	Where Captured	Prison	Remarks
Bishop, James M. Private	Unk	June 29, 1861, Wytheville, Virginia	Co. B, 50th Virginia Infantry	May 12, 1864, Spotsylvania Court House, Virginia	Point Lookout, Maryland, transferred to Elmira Prison, NY August 2, 1864	Oath of Allegiance June 30, 1865
Bishop, R. B. Private	21	July 3, 1861, Atlanta, Georgia	Co. D, 11th Georgia Infantry	May 6, 1864, Wilderness, Virginia	Point Lookout, Maryland, transferred to Elmira Prison, NY August 14, 1864	Oath of Allegiance June 23, 1865
Bishop, William F. Private	16	February 22, 1862, Greensboro, North Carolina	Co. C, 45th North Carolina Infantry	May 20, 1864, Spotsylvania Court House, Virginia	Point Lookout, Maryland, transferred to Elmira Prison, NY July 25, 1864	Exchanged March 14, 1865 on the James River, Virginia. Died April 13, 1865 at Jackson Hospital, Virginia.
Bissett, Philander J. Private	21	June 10, 1861, Garysburg, North Carolina	Co. E, 7th North Carolina Infantry	May 6, 1864, Wilderness, Virginia	Point Lookout, Maryland, transferred to Elmira Prison, NY July 8, 1864	Exchanged March 10, 1865 at Boulware's wharf on the James River, Virginia
Biter, John Private	Unk	January 10, 1862, Columbia, South Carolina	Co. C, 22nd South Carolina Infantry	July 30, 1864, Petersburg, Virginia	Point Lookout, Maryland, transferred to Elmira Prison, NY August 12, 1864	Died October 9, 1864 of Typhoid Fever, Grave No. 664. Headstone has Regiment as Cavalry.
Bivens, James Sergeant	25	April 30, 1862, Louisville, Alabama	Co. D, 59th Alabama Infantry	March 15, 1865, Hatchers Run, Virginia	Old Capital Prison, Washington D. C. Transferred to Elmira Prison, NY May 2, 1865.	Oath of Allegiance July 7, 1865
Bivins, James K. Private	16	September 10, 1861, Camp Clark, Marshall, Texas	Co. A, 7th Texas Infantry	February 12, 1863, Raymond, Mississippi	Point Lookout, Maryland, transferred to Elmira Prison, NY August 18, 1864	Oath of Allegiance June 14, 1865
Black, Alford Private	29	August 15, 1861, Jonesboro, North Carolina	Co. H, 30th North Carolina Infantry	May 12, 1864, Spotsylvania, Virginia	Point Lookout, Maryland, transferred to Elmira Prison, NY July 23, 1864	Oath of Allegiance May 19, 1865

Name & Rank	Age	Enlisted	Regiment and State	Where Captured	Prison	Remarks
Black, Andrew D. Private	Unk	August 1, 1861, Staunton, Virginia	Co. K, 52nd Virginia Infantry	May 20, 1864, Spotsylvania Court House, Virginia	Point Lookout, Maryland, transferred to Elmira Prison, NY July 3, 1864	Exchanged February 20, 1865 at Boulware's or Cox Wharf on the James River, Virginia
Black, Atchimon Perrin Private	19	January 25, 1862, Springfield, Missouri	Co. E, 1st Missouri Cavalry	May 17, 1863, Big Black Bridge, Champion Hill, Mississippi	Point Lookout, Maryland, transferred to Elmira Prison, NY August 18, 1864	Exchanged February 13, 1865 at Boulware's wharf on the James River, Virginia
Black, Daniel L. Private	24	September 3, 1862, Mocksville, North Carolina	Co. G, 7th Confederate States Cavalry	May 7, 1864, Cypress Bridge, Virginia	Point Lookout, Maryland, transferred to Elmira Prison, NY August 17, 1864	Died September 26, 1864 of Chronic Diarrhea, Grave No. 377
Black, David Sergeant	Unk	January 14, 1862, Camp Hampton, Columbia, South Carolina	Co. D, 17th South Carolina Infantry	July 30, 1864, Petersburg, Virginia	Point Lookout, Maryland, transferred to Elmira Prison, NY August 12, 1864	Exchanged February 13, 1865 at Boulware's Wharf on the James River, Virginia
Black, Ephraim Private	32	August 1, 1862, Raleigh, North Carolina	Co. K, 45th North Carolina Infantry	May 27, 1864, Hanover Junction, Virginia	Point Lookout, Maryland, transferred to Elmira Prison, NY July 8, 1864	Died November 7, 1864 of Pneumonia, Grave No. 777
Black, Eugene P. Private	Unk	May 2, 1861, Portsmouth, Georgia	Co. K, 4th Georgia Infantry	July 8, 1864, Near Harper's Ferry, Virginia	Old Capital Prison, Washington, DC, transferred to Elmira Prison, NY, July 25, 1864	Exchanged February 20, 1865 at Boulware's or Cox Wharf on the James River, Virginia
Black, James D. Private	Unk	August 24, 1861, White County, Georgia	Co. C, 24th Georgia Infantry	June 1, 1864, Cold Harbor, Virginia	Point Lookout, Maryland, transferred to Elmira Prison, NY July 17, 1864	Oath of Allegiance June 16, 1865
Black, John Private	Unk	Unknown	Co. K, 3rd North Carolina Infantry	May 12, 1864, Near Spotsylvania Court House, Virginia	Point Lookout, Maryland, transferred to Elmira Prison, NY August 12, 1864	Exchanged March 2, 1865 at Akins Landing on the James River, Virginia

Name & Rank	Age	Enlisted	Regiment and State	Where Captured	Prison	Remarks
Black, John D. Private	Unk	June 25, 1861, Wytheville, Virginia	Co. I, 50th Virginia Infantry	May 5, 1864, Wilderness, Virginia	Point Lookout, Maryland, transferred to Elmira Prison, NY August 14, 1864	Died October 10, 1864 of Chronic Diarrhea, Grave No. 653
Black, John M. Private	23	August 25, 1862, Fort Fisher, North Carolina	Co. G, 40th Regiment, 3rd North Carolina Artillery	January 15, 1865, Fort Fisher, North Carolina	February 1, 1865, Elmira Prison Camp, New York	Exchanged March 2, 1865 at Akins Landing on the James River, Virginia
Black, John W. Sergeant	30	May 1, 1862, Kinston, North Carolina	Co. C, 35th North Carolina Infantry	June 17, 1864, Petersburg, Virginia	Point Lookout, Maryland, transferred to Elmira Prison, NY July 30, 1864	Oath of Allegiance June 12, 1865
Black, John Y. Private	Unk	Unknown	Swansboro, North Carolina Home Guards	June 22, 1864, Jackson's Mills, Near Kinston, North Carolina	Point Lookout, Maryland, transferred to Elmira Prison, NY July 23, 1864	Oath of Allegiance May 13, 1865
Black, Samuel F. Private	Unk	September 3, 1862, Mocksville, North Carolina	Co. G, 7th Confederate Cavalry	May 7, 1864, Cypress Bridge, Virginia	Point Lookout, Maryland, transferred to Elmira Prison, NY August 17, 1864	Exchanged February 13, 1865 at Boulware's wharf on the James River, Virginia
Black, Willis Private	Unk	May 16, 1864, Jefferson County, Alabama	Co. G, 12th Alabama Infantry	July 28, 1864, Frederick, Virginia	Old Capitol Prison, Washington, D. C., transferred to Elmira October 27, 1864	Died April 19, 1865 of Chronic Diarrhea, Grave No. 1372
Blackburn, James Private	Unk	May 1, 1862, Fayetteville, Georgia	Co. C, 53rd Georgia Infantry	June 1, 1864, Gaines Farm, Cold Harbor, Virginia	Point Lookout, Maryland, transferred to Elmira Prison, NY July17, 1864	Oath of Allegiance July 7, 1865
Blackburn, James T. Private	18	January 23, 1864, Camp Holmes, North Carolina	Co. A, 34th North Carolina Infantry	May 12, 1864, Spotsylvania Court House, Virginia	Point Lookout, Maryland, transferred to Elmira Prison, NY July 25, 1864	Died September 13, 1864 of Chronic Diarrhea Grave No. 274

Name & Rank	Age	Enlisted	Regiment and State	Where Captured	Prison	Remarks
Blackburn, Kinnon Private	34	April 6, 1862, Fort Fisher, North Carolina	Co. J, 36th Regiment, 2nd North Carolina Artillery	January 15, 1865, Fort Fisher, North Carolina. Wounded.	February 1, 1865, Elmira Prison Camp, New York	Died February 28, 1865 of Variola (Smallpox), Grave No. 2116
Blackburn, Louis C. Private	19	June 11, 1861, Bledsoe's Store, Virginia	Co. K, 44th Virginia Infantry	May 12, 1864, Spotsylvania Court House, Virginia	Point Lookout, Maryland, transferred to Elmira Prison, NY August 2, 1864	Exchanged February 13, 1865 at Boulware's wharf on the James River, Virginia
Blackburn, M. E. L. Private	Unk	September 22, 1862, Waynesville, Georgia	Co. G, 7th Georgia Cavalry	June 11, 1864, Trevilian Station, Louisa Court House, Virginia	Point Lookout, Maryland, transferred to Elmira Prison, NY July 25, 1864	Died November 3, 1864 of Chronic Diarrhea, Grave No. 841
Blackman, A. M. Private	Unk	August 23, 1863, Talladega, Alabama	Jeff Davis Alabama Artillery	May 5, 1864, Wilderness, Virginia	Point Lookout, Maryland, transferred to Elmira Prison, NY August 17, 1864	Oath of Allegiance June 19, 1865
Blackman, James Private	Unk	February 19, 1863, Darlington District, South Carolina	Co. A, 21st South Carolina Infantry	June 24, 1864, Near Petersburg, Virginia	Point Lookout, Maryland, transferred to Elmira Prison, NY August 18, 1864	Died March 6, 1865 of Diarrhea, Grave No. 2416
Blackman, Joel W. Private	Unk	June 1, 1861, Lock's Creek, Fayetteville, North Carolina	Co. F, 24th North Carolina Infantry	May 16, 1864, Near Drury's Bluff, Virginia	Point Lookout, Maryland, transferred to Elmira Prison, NY July 23, 1864	Oath of Allegiance May 29, 1865
Blackmon, James Private	Unk	September 16, 1862, Lowndes, Alabama	Co. F, 1st Battalion Alabama Artillery	August 23, 1864, Fort Morgan, Alabama	Steam Press No. 4, New Orleans, Louisiana transferred to Elmira Prison, October 8, 1864.	Oath of Allegiance June 23, 1865
Blackmon, William Private	Unk	September 13, 1862, Calhoun, Georgia	Co. I, 4th Georgia Infantry	July 13, 1864, Near Washington, DC,	Old Capital Prison, Washington, DC, transferred to Elmira Prison, NY, July 25, 1864	Oath of Allegiance July 7, 1865

Name & Rank	Age	Enlisted	Regiment and State	Where Captured	Prison	Remarks
Blackmore, Buck L. Musician Private	15	September 15, 1861, Duplin County, North Carolina	Co. A, 36th Regiment, 2nd North Carolina Artillery	January 15, 1865, Fort Fisher, North Carolina. Wounded.	February 1, 1865, Elmira Prison Camp, New York	Exchanged February 20, 1865 at Boulware's or Cox Wharf on the James River, Virginia
Blackmore, Harold E. Private	21	September 15, 1861, Duplin County, North Carolina	Co. A, 36th Regiment, 2nd North Carolina Artillery	January 15, 1865, Fort Fisher, North Carolina. Wounded.	February 1, 1865, Elmira Prison Camp, New York	Oath of Allegiance July 7, 1865
Blackmore, Romulus A. Private	24	May 13, 1862, Duplin County, North Carolina	Co. A, 36th Regiment, 2nd North Carolina Artillery	January 15, 1865, Fort Fisher, North Carolina. Wounded.	February 1, 1865, Elmira Prison Camp, New York	Died June 3, 1865 of Chronic Diarrhea, Grave No. 2899. Headstone has R. A. Blackman.
Blackshear, Isaac Private	Unk	September 25, 1861, Twiggs County, Georgia	Co. J, 26th Georgia Infantry	May 20, 1864, Spotsylvania Court House, Virginia	Point Lookout, Maryland, transferred to Elmira Prison, NY July 3, 1864	Exchanged October 29, 1864 at Venus Point, Savannah River, GA.
Blackstock, Richard Private	Unk	May 15, 1862, Atlanta, Georgia	Co. J, 38th Georgia Infantry	July 14, 1864, Rockville, Maryland	Old Capital Prison, Washington, D. C. Transferred to Elmira Prison, NY August 12, 1864	Exchanged March 14, 1865 at Boulware's Wharf on the James River, Virginia
Blackwelder Adam M. Private	21	June 15, 1861, Cabarrus County, North Carolina	Co. B, 7th North Carolina Infantry	July 29, 1864, Petersburg, Virginia	Point Lookout, Maryland, transferred to Elmira Prison, NY August 12, 1864	Oath of Allegiance June 12, 1865
Blackwelder, John C. Private	19	April 18, 1861, Concord, Cabarrus County, North Carolina	Co. B, 20th North Carolina Infantry	May 12, 1864, Near Spotsylvania Court House, Virginia	Point Lookout Prison, Maryland. Transferred to Elmira Prison Camp New York August 14, 1864.	Oath of Allegiance June 30, 1865

Name & Rank	Age	Enlisted	Regiment and State	Where Captured	Prison	Remarks
Blackwell, James H. Private	Unk	May 27, 1861, Staunton, Virginia	Co. D, 25th Virginia Infantry	May 12, 1864, Spotsylvania, Virginia	Point Lookout, Maryland, transferred to Elmira Prison, NY July 23, 1864	Oath of Allegiance May 19, 1865
Blackwell, John O. Private	Unk	May 26, 1861, Heathsville, Virginia	Co. H, 40th Virginia Infantry	June 2, 1864, Old Church, Virginia	Point Lookout, Maryland, transferred to Elmira Prison, NY July 17,1864	Died November 21, 1864 of Typhoid Fever, Grave No. 973
Blackwell, M. Private	Unk	Unknown	Co. C, 23rd North Carolina Infantry	May 12, 1864, Near Spotsylvania Court House, Virginia	Point Lookout, Maryland, transferred to Elmira Prison, NY August 14, 1864	Transferred for Exchange 10/11/64. Died 10/24/64 of Unknown Causes at Point Lookout, MD.
Blackwell, M. C. Private	Unk	November 21, 1861, Spartanburg, South Carolina	Co. J, Holcombe Legion, South Carolina Infantry	May 7, 1864, Stony Creek, Virginia	Point Lookout, Maryland, transferred to Elmira Prison, NY August 17, 1864	Oath of Allegiance June 23, 1865
Blackwell, Samuel Private	Unk	October 1, 1863, Jacksonboro, South Carolina	Co. K, 6th South Carolina Cavalry	June 11, 1864, Trevilian Station, Louisa Court House, Virginia	Point Lookout, Maryland, transferred to Elmira Prison, NY July 25, 1864	Died February 3, 1865 of Chronic Diarrhea. Grave No. 1752
Blackwell, Uriah A. Private	24	November 14, 1861, Lynch Creek, Camden, South Carolina	Co. A, 7th Battalion South Carolina Infantry	August 21, 1864, Weldon Railroad, Virginia. Gunshot Wound Left Leg.	Old Capital Prison, Washington, DC, transferred to Elmira Prison, NY, December 17, 1864	Exchanged March 10, 1865 at Boulware's Wharf on the James River, Virginia
Blackwood, G. G. Corporal	Unk	January 8, 1863, Charleston, South Carolina	Co. A, 25th South Carolina Infantry	January 15, 1865, Fort Fisher, North Carolina	Elmira Prison Camp January 30, 1865	Oath of Allegiance July 26, 1865
Blackwood, John K. Private	Unk	May 1, 1862, Adam's Run, South Carolina	Co. K, Holcombe Legion, South Carolina Infantry	May 7, 1864, Stony Creek, Virginia	Point Lookout, Maryland, transferred to Elmira Prison, NY August 17, 1864	Died December 15, 1864 of Chronic Diarrhea, Grave No. 1118

Name & Rank	Age	Enlisted	Regiment and State	Where Captured	Prison	Remarks
Blackwood, Joseph Private	Unk	December 6, 1863, Camp Holmes, Raleigh, North Carolina	Co. H, 37th North Carolina Infantry	May 12, 1864, Spotsylvania Court House, Virginia. Gunshot Wound Left Thigh.	Point Lookout, Maryland, transferred to Elmira Prison, NY October 24, 1864	Died March 3, 1865 of Abscess, Grave No. 1993
Blackwood, William S. Corporal	17	March 18, 1862, Dobson, North Carolina	Co. A, 28th North Carolina Infantry	July 29, 1864, Petersburg, Virginia	Point Lookout, Maryland, transferred to Elmira Prison, NY August 12, 1864	Oath of Allegiance June 16, 1865
Blagg, John M. Sergeant	Unk	June 11, 1861, Hevener's Store, Virginia	Co. F, 25th Virginia Infantry	May 5, 1864, Wilderness, Virginia	Point Lookout, Maryland, transferred to Elmira Prison, NY August 14, 1864	Oath of Allegiance June 23, 1865
Blair, Benjamin S. Private	23	May 10, 1862, Macon, Georgia	Co. J, 61st Georgia Infantry	May 12, 1864, Spotsylvania Court House, Virginia	Point Lookout, Maryland, transferred to Elmira Prison, NY July 25, 1864	Oath of Allegiance June 30, 1865
Blair, William C. Private	Unk	Unknown	Co. C, 12th Alabama Infantry	July 13, 1864, near Washington, D. C.	Old Capital Prison Washington, D. C., transferred to Elmira Prison, NY July 23, 1864	Died October 9, 1864 of Chronic Diarrhea, Grave No. 657
Blake, George W. Private	Unk	October 30, 1862, Berryville, Virginia	Co. I, 42nd Virginia Infantry	May 12, 1864, Near Spotsylvania Court House, Virginia	Point Lookout, Maryland, transferred to Elmira Prison, NY August 2, 1864	Oath of Allegiance July 3, 1865
Blake, John H. Private	29	July 23, 1861, Matthews Court House, Virginia	Co. F, 5th Virginia Cavalry	May 11, 1864, Yellow Tavern, Hanover County, Virginia	Point Lookout, Maryland, transferred to Elmira Prison, NY August 17, 1864	Exchanged October 29, 1864, at Venus Point, Savannah River, GA.
Blake, Richard M. Private	16	May 19, 1863, Fort St. Phillips, North Carolina	Co. E, 36th Regiment, 2nd North Carolina Artillery	January 15, 1865, Fort Fisher, North Carolina. Wounded.	February 1, 1865, Elmira Prison Camp, New York	Oath of Allegiance July 3, 1865

Name & Rank	Age	Enlisted	Regiment and State	Where Captured	Prison	Remarks
Blake, Robert Private	18	August 6, 1863, Fort Branch, Martin County, North Carolina	Co. K, 40th Regiment, 3rd North Carolina Heavy Artillery	January 15, 1865, Fort Fisher, North Carolina	February 1, 1865, Elmira Prison Camp, New York	Died February 27, 1865 of Pneumonia, Grave No. 2129
Blake, W. C. Private	Unk	Unknown	Co. E, 42nd Virginia Cavalry	May 30, 1864, Cold Harbor, Virginia	Unknown	Exchanged October 11, 1864. Nothing Further.
Blakeley, J. K. Private	Unk	February 11, 1863, Charleston, South Carolina	Co. G, 27th South Carolina Infantry	June 24, 1864, Near Petersburg, Virginia	Point Lookout, Maryland, transferred to Elmira Prison, NY August 18, 1864	Exchanged October 29, 1864, at Venus Point, Savannah River, GA.
Blakely, Madison P. Private	Unk	March 25, 1862, Clinton, South Carolina	Co. F, 14th South Carolina Infantry	July 29, 1864, Petersburg, Virginia	Point Lookout, Maryland, transferred to Elmira Prison, NY August 12, 1864	Exchanged March 14, 1865 at Boulware's Wharf on the James River, Virginia
Blakely, Robert A. Private	29	December 31, 1861, Springfield, Missouri	Co. H, 1st Missouri Cavalry	May 17, 1863, Big Black Bridge, Champion Hill, Mississippi	Point Lookout, Maryland, transferred to Elmira Prison, NY August 18, 1864	Exchanged February 13, 1865 at Boulware's wharf on the James River, Virginia
Blakemore, William H. Sergeant	Unk	April 18, 1861, Harrisonburg, Virginia	Co. G, 10th Virginia Infantry	May 12, 1864, Spotsylvania Court House, Virginia	Point Lookout, Maryland, transferred to Elmira Prison, NY August 2, 1864	Oath of Allegiance June 16, 1865
Blalock, Arbert Private	38	March 17, 1863, Roxboro, North Carolina	Co. E, 35th North Carolina Infantry	June 17, 1864, Petersburg, Virginia	Point Lookout, Maryland, transferred to Elmira Prison, NY July 30, 1864	Died September 11, 1864 of Chronic Diarrhea, Grave No. 257
Blalock, Calvin Private	Unk	February 1, 1864, Albemarle, North Carolina	Co. H, 14th North Carolina Infantry	July 14, 1864, Near Washington, DC	Point Lookout, Maryland, transferred to Elmira Prison, NY August 29, 1864	Died March 29, 1865 of Variola (Smallpox), Grave No. 2506
Blalock, Zachariah D. Private	22	March 25, 1862, Albemarle, North Carolina	Co. I, 52nd North Carolina Infantry	May 12, 1864, Spotsylvania Court House, Virginia	Point Lookout, Maryland, transferred to Elmira Prison, NY August 12, 1864	Oath of Allegiance June 12, 1865

Name & Rank	Age	Enlisted	Regiment and State	Where Captured	Prison	Remarks
Blanchard, Abram W. Private	29	June 17, 1862, Warsaw, North Carolina	Co. G, 61st North Carolina Infantry	July 27, 1863, Morris Island, South Carolina	Point Lookout, Maryland, transferred to Elmira Prison, NY August 18, 1864	Exchanged March 10, 1865 at Boulware's Wharf on the James River, Virginia
Bland, Harmon Private	21	July 1, 1861, Wilmington, North Carolina	Co. I, 18th North Carolina Infantry	May 12, 1864, Spotsylvania Court House, Virginia	Point Lookout, Maryland, transferred to Elmira Prison, NY August 6, 1864	Oath of Allegiance June 21, 1865
Bland, James T. Private	Unk	September 22, 1862, New Hope, Virginia	Co. C, 24th Virginia Cavalry	July 28, 1864, Petersburg, Virginia	Point Lookout, Maryland, transferred to Elmira Prison, NY August 12, 1864	Exchanged March 10, 1865 at Boulware's Wharf on the James River, Virginia
Bland, John Private	28	October 3, 1861, Fort Fisher, North Carolina	Co. I, 18th North Carolina Infantry	May 12, 1864, Spotsylvania Court House, Virginia	Point Lookout, Maryland, transferred to Elmira Prison, NY August 6, 1864	Died September 19, 1864 of Chronic Diarrhea, Grave No. 518
Bland, John A. Sergeant	Unk	May 18, 1861, Franklin, Virginia	Co. K, 25th Virginia Infantry	May 5, 1864, Wilderness, Virginia	Point Lookout, Maryland, transferred to Elmira Prison, NY August 14, 1864	Oath of Allegiance June 23, 1865
Bland, R. Sergeant	Unk	June 2, 1861, Centerville, Virginia	Co. C, 24th Virginia Cavalry	July 28, 1864, Petersburg, Virginia	Point Lookout, Maryland, transferred to Elmira Prison, NY August 12, 1864	Exchanged March 10, 1865 at Boulware's Wharf on the James River, Virginia
Blande, Edward M. Private	Unk	March 8, 1862, Scooba, Mississippi	Co. C, Jeff Davis Legion, Mississippi Cavalry	June 21, 1864, White House Landing, Virginia	Point Lookout, Maryland, transferred to Elmira Prison, NY July 23, 1864	Oath of Allegiance May 29, 1865
Blandford, W. B. H. Private	Unk	Unknown	Engineers Corps, Confederate States Army	August 24, 1863, King George County, Virginia	Point Lookout, Maryland, transferred to Elmira Prison, NY August 18, 1864	Exchanged February 20, 1865 at Boulware's or Cox Wharf on the James River, Virginia

Name & Rank	Age	Enlisted	Regiment and State	Where Captured	Prison	Remarks
Blaney, John Private	Unk	Unknown	Co. A, Captain Norwood's Home Guard Florida	September 27, 1864, Marianna, Florida	New Orleans, Louisiana transferred to Elmira November 19, 1864.	Died December 15, 1864 of Pneumonia, Grave No. 1114. Headstone has Blarney.
Blankenship William T. Private	25	February 5, 1862, Alexandria County, North Carolina	Co. D, 18th North Carolina Infantry	May 12, 1864, Spotsylvania Court House, Virginia	Point Lookout, Maryland, transferred to Elmira Prison, NY August 6, 1864	Exchanged October 29, 1864 at Venus Point, Savannah River, GA.
Blankner, F. Private	Unk	May 13, 1864, Richmond, Virginia	Captain Lyneman's Co., Virginia Infantry	July 15, 1863, Shepherdstown, Virginia	Point Lookout, Maryland, transferred to Elmira Prison, NY August 18, 1864	Exchanged February 13, 1865 at Boulware's Wharf on the James River, Virginia
Blanks, Charles D. Private	Unk	March 12, 1862, Petersburg, Virginia	Co. E, 13th Virginia Cavalry	July 24, 1863, Front Royal, Virginia	Point Lookout, Maryland, transferred to Elmira Prison, NY August 18, 1864	Exchanged October 29, 1864, at Venus Point, Savannah River, GA.
Blann, Thomas W. Private	Unk	August 2, 1862, Dallas County, Alabama	Co. C, 21st Alabama Infantry	August 23, 1864, Fort Morgan, Alabama	Steam Press No. 4, New Orleans, Louisiana transferred to Elmira Prison, October 8, 1864.	Oath of Allegiance June 14, 1865
Blanton, Allen A. Sergeant	Unk	June 8, 1861, Amelia Court House, Virginia	Co. J, 21st Virginia Infantry	July 8, 1864, Near Harper's Ferry, Virginia	Old Capital Prison, Washington, DC, transferred to Elmira Prison, NY, July 23, 1864	Exchanged March 10, 1865 at Boulware's wharf on the James River, Virginia
Blanton, Blaney Private	19	March 25, 1862, Wilmington, North Carolina	Co. D, 40th Regiment, 3rd North Carolina Heavy Artillery	January 15, 1865, Fort Fisher, North Carolina. Wounded	February 1, 1865, Elmira Prison Camp, New York	Oath of Allegiance July 11, 1865
Blanton, J. L. Private	Unk	January 1, 1863, Charleston, South Carolina	Co. K, Holcombe Legion, South Carolina Infantry	May 7, 1864, Stony Creek, Virginia	Point Lookout, Maryland, transferred to Elmira Prison, NY August 17, 1864	Exchanged October 29, 1864, at Venus Point, Savannah River, GA.

Name & Rank	Age	Enlisted	Regiment and State	Where Captured	Prison	Remarks
Blanton, James Joseph Private	40	April 15, 1862, Wilmington, North Carolina	Co. G, 51st North Carolina Infantry	June 3, 1864, Gaines Mill, Cold Harbor, Virginia	Point Lookout, Maryland, transferred to Elmira Prison, NY July 17,1864	Died January 18, 1865 of Variola (Smallpox) Grave No. 1431
Blanton, Josiah S. Private	Unk	December 9, 1861, Shelby, North Carolina	Co. H, 28th North Carolina Infantry	May 7, 1864, Wilderness, Virginia	Point Lookout, Maryland, transferred to Elmira Prison, NY August 17, 1864	Exchanged October 29, 1864, at Venus Point, Savannah River, GA.
Blanton, William J. Private	Unk	October 13, 1863, McDowell, North Carolina	Co. A, 49th North Carolina Infantry	June 2, 1864, Bermuda Hundred, Virginia	Point Lookout, Maryland, transferred to Elmira Prison, NY July 9, 1864	Died October 10, 1864 of Anasarca, Grave No. 662
Blanton, William M. Private	Unk	January 1, 1864, Charleston, South Carolina	Co. K, Holcombe Legion, South Carolina Infantry	May 7, 1864, Stony Creek, Virginia	Point Lookout, Maryland, transferred to Elmira Prison, NY August 17, 1864	Transferred For Exchange October 11, 1864 to Point Lookout Prison, MD. Died November 7, 1864 of Unknown Causes at Fort Monroe, VA
Blarney, John Private	51	Unknown	Co. H, 11th Florida Infantry	September 26, 1864, Marianna, Florida	Point Lookout, Maryland, transferred to Elmira Prison, NY November 19, 1864	Died December 15, 1864 of Pneumonia, Grave No. 1114
Blaylock, Calvin Private	Unk	February 1, 1864, Albemarle, North Carolina	Co. H, 14th North Carolina Infantry	July 14, 1864, Near Washington, DC	Point Lookout, Maryland, transferred to Elmira Prison, NY August 29, 1864	Died March 29, 1865 of Variola (Smallpox), Grave No. 2506
Blaylock, John A. Corporal	26	May 15, 1862, Salisbury, North Carolina	Co. C, 42nd North Carolina Infantry	June 3, 1864, Cold Harbor, Virginia	Point Lookout, Maryland, transferred to Elmira Prison, NY July 17,1864	Exchanged October 29, 1864 at Venus Point, Savannah River, GA.
Blaylock, John H. Sergeant	25	April 27, 1861, Duplin County, North Carolina	Co. E, 20th North Carolina Infantry	July 8, 1864, Near Harper's Ferry, Virginia	Old Capital Prison, Washington, DC, transferred to Elmira Prison, NY, July 23, 1864	Oath of Allegiance June 27, 1865

Name & Rank	Age	Enlisted	Regiment and State	Where Captured	Prison	Remarks
Blaylock, John R. Corporal	22	May 31, 1861, Raleigh, North Carolina	Co. D, 1st North Carolina Infantry	May 12, 1864, Spotsylvania Court House, Virginia	Point Lookout, Maryland, transferred to Elmira Prison, NY August 6, 1864	Oath of Allegiance June 23, 1865
Bledsoe, Audley Private	Unk	October 1, 1862, Guiles County, Virginia	Co. E, 23rd Virginia Infantry	August 11, 1864, Winchester, Virginia	Point Lookout, Maryland, transferred to Elmira Prison, NY August 29, 1864	Exchanged February 13, 1865 at Boulware's Wharf on the James River, Virginia
Blevins, Henry Private	22	May 18, 1861, Seven Mile Ford, Virginia	Co. D, 48th Virginia Infantry	May 12, 1864, Spotsylvania Court House, Virginia	Point Lookout, Maryland, transferred to Elmira Prison, NY August 2, 1864	Exchanged October 29, 1864 at Venus Point, Savannah River, GA.
Blevins, Robert Private	32	August 15, 1862, Statesville, Iredell County, North Carolina	Co. B, 37 North Carolina Infantry	May 12, 1864, Near Spotsylvania Court House, Virginia	Point Lookout Prison, Maryland. Transferred to Elmira Prison Camp New York August 12, 1864.	Oath of Allegiance June 16, 1865
Blewitt, George W. Sergeant	Unk	May 14, 1861, Franklin, Virginia	Co. E, 25th Virginia Infantry	May 5, 1864, Wilderness, Virginia	Point Lookout, Maryland, transferred to Elmira Prison, NY August 14, 1864	Oath of Allegiance July 11, 1865
Blitch, Alonzo E. Private	17	July 13, 1861, Jacksonville, Florida	Co. E, 2nd Florida Infantry	May 6, 1864, Wilderness, Virginia	Point Lookout, Maryland, transferred to Elmira Prison, NY July 7, 1864	Exchanged October 29, 1864 at Venus Point, Savannah River, GA.
Blitch, Obadiah T. Private	Unk	September 22, 1862, Waynesville, Georgia	Co. G, 7th Georgia Cavalry	June 11, 1864, Trevilian Station, Louisa Court House, Virginia	Point Lookout, Maryland, transferred to Elmira Prison, NY July 25, 1864	Oath of Allegiance May 29, 1865
Blizzard, Blany Private	27	February 16, 1862, Lenoir County, North Carolina	Co. E, 61st North Carolina Infantry	August 27, 1863, Battery Wagner, Morris Island, South Carolina	Point Lookout, Maryland, transferred to Elmira Prison, NY August 18, 1864	Exchanged March 10, 1865 at Boulware's Wharf on the James River, Virginia

Name & Rank	Age	Enlisted	Regiment and State	Where Captured	Prison	Remarks
Blizzard, Jacob L. Private	36	April 5, 1862, Camp Shenandoah, Virginia	Co. E, 25th Virginia Infantry	May 5, 1864, Wilderness, Virginia	Point Lookout, Maryland, transferred to Elmira Prison, NY August 14, 1864	Oath of Allegiance June 19, 1865
Blizzard, John D. Private	Unk	May 28, 1863, Fayetteville, North Carolina	Co. B, 56th North Carolina Infantry	June 18, 1864, Petersburg, Virginia	Point Lookout, Maryland, transferred to Elmira Prison, NY July 23, 1864	Died December 4, 1864 of Pneumonia, Grave No. 882
Blocker, Joseph A. Private	Unk	September 1, 1861, Reidsville, Georgia	Co. B, 61st Georgia Infantry	May 12, 1864, Spotsylvania Court House, Virginia	Point Lookout, Maryland, transferred to Elmira Prison, NY July 25, 1864	Exchanged February 20, 1865 at Boulware's or Cox Wharf on the James River, Virginia
Bloodsworth James H. Private	Unk	August 30, 1862, Dale County, Alabama	Co. G, 5th Alabama Infantry	May 5, 1864, Wilderness, Virginia	Point Lookout, Maryland, transferred to Elmira Prison, NY August 17, 1864	Died January 26, 1865 of Chronic Diarrhea, Grave No. 1635
Bloudean, L. Private	25	March 1, 1862, Union, Virginia	Co. A, 6th Virginia Cavalry	July 14, 1864, Williamsport, Maryland	Point Lookout, Maryland, transferred to Elmira Prison, NY July 25, 1864	Exchanged October 29, 1864 at Venus Point, Savannah River, GA.
Blount, B. F. Private	Unk	March 6, 1864, Camp Watts, Alabama	Co. H, 12th Alabama Infantry	May 12, 1864, Spotsylvania Court House, Virginia	Point Lookout, Maryland, transferred to Elmira Prison, NY August 17, 1864	Exchanged October 29, 1864, at Venus Point, Savannah River, GA.
Blow, Robert Private	18	May 1, 1864, Albemarle County, Virginia	Co. A, Huger's Battalion Virginia Light Artillery	April 6, 1865, Sailor's Creek, Virginia. Saber Wound of Scalp.	Old Capital Prison, Washington D. C. Transferred to Elmira Prison, NY May 12, 1865.	Oath of Allegiance July 7, 1865
Blue, D. A. Sergeant	20	September 12, 1861, Carthage, North Carolina	Co. C, 35th North Carolina Infantry	June 17, 1864, Petersburg, Virginia	Point Lookout, Maryland, transferred to Elmira Prison, NY July 30, 1864	Exchanged October 29, 1864 at Venus Point, Savannah River, GA.

Name & Rank	Age	Enlisted	Regiment and State	Where Captured	Prison	Remarks
Blythe, Joseph Private	Unk	October 12, 1863, Montgomery, Alabama	Co. K, 3rd Alabama Infantry	June 12, 1864, Spotsylvania, Virginia	Point Lookout, Maryland, transferred to Elmira Prison, NY July 25, 1864	Exchanged February 12, 1865 at Akins Landing on the James River, Virginia
Blythe, Samuel W. Private	26	October 22, 1861, Charlotte, North Carolina	Co. J, 37th North Carolina Infantry	July 29, 1864, Gravel Hill, Near Petersburg, Virginia	Point Lookout, Maryland, transferred to Elmira Prison, NY August 12, 1864	Died September 20, 1864 of Chronic Diarrhea, Grave No. 498. Name L. W. Bythe on Headstone.
Boan, Archibald A. Corporal	19	December 20, 1861, Chesterfield District, South Carolina	Co. E, 21st South Carolina Infantry	June 24, 1864, Petersburg, Virginia	Point Lookout, Maryland, transferred to Elmira Prison, NY August 18, 1864	Exchanged October 29, 1864, at Venus Point, Savannah River, GA.
Boatright, Richard J. Private	Unk	April 4, 1862, Waynesville, Georgia	Co. D, 26th Georgia Infantry	May 20, 1864, Spotsylvania Court House, Virginia	Point Lookout, Maryland, transferred to Elmira Prison, NY July 6, 1864	Oath of Allegiance June 30, 1865
Boazman, William M. Private	21	April 10, 1862, Peninsula, Virginia	Co. G, 2nd South Carolina Infantry	September 13, 1863, Near Culpepper, Virginia	Point Lookout, Maryland, transferred to Elmira Prison, NY August 18, 1864	Exchanged October 29, 1864 at Venus Point, Savannah River, GA.
Bobbitt, Isham C. Private	18	September 7, 1861, Granville, North Carolina	Co. G, 30th North Carolina Infantry	July 13, 1864, Near Washington, DC,	Old Capital Prison, Washington, DC, transferred to Elmira Prison, NY, July 23, 1864	Exchanged March 14, 1865 at Boulware's Wharf on the James River, Virginia
Boblett, William R. Private	Unk	May 18, 1861, Lisbon, Virginia	Co. C, 42nd Virginia Infantry	May 12, 1864, Spotsylvania Court House, Virginia	Point Lookout, Maryland, transferred to Elmira Prison, NY August 2,1864	Exchanged March 2, 1865 at Akins Landing on the James River, Virginia
Bobo, Solomon Private	40	March 4, 1862, Hartwell, Georgia	Co. C, 16th Georgia Infantry	June 1, 1864, Gaines Farm, Cold Harbor, Virginia	Point Lookout, Maryland, transferred to Elmira Prison, NY July 17,1864	Oath of Allegiance July 7, 1865

Name & Rank	Age	Enlisted	Regiment and State	Where Captured	Prison	Remarks
Bobo, Solomon M. Sergeant	Unk	August 24, 1861, Hartwell, Georgia	Co. B, 24th Georgia Infantry	August 16, 1864, Front Royal, Virginia	Point Lookout, Maryland, transferred to Elmira Prison, NY August 29, 1864	Oath of Allegiance June 27, 1865
Boddie, Nicholas Private	Unk	May 8, 1862, Augusta, Georgia	Co. A, 7th Georgia Cavalry	June 11, 1864, Trevilian Station, Louisa Court House, Virginia	Point Lookout, Maryland, transferred to Elmira Prison, NY July 25, 1864	Oath of Allegiance July 7, 1865
Bodenhamer Randle Private	Unk	November 13, 1863, Raleigh, North Carolina	Co. K, 21st North Carolina Infantry	July 10, 1864, Near Harper's Ferry, Virginia	Old Capital Prison, Washington, DC, transferred to Elmira Prison, NY, July 23, 1864	Oath of Allegiance May 19, 1865
Bodkin, John Private	Unk	March 30, 1862, Camp Allegheny, Virginia	Co. F, 25th Virginia Infantry	May 5, 1864, Wilderness, Virginia	Point Lookout, Maryland, transferred to Elmira Prison, NY August 14, 1864	Exchanged February 20, 1865 at Boulware's or Cox Wharf on the James River, Virginia
Bodkin, Israel Private	Unk	June 11, 1861, Hevener's Store, Virginia	Co. F, 25th Virginia Infantry	May 5, 1864, Wilderness, Virginia	Point Lookout, Maryland, transferred to Elmira Prison, NY August 14, 1864	Oath of Allegiance June 23, 1865
Bodley, Thomas Private	Unk	March 4, 1861, Selma, Alabama	Co. C, 1st Battalion Alabama Artillery	August 23, 1864, Fort Morgan, Alabama	New Orleans, Louisiana transferred to Elmira December 4, 1864.	Exchanged March 14, 1865 at Boulware's Wharf on the James River, Virginia
Bogan, Benjamin G. Private	Unk	December 31, 1863, Columbia, South Carolina	Co. H, 1st South Carolina Infantry	July 29, 1864, Petersburg, Virginia	Point Lookout, Maryland, transferred to Elmira Prison, NY August 12, 1864	Died December 9, 1864 of Chronic Valvular Disease of Heart, Grave No. 1160
Bogar, Moses Private	22	March 24, 1862, Salisbury, North Carolina	Co. D, 42nd North Carolina Infantry	June 2, 1864, Cold Harbor, Virginia	Point Lookout, Maryland, transferred to Elmira Prison, NY July 17,1864	Oath of Allegiance May 29, 1865

Name & Rank	Age	Enlisted	Regiment and State	Where Captured	Prison	Remarks
Boger, Jacob Private	33	August 8, 1862, Raleigh, North Carolina	Co. B, 5th North Carolina Infantry	May 12, 1864, Spotsylvania Court House, Virginia	Point Lookout, Maryland, transferred to Elmira Prison, NY August 6, 1864	Died February 5, 1865 of Variola (Smallpox), Grave No. 1740, Name Boyer on Headstone.
Boggan, James N. Private	18	August 20, 1863, Fort Branch, Martin County, North Carolina	Co. G, 40th Regiment, 3rd North Carolina Artillery	January 15, 1865, Fort Fisher, North Carolina	Elmira Prison Camp January 30, 1865	Exchanged February 20, 1865 at Boulware's or Cox Wharf on the James River, Virginia
Boggs, William M. Private	Unk	March 24, 1862, Lewisburg, Virginia	Co. E, 26th Virginia Infantry	June 3, 1864, Gaines Farm, Cold Harbor, Virginia	Point Lookout, Maryland, transferred to Elmira Prison, NY July 17, 1864	Died December 19, 1864 of Chronic Diarrhea, Grave No. 1071
Bogle, George Washington Private	42	December 12, 1863, Weldon, North Carolina	Co. H, 56th North Carolina Infantry	May 14, 1864, Near Fort Darling, Virginia	Point Lookout, Maryland, transferred to Elmira Prison, NY August 17, 1864	Died August 23, 1864 of Chronic Diarrhea, Grave No. 42
Bogue, Francis Private	Unk	Unknown	Co. C, 1st Maryland Cavalry	July 13, 1864, Near Washington, DC,	Old Capital Prison, Washington, DC, transferred to Elmira Prison, NY, July 23, 1864	Exchanged February 20, 1865 at Boulware's or Cox Wharf on the James River, Virginia
Bogue, John J. Private	21	May 18, 1861, Edenton, North Carolina	Co. A, 1st North Carolina Infantry	May 12, 1864, Spotsylvania Court House, Virginia	Point Lookout, Maryland, transferred to Elmira Prison, NY August 6, 1864	Oath of Allegiance June 12, 1865
Bohannan, Andrew C. Private	Unk	February 18, 1862, Gloucester Point, Virginia	Co. E, 5th Virginia Cavalry	May 11, 1864, Yellow Tavern, Hanover County, Virginia	Point Lookout, Maryland, transferred to Elmira Prison, NY August 17, 1864	Exchanged October 29, 1864, at Venus Point, Savannah River, GA.
Bohannan, J. F. Corporal	Unk	February 24, 1862, Hawkinsville, Georgia	Co. G, 8th Georgia Infantry	May 6, 1864, Wilderness, Virginia	Point Lookout, Maryland, transferred to Elmira Prison, NY August 17, 1864	Oath of Allegiance June 14, 1865

Name & Rank	Age	Enlisted	Regiment and State	Where Captured	Prison	Remarks
Bohannon, J. C. Private	Unk	February 18, 1862, Glouchester Point, Virginia	Co. E, 5th Virginia Cavalry	May 31, 1864, Cold Harbor, Virginia	Point Lookout, Maryland, transferred to Elmira Prison, NY July 8, 1864	Exchanged October 29, 1864 at Venus Point, Savannah River, GA.
Bohler, James Bugler, Private	Unk	October 1, 1862, Augusta, Georgia	Co. A, 7th Georgia Cavalry	June 11, 1864, Trevilian Station, Louisa Court House, Virginia	Point Lookout, Maryland, transferred to Elmira Prison, NY July 25, 1864	Oath of Allegiance June 21, 1865
Bohn, W. H. Private	Unk	Unknown	Imboden's Signal Guard, Virginia	August 11, 1864, Summit Point, Virginia	Point Lookout, Maryland, transferred to Elmira Prison, NY August 29, 1864	Died September 8, 1864 of Typhoid Fever, Grave No. 209. Headstone has W. H. Boehur.
Bointer, J. F. Private	Unk	Unknown	Co. A, 26th Virginia Infantry	June 15, 1864, Near Petersburg, Virginia	Point Lookout, Maryland, transferred to Elmira Prison, NY July 30, 1864	Oath of Allegiance July 8, 1865
Boitnott, Lenard D. Private	Unk	June 17, 1861, Rocky Mount, Virginia	Co. K, 42nd Virginia Infantry	May 12, 1864, Spotsylvania Court House, Virginia	Point Lookout, Maryland, transferred to Elmira Prison, NY August 2, 1864	Oath of Allegiance June 19, 1865
Bolan, George W. Private	28	July 3, 1861, Atlanta, Georgia	Co. K, 11th Georgia Infantry	May 6, 1864, Wilderness, Virginia	Point Lookout, Maryland, transferred to Elmira Prison, NY August 14, 1864	Exchanged February 20, 1865 at Boulware's or Cox Wharf on the James River, Virginia
Bolden, Calvin Private	28	March 15, 1862, Albemarle, North Carolina	Co. D, 28th North Carolina Infantry	May 12, 1864, Spotsylvania Court House, Virginia	Point Lookout, Maryland, transferred to Elmira Prison, NY August 8, 1864	Died September 30, 1864 of Pneumonia, Grave No. 398
Bolemand, A. W. Private	Unk	September 7, 1863, Cobb County, Georgia	Co. A, 7th Georgia Cavalry	June 11, 1864, Trevilian Station, Louisa Court House, Virginia	Point Lookout, Maryland, transferred to Elmira Prison, NY July 25, 1864	Exchanged March 10, 1865 at Boulware's wharf on the James River, Virginia

Name & Rank	Age	Enlisted	Regiment and State	Where Captured	Prison	Remarks
Boles, Richard Private	Unk	July 19, 1861, Montgomery, Alabama	Co. B, 13th Alabama Infantry	May 6, 1864, Wilderness, Virginia	Point Lookout, Maryland, transferred to Elmira Prison, NY August 11, 1864	Died November 4, 1864 of Chronic Diarrhea, Grave No. 842
Bolick, Henry J. Private	Unk	March 10, 1864, Camp Holmes, Raleigh, North Carolina	Co. B, 32nd North Carolina Infantry	May 10, 1864, Spotsylvania, Virginia	Point Lookout, Maryland, transferred to Elmira Prison, NY August 6, 1864	Exchanged October 29, 1864, at Venus Point, Savannah River, GA.
Bolin, Daniel A. Private	27	July 9, 1861, Antioch, Georgia	Co. F, 21st Georgia Infantry	July 13, 1864, Near Washington DC	Old Capital Prison, Washington, DC transferred to Elmira Prison, NY August 27, 1864	Died April 2, 1865 of Variola (Smallpox), Grave No. 2582. Headstone has Danile A. Bowlin.
Bolin, Joseph Private	35	March 31, 1862, Alexander, North Carolina	Co. H, 56th North Carolina Infantry	May 14, 1864, Near Fort Darling, Virginia	Point Lookout, Maryland, transferred to Elmira Prison, NY August 17, 1864	Exchanged March 2, 1865 at Boulware's Wharf on the James River, Virginia
Boling, Andrew P. Private	Unk	Unknown	Co. E, 50th Virginia Infantry	May 12, 1864, Spotsylvania Court House, Virginia	Point Lookout, Maryland, transferred to Elmira Prison, NY August 2, 1864	Oath of Allegiance June 27, 1865
Boling, J. M. Private	Unk	October 28, 1861, Fort Henry, Tennessee	Co. L, Jackson's 1st Regiment, Tennessee Heavy Artillery	August 23, 1864, Fort Morgan, Alabama	New Orleans, Louisiana transferred to Elmira December 4, 1864.	Exchanged February 20, 1865 at Boulware's or Cox Wharf on the James River, Virginia
Boling, James A. Private	Unk	August 24, 1861, Homer, Georgia	Co. A, 24th Georgia Infantry	August 16, 1864, Front Royal, Virginia	Point Lookout, Maryland, transferred to Elmira Prison, NY August 29, 1864	Oath of Allegiance July 11, 1865
Bolling, James T. Private	Unk	April 1, 1861, Patrick Court House, Virginia	Co. A, 42nd Virginia Infantry	May 12, 1864, Spotsylvania Court House, Virginia	Point Lookout, Maryland, transferred to Elmira Prison, NY August 2, 1864	Exchanged October 29, 1864 at Venus Point, Savannah River, GA.

Name & Rank	Age	Enlisted	Regiment and State	Where Captured	Prison	Remarks
Bolling, John S. Private	Unk	May 16, 1861, Radfordsville, Parry County, Alabama	Co. K, 8th Alabama Infantry	July 3, 1863, Gettysburg, Pennsylvania	Point Lookout, Maryland, transferred to Elmira Prison, NY August 17, 1864	Exchanged October 29, 1864 at Venus Point, Savannah River, GA.
Bolls, Richard Private	Unk	Unknown	Co. B, 12th Alabama Infantry	May 6, 1864, Wilderness, Virginia	Point Lookout, Maryland, transferred to Elmira Prison, NY August 14, 1864	Died November 4, 1864 of Chronic Diarrhea, Grave No. 842
Bolston, J. Private	Unk	Unknown	Co. A, 1st Battalion Alabama Artillery	August 23, 1864, Fort Morgan, Alabama	New Orleans, Louisiana transferred to Elmira December 4, 1864.	No Further Information Available
Bolt, Dorroh Private	25	August 11, 1861, Lightwood Knot Springs, Near Columbia, South Carolina	Co. C, 14th South Carolina Infantry	July 29, 1864, Petersburg, Virginia	Point Lookout, Maryland, transferred to Elmira Prison, NY August 12, 1864	Oath of Allegiance June 21, 1865
Bolton, Calvin Private	28	March 15, 1862, Albemarle, North Carolina	Co. D, 28th North Carolina Infantry	May 12, 1864, Spotsylvania Court House, Virginia	Point Lookout, Maryland, transferred to Elmira Prison, NY August 12, 1864	Died September 30, 1864 of Pneumonia, Grave No. 398. Name Bolden on Headstone.
Bolton, James Private	Unk	Unknown	Co. G, 5th Louisiana Infantry	June 11, 1864, Orange County, Virginia	Old Capital Prison, Washington, DC, transferred to Elmira Prison, NY, July 23, 1864	Oath of Allegiance October 9, 1864
Bolton, James T. Corporal	37	June 4, 1861, Camp Moore, Louisiana	Co. A, 6th Louisiana Infantry	May 5, 1864, Wilderness, Virginia	Point Lookout, Maryland, transferred to Elmira Prison, NY August 17, 1864	Exchanged October 29, 1864 at Venus Point, Savannah River, GA.
Bolton, Major Thomas Private	18	February 12, 1862, Warrenton, North Carolina	Co. G, 43rd North Carolina Infantry	May 16, 1864, Near Drury's Bluff, Virginia	Point Lookout, Maryland, transferred to Elmira Prison, NY August 17, 1864	Oath of Allegiance June 19, 1865

Name & Rank	Age	Enlisted	Regiment and State	Where Captured	Prison	Remarks
Bolton, Terrel Private	25	July 29, 1861, Albemarle, North Carolina	Co. D, 28th North Carolina Infantry	May 6, 1864, Wilderness, Virginia	Old Capital Prison, Washington, DC transferred to Elmira Prison, NY August 27, 1864	Exchanged February 13, 1865 at Boulware's wharf on the James River, Virginia
Bomar, George W. Private	17	February 24, 1862, Charleston, South Carolina	Co. A, 25th South Carolina Infantry	January 15, 1865, Fort Fisher, North Carolina	Elmira Prison Camp January 30, 1865	Oath of Allegiance June 16, 1865
Bond, Balas H. Private	31	October 9, 1861, Enfield, North Carolina	Co. F, 36th Regiment, 2nd North Carolina Artillery	January 15, 1865, Fort Fisher, North Carolina. Wounded.	February 1, 1865, Elmira Prison Camp, New York	Exchanged March 14, 1865 at Boulware's Wharf on the James River, Virginia
Bond, James G. Private	Unk	August 5, 1861, Danielsville, Georgia	Co. B, 16th Georgia Infantry	August 16, 1864, Front Royal, Virginia	Point Lookout, Maryland, transferred to Elmira Prison, NY August 29, 1864	Oath of Allegiance June 19, 1865
Bond, John F. Private	21	April 22, 1861, Wilmington, North Carolina	Co. K, 10th Regiment, 1st North Carolina Artillery	January 15, 1865, Fort Fisher, North Carolina	Elmira Prison Camp January 30, 1865	Died February 18, 1865 of Chronic Diarrhea, Grave No. 2349
Bond, John H. Private	Unk	August 5, 1861, Danielsville, Georgia	Co. D, 16th Georgia Infantry	June 1, 1864, Gaines Farm, Cold Harbor, Virginia	Point Lookout, Maryland, transferred to Elmira Prison, NY July 17, 1864	Oath of Allegiance July 7, 1865
Boney, John B. Private	30	July 6, 1861, Piney Wood, North Carolina	Co. G, 61st North Carolina Infantry	June 16, 1864, Petersburg, Virginia	Point Lookout, Maryland, transferred to Elmira Prison, NY July 9, 1864	Died January 8, 1865 of Chronic Diarrhea, Grave No. 1499
Bonner, Adoniram J. Sergeant	23	July 29, 1861, Madison, Georgia	Co. G, Cobb's Legion Georgia	August 16, 1864, Front Royal, Virginia	Point Lookout, Maryland, transferred to Elmira Prison, NY August 29, 1864	Oath of Allegiance July 11, 1865
Bonner, J. M. Private	Unk	Unknown	Co. A, 60th Louisiana Infantry	May 20, 1864, Spotsylvania Court House, Virginia	Point Lookout, Maryland, transferred to Elmira Prison, NY July 6, 1864	Exchanged February 18, 1865 on the James River, Virginia

Name & Rank	Age	Enlisted	Regiment and State	Where Captured	Prison	Remarks
Bonnet, D. D. Private	Unk	March 1, 1864, Columbia, South Carolina	Co. D, 25th South Carolina Infantry	January 15, 1865, Fort Fisher, North Carolina	Elmira Prison Camp January 30, 1865	Exchanged February 20, 1865. Died March 7, 1865 of Chronic Diarrhea at Hospital No. 9, Richmond, VA
Bontz, Silas Private	Unk	Unknown	Co. C, 38th Virginia Cavalry	August 19, 1864, Waterford, Virginia	Old Capital Prison, Washington D. C. Transferred to Elmira Prison, NY October 27, 1864.	Oath of Allegiance July 19, 1865
Booher, A. C. Private	27	June 6, 1861, Lynchburg, Virginia	Co. E, 63rd Tennessee Infantry	June 17, 1864, Petersburg, Virginia	Point Lookout, Maryland, transferred to Elmira Prison, NY July 30, 1864	Exchanged February 25, 1865 at Boulware's or Cox Wharf on the James River, Virginia
Booher, Ellis Private	Unk	October 17 1862, Sullivan County, Tennessee	Co. K, 63rd Tennessee, Infantry	June 17, 1864, Petersburg, Virginia	Point Lookout, Maryland, transferred to Elmira Prison, NY July 30, 1864	Exchanged February 25, 1865 at Boulware's or Cox Wharf on the James River, Virginia
Booker, Benjamin H. Private	26	June 2, 1861, Centerville, Virginia	Co. J, 26th North Carolina Infantry	June 17, 1864, Near Petersburg, Virginia	Point Lookout, Maryland, transferred to Elmira Prison, NY July 30, 1864	Died September 27, 1864 of Chronic Diarrhea, Grave No. 391. Name Brooke, Benjamin H. on Headstone.
Booker, Edward H. Private	Unk	June 22, 1861, Henry County, Virginia	Co. F, 42nd Virginia Infantry	May 12, 1864, Near Spotsylvania Court House, Virginia	Point Lookout, Maryland, transferred to Elmira Prison, NY August 6, 1864	Oath of Allegiance June 23, 1865
Boon, Augustus A. Private	Unk	June 23, 1861, Camp Moore, Louisiana	Co. G, 8th Louisiana Infantry	June 2, 1864, Brown's Farm, Virginia	Point Lookout, Maryland, transferred to Elmira Prison, NY July 17,1864	Exchanged February 25, 1865 at Boulware's or Cox Wharf on the James River, Virginia

Name & Rank	Age	Enlisted	Regiment and State	Where Captured	Prison	Remarks
Boon, Francis M. Private	Unk	March 4, 1862, Waresboro, Georgia	Co. B, 50th Georgia Intantry	June 1, 1864, Gaines Mill, Cold Harbor, Virginia	Point Lookout, Maryland, transferred to Elmira Prison, NY July 17,1864	Oath of Allegiance May 29, 1865
Boon, Gibson Private	Unk	April 28, 1862, Jasper, Hamilton County, Florida	Co. F, 5th Florida Infantry	May 12, 1864, Near Spotsylvania Court House, Virginia	Point Lookout Prison, Maryland. Transferred to Elmira Prison Camp New York July 30, 1864.	Oath of Allegiance June 19, 1865
Boon, James W. Private	Unk	February 9, 1863, Lumberton, North Carolina	Co E, 51st North Carolina Infantry	June 1, 1864, Cold Harbor, Virginia	Point Lookout, Maryland, transferred to Elmira Prison, NY July 17,1864	Oath of Allegiance June 21, 1865
Boon, John H. Private	28	March 1, 1862, Magnolia, North Carolina	Co. B, 51st North Carolina Infantry	August 19, 1864, Petersburg, Virginia. Gunshot Wound in Back and Right Leg.	Old Capital Prison, Washington, DC, transferred to Elmira Prison, NY, December 17, 1864	Exchanged March 10, 1865 at Boulware's Wharf on the James River, Virginia
Boon, Nicholas Private	20	September 1, 1861, Sampson County, North Carolina	Co. A, 30th North Carolina Infantry	May 12, 1864, Spotsylvania Court House, Virginia	Point Lookout, Maryland, transferred to Elmira Prison, NY August 14, 1864	Oath of Allegiance June 30, 1865
Boon, Stephen Corporal	28	April 14, 1862, Clinton, North Carolina	Co. A, 30th North Carolina Infantry	May 12, 1864, Spotsylvania Court House, Virginia	Point Lookout, Maryland, transferred to Elmira Prison, NY August 14, 1864	Oath of Allegiance May 29, 1865
Boone, Gibson Private	Unk	May 7, 1862, Jasper, Hamilton County, Florida	Co. F, 5th Florida Infantry	May 12, 1864, Spotsylvania Court House, Virginia	Point Lookout, Maryland, transferred to Elmira Prison, NY July 30, 1864	Oath of Allegiance June 19, 1865
Boone, Sampson Sergeant	24	March 10, 1862, Wilmington, North Carolina	Co. G, 51st North Carolina Infantry	June 3, 1864, Gaines Mill, Cold Harbor, Virginia	Point Lookout, Maryland, transferred to Elmira Prison, NY July 17,1864	Died November 24, 1864 of Chronic Diarrhea Grave No. 913

Name & Rank	Age	Enlisted	Regiment and State	Where Captured	Prison	Remarks
Boone, Thomas E. Private	Unk	May 6, 1863, Sutton, Virginia	Co. C, 25th Virginia Infantry	May 6, 1864, Wilderness, Virginia	Old Capital Prison, Washington D. C. Transferred to Elmira Prison, NY July 14, 1864	Died September 20, 1864 of Chronic Diarrhea, Grave No. 352
Booth, Cornelius Private	27	March 13, 1862, Floyd Court House, Virginia	Co. B, 42nd Virginia Infantry	May 12, 1864, Spotsylvania Court House, Virginia	Point Lookout, Maryland, transferred to Elmira Prison, NY July 23, 1864	Died October 12, 1864 of Chronic Diarrhea, Grave No. 571
Booth, Thomas H. Private	Unk	June 12, 1861, Red Sulfur Springs, Virginia	Co. F, 26th Battalion, Virginia Infantry	June 3, 1864, Gaines Farm, Cold Harbor, Virginia	Point Lookout, Maryland, transferred to Elmira Prison, NY July 17,1864	Exchanged October 29, 1864 at Venus Point, Savannah River, GA.
Booth, William S. Private	21	September 5, 1862, Baton Rouge Barracks, Louisiana	Co. B, 1st Louisiana Cavalry	September 24, 1864, East Baton Rouge, Louisiana	New Orleans, Louisiana transferred to Elmira November 19, 1864.	No Further Information Available.
Borne, Zephirin Corporal	20	July 22, 1861, Camp Moore, Louisiana	Co. G, 10th Louisiana Infantry	May 12, 1864, Spotsylvania Court House, Virginia	Point Lookout, Maryland, transferred to Elmira Prison, NY July 25, 1864	Died September 11, 1864 of Chronic Diarrhea, Grave No. 253. Name Z. Barnes Appears on Headstone.
Borrow, Adam J. Private	27	June 2, 1862, Fort Smith, Arkansas	Co. C, 35th Arkansas Infantry	September 20, 1864, St. Joseph, Louisiana	New Orleans, Louisiana transferred to Elmira November 19, 1864.	Exchanged February 25, 1865 at Boulware's or Cox Wharf on the James River, Virginia
Borst, Addison D. Private	Unk	June 2, 1861, Luray, Virginia	Co. K, 10th Virginia Infantry	May 12, 1864, Spotsylvania Court House, Virginia	Point Lookout, Maryland, transferred to Elmira Prison, NY August 2, 1864	Exchanged October 29, 1864 at Venus Point, Savannah River, GA.

Name & Rank	Age	Enlisted	Regiment and State	Where Captured	Prison	Remarks
Boss, Henry Private	Unk	Unknown	Co. H, 1st Virginia Cavalry	October 28, 1864, Broomfield, Virginia	Old Capital Prison, Washington, DC, transferred to Elmira Prison, NY, December 17, 1864	Oath of Allegiance May 15, 1865
Bostian, Andrew A. Private	34	August 8, 1862, Statesville, North Carolina	Co. K, 5th North Carolina Infantry	May 20, 1864, Spotsylvania Court House, Virginia	Point Lookout, Maryland, transferred to Elmira Prison, NY July 6, 1864	Died September 16, 1864 of Chronic Diarrhea, Grave No. 302
Bostian, Eli Private	Unk	August 8, 1862, Statesville, North Carolina	Co. K, 5th North Carolina Infantry	May 20, 1864, Spotsylvania Court House, Virginia	Point Lookout, Maryland, transferred to Elmira Prison, NY July 3, 1864	Transferred for Exchange 10/11/64. Died 11/2/64 of Unknown Causes at Fort Monroe, VA.
Bostic, Benniah N. Private	Unk	May 1, 1862, White Sulfur Springs, Virginia	Co. G, 26th Battalion, Virginia Infantry	June 3, 1864, Gaines Farm, Cold Harbor, Virginia	Point Lookout, Maryland, transferred to Elmira Prison, NY July 17, 1864	Exchanged October 29, 1864 at Venus Point, Savannah River, GA.
Bostick, Addison Private	Unk	April 29, 1863, White Sulfur Springs, Virginia	Co. C, 26th Battalion, Virginia Infantry	June 3, 1864, Gaines Farm, Cold Harbor, Virginia	Point Lookout, Maryland, transferred to Elmira Prison, NY July 17, 1864	Died July 5, 1865 of Chronic Diarrhea, Grave No. 2836
Bostick, Daniel J. Private	Unk	April 15, 1862, Wilmington, North Carolina	Co. C, 51st North Carolina Infantry	June 1, 1864, Cold Harbor, Virginia	Point Lookout, Maryland, transferred to Elmira Prison, NY July 17,1864	Oath of Allegiance July 3, 1865
Bostick, Henry J. Private	Unk	June 14, 1861, Valdosta, Georgia	Co. J, 12th Georgia Infantry	May 6, 1864, Wilderness, Virginia	Point Lookout, Maryland, transferred to Elmira Prison, NY August 14, 1864	Died January 14, 1865 of Pneumonia, Grave No. 1464
Bostick, Thomas T. Private	21	April 4, 1862, Richmond County, North Carolina	Co. E, 52nd North Carolina Infantry	May 12, 1864, Spotsylvania Court House, Virginia	Point Lookout, Maryland, transferred to Elmira Prison, NY August 12, 1864	Oath of Allegiance June 12, 1865

Name & Rank	Age	Enlisted	Regiment and State	Where Captured	Prison	Remarks
Bostick, William Civilian	Unk	Unknown	Citizen of Franklin County, Tennessee	June 10, 1864, Newton, Virginia	Point Lookout, Maryland, transferred to Elmira Prison, NY July 25, 1864	Exchanged November 10, 1864 at Akins Landing on the James River, Virginia
Boston, Alexander L. Private	34	September 6, 1862, Camp Hill, North Carolina	Co. C, 18th North Carolina Infantry	July 29, 1864, Petersburg, Virginia	Point Lookout, Maryland, transferred to Elmira Prison, NY August 12, 1864	Oath of Allegiance July 3, 1865
Boston, James H. Sergeant	Unk	June 14, 1861, Valdosta, Georgia	Co. J, 12th Georgia Infantry	May 10, 1864, Spotsylvania Court House, Virginia	Point Lookout, Maryland, transferred to Elmira Prison, NY July 25, 1864	Exchanged March 10, 1865 at Boulware's Wharf on the James River, Virginia
Boston, John W. Private	Unk	October 8, 1861, Savannah, Georgia	Co. B, 7th Georgia Cavalry	June 11, 1864, Trevilian Station, Louisa Court House, Virginia	Point Lookout, Maryland, transferred to Elmira Prison, NY July 25, 1864	Exchanged October 29, 1864 at Venus Point, Savannah River, GA.
Boston, W. T. Corporal	Unk	October 8, 1861, Savannah, Georgia	Co. B, 7th Georgia Cavalry	June 11, 1864, Trevilian Station, Louisa Court House, Virginia	Point Lookout, Maryland, transferred to Elmira Prison, NY July 25, 1864	Exchanged October 29, 1864 at Venus Point, Savannah River, GA.
Boswell, A. F. Private	Unk	Unknown	Co. G, 2nd South Carolina Infantry	May 20, 1864, Spotsylvania Court House, Virginia	Point Lookout, Maryland, transferred to Elmira Prison, NY July 3, 1864	Oath of Allegiance June 30, 1865
Boswell, Hamilton L. Corporal	22	August 1, 1861, Livingston, Overton County, Tennessee	Co. D, 25th Tennessee Infantry	May 16, 1864, Near Drury's Bluff, Virginia	Point Lookout, Maryland, transferred to Elmira Prison, NY August 17, 1864	Died January 3, 1865 of Chronic Diarrhea, Grave No. 1259
Boswell, James C. Private	Unk	January 20, 1864, Orange Court House, Virginia	Co. C, 39th Virginia Cavalry	June 1, 1864, Stores Harbor, Virginia	Point Lookout, Maryland, transferred to Elmira Prison, NY July 17,1864	Died September 23, 1864 of Typhoid Fever, Grave No. 474
Boswell, John C. Sergeant	35	October 19, 1862, Elizabethtown, North Carolina	Co. H, 36th Regiment, 2nd North Carolina Artillery	January 15, 1865, Fort Fisher, North Carolina. Wounded.	February 1, 1865, Elmira Prison Camp, New York	Exchanged March 14, 1865 at Boulware's Wharf on the James River, Virginia

Elmira Prison Camp Roster Volume I

Name & Rank	Age	Enlisted	Regiment and State	Where Captured	Prison	Remarks
Botts, Charles A. Private	20	July 20, 1861, Camp Pickens, Anderson District, South Carolina	Co. G, 1st South Carolina Infantry	July 14, 1863, Falling Waters, Maryland	Point Lookout, Maryland, transferred to Elmira Prison, NY August 18, 1864	Exchanged October 29, 1864 at Venus Point, Savannah River, GA.
Botts, J. G. Corporal	Unk	December 28, 1861, Camp Hampton Legion, South Carolina	Co. F, Holcombe Legion, South Carolina	May 8, 1864, Jarrett's Depot, Virginia	Point Lookout, Maryland, transferred to Elmira Prison, NY August 17, 1864	Exchanged March 14, 1865 at Boulware's Wharf on the James River, Virginia
Botts, T. A. Private	Unk	December 28, 1861, Camp Hampton Legion, South Carolina	Co. F, Holcombe Legion, South Carolina	May 8, 1864, Jarrett's Depot, Virginia	Point Lookout, Maryland, transferred to Elmira Prison, NY August 17, 1864	Died May 14, 1865 of Rheumatism, Grave No. 2801. Headstone has F. A. Botts
Boughton, Thomas Private	18	March 1, 1862, Gloucester Point, Virginia	Co. C, 26th Virginia Infantry	June 15, 1864, Petersburg, Virginia	Point Lookout, Maryland, transferred to Elmira Prison, NY July 12, 1864	Died November 11, 1864 of Chronic Diarrhea, Grave No. 788
Boulware, B. F. Private	Unk	June 9, 1863, Camp Prichard, South Carolina	Co. B, 4th South Carolina Cavalry	May 30, 1864, Old Church, Virginia	Point Lookout, Maryland, transferred to Elmira Prison, NY July 11, 1864	Oath of Allegiance June 14, 1865
Bourdeaux, F. M. Corporal	19	August 22, 1861, Lillington, North Carolina	Co. C, 1st North Carolina Infantry	May 12, 1864, Spotsylvania Court House, Virginia	Point Lookout, Maryland, transferred to Elmira Prison, NY August 6, 1864	Oath of Allegiance June 19, 1865
Bourgeois, Adam D. Private	Unk	March 21, 1862, Terre Bonne, Louisiana	Co. H, 26th Louisiana Infantry	July 4, 1863, Vicksburg, Mississippi	New Orleans, Louisiana transferred to Elmira November 19, 1864.	Exchanged February 25, 1865 at Boulware's or Cox Wharf on the James River, Virginia
Bourn, George A. Private	Unk	March 20, 1862, Elk Creek, Virginia	Co. F, 4th Virginia Infantry	May 12, 1864 Spotsylvania Court House, Virginia	Point Lookout, Maryland, transferred to Elmira Prison, NY August 2, 1864	Oath of Allegiance June 23, 1865

Name & Rank	Age	Enlisted	Regiment and State	Where Captured	Prison	Remarks
Bourne, James	Unk	July 2, 1861, Wytheville, Virginia	Co. C, 5th Virginia Infantry	May 12, 1864, Spotsylvania Court House, Virginia	Point Lookout, Maryland, transferred to Elmira Prison, NY August 2, 1864	Died May 10, 1865 of Inflammation of Lungs, Grave No. 2785
Bousman, Henry Private	Unk	July 24, 1861, John Pasley's, Virginia	Co. E, 58th Virginia Infantry	May 20, 1864, Spotsylvania Court House, Virginia	Point Lookout, Maryland, transferred to Elmira Prison, NY July 3, 1864	Oath of Allegiance June 30, 1865
Boutet, A. M. Private	Unk	August 22, 1863, Decatur, Georgia	Co. A, 7th South Carolina Cavalry	May 30, 1864, Old Church, Virginia	Point Lookout, Maryland, transferred to Elmira Prison, NY July 25, 1864	Exchanged March 10, 1865 at Boulware's wharf on the James River, Virginia
Bowden, Joseph N. Private	18	January 17, 1863, Wilmington, North Carolina	Co. D, 1st Battalion North Carolina Heavy Artillery	January 15, 1865, Fort Fisher, North Carolina. Wounded.	February 1, 1865, Elmira Prison Camp, New York	Exchanged February 20, 1865 at Boulware's or Cox Wharf on the James River, Virginia
Bowden, Morris C. Private	18	June 1, 1861, Dogwood Grove, North Carolina	Co. K, 3rd North Carolina Infantry	May 12, 1864, Near Spotsylvania Court House, Virginia	Point Lookout, Maryland, transferred to Elmira Prison, NY August 12, 1864	Exchanged March 2, 1865 at Akins Landing on the James River, Virginia
Bowden, Thomas Private	25	May 27, 1861, Troy, North Carolina	Co. C, 23rd North Carolina Infantry	May 12, 1864, Near Spotsylvania Court House, Virginia	Point Lookout, Maryland, transferred to Elmira Prison, NY August 14, 1864	Oath of Allegiance June 27, 1865
Bowden, William Private	28	May 8, 1862, Fayetteville, North Carolina	Co. B, 56th North Carolina Infantry	June 18, 1864, Petersburg, Virginia	Point Lookout, Maryland, transferred to Elmira Prison, NY July 30, 1864	Exchanged March 2, 1865 at Akins Landing on the James River, Virginia
Bowen, Calvin Sergeant	21	June 23, 1861, Fort Caswell, Fair Bluff, North Carolina	Co. C, 20th North Carolina Infantry	May 12, 1864, Near Spotsylvania Court House, Virginia	Point Lookout Prison, Maryland. Transferred to Elmira Prison Camp New York August 14, 1864.	Oath of Allegiance June 12, 1865

Name & Rank	Age	Enlisted	Regiment and State	Where Captured	Prison	Remarks
Bowen, George W. Private	28	September 23, 1861, Camp Lamar, Georgia	Co. B, 61st Georgia Infantry	May 12, 1864, Spotsylvania Court House, Virginia	Point Lookout, Maryland, transferred to Elmira Prison, NY July 25, 1864	Exchanged October 29, 1864 at Venus Point, Savannah River, GA.
Bowen, John W. Private	Unk	March 9, 1864, Liberty Mills, North Carolina	Co. I, 18th North Carolina Infantry	May 12, 1864, Spotsylvania Court House, Virginia	Point Lookout, Maryland, transferred to Elmira Prison, NY August 6, 1864	Oath of Allegiance July 3, 1865
Bowen, Lawrence Private	42	February 1, 1862, Williamston, North Carolina	Co. H, 1st North Carolina Infantry	May 12, 1864, Spotsylvania, Virginia	Point Lookout Prison Camp, Maryland. Transferred to Elmira Prison Camp, New York August 6, 1864	Died September 21, 1864 of Chronic Diarrhea, Grave No. 348
Bowen, Lewis B. Private	Unk	March 24, 1862, Lewisburg, Virginia	Co. A, 26th Battalion, Virginia Infantry	June 3, 1864, Gaines Mill, Cold Harbor, Virginia	Point Lookout, Maryland, transferred to Elmira Prison, NY July 17, 1864	Exchanged February 13, 1865 at Boulware's wharf on the James River, Virginia
Bowen, William H. Private	Unk	May 16, 1862, Augusta, Georgia	Co. G, 49th Georgia Infantry	May 6, 1864, Wilderness, Virginia	Point Lookout, Maryland, transferred to Elmira Prison, NY August 14, 1864	Died October 22, 1864 of Pneumonia, Grave No. 869
Bowers, Anderson John Private	22	March 17, 1862, McDowell, North Carolina	Co. A, 49th North Carolina Infantry	June 2, 1864, Bermuda Hundred, Virginia	Point Lookout, Maryland, transferred to Elmira Prison, NY July 17,1864	Exchanged March 2, 1865 at Akins Landing on the James River, Virginia
Bowers, Anthony J. Sergeant	Unk	January 25, 1862, Columbia, South Carolina	Co. B, 22nd South Carolina Infantry	July 30, 1864, Petersburg, Virginia	Point Lookout, Maryland, transferred to Elmira Prison, NY August 12, 1864	Died March 7, 1865 of Chronic Diarrhea, Grave No. 2395
Bowers, Daniel Private	32	May 8, 1862, Camp Hill, Stanley County, North Carolina	Co. F, 5th North Carolina Infantry	May 6, 1864, Wilderness, Virginia	Point Lookout, Maryland, transferred to Elmira Prison, NY July 30, 1864	Oath of Allegiance May 27, 1865

Name & Rank	Age	Enlisted	Regiment and State	Where Captured	Prison	Remarks
Bowers, Joseph Private	Unk	July 25, 1861, Delps Muster Ground, Carroll County, Virginia	Co. C, 29th, Virginia Infantry	June 1, 1864, Gaines Mill, Cold Harbor, Virginia	Point Lookout, Maryland, transferred to Elmira Prison, NY July 17, 1864	Died September 4, 1864 of Chronic Diarrhea, Grave No. 231
Bowers, William Private	Unk	August 8, 1862, Davidson County, North Carolina	Co. B, 48th North Carolina Infantry	June 3, 1864, Near Talapatomoy Creek, Cold Harbor, Virginia	Transferred From Point Lookout Prison, MD, July 12, 1864. Train Never Arrived at Elmira Prison Camp, NY.	Died July 15, 1864 in Train Wreck at Shohola, Pennsylvania.
Bowie, Brune H. Sergeant	20	July 20, 1862, Richmond, Virginia	Co. D, 1st Virginia Cavalry	October 7, 1864, Montgomery County, Virginia	Old Capital Prison, Washington, DC transferred to Elmira Prison, NY August 27, 1864	Oath of Allegiance June 15, 1865
Bowie, Gillespie Private	18	May 9, 1861, Petersburg, Virginia	Co. C, 41st Virginia Infantry	June 24, 1864, North Anna, Virginia	Point Lookout, Maryland, transferred to Elmira Prison, NY July 8, 1864	Oath of Allegiance May 19, 1865
Bowie, William P. Private	Unk	May 11, 1861, New Orleans, Louisiana	Co. A, 2nd Louisiana Infantry	May 20, 1864, Spotsylvania Court House, Virginia	Point Lookout, Maryland, transferred to Elmira Prison, NY July 6, 1864	Died September 2, 1864 of Acute Bronchitis, Grave No. 62
Bowles, Alfred G. Private	27	April 6, 1862, Kinston, North Carolina	Co. G, 37th Virginia Infantry	May 20, 1864, Near Spotsylvania, Virginia	Point Lookout, Maryland, transferred to Elmira Prison, NY July 23, 1864	Oath of Allegiance May 29, 1865
Bowles, Bartlett Private	23	March 10, 1862, Roxboro, North Carolina	Co. A, 24th North Carolina Infantry	June 17, 1864, Near Petersburg, Virginia	Point Lookout, Maryland, transferred to Elmira Prison, NY July 23, 1864	Oath of Allegiance May 29, 1865
Bowles, Benjamin T. Private	Unk	November 1, 1863, Culpeper Court House, Virginia	Co. K, 5th Virginia Cavalry	May 31, 1864, Cold Harbor, Virginia	Point Lookout, Maryland, transferred to Elmira Prison, NY July 11, 1864	Oath of Allegiance June 14, 1865

Name & Rank	Age	Enlisted	Regiment and State	Where Captured	Prison	Remarks
Bowles, Jerome Private	35	March 8, 1862, Lynchburg, Virginia	Co. D, 20th Virginia Artillery	April 6, 1865, Sailor's Creek, Virginia. Gunshot Wound Right Thigh.	Old Capital Prison, Washington D. C. Transferred to Elmira Prison, NY May 12, 1865.	Oath of Allegiance July 11, 1865
Bowles, N. A. Private	Unk	June 10, 1862, Athens, Georgia	Co. C, 7th Georgia Cavalry	June 11, 1864, Trevilian Station, Louisa Court House, Virginia	Point Lookout, Maryland, transferred to Elmira Prison, NY July 25, 1864	Died November 29, 1864 of Pneumonia, Grave No. 992
Bowles, Richard Private	Unk	July 19, 1861, Montgomery, Alabama	Co. B, 13th Alabama Infantry	May 6, 1864, Wilderness, Virginia	Point Lookout, Maryland, transferred to Elmira Prison, NY August 14, 1864	Died November 4, 1864 of Chronic Diarrhea, Grave No. 842
Bowling, John W. Sergeant	Unk	July 2, 1861, Wytheville, Virginia	Co. C, 50th Virginia Infantry	May 12, 1864 Spotsylvania Court House, Virginia	Point Lookout, Maryland, transferred to Elmira Prison, NY August 2, 1864	Died January 11, 1865 of Variola (Smallpox), Grave No. 1494
Bowls, D. C. Corporal	Unk	Unknown	Co. C, 12th Arkansas Infantry	May 10, 1863, Champion Hill, Mississippi	Point Lookout, Maryland, transferred to Elmira Prison, NY August 18, 1864	Exchanged February 13, 1865 at Boulware's Wharf on the James River, Virginia
Bowman, Austin Private	Unk	Unknown	Co. K, 50th Virginia Infantry	May 12, 1864, Spotsylvania Court House, Virginia	Point Lookout, Maryland, transferred to Elmira Prison, NY August 2, 1864	Exchanged October 29, 1864 at Venus Point, Savannah River, GA.
Bowman, Calvin A. Private	21	September 12, 1861, Newton, North Carolina	Co. E, 32nd North Carolina Infantry	June 18, 1864, Petersburg, Virginia	Old Capital Prison, Washington, DC, transferred to Elmira Prison, NY, December 17, 1864	Oath of Allegiance June 27, 1865
Bowman, Calvin M. Private	18	March 15, 1862, Newton, North Carolina	Co. C, 28th North Carolina Infantry	May 12, 1864, Spotsylvania Court House, Virginia	Point Lookout, Maryland, transferred to Elmira Prison, NY August 12, 1864	Exchanged October 29, 1864 at Venus Point, Savannah River, GA.

Name & Rank	Age	Enlisted	Regiment and State	Where Captured	Prison	Remarks
Bowman, David Private	36	December 8, 1863, Newton, North Carolina	Co. E, 32nd North Carolina Infantry	May 10, 1864, Spotsylvania, Virginia	Lookout, Maryland, transferred to Elmira Prison, NY August 6, 1864	Exchanged October 29, 1864 at Venus Point, Savannah River, GA.
Bowman, J. Private	Unk	Unknown	Co. H, 5th Virginia Infantry	May 12, 1864, Spotsylvania Court House, Virginia	Point Lookout, Maryland, transferred to Elmira Prison, NY August 2, 1864	Transferred for Exchange 10/11/1864. Nothing Further.
Bowman, Jacob Private	Unk	December 8, 1863, Newton, North Carolina	Co. F, 32nd North Carolina Infantry	May 10, 1864, Wilderness, Virginia	Point Lookout, Maryland, transferred to Elmira Prison, NY August 6, 1864	Exchanged October 29, 1864, at Venus Point, Savannah River, GA.
Bowman, Jonas Private	19	September 12, 1861, Newton, North Carolina	Co. F, 32nd North Carolina Infantry	May 10, 1864, Wilderness, Virginia	Point Lookout, Maryland, transferred to Elmira Prison, NY August 6, 1864	Died September 12, 1864 of Chronic Diarrhea, Grave No. 177. Name Barman on Headstone.
Bowman, Lucius B. Private	Unk	June 15, 1861, Macon County, Georgia	Co. C, 12th Georgia Infantry	July 13, 1864, Silver Springs, Maryland. Gunshot Wound Back Near Scapula.	Old Capital Prison, Washington, DC transferred to Elmira Prison, NY August 27, 1864	Oath of Allegiance June 30, 1865
Bowman, Madison Private	Unk	August 20, 1863, Smyth County, Virginia	Co. K, 21st Virginia Cavalry	July 3, 1864, Leetown, Virginia	Old Capital Prison, Washington, DC, transferred to Elmira Prison, NY, July 23, 1864	Died September 1, 1864 of Chronic Diarrhea, Grave No. 90
Bowman, William C. Private	Unk	July 27, 1863, Culpepper County Court House, Virginia	Co. C, 34th North Carolina Infantry	May 6, 1864, Wilderness, Virginia	Point Lookout, Maryland, transferred to Elmira Prison, NY August 14, 1864	Oath of Allegiance June 19, 1865
Bowman, William H. Civilian	Unk	Mississippi	Citizen of Mississippi	August 3, 1864, Natchez, Mississippi	New Orleans, Louisiana transferred to Elmira November 19, 1864.	Died February 12, 1865 of Chronic Diarrhea, Grave No. 2050

Name & Rank	Age	Enlisted	Regiment and State	Where Captured	Prison	Remarks
Bowser, John B. Private	22	June 16, 1861, Washington County, Virginia	Co. J, 48th Virginia Infantry	May 12, 1864, Near Spotsylvania Court House, Virginia	Point Lookout, Maryland, transferred to Elmira Prison, NY August 6, 1864	Oath of Allegiance June 27, 1865
Boy, Philip Private	19	May 14, 1862, Zollicoffer, Sullivan County, Tennessee	Co. F, 63rd Tennessee Infantry	June 17, 1864, Petersburg, Virginia	Point Lookout, Maryland, transferred to Elmira Prison, NY July 30, 1864	Exchanged February 25, 1865 at Boulware's or Cox Wharf on the James River, Virginia
Boyce, John H. Private	19	February 21, 1862, Charleston, South Carolina	Co. E, 25th South Carolina Infantry	January 15, 1865, Fort Fisher, North Carolina	Elmira Prison Camp January 30, 1865	Oath of Allegiance May 15, 1865
Boyce, William A. Sergeant	23	April 2, 1862, South Mills, North Carolina	Co. C, 56th North Carolina Infantry	March 25, 1865, Fort Steadman, Virginia. Shell Contusion Left Side of Neck.	Old Capital Prison, Washington D. C. Transferred to Elmira Prison, NY May 12, 1865.	Oath of Allegiance July 11, 1865
Boyd, Enoch J. Corporal	Unk	February 22, 1862, Blockers, Alabama	Co. C, 1st Battalion Alabama Artillery	August 23, 1864, Fort Morgan, Alabama	New Orleans, Louisiana transferred to Elmira December 4, 1864.	Died December 29, 1864 of Variola (Smallpox), Grave No. 1309
Boyd, George A. Private	Unk	August 14, 1863, Cobb County, Georgia	Co. J, 7th Georgia Cavalry	June 11, 1864, Louisa Court House, Trevilian Station, Virginia	Point Lookout, Maryland, transferred to Elmira Prison, NY July 30, 1864	Oath of Allegiance May 19, 1865
Boyd, George W. Private	Unk	June 14, 1861, Valdosta, Georgia	Co. J, 12th Georgia Infantry	May 10, 1864, Spotsylvania Court House, Virginia	Point Lookout, Maryland, transferred to Elmira Prison, NY July 25, 1864	Oath of Allegiance June 14, 1865
Boyd, John B. S. Private	Unk	June 22, 1864, Camp Watts, Alabama	Co. F, 1st Battalion Alabama Artillery	August 23, 1864, Fort Morgan, Alabama	Steam Press No. 4, New Orleans, Louisiana transferred to Elmira Prison, October 8, 1864.	Died February 5, 1865 of Variola (Smallpox), Grave No. 1894

Name & Rank	Age	Enlisted	Regiment and State	Where Captured	Prison	Remarks
Boyett, Albert D. Private	28	May 1, 1862, South Mills, North Carolina	Co. D, 32nd North Carolina Infantry	May 10, 1864, Spotsylvania, Virginia	Point Lookout, Maryland, transferred to Elmira Prison, NY August 6, 1864	Exchanged March 2, 1865 at Akins Landing on the James River, Virginia
Boyle, George Private	27	July 20, 1861, Camp Pickens, Anderson District, South Carolina	Co. A, 1st South Carolina Infantry	June 1, 1864, Fairfax County, Virginia	Old Capital Prison, Washington, DC, transferred to Elmira Prison, NY, July 23, 1864	Oath of Allegiance May 15, 1865
Bozard, David T. Private	28	April 21, 1862, Orangeburg, South Carolina	Co. G, 25th South Carolina Infantry	January 15, 1865, Fort Fisher, North Carolina	Elmira Prison Camp January 30, 1865	Oath of Allegiance July 7, 1865
Bozeman, William R. Corporal	Unk	September 15, 1862, Lowndes, Alabama	Co. E, 1st Battalion Alabama Artillery	August 23, 1864, Fort Morgan, Alabama	Steam Press No. 4, New Orleans, Louisiana transferred to Elmira Prison, October 8, 1864.	Exchanged February 13, 1865 at Boulware's wharf on the James River, Virginia
Brackman, Archibald Private	Unk	Unknown	Co. B, 44th Alabama Infantry	May 23, 1864, Hanover Court House, Virginia	Point Lookout, Maryland, transferred to Elmira Prison, NY July 8, 1864	Exchanged October 29, 1864 at Venus Point, Savannah River, GA.
Bradberry, J. H. Private	Unk	July 29, 1861, Bell's Landing, Alabama	Co. C, 5th Alabama Infantry	May 13, 1864, Spotsylvania Court House, Virginia	Point Lookout, Maryland, transferred to Elmira Prison, NY August 17, 1864	Died April 13, 1865 of Pneumonia, Grave No. 2678
Bradburn, J. B. Private	38	March 31, 1863, Newton, North Carolina	Co. E, 32nd North Carolina Infantry	May 10, 1864, Wilderness, Virginia	Point Lookout, Maryland, transferred to Elmira Prison, NY August 6, 1864	Exchanged October 29, 1864, at Venus Point, Savannah River, GA.
Braddock, Frankling Private	32	April 21, 1862, Camp Manigault, Chesterfield, South Carolina	Co. D, 21st South Carolina Infantry	July 10, 1863, Morris Island, South Carolina	Point Lookout, Maryland, transferred to Elmira Prison, NY August 18, 1864	Exchanged October 29, 1864, at Venus Point, Savannah River, GA.
Braddock, Henry T. Private	21	August 6, 1861, Camp Pulaski, Louisiana	Co. G, 15th Louisiana Infantry	May 20, 1864, Spotsylvania Court House, Virginia	Point Lookout, Maryland, transferred to Elmira Prison, NY July 6, 1864	Exchanged February 16, 1865 on the James River, Virginia

Name & Rank	Age	Enlisted	Regiment and State	Where Captured	Prison	Remarks
Braddock, John Private	25	January 1, 1862, Camp Hardee, Chesterfield, South Carolina	Co. D, 21st South Carolina Infantry	June 17, 1864, Petersburg, Virginia	Point Lookout, Maryland, transferred to Elmira Prison, NY July 30, 1864	Exchanged March 2, 1865 at Akins Landing on the James River, Virginia
Braddock, Ralph Private	27	December 20, 1861, Cheraw, South Carolina	Co. D, 21st South Carolina Infantry	January 15, 1865, Fort Fisher, North Carolina	Elmira Prison Camp January 30, 1865	Exchanged February 20, 1865 at Boulware's or Cox Wharf on the James River, Virginia
Braddock, T. Private	17	January 1, 1862, Chesterfield, South Carolina	Co. D, 21st South Carolina Infantry	January 15, 1865, Fort Fisher, North Carolina	Elmira Prison Camp January 30, 1865	Oath of Allegiance July 7, 1865
Braddock, William A. Private	Unk	October 1, 1861, Macon, Georgia	Co. I, 61st Georgia Infantry	July 13, 1864, Near Washington, DC,	Old Capital Prison, Washington, DC, transferred to Elmira Prison, NY, July 23, 1864	Oath of Allegiance May 29, 1865
Bradford, David F. Sergeant	18	July 31, 1861, Livingston, Tennessee	Co. F, 25th Tennessee Infantry	May 16, 1864, Near Drury's Bluff, Virginia	Point Lookout, Maryland, transferred to Elmira Prison, NY August 17, 1864	Exchanged February 13, 1865 at Boulware's wharf on the James River, Virginia
Bradford, John A. Private	Unk	February 10, 1863, Choctaw Bluff, Alabama	Co. A, 21st Alabama Infantry	August 23, 1864, Fort Morgan, Alabama	Steam Press No. 4, New Orleans, Louisiana transferred to Elmira Prison, October 8, 1864.	Oath of Allegiance June 14, 1865
Bradham, Benjamin Private	Unk	April 21, 1862, Woodville, Texas	Co. F, 1st Texas Infantry	May 12, 1864, Spotsylvania Court House, Virginia	Point Lookout, Maryland, transferred to Elmira Prison, NY August 12, 1864	Oath of Allegiance June 16, 1865
Bradham, T. A. Corporal	Unk	September 15, 1863, Pocataligo, South Carolina	Co. D, 4th South Carolina Cavalry	May 30, 1864, Old Church, Virginia	Point Lookout, Maryland, transferred to Elmira Prison, NY July 11, 1864	Oath of Allegiance June 16, 1865

Name & Rank	Age	Enlisted	Regiment and State	Where Captured	Prison	Remarks
Bradley, Augusta Marine	Unk	Unknown	Confederate States Navy, assigned to CSS Chattahoochee	January 15, 1865, Fort Fisher, North Carolina	February 1, 1865, Elmira Prison Camp, New York	Oath of Allegiance May 15, 1865
Bradley, Benton W. Private	22	May 9, 1861, Rutherford, North Carolina	Co. G, 16th North Carolina Infantry	May 6, 1864, Wilderness, Virginia	Point Lookout, Maryland, transferred to Elmira Prison, NY August 14, 1864	Oath of Allegiance June 19, 1865
Bradley, J. N. Private	Unk	March 12, 1862, Greenville, Alabama	Co. F, 1st Battalion Alabama Artillery	August 23, 1864, Fort Morgan, Alabama	Steam Press No. 4, New Orleans, Louisiana transferred to Elmira Prison, October 8, 1864.	Oath of Allegiance June 19, 1865
Bradley, James M. Sergeant	27	July 26, 1861, Gallatin, Tennessee	Co. A, 23rd Tennessee Infantry	June 17, 1864, Petersburg, Virginia	Point Lookout, Maryland, transferred to Elmira Prison, NY July 30, 1864	Exchanged February 13, 1865 at Boulware's wharf on the James River, Virginia
Bradley, John H. Private	Unk	August 20, 1864, Fort Fisher, North Carolina	Co. F, 36th Regiment, 2nd North Carolina Artillery	January 15, 1865, Fort Fisher, North Carolina. Wounded.	February 1, 1865, Elmira Prison Camp, New York	Died February 21, 1865, Variola (Smallpox), Grave No. 2313. Headstone has H. H. Brady.
Bradley, Johnston T. Private	Unk	May 10, 1861, Richmond, Virginia	Co. C, 38th Read's Battalion, Virginia Light Artillery	June 3, 1864, Gaines Farm, Cold Harbor, Virginia	Point Lookout, Maryland, transferred to Elmira Prison, NY July 17,1864	Exchanged March 10, 1865 at Boulware's Wharf on the James River, Virginia
Bradley, Rufus H. Sergeant	Unk	June 17, 1861, Rocky Mount, Virginia	Co. K, 4th Virginia Infantry	May 12, 1864, Spotsylvania Court House, Virginia	Point Lookout, Maryland, transferred to Elmira Prison, NY August 2, 1864	Oath of Allegiance June 27, 1865
Bradley, Stephen B. Private	Unk	September 16, 1862, Lowndes, Alabama	Co. F, 1st Battalion Alabama Artillery	August 23, 1864, Fort Morgan, Alabama	Steam Press No. 4, New Orleans, Louisiana transferred to Elmira Prison, October 8, 1864.	Exchanged February 13, 1865 at Boulware's wharf on the James River, Virginia

Name & Rank	Age	Enlisted	Regiment and State	Where Captured	Prison	Remarks
Bradley, Thomas J. Private	Unk	Unknown	Co. D, 16th Georgia Infantry	Unknown	Unknown	Died June 6, 1865 of Unknown Disease, Grave No. 2891
Bradley, William S. Corporal	Unk	September 16, 1862, Lowndes, Alabama	Co. E, 1st Battalion Alabama Artillery	August 23, 1864, Fort Morgan, Alabama	Steam Press No. 4, New Orleans, Louisiana transferred to Elmira Prison, October 8, 1864.	Exchanged March 14, 1865 at Boulware's Wharf on the James River, Virginia
Bradner, James A. Private	Unk	May 24, 1863, Danville, Virginia	Co. D, 39th Battalion Virginia Cavalry	May 9, 1864, Caroline County, Virginia	Point Lookout, Maryland, transferred to Elmira Prison, NY August 17, 1864	Died October 9, 1864 of Chronic Diarrhea, Grave No. 663. Headstone has Bradnor.
Bradner, William H. Private	Unk	June 22, 1861, Richmond, Virginia	Co. C, 46th Virginia Infantry	June 16, 1864, Petersburg, Virginia	Point Lookout, Maryland, transferred to Elmira Prison, NY July 25, 1864	Exchanged February 13, 1865 at Boulware's wharf on the James River, Virginia
Bradshaw, Ashley Private	21	Unknown	Co K, 20th North Carolina Infantry	May 12, 1864, Near Spotsylvania Court House, Virginia	Point Lookout, Maryland, transferred to Elmira Prison, NY August 14, 1864	Oath of Allegiance June 14, 1865
Bradshaw, Jesse Private	21	October 24, 1861, Fayetteville, North Carolina	Co. G, 33rd North Carolina Infantry	May 6, 1864, Wilderness, Virginia	Old Capital Prison, Washington D. C. Transferred to Elmira Prison, NY July 14, 1864	Exchanged March 2, 1865 at Akins Landing on the James River, Virginia
Bradshaw, William D. Private	28	June 8, 1861, Duplin County, North Carolina	Co. B, 3rd North Carolina Infantry	June 10, 1864, Spotsylvania, Virginia	Point Lookout, Maryland, transferred to Elmira Prison, NY July 25, 1864	Oath of Allegiance June 10, 1865
Brady, Alven Private	Unk	March 10, 1864, Cooke County, Tennessee	Co. D, 7th Tennessee Infantry	May 5, 1864, Wilderness, Virginia	Point Lookout, Maryland, transferred to Elmira Prison, NY July 25, 1864	Oath of Allegiance November 16, 1864. Early Release per Lincoln's Proclamation, 12/8/1863.

Name & Rank	Age	Enlisted	Regiment and State	Where Captured	Prison	Remarks
Brady, C. C. Private	Unk	Unknown	Co. B, 35th Virginia Infantry	August 10, 1864, Leesburg, Virginia	Old Capital Prison, Washington, D. C. Transferred to Elmira Prison, NY August 12, 1864	Oath of Allegiance June 14, 1865
Brady, Daniel Private	Unk	December 9, 1863, Petersburg, Virginia	Co. C, 38th Read's Battalion, Virginia Light Artillery	June 3, 1864, Gaines Farm, Cold Harbor, Virginia	Point Lookout, Maryland, transferred to Elmira Prison, NY July 17, 1864	Exchanged February 20, 1865 at Boulware's or Cox Wharf on the James River, Virginia
Brady, Eugene Private	Unk	May 14, 1861, Todd's Tavern, Leesburg, Virginia	Co. K, 1st Virginia Cavalry	May 8, 1864, Wilderness, Virginia	Point Lookout, Maryland, transferred to Elmira Prison, NY July 8, 1864	Exchanged October 29, 1864 at Venus Point, Savannah River, GA.
Brady, George W. Private	21	May 24, 1861, Raleigh, North Carolina	Co. A, 5th North Carolina Infantry	July 13, 1864, Near Washington, DC,	Old Capital Prison, Washington, DC, transferred to Elmira Prison, NY, July 23, 1864	Oath of Allegiance May 13, 1865
Brady, James Private	Unk	March 12, 1863, Augusta, Georgia	Co. D, 12th Battalion Georgia Light Artillery	July 8, 1864, Near Harper's Ferry, Virginia	Old Capital Prison, Washington, DC, transferred to Elmira Prison, NY, July 23, 1864	Oath of Allegiance May 15, 1865
Brady, Joseph M. Private	21	July 17, 1862, Raleigh, North Carolina	Co. H, 3rd North Carolina Infantry	May 12, 1864, Near Spotsylvania Court House, Virginia	Point Lookout Prison, Maryland. Transferred to Elmira Prison Camp New York August 14, 1864.	Oath of Allegiance June 30, 1865
Brady, Robert N. Private	Unk	March 4, 1862, Homersville, Georgia	Co. G, 50th Georgia Infantry	July 5, 1863, Gettysburg, Pennsylvania	Point Lookout, Maryland, transferred to Elmira Prison, NY August 18, 1864	Exchanged October 29, 1864, at Venus Point, Savannah River, GA.

Name & Rank	Age	Enlisted	Regiment and State	Where Captured	Prison	Remarks
Brady, S. B. Private	Unk	Unknown	Co. A, 6th North Carolina Infantry	May 29, 1864, Chickahominy, Cold Harbor, Virginia	Point Lookout, Maryland, transferred to Elmira Prison, NY July 25, 1864	Exchanged October 29, 1864 at Venus Point, Savannah River, GA.
Brady, William J. Private	Unk	February 26, 1861, Eufaula, Alabama	Co. A, 1st Alabama Artillery	August 23, 1864, Fort Morgan, Alabama	New Orleans, Louisiana transferred to Elmira December 4, 1864.	No Further Information Available
Brafford, Edward Private	35	July 15, 1862, Wayne County, North Carolina	Co. F, 3rd North Carolina Infantry	May 12, 1864, Near Spotsylvania Court House, Virginia	Point Lookout Prison, Maryland. Transferred to Elmira Prison Camp New York August 14, 1864.	Oath of Allegiance June 19, 1865
Brafford, Joshua Private	51	April 9, 1864, Wilmington, North Carolina	Co. F, 1st North Carolina Artillery	January 15, 1865, Fort Fisher, North Carolina	Elmira Prison Camp January 30, 1865	Died April 21, 1865 of Variola (Smallpox), Grave No. 1392
Brafford, Wesley Private	17	September 20, 1862, Goldsboro, North Carolina	Co. F, 1st North Carolina Artillery	January 15, 1865, Fort Fisher, North Carolina	Elmira Prison Camp January 30, 1865	Died April 10, 1865 of Variola (Smallpox), Grave No. 2671
Bragg, Joseph H. Private	Unk	June 24, 1861, Beverly, Virginia	Co. G, 25th Virginia Infantry	May 5, 1864, Wilderness, Virginia	Point Lookout, Maryland, transferred to Elmira Prison, NY August 14, 1864	Oath of Allegiance June 27, 1865
Brake, Jesse Private	19	October 9, 1861, Enfield, North Carolina	Co. F, 36th Regiment, 2nd North Carolina Artillery	January 15, 1865, Fort Fisher, North Carolina. Wounded.	February 1, 1865, Elmira Prison Camp, New York	Oath of Allegiance June 12, 1865
Branch, A. J. Private	Unk	May 1, 1862, Camp Holmes, New Hanover, North Carolina	Co. E, 51st North Carolina Infantry	June 1, 1864, Cold Harbor, Virginia	Point Lookout, Maryland, transferred to Elmira Prison, NY July 17, 1864	Oath of Allegiance July 3, 1865
Branch, Bryant W. Private	29	September 9, 1861, Fayetteville, North Carolina	Co. E, 8th North Carolina Infantry	May 31, 1864, Cold Harbor, Virginia	Point Lookout, Maryland, transferred to Elmira Prison, NY July 17,1864	Exchanged October 29, 1864, at Venus Point, Savannah River, GA.

Name & Rank	Age	Enlisted	Regiment and State	Where Captured	Prison	Remarks
Branch, Pinkney Private	Unk	March 15, 1864, Morganton, North Carolina	Co. B, 54th North Carolina Infantry	May 16, 1864, Near Drury's Bluff, Virginia	Point Lookout, Maryland, transferred to Elmira Prison, NY August 18, 1864	Oath of Allegiance June 14, 1865
Branch, Thad Private	21	May 15, 1862, Halifax County, North Carolina	Co. F, 43rd North Carolina Infantry	July 20, 1864, Snickers Gap, Virginia	Old Capital Prison, Washington, D. C. Transferred to Elmira Prison, NY August 12, 1864	Oath of Allegiance July 3, 1865
Branch, William H. Private	25	April 25, 1861, Halifax County, North Carolina	Co. G, 12th North Carolina Infantry	July 13, 1864, Near Washington, DC,	Old Capital Prison, Washington, DC, transferred to Elmira Prison, NY, July 23, 1864	Exchanged February 13, 1865 at Boulware's wharf on the James River, Virginia
Brand, A. R. Firemen	Unk	Unknown	Confederate States Navy	May 5, 1864, Albemarle Sound on Steamer CSS Bombshell	Point Lookout, Maryland, transferred to Elmira Prison, NY August 17, 1864	Died January 4, 1865 of Typhoid Fever, Grave No. 1263
Brand, Benjamin H. Private	Unk	February 28, 1862, West Point, Georgia	Co. F, 14th Alabama Infantry	June 24, 1864, Hanover Junction, Virginia	Point Lookout, Maryland, transferred to Elmira Prison, NY July 8, 1864	Oath of Allegiance June 14, 1865
Brandeburg, John Private	21	March 23, 1863, Ponchatoula, Louisiana	Co. K, 7th Louisiana Infantry	May 5, 1864, Wilderness, Virginia	Point Lookout, Maryland, transferred to Elmira Prison, NY August 17, 1864	Died February 9, 1865 of Chronic Diarrhea, Grave No. 1940
Brandley, James A. Private	Unk	May 10, 1862, Butler, Georgia	Co. C, 59th Georgia Infantry	May 6, 1864, Wilderness, Virginia	Point Lookout, Maryland, transferred to Elmira Prison, NY August 14, 1864	Oath of Allegiance June 19, 1865
Brandon, Hugh Private	Unk	February 27, 1864, Florida	Co. H, 18th South Carolina Infantry	July 30, 1864, Petersburg, Virginia	Point Lookout, Maryland, transferred to Elmira Prison, NY August 12, 1864	Died September 7, 1864 of Chronic Diarrhea, Grave No. 219, Name Brannon on Headstone.

Name & Rank	Age	Enlisted	Regiment and State	Where Captured	Prison	Remarks
Brandon, W. A. Private	Unk	July 10, 1862, Farmington, North Carolina	Co. H, 5th North Carolina Cavalry	May 31, 1864, Hanover Court House, Cold Harbor, Virginia	Point Lookout, Maryland, transferred to Elmira Prison, NY July 17, 1864	Exchanged March 10, 1865 at Boulware's wharf on the James River, Virginia
Brandt, Augusto Private	21	August 1, 1861, Galveston, Texas	Co. L, 1st Texas Infantry	May 12, 1864, Spotsylvania Court House, Virginia	Point Lookout, Maryland, transferred to Elmira Prison, NY August 12, 1864	Oath of Allegiance June 16, 1865
Brandt, William Private	26	September 13, 1862, Richmond, Virginia	Co. E, 1st Battalion Maryland Infantry	July 15, 1864, Leesburg, Virginia	Old Capital Prison, Washington, D. C. Transferred to Elmira Prison, NY August 12, 1864	Oath of Allegiance February 13, 1865. Early Release per Lincoln's Proclamation, 12/8/1863.
Brannan, R. H. Private	Unk	Unknown	Co. H, 6th Florida Infantry	June 3, 1864, Gaines Mill, Cold Harbor, Virginia	Point Lookout, Maryland, transferred to Elmira Prison, NY July 17, 1864	Died November 28, 1864 of Chronic Diarrhea, Grave No. 984
Brannen, John T. Private	Unk	May 15, 1862, Savannah, Georgia	Co. B, 7th Georgia Cavalry	June 11, 1864, Trevilian Station, Louisa Court House, Virginia	Point Lookout, Maryland, transferred to Elmira Prison, NY July 25, 1864	Exchanged March 2, 1865 at Akins Landing on the James River, Virginia
Brannon, Fletcher J. Private	Unk	March 4, 1862, Hamilton, Georgia	Co. K, 35th Georgia Infantry	May 27, 1864, Hanover Junction, Virginia	Point Lookout, Maryland, transferred to Elmira Prison, NY July 12, 1864	Died March 30, 1865 of Chronic Diarrhea, Grave No. 2520
Branson, Absalom Private	19	June 16, 1861, Washington County, Virginia	Co. J, 48th Virginia Infantry	May 12, 1864, Near Spotsylvania Court House, Virginia	Point Lookout, Maryland, transferred to Elmira Prison, NY August 6, 1864	Exchanged March 2, 1865 at Akins Landing on the James River, Virginia
Brantley, George W. Private	26	June 10, 1861, Wilmington, North Carolina	Co. F, 3rd North Carolina Infantry	May 12, 1864, Spotsylvania Court House, Virginia	Point Lookout, Maryland, transferred to Elmira Prison, NY July 17, 1864	Exchanged March 2, 1865 at Akins Landing on the James River, Virginia

Name & Rank	Age	Enlisted	Regiment and State	Where Captured	Prison	Remarks
Brantley, James D. Sergeant	Unk	August 26, 1861, Waresboro, Georgia	Co. F, 26th Georgia Infantry	May 10, 1864, Spotsylvania, Virginia	Old Capital Prison, Washington, DC, transferred to Elmira Prison, NY, December 17, 1864	Exchanged February 13, 1865 at Boulware's Wharf on the James River, Virginia
Brantley, Redmen Private	Unk	Unknown	Co. E, 32nd North Carolina Infantry	November 7, 1863, Kelly Ford, Virginia	Old Capital Prison, Washington, DC, transferred to Elmira Prison, NY, December 17, 1864	Exchanged February 13, 1865 at Boulware's Wharf on the James River, Virginia
Brantley, William Private	Unk	March 4, 1862, Wrightsville, Georgia	Co. F, 14th Georgia Infantry	May 6, 1864, Wilderness, Virginia	Point Lookout, Maryland, transferred to Elmira Prison, NY August 17, 1864	Exchanged February 13, 1865 at Boulware's wharf on the James River, Virginia
Branton, Henry H. Private	21	July 15, 1862, Raleigh, North Carolina	Co. I, 3rd North Carolina Infantry	May 12, 1864, Near Spotsylvania Court House, Virginia	Point Lookout, Maryland, transferred to Elmira Prison, NY August 12, 1864	Died November 24, 1864 of Chronic Diarrhea, Grave No. 911
Branton, John Private	50	September 1, 1862, Richmond, Virginia	Co. E, 59th Virginia Infantry	June 18, 1864, Petersburg, Virginia	Point Lookout Prison Camp, Maryland. Transferred to Elmira Prison, July 26, 1864	Died February 2, 1865 of Chronic Diarrhea, Grave No. 1758
Braswell, Bullock Private	18	May 1, 1862, Edgecombe County, North Carolina	Co. B, 33rd North Carolina Infantry	July 14, 1863, Falling Waters, Maryland	Point Lookout, Maryland, transferred to Elmira Prison, NY August 18, 1864	Exchanged March 10, 1865 at Boulware's Wharf on the James River, Virginia
Braswell, James A. Corporal	Unk	March 4, 1862, Millen County, Georgia	Co. D, 51st Georgia Infantry	June 3, 1864, Gaines Farm, Cold Harbor, Virginia	Point Lookout, Maryland, transferred to Elmira Prison, NY July 17,1864	Exchanged March 2, 1865 at Akins Landing on the James River, Virginia
Braswell, Joel H. Private	Unk	August 11, 1861, Gwinnett, Georgia	Co. B, 16th Georgia Infantry	August 16, 1864, Front Royal, Virginia	Point Lookout, Maryland, transferred to Elmira Prison, NY August 29, 1864	Exchanged March 14, 1865 at Boulware's Wharf on the James River, Virginia

Name & Rank	Age	Enlisted	Regiment and State	Where Captured	Prison	Remarks
Braswell, Samuel D. Corporal	19	March 1, 1861, Nashville, North Carolina	Co. H, 32nd North Carolina Infantry	May 10, 1864, Spotsylvania, Virginia	Point Lookout, Maryland, transferred to Elmira Prison, NY August 6, 1864	Oath of Allegiance June 27, 1865
Braswell, Sydney Private	18	October 10, 1862, Nashville, North Carolina	Co. H, 32nd North Carolina Infantry	May 10, 1864, Wilderness, Virginia	Point Lookout, Maryland, transferred to Elmira Prison, NY August 6, 1864	Died March 9, 1865 of Chronic Diarrhea, Grave No. 2367
Brawley, J. B. Sergeant	Unk	February 1, 1863, Spartanburg, South Carolina	Co. K, Holcombes Legion South Carolina Infantry	May 7, 1864, Stony Creek, Virginia	Point Lookout, Maryland, transferred to Elmira Prison, NY August 17, 1864	Exchanged October 29, 1864, at Venus Point, Savannah River, GA.
Brawner, H. M. Private	Unk	June 11, 1861, Camp McDonald, Georgia	Co. G, 18th Georgia Infantry	June 1, 1864, Cold Harbor, Virginia	Point Lookout, Maryland, transferred to Elmira Prison, NY July 17, 1864	Oath of Allegiance June 21, 1865
Bray, D. C. K. Private	28	March 5, 1862 Wilmington, North Carolina	Co. D, 1st Battalion, 3rd North Carolina Heavy Artillery	January 15, 1865, Fort Fisher, North Carolina	February 1, 1865, Elmira Prison Camp, New York	Exchanged February 20, 1865. Died March 6, 1865 of Chronic Diarrhea at CSA Hospital, Richmond, VA.
Bray, James C. Private	Unk	August 24, 1861, Hartwell, Hart County, Georgia	Co. B, 16th Georgia Infantry	August 16, 1864, Front Royal, Virginia	Point Lookout, Maryland, transferred to Elmira Prison, NY August 29, 1864	Oath of Allegiance June 27, 1865
Bray, James H. Private	Unk	June 29, 1861, Pittsylvania, Virginia	Co. J, 21st Virginia Infantry	July 9, 1864, Near Harper's Ferry, Virginia	Old Capital Prison, Washington, DC, transferred to Elmira Prison, NY, July 23, 1864	Oath of Allegiance May 13, 1865
Bray, J. R. Private	Unk	April 1, 1864, Ashland, Virginia	Co. E, 5th Virginia Cavalry	May 11, 1864, Yellow Tavern, Hanover County, Virginia	Point Lookout, Maryland, transferred to Elmira Prison, NY August 17, 1864	Died September 21, 1864 of Chronic Diarrhea, Grave No. 334

Name & Rank	Age	Enlisted	Regiment and State	Where Captured	Prison	Remarks
Bray, John W. Private	21	July 1, 1862, Camp Holmes, North Carolina	Co. E, 30th North Carolina Infantry	May 8, 1864, Wilderness, Virginia	Point Lookout, Maryland, transferred to Elmira Prison, NY July 25, 1864	Oath of Allegiance May 29, 1865
Bray, Robert F. Private	25	August 2, 1861, Dobson, Surrey County, North Carolina	Co. B, 2nd Battalion North Carolina Infantry	July 13, 1864, Near Washington, DC,	Old Capital Prison, Washington, DC, transferred to Elmira Prison, NY, July 23, 1864	Exchanged March 2, 1865 at Akins Landing on the James River, Virginia
Braziel, Richard V. Private	23	August 20, 1861, Ridgeway, South Carolina	Co. C, 12th South Carolina Infantry	July 28, 1864, Deep Bottom, Virginia. Gunshot Wound Left Thigh.	November 11, 1864, Old Capital Prison, Washington, DC. February 4, 1865 Elmira, Prison Camp, NY	Exchanged February 13, 1865 at Boulware's wharf on the James River, Virginia
Breard, D. A. Private	Unk	August 14, 1861, Camp Magruder, Louisiana	Co. F, 2nd Louisiana Infantry	May 12, 1864, Spotsylvania Court House, Virginia	Point Lookout, Maryland, transferred to Elmira Prison, NY August 17, 1864	Exchanged February 25, 1865 at Boulware's or Cox Wharf on the James River, Virginia
Breckenridge, Joseph F. Private	Unk	May 29, 1863, Macon County, Alabama	Co. J, 61st Alabama Infantry	May 12, 1864, Near Spotsylvania Court House, Virginia	Point Lookout, Maryland, transferred to Elmira Prison, NY August 17, 1864	Died March 23, 1865 of Variola (Smallpox), Grave No. 1671
Bredhause, James K. Private	Unk	Unknown	Co. G, 27th Virginia Cavalry	July 16, 1864, Loudoun County, Virginia	Old Capital Prison, Washington, DC, transferred to Elmira Prison, NY, July 23, 1864	Oath of Allegiance May 19, 1865
Breece, James Corporal	29	July 14, 1862, Camp Holmes, North Carolina	Co. E, 8th North Carolina Infantry	May 31, 1864, Cold Harbor, Virginia	Point Lookout, Maryland, transferred to Elmira Prison, NY July 11, 1864	Oath of Allegiance June 12, 1865
Breeden, James Private	Unk	February 18, 1864, Greenville, Tennessee	Co. B, 1st Tennessee Infantry	May 6, 1864, Wilderness, Virginia	Point Lookout, Maryland, transferred to Elmira Prison, NY July 23, 1864	Died, November 14, 1864 of Chronic Diarrhea, Grave No. 805.

Name & Rank	Age	Enlisted	Regiment and State	Where Captured	Prison	Remarks
Breeden, Thomas F. Private	Unk	February 1, 1864, Charleston, South Carolina	Co. D, 34th, Virginia Infantry	June 15, 1864, Near Petersburg, Virginia	Point Lookout, Maryland, transferred to Elmira Prison, NY July 17,1864	Oath of Allegiance July 3, 1865
Breeding, James L. Private	Unk	Unknown	Co. I, 50th Virginia Infantry	May 12, 1864, Spotsylvania Court House, Virginia	Point Lookout, Maryland, transferred to Elmira Prison, NY August 2, 1864	Died November 26, 1864 of Pneumonia, Grave No. 906
Breedlove, Willis M. Private	22	May 20, 1861, Louisburg, North Carolina	Co. K, 32nd North Carolina Infantry	May 10, 1864, Spotsylvania, Virginia	Point Lookout, Maryland, transferred to Elmira Prison, NY August 6, 1864	Oath of Allegiance June 30, 1865
Breen, R. F. Private	35	January 21, 1864, Eutaw, Alabama	Co. C, 1st Battalion Alabama Artillery	August 23, 1864, Fort Morgan, Alabama	New Orleans, Louisiana transferred to Elmira December 4, 1864.	Oath of Allegiance June 21, 1865
Brenan, Michael Firemen	Unk	Unknown	Confederate States Navy	May 5, 1864, Albemarle Sound on Steamer CSS Bombshell	Point Lookout, Maryland, transferred to Elmira Prison, NY August 17, 1864	Oath of Allegiance June 19, 1865
Brenner, John E. Private	22	April 22, 1861, Leesburg, Virginia	Co. C, 17th Virginia Infantry	July 21, 1863, Manassas Gap, Virginia	Point Lookout, Maryland, transferred to Elmira Prison, NY August 18, 1864	Exchanged March 10, 1865 at Boulware's Wharf on the James River, Virginia
Brewer, Martin Private	22	July 15, 1862, County, North Carolina	Co. F, 3rd North Carolina Infantry	May 12, 1864, Near Spotsylvania Court House, Virginia	Point Lookout Prison, Maryland. Transferred to Elmira Prison Camp New York August 14, 1864.	Oath of Allegiance June 19, 1865
Brewer, Morean Private	Unk	April 10, 1864, Fort Morgan, Alabama	Co. A, Jackson's 1st Regiment, Tennessee Heavy Artillery	August 23, 1864, Fort Morgan, Alabama	New Orleans, Louisiana transferred to Elmira December 4, 1864.	Oath of Allegiance April 11, 1865

Name & Rank	Age	Enlisted	Regiment and State	Where Captured	Prison	Remarks
Brewer, Samuel B. Private	Unk	June 12, 1861, Tuskegee, Macon County, Alabama	Co. B, 12th Alabama Infantry	May 12, 1864, Spotsylvania Court House, Virginia	Point Lookout, Maryland, transferred to Elmira Prison, NY August 6, 1864	Oath of Allegiance June 21, 1865
Brewer, Thomas Private	25	May 10, 1862, Wadesboro, North Carolina	Co. K, 26th North Carolina Infantry	May 12, 1864, Spotsylvania Court House, Virginia	Point Lookout, Maryland, transferred to Elmira Prison, NY July 30, 1864	Oath of Allegiance June 23, 1865
Brewer, Wiley Private	Unk	October 26, 1863, Camp Homes, Near Raleigh, North Carolina	Co. A, 3rd North Carolina Infantry	May 12, 1864, Near Spotsylvania Court House, Virginia	Point Lookout Prison, Maryland. Transferred to Elmira Prison Camp New York August 14, 1864.	Died November 15, 1864 of Chronic Diarrhea, Grave No. 806
Brewer, William J. Private	Unk	March 16, 1862, Autauga, Alabama	Co. B, 59th Alabama Infantry	June 17, 1864, Petersburg, Virginia	Point Lookout, Maryland, transferred to Elmira Prison, NY July 30, 1864	Exchanged March 14, 1865 at Boulware's Wharf on the James River, Virginia
Brewster, Benjamin C. M. Private	Unk	June 4, 1861, Cropwell, St. Clair County, Alabama	Co. F, 10th Alabama Infantry	May 12, 1864, Spotsylvania Court House, Virginia	Point Lookout, Maryland, transferred to Elmira Prison, NY August 17, 1864	Transferred For Exchange October 11, 1864 to Point Lookout Prison, MD. Died. Unknown Date and Cause on U. S. Steamer Northern Light.
Brewster, William D. Private	Unk	Unknown	Co. D, 6th Georgia Infantry	July 16, 1863, James Island, South Carolina	Point Lookout, Maryland, transferred to Elmira Prison, NY August 18, 1864	Died October 17, 1864 of Typhoid-Pneumonia, Grave No. 548
Brewster, Young Private	Unk	May 9, 1861, Camp Walker, New Orleans, Louisiana	Co. E, 2nd Louisiana Infantry	May 12, 1864, Spotsylvania, Virginia	Point Lookout, Maryland, transferred to Elmira Prison, NY August 17, 1864	Exchanged February 25, 1865 at Boulware's or Cox Wharf on the James River, Virginia

Name & Rank	Age	Enlisted	Regiment and State	Where Captured	Prison	Remarks
Briant, Andrew Bachus Private	21	August 13, 1861, New Orleans, Louisiana	Co. B, 7th Louisiana Infantry	May 11, 1864, Near Spotsylvania Court House, Virginia	Point Lookout, Maryland, transferred to Elmira Prison, NY August 17, 1864	Exchanged February 13, 1865 at Doulware's wharf on the James River, Virginia
Bricker, Abner Private	Unk	April 18, 1861, Harrisonburg, Virginia	Co. D, 10th Virginia Infantry	May 12, 1864, Spotsylvania Court House, Virginia	Point Lookout, Maryland, transferred to Elmira Prison, NY August 2, 1864	Oath of Allegiance June 19, 1865
Bricker, George W. Private	Unk	June 25, 1861, Winchester, Virginia	Co. D, 10th Virginia Infantry	May 12, 1864, Spotsylvania Court House, Virginia	Point Lookout, Maryland, transferred to Elmira Prison, NY August 2, 1864	Oath of Allegiance June 21, 1865
Brickey, John Private	Unk	Unknown	Co. E, 22nd Virginia Infantry	July 16, 1864, Poolesville, Maryland	Old Capital Prison, Washington, DC, transferred to Elmira Prison, NY, July 23, 1864	Oath of Allegiance September 11, 1865
Brickett, Joseph H. Sergeant	Unk	April 11, 1862, Coles Island, South Carolina	Co. H, 25th South Carolina Infantry	January 15, 1865, Fort Fisher, North Carolina	Elmira Prison Camp, New York, January 30, 1865	Died of Chronic Diarrhea, June 15, 1865. Grave No. 2880
Bridge, Joseph S. Private	21	May 27, 1861, Staunton, Virginia	Co. D, 25th Virginia Infantry	May 12, 1864, Spotsylvania Court House, Virginia	Point Lookout, Maryland, transferred to Elmira Prison, NY August 2, 1864	Oath of Allegiance June 27, 1865
Bridgeman, Lewis J. Private	Unk	Unknown	Co. D, 36th Regiment, 2nd North Carolina Artillery	January 15, 1865, Fort Fisher, North Carolina. Wounded.	February 1, 1865, Elmira Prison Camp, New York	Oath of Allegiance July 7, 1865
Bridgeman, Lorenzo D. Private	Unk	January 1, 1862, Smyth County, Virginia	Co. J, 23rd Battalion Virginia Infantry	July 9, 1864, Near Harper's Ferry, Virginia	Old Capital Prison, Washington, DC, transferred to Elmira Prison, NY, July 23, 1864	Exchanged February 13, 1865 at Boulware's wharf on the James River, Virginia

Name & Rank	Age	Enlisted	Regiment and State	Where Captured	Prison	Remarks
Bridgers, John C. Private	18	February 7, 1864, Fort Holmes, Near Raleigh, North Carolina	Co. E, 40th Regiment, 3rd North Carolina Heavy Artillery	January 15, 1865, Fort Fisher, North Carolina	February 1, 1865, Elmira Prison Camp, New York	Exchanged March 14, 1865 at Boulware's Wharf on the James River, Virginia
Bridgers, John E. Corporal	Unk	July 8, 1861, Griffin, Georgia	Co. E, 13th Georgia Infantry	August 12, 1864, Newtown, Virginia	Point Lookout, Maryland, transferred to Elmira Prison, NY August 29, 1864	Oath of Allegiance June 27, 1865
Bridgers, Lemuel H. Sergeant	21	May 1, 1862, South Mills, North Carolina	Co. L, 32nd North Carolina Infantry	May 10, 1864, Spotsylvania, Virginia	Point Lookout, Maryland, transferred to Elmira Prison, NY August 6, 1864	Oath of Allegiance June 27, 1865
Bridges, Daniel E. Private	17	May 1, 1862, South Mills, North Carolina	Co. D, 32nd North Carolina Infantry	May 10, 1864, Spotsylvania, Virginia	Point Lookout, Maryland, transferred to Elmira Prison, NY August 6, 1864	Oath of Allegiance June 27, 1865
Bridges, Hosea W. Private	20	August 14, 1861, Newton, North Carolina	Co. E, 32nd North Carolina Infantry	May 10, 1864, Spotsylvania, Virginia	Point Lookout, Maryland, transferred to Elmira Prison, NY August 6, 1864	Exchanged October 29, 1864, at Venus Point, Savannah River, GA.
Bridges, John W. Private	23	June 20, 1861, Yorktown, Virginia	Co. K, 6th Georgia Infantry	August 19, 1864, Weldon Railroad, Virginia. Gunshot Wound Left Leg. Leg Amputated.	Old Capital Prison, Washington D. C. Transferred to Elmira Prison, NY May 12, 1865.	Oath of Allegiance June 14, 1865
Bridges, William Private	15	September 2, 1861, Rutherford County, North Carolina	Co. B, 34th North Carolina Infantry	June 16, 1864, Petersburg, Virginia	Point Lookout, Maryland, transferred to Elmira Prison, NY July 25, 1864	Oath of Allegiance July 3, 1865
Bridgewater, James C. Private	Unk	Unknown	Co. B, Hood's Battalion, Virginia Reserve Infantry	June 15, 1864, Petersburg, Virginia	Point Lookout, Maryland, transferred to Elmira Prison, NY July 30, 1864	Exchanged March 14, 1865 at Boulware's Wharf on the James River, Virginia

Name & Rank	Age	Enlisted	Regiment and State	Where Captured	Prison	Remarks
Briggs, Daniel, Private	32	May 9, 1861, Camp Walker, New Orleans, Louisiana	Co. H, 2nd Louisiana Infantry	May 12, 1864, Spotsylvania Court House, Virginia	Point Lookout, Maryland, transferred to Elmira Prison, NY August 17, 1864	Exchanged February 13, 1865 at Boulware's wharf on the James River, Virginia
Briggs, John, Private	18	July 24, 1862, Lumberton, North Carolina	Co. D, 18th North Carolina Infantry	May 12, 1864, Spotsylvania, Virginia	Old Capital Prison, Washington, DC, transferred to Elmira Prison, NY, July 23, 1864	Exchanged October 29, 1864, at Venus Point, Savannah River, GA.
Briggs, John W., Corporal	23	March 15, 1862, Gaston County, North Carolina	Co. A, 49th North Carolina Infantry	June 9, 1864, Chickahominy Swamp, Cold Harbor, Virginia	Old Capital Prison, Washington, DC, transferred to Elmira Prison, NY, July 23, 1864	Oath of Allegiance September 19, 1864
Briggs, Rufus, Private	21	March 13, 1863, Knoxville, Tennessee	Co. F, 63rd Tennessee Infantry	June 17, 1864, Petersburg, Virginia	Point Lookout, Maryland, transferred to Elmira Prison, NY July 30, 1864	Exchanged February 25, 1865 at Boulware's or Cox Wharf on the James River, Virginia
Bright, Andrew J., Private	Unk	January 10, 1862, Columbia, South Carolina	Co. C, 22nd South Carolina Infantry	July 30, 1864, Petersburg, Virginia	Point Lookout, Maryland, transferred to Elmira Prison, NY August 12, 1864	Oath of Allegiance July 3, 1865
Bright, Cornelius Q., Private	30	July 15, 1862, Raleigh, Carolina	Co. G, 1st North Carolina Infantry	May 12, 1864, Spotsylvania Court House, Virginia	Point Lookout, Maryland, transferred to Elmira Prison, NY August 6, 1864	Oath of Allegiance June 12, 1865
Bright, Jesse T., Private	Unk	March 27, 1862, Ocean View, Virginia	Co. C, 15th Virginia Cavalry	May 11, 1864, Near Ashland, Virginia	Point Lookout, Maryland, transferred to Elmira Prison, NY August 17, 1864	Oath of Allegiance June 19, 1865
Bright, John, Private	Unk	September 19, 1863, Swift Creek, North Carolina	Co. F, 67th North Carolina Infantry	June 1, 1864, Near Newbern, North Carolina	Point Lookout, Maryland, transferred to Elmira Prison, NY July 25, 1864	Exchanged February 13, 1865 at Boulware's wharf on the James River, Virginia

Name & Rank	Age	Enlisted	Regiment and State	Where Captured	Prison	Remarks
Bright, John W. Private	Unk	April 30, 1864, Lewisburg, Virginia	Co. A, 26th Battalion, Virginia Infantry	June 3, 1864, Gaines Mill, Cold Harbor, Virginia	Transferred From Point Lookout Prison, MD, July 12, 1864. Train Never Arrived at Elmira Prison Camp, NY.	Died July 15, 1864 in Train Wreck at Shohola, Pennsylvania
Bright, Jonathan Private	19	September 17, 1861, Camden, North Carolina	Co. J, 8th North Carolina Infantry	May 31, 1864, Cold Harbor, Virginia	Point Lookout, Maryland, transferred to Elmira Prison, NY July 12,1864	Died September 12, 1864 of Chronic Bronchitis, Grave No. 250
Bright, Robert B. Private	Unk	December 20, 1863, Greenville, South Carolina	Co. H, 22nd South Carolina Infantry	July 30, 1864, Petersburg, Virginia	Point Lookout, Maryland, transferred to Elmira Prison, NY August 12, 1864	Died September 13, 1864 of Typhoid Fever, Grave No. 262
Bright, Samuel S. Private	25	December 26, 1861, Bladen County, North Carolina	Co. E, 36th Regiment, 2nd North Carolina Artillery	January 15, 1865, Fort Fisher, North Carolina. Wounded.	February 1, 1865, Elmira Prison Camp, New York	Died March 2, 1865 of Diarrhea, Grave No. 2008
Bright, William I. Private	Unk	January 10, 1862, Columbia, South Carolina	Co. C, 22nd South Carolina Infantry	July 30, 1864, Petersburg, Virginia	Point Lookout, Maryland, transferred to Elmira Prison, NY August 12, 1864	Died September 23, 1864 of Pneumonia, Grave No. 469
Brightwell, Charles W. Private	Unk	October 7, 1863, Camp Lee, Virginia	Co. D, 18th Virginia Infantry	June 3, 1864, Gaines Mill, Cold Harbor, Virginia	Point Lookout, Maryland, transferred to Elmira Prison, NY July 17,1864	Exchanged October 29, 1864 at Venus Point, Savannah River, GA.
Brigman, John Private	44	September 16, 1863, Union County, North Carolina	Co. E, 30th North Carolina Infantry	May 31, 1864, Old Church, Virginia	Point Lookout, Maryland, transferred to Elmira Prison, NY July 8, 1864	Transferred for Exchange 10/11/64. Died 10/24/64 of Chronic Diarrhea at Point Lookout, MD.
Brigman, Robert Private	Unk	January 16, 1862, Chesterfield, South Carolina	Co. B, 26th South Carolina Infantry	July 30, 1864, Petersburg, Virginia	Point Lookout, Maryland, transferred to Elmira Prison, NY August 12, 1864	Exchanged October 29, 1864 at Venus Point, Savannah River, GA.

Name & Rank	Age	Enlisted	Regiment and State	Where Captured	Prison	Remarks
Brim, E. Oscar Private	26	September 1, 1862, Bovina, Mississippi	Co. H, 21st Mississippi Infantry	May 20, 1864, Wilderness, Virginia	Point Lookout, Maryland, transferred to Elmira Prison, NY July 8, 1864	Oath of Allegiance May 13, 1865
Brimm, Richard Private	18	September 15, 1863, Richmond, Virginia	Co. G, 45th North Carolina Infantry	May 10, 1864, Spotsylvania Court House, Virginia	Point Lookout, Maryland, transferred to Elmira Prison, NY August 6, 1864	Died November 11, 1864 of Gastritis, Grave No. 793
Brinegar, M. H. Private	Unk	April 1, 1864, Mocksville, North Carolina	Co. H, 5th North Carolina Cavalry	May 31, 1864, Hanover Court House, Virginia	Point Lookout, Maryland, transferred to Elmira Prison, NY July 17, 1864	Died August 24, 1864 of Chronic Diarrhea, Grave No. 39
Brinkley, A. S. Private	Unk	January 31, 1864, Bath, Virginia	Co. G, 5th Virginia Cavalry	May 11, 1864, Yellow Tavern, Hanover County, Virginia	Point Lookout, Maryland, transferred to Elmira Prison, NY August 17, 1864	Oath of Allegiance June 19, 1865
Brinkley, Frederick K. Private	21	June 23, 1861, Nausemond, Virginia	Co. J, 41st Virginia Infantry	October 27, 1864, Petersburg, Virginia. Cannon Ball Contusion Right Hip, Severe.	Old Capital Prison, Washington, DC, transferred to Elmira Prison, NY, December 17, 1864	Exchanged March 14, 1865 at Boulware's Wharf on the James River, Virginia
Brinkley, Jethro K. Private	32	August 29, 1861, Gates County, North Carolina	Co. E, 33rd North Carolina Infantry	May 6, 1864, Wilderness, Virginia	Point Lookout, Maryland, transferred to Elmira Prison, NY August 14, 1864	Died November 26, 1864 of Acute Pleuritis, Grave No. 908. Name Fetherd Brinkley on Headstone.
Brinkley, Thomas H. Private	28	July 1, 1863, Raleigh, North Carolina	Co. I, 1st North Carolina Infantry	May 12, 1864, Spotsylvania Court House, Virginia	Point Lookout, Maryland, transferred to Elmira Prison, NY August 6, 1864	Oath of Allegiance June 12, 1865
Brinkley, William Private	26	March 31, 1862, Pfafftown, North Carolina	Co. J, 33rd North Carolina Infantry	May 6, 1864, Wilderness, Virginia	Point Lookout, Maryland, transferred to Elmira Prison, NY August 14, 1864	Died September 28, 1864 of Chronic Diarrhea, Grave No. 396

Name & Rank	Age	Enlisted	Regiment and State	Where Captured	Prison	Remarks
Brinkley, William S. Private	32	July 15, 1862, Raleigh, North Carolina	Co. I, 3rd North Carolina Infantry	May 12, 1864, Near Spotsylvania Court House, Virginia	Point Lookout, Maryland, transferred to Elmira Prison, NY August 12, 1864	Exchanged February 13, 1865 at Boulware's wharf on the James River, Virginia
Brinson, Calvin G. Corporal	25	May 29, 1861, Corinth, Mississippi	Co. B, 16th Mississippi Infantry	May 13, 1864, Spotsylvania Court House, Virginia	Old Capital Prison, Washington, DC transferred to Elmira Prison, NY August 27, 1864	Exchanged February 13, 1865 at Boulware's Wharf on the James River, Virginia
Brinson, Field S. Private	19	June 17, 1861, Duplin County, North Carolina	Co. B, 3rd North Carolina Infantry	May 12, 1864, Near Spotsylvania Court House, Virginia	Point Lookout Prison, Maryland. Transferred to Elmira Prison Camp New York August 14, 1864.	Died March 23, 1865 of Pneumonia, Grave No. 1519.
Brinson, G. W. Private	Unk	July 15, 1862, Raleigh, North Carolina	Co. E, 3rd North Carolina Infantry	May 12, 1864, Near Spotsylvania Court House, Virginia	Point Lookout, Maryland, transferred to Elmira Prison, NY August 14, 1864	Exchanged February 20, 1865 at Boulware's or Cox Wharf on the James River, Virginia
Brinson, Jasper S. Sergeant	Unk	May 15, 1862, Savannah, Georgia	Co. B, 7th Georgia Cavalry	June 11, 1864, Trevilian Station, Louisa Court House, Virginia	Point Lookout, Maryland, transferred to Elmira Prison, NY July 9, 1864	Died December 11, 1864 of Pneumonia, Grave No. 1049
Brinson, John E. Private	Unk	March 1, 1862, Charleston, South Carolina	Co. B, 7th Georgia Cavalry	June 11, 1864, Trevilian Station, Louisa Court House, Virginia	Point Lookout, Maryland, transferred to Elmira Prison, NY July 25, 1864	Oath of Allegiance June 21, 1865
Brinson, William G. Sergeant	Unk	July 8, 1862, Wilmington, North Carolina	Co. K, 10th Regiment, 1st North Carolina Artillery	January 15, 1865, Fort Fisher, North Carolina	Old Capital Prison, Washington, DC, transferred to Elmira Prison, January 30, 1865	Exchanged February 25, 1865 at Boulware's or Cox Wharf on the James River, Virginia

Name & Rank	Age	Enlisted	Regiment and State	Where Captured	Prison	Remarks
Brinson, William R. Private	Unk	August 3, 1861, Richmond, Virginia	Co. C, 1st North Carolina Infantry	May 20, 1864, Spotsylvania Court House, Virginia	Point Lookout, Maryland, transferred to Elmira, New York, July 6, 1864.	Oath of Allegiance May 15, 1865
Brinson, William T. Private	Unk	September 20, 1862, Charleston, South Carolina	Co. B, 7th Georgia Cavalry	June 11, 1864, Trevilian Station, Louisa Court House, Virginia	Point Lookout, Maryland, transferred to Elmira Prison, NY July 25, 1864	Exchanged March 2, 1865 at Akins Landing on the James River, Virginia
Brisclair, H. Private	Unk	Unknown	Co. F, 27th Mississippi Infantry	May 8, 1864, Wilderness, Virginia	Point Lookout, Maryland, transferred to Elmira Prison, NY August 14, 1864	Oath of Allegiance June 30, 1865
Briscoe, Lafayette F. Private	34	July 18, 1862, Camp Hill, Statesville, North Carolina	Co. E, 18th North Carolina Infantry	May 12, 1864, Spotsylvania Court House, Virginia	Point Lookout, Maryland, transferred to Elmira Prison, NY August 6, 1864	Oath of Allegiance June 19, 1865
Brissaw, James Private	Unk	May 4, 1864, Petersburg, Virginia	Co. A, 3rd Archer's Battalion, Virginia Reserves Infantry	June 9, 1864, Petersburg, Virginia	Point Lookout, Maryland, transferred to Elmira Prison, NY July 12, 1864	Transferred for Exchange October 11, 1864. No Further Information
Bristow, Daniel M. Private	22	April 6, 1862, Marlboro District, South Carolina	Co. F, 21st South Carolina Infantry	January 15, 1865, Fort Fisher, North Carolina	Elmira Prison Camp January 30, 1865	Died March 3, 1865 of Pneumonia, Grave No. 1998
Bristow, James A. Private	31	February 1, 1862, Rich Square, North Carolina	Co. F, 1st North Carolina Infantry	May 12, 1864, Spotsylvania, Virginia	Point Lookout Prison Camp, Maryland. Transferred to Elmira Prison Camp, NY, August 6, 1864	Died April 6, 1865, of Chronic Diarrhea, Grave No. 2653
Bristow, James T. Private	20	April 23, 1861, Gloucester Court House, Virginia	Co. B, 26th Virginia Infantry	June 15, 1864, Near Petersburg, Virginia	Point Lookout, Maryland, transferred to Elmira Prison, NY July 12, 1864	Died October 10, 1864 of Chronic Diarrhea, Grave No. 671
Bristow, Joseph A. Sergeant	Unk	July 18, 1861, Urbana, Virginia	Co. C, 24th Virginia Cavalry	July 28, 1864, Petersburg, Virginia	Point Lookout, Maryland, transferred to Elmira Prison, NY August 12, 1864	Exchanged February 25, 1865 at Boulware's or Cox Wharf on the James River, Virginia

Name & Rank	Age	Enlisted	Regiment and State	Where Captured	Prison	Remarks
Bristow, Robert N. Private	29	April 3, 1862, Bennettsville, South Carolina	Co. F, 21st South Carolina Infantry	January 15, 1865, Fort Fisher, North Carolina	Elmira Prison Camp January 30, 1865	Died March 18, 1865 of Typhoid Fever, Grave No. 1719
Brit, Thomas Private	Unk	Unknown	Co. K, 12th Georgia Infantry	August 20, 1864, Front Royal, Virginia	Old Capital Prison, Washington, DC transferred to Elmira Prison, NY August 27, 1864	Oath of Allegiance May 19, 1865
Britnal, W. W. Private	Unk	March 16, 1862, Autauga, Alabama	Co. B, 59th Alabama Infantry	June 17, 1864, Petersburg, Virginia	Point Lookout, Maryland, transferred to Elmira Prison, NY July 30, 1864	Oath of Allegiance July 7, 1865
Britt, Caswell Private	Unk	May 9, 1863, Lumberton, North Carolina	Co. E, 51st North Carolina Infantry	June 1, 1864, Cold Harbor, Virginia	Point Lookout, Maryland, transferred to Elmira Prison, NY July 17,1864	Oath of Allegiance July 3, 1865
Britt, Ellis Corporal	22	August 9, 1861, Lumberton, North Carolina	Co. D, 37th North Carolina Infantry	July 29, 1864, Petersburg, Virginia	Point Lookout, Maryland, transferred to Elmira Prison, NY August 12, 1864	Died September 28, 1864 of Chronic Diarrhea, Grave No. 428
Britt, George W. Corporal	31	January 13, 1862, Newbern, North Carolina	Co. F, 36th Regiment, 2nd North Carolina Artillery	January 15, 1865, Fort Fisher, North Carolina. Wounded.	February 1, 1865, Elmira Prison Camp, New York	Oath of Allegiance June 12, 1865
Britt, Isham N. Private	17	May 18, 1861, Lumberton, North Carolina	Co. B, 18th North Carolina Infantry	May 6, 1864, Wilderness, Virginia	Point Lookout, Maryland, transferred to Elmira Prison, NY August 14, 1864	Oath of Allegiance June 14, 1865
Britt, Jonathan M. Private	33	July 15, 1862, Johnston County, North Carolina	Co. F, 24th North Carolina Infantry	June 17, 1864, Near Petersburg, Virginia	Point Lookout, Maryland, transferred to Elmira Prison, NY July 30, 1864	Died July 7, 1865 of General Debility, Grave No. 2840. Name J. A. Butts on Headstone.
Britt, Lemuel H. Private	Unk	November 29, 1863, Goldsboro, North Carolina	Co. F, 10th Regiment 1st North Carolina Artillery	January 15, 1865, Fort Fisher, North Carolina	Elmira Prison Camp January 30, 1865	Oath of Allegiance June 23, 1865

Name & Rank	Age	Enlisted	Regiment and State	Where Captured	Prison	Remarks
Britt, William H. Private	24	May 8, 1862, Green County, North Carolina	Co. E, 61st North Carolina Infantry	August 27, 1863, Battery Wagner, Morris Island, South Carolina	Point Lookout, Maryland, transferred to Elmira Prison, NY August 18, 1864	Exchanged March 10, 1865 at Boulware's Wharf on the James River, Virginia
Brittain, William J. Private	Unk	September 5, 1861, Athens, Georgia	Co. D, Cobb's Legion Georgia	August 16, 1864, Front Royal, Virginia	Point Lookout, Maryland, transferred to Elmira Prison, NY August 29, 1864	Died March 2, 1865 of Pneumonia, Grave No. 2019. Headstone has Britton.
Brittingham, W. F. Gunner Sailor	Unk	Unknown	Confederate States Navy	April 6, 1865, Sailor's Creek, Virginia	Old Capital Prison, Washington D. C. Transferred to Elmira Prison, NY May 2, 1865.	Oath of Allegiance June 23, 1865
Britton, John F. Private	Unk	June 11, 1863, James Island, South Carolina	Co. A, 27th South Carolina Infantry	June 24, 1864, Near Petersburg, Virginia	Point Lookout, Maryland, transferred to Elmira Prison, NY August 18, 1864	Exchanged October 29, 1864, at Venus Point, Savannah River, GA.
Britton, Noah J. Private	30	February 1, 1862, Rich Square, North Carolina	Co. F, 1st North Carolina Infantry	May 12, 1864, Spotsylvania Court House, Virginia	Point Lookout, Maryland, transferred to Elmira Prison, NY August 6, 1864	Oath of Allegiance May 29, 1865
Britton, Thomas G. Private	19	February 22, 1863, Georgetown, South Carolina	Co. I, 4th South Carolina Cavalry	May 28, 1864, Old Church, Virginia. Gunshot Wound Left Hip.	Old Capital Prison, Washington, DC, transferred to Elmira Prison, NY, July 25, 1864	Oath of Allegiance June 30, 1865
Broadway, David T. Private	25	March 6, 1862, Davidson County, North Carolina	Co. A, 54th North Carolina Infantry	May 16, 1864, Near Drury's Bluff, Virginia	Point Lookout, Maryland, transferred to Elmira Prison, NY August 17, 1864	Died February 6, 1865 of Intussusception (Twisting of the of the Bowel Causing an Obstruction), Grave No. 1914
Broadwell, Ruffin Private	39	February 4, 1863, Wake County, North Carolina	Co. K, 12th North Carolina Infantry	May 12, 1864, Near Spotsylvania Court House, Virginia	Point Lookout, Maryland, transferred to Elmira Prison, NY August 14, 1864	Died November 10, 1864 of Pneumonia, Grave No. 833

Name & Rank	Age	Enlisted	Regiment and State	Where Captured	Prison	Remarks
Brock, Benjamin F. Corporal	20	June 22, 1861, Henry County, Virginia	Co. F, 42nd Virginia Infantry	May 12, 1864, Near Spotsylvania Court House, Virginia	Point Lookout, Maryland, transferred to Elmira Prison, NY August 6, 1864	Exchanged October 29, 1864 at Venus Point, Savannah River, GA.
Brock, George W. Private	Unk	December 15, 1863, Mount Pleasant, South Carolina	Co. G, 27th South Carolina Infantry	June 24, 1864, Near Petersburg, Virginia	Point Lookout, Maryland, transferred to Elmira Prison, NY August 18, 1864	Exchanged October 29, 1864, at Venus Point, Savannah River, GA.
Brock, John R. Sergeant	Unk	August 24, 1861, Habersham County, Georgia	Co. H, 24th Georgia Infantry	June 3, 1864, Gaines Mill, Cold Harbor, Virginia	Point Lookout, Maryland, transferred to Elmira Prison, NY July 17,1864	Oath of Allegiance July 7, 1865
Brockwell, Benjamin Private	36	March 5, 1862, Orange County, North Carolina	Co. G, 28th North Carolina Infantry	May 12, 1864, Spotsylvania Court House, Virginia	Point Lookout, Maryland, transferred to Elmira Prison, NY August 12, 1864	Oath of Allegiance June 19, 1865
Brockwell, H. C. Civilian	Unk	Date Unknown, Chesterfield County, Virginia	Citizen of Virginia	May 6, 1864, Chesterfield County, Virginia	Point Lookout, Maryland, transferred to Elmira Prison, NY July 23, 1864	Exchanged October 29, 1864, at Venus Point, Savannah River, GA.
Brodnax, E. A. Private	Unk	May 4, 1864, Petersburg, Virginia	Co. B, 3rd Archer's Battalion, Virginia Reserves Infantry	June 9, 1864, Petersburg, Virginia	Point Lookout, Maryland, transferred to Elmira Prison, NY July 12, 1864	Exchanged October 29, 1864 at Venus Point, Savannah River, GA.
Brookes, David M. Private	23	April 22, 1864, Shelby, North Carolina	Co. E, 12th North Carolina Infantry	May 12, 1864, Spotsylvania Court House, Virginia	Point Lookout, Maryland, transferred to Elmira Prison, NY August 14, 1864	Exchanged February 20, 1865 at Boulware's or Cox Wharf on the James River, Virginia
Brooking, John W. Private	Unk	June 25, 1862, Gloucester Point, Virginia	Co. B, 26th Virginia Infantry	June 15, 1864, Near Petersburg, Virginia	Point Lookout, Maryland, transferred to Elmira Prison, NY July 12,1864	Oath of Allegiance June 28, 1865

Name & Rank	Age	Enlisted	Regiment and State	Where Captured	Prison	Remarks
Brooking, William C. Private	18	February 21, 1862, Gloucester Point, Virginia	Co. B, 26th Virginia Infantry	June 15, 1864, Near Petersburg, Virginia	Point Lookout, Maryland, transferred to Elmira Prison, NY July 12, 1864	Oath of Allegiance June 30, 1865
Brookman, G. Private	Unk	Unknown	Co. H, 5th Virginia Infantry	May 12, 1864, Spotsylvania Court House, Virginia	Point Lookout, Maryland, transferred to Elmira Prison, NY August 2, 1864	Oath of Allegiance June 27, 1865
Brooks, Andrew P. Private	23	July 20, 1861, Camp Pickens, Anderson District, South Carolina	Co. G, 1st South Carolina Infantry	July 14, 1863, Falling Waters, Maryland	Point Lookout, Maryland, transferred to Elmira Prison, NY August 18, 1864	Died June 15, 1865 of Chronic Diarrhea, Grave No. 2879
Brooks, Andrew T. Private	Unk	March 1, 1864, Williamsburg, Virginia	Co. G, 19th Virginia Cavalry	July 16, 1864, Loudoun County, Virginia	Old Capital Prison, Washington, DC, transferred to Elmira Prison, NY, July 23, 1864	Died January 31, 1865 of Chronic Diarrhea, Grave No. 1775
Brooks, Archibald Private	Unk	May 30, 1863, Columbus, Georgia	Co. F, 64th Georgia Infantry	August 16, 1864, New Market, Virginia	Old Capital Prison, Washington, DC transferred to Elmira Prison, NY August 27, 1864	Oath of Allegiance May 19, 1865
Brooks, Archibald G. Corporal	Unk	July 25, 1863, Dawson, Georgia	Co. H, 64th Georgia Infantry	June 17, 1864, Petersburg, Virginia	Point Lookout, Maryland, transferred to Elmira Prison, NY July 30, 1864	Died August 10, 1864 of Continued Fever, Grave No. 135
Brooks, David H. Private	Unk	April 29, 1862, Tunnel Hill, Georgia	Co. G, 11th Georgia Infantry	May 6, 1864, Wilderness, Virginia	Point Lookout, Maryland, transferred to Elmira Prison, NY August 14, 1864	Died April 10, 1865 of Pneumonia, Grave No. 2542
Brooks, E. P. Private	Unk	August 11, 1861, Gwinnett, Georgia	Co. H, 16th Georgia Infantry	August 16, 1864, Front Royal, Virginia	Point Lookout, Maryland, transferred to Elmira Prison, NY August 29, 1864	Exchanged March 14, 1865 at Boulware's Wharf on the James River, Virginia

Name & Rank	Age	Enlisted	Regiment and State	Where Captured	Prison	Remarks
Brooks, George W. Private	Unk	Unknown	Co. A, 49th Louisiana Infantry	March 25, 1865, Fort Steadman, Petersburg, Virginia	Old Capital Prison, Washington D. C. Transferred to Elmira Prison, NY May 2, 1865.	Transferred to Elmira Post Hospital July 13, 1865. No Additional Information Available.
Brooks, J. H. Private	Unk	Unknown	Co. G, 11th Georgia Infantry	Unknown	Unknown	Died April 10, 1865 of Unknown Disease, Grave No. 2663
Brooks, John Sergeant	Unk	Unknown	Co. D, 4th Virginia Cavalry	June 5, 1864, West Point, Virginia	Point Lookout, Maryland, transferred to Elmira Prison, NY July 8, 1864	Oath of Allegiance May 13, 1865
Brooks, John D. Sergeant	19	March 7, 1862, Wilmington, North Carolina	Co. H, 51st North Carolina Infantry	June 1, 1864, Cold Harbor, Virginia	Point Lookout, Maryland, transferred to Elmira Prison, NY July 17,1864	Exchanged February 20, 1865 at Boulware's or Cox Wharf on the James River, Virginia
Brooks, John R. Corporal	19	May 1, 1862, Fayetteville, Georgia	Co. C, 53rd Georgia Infantry	June 1, 1864, Gaines Mill, Cold Harbor, Virginia	Point Lookout, Maryland, transferred to Elmira Prison, NY July 17,1864	Oath of Allegiance June 16, 1865
Brooks, Joseph H. Sergeant	Unk	June 15, 1861, Columbus, Georgia	Co. E, 12th Georgia Infantry	May 10, 1864, Spotsylvania Court House, Virginia	Point Lookout, Maryland, transferred to Elmira Prison, NY July 25, 1864	Exchanged February 20, 1865 at Boulware's or Cox Wharf on the James River, Virginia
Brooks, Richard H. Private	Unk	May 7, 1862, Blakely, Georgia	Co. A, 51st Georgia Infantry	June 3, 1864, Gaines Farm, Cold Harbor, Virginia	Point Lookout, Maryland, transferred to Elmira Prison, NY July 17,1864	Exchanged March 2, 1865 at Akins Landing on the James River, Virginia
Brooks, Richard R. Private	Unk	March 10, 1862, Fort Lowry, Virginia	Co. F, 55th Virginia Infantry	May 6, 1864, Wilderness, Virginia	Point Lookout, Maryland, transferred to Elmira Prison, NY August 14, 1864	Oath of Allegiance June 23, 1865

Name & Rank	Age	Enlisted	Regiment and State	Where Captured	Prison	Remarks
Brooks, Robert Private	25	March 14, 1862, Wilkesboro, North Carolina	Co. F, 52nd North Carolina Infantry	May 12, 1864, Spotsylvania Court House, Virginia	Point Lookout, Maryland, transferred to Elmira Prison, NY August 12, 1864	Exchanged February 20, 1865 at Doulware's or Cox Wharf on the James River, Virginia. Died on the Route.
Brooks, Thomas Private	46	October 4, 1861, Raleigh, North Carolina	Co. G, 33rd North Carolina Infantry	May 12, 1864, Spotsylvania Court House, Virginia	Point Lookout, Maryland, transferred to Elmira Prison, NY August 12, 1864	Died December 24, 1864 of Valvular disease of the Heart. Grave No. 1103
Brooks, Thomas D. Private	42	August 18, 1863, Chatham County, North Carolina	Co. G, 40th Regiment, 3rd North Carolina Artillery	January 15, 1865, Fort Fisher, North Carolina	Elmira Prison Camp January 30, 1865	Died March 8, 1865 of Diarrhea, Grave No. 2409
Brooks, Thomas G. Private	Unk	August 13, 1863, Burton's Farm, Virginia	Co. C, 26th Virginia Infantry	June 15, 1864, Petersburg, Virginia	Point Lookout, Maryland, transferred to Elmira Prison, NY July 12,1864	Died October 16, 1864 of Scorbutus (Scurvy), Grave No. 554
Brooks, Wesley B. Private	Unk	December 20, 1861, Urbanna, Virginia	Co. D, 55th Virginia Infantry	May 5, 1864, Wilderness, Virginia	Point Lookout, Maryland, transferred to Elmira Prison, NY August 14, 1864	Oath of Allegiance June 23, 1865
Brooks, William Private	Unk	July 1, 1863, Charlotte, North Carolina	Co. F, 5th North Carolina Cavalry	September 22, 1863, Near Madison Court House, Virginia	Point Lookout, Maryland, transferred to Elmira Prison, NY August 18, 1864	Died February 24, 1865 of Pneumonia, Grave No. 2260
Brookshier, Joseph J. Private	Unk	June 3, 1862, Clarksville, Georgia	Co. K, 24th Georgia Infantry	August 16, 1864, Front Royal, Virginia	Old Capitol Prison, Washington, D. C., transferred to Elmira October 28, 1864	Oath of Allegiance July 7, 1865
Broom, Levi Private	Unk	August 24, 1861, Poplar Springs, Hall County, Georgia	Co. J, 24th Georgia Infantry	August 16, 1864, Front Royal, Virginia	Point Lookout, Maryland, transferred to Elmira Prison, NY August 29, 1864	Oath of Allegiance July 11, 1865

Name & Rank	Age	Enlisted	Regiment and State	Where Captured	Prison	Remarks
Broom, Wilson Private	24	January 3, 1862, Monroe, North Carolina	Co. B, 43rd North Carolina Infantry	July 13, 1864, Near Washington, DC. Gunshot Wound Wound Left Shoulder.	Old Capital Prison, Washington, DC, transferred to Elmira Prison, NY, July 23, 1864	Died April 10, 1865 of Chronic Diarrhea, Grave No 2603, Name W. B. Brown on Headstone.
Brotherton, Elias M. Private	35	March 4, 1862, Salisbury, North Carolina	Co. D, 42nd North Carolina Infantry	June 3, 1864, Gaines Farm, Cold Harbor, Virginia	Point Lookout, Maryland, transferred to Elmira Prison, NY July 17, 1864	Died August 29, 1864 of Chronic Diarrhea, Grave No. 436
Broughton, William S. Private	Unk	July 3, 1861, Fort Mitchell, Alabama	Co. A, 15th Alabama Infantry	May 6, 1864, Wilderness, Virginia	Point Lookout, Maryland, transferred to Elmira Prison, NY August 18, 1864	Oath of Allegiance June 23, 1865
Browder, Benjamin R. Private	39	December 29, 1861, Williamsburg, South Carolina	Co. K, 25th South Carolina Infantry	January 15, 1865, Fort Fisher, North Carolina	January 30, 1865, Elmira Prison Camp, NY	Oath of Allegiance July 11, 1865
Browder, Gadsden W. Private	36	December 29, 1861, Williamsburg, South Carolina	Co. K, 25th South Carolina Infantry	January 15, 1865, Fort Fisher, North Carolina	January 30, 1865, Elmira Prison Camp, NY	Oath of Allegiance June 23, 1865
Browder, John J. Private	Unk	May 27, 1862, Mars Bluff, South Carolina	Co. G, 21st South Carolina Infantry	January 15, 1865, Fort Fisher, North Carolina	Elmira Prison Camp January 30, 1865	Oath of Allegiance July 7, 1865
Browder, S. W. Private	Unk	May 1, 1863, James Island, South Carolina	Co. C, 25th South Carolina Infantry	May 14, 1864, Near Fort Darling, Virginia	Point Lookout, Maryland, transferred to Elmira Prison, NY August 17, 1864	Died May 17, 1865 of Rheumatism, Grave No. 2954. Headstone has J. W. Bromder.
Browder, William T. Private	39	December 29, 1861, Williamsburg, South Carolina	Co. K, 25th South Carolina Infantry	January 15, 1865, Fort Fisher, North Carolina	January 30, 1865, Elmira Prison Camp, NY	Oath of Allegiance July 19, 1865
Browen, Jesse Drummer Private	17	March 17, 1864, Duplin County, North Carolina	Co. D, 1st Battalion North Carolina Heavy Artillery	January 15, 1865, Fort Fisher, North Carolina	February 1, 1865, Elmira Prison Camp, New York	Exchanged March 2, 1865 at Akins Landing on the James River, Virginia

Name & Rank	Age	Enlisted	Regiment and State	Where Captured	Prison	Remarks
Browlee, F. L. Private	16	August 20, 1861, Ridgeville, South Carolina	Co. G, 11th South Carolina Infantry	May 16, 1864, Near Drury's Bluff, Virginia	Point Lookout, Maryland, transferred to Elmira Prison, NY August 17, 1864	Died May 16, 1865 of Pneumonia, Grave No. 2961. Headstone has L. Brownlee.
Brown, A. B. Private	Unk	Unknown	Co. G, 25th Virginia Infantry	May 5, 1864, Wilderness, Virginia	Point Lookout, Maryland, transferred to Elmira Prison, NY August 17, 1864	Died March 29, 1865 of Variola (Smallpox), Grave No. 2493
Brown, Adam L. Private	Unk	Unknown	Co. H, 22nd Virginia Infantry	May 5, 1864, Wilderness, Virginia	Point Lookout, Maryland, transferred to Elmira Prison, NY August 14, 1864	Exchanged March 10, 1865 at Boulware's Wharf on the James River, Virginia
Brown, Alexander G. Private	23	January 1, 1862, Camp Stephens, Whiteville, North Carolina	Co. H, 18th North Carolina Infantry	May 12, 1864, Spotsylvania Court House, Virginia	Point Lookout, Maryland, transferred to Elmira Prison, NY August 6, 1864	Oath of Allegiance June 30, 1865
Brown, Andrew Charles Private	29	April 25, 1861, New Orleans, Louisiana	Co. A, 1st Louisiana Infantry	May 5, 1864, Wilderness, Virginia	Point Lookout, Maryland, transferred to Elmira Prison, NY August 17, 1864	Exchanged February 25, 1865 at Boulware's or Cox Wharf on the James River, Virginia
Brown, Andrew D. Corporal	Unk	May 8, 1861, Charleston, Virginia	Co. A, 26th Virginia Infantry	June 3, 1864, Gaines Farm, Cold Harbor, Virginia	Point Lookout, Maryland, transferred to Elmira Prison, NY July 17,1864	Oath of Allegiance June 23, 1865
Brown, Andrew J. Private	Unk	August 13, 1861, Camp Moore, Louisiana	Co. C, 12th Louisiana Infantry	May 16, 1863, Baker's Creek, Champion Hill, Mississippi	Point Lookout, Maryland, transferred to Elmira Prison, NY August 18, 1864	Exchanged October 29, 1864 at Venus Point, Savannah River, GA.
Brown, Asa Private	Unk	May 1, 1862, Georgetown, South Carolina	Co. F, 4th South Carolina Cavalry	June 11, 1864, Trevilian Station, Louisa Court House, Virginia	Point Lookout, Maryland, transferred to Elmira Prison, NY July 25, 1864	Died October 10, 1864 of Chronic Diarrhea, Grave No. 672

Name & Rank	Age	Enlisted	Regiment and State	Where Captured	Prison	Remarks
Brown, Austin Sergeant	Unk	March 2, 1862, Scott County, Virginia	Co. A, 48th Virginia Infantry	May 12, 1864 Spotsylvania Court House, Virginia	Point Lookout, Maryland, transferred to Elmira Prison, NY August 2, 1864	Oath of Allegiance June 16, 1865
Brown, Bryant Private	22	April 22, 1862, Wilmington, North Carolina	Co. D, 1st Battalion North Carolina Heavy Artillery	January 15, 1865, Fort Fisher, North Carolina. Wounded.	February 1, 1865, Elmira Prison Camp, New York	Died April 16, 1865 of Chronic Diarrhea, Grave No. 2718
Brown, C. N. Private	26	April 1, 1862, Newton, North Carolina	Co. A, 12th North Carolina Infantry	May 12, 1864, Near Spotsylvania Court House, Virginia	Point Lookout, Maryland, transferred to Elmira Prison, NY August 14, 1864	Oath of Allegiance June 12, 1865
Brown, Calvin F. Private	Unk	December 18, 1861, Davis Old Field, Union District, South Carolina	Co. F, 18th South Carolina Infantry	July 30, 1864, Petersburg, Virginia	Point Lookout, Maryland, transferred to Elmira Prison, NY August 12, 1864	Exchanged March 14, 1865 at Boulware's Wharf on the James River, Virginia
Brown, Christopher J. Private	26	July 6, 1861, Pleasant Home, North Carolina	Co. D, 1st North Carolina Infantry	May 12, 1864, Spotsylvania Court House, Virginia	Point Lookout, Maryland, transferred to Elmira Prison, NY August 6, 1864	Oath of Allegiance June 30, 1865
Brown, Daniel Private	24	May 12, 1861, Corinth, Mississippi	Co. C, 16th Mississippi Infantry	May 30, 1864, Cold Harbor, Virginia	Old Capital Prison, Washington D. C. Transferred to Elmira Prison, NY March 3, 1865.	Exchanged March 14, 1865 at Boulware's Wharf on the James River, Virginia
Brown, C. Edward Private	19	July 18, 1861, Bay Point, Coosawhatchie, South Carolina	Co. E, 11th South Carolina Infantry	June 24, 1864, Near Petersburg, Virginia	Point Lookout Prison Camp, Maryland. Transferred to Elmira Prison, August 18, 1864	Died January 23, 1865 Pneumonia, Grave No. 1607
Brown, F. B. Private	Unk	Unknown	Co. A, Powers' Regiment Mississippi Cavalry	October 8, 1864, Natchez, Mississippi	New Orleans, Louisiana transferred to Elmira November 19, 1864.	Exchanged February 25, 1865 at Boulware's or Cox Wharf on the James River, Virginia

Name & Rank	Age	Enlisted	Regiment and State	Where Captured	Prison	Remarks
Brown, Felix Sergeant	17	April 10, 1862, Des Arc, Arkansas	Co. D, 3rd Battalion Missouri Cavalry	May 17, 1863, Big Black Bridge, Champion Hill, Mississippi	Point Lookout, Maryland, transferred to Elmira Prison, NY August 18, 1864	Exchanged February 13, 1865 at Boulware's wharf on the James River, Virginia
Brown, Frederick Private	Unk	July 2, 1861, New Orleans, Louisiana	Co. H, 15th Louisiana Infantry	May 12, 1864, Spotsylvania Court House, Virginia	Point Lookout, Maryland, transferred to Elmira Prison, NY July 25, 1864	Exchanged February 25, 1865 at Boulware's or Cox Wharf on the James River, Virginia
Brown, George M. Private	Unk	March 19, 1861, Tallapoosa, Alabama	Co. C, 1st Battalion Alabama Artillery	August 23, 1864, Fort Morgan, Alabama	New Orleans, Louisiana transferred to Elmira December 4, 1864.	Exchanged February 20, 1865 at Boulware's or Cox Wharf on the James River, Virginia
Brown, George M. Sergeant	29	March 7, 1862, Wilmington, North Carolina	Co. I, 51st North Carolina Infantry	June 15, 1864, Petersburg, Virginia	Point Lookout, Maryland, transferred to Elmira Prison, NY July 9, 1864	Exchanged February 25, 1865 at Boulware's or Cox Wharf on the James River, Virginia
Brown, H. H. Sergeant	Unk	May 15, 1862, Randolph County, Alabama	Co. F, 59th Alabama Infantry	June 17, 1864, Petersburg, Virginia	Point Lookout, Maryland, transferred to Elmira Prison, NY July 30, 1864	Died December 13, 1864 of Pneumonia, Grave No. 1133
Brown, H. J. Private	20	April 12, 1862, Battery Island, South Carolina	Co. A, 25th South Carolina Infantry	January 15, 1865, Fort Fisher, North Carolina	Elmira Prison Camp January 30, 1865	Oath of Allegiance June 23, 1865
Brown, Henry G. Private	18	September 1, 1862, Yadkinville, North Carolina	Co. B, 38th North Carolina Infantry	July 12, 1863, Funktown, Jamestown, Maryland	Point Lookout, Maryland, transferred to Elmira Prison, NY August 18, 1864	Exchanged October 29, 1864 at Venus Point, Savannah River, GA.
Brown, Henry M. Private	20	July 3, 1861, Salisbury, North Carolina	Co. E, 5th North Carolina Infantry	May 12, 1864, Spotsylvania Court House, Virginia	Point Lookout, Maryland, transferred to Elmira Prison, NY August 6, 1864	Oath of Allegiance May 19, 1865

Name & Rank	Age	Enlisted	Regiment and State	Where Captured	Prison	Remarks
Brown, Henry M. Private	18	August 19, 1862, Fort Branch, Brunswick County, North Carolina	Co. H, 36th Regiment North Carolina, 2nd Artillery	January 15, 1865, Fort Fisher, North Carolina	February 1, 1865, Elmira Prison Camp, New York	Oath of Allegiance July 11, 1865
Brown, Hiram Private	Unk	January 25, 1862, Columbia, South Carolina	Co. B, 22nd South Carolina Infantry	July 30, 1864, Petersburg, Virginia	Point Lookout, Maryland, transferred to Elmira Prison, NY August 12, 1864	Died March 11, 1865 of Diarrhea, Grave No. 1842
Brown, Isaac Private	Unk	May 15, 1862, Randolph County, Alabama	Co. F, 59th Alabama Infantry	June 17, 1864, Petersburg, Virginia	Point Lookout, Maryland, transferred to Elmira Prison, NY July 30, 1864	Oath of Allegiance July 7, 1865
Brown, J. G. G. Private	Unk	February 15, 1864, Mobile, Alabama	Co. A, 12th Alabama Infantry	May 27, 1864, Came Into Union Lines	Point Lookout, Maryland, transferred to Elmira Prison, NY July 17, 1864	Exchanged October 29, 1864, at Venus Point, Savannah River, GA.
Brown, J. H. Private	Unk	Unknown	Co. A, 3rd North Carolina Infantry	May 20, 1864, Spotsylvania Court House, Virginia	Point Lookout, Maryland, transferred to Elmira Prison, NY July 3, 1864	Transferred for Exchange October 11, 1864. Nothing Further.
Brown, James Private	Unk	May 10, 1861, Virginia	Co. M, 23rd Virginia Cavalry	July 11, 1864 Rockville, Maryland	Old Capital Prison, Washington, DC, transferred to Elmira Prison, NY, July 23, 1864	Oath of Allegiance May 14, 1865
Brown, James A. Private	22	February 15, 1862, Warsaw, North Carolina	Co. B, 51st North Carolina Infantry	June 1, 1864, Cold Harbor, Virginia	Point Lookout, Maryland, transferred to Elmira Prison, NY July 17, 1864	Died November 29, 1864 of Pneumonia, Grave No. 999
Brown, James H. Private	Unk	March 1, 1862, Vicksburg, Mississippi	Co. A, Jackson's 1st Regiment, Tennessee Heavy Artillery	August 23, 1864, Fort Morgan, Alabama	New Orleans, Louisiana transferred to Elmira December 4, 1864.	Exchanged February 13, 1865 at Boulware's wharf on the James River, Virginia

Name & Rank	Age	Enlisted	Regiment and State	Where Captured	Prison	Remarks
Brown, James R. Private	18	May 9, 1862, Monroe, Louisiana	Co. F, 2nd Louisiana Infantry	May 12, 1864, Spotsylvania Court House, Virginia	Point Lookout, Maryland, transferred to Elmira Prison, NY August 17, 1864	Exchanged February 25, 1865 at Boulware's or Cox Wharf on the James River, Virginia
Brown, James W. Private	20	April 8, 1864, Decatur, Georgia	Co. B, Jackson's 1st Regiment, Tennessee Heavy Artillery	August 23, 1864, Fort Morgan, Alabama	New Orleans, Louisiana transferred to Elmira December 4, 1864.	Died December 20, 1864 of Pneumonia and Chronic Diarrhea, Grave No. 1075
Brown, Jesse Drummer Private	17	March 17, 1864, Duplin County, North Carolina	Co. D, 1st Battalion North Carolina Heavy Artillery Battery	January 15, 1865, Fort Fisher, North Carolina	February 1, 1865, Elmira Prison Camp, New York	Exchanged March 2, 1865 On the James River, Virginia
Brown, Jesse C. Private	21	July 25, 1861, Tullahoma, Tennessee	Co. K, 25th Tennessee Infantry	May 16, 1864, Near Drury's Bluff, Virginia	Point Lookout, Maryland, transferred to Elmira Prison, NY August 17, 1864	Exchanged February 13, 1865 at Boulware's wharf on the James River, Virginia
Brown, Jesse J. Private	Unk	February 23, 1864, Columbia, South Carolina	Co. L, McCreary's 1st South Carolina Infantry	May 25, 1864, Hanover Junction, Virginia	Point Lookout, Maryland, transferred to Elmira Prison, NY July 11, 1864	Died April 29, 1865 of Chronic Diarrhea, Grave No. 2731
Brown, John Private	Unk	Unknown	Co. B, 62nd Georgia Infantry	July 16, 1864, Loudoun County, Virginia	Old Capital Prison, Washington, DC, transferred to Elmira Prison, NY, July 23, 1864	Exchanged March 10, 1865 at Boulware's wharf on the James River, Virginia
Brown, John Private	20	July 4, 1861, New Orleans, Louisiana	Co. H, 14th Louisiana Infantry	May 5, 1864, Wilderness, Virginia	Point Lookout, Maryland, transferred to Elmira Prison, NY July 25, 1864	Exchanged February 13, 1865 at Boulware's wharf on the James River, Virginia
Brown, John Private	Unk	August 7, 1861, Baton Rouge, Louisiana	Co. C, 15th Louisiana Infantry	May 12, 1864, Spotsylvania Court House, Virginia	Point Lookout, Maryland, transferred to Elmira Prison, NY July 25, 1864	Oath of Allegiance May 15, 1865

Name & Rank	Age	Enlisted	Regiment and State	Where Captured	Prison	Remarks
Brown, John F. Private	Unk	June 20, 1864, Bronson, Florida	Co. A, 1st Reserves Florida Infantry	September 27, 1864, Marianna, Florida	New Orleans, Louisiana transferred to Elmira November 19, 1864.	Died March 9, 1865 of Diarrhea, Grave No. 1882. Headstone has Joel Brown.
Brown, John H. Private	Unk	August 7, 1861, Baton Rouge, Louisiana	Co. C, 15th Louisiana Infantry	May 12, 1864, Near Spotsylvania, Virginia	Point Lookout, Maryland, transferred to Elmira Prison, NY July 23, 1864	Oath of Allegiance May 15, 1865
Brown, John H. C. Corporal	19	March 13, 1862, Concord, North Carolina	Co. A, 52nd North Carolina Infantry	May 12, 1864, Spotsylvania Court House, Virginia	Point Lookout, Maryland, transferred to Elmira Prison, NY August 12, 1864	Died June 6, 1865 of Chronic Diarrhea, Grave No. 2892
Brown, John M. Private	18	September 4, 1863, Ocala, Florida	Co. K, 9th Florida Infantry	August 14, 1864, Petersburg, Virginia. Gunshot Wound in Back.	Old Capital Prison, Washington, DC transferred to Elmira Prison, NY August 27, 1864	Oath of Allegiance January 25, 1865. Early Release per Lincoln's Proclamation, 12/8/1863.
Brown, John T. Private	28	April 5, 1862, Wilkesboro, North Carolina	Co. F, 52nd North Carolina Infantry	May 12, 1864, Spotsylvania Court House, Virginia	Point Lookout Prison Camp, Maryland. Transferred to Elmira Prison, NY, August 12, 1864	Died February 9, 1865 of Pneumonia, Grave No. 1943
Brown, John T. Private	Unk	April 2, 1862, Orange County, Virginia	Co. C, 49th Virginia Infantry	June 30, 1864, Gaines Mill, Cold Harbor, Virginia	Point Lookout, Maryland, transferred to Elmira Prison, NY July 8, 1864	Oath of Allegiance March 14, 1865
Brown, John W. Sergeant	Unk	April 5, 1861, Mount Sterling, Alabama	Co. E, 1st Battalion Alabama Artillery	August 23, 1864, Fort Morgan, Alabama	Steam Press No. 4, New Orleans, Louisiana transferred to Elmira Prison, October 8, 1864.	Oath of Allegiance July 11, 1865
Brown, John W. Private	Unk	March 4, 1862, Scottsville, Virginia	Co. F, 46th Virginia Infantry	June 17, 1864, Petersburg, Virginia	Point Lookout, Maryland, transferred to Elmira Prison, NY July 30, 1864	Oath of Allegiance July 11, 1865

Name & Rank	Age	Enlisted	Regiment and State	Where Captured	Prison	Remarks
Brown, John W. Corporal	Unk	June 25, 1861, Wytheville, Virginia	Co. K, 50th Virginia Infantry	May 12, 1864 Spotsylvania Court House, Virginia	Point Lookout, Maryland, transferred to Elmira Prison, NY August 2, 1864	Oath of Allegiance July 10, 1865
Brown, Joseph A. Private	22	December 27, 1861, Springfield, Missouri	Co. H, 1st Missouri Cavalry	May 17, 1863, Big Black Bridge, Champion Hill, Mississippi	Point Lookout, Maryland, transferred to Elmira Prison, NY August 18, 1864	Oath of Allegiance October 16, 1864. Early Release per Lincoln's Proclamation, 12/8/1863.
Brown, Joshua B. Corporal	23	May 1, 1862, South Mills, North Carolina	Co. D, 32nd North Carolina Infantry	May 10, 1864, Spotsylvania, Virginia	Point Lookout, Maryland, transferred to Elmira Prison, NY August 6, 1864	Oath of Allegiance June 27, 1865
Brown, Josiah Private	Unk	January 10, 1862, Lexington, South Carolina	Co. A, 27th South Carolina Infantry	June 18, 1864, Near Petersburg, Virginia	Point Lookout, Maryland, transferred to Elmira Prison, NY July 30, 1864	Exchanged March 14, 1865 at Boulware's Wharf on the James River, Virginia
Brown, Julius F. Private	Unk	July 7, 1862, Concord, North Carolina	Co. F, 57th North Carolina Infantry	July 8, 1864, Near Harper's Ferry, Virginia	Old Capital Prison, Washington, DC, transferred to Elmira Prison, NY, July 23, 1864	Exchanged March 2, 1865 at Akins Landing on the James River, Virginia
Brown, Malcom Private	21	November 25, 1863, Cumberland County, North Carolina	Co. B, 36th Regiment, 2nd North Carolina Artillery	January 15, 1865, Fort Fisher, North Carolina. Wounded.	February 1, 1865, Elmira Prison Camp, New York	Oath of Allegiance June 24, 1865
Brown, Nathan Sergeant	Unk	April 3, 1862, Bryan County, Georgia	Co. H, 7th Georgia Cavalry	June 11, 1864, Trevilian Station, Louisa Court House, Virginia	Point Lookout, Maryland, transferred to Elmira Prison, NY July 25, 1864	Died September 26, 1864 of Typhoid Fever, Grave No. 450
Brown, Neill W. Private	20	June 1, 1861, Richmond County, North Carolina	Co. F, 18th North Carolina Infantry	May 12, 1864, Spotsylvania Court House, Virginia	Point Lookout, Maryland, transferred to Elmira Prison, NY August 6, 1864	Died October 16, 1864 of Typhoid Fever, Grave No. 557. Name William on Headstone.

Name & Rank	Age	Enlisted	Regiment and State	Where Captured	Prison	Remarks
Brown, Peter A. Private	Unk	September 8, 1861, Statesville, North Carolina	Co. A, 18th North Carolina Infantry	May 12, 1864, Spotsylvania Court House, Virginia	Point Lookout, Maryland, transferred to Elmira Prison, NY August 6, 1864	Died January 31, 1865 of Pneumonia, Grave No. 1783
Brown, Richard E. Private	Unk	November 1, 1862, Morris Island, South Carolina	Co. J, 21st South Carolina Infantry	May 9, 1864, Petersburg, Virginia	Point Lookout Prison Camp, Maryland. Transferred to Elmira Prison Camp, New York August 18, 1864	Died October 1, 1864 of Chronic Diarrhea, Grave No. 404
Brown, Robert Private	Unk	April 20, 1864, Raleigh, North Carolina	Co. G, 7th North Carolina Infantry	July 29, 1864, Petersburg, Virginia	Point Lookout, Maryland, transferred to Elmira Prison, NY August 12, 1864	Oath of Allegiance June 12, 1865
Brown, Robert F. Private	32	January 26, 1862, Mount Vernon, Lincoln County, North Carolina	Co. D, 1st North Carolina Infantry	May 12, 1864, Spotsylvania Court House, Virginia	Point Lookout, Maryland, transferred to Elmira Prison, NY August 6, 1864	Exchanged October 29, 1864 at Venus Point, Savannah River, GA.
Brown, Ruffin Private	19	March 19, 1862, Greensboro, North Carolina	Co. G, 45th North Carolina Infantry	May 10, 1864, Spotsylvania Court House, Virginia	Point Lookout, Maryland, transferred to Elmira Prison, NY August 6, 1864	Oath of Allegiance June 19, 1865
Brown, Rufus D. Private	Unk	July 29, 1861, Madison, Georgia	Co. D, 3rd Battalion Georgia Sharp shooters	August 16, 1864, Front Royal, Virginia	Point Lookout, Maryland, transferred to Elmira Prison, NY August 29, 1864	Oath of Allegiance July 7, 1865
Brown, S. R. Private	Unk	October 1, 1862, Augusta, Georgia	Co. A, 7th Georgia Cavalry	June 11, 1864, Trevilian Station, Louisa Court House, Virginia	Point Lookout, Maryland, transferred to Elmira Prison, NY July 25, 1864	Exchanged March 10, 1865 at Boulware's wharf on the James River, Virginia
Brown, Thomas J. Private	Unk	September 7, 1862, North Carolina	Co. H, 37th North Carolina Infantry	July 29, 1864, Petersburg, Virginia	Point Lookout, Maryland, transferred to Elmira Prison, NY August 12, 1864	Died February 8, 1865 of Chronic Diarrhea, Grave No. 1938

Name & Rank	Age	Enlisted	Regiment and State	Where Captured	Prison	Remarks
Brown, Thomas K. Private	23	August 2, 1861, Camp McDonald, Cobb County, Georgia	Co. C, Phillips Legion Georgia Infantry	June 11, 1864, Trevilian Station, Louisa Court House, Virginia	Point Lookout, Maryland, transferred to Elmira Prison, NY July 25, 1864	Died March 13, 1865 of Variola (Smallpox), Grave No. 2435
Brown, Thomas S. Private	Unk	March 4, 1862, Camp Davis, Georgia	Co. B, 7th Georgia Cavalry	June 11, 1864, Trevilian Station, Louisa Court House, Virginia	Point Lookout, Maryland, transferred to Elmira Prison, NY July 25, 1864	Died January 14, 1865 of Chronic Diarrhea, Grave No. 1472
Brown, W. A. Private	Unk	Unknown	Co. D, 26th Battalion Virginia Infantry	June 3, 1864, Gaines Farm, Cold Harbor, Virginia	Point Lookout, Maryland, transferred to Elmira Prison, NY July 17,1864	Oath of Allegiance May 29, 1865
Brown, W. E. Private	17	September 5, 1861, Baton Rouge Barracks, Louisiana	Co. B, 1st Louisiana Cavalry	October 6, 1864, Clinton, Louisiana	New Orleans, Louisiana transferred to Elmira November 19, 1864.	Exchanged February 13, 1865 at Boulware's wharf on the James River, Virginia
Brown, W. H. Private	Unk	Unknown	2nd Battalion Maryland Artillery	May 11, 1864, Yellow Tavern, Hanover County, Virginia	Point Lookout, Maryland, transferred to Elmira Prison, NY August 17, 1864	Transferred For Exchange October 11, 1864 to Point Lookout Prison Camp, MD. Nothing Further.
Brown, William Marine	Unk	Unknown	Confederate States Navy, assigned to ships CSS Arctic and CSS Raleigh.	January 15, 1865, Fort Fisher, North Carolina	February 1, 1865, Elmira Prison Camp, New York	Died April 4, 1865 of Chronic Diarrhea, Grave No. 2562
Brown, William Private	Unk	December 16, 1863, Raleigh, North Carolina	Co. G, 13th North Carolina Infantry	June 9, 1864, Beaver Dam Station, Virginia	Point Lookout Prison Camp, Maryland. Transferred to Elmira Prison, July 28, 1864	Died February 28, 1865 of Variola (Smallpox), Grave No. 2127
Brown, William Private	Unk	March 1, 1862, Heathsville, Virginia	Co. C, 40th Virginia Infantry	June 14, 1864, Edward's Ferry, Virginia	Old Capital Prison, Washington, DC, transferred to Elmira Prison, NY, July 23, 1864	Joined US Army and deserted.

Name & Rank	Age	Enlisted	Regiment and State	Where Captured	Prison	Remarks
Brown, William A. Private	Unk	October 15, 1861, Haley's Store, Georgia	Co. F, 38th Georgia Infantry	July 3, 1863, Gettysburg, Pennsylvania	Point Lookout, Maryland, transferred to Elmira Prison, NY July 17, 1864	Exchanged February 24, 1865 at Akins Landing on the James River, Virginia
Brown, William A. Private	Unk	December 7, 1861, Camp Trousdale, Tennessee	Co. B, 44th Tennessee Infantry	June 17, 1864, Petersburg, Virginia	Point Lookout, Maryland, transferred to Elmira Prison, NY July 23, 1864	Died February 20, 1865 of Pneumonia, Grave No. 2305
Brown, William D. Private	24	June 12, 1861, Weldon, North Carolina	Co. B, 5th North Carolina Infantry	May 12, 1864, Spotsylvania Court House, Virginia	Point Lookout, Maryland, transferred to Elmira Prison, NY August 6, 1864	Oath of Allegiance June 21, 1865
Brown, William G. Private	21	June 26, 1861, Atlanta, Georgia	Co. C, 21st Georgia Infantry	May 21, 1864, Spotsylvania Court House, Virginia	Point Lookout, Maryland, transferred to Elmira Prison, NY July 25, 1864	Oath of Allegiance June 30, 1865
Brown, William G. Private	Unk	August 1, 1862, Gordonsville, Virginia	Co. G, 10th Virginia Infantry	May 12, 1864, Spotsylvania Court House, Virginia	Point Lookout, Maryland, transferred to Elmira Prison, NY August 2, 1864	Oath of Allegiance June 27, 1865
Brown, William J. Private	Unk	May 1, 1863, Fetterman, Virginia	Co. A, 25th Virginia Infantry	May 12, 1864, Spotsylvania Court House, Virginia	Point Lookout, Maryland, transferred to Elmira Prison, NY August 2, 1864	Oath of Allegiance June 30, 1865
Brown, William L. Private	18	July 17, 1862, Raleigh, North Carolina	Co. B, 56th North Carolina Infantry	June 18, 1864, Petersburg, Virginia	Point Lookout, Maryland, transferred to Elmira Prison, NY July 30, 1864	Died September 18, 1864 of Chronic Diarrhea, Grave No. 311
Brown, William R. Private	18	May 1, 1862, Williamston, North Carolina	Co. H, 1st North Carolina Infantry	May 12, 1864, Spotsylvania Court House, Virginia	Point Lookout, Maryland, transferred to Elmira Prison, NY August 6, 1864	Exchanged March 2, 1865 at Akins Landing on the James River, Virginia
Brown, William W. Sergeant	20	March 1, 1862, Cerogordo, North Carolina	Co. E, 36th Regiment, 2nd North Carolina Artillery	January 15, 1865, Fort Fisher, North Carolina. Wounded.	February 1, 1865, Elmira Prison Camp, New York	Exchanged March 2, 1865 at Akins Landing on the James River, Virginia

Name & Rank	Age	Enlisted	Regiment and State	Where Captured	Prison	Remarks
Brown, Yelven Private	Unk	March 18, 1862, Salem, Virginia	Co. E, 42nd Virginia Infantry	May 12, 1864, Near Spotsylvania Court House, Virginia	Point Lookout, Maryland, transferred to Elmira Prison, NY August 2, 1864	Exchanged March 14, 1865 at Boulware's Wharf on the James River, Virginia
Browning, Alexander M. Corporal	31	March 8, 1862, Lake City, Florida	Co. B, 5th Florida Infantry	May 12, 1864, Spotsylvania Court House, Virginia	Point Lookout, Maryland, transferred to Elmira Prison, NY August 12, 1864	Exchanged October 29, 1864 at Venus Point, Savannah River, GA.
Browning, George W. Sergeant	Unk	September 13, 1861, Whitesville, Georgia	Co. E, 61st Georgia Infantry	May 12, 1864, Spotsylvania Court House, Virginia	Point Lookout, Maryland, transferred to Elmira Prison, NY July 30, 1864	Oath of Allegiance May 29, 1865
Browning, Lewis R. Private	23	July 16, 1861, Forestville, North Carolina	Co. I, 1st North Carolina Infantry	May 12, 1864, Spotsylvania Court House, Virginia	Point Lookout, Maryland, transferred to Elmira Prison, NY August 6, 1864	Oath of Allegiance June 12, 1865
Browning, Thomas Jefferson Corporal	21	December 20, 1862, Fort Fisher, North Carolina	Co. J, 36th Regiment, 2nd North Carolina Artillery	January 15, 1865, Fort Fisher, North Carolina. Wounded.	February 1, 1865, Elmira Prison Camp, New York	Oath of Allegiance June 12, 1865
Browning, William H. Sergeant	28	June 28, 1862, Wilmington, North Carolina	Co. C, 8th North Carolina Infantry	June 1, 1864, Cold Harbor, Virginia	Point Lookout, Maryland, transferred to Elmira Prison, NY July 17,1864	Exchanged March 10, 1865 at Boulware's wharf on the James River, Virginia
Brownlee, Elijah J. Private	Unk	June 1, 1864, Petersburg, Virginia	Co. C, 11th South Carolina Infantry	June 18, 1864, Petersburg, Virginia	Point Lookout, Maryland, transferred to Elmira Prison, NY July 30, 1864	Oath of Allegiance July 7, 1865
Brownlee, Horatio H. Private	20	May 3, 1861, Brownsburg, Virginia	Co. H, 25th Virginia Infantry	May 5, 1864, Wilderness, Virginia	Point Lookout, Maryland, transferred to Elmira Prison, NY August 2, 1864	Exchanged October 29, 1864, at Venus Point, Savannah River, GA.

Name & Rank	Age	Enlisted	Regiment and State	Where Captured	Prison	Remarks
Brownlee, Thomas W. Private	19	August 20, 1861, Ridgeville, South Carolina	Co. G, 11th South Carolina Infantry	August 21, 1864, Weldon Railroad, Near Petersburg, Virginia. Gunshot Wound Left Leg.	DeCamp General Hospital, David's Island New York Harbor.	Exchanged March 14, 1865 at Boulware's Wharf on the James River, Virginia
Broyles, John Sergeant	Unk	April 29, 1862, White Sulfur Springs, Virginia	Co. H, 26th Battalion, Virginia Infantry	June 3, 1864, Gaines Mill, Cold Harbor, Virginia	Point Lookout, Maryland, transferred to Elmira Prison, NY July 17, 1864	Died September 26, 1864 of Chronic Diarrhea, Grave No. 448
Brubaker, Isaac Private	Unk	Unknown	Co. D, 12th Virginia Cavalry	July 10, 1864, Near Frederick, Maryland	Old Capital Prison, Washington, DC, transferred to Elmira Prison, NY, July 23, 1864	Oath of Allegiance September 13, 1864, Joined US Army and Deserted
Bruin, Dulany Private	20	April 17, 1861, Alexandria, Virginia	Co. E, 17th Virginia Infantry	July 21, 1863, Manassas Gap, Virginia	Point Lookout, Maryland, transferred to Elmira Prison, NY August 18, 1864	Exchanged February 25, 1865 at Boulware's or Cox Wharf on the James River, Virginia
Brumbeloe, N. D. Private	Unk	July 31, 1861, Hickory Flat, Alabama	Co. F, 14th Alabama Infantry	May 24, 1864, North Anna River, Hanover Junction, Virginia	Point Lookout, Maryland, transferred to Elmira Prison, NY July 12, 1864	Oath of Allegiance June 19, 1865
Brusan, John Private	Unk	October 12, 1862, Charlottesville, Virginia	Co. B, 35th Battalion Virginia Cavalry	June 26, 1864 Leesburg, Virginia	Old Capital Prison, Washington, DC, transferred to Elmira Prison, NY, July 23, 1864	Oath of Allegiance May 17, 1865
Bruton, Atlas J. Private	36	July 22, 1863, Fort Branch, Martin County, North Carolina	Co. G, 40th Regiment, 3rd North Carolina Artillery	January 15, 1865, Fort Fisher, North Carolina	February 1, 1865, Elmira Prison Camp, New York	Exchanged February 20, 1865 at Boulware's or Cox Wharf on the James River, Virginia
Bruton, Richard N. Private	30	July 25, 1863, Fort Branch, Martin County, North Carolina	Co. G, 40th Regiment, 3rd North Carolina Artillery	January 15, 1865, Fort Fisher, North Carolina	February 1, 1865, Elmira Prison Camp, New York	Died March 20, 1865 of Intermittent Fever, Grave No. 1573

Name & Rank	Age	Enlisted	Regiment and State	Where Captured	Prison	Remarks
Bryan, Angus R. Private	21	May 30, 1861, Rockingham, North Carolina	Co. D, 23rd North Carolina Infantry	May 12, 1864, Near Spotsylvania Court House, Virginia	Point Lookout, Maryland, transferred to Elmira Prison, NY August 14, 1864	Oath of Allegiance June 19, 1865
Bryan, Carney J. Private	Unk	June 28, 1862, Kinston, Lenoir County, North Carolina	Co. D, 13th Battalion North Carolina Light Artillery	January 15, 1865, Fort Fisher, North Carolina. Wounded	February 1, 1865, Elmira Prison Camp, New York	Exchanged March 2, 1865 at Akins Landing on the James River, Virginia
Bryan, James H. Private	19	July 15, 1862, Raleigh, North Carolina	Co. A, 3rd North Carolina Infantry	May 12, 1864, Near Spotsylvania Court House, Virginia	Point Lookout Prison, Maryland. Transferred to Elmira Prison, NY, August 14, 1864.	Oath of Allegiance June 30, 1865
Bryan, Robert S. Private	Unk	January 22, 1862, Columbia, South Carolina	Co. A, 22nd South Carolina Infantry	June 2, 1864, Near Bermuda Hundred, Cold Harbor, Virginia	Point Lookout Prison Camp, Maryland. Transferred to Elmira Prison, NY, July 28, 1864	Died November 28, 1864 of Chronic Diarrhea, Grave No. 991
Bryan, William T. Private	41	September 5, 1863, Fort Caswell, Brunswick County, North Carolina	Co. G, 36th Regiment North Carolina, 2nd Artillery	January 15, 1865, Fort Fisher, North Carolina	February 1, 1865, Elmira Prison Camp, New York	Exchanged March 2, 1865 On the James River, Virginia
Bryant, Alfred T. Private	Unk	December 28, 1861, Columbia, South Carolina	Co. F, 18th South Carolina Infantry	July 30, 1864, Petersburg, Virginia	Point Lookout, Maryland, transferred to Elmira Prison, NY August 12, 1864	Died December 16, 1864 of Typhoid Fever, Grave No. 1275
Bryant, Andrew J. Private	17	Unknown	Co. E, 50th Virginia Infantry	May 12, 1864, Spotsylvania Court House, Virginia	Point Lookout, Maryland, transferred to Elmira Prison, NY August 2, 1864	Exchanged March 14, 1865 at Boulware's Wharf on the James River, Virginia
Bryant, Augustus M. Corporal	19	May 1, 1862, South Mills, North Carolina	Co. D, 32nd North Carolina Infantry	May 10, 1864, Spotsylvania, Virginia	Point Lookout, Maryland, transferred to Elmira Prison, NY August 6, 1864	Oath of Allegiance July 26, 1865

Name & Rank	Age	Enlisted	Regiment and State	Where Captured	Prison	Remarks
Bryant, Benjamin W. Private	19	May 1, 1862, South Mills, North Carolina	Co. D, 32nd North Carolina Infantry	May 10, 1864, Spotsylvania, Virginia	Point Lookout, Maryland, transferred to Elmira Prison, NY August 6, 1864	Oath of Allegiance July 27, 1865
Bryant, Ferdinand D. Private	15	April 6, 1862, Camp Wyatt, New Hanover County, North Carolina	Co. D, 20th North Carolina Infantry	May 12, 1864, Near Spotsylvania Court House, Virginia	Point Lookout Prison, Maryland. Transferred to Elmira Prison Camp New York August 14, 1864.	Oath of Allegiance June 19, 1865
Bryant, Francis M. Private	17	August 5, 1861, Lumberton, North Carolina	Co. D, 18th North Carolina Infantry	May 12, 1864, Spotsylvania Court House, Virginia	Point Lookout, Maryland, transferred to Elmira Prison, NY August 6, 1864	Died February 1, 1865 of Pneumonia, Grave No. 1777
Bryant, George T. Private	18	August 20, 1863, Fort Branch, Martin County, North Carolina	Co. G, 3rd North Carolina Artillery	January 15, 1865, Fort Fisher, North Carolina	Elmira Prison Camp January 30, 1865	Oath of Allegiance June 12, 1865
Bryant, H. W. Private	18	February 21, 1862, Lillington, North Carolina	Co. C, 1st North Carolina Infantry	May 12, 1864, Spotsylvania Court House, Virginia	Point Lookout, Maryland, transferred to Elmira Prison, NY August 6, 1864	Oath of Allegiance June 12, 1865
Bryant, Jackson W. Private	Unk	December 12, 1861, Suffolk, Virginia	Co. G, 1st South Carolina Infantry	July 29, 1864, Petersburg, Virginia	Point Lookout, Maryland, transferred to Elmira Prison, NY August 12, 1864	Oath of Allegiance July 3, 1865
Bryant, John H. Private	Unk	Unknown	Petersburg City Guard, Virginia Infantry	June 9, 1864, Captured at Plank Road, Petersburg, Virginia	Point Lookout, Maryland, transferred to Elmira Prison, NY July 12, 1864	Oath of Allegiance July 3, 1865
Bryant, John W. Private	Unk	January 9, 1864, Henry County, Alabama	Captain Chisholm's Co., Alabama Cavalry	September 23, 1864, Euchee Anna, Louisiana	New Orleans, Louisiana transferred to Elmira November 19, 1864.	Oath of Allegiance June 19, 1865

Name & Rank	Age	Enlisted	Regiment and State	Where Captured	Prison	Remarks
Bryant, Marcellus Corporal	Unk	June 15, 1861, Columbus, Georgia	Co. E, 12th Georgia Infantry	May 10, 1864, Spotsylvania Court House, Virginia	Point Lookout, Maryland, transferred to Elmira Prison, NY July 25, 1864	Oath of Allegiance June 19, 1865
Bryant, Martin Private	Unk	December 7, 1861, Camp Trousdale, Tennessee	Co. E, 44th Tennessee Infantry	June 17, 1864, Petersburg, Virginia	Point Lookout, Maryland, transferred to Elmira Prison, NY July 30, 1864	Exchanged February 25, 1865 at Boulware's or Cox Wharf on the James River, Virginia
Bryant, Richard Private	Unk	Unknown	Co. C, 17th Tennessee Infantry	June 17, 1864, Petersburg, Virginia	Point Lookout, Maryland, transferred to Elmira Prison, NY July 30, 1864	Exchanged October 29, 1864, at Venus Point, Savannah River, GA.
Bryant, Richard B. Private	Unk	February 8, 1862, Lumberton, North Carolina	Co. D, 18th North Carolina Infantry	May 12, 1864, Spotsylvania Court House, Virginia	Point Lookout, Maryland, transferred to Elmira Prison, NY August 6, 1864	Exchanged February 13, 1865 at Boulware's wharf on the James River, Virginia
Bryant, Richard R. Private	Unk	Unknown	Co. E, 50th Virginia Infantry	May 12, 1864, Spotsylvania Court House, Virginia	Point Lookout, Maryland, transferred to Elmira Prison, NY August 2, 1864	Exchanged March 2, 1865 at Akins Landing on the James River, Virginia
Bryant, Travis Private	Unk	March 5, 1862, Cumberland County, North Carolina	Co. J, 51st North Carolina Infantry	June 1, 1864, Cold Harbor, Virginia	Transferred From Point Lookout Prison, MD, July 12, 1864. Train Never Arrived at Elmira Prison Camp, NY.	Died July 15, 1864 in Train Wreck at Shohola, Pennsylvania
Bryant, William Private	Unk	April 15, 1861, Livingston, Alabama	Co. G, 5th Alabama Infantry	August 12, 1864, Bristow, Virginia	Point Lookout, Maryland, transferred to Elmira Prison, NY August 29, 1864	Oath of Allegiance July 26, 1865
Bryant, William Private	28	May 7, 1862, Stanhope, North Carolina	Co. A, 47th North Carolina Infantry	June 2, 1864, Cold Harbor, Virginia. Gunshot Wound Right Arm.	Old Capital Prison, Washington, DC, transferred to Elmira Prison, NY, July 23, 1864	Exchanged March 2, 1865 at Akins Landing on the James River, Virginia

Name & Rank	Age	Enlisted	Regiment and State	Where Captured	Prison	Remarks
Bryant, William A. Private	Unk	May 1, 1862, Macon County, Georgia	Co. C, 12th Georgia Infantry	May 10, 1864, Spotsylvania Court House, Virginia	Point Lookout, Maryland, transferred to Elmira Prison, NY July 25, 1864	Oath of Allegiance June 19, 1865
Bryant, William J. Private	Unk	October 10, 1861, Cumberland Ford, Kentucky	Co. C, 17th Tennessee Infantry	June 17, 1864, Petersburg, Virginia	Point Lookout, Maryland, transferred to Elmira Prison, NY July 30, 1864	Exchanged February 13, 1865 at Boulware's wharf on the James River, Virginia
Bryant, William M. Sergeant	18	April 23, 1861, Snow Hill, North Carolina	Co. A, 3rd North Carolina Infantry	May 12, 1864, Near Spotsylvania Court House, Virginia	Point Lookout, Maryland, transferred to Elmira Prison, NY August 12, 1864	Exchanged March 14, 1865 at Boulware's Wharf on the James River, Virginia
Bryant, William T. Private	41	September 5, 1863, Fort Caswell, North Carolina	Co. F, 36th Regiment, 2nd North Carolina Artillery	January 15, 1865, Fort Fisher, North Carolina. Wounded.	February 1, 1865, Elmira Prison Camp, New York	Exchanged March 2, 1865 at Akins Landing on the James River, Virginia
Bryant, William T. Sergeant	Unk	December 4, 1861, Mountain Spring, Anderson District, South Carolina	Co. D, 18th South Carolina Infantry	July 30, 1864, Petersburg, Virginia	Point Lookout, Maryland, transferred to Elmira Prison, NY August 12, 1864	Died May 9, 1865 of Chronic Diarrhea, Grave No. 1652
Bryson, Stephen Private	Unk	June 25, 1861, Wytheville, Virginia	Co. I, 50th Virginia Infantry	May 12, 1864, Spotsylvania Court House, Virginia	Point Lookout, Maryland, transferred to Elmira Prison, NY August 2, 1864	Oath of Allegiance July 3, 1865
Bryson, Wesley Private	Unk	March 17, 1862, Charleston, South Carolina	Co. G, 27th South Carolina Infantry	June 24, 1864, Near Petersburg, Virginia	Point Lookout, Maryland, transferred to Elmira Prison, NY August 18, 1864	Exchanged October 29, 1864, at Venus Point, Savannah River, GA.
Buchanan, John S. Private	22	August 28, 1861, Walterboro, South Carolina	Co. K, 11th South Carolina Infantry	August 21, 1864, Weldon Railroad, Virginia. Gunshot Wound Shoulder and Left thigh. Leg Amputated.	Old Capital Prison, Washington D. C. Transferred to Elmira Prison, NY March 3, 1865.	Oath of Allegiance June 21, 1865

Name & Rank	Age	Enlisted	Regiment and State	Where Captured	Prison	Remarks
Buchanan, John W. Private	26	April 17, 1861, Augusta County, Virginia	Co. D, 5th Virginia Infantry	May 12, 1864, Spotsylvania Court House, Virginia. Gunshot Wound Left Thigh.	Old Capital Prison, Washington, DC transferred to Elmira Prison, NY August 27, 1864	Exchanged March 2, 1865 at Akins Landing on the James River, Virginia
Buchanan, Joseph Private	21	May 18, 1861, Seven Mile Ford, Virginia	Co. D, 48th Virginia Infantry	May 12, 1864, Spotsylvania Court House, Virginia	Point Lookout, Maryland, transferred to Elmira Prison, NY August 2, 1864	Transferred for Exchange 10/11/64. Died 11/4/64 of Unknown Causes at Fort Munroe, VA
Buchanan, Lorenzo D. Private	21	May 30, 1861, Webster, North Carolina	Co. B, 25th North Carolina	June 2, 1864, Near Petersburg, Virginia	Point Lookout, Maryland, transferred to Elmira Prison, NY July 12, 1864	Died September 12, 1864 of Chronic Diarrhea, Grave No. 183
Buchanan, Micajah T. Private	19	April 26, 1861, Townsville, North Carolina	Co. B, 12th North Carolina Infantry	May 20, 1864, Spotsylvania Court House, Virginia	Point Lookout Prison. Transferred to Elmira Prison, New York, July 6, 1864.	Oath of Allegiance June 30, 1865
Buchanan, Thomas T. Private	Unk	Unknown	Co. E, 50th Virginia Infantry	May 12, 1864, Spotsylvania Court House, Virginia	Point Lookout, Maryland, transferred to Elmira Prison, NY August 2, 1864	Died December 31, 1864 of Variola (Smallpox), Grave No. 1328
Buchanan, William Sergeant	19	June 1, 1861, Richmond County, North Carolina	Co. F, 18th North Carolina Infantry	May 12, 1864, Spotsylvania Court House, Virginia	Point Lookout, Maryland, transferred to Elmira Prison, NY August 6, 1864	Exchanged February 20, 1865 at Boulware's or Cox Wharf on the James River, Virginia
Buchanan, William H. Private	Unk	July 4, 1861, Talladega, Alabama	Co. B, 5th Alabama Infantry	May 5, 1864, Wilderness, Virginia	Point Lookout, Maryland, transferred to Elmira Prison, NY August 17, 1864	Oath of Allegiance June 23, 1865
Buck, Samuel R. Private	Unk	August 6, 1862, Pitt County, North Carolina	Co. E, 3rd North Carolina Cavalry	May 27, 1862, Hanover Junction, Virginia	Point Lookout Prison Camp, Maryland. Transferred to Elmira Prison, July 12, 1864	Died December 10, 1864 of General Debility, Grave No. 1153

Name & Rank	Age	Enlisted	Regiment and State	Where Captured	Prison	Remarks
Buckalew, Ansel M. Private	Unk	August 11, 1861, Auburn, Alabama	Co. F, 14th Alabama Infantry	May 24, 1864, North Anna River, Hanover Junction, Virginia	Point Lookout, Maryland, transferred to Elmira Prison, NY July 12, 1864	Exchanged February 25, 1865 at Boulware's or Cox Wharf on the James River, Virginia
Buckalew, William Private	Unk	March 16, 1862, Grove Hill, Alabama	Co. I, 5th Alabama Infantry	May 5, 1864, Wilderness, Virginia. Gunshot Wound of Neck and Left Shoulder.	Old Capital Prison, Washington, DC, transferred to Elmira Prison, NY, July 23, 1864	Oath of Allegiance June 16, 1865
Buckley, Eppa Civilian	Unk	Unknown	Citizen of Fairfax County, Virginia	November 26, 1863, Fairfax County, Virginia	Point Lookout, Maryland, transferred to Elmira Prison, NY July 25, 1864	Exchanged March 10, 1865 at Boulware's wharf on the James River, Virginia
Buckley, J. Sergeant	22	June 4, 1861, Camp Moore, Louisiana	Co. C, 6th Louisiana Infantry	May 5, 1864, Wilderness, Virginia	Point Lookout, Maryland, transferred to Elmira Prison, NY August 17, 1864	Exchanged February 25, 1865 at Boulware's or Cox Wharf on the James River, Virginia
Buckley, John Sergeant	16	June 6, 1861, New Orleans, Louisiana	Co. C, 14th Louisiana Infantry	August 12, 1864, Cedar Creek, Virginia	Point Lookout, Maryland, transferred to Elmira Prison, NY August 29, 1864	Exchanged February 25, 1865 at Boulware's or Cox Wharf on the James River, Virginia
Buckner, John J. Private	18	March 10, 1862, Northampton, North Carolina	Co. C, 3rd Battalion North Carolina Light Artillery	January 15, 1865, Fort Fisher, North Carolina	February 1, 1865, Elmira Prison Camp, New York	Died April 14, 1865 of Chronic Diarrhea, Grave No. 2708
Buckner, Thomas S. Sergeant	29	March 10, 1862, Milton, North Carolina	Co. I, 45th North Carolina Infantry	May 10, 1864, Spotsylvania Court House, Virginia	Point Lookout, Maryland, transferred to Elmira Prison, NY August 6, 1864	Died April 25, 1865 of Pneumonia, Grave No. 1414
Buffaloe, David B. Private	19	March 4, 1862, Raleigh, North Carolina	Co. I, 1st North Carolina Infantry	May 12, 1864, Spotsylvania Court House, Virginia	Point Lookout, Maryland, transferred to Elmira Prison, NY August 6, 1864	Exchanged February 13,1865 at Boulware's wharf on the James River, Virginia

Name & Rank	Age	Enlisted	Regiment and State	Where Captured	Prison	Remarks
Buffaloe, W. Calvin Private	18	March 3, 1862, Raleigh, North Carolina	Co. I, 1st North Carolina Infantry	May 12, 1864, Spotsylvania Court House, Virginia	Point Lookout, Maryland, transferred to Elmira Prison, NY August 6, 1864	Oath of Allegiance July 12, 1865
Buffaloe, William H. Private	22	May 12, 1862, Camp McIntosh, North Carolina	Co. I, 1st North Carolina Infantry	May 12, 1864, Spotsylvania Court House, Virginia	Point Lookout, Maryland, transferred to Elmira Prison, NY August 6, 1864	Exchanged February 13,1865 at Boulware's wharf on the James River, Virginia
Buffkin, Jordan W. Private	23	May 4, 1861, Elizabeth City, North Carolina	Co. A, 8th North Carolina Infantry	June 1, 1864, Cold Harbor, Virginia	Point Lookout, Maryland, transferred to Elmira Prison, NY July 17,1864	Died September 20, 1864 of Pneumonia, Grave No. 324
Bugg, Hett Sergeant	Unk	June 5, 1861, Memphis, Tennessee	Co. A, Jackson's 1st Regiment, Tennessee Heavy Artillery	August 23, 1864, Fort Morgan, Alabama	New Orleans, Louisiana transferred to Elmira December 4, 1864.	Exchanged February 13, 1865 at Boulware's wharf on the James River, Virginia
Bugg, Jeremiah H. Private	20	June 29, 1861, Haywood County, North Carolina	Co. F, 25th North Carolina Infantry	March 25, 1865, Fort Steadman, Petersburg, Virginia. Gunshot Wound Right Elbow, Severe.	Old Capital Prison, Washington D. C. Transferred to Elmira Prison, NY May 12, 1865.	Oath of Allegiance August 7, 1865
Buie, Hayes M. Private	16	May 15, 1862, Fort St. Philip, Brunswick County, North Carolina	Co. K, 40th Regiment, 3rd North Carolina Artillery	January 15, 1865, Fort Fisher, North Carolina	February 1, 1865, Elmira Prison Camp, New York	Exchanged March 14, 1865 at Boulware's Wharf on the James River, Virginia
Buie, James A. Private	Unk	March 5, 1862, Columbia, Alabama	Co. A, 6th Alabama Infantry	May 8, 1864, near Spotsylvania Court House, Virginia	Point Lookout, Maryland, transferred to Elmira Prison, NY August 17, 1864	Oath of Allegiance June 14, 1865
Buie, Mitchell Private	22	April 26, 1861, Elizabethtown, North Carolina	Co. K, 18th North Carolina Infantry	May 12, 1864, Spotsylvania Court House, Virginia	Point Lookout, Maryland, transferred to Elmira Prison, NY August 6, 1864	Died January 23, 1865 of Variola (Smallpox), Grave No. 1594

Name & Rank	Age	Enlisted	Regiment and State	Where Captured	Prison	Remarks
Buie, William N. Sergeant	18	Wilmington, New Hanover County NC, 11/5/1861, Volunteer	3rd Co. B, 36th Regiment North Carolina, 2nd Artillery	January 15, 1865, Fort Fisher, North Carolina	January 30, 1865, Elmira Prison Camp, New York	Exchanged on the James River, VA, 2/20/1865, Died of Variola (Smallpox), 4/27/1865, Marine USA Hospital, Baltimore, MD
Buie, William W. Private	35	February 12, 1862, Camp Price, North Carolina	Co. H, 3rd North Carolina Infantry	May 12, 1864, Near Spotsylvania Court House, Virginia	Point Lookout Prison, Maryland. Transferred to Elmira Prison Camp New York August 14, 1864.	Oath of Allegiance June 30, 1865
Buis, William A. Private	30	June 14, 1861, Camp Hill, North Carolina	Co. K, 4th North Carolina Infantry	July 4, 1863, Gettysburg, Pennsylvania	Point Lookout, Maryland, transferred to Elmira Prison, NY July 17,1864	Exchanged March 2, 1865 at Akins Landing on the James River, Virginia
Bulger, James Private	Unk	August 4, 1863, Talladega, Alabama	Jeff Davis Alabama Artillery	May 5, 1864, Wilderness, Virginia	Point Lookout, Maryland, transferred to Elmira Prison, NY August 17, 1864	Exchanged October 29, 1864, at Venus Point, Savannah River, GA.
Bull, William Private	Unk	Unknown	Co. B, Jackson's 1st Regiment, Tennessee Heavy Artillery	August 23, 1864, Fort Morgan, Alabama	New Orleans, Louisiana transferred to Elmira December 4, 1864.	Exchanged February 25, 1865 at Boulware's or Cox Wharf on the James River, Virginia
Bullard, J. J. Private	Unk	Unknown	Co. E, 30th North Carolina Infantry	Unknown	Unknown	Died February 16, 1865 of Unknown Disease, Grave No. 2206
Bullard, Jesse F. Private	Unk	March 1, 1862, Cerogordo, North Carolina	Co. E, 36th Regiment, 2nd North Carolina Artillery	January 15, 1865, Fort Fisher, North Carolina	February 1, 1865, Elmira Prison Camp, New York	Died February 15, 1865 of Pneumonia, Grave No. 2182

Name & Rank	Age	Enlisted	Regiment and State	Where Captured	Prison	Remarks
Bullard, John Isom Private	17	March 7, 1862, Cerro Gordo, Columbus County, North Carolina	Co. F, 36th Regiment 2nd North Carolina Artillery	January 15, 1865, Fort Fisher, North Carolina	February 1, 1865, Elmira Prison Camp, New York	Died February 27, 1865 of Pneumonia, No Grave Found in Woodlawn Cemetery, Elmira, NY
Bullard, Moses D. Private	Unk	March 4, 1862, Baker County, Georgia	Co. E, 51st Georgia Infantry	June 3, 1864, Gaines Farm, cold Harbor, Virginia	Point Lookout, Maryland, transferred to Elmira Prison, NY July 17,1864	Transferred for Exchange October 11, 1864. No Additional Information.
Bullard, William J. Private	18	August 16, 1862, Fort St. Philip, North Carolina	Co. K, 40th Regiment, 3rd North Carolina Artillery	January 15, 1865, Fort Fisher, North Carolina	February 1, 1865, Elmira Prison Camp, New York	Died February 27, 1865 of Pneumonia, Grave No. 2154
Bullis, James E. Private	Unk	September 9, 1862, Raleigh, North Carolina	Co. H, 18th North Carolina Infantry	May 12, 1864, Spotsylvania Court House, Virginia	Point Lookout, Maryland, transferred to Elmira Prison, NY August 6, 1864	Oath of Allegiance June 30, 1865
Bullock, James H. Private	Unk	July 11, 1861, Athens, Georgia	Co. E, 3rd Battalion Georgia Sharp shooters	August 16, 1864, Front Royal, Virginia	Point Lookout, Maryland, transferred to Elmira Prison, NY August 29, 1864	Oath of Allegiance July 7, 1865
Bullock, John H. Private	Unk	April 2, 1862, Fredericksburg, Virginia	Co. E, 47th Virginia Infantry	May 24, 1864, Hanover Junction, Virginia	Point Lookout, Maryland, transferred to Elmira Prison, NY July 11,1864	Died October 6, 1864 of Remittent Fever, Grave No. 645
Bullock, Joseph A. Private	Unk	March 12, 1862, Norfolk County, Virginia	Co. F, 15th Virginia Cavalry	September 14, 1863, Near Culpepper, Virginia	Point Lookout, Maryland, transferred to Elmira Prison, NY August 18, 1864	Oath of Allegiance June 14, 1865
Bulman, J. L. Private	Unk	January 14, 1862, Camp Walsh, South Carolina	Co. J, Holcombe Legion, South Carolina Infantry	May 7, 1864, Stony Creek, Virginia	Point Lookout, Maryland, transferred to Elmira Prison, NY August 17, 1864	Died in February 4, 1865 of Variola (Smallpox), Grave No. 1748

Name & Rank	Age	Enlisted	Regiment and State	Where Captured	Prison	Remarks
Bumbough, Thomas C. Private	Unk	March 1, 1862, New Madrid, Tennessee	Co. L, Jackson's 1st Regiment, Tennessee Heavy Artillery	August 23, 1864, Fort Morgan, Alabama	New Orleans, Louisiana transferred to Elmira December 4, 1864.	Died January 14, 1865 of Typhoid Fever, Grave No. 1469. Headstone has Bunbough.
Bumpass, Simeon Private	17	September 25, 1861, Camp Branch, Roxboro, North Carolina	Co. E, 35th North Carolina Infantry	June 17, 1864, Petersburg, Virginia	Point Lookout, Maryland, transferred to Elmira Prison, NY July 30, 1864	Exchanged March 14, 1865 at Boulware's Wharf on the James River, Virginia
Bunch, E. C. Private	34	May 28, 1862, Charleston, South Carolina	Co. D, 6th South Carolina Cavalry	June 11, 1864, Trevilian Station, Louisa Court House, Virginia	Point Lookout, Maryland, transferred to Elmira Prison, NY July 25, 1864	Oath of Allegiance June 11, 1865
Bunch, M. A. Private	Unk	May 15, 1862, Dawson, Georgia	Co. F, 51st Georgia Infantry	June 1, 1864, Gaines Mill, Cold Harbor, Virginia	Point Lookout, Maryland, transferred to Elmira Prison, NY July 17,1864	Oath of Allegiance June 16, 1865
Bunch, William H. Private	25	July 15, 1862, Guilford County, North Carolina	Co. A, 1st North Carolina Infantry	May 12, 1864, Spotsylvania Court House, Virginia	Point Lookout, Maryland, transferred to Elmira Prison, NY August 6, 1864	Oath of Allegiance June 12, 1865
Bundy, George W. Private	Unk	October 11, 1864, Bennettsville, South Carolina	Co. F, 21st South Carolina Infantry	January 15, 1865, Fort Fisher, North Carolina	Elmira Prison Camp January 30, 1865	Died March 5, 1865, Chronic Diarrhea, Grave No. 2377
Bunn, Sidney Private	Unk	March 1, 1864, Raleigh, North Carolina	Co. H, 32nd North Carolina Infantry	May 10, 1864, Spotsylvania, Virginia	Point Lookout, Maryland, transferred to Elmira Prison, NY August 6, 1864	Died April 6, 1865 of Chronic Diarrhea, Grave No. 2642
Bunn, W. J. Private	Unk	July 29, 1861, Lineville, Talladega County, Alabama	Co. F, 14th Alabama Infantry	May 12, 1864, Spotsylvania Court House, Virginia	Point Lookout, Maryland, transferred to Elmira Prison, NY August 17, 1864	Exchanged October 29, 1864, at Venus Point, Savannah River, GA.
Bunnel, Rueben B. Private	Unk	March 28, 1862, Pickensville, Alabama	Co. C, 41th Alabama Infantry	June 16, 1864, Bermuda Hundred, Virginia	Point Lookout, Maryland, transferred to Elmira Prison, NY July 12,1864	Oath of Allegiance June 21, 1865

Name & Rank	Age	Enlisted	Regiment and State	Where Captured	Prison	Remarks
Bunnell, Kenneth Private	Unk	August 8, 1861, Oak Grove, Virginia	Co. F, 61st Virginia Infantry	June 1, 1864, Cold Harbor, Virginia	Point Lookout, Maryland, transferred to Elmira Prison, NY July 17, 1864	Died October 7, 1864 of Chronic Diarrhea, Grave No. 650
Buntin, R. H. Sergeant	Unk	Unknown	Co. H, 26th Virginia Infantry	June 15, 1864, Near Petersburg, Virginia	Point Lookout, Maryland, transferred to Elmira Prison, NY July 12, 1864	Exchanged March 10, 1865 at Boulware's Wharf on the James River, Virginia
Burcham, Shubal W. Private	25	October 4, 1863, Raleigh, North Carolina	Co. D, 33rd North Carolina Infantry	May 12, 1864, Spotsylvania Court House, Virginia	Point Lookout, Maryland, transferred to Elmira Prison, NY July 8, 1864	Died February 25, 1865 of Rheumatism, Grave No. 2275
Burdeaux, Enoch Private	18	September 2, 1863, Fort Pender, North Carolina	Co. H, 36th 2nd North Carolina Artillery	January 15, 1865, Fort Fisher, North Carolina	February 1, 1865, Elmira Prison Camp, New York	Died April 10, 1865 of Variola (Smallpox), Grave No. 2666. Headstone has Enoch Mindex.
Burdeshaw, John T. Private	Unk	September 26, 1862, Henry County, Alabama	Co. K, 3rd Alabama Infantry	May 12, 1864, Spotsylvania Court House, Virginia	Point Lookout, Maryland, transferred to Elmira Prison, NY August 6, 1864	Died March 23, 1865 of Diarrhea, Grave No. 1518
Burdett, Alfred W. Private	Unk	Unknown	Co. B, 13th Alabama Infantry	May 5, 1864, Wilderness, Virginia	Point Lookout, Maryland, transferred to Elmira Prison, NY July 30, 1864	Died September 5, 1864 of Chronic Diarrhea, Grave No. 233
Burdon, W. H. Private	Unk	April 30, 1862, Haralson, Georgia	Co. G, 53rd Georgia Infantry	June 1, 1864, Gaines Mill, Cold Harbor, Virginia	Point Lookout, Maryland, transferred to Elmira Prison, NY July 17, 1864	Died September 7, 1864 of Chronic Diarrhea, Grave No. 247. Name Burton on Headstone.
Buress, John W. Private	Unk	May 2, 1862, Guineas, Virginia	Co. J, 5th Virginia Cavalry	May 11, 1864, Yellow Tavern, Hanover County, Virginia	Point Lookout, Maryland, transferred to Elmira Prison, NY July 8, 1864	Died October 6, 1864 of Typhoid-Pneumonia, Grave No. 590

Name & Rank	Age	Enlisted	Regiment and State	Where Captured	Prison	Remarks
Burford, John T. Sergeant	Unk	July 11, 1861, Lynchburg, Virginia	Co. I, 42nd Virginia Infantry	May 12, 1864, Spotsylvania Court House, Virginia	Point Lookout, Maryland, transferred to Elmira Prison, NY August 2, 1864	Exchanged February 25, 1865 at Boulware's or Cox Wharf on the James River, Virginia
Burford, Robert H. Corporal	Unk	March 22, 1864, Battery No. 6, Virginia	Co. D, 18th Battalion Virginia Heavy Artillery	April 6, 1865, Sailor's Creek, Virginia	Old Capital Prison, Washington D. C. Transferred to Elmira Prison, NY May 12, 1865.	Oath of Allegiance September 11, 1865
Burgamy, William H. Private	Unk	June 15, 1861, Buena Vista, Georgia	Co. K, 12th Georgia Infantry	May 10, 1864, Spotsylvania Court House, Virginia	Point Lookout, Maryland, transferred to Elmira Prison, NY July 25, 1864	Died February 22, 1865 of Variola (Smallpox), Grave No. 2248
Burge, William Private	Unk	Unknown	Co. E, 50th Virginia Infantry	May 5, 1864, Wilderness, Virginia	Point Lookout, Maryland, transferred to Elmira Prison, NY August 14, 1864	Oath of Allegiance June 23, 1865
Burgen, John M. Private	Unk	Unknown	Co. I, 50th Virginia Infantry	May 12, 1864, Near Spotsylvania Court House, Virginia	Point Lookout, Maryland, transferred to Elmira Prison, NY August 2, 1864	Exchanged October 29, 1864, at Venus Point, Savannah River, GA.
Burgess, J. H. Orderly Private	Unk	Unknown	Orderly to Confederate General Richard S. Ewell	April 6, 1865, Sailor's Creek, Virginia	Old Capital Prison, Washington D. C. Transferred to Elmira Prison, NY May 2, 1865.	Oath of Allegiance June 23, 1865
Burgess, John H. Private	19	April 12, 1862, Battery Island, South Carolina	Co. J, 25th South Carolina Infantry	January 15, 1865, Fort Fisher, North Carolina	Elmira Prison Camp January 30, 1865	Oath of Allegiance July 26, 1865
Burgess, Joseph Private	Unk	April 15, 1862, Charleston, South Carolina	Co. B, 18th South Carolina Infantry	July 30, 1864, Petersburg, Virginia	Point Lookout, Maryland, transferred to Elmira Prison, NY August 12, 1864	Died February 20, 1865 of Diarrhea, Grave No. 2307. Headstone has NC Regiment.

Name & Rank	Age	Enlisted	Regiment and State	Where Captured	Prison	Remarks
Burgess, Joseph C. Private	Unk	May 28, 1863, Secessionville, James Island, South Carolina	Co. J, 25th South Carolina Infantry	January 15, 1865, Fort Fisher, North Carolina	Elmira Prison Camp January 30, 1865	Died July 10, 1865 of Chronic Diarrhea, Grave No. 2844
Burgess, Shelton H. Corporal	19	January 1, 1862, Camp Harley, Georgetown, South Carolina	Co. J, 25th South Carolina Infantry	January 15, 1865, Fort Fisher, North Carolina	Elmira Prison Camp January 30, 1865	Exchanged March 2, 1865 at Boulware's Wharf on the James River, Virginia
Burgess, William J. Corporal	20	May 2, 1862, Guineas, Virginia	Co. J, 5th Virginia Cavalry	May 11, 1864, Yellow Tavern, Hanover County, Virginia	Point Lookout, Maryland, transferred to Elmira Prison, NY July 8, 1864	Exchanged October 29, 1864, at Venus Point, Savannah River, GA.
Burk, Isaac Private	Unk	February 22, 1862, Blockers, Alabama	Co. C, 1st Battalion Alabama Artillery	August 23, 1864, Fort Morgan, Alabama	New Orleans, Louisiana transferred to Elmira December 4, 1864.	Died June 25, 1865 of Remittent Fever, Grave No. 2822
Burk, Joseph Private	Unk	February 9, 1864, Centerville, Alabama	Co. C, 1st Battalion Alabama Artillery	August 23, 1864, Fort Morgan, Alabama	New Orleans, Louisiana transferred to Elmira December 4, 1864.	Died January 22, 1865 of Pneumonia, Grave No. 1601
Burke, J. J. Private	Unk	July 1, 1862, Orangeburg, South Carolina	Co. G, 27th South Carolina Infantry	June 24, 1864, Near Petersburg, Virginia	Point Lookout, Maryland, transferred to Elmira Prison, NY August 18, 1864	Died April 11, 1865 of Pneumonia, Grave No. 2675.
Burke, Thomas Quartermaster Sergeant	28	March 15, 1861, Mobile, Alabama	Field and Staff, 1st Alabama Artillery	August 23, 1864, Fort Morgan, Alabama.	New Orleans, Louisiana transferred to Elmira December 4, 1864.	Oath of Allegiance May 17, 1865
Burke, William Private	Unk	September 5, 1862, Butler County, Alabama	Co. B, 3rd Alabama Infantry	May 8, 1864, Spotsylvania Court House, Virginia	Point Lookout, Maryland, transferred to Elmira Prison, NY July 30, 1864	Died December 7, 1864 of Pneumonia, Grave No. 1184
Burket, Joshua Private	Unk	September 2, 1862, Butler County, Alabama	Co. A, 1st Battalion Alabama Artillery	August 23, 1864, Fort Morgan, Alabama	Old Capital Prison, Washington, DC, transferred to Elmira Prison, December 4, 1864	Died January 4, 1865 of Typhoid Fever, Grave No. 1248

Name & Rank	Age	Enlisted	Regiment and State	Where Captured	Prison	Remarks
Burkett, Bartilla Private	Unk	September 2, 1862, Butler County, Alabama	Co. A, 1st Alabama Artillery	August 23, 1864, Fort Morgan, Alabama	New Orleans, Louisiana transferred to Elmira December 4, 1864.	Oath of Allegiance June 21, 1865
Burkett, Christian Private	21	May 17, 1861, Jefferson, North Carolina	Co. A, 26th North Carolina Infantry	July 14, 1863, Falling Waters, Maryland	Point Lookout, Maryland, transferred to Elmira Prison, NY August 18, 1864	Exchanged October 29, 1864 at Venus Point, Savannah River, GA.
Burkett, George H. Private	19	October 27, 1863, Starlington, Butler County, Alabama	Co. A, 1st Alabama Artillery	August 23, 1864, Fort Morgan, Alabama	New Orleans, Louisiana transferred to Elmira December 4, 1864.	Died March 11, 1865 of Chronic Diarrhea, Grave No. 1845
Burkett, John W. Private	40	April 19, 1863, Wilmington, North Carolina	Co. C, 40th Regiment, 3rd North Carolina Heavy Artillery	January 15, 1865, Fort Fisher, North Carolina	February 1, 1865, Elmira Prison Camp, New York	Died February 25, 1865 of Chronic Diarrhea, Grave No. 2289
Burkett, Manuel Private	Unk	February 22, 1863, Fort Morgan, Alabama	Co. A, 1st Alabama Artillery	August 23, 1864, Fort Morgan, Alabama	New Orleans, Louisiana transferred to Elmira December 4, 1864.	Oath of Allegiance May 29, 1865
Burkett, William H. Sergeant	Unk	September 14, 1861, Smythe County, Virginia	Co. E, 23rd Battalion Virginia Infantry	June 2, 1864, Gaines Farm, Cold Harbor, Virginia	Point Lookout, Maryland, transferred to Elmira Prison, NY July 17,1864	Exchanged March 10, 1865 at Boulware's Wharf on the James River, Virginia
Burkhalter, Bryant Private	Unk	May 9, 1861, Reidsville, Georgia	Co. H, 61st Georgia Infantry	May 12, 1864, Spotsylvania Court House, Virginia	Point Lookout, Maryland, transferred to Elmira Prison, NY July 25, 1864	Transferred for Exchange 10/11/64. Died 10/21/64 of Chronic Diarrhea at Point Lookout, MD.
Burkhalter, John Private	Unk	September 1, 1861, Reidsville, Tattnall County, Georgia	Co. B, 61st Georgia Infantry	May 12, 1864, Spotsylvania Court House, Virginia	Point Lookout, Maryland, transferred to Elmira Prison, NY July 30, 1864	Exchanged October 29, 1864, at Venus Point, Savannah River, GA.

Name & Rank	Age	Enlisted	Regiment and State	Where Captured	Prison	Remarks
Burkhart, James M. Private	Unk	July 23, 1861, Mount Airy, Wythe County, Virginia	Co. B, 29th Virginia Infantry	June 3, 1864, Cold Harbor, Virginia	Point Lookout, Maryland, transferred to Elmira Prison, NY July 12, 1864	Exchanged March 10, 1865 at Boulware's Wharf on the James River, Virginia
Burks, Charles L. Sergeant	Unk	August 9. 1861, Cumberland Gap, Tennessee	Co. D, 17th Tennessee Infantry	June 17, 1864, Petersburg, Virginia	Point Lookout, Maryland, transferred to Elmira Prison, NY July 30, 1864	Exchanged February 13, 1865 at Boulware's wharf on the James River, Virginia
Burks, William J. Corporal	23	July 17, 1861, Stewart County, Georgia	Co. J, 21st Georgia Infantry	July 13, 1864, Silver Spring, Maryland. Gunshot Fracture of Right Forearm.	Point Lookout, Maryland, transferred to Elmira Prison, NY August 29, 1864	Exchanged October 29, 1864, at Venus Point, Savannah River, GA.
Burleyson, William Private	20	May 8, 1862, Salisbury, North Carolina	Co. C, 42nd North Carolina Infantry	June 3, 1864, Cold Harbor, Virginia	Point Lookout, Maryland, transferred to Elmira Prison, NY July 17,1864	Died March 9, 1865 of Variola (Smallpox) Grave No. 1871
Burlong, James I. Private	Unk	August 31, 1861, Reidsville, Georgia	Co. B, 61st Georgia Infantry	May 12, 1864, Spotsylvania Court House, Virginia	Point Lookout, Maryland, transferred to Elmira Prison, NY July 25, 1864	Oath of Allegiance June 30, 1865
Burnett, Decatur Private	24	May 14, 1862, Zollicoffer, Sullivan County, Tennessee	Co. F, 63rd Tennessee Infantry	June 17, 1864, Petersburg, Virginia	Point Lookout, Maryland, transferred to Elmira Prison, NY July 30, 1864	Exchanged February 25, 1865 at Boulware's or Cox Wharf on the James River, Virginia
Burnett, J. G. Corporal	Unk	Unknown	Co. B, 7th South Carolina Cavalry	May 6, 1864, Cypress Bridge, Virginia	Point Lookout, Maryland, transferred to Elmira Prison, NY August 17, 1864	Transferred For Exchange October 11, 1864 to Point Lookout Prison Camp, MD. Nothing Further.
Burnett, James C. Private	Unk	July 24, 1861, John Pasley's, Virginia	Co. E, 58th Virginia Infantry	May 20, 1864, Spotsylvania Court House, Virginia	Point Lookout, Maryland, transferred to Elmira Prison, NY July 3, 1864	Exchanged October 29, 1864, at Venus Point, Savannah River, GA.

Name & Rank	Age	Enlisted	Regiment and State	Where Captured	Prison	Remarks
Burnett, John Private	Unk	October 9, 1863, Columbia, South Carolina	Co. C, 22nd South Carolina Infantry	July 30, 1864, Petersburg, Virginia	Point Lookout, Maryland, transferred to Elmira Prison, NY August 12, 1864	Died December 7, 1864 of Pneumonia, Grave No. 1182
Burnett, P. L. Private	Unk	Unknown	Co. C, 3rd Virginia Infantry	June 16, 1864, Near Petersburg, Virginia	Point Lookout, Maryland, transferred to Elmira Prison, NY August 18, 1864	Exchanged March 10, 1865 at Boulware's wharf on the James River, Virginia
Burnett, Samuel H. Private	Unk	March 13, 1862, Kentuck, Virginia	Co. A, 38th Virginia Infantry	May 10, 1864, Near Petersburg, Virginia	Point Lookout, Maryland, transferred to Elmira Prison, NY August 17, 1864	Died December 21, 1864 of Disease of the Heart, Grave No. 1087. Headstone has Bennett.
Burnett, Samuel P. Private	Unk	August 24, 1861, Atlanta, Georgia	Co. E, 3rd Battalion Georgia Sharp shooters	August 16, 1864, Front Royal, Virginia	Point Lookout, Maryland, transferred to Elmira Prison, NY August 29, 1864	Oath of Allegiance July 7, 1865
Burnett, T. Private	Unk	May 10, 1864, Petersburg, Virginia	Co. F, 31st North Carolina Infantry	June 1, 1864, Gaines Farm, Cold Harbor, Virginia	Point Lookout, Maryland, transferred to Elmira Prison, NY July 17, 1864	Died November 7, 1864 of Diphtheria, Grave No. 769
Burnett, William Private	27	April 24, 1861, Fancy Grove, Virginia	Co. B, 14th Virginia Infantry	July 1, 1864, Plank Road, Near Petersburg, Virginia	Point Lookout, Maryland, transferred to Elmira Prison, NY July 23, 1864	Oath of Allegiance May 15, 1865
Burnette, John R. Private	Unk	October 11, 1861, Pig Point, Virginia	Co. H, 59th Virginia Infantry	May 8, 1864, Nottoway Bridge, Virginia	Point Lookout, Maryland, transferred to Elmira Prison, NY August 17, 1864	Exchanged February 13, 1865 at Boulware's wharf on the James River, Virginia
Burney, Daniel Private	46	March 7, 1862, Wilmington, North Carolina	Co. H, 51st North Carolina Infantry	June 15, 1864, Petersburg, Virginia	Point Lookout, Maryland, transferred to Elmira Prison, NY July 12, 1864	Died February 27, 1864 of Chronic Diarrhea, Grave No. 2160. Name Burnell on Headstone.

Name & Rank	Age	Enlisted	Regiment and State	Where Captured	Prison	Remarks
Burney, William James Private	23	March 5, 1862, Elizabethtown, Bladen County, North Carolina	Co. B, 36th Regiment, 2nd North Carolina Artillery	January 15, 1865, Fort Fisher, North Carolina. Wounded	February 1, 1865, Elmira Prison Camp, New York	Exchanged March 2, 1865. Died April 3, 1865 of Debility at Charlotte, North Carolina
Burnley, Charles F. Private	Unk	March 8, 1864, Boydton, Virginia	Co. 3rd Virginia Cavalry	May 12, 1864, Near Mechanics-ville, Virginia	Point Lookout, Maryland, transferred to Elmira Prison, NY August 17, 1864	Oath of Allegiance May 29, 1865
Burns, Edward Sergeant	24	June 4, 1861, Camp Moore, Louisiana	Co. H, 6th Louisiana Infantry	May 12, 1864, Near Spotsylvania Court House, Virginia	Point Lookout, Maryland, transferred to Elmira Prison, NY August 17, 1864	Exchanged February 25, 1865 at Boulware's or Cox Wharf on the James River, Virginia
Burns, George Private	Unk	May 18, 1861, Franklin, Virginia	Co. K, 25th Virginia Infantry	May 12, 1864, Spotsylvania Court House, Virginia	Point Lookout, Maryland, transferred to Elmira Prison, NY August 12, 1864	Exchanged October 29, 1864 at Venus Point, Savannah River, GA.
Burns, Giles M. Private	27	March 1, 1862, Jacinto, Mississippi	Co. A, 2nd Mississippi Infantry	October 1, 1864, Petersburg, Virginia	Old Capital Prison, Washington, DC, transferred to Elmira Prison, NY, December 17, 1864	Oath of Allegiance June 14, 1865
Burns, James N. Private	21	October 1, 1862, Snickersville, Virginia	Co. K, 6th Virginia Cavalry	October 17, 1864, Farquier County, Virginia	Old Capital Prison, Washington, DC, transferred to Elmira Prison, NY, December 17, 1864	Exchanged March 14, 1865 at Boulware's Wharf on the James River, Virginia
Burns, John H. Private	Unk	Unknown	Co. M, 1st Virginia Cavalry	September 23, 1863, Middleburg, Virginia	Point Lookout, Maryland, transferred to Elmira Prison, NY August 18, 1864	Exchanged February 20, 1865 at Boulware's or Cox Wharf on the James River, Virginia

Name & Rank	Age	Enlisted	Regiment and State	Where Captured	Prison	Remarks
Burns, Samuel Private	Unk	January 1, 1863, Baton Rouge, Louisiana	Co. A, Miles' Legion Louisiana	October 2, 1864, Hermitage Plantation Amite, River, Louisiana	New Orleans, Louisiana transferred to Elmira November 19, 1864.	Oath of Allegiance May 17, 1865
Burns, Samuel A. Sergeant	31	October 22, 1861, Charlotte, North Carolina	Co. A, 37th North Carolina Infantry	May 6, 1864, Wilderness, Virginia	Point Lookout, Maryland, transferred to Elmira Prison, NY August 14, 1864	Oath of Allegiance May 15, 1865
Burns, William H. Corporal	Unk	November 1, 1861, Lebanon, Tennessee	Co. B, Jackson's 1st Regiment, Tennessee Heavy Artillery	August 23, 1864, Fort Morgan, Alabama	New Orleans, Louisiana transferred to Elmira December 4, 1864.	Exchanged February 13, 1865 at Boulware's wharf on the James River, Virginia
Burress, D. L. Private	Unk	Unknown	Co. D, 1st North Carolina Infantry	May 20, 1864, Spotsylvania Court House, Virginia	Point Lookout, Maryland, transferred to Elmira Prison, NY July 3, 1864	Exchanged March 14, 1865 at Boulware's Wharf on the James River, Virginia
Burris, G. W. Sergeant Major	Unk	December 25, 1861, Charleston, South Carolina	Field & Staff, 17th South Carolina Infantry	July 30, 1864, Petersburg, Virginia	Point Lookout, Maryland, transferred to Elmira Prison, NY August 12, 1864	Oath of Allegiance July 26, 1865
Burris, William R. Private	20	August 24, 1862, Charlotte, North Carolina	Co. F, 5th North Carolina Cavalry	May 20, 1864, Spotsylvania Court House, Virginia	Point Lookout, Maryland, transferred to Elmira Prison, NY July 6, 1864	Oath of Allegiance June 30, 1865
Burroughs, J. W. Private	Unk	June 1, 1863, Culpepper Court House, Virginia	Co. D, 5th Virginia Cavalry	May 11, 1864, Yellow Tavern, Hanover County, Virginia	Point Lookout, Maryland, transferred to Elmira Prison, NY July 8, 1864	Exchanged March 10, 1865 at Boulware's wharf on the James River, Virginia
Burroughs, Thomas J. Private	18	July 18, 1861, Camp Pickens, Stanardsville, Virginia	Co. D, 34th, Virginia Infantry	June 15, 1864, Near Petersburg, Virginia	Point Lookout, Maryland, transferred to Elmira Prison, NY July 17,1864	Exchanged 3/2/65. Died of Scurvy 3/16/65 at Chimborazo Hospital, No. 2, Richmond, VA

Name & Rank	Age	Enlisted	Regiment and State	Where Captured	Prison	Remarks
Burt, J. G. Private	Unk	April 5, 1862, Luka, Mississippi	Co. A, 17th Tennessee Infantry	June 17, 1864, Petersburg, Virginia	Point Lookout, Maryland, transferred to Elmira Prison, NY July 30, 1864	Exchanged February 13, 1865 at Boulware's wharf on the James River, Virginia
Burt, William E. Private	21	February 25, 1863, Halifax County, North Carolina	Co. J, 12th North Carolina Infantry	May 12, 1864, Near Spotsylvania Court House, Virginia	Point Lookout, Maryland, transferred to Elmira Prison, NY August 14, 1864	Died November 21, 1864 of Pneumonia, Grave No. 940.
Burton, George H. Private	Unk	July 25, 1861, Camp Jackson, Virginia	Co. F, 50th Virginia Infantry	May 12, 1864, Spotsylvania Court House, Virginia	Point Lookout, Maryland, transferred to Elmira Prison, NY July 30, 1864	Exchanged February 20, 1865 at Boulware's or Cox Wharf on the James River, Virginia
Burton, Horace Private	26	April 24, 1861, Mobile, Alabama	Co. K, 3rd Alabama Infantry	May 12, 1864, Spotsylvania Court House, Virginia	Point Lookout, Maryland, transferred to Elmira Prison, NY August 12, 1864	Exchanged March 10, 1865 at Boulware's Wharf on the James River, Virginia
Burton, John E. Private	Unk	Unknown	Co. B, Hood's Battalion, Virginia Reserves	June 15, 1864, Petersburg, Virginia	Point Lookout, Maryland, transferred to Elmira Prison, NY July 30, 1864	Transferred for Exchange 10/11/64. Died 10/17/64 of Unknown Causes at Point Lookout Prison Camp, MD.
Burton, John T. Private	30	August 5, 1861, Currituck County, North Carolina	Co. B, 8th North Carolina Infantry	May 31, 1864, Cold Harbor, Virginia	Point Lookout, Maryland, transferred to Elmira Prison, NY July 12, 1864	Died November 5, 1864 of Chronic Diarrhea, Grave No. 837
Burton, P. O. Sergeant	Unk	July 2, 1861, Bethel Am., Virginia	Co. F, 50th Virginia Infantry	May 12, 1864, Spotsylvania Court House, Virginia	Point Lookout, Maryland, transferred to Elmira Prison, NY August 2, 1864	Exchanged March 2, 1865 at Akins Landing on the James River, Virginia
Burton, Peter L. Sergeant Major	Unk	June 8, 1861, Amelia County Court House, Virginia	Co. H, 44th Virginia Infantry	May 12, 1864, Spotsylvania Court House, Virginia	Point Lookout, Maryland, transferred to Elmira Prison, NY August 2, 1864	Exchanged October 29, 1864, at Venus Point, Savannah River, GA.

Name & Rank	Age	Enlisted	Regiment and State	Where Captured	Prison	Remarks
Burton, Thomas B. Sergeant	Unk	June 27, 1861, Shady Grove, Caswell County, North Carolina	Co. I, 5th North Carolina Infantry	May 12, 1864, Spotsylvania Court House, Virginia	Point Lookout, Maryland, transferred to Elmira Prison, NY August 6, 1864	Exchanged March 10, 1865 at Boulware's Wharf on the James River, Virginia
Burton, William T. Private	Unk	April 3, 1862, Richmond, Virginia	Co. A, 10th Battalion Virginia Heavy Artillery	April 3, 1865, Henrico County, Virginia	Old Capital Prison, Washington D. C. Transferred to Elmira Prison, NY May 12, 1865.	Oath of Allegiance July 7, 1865
Bush, Albert G. Corporal	Unk	Unknown	Co. A, Captain Norwood's Home Guard Florida	September 27, 1864, Marianna, Florida	New Orleans, Louisiana transferred to Elmira November 19, 1864.	Died February 2, 1865 of Acute Bronchitis, Grave No. 1766
Bush, Dionishus W. Sergeant	Unk	July 13, 1861, Barnwell District, South Carolina	Co. A, 1st South Carolina Infantry	May 24, 1864, North Anna, Virginia	Point Lookout, Maryland, transferred to Elmira Prison, NY August 17, 1864	Exchanged March 14, 1865 at Boulware's Wharf on the James River, Virginia
Bush, James S. Private	18	June 1, 1861, Harper's Ferry, Virginia	Co. H, 5th Virginia Infantry	May 20, 1864, Spotsylvania Court House, Virginia	Point Lookout, Maryland, transferred to Elmira Prison, NY July 6, 1864	Died October 6, 1864 of Remittent Fever, Grave No. 647
Bush, Jehu Private	Unk	March 13, 1863, Frankford, Virginia	Co. E, 19th Virginia Cavalry	July 15, 1864, Loudoun County, Virginia	Old Capital Prison, Washington, DC, transferred to Elmira Prison, NY, July 23, 1864	Oath of Allegiance May 13, 1865
Bush, Lolder W. J. Private	Unk	Unknown	Co. D, 58th Virginia Infantry	May 20, 1864, Spotsylvania Court House, Virginia	Point Lookout, Maryland, transferred to Elmira Prison, NY July 3, 1864	Oath of Allegiance June 30, 1865
Bushman, N. T. Private	Unk	Unknown	Co. P, 12th North Carolina Infantry	May 20, 1864, Spotsylvania Court House, Virginia	Point Lookout, Maryland, transferred to Elmira Prison, NY July 3, 1864	Oath of Allegiance June 30, 1865

Name & Rank	Age	Enlisted	Regiment and State	Where Captured	Prison	Remarks
Bushong, J. M. Private	Unk	May 9, 1861, Camp Walker, New Orleans, Louisiana	Co. E, 2nd Louisiana Infantry	May 12, 1864, Spotsylvania, Virginia	Point Lookout, Maryland, transferred to Elmira Prison, NY August 17, 1864	Exchanged 2/20/65. Died 3/14/65 of Unknown Causes at Howard Grove Hospital, VA.
Bushong, John Private	Unk	September 22, 1862, Bristol, Tennessee	Co. E, 63rd Tennessee Infantry	June 17, 1864, Petersburg, Virginia	Point Lookout, Maryland, transferred to Elmira Prison, NY July 30, 1864	Died January 29, 1865 of Chronic Diarrhea, Grave No. 1802
Buskill, John W. Private	24	Unknown	Co. E, 50th Virginia Infantry	May 12, 1864, Spotsylvania Court House, Virginia	Point Lookout, Maryland, transferred to Elmira Prison, NY August 2, 1864	Died April 13, 1865 of Chronic Diarrhea, Grave No. 2680. Name Buskett on Headstone.
Bussard, Samuel Private	17	April 8, 1861, Columbia, South Carolina	Co. E, 2nd South Carolina Infantry	May 24, 1864, Hanover Junction, Virginia	Point Lookout, Maryland, transferred to Elmira Prison, NY July 11, 1864	Exchanged October 29, 1864, at Venus Point, Savannah River, GA.
Buster, William M. Private	23	December 25, 1861, Springfield, Greene County, Missouri	Co. F, 1st Missouri Cavalry	May 17, 1863, Big Black River, Mississippi	Point Lookout, Maryland, transferred to Elmira Prison, NY August 18, 1864	Exchanged February 13, 1865 at Boulware's Wharf on the James River, Virginia
Butcher, James E. Private	25	July 17, 1862, Joyner's Depot, Wilson, North Carolina	Co. C, 8th North Carolina Infantry	June 1, 1864, Cold Harbor, Virginia	Point Lookout, Maryland, transferred to Elmira Prison, NY July 25, 1864	Died January 19, 1865 of Chronic Diarrhea, Grave No. 1202
Butler, David Private	Unk	April 1, 1862, Baker County, Georgia	Co. E, 51st Georgia Infantry	June 3, 1864, Gaines Farm, Cold Harbor, Virginia	Point Lookout, Maryland, transferred to Elmira Prison, NY July 17,1864	Died September 28, 1864 of Chronic Diarrhea, Grave No. 433
Butler, E. L. Private	Unk	Unknown	Co. B, Hood's Battalion, Virginia Reserves	June 15, 1864, Petersburg, Virginia	Point Lookout, Maryland, transferred to Elmira Prison, NY July 30, 1864	Exchanged February 13, 1865 at Boulware's wharf on the James River, Virginia

Name & Rank	Age	Enlisted	Regiment and State	Where Captured	Prison	Remarks
Butler, Emmett A. Private	19	June 4, 1861, Corinth, Mississippi	Co. H, 18th Mississippi Infantry	May 8, 1864, Wilderness, Virginia	Point Lookout, Maryland, transferred to Elmira Prison, NY August 14, 1864	Oath of Allegiance June 30, 1865
Butler, Fountain M. Private	Unk	May 27, 1863, Richmond, Virginia	Co. E, 25th Battalion Virginia Infantry	July 12, 1864, Cox's Farm, Virginia	Point Lookout, Maryland, transferred to Elmira Prison, NY August 6, 1864	Died August 30, 1864 of Rubeola (Measles), Grave No. 54
Butler, George A. Private	Unk	Unknown	Conscript Regiment State Unknown	September 27, 1864, Marianna, Florida	New Orleans, Louisiana transferred to Elmira November 19, 1864.	Died January 23, 1865 of Variola (Smallpox), Grave No. 1610
Butler, Isaac A. Private	20	February 22, 1862, Greenville, Virginia	Co. I, 12th Virginia Infantry	August 21, 1864, Weldon Railroad, Virginia. Gunshot Wound Left Thigh.	Old Capital Prison, Washington D. C. Transferred to Elmira Prison, NY March 3, 1865.	Oath of Allegiance July 7, 1865
Butler, Jerry F. Private	17	August 22, 1861, Charleston, South Carolina	Co. H, 1st South Carolina Infantry	July 13, 1864, Deep Bottom, Virginia, Gunshot Wound Right Knee.	Old Capital Prison, Washington, DC transferred to Elmira Prison, NY August 27, 1864	Exchanged February 13, 1865 at Boulware's Wharf on the James River, Virginia
Butler, John Corporal	30	June 9, 1861, Richmond, Virginia	Co. A, 10th Virginia Cavalry	October 11, 1863, Brandy Station, Virginia	Point Lookout, Maryland, transferred to Elmira Prison, NY July 23, 1864	Oath of Allegiance April 1, 1865
Butler, John C. Private	21	July 18, 1861, Camp Howard, North Carolina	Co. C, 23rd North Carolina Infantry	May 12, 1864, Spotsylvania Court House, Virginia	Point Lookout, Maryland, transferred to Elmira Prison, NY August 14, 1864	Died January 4, 1865 of Variola (Smallpox) Grave No. 1247
Butler, John E. Private	Unk	June 4, 1861, Drayton, Georgia	Co. J, 12th Georgia Infantry	May 10, 1864, Spotsylvania Court House, Virginia	Point Lookout, Maryland, transferred to Elmira Prison, NY July 25, 1864	Oath of Allegiance June 30, 1865

Name & Rank	Age	Enlisted	Regiment and State	Where Captured	Prison	Remarks
Butler, John K. Corporal	Unk	October 6, 1861, Camp Kirkpatrick, Milton County, Georgia	Co. B, 38th Georgia Infantry	May 20, 1864, Spotsylvania Court House, Virginia	Point Lookout, Maryland, transferred to Elmira Prison, NY July 6, 1864	Oath of Allegiance June 19, 1865
Butler, Luke H. Private	28	March 2, 1862, Wilmington, North Carolina	Co. H, 51st North Carolina Infantry	June 16, 1864, Bermuda Hundred, Virginia	Point Lookout, Maryland, transferred to Elmira Prison, NY July 12, 1864	Exchanged March 2, 1865 at Akins Landing on the James River, Virginia
Butler, Patrick 1st Sergeant	23	June 7, 1861, Camp Moore, Louisiana	Co. C, 7th Louisiana Infantry	May 11, 1864, Spotsylvania Court House, Virginia	Point Lookout, Maryland, transferred to Elmira Prison, NY August 17, 1864	Exchanged February 25, 1865 at Boulware's or Cox Wharf on the James River, Virginia
Butler, Raiford D. Private	17	September 1, 1861, Sampson County, North Carolina	Co. A, 30th North Carolina Infantry	May 12, 1864, Spotsylvania Court House, Virginia	Point Lookout, Maryland, transferred to Elmira Prison, NY August 14, 1864	Oath of Allegiance June 30, 1865
Butler, Thomas E. Private	21	February 26, 1862, Camp Leon, Madison, Florida	Co. D, 5th Florida Infantry	May 12, 1864, Spotsylvania Court House, Virginia	Point Lookout, Maryland, transferred to Elmira Prison, NY July 30, 1864	Exchanged October 29, 1864, at Venus Point, Savannah River, GA.
Butler, William F. Private	32	July 18, 1862, Camp Hill, Statesville, North Carolina	Co. E, 18th North Carolina Infantry	May 12, 1864, Spotsylvania Court House, Virginia	Point Lookout, Maryland, transferred to Elmira Prison, NY August 6, 1864	Exchanged February 13, 1865 at Boulware's wharf on the James River, Virginia
Butler, William H. Private	Unk	March 10, 1862, Montross, Virginia	Co. A, 15th Virginia Cavalry	September 14, 1863, Near Culpepper, Virginia	Point Lookout, Maryland, transferred to Elmira Prison, NY August 18, 1864	Exchanged March 2, 1865 at Akins Landing on the James River, Virginia
Butram, William E. Private	25	August 1, 1861, Livingston, Overton County, Tennessee	Co. D, 25th Tennessee Infantry	May 16, 1864, Near Drury's Bluff, Virginia	Point Lookout, Maryland, transferred to Elmira Prison, NY August 17, 1864	Died September 21, 1864 of Chronic Diarrhea, Grave No. 351. Headstone has Bertram.

Name & Rank	Age	Enlisted	Regiment and State	Where Captured	Prison	Remarks
Butt, W. F. Private	Unk	Unknown	Co. B, 48th Virginia Infantry	May 12, 1864, Spotsylvania Court House, Virginia	Point Lookout, Maryland, transferred to Elmira Prison, NY August 2, 1864	Died October 5, 1864 of Chronic Diarrhea, Grave 604. Name Britton on Headstone.
Butterton, James H. Corporal	18	January 23, 1862, Purdy County, North Carolina	Co. A, 3rd Battalion North Carolina Light Artillery	January 15, 1865, Fort Fisher, North Carolina	February 1, 1865, Elmira Prison Camp, New York	Oath of Allegiance June 12, 1865
Butts, Augustus Private	40	May 25, 1861, Pensacola, Florida	Co. A, 2nd Florida Infantry	May 7, 1864, Wilderness, Virginia. Gunshot Wound Hip.	Old Capital Prison, Washington, DC, transferred to Elmira Prison, NY, July 23, 1864	Oath of Allegiance May 11, 1865
Butts, B. H. Private	Unk	May 4, 1864, Petersburg, Virginia	Co. A, 3rd Archer's Battalion, Virginia Reserves Infantry	June 9, 1864, Petersburg, Virginia	Point Lookout, Maryland, transferred to Elmira Prison, NY July 12, 1864	Exchanged October 29, 1864 at Venus Point, Savannah River, GA.
Butts, Mathew W. Private	35	July 15, 1862, Raleigh, North Carolina	Co. D, 1st North Carolina Infantry	May 12, 1864, Spotsylvania Court House, Virginia	Point Lookout, Maryland, transferred to Elmira Prison, NY August 6, 1864	Died November 11, 1864 of Chronic Diarrhea, Grave No. 826
Butts, Thomas J. Sergeant	Unk	February 23, 1861, Montgomery, Alabama	Co. A, 1st Alabama Artillery	August 23, 1864, Fort Morgan, Alabama.	New Orleans, Louisiana transferred to Elmira December 4, 1864.	Died January 14, 1865, Pneumonia, Grave No. 1456
Byers, Samuel R. Private	Unk	July 29, 1861, Columbia, South Carolina	Co. C, 1st South Carolina Infantry	May 23, 1864, North Anna, Virginia	Point Lookout, Maryland, transferred to Elmira Prison, NY July 25, 1864	Oath of Allegiance June 19, 1865
Bynum, John G. Sergeant	39	August 14, 1861, Catawba Station, North Carolina	Co. F, 32nd North Carolina Infantry	May 10, 1864, Wilderness, Virginia	Point Lookout, Maryland, transferred to Elmira Prison, NY August 6, 1864	Oath of Allegiance June 21, 1865

Name & Rank	Age	Enlisted	Regiment and State	Where Captured	Prison	Remarks
Byrd, John F. Sergeant	23	May 28, 1861, Corinth, Mississippi	Co. D, 17th Mississippi Infantry	May 8, 1864, Spotsylvania Court House, Virginia	Point Lookout, Maryland, transferred to Elmira Prison, NY August 17, 1864	Died December 2, 1864 of Pneumonia, Grave No. 1007
Byrd, John O. Private	25	May 12, 1862, Elizabethtown, North Carolina	Co. K, 40th Regiment, 3rd North Carolina Heavy Artillery	January 15, 1865, Fort Fisher, North Carolina	February 1, 1865, Elmira Prison Camp, New York	Oath of Allegiance July 11, 1865
Byrd, Lemuel Private	28	May 13, 1862, Green County, North Carolina	Co. E, 61st North Carolina Infantry	August 27, 1863, Battery Wagner, Morris Island, South Carolina	Point Lookout, Maryland, transferred to Elmira Prison, NY August 18, 1864	Exchanged March 10, 1865 at Boulware's Wharf on the James River, Virginia
Byrd, Leroy Private	Unk	July 15, 1862, Raleigh, North Carolina	Co. C, 5th North Carolina Infantry	May 12, 1864, Spotsylvania Court House, Virginia	Point Lookout, Maryland, transferred to Elmira Prison, NY August 6, 1864	Exchanged October 29, 1864, at Venus Point, Savannah River, GA.
Byrd, Lewis S. Private	Unk	April 15, 1864, Rudes Hill, Virginia	Co. A, 2nd Virginia Infantry	May 12, 1864, Near Spotsylvania Court House, Virginia	Point Lookout, Maryland, transferred to Elmira Prison, NY August 6, 1864	Oath of Allegiance June 14, 1865
Byrd, Matthew Private	18	January 13, 1862, Darlington District, South Carolina	Co. G, 21st South Carolina Infantry	January 15, 1865, Fort Fisher, North Carolina	Elmira Prison Camp, NY, January 30, 1865	Died March 28, 1865 of Chronic Diarrhea, Grave No. 2508
Byrd, Robert Private	40	July 4, 1863, Fort Fisher, North Carolina	Co. K, 40th Regiment, 3rd North Carolina Heavy Artillery	January 15, 1865, Fort Fisher, North Carolina	February 1, 1865, Elmira Prison Camp, New York	Died March 21, 1865 of Chronic Diarrhea, Grave No. 1534
Byrd, Solomon S. Sergeant	Unk	February 5, 1862, Norfolk, Virginia	Co. F, 46th Virginia Infantry	June 17, 1864, Petersburg, Virginia	Point Lookout, Maryland, transferred to Elmira Prison, NY July 30, 1864	Oath of Allegiance June 14, 1865
Byrd, W. C. Private	Unk	March 23, 1862, Charleston, South Carolina	Co. A, 25th South Carolina Infantry	January 15, 1865, Fort Fisher, North Carolina	Elmira Prison Camp January 30, 1865	Oath of Allegiance July 7, 1865

Name & Rank	Age	Enlisted	Regiment and State	Where Captured	Prison	Remarks
Byrd, Wiley Private	20	January 13, 1862, Darlington District, South Carolina	Co. G, 21st South Carolina Infantry	January 15, 1865, Fort Fisher, North Carolina	Elmira Prison Camp January 30, 1865	Oath of Allegiance June 23, 1865
Byrnes, William Private	Unk	Unknown	Co. A, 6th Georgia Infantry	Deserted from Richmond and Surrendered April 28, 1864 at Eastville, Virginia	Point Lookout, Maryland, transferred to Elmira Prison, NY August 18, 1864	Exchanged October 29, 1864, at Venus Point, Savannah River, GA.
Byron, John H. Private	Unk	May 1, 1864, Decatur, Georgia	Co. I, 12th Georgia Infantry	July 13, 1864, Near Washington, DC.	Old Capital Prison, Washington, DC, transferred to Elmira Prison, NY, July 23, 1864	Oath of Allegiance May 17, 1865
Byrum, James H. Private	22	April 1, 1862, Windsor, North Carolina	Co. G, 32nd North Carolina Infantry	July 13, 1864, Near Washington, DC,	Old Capital Prison, Washington, DC, transferred to Elmira Prison, NY, July 23, 1864	Oath of Allegiance June 12, 1865

Name & Rank	Age	Enlisted	Regiment and State	Where Captured	Prison	Remarks
Cabaniss, Joseph W. Private	23	May 17, 1862, Guineas, Virginia	Co. B, 45th Georgia Infantry	April 2, 1865, Fort Gregg, Virginia. Gunshot Wound of Head and Back of Neck.	Old Capital Prison, Washington D. C. Transferred to Elmira Prison, NY May 2, 1865.	Oath of Allegiance July 7, 1865
Cable, Alexander L. Private	19	September 8, 1861, Boone, North Carolina	Co. A, 37th North Carolina Infantry	May 12, 1864, Near Spotsylvania Court House, Virginia	Point Lookout, Maryland, transferred to Elmira Prison, NY August 14, 1864	Oath of Allegiance June 23, 1865
Cable, Eli G. Private	23	July 17, 1862, Randolph County, North Carolina	Co. H, 3rd North Carolina Infantry	May 12, 1864, Near Spotsylvania Court House, Virginia	Point Lookout, Maryland, transferred to Elmira Prison, NY August 14, 1864	Oath of Allegiance June 30, 1865
Cade, Bonyer Private	Unk	February 24, 1864, Richmond, Virginia	Co. B, 14th Virginia Cavalry	May 2, 1864, Ely's Ford, Wilderness, Virginia	Point Lookout, Maryland, transferred to Elmira Prison, NY August 17, 1864	Died October 29, 1864 of Pneumonia, Grave No. 734. Headstone has Bonger.

Name & Rank	Age	Enlisted	Regiment and State	Where Captured	Prison	Remarks
Cade, John L. Sergeant	Unk	January 1, 1862, Georgetown, South Carolina	Co. K, 21st South Carolina Infantry	January 15, 1865, Fort Fisher, North Carolina	Elmira Prison Camp January 30, 1865	Oath of Allegiance July 16, 1865
Cade, John W. Sergeant	Unk	May 11, 1861, New Orleans, Louisiana	Co. A, 2nd Louisiana Infantry	May 5, 1864, Wilderness, Virginia	Point Lookout, Maryland, transferred to Elmira Prison, NY August 17, 1864	Exchanged February 25, 1865 at Boulware's or Cox Wharf on the James River, Virginia
Cade, R. J. Y. Private	Unk	May 1, 1862, Cat Island, South Carolina	Co. J, 4th South Carolina Cavalry	June 11, 1864, Trevilian Station, Louisa Court House, Virginia	Point Lookout, Maryland, transferred to Elmira Prison, NY July 25, 1864	Oath of Allegiance June 30, 1865
Cahoon, Jesse S. Private	23	May 16, 1861, Columbia, North Carolina	Co. A, 32nd North Carolina Infantry	May 10, 1864, Spotsylvania, Virginia	Point Lookout, Maryland, transferred to Elmira Prison, NY August 6, 1864	Oath of Allegiance June 27, 1865
Cain, Cicero C. Sergeant	Unk	December 24, 1861, Lawrenceville, Georgia	Co. F, 24th Georgia Infantry	August 16, 1864, Front Royal, Virginia	Old Capital Prison, Washington, DC transferred to Elmira Prison, NY August 29, 1864	Exchanged March 14, 1865 at Boulware's Wharf on the James River, Virginia
Cain, John S. Corporal	22	May 6, 1862, Bladen County, North Carolina	Co. H, 36th Regiment, 2nd North Carolina Artillery	January 15, 1865, Fort Fisher, North Carolina. Wounded	February 1, 1865, Elmira Prison Camp, New York	Oath of Allegiance July 7, 1865
Cain, Joshua Private	20	March 8, 1862, Fort Fisher, North Carolina	Co. I, 36th Regiment, 2nd North Carolina Artillery	January 15, 1865, Fort Fisher, North Carolina. Wounded	February 1, 1865, Elmira Prison Camp, New York	Died April 20, 1865 of Variola (Smallpox), Grave No. 1384
Cain, Patrick Private	Unk	February 21, 1863, Pine Bluff, Arkansas	Edgar's Co. 1st Texas Field Battery	March 21, 1864, Natchitoches, Louisiana	New Orleans, Louisianna Transferred to Elmira Prison, New York, November 19, 1864	Oath of Allegiance May 17, 1865

Name & Rank	Age	Enlisted	Regiment and State	Where Captured	Prison	Remarks
Cain, Travis H. Private	34	May 6, 1862, Elizabethtown, North Carolina	Co. K, 40th Regiment, 3rd North Carolina Artillery	January 15, 1865, Fort Fisher, North Carolina. Wounded	February 1, 1865, Elmira Prison Camp, New York	Exchanged February 20, 1865 at Boulware's or Cox Wharf on the James River, Virginia
Cain, Wiley Private	38	October 24, 1863, Cumberland County, North Carolina	Co. E, 36th Regiment, 2nd North Carolina Artillery	January 15, 1865, Fort Fisher, North Carolina. Wounded	February 1, 1865, Elmira Prison Camp, New York	Oath of Allegiance June 30, 1865
Cain, William Private	Unk	August 30, 1863, Saltville, Virginia	Co. E, 45th Virginia Infantry	July 14, 1864, Rockville, Maryland	Old Capital Prison, Washington, DC, transferred to Elmira Prison, NY, July 23, 1864	Oath of Allegiance May 17, 1865
Calahan, C. Private	Unk	Unknown	Co. C, 10th Virginia Cavalry	June 3, 1864, Gaines Farm, Cold Harbor, Virginia	Transferred From Point Lookout Prison, MD, July 12, 1864. Train Never Arrived at Elmira Prison Camp, NY.	Died July 15, 1864 in Train Wreck at Shohola, Pennsylvania.
Calaway, P. G. Private	Unk	June 12, 1861, Red Sulphur Springs, Virginia	Co. F, 26th Battalion, Virginia Infantry	June 3, 1864, Gaines Farm, Cold Harbor, Virginia	Point Lookout, Maryland, transferred to Elmira Prison, NY July 17, 1864	Oath of Allegiance July 3, 1865
Calcote, John S. Private	19	October 5, 1863, Reidsville, Mississippi	Co. J, 14th Confederate States Cavalry	April 16, 1864, Franklin County, Mississippi	New Orleans, Louisiana, Transferred to Fort Columbus, NY Harbor Transferred to Elmira Prison, NY, November 19, 1864	Exchanged March 10, 1865 at Boulware's Wharf on the James River, Virginia
Calcutt, George T. Private	48	February 19, 1862, Fayetteville, North Carolina	Co. C, 3rd North Carolina Infantry	May 12, 1864, Near Spotsylvania Court House, Virginia	Point Lookout Prison, Maryland. Transferred to Elmira Prison Camp New York August 14, 1864.	Exchanged February 13, 1865 at Boulware's wharf on the James River, Virginia

Name & Rank	Age	Enlisted	Regiment and State	Where Captured	Prison	Remarks
Calder, Alex Private	46	February 10, 1864, Charleston, South Carolina	Co. A, 27th South Carolina Infantry	June 18, 1864, Near Petersburg, Virginia	Point Lookout, Maryland, transferred to Elmira Prison, NY July 30, 1864	Exchanged October 29, 1864, at Venus Point, Savannah River, GA.
Calder, Edwin E. Private	Unk	February 20, 1862, Charleston, South Carolina	Co. A, 25th South Carolina Infantry	January 15, 1865, Fort Fisher, North Carolina	Elmira Prison Camp January 30, 1865	Oath of Allegiance May 17, 1865
Calder, William Private	26	September 7, 1862, Fayettevile, North Carolina	Co. E, 8th North Carolina Infantry	May 31, 1864, Cold Harbor, Virginia	Point Lookout, Maryland, transferred to Elmira Prison, NY July 11, 1864	Exchanged February 13, 1865 at Boulware's wharf on the James River, Virginia
Calder, William Private	22	April 21, 1862, Marion, South Carolina	Co. F, 27th South Carolina Infantry	August 21, 1864, Petersburg, Virginia. Gunshot Wound Right Leg.	November 11, 1864, Old Capital Prison, Washington, DC. February 4, 1865 Elmira, Prison Camp, NY	Oath of Allegiance July 11, 1865
Caldwell, David Private	25	March 12, 1862, Salem, Virginia	Co. E, 42nd Virginia Infantry	July 20, 1864, Snickers' Gap, Virginia	Old Capital Prison, Washington D. C. Transferred to Elmira Prison, NY August 12, 1864	Died February 27, 1865 of Diarrhea, Grave No. 2145. Headstone has 45th VA
Caldwell, David S. P. Private	Unk	May 7, 1862, Hartwell, Georgia	Co. B, 24th Georgia Infantry	June 1, 1864, Cold Harbor, Virginia	Point Lookout, Maryland, transferred to Elmira Prison, NY July 17,1864	Oath of Allegiance June 19, 1865
Caldwell, J. J. Private	29	September 25, 1862, Newton, North Carolina	Co. E, 32nd North Carolina Infantry	May 10, 1864, Wilderness, Virginia	Point Lookout, Maryland, transferred to Elmira Prison, NY August 6, 1864	Oath of Allegiance June 27, 1865
Caldwell, John A. Private	32	May 13, 1862, Churchville, Highland County, Virginia	Co. J, 14th Virginia Cavalry	July 10, 1864, Frederick, Maryland	Old Capital Prison, Washington, DC, transferred to Elmira Prison, NY, July 23, 1864	Exchanged March 2, 1865 at Akins Landing on the James River, Virginia

Name & Rank	Age	Enlisted	Regiment and State	Where Captured	Prison	Remarks
Caldwell, John M. Private	25	September 15, 1862, Allegheny County, North Carolina	Co. K, 37th North Carolina Infantry	May 12, 1864, Spotsylvania Court House, Virginia Gunshot Wound Right Leg. Leg Amputated.	Old Capital Prison, Washington, DC transferred to Elmira Prison, NY August 27, 1864	Exchanged February 13, 1865 at Boulware's Wharf on the James River, Virginia
Caldwell, L. J. Private	20	September 25, 1862, Newton, North Carolina	Co. E, 32nd North Carolina Infantry	May 10, 1864, Wilderness, Virginia	Point Lookout, Maryland, transferred to Elmira Prison, NY August 6, 1864	Exchanged October 29, 1864, at Venus Point, Savannah River, GA.
Caldwell, R. Pinkney Private	Unk	November 27, 1861, Columbia, South Carolina	Co. F, 17th South Carolina Infantry	July 30, 1864, Petersburg, Virginia	Point Lookout, Maryland, transferred to Elmira Prison, NY August 12, 1864	Oath of Allegiance July 3, 1865
Caldwell, W. H. Private	Unk	Unknown	Co. D, 12th Georgia Infantry	July 15, 1864, Leesburg, Virginia	Old Capital Prison, Washington D. C. Transferred to Elmira Prison, NY August 12, 1864	Oath of Allegiance May 17, 1865
Caldwell, William T. Private	Unk	September 28, 1862, Jefferson County, Alabama	Co. A, 21st Alabama Infantry	August 23, 1864, Fort Morgan, Alabama	Steam Press No. 4, New Orleans, Louisiana transferred to Elmira Prison, October 8, 1864.	Died December 29, 1864 of Chronic Diarrhea, Grave No. 1307
Caldwell, William W. Private	24	August 15, 1862, Mecklenburg County, North Carolina	Co. C, 37th North Carolina Infantry	May 12, 1864, Near Spotsylvania Court House, Virginia	Point Lookout, Maryland, transferred to Elmira Prison, NY August 14, 1864	Transferred for Exchange 10/11/64. Died 10/21/64 of Chronic Diarrhea at US Army Hospital, Baltimore, MD
Cale, James Private	Unk	November 5, 1861, Marlboro District, South Carolina	Co. G, 23rd South Carolina Infantry	June 17, 1864, Near Petersburg, Virginia	Point Lookout, Maryland, transferred to Elmira Prison, NY July 30, 1864	Exchanged February 13, 1865 at Boulware's wharf on the James River, Virginia

Name & Rank	Age	Enlisted	Regiment and State	Where Captured	Prison	Remarks
Caler, J. E. Private	Unk	April 12, 1862, Battery Island, South Carolina	Co. C, 25th South Carolina Infantry	January 15, 1865, Fort Fisher, North Carolina	January 30, 1865, Elmira Prison Camp, NY	Died on the Route to be Exchanged February 20, 1865
Calhoun, Henry A. Sergeant	Unk	September 13, 1861, Whitesville, Georgia	Co. E, 61st Georgia Infantry	May 12, 1864, Spotsylvania Court House, Virginia	Point Lookout, Maryland, transferred to Elmira Prison, NY July 30, 1864	Exchanged March 10, 1865 at Boulware's Wharf on the James River, Virginia
Calhoun, Hugh C. Private	Unk	June 1, 1861, Richmond County, North Carolina	Co. F, 18th North Carolina Infantry	May 12, 1864, Spotsylvania Court House, Virginia	Point Lookout, Maryland, transferred to Elmira Prison, NY August 6, 1864	Died February 8, 1865 of Pneumonia, Grave No. 1929
Calhoun, Jesse S. Private	23	May 16, 1861, Columbia, North Carolina	Co. A, 32nd North Carolina Infantry	May 10, 1864, Spotsylvania, Virginia	Point Lookout, Maryland, transferred to Elmira Prison, NY August 6, 1864	Oath of Allegiance June 27, 1865
Calhoun, John C. Private	Unk	September 15, 1862, Coffee County, Alabama	Co. F, 3rd Alabama Infantry	May 12, 1864, Spotsylvania Court House, Virginia	Point Lookout, Maryland, transferred to Elmira Prison, NY August 12, 1864	Exchanged October 29, 1864 at Venus Point, Savannah River, GA.
Calhoun, Nathan Private	Unk	September 30, 1863, Mt. Pleasant, South Carolina	Co. F, Holcombe Legion, South Carolina	May 8, 1864, Jarrett's Depot, Virginia	Point Lookout, Maryland, transferred to Elmira Prison, NY August 17, 1864	Died September 14, 1865 of Typhoid Fever, Grave No. 264
Call, James H. Private	18	September 27, 1862, Raleigh, North Carolina	Co. L, 13th North Carolina Infantry	May 6, 1864, Wilderness, Virginia	Point Lookout, Maryland, transferred to Elmira Prison, NY August 14, 1864	Died December 10, 1864 of Pneumonia, Grave No. 1159
Call, Richard R. Private	Unk	Unknown	Co. E, 50th Virginia Infantry	May 5, 1864, Wilderness, Virginia	Point Lookout, Maryland, transferred to Elmira Prison, NY August 14, 1864	Oath of Allegiance June 23, 1865

Name & Rank	Age	Enlisted	Regiment and State	Where Captured	Prison	Remarks
Callahan, Erastus J. Private	Unk	September 10, 1861, Covington, Georgia	Co. F, Cobb's Legion Georgia	August 16, 1864, Front Royal, Virginia	Old Capital Prison, Washington, DC transferred to Elmira Prison, NY August 29, 1864	Oath of Allegiance July 11, 1865
Callahan, F. M. Private	Unk	August 15, 1863, Pleasant Hill, Alabama	Jeff Davis Alabama Artillery	May 5, 1864, Wilderness, Virginia	Point Lookout, Maryland, transferred to Elmira Prison, NY August 17, 1864	Exchanged October 29, 1864, at Venus Point, Savannah River, GA.
Callahan, John B. Sergeant	29	April 29, 1861, Marshall, North Carolina	Co. E, 16th North Carolina Infantry	May 6, 1864, Wilderness, Virginia	Point Lookout, Maryland, transferred to Elmira Prison, NY August 14, 1864	Oath of Allegiance June 27, 1865
Callahan, Thomas Private	34	May 10, 1862, Charleston, South Carolina	Co. E, 25th South Carolina Infantry	January 15, 1865, Fort Fisher, North Carolina	Elmira Prison Camp January 30, 1865	Oath of Allegiance July 13, 1865
Callahan, William J. Private	18	November 5, 1861, Wilmington, New Hanover County, North Carolina	Co. B, 36th Regiment North Carolina Artillery	January 15, 1865, Fort Fisher, North Carolina	February 1, 1865, Elmira Prison Camp, New York	Died March 14, 1865 of Gangrene of Feet, Grave No. 1661
Callaway, John C. Private	25	March 25, 1862, Albemarle, North Carolina	Co. J, 52nd North Carolina Infantry	July 14, 1863, Falling Waters, Maryland	Point Lookout Prison Camp, Maryland. Transferred to Elmira Prison Camp, NY, Date Unknown	Died April 8, 1865 of Pneumonia, Grave No. 2637
Callis, John Hiram Private	Unk	July 20, 1861, Matthews Court House, Virginia	Co. D, 26th Virginia Infantry	May 8, 1864, Nollorrary, Virginia	Point Lookout, Maryland, transferred to Elmira Prison, NY August 17, 1864	Exchanged March 2, 1865 at Akins Landing on the James River, Virginia
Callis, John R. Private	46	December 5, 1863, Mathews, Virginia	Co. F, 5th Virginia Infantry	May 20, 1864, Spotsylvania Court House, Virginia	Point Lookout, Maryland, transferred to Elmira Prison, NY July 25, 1864	Died November 19, 1864 of Chronic Diarrhea, Grave No. 969. Name Collins on Headstone.

Name & Rank	Age	Enlisted	Regiment and State	Where Captured	Prison	Remarks
Callis, R, M, Private	Unk	Unknown	Co. A, 3rd Virginia Cavalry	August 16, 1864, Front Royal, Virginia	Old Capital Prison, Washington, DC transferred to Elmira Prison, NY August 29, 1864	Exchanged March 2, 1865 at Akins Landing on the James River, Virginia
Calloway, William T. Private	Unk	April 8, 1864, Dublin, Virginia	Co. C, 4th Virginia Infantry	May 5, 1864, Wilderness, Virginia	Point Lookout, Maryland, transferred to Elmira Prison, NY July 25, 1864	Oath of Allegiance January 21, 1865. Early Release per Lincoln's Proclamation, 12/8/1863.
Calvin, John Private	Unk	August 31, 1861, Place Unknown	Co. F, 23rd Georgia Infantry	June 23, 1864, Between Petersburg and Richmond, Virginia	Point Lookout, Maryland, transferred to Elmira Prison, NY July 23, 1864	Died December 17, 1864 of Pneumonia, Grave No. 1280
Cameron, E. Private		Unknown	Co. M, 1st South Carolina Infantry	May 10, 1864, Spotsylvania, Virginia	Point Lookout, Maryland, transferred to Elmira Prison, NY July 3, 1864	Transferred for Exchange October 11, 1864. Nothing Further.
Cameron, George Private	Unk	May 29, 1864, Petersburg, Virginia	Co. B, 3rd Archer's Battalion, Virginia Reserves Infantry	June 9, 1864, Plank Road, Petersburg, Virginia	Point Lookout, Maryland, transferred to Elmira Prison, NY July 12, 1864	Exchanged October 29, 1864 at Venus Point, Savannah River, GA.
Cameron, William R. Private	Unk	February 24, 1862, Abbeville, Alabama	Co. B, 6th Alabama Infantry	May 4, 1864, Wilderness, Virginia	Point Lookout, Maryland, transferred to Elmira Prison, NY August 17, 1864	Died March 12, 1865 of Diarrhea, Grave No. 1840
Cameson, R. F. Private	Unk	Unknown	Co. B, 4th South Carolina Infantry	May 28, 1864, Hall's Shop, Virginia	Point Lookout, Maryland, transferred to Elmira Prison, NY July 12, 1864	Died December 28, 1864, of Pneumonia, Grave No. 1092
Camp, Charles C. Private	35	July 27, 1863, Camp Randolph, Georgia	Co. B, 7th Georgia Infantry	May 6, 1864, Wilderness, Virginia	Point Lookout, Maryland, transferred to Elmira Prison, NY August 14, 1864	Oath of Allegiance April 18, 1865. Early Release per Lincoln's Proclamation, 12/8/1863.

Name & Rank	Age	Enlisted	Regiment and State	Where Captured	Prison	Remarks
Camp, J. M. Private	Unk	January 14, 1862, Camp Walsh, South Carolina	Co. J, Holcombe Legion, South Carolina Infantry	May 7, 1864, Stony Creek, Virginia	Point Lookout, Maryland, transferred to Elmira Prison, NY August 17, 1864	Exchanged October 29, 1864, at Venus Point, Savannah River, GA.
Camp, J. R. Corporal	Unk	Unknown	Co. H, 3rd North Carolina Infantry	May 12, 1864, Near Spotsylvania Court House, Virginia	Point Lookout Prison Camp, Maryland. Transferred to Elmira Prison, August 24, 1864	Died February 15, 1865 of Variola (Smallpox), Grave No. 2177
Camp, John Corporal	Unk	March 5, 1861, Six Mile Bridge, Alabama	Co. C, 1st Battalion Alabama Artillery	August 23, 1864, Fort Morgan, Alabama	New Orleans, Louisiana transferred to Elmira December 4, 1864.	Oath of Allegiance May 17, 1865
Camp, John L. Private	Unk	January 29, 1864, Cobb County, Georgia	Co. D, 7th Georgia Cavalry	June 11, 1864, Trevilian Station, Louisa Court House, Virginia	Point Lookout, Maryland, transferred to Elmira Prison, NY July 25, 1864	Exchanged March 2, 1865 at Akins Landing on the James River, Virginia
Camp, Milton Private	Unk	February 16, 1862, Scottsville, Alabama	Co. C, 1st Battalion Alabama Artillery	August 23, 1864, Fort Morgan, Alabama	New Orleans, Louisiana transferred to Elmira December 4, 1864.	Oath of Allegiance June 21, 1865
Campbell, A. J. Civilian	Unk	Unknown	Citizen of Louisiana	September 19, 1864, Fenson Parish, Louisiana	Old Capital Prison, Washington, DC transferred to Elmira Prison, NY August 27, 1864	Exchanged March 14, 1865 at Boulware's Wharf on the James River, Virginia
Campbell, A. T. Private	32	August 15, 1861, Jonesboro, North Carolina	Co. H, 30th North Carolina Infantry	May 12, 1864, Spotsylvania Court House, Virginia	Point Lookout, Maryland, transferred to Elmira Prison, NY August 14, 1864	Died March 22, 1865 of Pneumonia, Grave No. 2441. Name A. P. Campbell on Headstone.
Campbell, Alan J. Private	Unk	May 25, 1861, Montevallo, Alabama	Co. F, 1st Battalion Alabama Artillery	August 23, 1864, Fort Morgan, Alabama	Steam Press No. 4, New Orleans, Louisiana transferred to Elmira Prison, October 8, 1864.	Died January 3, 1865 of Remittent Fever, Grave No. 1344

Name & Rank	Age	Enlisted	Regiment and State	Where Captured	Prison	Remarks
Campbell, Andrew Jackson Private	Unk	April 23, 1864, Jasper County, Georgia	Co. B, 44th Georgia Infantry	May 10, 1864, Spotsylvania Court House, Virginia Gunshot Wound Left Shoulder.	Old Capital Prison, Washington D. C. Transferred to Elmira Prison, NY August 12, 1864	Died October 5, 1864 of Chronic Diarrhea, Grave No. 605. Name James Campbell on Headstone.
Campbell, Archibald Private	30	October 19, 1861, Elizabethtown, Bladen County, North Carolina	Co. I, 36th Regiment 2nd North Carolina Artillery	January 15, 1865, Fort Fisher, North Carolina	February 1, 1865, Elmira Prison Camp, New York	Exchanged February 20, 1865 at Boulware's or Cox Wharf on the James River, Virginia
Campbell, Charles J. E. Private	18	March 11, 1863, Moore County, North Carolina	Co. B, 36th Regiment, 2nd North Carolina Artillery	January 15, 1865, Fort Fisher, North Carolina. Wounded	February 1, 1865, Elmira Prison Camp, New York	Died February 19, 1865 of Chronic Diarrhea, Grave No. 2316
Campbell, Charles William Private	Unk	March 10, 1862, Lexington, Virginia	Co. C, 1st Virginia Cavalry	May 12, 1864, Spotsylvania Court House, Virginia	Point Lookout, Maryland, transferred to Elmira Prison, NY August 18, 1864	Exchanged March 10, 1865 at Boulware's wharf on the James River, Virginia
Campbell, Colen Private	41	August 15, 1863, Fort Branch, Martin County, North Carolina	Co. G, 40th Regiment, 3rd North Carolina Artillery	January 15, 1865, Fort Fisher, North Carolina	Elmira Prison Camp January 30, 1865	Died March 2, 1865 of Diarrhea, Grave No. 1999
Campbell, Duncan D. Private	18	September 25, 1862, Bladen County, North Carolina	Co. B, 36th Regiment, 2nd North Carolina Artillery	January 15, 1865, Fort Fisher, North Carolina. Wounded	February 1, 1865, Elmira Prison Camp, New York	Died March 9, 1865 of Diarrhea, Grave No. 1885
Campbell, Eugene Private	16	October 3, 1861, Vidalia, Louisiana	Co. F, 1st Louisiana Cavalry	September 14, 1864, Tunica, Louisiana	New Orleans, Louisiana transferred to Elmira November 19, 1864.	Died January 10, 1865 of Variola (Smallpox), Grave No. 1214
Campbell, George Private	Unk	April 24, 1864, Bristol, Tennessee	Co. A, 14th Tennessee Infantry	May 6, 1864, Wilderness, Virginia	Point Lookout, Maryland, transferred to Elmira Prison, NY July 23, 1864	Died December 7, 1864 of Chronic Diarrhea, Grave No. 1181

Name & Rank	Age	Enlisted	Regiment and State	Where Captured	Prison	Remarks
Campbell, H. B. Corporal	Unk	October 1, 1863, Camp Harlee, South Carolina	Co. D, 21st South Carolina Infantry	January 15, 1865, Fort Fisher, North Carolina	Elmira Prison Camp January 30, 1865	Oath of Allegiance July 11, 1865
Campbell, J. P. Private	Unk	June 18, 1864, Raleigh, North Carolina	Co. E, 12th North Carolina Infantry	May 12, 1864, Spotsylvania Court House, Virginia	Old Capital Prison, Washington, DC transferred to Elmira Prison, NY August 29, 1864	Oath of Allegiance July 11, 1865
Campbell, J. W. Private	Unk	March 7, 1862, Lebanon, Alabama	Co. E, 12th Alabama Infantry	June 10, 1864, Spotsylvania Court House, Virginia	Point Lookout, Maryland, transferred to Elmira Prison, NY July 25, 1864	Oath of Allegiance May 11, 1865
Campbell, James R. Sergeant	25	March 8, 1862, Camp Leon, Madison, Florida	Co. D, 5th Florida Infantry	May 12, 1864, Spotsylvania Court House, Virginia	Point Lookout, Maryland, transferred to Elmira Prison, NY July 30, 1864	Oath of Allegiance June 19, 1865
Campbell, John Private	25	June 19, 1861, Camp Moore, Tangipaho, Louisiana	Co. D, 8th Louisiana Infantry	May 12, 1864, Spotsylvania Court House, Virginia	Transferred From Point Lookout Prison, MD, July 12, 1864. Train Never Arrived at Elmira Prison Camp, NY.	Died July 15, 1864 in Train Wreck at Shohola, Pa. Grave No. 2852. Headstone has 3rd Regiment
Campbell, John A. Private	Unk	May 21, 1861, Brownsburg, Virginia	Co. H, 25th Virginia Infantry	May 6, 1864, Wilderness, Virginia	Point Lookout, Maryland, transferred to Elmira Prison, NY August 14, 1864	Exchanged October 29, 1864, at Venus Point, Savannah River, GA.
Campbell, John C. Sergeant	17	December 20, 1861, Camp Harlee, South Carolina	Co. D, 21st South Carolina Infantry	January 15, 1865, Fort Fisher, North Carolina	Elmira Prison Camp January 30, 1865	Oath of Allegiance July 11, 1865
Campbell, John D. Private	18	March 19, 1863, Chatham County, North Carolina	Co. K, 12th North Carolina Infantry	May 12, 1864, Near Spotsylvania County Court House, Virginia	Point Lookout, Maryland, transferred to Elmira Prison, NY August 14, 1864	Died August 28, 1865 of Chronic Diarrhea, Grave No. 2856. Headstone has John N. Campbell, 25th NC.

Name & Rank	Age	Enlisted	Regiment and State	Where Captured	Prison	Remarks
Campbell, John H. Private	Unk	May 10, 1862, Henry County, Virginia	Co. G, 42nd Virginia Infantry	May 12, 1864, Near Spotsylvania Court House, Virginia	Point Lookout, Maryland, transferred to Elmira Prison, NY August 6, 1864	Oath of Allegiance June 27, 1865
Campbell, Leonard Private	25	December 17, 1861, Unionville, South Carolina	Co. C, 18th South Carolina Infantry	July 30, 1864, Petersburg, Virginia	Point Lookout, Maryland, transferred to Elmira Prison, NY August 12, 1864	Died March 28, 1865 of Diarrhea, Grave No. 2485
Campbell, Martin Private	21	July 9, 1861, Camp McDonald, Cobb County, Georgia	Co. E, Phillips Legion, Georgia	June 2, 1864, Gaines Farm, Cold Harbor, Virginia	Point Lookout, Maryland, transferred to Elmira Prison, NY July 17,1864	Exchanged March 14, 1865 on the James River, Virginia. Died March 20th of Unknown Disease.
Campbell, Morgan B. Private	23	July 30, 1861, Allegheny County, Virginia	Co. E, 31st Virginia Infantry	May 30, 1864, Below Richmond, Virginia	Old Capital Prison, Washington, DC, transferred to Elmira Prison, NY, July 23, 1864	Exchanged October 29, 1864, at Venus Point, Savannah River, GA.
Campbell, Neill A. Private	25	April 1, 1862, St. Paul's, Floral, North Carolina	Co. G, 24th North Carolina Infantry	June 17, 1864, Near Petersburg, Virginia	Point Lookout, Maryland, transferred to Elmira Prison, NY July 30, 1864	Died January 5, 1865 of Typhoid-Pneumonia, Grave No. 1239. Name W. A. Campbell on Headstone.
Campbell, Robert G. Private	38	October 25, 1864, Rockbridge, Virginia	Co. D, 25th Virginia Infantry	March 25, 1865, Fort Steadman, Virginia. Gunshot Wound Right Shoulder and Arm.	Old Capital Prison, Washington D. C. Transferred to Elmira Prison, NY May 12, 1865.	Oath of Allegiance June 21, 1865
Campbell, Robert P. Sergeant	21	May 14, 1862, Loachapoka, Tallapoosa County, Alabama	Co. F, 47th Alabama Infantry	May 6, 1864, Wilderness, Virginia	Point Lookout, Maryland, transferred to Elmira Prison, NY August 17, 1864	Oath of Allegiance June 14, 1865

Name & Rank	Age	Enlisted	Regiment and State	Where Captured	Prison	Remarks
Campbell, Thomas Private	36	March 20, 1862, Danbury, North Carolina	Co. G, 53rd North Carolina Infantry	July 13, 1864, Near Washington, DC	Old Capital Prison, Washington, DC, transferred to Elmira Prison, NY, July 23, 1864	Died January 4, 1865 of Pneumonia, Grave 1250
Campbell, Thomas C. Private	19	May 13, 1862, Pittsboro, North Carolina	Co. D, 61st North Carolina Infantry	August 27, 1863, Battery Wagner, Morris Island, South Carolina	Point Lookout, Maryland, transferred to Elmira Prison, NY August 18, 1864	Exchanged October 29, 1864, at Venus Point, Savannah River, GA.
Campbell, William Private	20	December 1, 1861, Cleveland, Tennessee	Co. D, 63rd Tennessee Infantry	June 17, 1864, Petersburg, Virginia	Point Lookout, Maryland, transferred to Elmira Prison, NY July 30, 1864	Exchanged February 25, 1865 at Boulware's or Cox Wharf on the James River, Virginia
Campbell, William A. Private	24	November 5, 1861, Bladen County, North Carolina	Co. B, 36th Regiment, 2nd North Carolina Artillery	January 15, 1865, Fort Fisher, North Carolina. Wounded	February 1, 1865, Elmira Prison Camp, New York	Exchanged March 2, 1865. Died March 10, 1865 at General Hospital No. 9, Richmond, Virginia.
Campbell, William L. Private	Unk	May 10, 1861, New Orleans, Louisiana	Co. A, 5th Louisiana Infantry	May 5, 1864, Wilderness, Virginia	Point Lookout, Maryland, transferred to Elmira Prison, NY July 17,1864	Oath of Allegiance June 14, 1865
Campion, Benjamin Franklin Private	18	December 20, 1861, Camp Harlee, Cheraw, South Carolina	Co. D, 21st South Carolina Infantry	January 15, 1865, Fort Fisher, North Carolina	Elmira Prison Camp January 30, 1865	Oath of Allegiance May 29, 1865
Canaday, William J. Private	39	March 15 863, Fort Fisher, New Hanover County, North Carolina	Co. C, 36th Regiment North Carolina, 2nd Artillery	January 15, 1865, Fort Fisher, North Carolina	February 1, 1865, Elmira Prison Camp, New York	Oath of Allegiance June 12, 1865
Canady, Evander Private	16	April 24, 1861, Bug Hill, North Carolina	Co. C, 18th North Carolina Infantry	May 12, 1864, Spotsylvania Court House, Virginia	Point Lookout, Maryland, transferred to Elmira Prison, NY August 6, 1864	Oath of Allegiance May 13, 1865

Name & Rank	Age	Enlisted	Regiment and State	Where Captured	Prison	Remarks
Canady, Laban Private	23	October 6, 1861, Dallas, Gaston County, North Carolina	Co. H, 37th North Carolina Infantry	May 12, 1864, Spotsylvania Court House, Virginia	Point Lookout, Maryland, transferred to Elmira Prison, NY August 12, 1864	Oath of Allegiance May 19, 1865
Canarny, James Private	Unk	May 26, 1863, Fort Morgan, Alabama	Co. B, 1st Battalion Alabama Artillery	August 8, 1864, Fort Gaines, Alabama	Old Capital Prison, Washington, DC transferred to Elmira Prison, NY August 27, 1864	Died March 27, 1865 of Diarrhea, Grave No. 2491. Headstone has James Kanan.
Candler, John N. Private	19	March 8, 1862, Mt. Lebanon, Louisiana	Co. C, 9th Louisiana Infantry	May 12, 1864, Spotsylvania Court House, Virginia	Point Lookout, Maryland, transferred to Elmira Prison, NY August 17, 1864	Oath of Allegiance July 7, 1865
Canfield, Ashur Private	Unk	March 20, 1863, King and Queen Court House, Virginia	Co. F, 24th Virginia Cavalry	May 12, 1864, Savage Station, Virginia	Point Lookout, Maryland, transferred to Elmira Prison, NY July 17,1864	Exchanged February 13, 1865 at Boulware's wharf on the James River, Virginia
Canley, Samuel L. Private	Unk	May 10, 1862, Dallas, Gaston County, North Carolina	Co. H, 37th North Carolina Infantry	May 12, 1864, Spotsylvania Court House, Virginia	Point Lookout, Maryland, transferred to Elmira Prison, NY August 12, 1864	Oath of Allegiance June 14, 1865
Cannon, Archibald Private	25	February 27, 1862, Wilmington, North Carolina	Co. D, 36th Regiment, 2nd North Carolina Artillery	January 15, 1865, Fort Fisher, North Carolina. Wounded	February 1, 1865, Elmira Prison Camp, New York	Exchanged February 20, 1865. Died March 11, 1865 at Howard's Grove General Hospital, Richmond, VA.
Cannon, Elkanah Private	Unk	July 1, 1862, Spartanburg, South Carolina	Co. M, McCreary's 1st South Carolina Infantry	May 12, 1864, Spotsylvania, Virginia	Point Lookout, Maryland, transferred to Elmira Prison, NY July 17,1864	Exchanged October 29, 1864, at Venus Point, Savannah River, GA.
Cannon, James Private	41	July 21, 1863, Duplin County, North Carolina	Co. G, 40th Regiment, 3rd North Carolina Artillery	January 15, 1865, Fort Fisher, North Carolina	Elmira Prison Camp January 30, 1865	Died April 10, 1865, Pneumonia, Grave No. 2667

Name & Rank	Age	Enlisted	Regiment and State	Where Captured	Prison	Remarks
Cannon, R. J. Private	26	May 11, 1862, Williamsburg, South Carolina	Co. K, 25th South Carolina Infantry	January 15, 1865, Fort Fisher, North Carolina	Elmira Prison Camp January 30, 1865	Died March 9, 1865 of Diarrhea, Grave No. 1872
Canoy, John H. Private	Unk	March 23, 1863, Randolph County, North Carolina	Co. K, 10th Regiment, 1st North Carolina Artillery	January 15, 1865, Fort Fisher, North Carolina	January 30, 1865, Elmira Prison Camp, NY	Oath of Allegiance August 7, 1865
Cansler, Abel J. Private	20	August 14, 1861, Newton, North Carolina	Co. E, 32nd North Carolina Infantry	May 10, 1864, Wilderness, Virginia	Point Lookout, Maryland, transferred to Elmira Prison, NY August 6, 1864	Oath of Allegiance August 7, 1865
Canterbury, James D. Private	Unk	Unknown	Co. G, 8th Virginia Cavalry	July 10, 1864, Frederick, Maryland	Old Capital Prison, Washington, DC, transferred to Elmira Prison, NY, July 23, 1864	Exchanged March 14, 1865 at Boulware's Wharf on the James River, Virginia
Cantor, William J. Private	25	April 21, 1861, Memphis, Tennessee	Co. E, 1st Missouri Cavalry	May 17, 1863, Big Black Bridge, Champion Hill, Mississippi	Point Lookout, Maryland, transferred to Elmira Prison, NY August 18, 1864	Exchanged February 13, 1865 at Boulware's wharf on the James River, Virginia
Cantrell, Cornelius W. Private	Unk	March 1, 1861, Wetumpka, Alabama	Co. E, 1st Battalion Alabama Artillery	August 23, 1864, Fort Morgan, Alabama	New Orleans, Louisiana transferred to Elmira December 4, 1864.	Oath of Allegiance May 29, 1865
Cantrell, George W. Private	17	February 27, 1862, Reidsville, North Carolina	Co. E, 45th North Carolina Infantry	May 10, 1864, Spotsylvania Court House, Virginia	Point Lookout, Maryland, transferred to Elmira Prison, NY August 6, 1864	Died December 12, 1864 of Pneumonia, Grave No. 1144
Cantrell, Lorenzo A. Private	Unk	July 10, 1861, Spartanburg Court House, South Carolina	Co. J, 5th South Carolina Infantry	August 8, 1864, Deserted Near Deep Bottom, Virginia	Point Lookout, Maryland, transferred to Elmira Prison, NY August 18, 1864	Oath of Allegiance May 17, 1865
Canup, Benjamin F. Private	Unk	April 13, 1863, Salisbury, North Carolina	Co. K, 8th North Carolina Infantry	May 31, 1864, Cold Harbor, Virginia	Point Lookout, Maryland, transferred to Elmira Prison, NY July 11, 1864	Transferred for Exchange October 11, 1864. Died 10/13/64 at US Army Hospital, Baltimore, MD.

Name & Rank	Age	Enlisted	Regiment and State	Where Captured	Prison	Remarks
Canup, Miles A. Private	Unk	April 14, 1863, Salisbury, North Carolina	Co. K, 8th North Carolina Infantry	June 16, 1864, Petersburg, Virginia	Point Lookout, Maryland, transferred to Elmira Prison, NY July 12, 1864	Died November 2, 1864 of Pneumonia, Grave No. 760
Cape, Enoch A. Private	Unk	April 13, 1864, Homer, Georgia	Co. A, 24th Georgia Infantry	August 16, 1864, Front Royal, Virginia	Old Capital Prison, Washington, DC transferred to Elmira Prison, NY August 29, 1864	Died February 9, 1865 of Variola (Smallpox), Grave No. 1955
Capehart, Francis M. Private	24	August 27, 1861, Jefferson County, North Carolina	Co. A, 37th North Carolina Infantry	May 12, 1864, Near Spotsylvania Court House, Virginia	Point Lookout, Maryland, transferred to Elmira Prison, NY August 14, 1864	Oath of Allegiance June 30, 1865
Capel, Jesse A. Private	Unk	May 20, 1864, Fort Fisher, North Carolina	Co. H, 36th Regiment, 2nd North Carolina Artillery	January 15, 1865, Fort Fisher, North Carolina. Wounded	February 1, 1865, Elmira Prison Camp, New York	Oath of Allegiance July 11, 1865
Capps, Abner Private	29	July 15, 1862, Place Unknown, North Carolina	Co. G, 3rd North Carolina Infantry	May 7, 1864, Wilderness, Virginia	Point Lookout, Maryland, transferred to Elmira Prison, NY August 12, 1864	Oath of Allegiance June 30, 1865
Capps, Charles W. Private	30	July 15, 1862, Raleigh, North Carolina	Co. D, 1st North Carolina Infantry	May 12, 1864, Spotsylvania Court House, Virginia	Point Lookout, Maryland, transferred to Elmira Prison, NY August 6, 1864	Died June 30, 1865 of Pneumonia, Grave No. 2831
Capps, John M. Private	30	July 15, 1862, Raleigh, North Carolina	Co. E, 1st North Carolina Infantry	May 12, 1864, Spotsylvania Court House, Virginia	Point Lookout, Maryland, transferred to Elmira Prison, NY August 6, 1864	Died January 1, 1865 of Pneumonia, Grave No. 1331
Capps, William C. Private	Unk	August 29, 1864, Henry County, Alabama	Co. D, 3rd Alabama Infantry	May 12, 1864, Spotsylvania Court House, Virginia	Point Lookout, Maryland, transferred to Elmira Prison, NY August 12, 1864	Died January 27, 1865 of Pneumonia, Grave No. 1631

Name & Rank	Age	Enlisted	Regiment and State	Where Captured	Prison	Remarks
Carden, John W. Private	Unk	March 1, 1864, Orange County, North Carolina	Co. G, 28th North Carolina Infantry	July 29, 1864, Petersburg, Virginia	Point Lookout, Maryland, transferred to Elmira Prison, NY August 12, 1864	Died October 1, 1864 of Chronic Dysentery, Grave No. 418. Name Corder on Headstone.
Cardwell, James Private	Unk	February 7, 1863, Little Plymouth, Virginia	Co. G, 26th Virginia Infantry	June 15, 1864, Petersburg, Virginia	Point Lookout, Maryland, transferred to Elmira Prison, NY July 30, 1864	Died September 5, 1864 of Rubeola (Measles), Grave No. 235
Cardwell, Joseph B. Private	41	May 7, 1861, New Prospect, Virginia	Co. C, 26th North Carolina Infantry	May 12, 1864, Spotsylvania Court House, Virginia	Point Lookout, Maryland, transferred to Elmira Prison, NY July 30, 1864	Died October 20, 1864 of Pneumonia, Grave No. 878
Carey, James E. Private	26	September 17, 1863, Chaffin's Farm, Virginia	Co. F, 46th Virginia Infantry	March 17, 1864, Pungo Teague, Accomac County, Virginia	Point Lookout, Maryland, transferred to Elmira Prison, NY July 25, 1864	Oath of Allegiance April 1, 1865
Carfield, Henry L. Private	Unk	Unknown	Co. F, 6th North Carolina Infantry	July 10, 1864, Frederick, Maryland	Old Capital Prison, Washington, DC, transferred to Elmira Prison, NY, July 23, 1864	Oath of Allegiance June 12, 1865
Carickhoff, Peter C. Private	Unk	April 10, 1862, Harrisonburg, Virginia	Co. E, 10th Virginia Infantry	May 12, 1864, Spotsylvania Court House, Virginia	Point Lookout, Maryland, transferred to Elmira Prison, NY August 2, 1864	Oath of Allegiance June 27, 1865
Carico, Martin Private	Unk	July 25, 1862, Delps Muster Ground, Carroll County, Virginia	Co. C, 29th, Virginia Infantry	June 1, 1864, Gaines Mill, Cold Harbor, Virginia	Point Lookout, Maryland, transferred to Elmira Prison, NY July 12, 1864	Exchanged March 14, 1865 at Boulware's Wharf on the James River, Virginia
Carithers, J. D. Corporal	Unk	September 18, 1862, Danielsville, Georgia	Co. D, 16th Georgia Infantry	August 16, 1864, Front Royal, Virginia	Old Capital Prison, Washington, DC transferred to Elmira Prison, NY August 29, 1864	Oath of Allegiance July 11, 1865

Name & Rank	Age	Enlisted	Regiment and State	Where Captured	Prison	Remarks
Carithers, William A. Private	Unk	August 5, 1861, Danielsville, Georgia	Co. D, 16th Georgia Infantry	August 16, 1864, Front Royal, Virginia	Old Capital Prison, Washington, DC transferred to Elmira Prison, NY August 29, 1864	Oath of Allegiance July 11, 1865
Carithers, William H. Private	Unk	Unknown	Co. A, 16th Georgia Infantry	August 16, 1864, Front Royal, Virginia	Old Capital Prison, Washington, DC transferred to Elmira Prison, NY August 29, 1864	Oath of Allegiance July 7, 1865
Carlen, Philip Private	Unk	July 29, 1863, Mobile, Louisiana	Co. G, 5th Louisiana Infantry	June 3, 1864, Old Church, Virginia	Point Lookout, Maryland, transferred to Elmira Prison, NY July 17, 1864	Oath of Allegiance May 29, 1865
Carlisle, Dennis L. Corporal	39	April 7, 1862, Fayetteville, North Carolina	Co. D, 51st North Carolina Infantry	June 16, 1864, Near Petersburg, Virginia	Point Lookout, Maryland, transferred to Elmira Prison, NY July 9, 1864	Died September 29, 1864 of Chronic Diarrhea, Grave No. 400
Carlisle, S. S. Private	Unk	April 29, 1863, White Sulfur Springs, Virginia	Co. C, 26th Battalion, Virginia Infantry	June 3, 1864, Gaines Farm, Cold Harbor, Virginia	Point Lookout, Maryland, transferred to Elmira Prison, NY July 17, 1864	Exchanged February 13, 1865 at Boulware's wharf on the James River, Virginia
Carlton, George Private	Unk	Unknown	Co. E, 24th Alabama Infantry	July 4, 1864, Alexandria, Virginia	Old Capital Prison, Washington, DC, transferred to Elmira Prison, NY, July 23, 1864	Joined US Army and Deserted.
Carlton, George W. Private	22	September 8, 1862, Statesville, North Carolina	Co. G, 18th North Carolina Infantry	May 12, 1864, Spotsylvania Court House, Virginia	Point Lookout, Maryland, transferred to Elmira Prison, NY August 6, 1864	Died February 6, 1865 of Variola (Smallpox), Grave No. 1905
Carlton, J. B. Private	Unk	July 16, 1861, Monroe, Georgia	Co. F, 16th Georgia Infantry	June 1, 1864, Cold Harbor, Virginia	Point Lookout, Maryland, transferred to Elmira Prison, NY July 17,1864	Died September 18, 1864 of Chronic Diarrhea, Grave No. 162

Name & Rank	Age	Enlisted	Regiment and State	Where Captured	Prison	Remarks
Carlton, William B. Private	33	May 7, 1861, New Prospect, Virginia	Co. G, 26th Virginia Infantry	June 15, 1864, Petersburg, Virginia	Point Lookout, Maryland, transferred to Elmira Prison, NY July 30, 1864	Transferred For Exchange October 11, 1864 to Point Lookout Prison Camp, MD. Nothing Further.
Carman, John Private	Unk	June 13, 1861, Lebanon, Alabama	Co. C, 12th Alabama Infantry	May 12, 1864, Spotsylvania Court House, Virginia	Point Lookout, Maryland, transferred to Elmira Prison, NY July 6, 1864	Died February 5, 1865 of Variola (Smallpox), Grave No. 1908
Carmichael, J. T. Private	Unk	March 28, 1862, Marion District, South Carolina	Co. L, 21st South Carolina Infantry	January 15, 1865, Fort Fisher, North Carolina	Elmira Prison Camp January 30, 1865	Died March 30, 1865 of Pneumonia, Grave No. 2592
Carmichael, J. Wiseman Private	34	October 21, 1862, Camp French, North Carolina	Co. D, 52nd North Carolina Infantry	May 6, 1864, Wilderness, Virginia	Point Lookout, Maryland, transferred to Elmira Prison, NY July 25, 1864	Oath of Allegiance May 15, 1865
Carmina, Leroy Private	Unk	Unknown	Co. K, 2nd Louisiana Cavalry	September 9, 1864, Near Houma, Louisiana	New Orleans, Louisiana. Transferred to Elmira November 5, 1864	Exchanged February 13, 1865 at Boulware's Wharf on the James River, Virginia
Carmonche, Alcide Private	Unk	September 1, 1862, New Road, Louisiana	Co. K, 2nd Louisiana Cavalry	July 1, 1864, Near Morganza, Florida	Fort Columbus, New York Harbor. Transferred to Elmira November 19, 1864.	Died December 12, 1864 of Variola (Smallpox), Grave No. 1143
Carmonche, E. Avelaid Private	Unk	September 1, 1862, New Road, Louisiana	Co. K, 2nd Louisiana Cavalry	October 20, 1864, False River, Pointe Coupee Parish, Louisiana	New Orleans, Louisiana transferred to Elmira November 19, 1864.	Exchanged February 25, 1865 at Boulware's or Cox Wharf on the James River, Virginia
Carnard, L. Private	Unk	Unknown	Co. G, 4th South Carolina Infantry	May 28, 1864, Hall's Shop, Virginia	Point Lookout, Maryland, transferred to Elmira Prison, NY July 12, 1864	Transferred for Exchange October 11, 1864. Nothing Further.

Name & Rank	Age	Enlisted	Regiment and State	Where Captured	Prison	Remarks
Carnes, Henry Private	Unk	April 26, 1861, Talbotton, Georgia	Co. A, 4th Georgia Infantry	May 5, 1864, Wilderness, Virginia	Point Lookout, Maryland, transferred to Elmira Prison, NY August 17, 1864	Exchanged March 14, 1865 at Boulware's Wharf on the James River, Virginia
Carnes, James Nicholas Private	Unk	January 9, 1862, Columbia, South Carolina	Co. E, 22nd South Carolina Infantry	July 29, 1864, Petersburg, Virginia	Point Lookout, Maryland, transferred to Elmira Prison, NY August 12, 1864	Died April 17, 1865 of Pneumonia, Grave No. 1356
Carney, Lewis Private	Unk	July 1, 1861, Prints William County, Virginia	Co. B, 49th Virginia Infantry	September 14, 1863, Dumpries, Virginia	Point Lookout, Maryland, transferred to Elmira Prison, NY August 18, 1864	Exchanged March 10, 1865 at Boulware's Wharf on the James River, Virginia
Carnline, Richard P. Private	Unk	June 15, 1861, Columbus, Georgia	Co. E, 12th Georgia Infantry	May 10, 1864, Spotsylvania Court House, Virginia	Point Lookout, Maryland, transferred to Elmira Prison, NY July 3, 1864	Oath of Allegiance June 30, 1865
Carnochan, Nicholas Private	Unk	April 27, 1861, Wetumpka, Alabama	Co. C, 13th Alabama Infantry	May 12, 1864, Spotsylvania Court House, Virginia	Point Lookout, Maryland, transferred to Elmira Prison, NY July 30, 1864	Oath of Allegiance June 16, 1865
Carpenter, Churchwell Private	21	March 24, 1862, Salisbury, North Carolina	Co. C, 42nd North Carolina Infantry	June 3, 1864, Cold Harbor, Virginia	Point Lookout, Maryland, transferred to Elmira Prison, NY July 17,1864	Oath of Allegiance June 19, 1865
Carpenter, Eleazer Private	Unk	March 25, 1863, Macon, Georgia	Co. B, 64th Georgia Infantry	June 15, 1864, Near Petersburg, Virginia	Point Lookout, Maryland, transferred to Elmira Prison, NY July 25, 1864	Transferred for Exchange 10/11/64. Died 10/31/64 of Chronic Diarrhea at US Army Hospital, Baltimore, MD
Carpenter, Franklin H. Private	33	March 24, 1862, Salisbury, North Carolina	Co. C, 42nd North Carolina Infantry	June 3, 1864, Cold Harbor, Virginia	Point Lookout, Maryland, transferred to Elmira Prison, NY July 17,1864	Oath of Allegiance June 19, 1865

Name & Rank	Age	Enlisted	Regiment and State	Where Captured	Prison	Remarks
Carpenter, Jacob M. Private	28	February 26, 1863, Cleveland County, North Carolina	Co. D, 12th North Carolina Infantry	May 12, 1864, Near Spotsylvania, Virginia	Point Lookout, Maryland, transferred to Elmira Prison, NY August 14, 1864	Exchanged October 29, 1864, at Venus Point, Savannah River, GA.
Carpenter, Jonas Private	29	March 15, 1862, Lincolnton, North Carolina	Co. D, 1st North Carolina Infantry	May 12, 1864, Spotsylvania Court House, Virginia	Point Lookout, Maryland, transferred to Elmira Prison, NY August 6, 1864	Died October 18, 1864 of Typhoid Fever, Grave No. 546
Carpenter, Levi Private	32	August 15, 1862, Iredell County, North Carolina	Co. I, 37th North Carolina Infantry	July 29, 1864, Gravel Hill, Near Petersburg, Virginia	Point Lookout, Maryland, transferred to Elmira Prison, NY August 12, 1864	Died May 9, 1865 of Chronic Diarrhea, Grave No. 2740.
Carpenter, Marcus Private	24	August 15, 1862, Iredell County, North Carolina	Co. J, 37th North Carolina Infantry	May 12, 1864, Spotsylvania Court House, Virginia	Point Lookout, Maryland, transferred to Elmira Prison, NY August 12, 1864	Exchanged October 29, 1864 at Venus Point, Savannah River, GA.
Carpenter, Peter H. Private	26	February 26, 1863, Cleveland County, North Carolina	Co. E, 12th North Carolina Infantry	May 12, 1864, Near Spotsylvania County Court House, Virginia	Point Lookout, Maryland, transferred to Elmira Prison, NY August 14, 1864	Died March 3, 1865 of Typhoid Fever, Grave No. 2011
Carr, C. Corporal	Unk	Unknown	Co. G, 7th Louisiana Infantry	May 12, 1864, Spotsylvania Court House, Virginia	Point Lookout, Maryland, transferred to Elmira Prison, NY August 17, 1864	Exchanged February 25, 1865 at Boulware's or Cox Wharf on the James River, Virginia
Carr, Thomas D. Private	Unk	February 26, 1864, Dublin, Virginia	Co. F, 4th Virginia Infantry	May 12, 1864 Spotsylvania Court House, Virginia	Point Lookout, Maryland, transferred to Elmira Prison, NY August 2, 1864	Exchanged 3/2/65. Died 3/18/65 of Chronic Pneumonia at Chimborazo Hospital No. 2, Richmond, VA
Carraway, J. H. Private	Unk	December 20, 1861, Sumter District, South Carolina	Co. K, 23rd South Carolina Infantry	June 15, 1864, Petersburg, Virginia	Point Lookout, Maryland, transferred to Elmira Prison, NY July 25, 1864	Died November 24, 1864 of Unknown Disease, Grave No. 914

Name & Rank	Age	Enlisted	Regiment and State	Where Captured	Prison	Remarks
Carrell, Alfred T. Private	32	May 10, 1862, Rockingham County, North Carolina	Co. E, 45th North Carolina Infantry	May 10, 1864, Spotsylvania Court House, Virginia	Point Lookout, Maryland, transferred to Elmira Prison, NY August 6, 1864	Oath of Allegiance June 14, 1865
Carrell, James Private	17	May 15, 1862, Clayton, Johnston County, North Carolina	Co. C, 24th North Carolina Infantry	June 17, 1864, Petersburg, Virginia	Point Lookout, Maryland, transferred to Elmira Prison, NY July 30, 1864	Oath of Allegiance July 3, 1865
Carrell, Lee W. Corporal	25	February 27, 1862, Reidsville, North Carolina	Co. E, 45th North Carolina Infantry	May 10, 1864, Spotsylvania Court House, Virginia	Point Lookout, Maryland, transferred to Elmira Prison, NY August 6, 1864	Died May 9, 1865 of Chronic Diarrhea, Grave No. 2780. Name Carroll on Headstone.
Carrell, Rufus Private	!8	February 27, 1862, Reidsville, North Carolina	Co. E, 45th North Carolina Infantry	May 10, 1864, Spotsylvania Court House, Virginia	Point Lookout, Maryland, transferred to Elmira Prison, NY August 6, 1864	Oath of Allegiance June 27, 1865
Carroll, Benjamin F. Private	22	August 8, 1862, Davidson County, North Carolina	Co. B, 48th North Carolina Infantry	June 3, 1864, Near Talapatomoy Creek, Cold Harbor, Virginia	Point Lookout, Maryland, transferred to Elmira Prison, NY July 17, 1864	Oath of Allegiance May 13, 1865
Carroll, Haywood Private	42	April 16, 1862, Old Brunswick, North Carolina	Co. G, 36th Regiment, 2nd North Carolina Artillery	January 15, 1865, Fort Fisher, North Carolina. Wounded	February 1, 1865, Elmira Prison Camp, New York	Died March 25, 1865 of Variola (Smallpox), Grave No. 2467
Carroll, Henry W. Private	Unk	Unknown	Co. B, Hood's Battalion, Virginia Reserves	June 15, 1864, Petersburg, Virginia	Point Lookout, Maryland, transferred to Elmira Prison, NY July 30, 1864	Died February 2, 1865 of Chronic Diarrhea, Grave No. 1926
Carroll, James A. Private	44	April 16, 1862, Old Brunswick, North Carolina	Co. G, 36th Regiment, 2nd North Carolina Artillery	January 15, 1865, Fort Fisher, North Carolina. Wounded	February 1, 1865, Elmira Prison Camp, New York	Died May 16, 1865 of Chronic Diarrhea, Grave No. 2962
Carroll, Joel Private	35	April 16, 1862, Old Brunswick, North Carolina	Co. G, 36th Regiment, 2nd North Carolina Artillery	January 15, 1865, Fort Fisher, North Carolina. Wounded	February 1, 1865, Elmira Prison Camp, New York	Died March 10, 1865 of Pneumonia, Grave No. 1879

Name & Rank	Age	Enlisted	Regiment and State	Where Captured	Prison	Remarks
Carroll, John Private	20	May 30, 1861 Webster, North Carolina	Co. B, 25th North Carolina Infantry	June 17, 1864, Petersburg, Virginia	Point Lookout, Maryland, transferred to Elmira Prison, NY July 30, 1864	Oath of Allegiance July 11, 1865
Carroll, John Private	Unk	February 15, 1862, Atlanta, Georgia	Co. J, 1st South Carolina Artillery	July 10, 1863, Morris Island, South Carolina	Point Lookout, Maryland, transferred to Elmira Prison, NY August 18, 1864	Exchanged March 10, 1865 at Boulware's Wharf on the James River, Virginia
Carroll, John W. Private	25	April 4, 1862, Cumberland County, North Carolina	Co. I, 51st North Carolina Infantry	June 1, 1864, Cold Harbor, Virginia	Point Lookout, Maryland, transferred to Elmira Prison, NY July 17,1864	Died July 15, 1864 in Train Wreck at Shohola, Pennsylvania
Carroll, Joseph Corporal	21	May 6, 1862, Elizabethtown, North Carolina	Co. K, 40th Regiment, 3rd North Carolina Artillery	January 15, 1865, Fort Fisher, North Carolina	Elmira Prison Camp, New York, February 1, 1865	Died March 9, 1865 of Gangrene of Feet, Grave No. 1874
Carroll, Lewis H. Private	19	May 15, 1862, Fort Johnson, North Carolina	Co. J, 20th North Carolina Infantry	May 20, 1864, Spotsylvania Court House, Virginia	Point Lookout, Maryland, transferred to Elmira Prison, NY July 6, 1864	Exchanged February 13, 1865 at Boulware's wharf on the James River, Virginia
Carroll, Nathanial Private	38	June 1, 1863, Fort Fisher, New Hanover County, North Carolina	Co. K, 40th Regiment, 3rd North Carolina Artillery	January 15, 1865, Fort Fisher, North Carolina. Wounded	February 1, 1865, Elmira Prison Camp, New York	Exchanged February 20, 1865 at Boulware's or Cox Wharf on the James River, Virginia
Carroll, Peter Private	24	July 22, 1861, Camp Moore, Louisiana	Co. C, 10th Louisiana Infantry	May 12, 1864, Spotsylvania Court House, Virginia	Point Lookout, Maryland, transferred to Elmira Prison, NY July 25, 1864	Exchanged February 13, 1865 at Boulware's wharf on the James River, Virginia
Carroll, Samuel Private	Unk	April 8, 1862, Ocean View, Virginia	Co. C, 15th Virginia Infantry	May 11, 1864, Near Mechanicsville, Virginia	Point Lookout, Maryland, transferred to Elmira Prison, NY August 17, 1864	Died March 23, 1865 of Remittent Fever, Grave No. 1520

Name & Rank	Age	Enlisted	Regiment and State	Where Captured	Prison	Remarks
Carroll, Thomas Private	36	May 3, 1862, Macon, Georgia	Captain Slaten's Battery, Georgia Light Artillery	June 17, 1864, Petersburg, Virginia	Point Lookout, Maryland, transferred to Elmira Prison, NY July 25, 1864	Oath of Allegiance May 15, 1865
Carroll, Virgil Private	21	January 7, 1862, Centreville, Virginia	Captain Montgomery's Battery Virginia Light Artillery	May 12, 1864, Spotsylvania Court House, Virginia	Old Capital Prison, Washington, DC, transferred to Elmira Prison, NY, July 23, 1864	Exchanged October 29, 1864, at Venus Point, Savannah River, GA.
Carroll, William H. Private	44	November 10, 1864, Columbia, South Carolina	Co. F, 17th South Carolina Infantry	April 2, 1865, Fort Steadman, Virginia. Gunshot Wound of Abdomen, Above Pubis.	Old Capital Prison, Washington D. C. Transferred to Elmira Prison, NY May 2, 1865.	Oath of Allegiance July 7, 1865
Carroll, William J. Private	Unk	September 1, 1861, Lynnhaven Beach, Virginia	Co. I, 15th Virginia Cavalry	May 11, 1864, Near Ashland, Virginia	Point Lookout Prison Camp, Maryland. Transferred to Elmira Prison, August 17, 1864	Died January 29, 1865 of Variola (Smallpox), Grave No. 1800
Carruthers, J. J. Private	Unk	July 6, 1861, Corinth, Mississippi	Co. B, Jackson's 1st Regiment, Tennessee Heavy Artillery	August 23, 1864, Fort Morgan, Alabama	New Orleans, Louisiana transferred to Elmira December 4, 1864.	Exchanged February 25, 1865 at Boulware's or Cox Wharf on the James River, Virginia
Carson, Andrew M. Private	Unk	January 29, 1862, Charleston, South Carolina	Co. J, 1st South Carolina Artillery	July 10, 1863, Morris Island, South Carolina	Point Lookout, Maryland, transferred to Elmira Prison, NY August 18, 1864	Exchanged March 10, 1865 at Boulware's Wharf on the James River, Virginia
Carson, G. W. Private	25	March 7, 1862, Union Parish, Louisiana	Co. A, 6th Louisiana Infantry	May 5, 1864, Wilderness, Virginia	Point Lookout, Maryland, transferred to Elmira Prison, NY August 17, 1864	Exchanged February 25, 1865 at Boulware's or Cox Wharf on the James River, Virginia

Name & Rank	Age	Enlisted	Regiment and State	Where Captured	Prison	Remarks
Carson, Henry Private	32	September 3, 1862, Statesville, North Carolina	Co, H, 23rd North Carolina Infantry	May 12, 1864, Spotsylvania Court House, Virginia. Gunshot Wound Right Shoulder.	Old Capital Prison, Washington, DC transferred to Elmira Prison, NY August 29, 1864	Died March 18, 1865 Chronic Diarrhea, Grave No. 1702
Carson, John L. Private	Unk	April 27, 1863, Fort Sumter, South Carolina	Co. J, 1st South Carolina Heavy Artillery	July 10, 1863, Morris Island, South Carolina	Fort Columbus, NY Harbor, transferred to Elmira December 4, 1864.	Died February 21, 1865 of Diarrhea, Grave No. 2238
Carson, John M. Private	31	July 23, 1861, Democrat, North Carolina	Co. K, 25th North Carolina Infantry	June 17, 1864, Petersburg, Virginia	Point Lookout, Maryland, transferred to Elmira Prison, NY July 30, 1864	Died September 2, 1864 of Chronic Diarrhea, Grave No. 81
Carswell, J. D. Private	Unk	March 11, 1864, Dorchester, Georgia	Co. B, 7th Georgia Cavalry	June 11, 1864, Louisa Court House, Trevilian Station, Virginia	Point Lookout, Maryland, transferred to Elmira Prison, NY July 17,1864	Exchanged March 10, 1865 at Boulware's wharf on the James River, Virginia
Carter, Alexander Private	Unk	May 17, 1861, Rectortown, Virginia	Co. B, 8th Virginia Infantry	July 24, 1864, Berlin, Virginia. Deserted to Union Lines.	Old Capital Prison, Washington D. C. Transferred to Elmira Prison, NY August 12, 1864	Oath of Allegiance December 2, 1864. Early Release per Lincoln's Proclamation, 12/8/1863.
Carter, Allen Private	Unk	May 18, 1861, Lisbon, Virginia	Co. C, 42nd Virginia Infantry	May 12, 1864, Spotsylvania Court House, Virginia	Point Lookout, Maryland, transferred to Elmira Prison, NY August 2,1864	Exchanged February 20, 1865 at Boulware's or Cox Wharf on the James River, Virginia
Carter, Caleb Private	Unk	March 22, 1862, Sparks, North Carolina	Co. D, 33rd North Carolina Infantry	May 12, 1864, Spotsylvania, Virginia	Point Lookout, Maryland, transferred to Elmira Prison, NY August 12, 1864	Oath of Allegiance June 27, 1865
Carter, Columbus Private	18	March 22, 1862, Sparks, North Carolina	Co. D, 33rd North Carolina Infantry	May 12, 1864, Spotsylvania, Virginia	Point Lookout, Maryland, transferred to Elmira Prison, NY August 12, 1864	Oath of Allegiance June 27, 1865

Name & Rank	Age	Enlisted	Regiment and State	Where Captured	Prison	Remarks
Carter, Elliott Private	Unk	November 12, 1863, Orange County Court House, Virginia	Co. G, 47th Virginia Infantry	May 5, 1864, Wilderness, Virginia	Point Lookout, Maryland, transferred to Elmira Prison, NY July 23, 1864	Oath of Allegiance July 3, 1865
Carter, George W. Sergeant	28	February 27, 1862, Reidsville, North Carolina	Co. E, 45th North Carolina Infantry	May 10, 1864, Spotsylvania Court House, Virginia	Point Lookout, Maryland, transferred to Elmira Prison, NY August 6, 1864	Oath of Allegiance June 30, 1865
Carter, Gustavus A. Private	28	April 27, 1861, Union, Virginia	Co. H, 1st Virginia Cavalry	December 3, 1864, Luray Valley, Fauquier County, Virginia	Old Capital Prison, Washington, DC, transferred to Elmira Prison, NY, December 17, 1864	Exchanged March 10, 1865 at Boulware's Wharf on the James River, Virginia
Carter, Henry Private	18	March 15, 1863, Fort Fisher, North Carolina	Co. B, 36th Regiment, 2nd North Carolina Artillery	January 15, 1865, Fort Fisher, North Carolina. Wounded	February 1, 1865, Elmira Prison Camp, New York	Oath of Allegiance June 12, 1865
Carter, Henry Z. M. Sergeant	Unk	June 10, 1861, Richmond, Virginia	Co. E, 44th Virginia Infantry	May 12, 1864, Spotsylvania Court House, Virginia	Point Lookout, Maryland, transferred to Elmira Prison, NY August 2, 1864	Exchanged March 14, 1865 at Boulware's Wharf on the James River, Virginia
Carter, James H. Private	18	February 1, 1862, Salisbury, North Carolina	Co. C, 42nd North Carolina Infantry	June 1, 1864, Gaines Farm, Cold Harbor, Virginia	Point Lookout, Maryland, transferred to Elmira Prison, NY July 17,1864	Exchanged March 2, 1865 at Akins Landing on the James River, Virginia
Carter, James M. Private	Unk	April 30, 1862, Camp Leon, Florida	Co. K, 5th Florida Infantry	May 12, 1864, Spotsylvania Court House, Virginia	Point Lookout, Maryland, transferred to Elmira Prison, NY July 30, 1864	Died October 11, 1864 of Chronic Diarrhea, Grave No. 691
Carter, James M. Private	32	February 24, 1862, Harrisburg, North Carolina	Co. H, 7th North Carolina Infantry	July 21, 1864, Deep Bottom, Virginia	Point Lookout, Maryland, transferred to Elmira Prison, NY August 18, 1864	Exchanged February 20, 1865 at Boulware's or Cox Wharf on the James River, Virginia

Name & Rank	Age	Enlisted	Regiment and State	Where Captured	Prison	Remarks
Carter, James R. P. Private	Unk	March 21, 1863, Camp Tucker, South Carolina	Co. F, 4th South Carolina Cavalry	May 31, 1864, Old Church, Virginia	Point Lookout, Maryland, transferred to Elmira Prison, NY July 11, 1864	Died October 17, 1864, of Cerebral Spinal Meningitis, Grave No. 543
Carter, James W. Private	Unk	Unknown	Co. D, 4th Virginia Cavalry	September 1, 1863, Middleburg, Virginia	Point Lookout, Maryland, transferred to Elmira Prison, NY August 18, 1864	Oath of Allegiance May 19, 1865
Carter, Jonathan Private	16	August 14, 1861, Fayetteville, North Carolina	Co. D, 2nd North Carolina Cavalry	September 22, 1863, Jack's Shope, Near Madison Court House, Virginia	Point Lookout, Maryland, transferred to Elmira Prison, NY August 18, 1864	Exchanged March 10, 1865 at Boulware's wharf on the James River, Virginia
Carter, Joseph P. Private	26	May 18, 1861, Lisbon, Virginia	Co. C, 42nd Virginia Infantry	May 12, 1864, Spotsylvania Court House, Virginia	Point Lookout, Maryland, transferred to Elmira Prison, NY August 2,1864	Exchanged October 29, 1864, at Venus Point, Savannah River, GA.
Carter, Nicholas Private	25	July 15, 1862, Wayne County, North Carolina	Co. F, 3rd North Carolina Infantry	May 12, 1864, Near Spotsylvania, Virginia	Point Lookout, Maryland, transferred to Elmira Prison, NY August 14, 1864	Oath of Allegiance June 27, 1865
Carter, Peter Private	Unk	March 8, 1862, Ridgeway, Virginia	Co. A, 42nd Virginia Infantry	May 12, 1864, Spotsylvania Court House, Virginia	Point Lookout, Maryland, transferred to Elmira Prison, NY August 2, 1864	Transferred for Exchange 10/17/64. Died 10/17/64 of Inflammation of Lungs at Point Lookout Prison, MD
Carter, Richard Private	17	March 4, 1864, Wilmington, North Carolina	Co. C, 42nd North Carolina Infantry	June 1, 1864, Gaines Farm, Cold Harbor, Virginia	Point Lookout, Maryland, transferred to Elmira Prison, NY July 17,1864	Died January 23, 1865 of Pneumonia, Grave No. 1599
Carter, Richard Private	Unk	July 25, 1861, Camp Jackson, Virginia	Co. F, 50th Virginia Infantry	May 12, 1864, Spotsylvania Court House, Virginia	Point Lookout, Maryland, transferred to Elmira Prison, NY August 2, 1864	Exchanged October 29, 1864, at Venus Point, Savannah River, GA.

Name & Rank	Age	Enlisted	Regiment and State	Where Captured	Prison	Remarks
Carter, Samuel Private	Unk	July 1, 1861, Prince William County, Virginia	Co. B, 49th Virginia Infantry	June 7, 1864, Prince William County, Virginia	Old Capital Prison, Washington, DC, transferred to Elmira Prison, NY, July 23, 1864	Died January 26, 1865 of Chronic Diarrhea, Grave No. 1629
Carter, Solomon C. Private	28	August 8, 1862, Camp Hill, Stanly County, North Carolina	Co. F, 32nd North Carolina Infantry	May 12, 1864, Spotsylvania Court House, Virginia	Point Lookout, Maryland, transferred to Elmira Prison, NY August 6, 1864. Ward No. 44	Died August 12, 1864 of Chronic Diarrhea, Grave No. 132. Name C. L. Carter on Headstone.
Carter, Thomas P. Private	Unk	July 2, 1861, Bethel Am., Virginia	Co. F, 50th Virginia Infantry	May 12, 1864, Spotsylvania Court House, Virginia	Point Lookout, Maryland, transferred to Elmira Prison, NY August 2, 1864	Died April 12, 1865 of Acute Bronchitis, Grave No. 2681
Carter, William M. Private	21	September 7, 1861, Barnwell, South Carolina	Co. K, 11th South Carolina Infantry	June 18, 1864, Petersburg, Virginia	Point Lookout, Maryland, transferred to Elmira Prison, NY July 30, 1864	Oath of Allegiance July 3, 1865
Cartledge, John D. Private	Unk	March 4, 1862, Choctan County, Mississippi	Co. B, 31st Mississippi Infantry	May 14, 1862, Raymond, Mississippi	Point Lookout, Maryland, transferred to Elmira Prison, NY August 18, 1864	Exchanged March 10, 1865 at Boulware's wharf on the James River, Virginia
Cartmell, H. M. Commissary Sergeant	Unk	December 7, 1862, Lebanon, Tennessee	Field & Staff Jackson's 1st Regiment, Tennessee Heavy Artillery	August 23, 1864, Fort Morgan, Alabama	New Orleans, Louisiana transferred to Elmira December 4, 1864.	Exchanged February 13, 1865 at Boulware's wharf on the James River, Virginia
Cartwright, G. R. Private	Unk	July 4, 1863, Carrollton, Georgia	Co. F, Cobb's Legion Georgia	August 16, 1864, Front Royal, Virginia	Old Capital Prison, Washington, DC transferred to Elmira Prison, NY August 29, 1864	Exchanged October 29, 1864, at Venus Point, Savannah River, GA.
Caruth, F. A. Private	Unk	September 10, 1862, Camp Randolph, Georgia	Co. A, 38th Georgia Infantry	May 20, 1864, Spotsylvania Court House, Virginia	Point Lookout, Maryland, transferred to Elmira Prison, NY July 6, 1864	Exchanged March 10, 1865 at Boulware's Wharf on the James River, Virginia

Name & Rank	Age	Enlisted	Regiment and State	Where Captured	Prison	Remarks
Carver, H. W. Private	Unk	April 22, 1862, Lake City, Florida	Co. B, 5th Florida Infantry	May 30, 1864, Mechanics-ville, Virginia	Point Lookout, Maryland, transferred to Elmira Prison, NY July 17,1864	Exchanged March 2, 1865 at Akins Landing on the James River, Virginia
Carver, James B. Private	Unk	Junw 21, 1861, Cumberland County, North Carolina	Co. E, 36th Regiment, 2nd North Carolina Artillery	January 15, 1865, Fort Fisher, North Carolina. Wounded	February 1, 1865, Elmira Prison Camp, New York	Oath of Allegiance July 11, 1865
Carver, Joshua Private	37	February 24, 1862, Fayetteville, North Carolina	Co. D, 51st North Carolina Infantry	June 1, 1864, Cold Harbor, Virginia	Point Lookout, Maryland, transferred to Elmira Prison, NY July 17,1864	Exchanged October 29, 1864, at Venus Point, Savannah River, GA.
Cary, George W. Private	Unk	April 26, 1863, Lewisburg, Virginia	Co. A, 26th Virginia Infantry	June 3, 1864, Gaines Farm, Cold Harbor, Virginia	Point Lookout, Maryland, transferred to Elmira Prison, NY July 17,1864	Exchanged March 14, 1865 at Boulware's Wharf on the James River, Virginia
Casell, John Private	Unk	September 14, 1863, Mobile, Alabama	Co. A, 1st Alabama Artillery	August 23, 1864, Fort Morgan, Alabama	New Orleans, Louisiana transferred to Elmira December 4, 1864.	Oath of Allegiance May 29, 1865
Casey, Benjamin Private	18	April 14, 1863, Wayne County, North Carolina	Co. G, 40th Regiment, 3rd North Carolina Light Artillery	January 15, 1865, Fort Fisher, North Carolina	February 1, 1865, Elmira Prison Camp, New York	Oath of Allegiance June 12, 1865
Casey, Benjamin D. Private	17	July 24, 1863, Wayne County, North Carolina	Co. G, 40th Regiment, 3rd North Carolina Artillery	January 15, 1865, Fort Fisher, North Carolina	February 1, 1865, Elmira Prison Camp, New York	Died February 28, 1865 of Diarrhea, Grave No. 2139
Casey, Benjamin F. Private	17	October 16, 1861, Wayne County, North Carolina	Co. G, 40th Regiment, 3rd North Carolina Artillery	January 15, 1865, Fort Fisher, North Carolina	Elmira Prison Camp January 30, 1865	Oath of Allegiance June 12, 1865
Casey, James Sergeant	30	June 25, 1861, New Orleans, Louisiana	Co. F, 14th Louisiana Infantry	May 5, 1864, Wilderness, Virginia	Point Lookout, Maryland, transferred to Elmira Prison, NY July 25, 1864	Exchanged February 25, 1865 at Boulware's or Cox Wharf on the James River, Virginia

Name & Rank	Age	Enlisted	Regiment and State	Where Captured	Prison	Remarks
Casey, James A. Private	23	June 20, 1861, Abingdon, Virginia	Co. B, 48th Virginia Infantry	May 12, 1864, Spotsylvania Court House, Virginia	Point Lookout, Maryland, transferred to Elmira Prison, NY August 2, 1864	Died October 11, 1864 of Pneumonia, Grave 681
Casey, William Civilian	Unk	Unknown	Louisiana Citizen	September 13, 1864, Tensan Parish, Louisiana	New Orleans, Louisiana. Transferred to Elmira November 5, 1864	Oath of Allegiance March 6, 1865. Early Release per Lincoln's Proclamation, 12/8/1863.
Casey, Willis Private	Unk	July 2, 1861, Bethel Am., Virginia	Co. F, 50th Virginia Infantry	May 12, 1864, Spotsylvania Court House, Virginia	Point Lookout, Maryland, transferred to Elmira Prison, NY August 2, 1864	Transferred for Exchange 10/11/1864. Exchanged at Venus Point, Savannah River, GA, 11/15/1864
Casey, Wright Private	24	April 14, 1863, Wayne County, North Carolina	Co. G, 40th Regiment, 3rd North Carolina Artillery	January 15, 1865, Fort Fisher, North Carolina	February 1, 1865, Elmira Prison Camp, New York	Exchanged February 20, 1865 at Boulware's or Cox Wharf on the James River, Virginia
Cash, Green Private	16	March 6, 1862, Roxboro, North Carolina	Co. A, 24th North Carolina Infantry	June 17, 1864, Petersburg, Virginia	Point Lookout, Maryland, transferred to Elmira Prison, NY July 30, 1864	Died December 19, 1864 of Chronic Diarrhea, Grave No. 1064
Cash, J. Private	Unk	Unknown	Co. B, 5th Virginia Infantry	May 20, 1864, Spotsylvania Court House, Virginia	Point Lookout, Maryland, transferred to Elmira Prison, NY July 6, 1864	Transferred for Exchange October 11, 1864. Nothing Further.
Cashwell, Marshall Corporal	20	February 20, 1862, Fayetteville, Cumberland County, North Carolina	Co. C, 36th Regiment, 2nd North Carolina Artillery	January 15, 1865, Fort Fisher, North Carolina. Wounded	February 1, 1865, Elmira Prison Camp, New York	Oath of Allegiance July 12, 1865
Cashwell, Nathanial Private	Unk	July 15, 1863, Camp Vance, North Carolina	Co. H, 13th North Carolina Infantry	May 6, 1864, Wilderness, Virginia	Point Lookout, Maryland, transferred to Elmira Prison, NY July 23, 1864	Died March 6, 1865 of Pneumonia, Grave No. 2379

Name & Rank	Age	Enlisted	Regiment and State	Where Captured	Prison	Remarks
Cashwell, Noah Private	31	June 1, 1861, Cedar Creek, Cumberland County, North Carolina	Co. F, 24th North Carolina Infantry	June 17, 1864, Petersburg, Virginia	Point Lookout, Maryland, transferred to Elmira Prison, NY July 25, 1864	Died March 6, 1865 of Pneumonia. Grave No. 2379. Headstone has 15th NC.
Cashwell, Saunders Private	Unk	Unknown	Co. F, 24th North Carolina Infantry	July 30, 1861, Weldon, North Carolina	Point Lookout, Maryland, transferred to Elmira Prison, NY July 23, 1864	Oath of Allegiance May 29, 1865
Cason, Benjamin F. Private	Unk	March 16, 1862, Lynhaven Beach, Virginia	Co. J, 15th Virginia Cavalry	September 14, 1863, Near Culpepper, Virginia	Point Lookout, Maryland, transferred to Elmira Prison, NY August 18, 1864	Oath of Allegiance June 14, 1865
Cason, Henry Private	Unk	Unknown	Co. A, Powers' Regiment Mississippi Cavalry	October 2, 1864, Washington, Mississippi	New Orleans, Louisiana transferred to Elmira November 19, 1864.	Died December 19, 1864 of Chronic Diarrhea, Grave No. 1065
Casper, Adam M. Private	30	July 4, 1862, Salisbury, North Carolina	Co. C, 57th North Carolina Infantry	July 8, 1864, Near Harper's Ferry, Virginia	Old Capital Prison, Washington, DC, transferred to Elmira Prison, NY, July 23, 1864	Exchanged February 20, 1865 at Boulware's or Cox Wharf on the James River, Virginia
Casper, Ambrose Private	20	March 1864, Salisbury, North Carolina	Co. K, 4th North Carolina Infantry	May 30, 1864, Near Old Church, Virginia	Point Lookout, Maryland, transferred to Elmira Prison, NY July 12, 1864	Oath of Allegiance June 12, 1865
Casper, James C. Private	26	June 29, 1861, Rowan County, North Carolina	Co. K, 4th North Carolina Infantry	May 20, 1864, Spotsylvania Court House, Virginia	Point Lookout, Maryland, transferred to Elmira Prison, NY July 6, 1864	Oath of Allegiance June 12, 1865
Cassell, M. Browne Private	Unk	March 10, 1862, Wytheville, Virginia	Co. A, 4th Virginia Infantry	May 12, 1864, Spotsylvania Court House, Virginia	Point Lookout, Maryland, transferred to Elmira Prison, NY August 2, 1864	Oath of Allegiance June 21, 1865

Name & Rank	Age	Enlisted	Regiment and State	Where Captured	Prison	Remarks
Cassily, Albert D. Private	18	April 30, 1861, Corinth, Mississippi	Co. A, 12th Mississippi Infantry	July 29, 1864, Deserted to Union Lines, Petersburg, Virginia	Point Lookout, Maryland, transferred to Elmira Prison, NY August 12, 1864	Oath of Allegiance September 30, 1864. Early Release per Lincoln's Proclamation, 12/8/1863.
Cassily, John J. Corporal	20	April 30, 1861, Corinth, Mississippi	Co. A, 12th Mississippi Infantry	July 29, 1864, Petersburg, Virginia, Deserted while on Picket near Petersburg.	Point Lookout, Maryland, transferred to Elmira Prison, NY August 12, 1864	Oath of Allegiance September 30, 1864. Early Release per Lincoln's Proclamation, 12/8/1863.
Casteen, John Sergeant	33	June 12, 1861, Wilmington, North Carolina	Co. E, 1st North Carolina Infantry	May 12, 1864, Spotsylvania Court House, Virginia	Point Lookout, Maryland, transferred to Elmira Prison, NY August 6, 1864	Oath of Allegiance June 21, 1865
Casteen, John Sergeant	19	May 27, 1861, Wilmington, North Carolina	Co. D, 3rd North Carolina Infantry	May 12, 1864, Near Spotsylvania Court House, Virginia	Point Lookout, Maryland, transferred to Elmira Prison, NY August 14, 1864	Oath of Allegiance July 3, 1865
Caster, J. R. Private	Unk	April 5, 1864, Camp Holmes, North Carolina	Co. G, 32nd North Carolina Infantry	May 10, 1864, Wilderness, Virginia	Point Lookout, Maryland, transferred to Elmira Prison, NY August 6, 1864	Died September 22, 1864 from Jaundice, Grave No. 488
Castleberry, Jeremiah M. Private	Unk	March 26, 1862, Rockford, Alabama	Co. B, 59th Alabama Infantry	June 17, 1864, Petersburg, Virginia	Point Lookout, Maryland, transferred to Elmira Prison, NY July 30, 1864	Exchanged March 14, 1865 at Boulware's Wharf on the James River, Virginia
Castleman, James R. Private	20	August 1, 1863, Culpepper County, Virginia	Co. D, 6th Virginia Cavalry	July 2, 1864, Snickers Ferry, Virginia	Old Capital Prison, Washington, DC, transferred to Elmira Prison, NY, July 23, 1864	Exchanged February 13, 1865 at Boulware's wharf on the James River, Virginia

Name & Rank	Age	Enlisted	Regiment and State	Where Captured	Prison	Remarks
Cates, Archibald Private	25	July 8, 1862, Hillsboro, North Carolina	Co. F, 33rd North Carolina Infantry	May 6, 1864, Wilderness, Virginia	Old Capital Prison, Washington D. C. Transferred to Elmira Prison, NY July 12, 1864	Oath of Allegiance June 23, 1865
Cates, Dennis M. Private	22	December 20, 1861, Orange County Court House, North Carolina	Co. G, 28th North Carolina Infantry	May 6, 1864, Wilderness, Virginia	Point Lookout, Maryland, transferred to Elmira Prison, NY August 14, 1864	Oath of Allegiance June 19, 1865
Cates, Henry F. Private	20	February 24, 1862, Hillsboro, North Carolina	Co. D, 1st North Carolina Infantry	May 12, 1864, Spotsylvania Court House, Virginia	Point Lookout, Maryland, transferred to Elmira Prison, NY August 6, 1864	Oath of Allegiance June 27, 1865
Cather, George R. Private	Unk	September 20, 1862, Winchester, Virginia	Co. D, 1st Maryland Cavalry	July 13, 1864, Near Washington, DC	Old Capital Prison, Washington, DC, transferred to Elmira Prison, NY, July 23, 1864	Oath of Allegiance June 14, 1865
Caton, Elijah Private	26	April 3, 1862, Charlotte, North Carolina	Co. B, 53rd North Carolina Infantry	July 17, 1864, Near Washington, DC	Old Capital Prison, Washington, DC, transferred to Elmira Prison, NY, July 23, 1864	Died February 26, 1865 of Variola (Smallpox), Grave No. 2136
Caton, John C. Private	20	April 25, 1861, Fairfax Court House, Virginia	Co. D, 17th Virginia Infantry	October 4, 1863, Loudoun County, Virginia	Point Lookout, Maryland, transferred to Elmira Prison, NY July 23, 1864	Oath of Allegiance May 17, 1865
Caton, Richard H. Private	16	April 18, 1861, Conrad's Store, Virginia	Co. I, 10th Virginia Infantry	May 12, 1864, Spotsylvania Court House, Virginia	Point Lookout, Maryland, transferred to Elmira Prison, NY August 2, 1864	Exchanged 11/15/64 at Venus Point, Savannah River, GA.
Catrett, Luke R. Private	Unk	October 1, 1862, Columbus County, North Carolina	Co. H, 61st North Carolina Infantry	June 16, 1864, Near Petersburg, Virginia	Point Lookout, Maryland, transferred to Elmira Prison, NY July 12, 1864	Oath of Allegiance July 11, 1865

Name & Rank	Age	Enlisted	Regiment and State	Where Captured	Prison	Remarks
Catron, J. M. C. Sergeant	Unk	July 1, 1862, Giles County, Virginia	Co. A, 23rd Battalion, Virginia Infantry	June 3, 1864, Gaines Mill, Cold Harbor, Virginia	Point Lookout, Maryland, transferred to Elmira Prison, NY July 17,1864	Exchanged 11/15/64 at Venus Point, Savannah River, GA.
Catron, William P. Private	21	June 26, 1861, Scott County, Virginia	Co. H, 48th Virginia Infantry	May 12, 1864, Near Spotsylvania Court House, Virginia	Point Lookout, Maryland, transferred to Elmira Prison, NY August 6, 1864	Oath of Allegiance June 19, 1865
Cauble, Franklin Private	Unk	February 28, 1862, Salisbury, North Carolina	Co. C, 42nd North Carolina Infantry	June 3, 1864, Cold Harbor, Virginia	Point Lookout, Maryland, transferred to Elmira Prison, NY July 17,1864	Died October 28, 1864 of Chronic Diarrhea, Grave No. 718
Causey, Charles Private	Unk	Unknown	Co. D, 1st Alabama Infantry	May 12, 1864, Near Spotsylvania Court House, Virginia	Point Lookout, Maryland, transferred to Elmira Prison, NY July 11, 1864	Escaped December 30, 1864
Cavanaugh, John Sergeant	Unk	July 1, 1861, Nelson County Court House, Virginia	Co. E, 51st Virginia Infantry	July 15, 1864, Leesburg, Virginia	Old Capital Prison, Washington, D. C. Transferred to Elmira Prison, NY August 12, 1864	Died December 5, 1864 of Chronic Diarrhea, Grave No. 1030
Cawthorn, Lafayette Private	Unk	April 21, 1864, Walton, Florida	Co. J, 15th Confederate Cavalry	September 22, 1864, Shoe River, Florida	New Orleans, Louisiana transferred to Elmira November 19, 1864.	Oath of Allegiance June 23, 1865
Cawthorn, William J. Private	34	April 21, 1864, Walton, Florida	Co. J, 15th Confederate Cavalry	September 22, 1864, Shoe River, Florida	New Orleans, Louisiana transferred to Elmira November 19, 1864.	Died February 16, 1865 of Typhoid Fever, Grave No. 2279. Headstone has W. J. Cauthorn.
Cay, Henry T. Private	21	March 11, 1862, Tallahassee, Florida	Co. K, 5th Florida Infantry	May 6, 1864, Wilderness, Virginia	Point Lookout, Maryland, transferred to Elmira Prison, NY July 30, 1864	Oath of Allegiance June 19, 1865

Name & Rank	Age	Enlisted	Regiment and State	Where Captured	Prison	Remarks
Cayler, John Private	Unk	May 2, 1864, Camp Vance, North Carolina	Co. B, 32nd North Carolina Infantry	July 14, 1864, Near Washington, DC	Old Capital Prison, Washington DC. Transferred to Elmira Prison Camp, New York July 25, 1864.	Died March 27, 1865 of Pneumonia, Grave No. 2500. Headstone has Kaylor.
Cazorte, John L. Private	30	July 15, 1861, Raleigh, North Carolina	Co. H, 56th North Carolina Infantry	May 14, 1864, Near Fort Darling, Virginia	Point Lookout, Maryland, transferred to Elmira Prison, NY August 17, 1864	Exchanged February 13, 1865 at Boulware's Wharf on the James River, Virginia
Cecil, James L. Private	Unk	April 3, 1862, Saltville, Virginia	Co. F, 29th Virginia Infantry	June 1, 1864, Gaines Mill, Cold Harbor, Virginia	Point Lookout, Maryland, transferred to Elmira Prison, NY July 17,1864	Died September 23, 1864 of Chronic Diarrhea, Grave No. 353
Ceherr, J. C. Private	Unk	Unknown	Co. D, 14th North Carolina Infantry	May 30, 1864, Mechanics-ville, Virginia	Point Lookout, Maryland, transferred to Elmira Prison, NY July 12, 1864	Oath of Allegiance May 29, 1865
Cerseley, Thomas B. Private	20	May 9, 1861, Manchester, Virginia	Co. J, 6th Virginia Infantry	May 12, 1864, Near Spotsylvania Court House, Virginia	Point Lookout, Maryland, transferred to Elmira Prison, NY August 6, 1864	Oath of Allegiance June 17, 1865
Cesoch, J. T. Private	Unk	Unknown	Co. K, 26th South Carolina Infantry	July 30, 1864, Petersburg, Virginia	Point Lookout, Maryland, transferred to Elmira Prison, NY August 12, 1864	Transferred for Exchange 10/11/64. Nothing Further.
Cessums, Peter T. Private	19	January 5, 1862, Raleigh, North Carolina	Co. H, 55th North Carolina Infantry	May 12, 1864, Spotsylvania Court House, Virginia	Point Lookout, Maryland, transferred to Elmira Prison, NY July 17,1864	Died October 12, 1864 of Chronic Diarrhea, Grave No. 573
Chadwell, Miller Private	Unk	March 2, 1864, Greenville, Tennessee	Co. G, 1st Tennessee Infantry	May 6, 1864, Wilderness, Virginia	Point Lookout, Maryland, transferred to Elmira Prison, NY July 23, 1864	Oath of Allegiance May 29, 1865

Name & Rank	Age	Enlisted	Regiment and State	Where Captured	Prison	Remarks
Chadwick, Robert Private	18	June 5, 1861, Dogwood Grove, North Carolina	Co. K, 3rd North Carolina Infantry	May 12, 1864, Near Spotsylvania Court House, Virginia	Point Lookout Prison, Maryland. Transferred to Elmira Prison Camp New York August 14, 1864.	Oath of Allegiance June 12, 1865
Chafin, J. L. Private	Unk	June 24, 1862, Camp Randolph, Georgia	Co. K, 10th Georgia Infantry	May 6, 1864, Wilderness, Virginia	Point Lookout, Maryland, transferred to Elmira Prison, NY August 14, 1864	Oath of Allegiance June 16, 1865
Chalker, B. C. Private	Unk	March 16, 1864, Newton, Alabama	Co. G, 13th Georgia Infantry	May 10, 1864, Spotsylvania Court House, Virginia	Point Lookout, Maryland, transferred to Elmira Prison, NY July 30, 1864	Oath of Allegiance June 30, 1865
Chambers, James G. Private	Unk	October 4, 1864, Wilmington, North Carolina	Co. K, 10th Regiment, 1st North Carolina Artillery	January 15, 1865, Fort Fisher, North Carolina	January 30, 1865, Elmira Prison Camp, NY	Died on the Route to be Exchanged February 20, 1865.
Chambers, James M. Private	Unk	March 16, 1863, Sumpter, Texas	Co. E, 7th Texas Cavalry	August 5, 1864, Cross Bay, Virginia	Old Capital Prison, Washington, DC transferred to Elmira Prison, NY August 27, 1864	Died February 22, 1865 of Pneumonia, Grave No. 2253
Chambers, John W. Private	Unk	May 8, 1861, Kanawha Court House, Virginia	Co. H, 22nd Virginia Infantry	June 3, 1864, Gaines Farm, Cold Harbor, Virginia	Point Lookout, Maryland, transferred to Elmira Prison, NY July 17, 1864	Oath of Allegiance June 16, 1865
Chambers, Joseph V. Private	Unk	February 1, 1864, Fayetteville, Georgia	Co. C, 53rd Georgia Infantry	June 1, 1864, Gaines Mill, Cold Harbor, Virginia	Point Lookout, Maryland, transferred to Elmira Prison, NY July 17, 1864	Exchanged February 20, 1865 at Boulware's or Cox Wharf on the James River, Virginia
Chambers, Pleasant Private	Unk	December 30, 1861, Nashville, Tennessee	Co. I, 44th Tennessee Infantry	June 17, 1864, Petersburg, Virginia	Point Lookout, Maryland, transferred to Elmira Prison, NY July 30, 1864	Died December 10, 1864 of Pneumonia, Grave No. 1053

Name & Rank	Age	Enlisted	Regiment and State	Where Captured	Prison	Remarks
Chambers, R. T. Private	Unk	March 4, 1862, Perry, Georgia	Co. K, 11th Georgia Infantry	May 6, 1864, Wilderness, Virginia	Point Lookout, Maryland, transferred to Elmira Prison, NY August 14, 1864	Oath of Allegiance June 16, 1865
Chambers, Rueben P. Corporal	Unk	March 18, 1862, Homer, Georgia	Co. A, 24th Georgia Infantry	August 16, 1864, Front Royal, Virginia	Old Capital Prison, Washington, DC transferred to Elmira Prison, NY August 29, 1864	Died May 19, 1865 of Variola (Smallpox). No Grave Found in Woodlawn Cemetery.
Chambers, William D. Private	18	June 25, 1861, Duplin County, North Carolina	Co. B, 3rd North Carolina Infantry	May 12, 1864, Near Spotsylvania, Virginia	Point Lookout, Maryland, transferred to Elmira Prison, NY August 14, 1864	Oath of Allegiance July 19, 1865
Chamblee, Robert Private	23	October 14, 1861, High House, Wake County, North Carolina	Co. H, 31st North Carolina Infantry	June 1, 1864, Gaines Mill, Cold Harbor, Virginia	Point Lookout, Maryland, transferred to Elmira Prison, NY July 17,1864	Oath of Allegiance July 3, 1865
Chambliss, David E. Private	Unk	January 16, 1864, Mobile, Alabama	Co. E, 1st Battalion Alabama Artillery	August 23, 1864, Fort Morgan, Alabama	New Orleans, Louisiana transferred to Elmira December 4, 1864.	Died February 18, 1865 of Variola (Smallpox), Grave No. 2347
Champion, Levi Private	48	October 7, 1862, Wake County, North Carolina	Co. G, 8th North Carolina Infantry	May 31, 1864, Cold Harbor, Virginia	Point Lookout, Maryland, transferred to Elmira Prison, NY July 12, 1864	Oath of Allegiance June 30, 1865
Chance, Alfred N. Private	Unk	August 1, 1861, Waynesboro, Georgia	Co. E, Cobb's Legion Georgia	August 16, 1864, Front Royal, Virginia	Old Capital Prison, Washington, DC transferred to Elmira Prison, NY August 29, 1864	Exchanged February 20, 1865 at Boulware's or Cox Wharf on the James River, Virginia
Chance, John A. Private	Unk	March 1, 1864, Liberty Mills, Virginia	Co. F, 18th North Carolina Infantry	May 10, 1864, Spotsylvania Court House, Virginia	Point Lookout, Maryland, transferred to Elmira Prison, NY August 6, 1864	Exchanged February 13, 1865 at Boulware's wharf on the James River, Virginia

Name & Rank	Age	Enlisted	Regiment and State	Where Captured	Prison	Remarks
Chanceller, Gillam L. Private	Unk	March 8, 1862, Claiborne Parish, Louisiana	Co. G, 12th Louisiana Infantry	May 16, 1863, Baker's Creek, Champion Hill, Mississippi	Point Lookout, Maryland, transferred to Elmira Prison, NY August 18, 1864	Exchanged February 25, 1865 at Boulware's wharf on the James River, Virginia
Chancey, John N. Sergeant	22	April 30, 1862, Louisville, Alabama	Co. E, 59th Alabama Infantry	March 25, 1865, Hatchers Run, Virginia. Gunshot Wound Left Leg.	Old Capital Prison, Washington D. C. Transferred to Elmira Prison, NY May 2, 1865.	Oath of Allegiance June 23, 1865
Chancy, David Civilian	Unk	Boy Camp Follower.	Citizen of Virginia	April 6, 1865, Sailor's Creek, Virginia	Old Capital Prison, Washington D. C. Transferred to Elmira Prison, NY May 12, 1865.	Oath of Allegiance May 15, 1865
Chandler, George H. Private	23	March 1, 1862, Person County, North Carolina	Co. H, 24th North Carolina Infantry	June 17, 1864, Petersburg, Virginia	Point Lookout, Maryland, transferred to Elmira Prison, NY July 30, 1864	Died October 6, 1864 of Chronic Diarrhea, Grave No. 648
Chandler, George W. Private	Unk	December 17, 1861, Camp Hampton, South Carolina	Co. D, Holcombe Legion South Carolina	August 27, 1863, Captured as Courier Near Slatersville, Virginia	Point Lookout, Maryland, transferred to Elmira Prison, NY August 18, 1864	Exchanged October 29, 1864, at Venus Point, Savannah River, GA.
Chandler, J. F. Private	Unk	July 17, 1861, Kingston, South Carolina	Co. K, 6th South Carolina Infantry	May 23, 1864, North Anna, Virginia	Point Lookout, Maryland, transferred to Elmira Prison, NY August 17, 1864	Oath of Allegiance June 14, 1865
Chandler, Obed H. Private	21	April 18, 1861, Strasburg, Virginia	Co. A, 10th Virginia Infantry	May 12, 1864, Spotsylvania Court House, Virginia	Point Lookout, Maryland, transferred to Elmira Prison, NY August 2, 1864	Exchanged March 14, 1865 at Boulware's Wharf on the James River, Virginia
Chandler, Thomas Private	31	March 20, 1862, Danville, Virginia	Co. C, 5th Virginia Cavalry	May 10, 1864, Beaver Dam Station, Virginia	Point Lookout, Maryland, transferred to Elmira Prison, NY August 17, 1864	Exchanged October 29, 1864 at Venus Point, Savannah River, GA.

Name & Rank	Age	Enlisted	Regiment and State	Where Captured	Prison	Remarks
Chapin, Hiram L. Private	22	February 6, 1862, Gainsboro, Tennessee	Co. J, 25th Tennessee Infantry	June 17, 1864, Petersburg, Virginia	Point Lookout, Maryland, transferred to Elmira Prison, NY July 25, 1864	Oath of Allegiance May 21, 1865
Chaplin, D. J. Private	Unk	May 9, 1861, Charleston, South Carolina	Co. D, 5th South Carolina Cavalry	June 11, 1864, Trevilian Station, Louisa Court House, Virginia	Point Lookout, Maryland, transferred to Elmira Prison, NY July 25, 1864	Exchanged March 2, 1865 at Akins Landing on the James River, Virginia
Chapman, Abner A. A. Private	Unk	December 19, 1863, Charleston, South Carolina	Co. J, 18th South Carolina Infantry	July 30, 1864, Petersburg, Virginia	Point Lookout, Maryland, transferred to Elmira Prison, NY August 12, 1864	Died April 6, 1865 of Chronic Diarrhea, Grave No. 2655
Chapman, Daniel Civilian	Unk	Unknown	Citizen of Frederick County, Virginia	August 2, 1863, Near Winchester, Virginia	Point Lookout, Maryland, transferred to Elmira Prison, NY July 25, 1864	Exchanged October 11, 1864. Nothing Further.
Chapman, George Private	Unk	Unknown	Co. B, 1st Alabama Artillery	August 23, 1864, Fort Morgan, Alabama	New Orleans, Louisiana transferred to Elmira November 19, 1864.	Died June 9, 1865 of Chronic Diarrhea, Grave No. 2889
Chapman, James T. Private	Unk	April 27, 1862, Charleston, South Carolina	Co. C, 22nd South Carolina Infantry	July 30, 1864, Petersburg, Virginia	Point Lookout, Maryland, transferred to Elmira Prison, NY August 12, 1864	Exchanged February 20, 1865 at Boulware's or Cox Wharf on the James River, Virginia
Chapman, John C. Sergeant	Unk	May 31, 1861, Yellow Branch, Virginia	Co. D, 42nd Virginia Infantry	May 12, 1864, Near Spotsylvania Court House, Virginia	Point Lookout, Maryland, transferred to Elmira Prison, NY August 6, 1864	Transferred for Exchange 10/11/64. Exchanged 11/15/64 at Venus Point, Savannah River, GA.
Chapman, Liberty Private	20	July 15, 1862, Fayetteville, Trenton, North Carolina	Co. J, 2nd North Carolina Cavalry	June 3, 1864, Near Talapatomoy Creek, Cold Harbor, Virginia	Point Lookout, Maryland, transferred to Elmira Prison, NY July 17, 1864	Oath of Allegiance June 19, 1865

Name & Rank	Age	Enlisted	Regiment and State	Where Captured	Prison	Remarks
Chapman, Pat H. Private	Unk	May 3, 1861, Yellow Branch, Virginia	Co. D, 42nd Virginia Infantry	May 12, 1864, Near Spotsylvania Court House, Virginia	Point Lookout, Maryland, transferred to Elmira Prison, NY August 6, 1864	Died February 27, 1865 of Pneumonia, Grave No. 2119
Chapman, Robert Private	Unk	April 20, 1864, Camp Holmes, North Carolina	Co. H, 34th North Carolina Infantry	May 6, 1864, Wilderness, Virginia	Point Lookout, Maryland, transferred to Elmira Prison, NY August 14, 1864	Died September 29, 1864 of Chronic Diarrhea, Grave No. 425
Chapman, Thomas Private	30	August 12, 1864, Warren County, North Carolina	Co. F, 8th North Carolina Infantry	May 16, 1864, Near Drury's Bluff, Virginia	Point Lookout Prison Camp, Maryland. Transferred to Elmira Prison, August 18, 1864	Died April 26, 1865 of Scorbutis (Scurvy), Grave No. 1418
Chapman, W. S. Private	Unk	August 22, 1862, Coffee County, Alabama	Co. G, 8th Alabama Infantry	May 6, 1864, Wilderness, Virginia	Point Lookout, Maryland, transferred to Elmira Prison, NY August 17, 1864	Died December 8, 1864 of Typhoid Fever, Grave No.1161
Chapman, Walter F. Private	Unk	March 10, 1862, Caroline County, Virginia	Co. B, 9th Virginia Cavalry	May 9, 1864, Childburg, Virginia	Point Lookout, Maryland, transferred to Elmira Prison, NY August 18, 1864	Oath of Allegiance June 14, 1865
Chapman, William Private	Unk	Unknown	Co. F, 48th Georgia Infantry	August 16, 1864, New Market, Virginia	Old Capital Prison, Washington, DC transferred to Elmira Prison, NY August 29, 1864	Released February 1, 1865, on Orders from L. C. Turner, Judge Advocate.
Chappell, John R. Private	18	June 3, 1864, Petersburg, Virginia	Co. B, Hood's Battalion, Virginia Reserve Infantry	June 15, 1864, Petersburg, Virginia	Point Lookout, Maryland, transferred to Elmira Prison, NY July 30, 1864	Oath of Allegiance May 13, 1865
Charles, Andrew Private	Unk	October 18, 1862, Davidson County, North Carolina	Co. F, 3rd North Carolina Infantry	May 12, 1864, Near Spotsylvania Court House, Virginia	Point Lookout, Maryland, transferred to Elmira Prison, NY August 14, 1864	Died September 9, 1865 of Chronic Diarrhea, Grave No. 207

Name & Rank	Age	Enlisted	Regiment and State	Where Captured	Prison	Remarks
Charlton, Henry W. Private	Unk	January 1, 1864, Orange County, Virginia	Co. F, 15th Virginia Cavalry	May 12, 1864, Mechanics-ville, Virginia	Point Lookout, Maryland, transferred to Elmira Prison, NY August 17, 1864	Exchanged October 29, 1864. Died November 10, 1864 of Unknown Causes at Sea.
Charlton, Waddy C. Private	21	April 17, 1861, Christians-burg, Virginia	Co. G, 4th Virginia Infantry	May 12, 1864, Spotsylvania Court House, Virginia	Point Lookout, Maryland, transferred to Elmira Prison, NY August 2, 1864	Oath of Allegiance June 30, 1865
Chase, Robert Private	18	May 27, 1861, Wilmington, North Carolina	Co. D, 3rd North Carolina Infantry	May 12, 1864, Near Spotsylvania, Virginia	Point Lookout, Maryland, transferred to Elmira Prison, NY August 14, 1864	Oath of Allegiance June 27, 1865
Chatham, F. M. Private	Unk	Unknown	Co. C, 7th Georgia Cavalry	June 11, 1864, Trevilian Station, Louisa Court House, Virginia	Point Lookout, Maryland, transferred to Elmira Prison, NY July 25, 1864	Died March 24, 1865 of Pneumonia, Grave No. 2444
Chatham, W. J. Private	Unk	September 29, 1864, Tallapoosa County, Alabama	Co. L, 3rd Alabama Infantry	May 12, 1864, Spotsylvania Court House, Virginia	Point Lookout, Maryland, transferred to Elmira Prison, NY August 12, 1864	Oath of Allegiance June 16, 1865
Chatman, Israel Private	Unk	April 1, 1863, Wytheville, Virginia	Co. H, 23rd Virginia Infantry	July 8, 1864, Near Harper's Ferry, Virginia	Old Capital Prison, Washington, DC, transferred to Elmira Prison, NY, July 23, 1864	Died October 25, 1864 of Chronic Diarrhea, Grave No. 858
Cheatham, James T. Private	17	September 7, 1862, Oxford, North Carolina	Co. F, 30th North Carolina Infantry	July 13, 1864, Near Washington, DC	Old Capital Prison, Washington, DC, transferred to Elmira Prison, NY, July 23, 1864	Oath of Allegiance June 12, 1865
Cheek, James Private	Unk	June 29, 1861, Wytheville, Virginia	Co. B, 50th Virginia Infantry	May 12, 1864, Spotsylvania Court House, Virginia	Point Lookout, Maryland, transferred to Elmira Prison, NY August 2, 1864	Oath of Allegiance June 30, 1865

Name & Rank	Age	Enlisted	Regiment and State	Where Captured	Prison	Remarks
Cheek, John D. Private	37	March 26, 1863, Chatham County, North Carolina	Co. G, 40th Regiment, 3rd North Carolina Artillery	January 15, 1865, Fort Fisher, North Carolina	Elmira Prison Camp January 30, 1865	Oath of Allegiance June 12, 1865
Cheek, Nathaniel W. Private	Unk	March 13, 1864, Graham, North Carolina	Co. B, 1st North Carolina Infantry	May 12, 1864, Spotsylvania Court House, Virginia	Point Lookout, Maryland, transferred to Elmira Prison, NY August 6, 1864	Died December 1, 1864 of Pleuro-Pneumonia, Grave No. 1005
Cheek, Robert G. Private	Unk	August 1, 1861, Covington, Georgia	Co. B, 1st North Carolina Infantry	May 12, 1864, Spotsylvania Court House, Virginia	Point Lookout, Maryland, transferred to Elmira Prison, NY August 6, 1864	Oath of Allegiance May 19, 1865
Cheek, Thomas S. Private	Unk	August 1, 1861, Covington, Georgia	Co. D, 3rd Battalion Georgia Sharp Shooters	August 16, 1864, Front Royal, Virginia	Old Capital Prison, Washington, DC transferred to Elmira Prison, NY August 29, 1864	Exchanged October 29, 1864, at Venus Point, Savannah River, GA.
Cheek, William J. A. Private	18	September 2, 1861, Orange County, North Carolina	Co. G, 28th North Carolina Infantry	May 12, 1864, Spotsylvania, Virginia	Point Lookout, Maryland, transferred to Elmira Prison, NY August 12, 1864	Oath of Allegiance June 19, 1865
Cheney, L. R. Private	Unk	May 25, 1862, Camp Moore, Louisiana	Co. A, 4th Louisiana Cavalry	October 6, 1864, Clinton, Louisiana	New Orleans, Louisiana transferred to Elmira November 19, 1864.	Exchanged February 13, 1865 at Boulware's wharf on the James River, Virginia
Cheney, S. Private	Unk	March 17, 1862, Charleston, South Carolina	Co. G, 27th South Carolina Infantry	June 24, 1864, Near Petersburg, Virginia	Point Lookout, Maryland, transferred to Elmira Prison, NY August 18, 1864	Died September 28, 1864 of Pneumonia, Grave No. 395
Cherry, Elisha J. Private	21	April 27, 1861, Duplin County, North Carolina	Co. E, 20th North Carolina Infantry	May 20, 1864, Spotsylvania Court House, Virginia	Point Lookout, Maryland, transferred to Elmira Prison, NY July 6, 1864	Oath of Allegiance June 12, 1865

Name & Rank	Age	Enlisted	Regiment and State	Where Captured	Prison	Remarks
Cherry, George T. Private	23	November 7, 1861, Duplin County, North Carolina	Co. G, 40th Regiment, 3rd North Carolina Artillery	January 15, 1865, Fort Fisher, North Carolina	Elmira Prison Camp January 30, 1865	Oath of Allegiance June 12, 1865
Cherry, Oliver Sergeant	20	May 30, 1861, Camden County, North Carolina	Co. B, 32nd North Carolina Infantry	May 10, 1864, Spotsylvania, Virginia	Point Lookout, Maryland, transferred to Elmira Prison, NY August 6, 1864	Died August 23, 1865 of Unknown Causes, Grave No. 2858
Chester, John Private	Unk	Unknown	Co. G, 4th Virginia Cavalry	October 17, 1864, Warrenton, Virginia	Old Capital Prison, Washington, DC, transferred to Elmira Prison, NY, December 17, 1864	Exchanged March 2, 1865 at Boulware's Wharf on the James River, Virginia
Chevalier, S. A. Private	Unk	Unknown	Co. J, 23rd Texas Cavalry	August 18, 1864, Near Morganza, Louisiana	New Orleans, Louisiana, Transferred to Elmira Prison, NY, November 19, 1864	Exchanged February 20, 1865 at Boulware's or Cox Wharf on the James River, Virginia
Chewning, Booker P. Private	26	March 2, 1863, Centreville Virginia	Co. F, 26th Battalion, Virginia Infantry	June 3, 1864, Gaines Farm, Cold Harbor, Virginia	Point Lookout, Maryland, transferred to Elmira Prison, NY July 17, 1864	Transferred for Exchange 10/11/64. Died of Unknown Causes 10/13/64 at U. S. Army Hospital, Baltimore, MD
Chewning, John A. Private	Unk	February 1, 1862, Decatur, Georgia	Co. D, 3rd Battalion Georgia Sharp Shooters	August 16, 1864, Front Royal, Virginia	Old Capital Prison, Washington, DC transferred to Elmira Prison, NY August 29, 1864	Oath of Allegiance July 7, 1865
Chewning, John S. Private	26	July 3, 1861, Peterstown, Virginia	Co. D, 26th Battalion, Virginia Infantry	June 3, 1864, Gaines Farm, Cold Harbor, Virginia	Point Lookout, Maryland, transferred to Elmira Prison, NY July 17, 1864	Died December 12, 1864 of Pneumonia Grave No. m
Chewning, Nelson S. Private	Unk	March 13, 1862, Fredericksburg, Virginia	Co. M, 55th Virginia Infantry	July 14, 1863, Falling Waters, Maryland	Point Lookout, Maryland, transferred to Elmira Prison, NY August 18, 1864	Exchanged March 10, 1865 at Boulware's Wharf on the James River, Virginia

Name & Rank	Age	Enlisted	Regiment and State	Where Captured	Prison	Remarks
Chick, H. N. Private	Unk	Unknown	Co. D, 4th Georgia Infantry	May 12, 1864, Spotsylvania Court House, Virginia	Point Lookout, Maryland, transferred to Elmira Prison, NY August 2, 1864	Oath of Allegiance June 23, 1865
Chighizola, John Private	Unk	April 23, 1861, Mobile, Alabama	Co. A, 3rd Alabama Infantry	July 13, 1864, Silver Springs, Maryland	Old Capital Prison, Washington, DC transferred to Elmira Prison, NY August 27, 1864	Oath of Allegiance June 16, 1865
Chilcutt, James R. Private	28	December 30, 1861, Camp Weakly, Nashville, Tennessee	Co. J, 44th Tennessee Infantry	June 17, 1864, Petersburg, Virginia	Point Lookout, Maryland, transferred to Elmira Prison, NY July 30, 1864	Oath of Allegiance April 3, 1865. Early Release per Lincoln's Proclamation, 12/8/1863.
Childers, A. Crowell Corporal	Unk	January 10, 1862, Columbia, South Carolina	Co. C, 22nd South Carolina Infantry	July 30, 1864, Petersburg, Virginia	Point Lookout, Maryland, transferred to Elmira Prison, NY August 12, 1864	Oath of Allegiance July 3, 1865
Childers, Ison M. Sergeant Major	Unk	July 15, 1864, Lynchburg, Virginia	Staff, 42nd Virginia Infantry	May 12, 1864, Near Spotsylvania Court House, Virginia	Point Lookout, Maryland, transferred to Elmira Prison, NY August 6, 1864	Exchanged March 2, 1865 at Akins Landing on the James River, Virginia
Childress, David D. Private	Unk	May 21, 1861, Brownsburg, Virginia	Co. H, 25th Virginia Infantry	May 6, 1864, Wilderness, Virginia	Point Lookout, Maryland, transferred to Elmira Prison, NY August 14, 1864	Exchanged October 29, 1864, at Venus Point, Savannah River, GA.
Childress, Edward T. Private	Unk	May 5, 1864, Talladega, Alabama	Co. A, 12th Alabama Infantry	May 30, 1864, Cold Harbor, Virginia	Point Lookout, Maryland, transferred to Elmira Prison, NY July 23, 1864	Exchanged February 13, 1865 at Boulware's wharf on the James River, Virginia
Childs, F. M. Private	Unk	September 7, 1863, Fauquier County, Virginia	Co. C, Mosby's Virginia, Cavalry	September 22, 1863, Near Madison Court House, Virginia	Point Lookout, Maryland, transferred to Elmira Prison, NY August 18, 1864	Exchanged February 20, 1865 at Boulware's or Cox Wharf on the James River, Virginia

288

Name & Rank	Age	Enlisted	Regiment and State	Where Captured	Prison	Remarks
Childs, William H. Sergeant	Unk	March 4, 1862, Clinton, Georgia	Co. F, 45th Georgia Infantry	May 6, 1864, Wilderness, Virginia	Point Lookout, Maryland, transferred to Elmira Prison, NY August 14, 1864	Oath of Allegiance June 14, 1865
Chiles, John F. Private	Unk	April 15, 1861, Livingston, Alabama	Co. G, 5th Alabama Infantry	May 5, 1864, Wilderness, Virginia	Point Lookout, Maryland, transferred to Elmira Prison, NY August 17, 1864	Exchanged February 13, 1865 at Boulware's wharf on the James River, Virginia
Chiles, T. J. Corporal	Unk	August 30, 1862, Dale County, Alabama	Co. G, 5th Alabama Infantry	May 5, 1864, Wilderness, Virginia	Point Lookout, Maryland, transferred to Elmira Prison, NY August 17, 1864	Exchanged October 29, 1864. Died November 11, 1864 of Unknown Causes at Port Royal, South Carolina.
Chilton, James V. Private	Unk	Unknown	Co. D, Mosby's Regiment Virginia Cavalry	April 6, 1865, Sailor's Creek, Virginia	Old Capital Prison, Washington D. C. Transferred to Elmira Prison, NY May 12, 1865.	Oath of Allegiance June 9, 1865
Chilton, Samuel H. Private	21	March 1, 1862, Reidsville, North Carolina	Co. H, 45th North Carolina Infantry	March 25, 1865, Fort Steadman, Virginia. Gunshot Wound Left Hand.	Old Capital Prison, Washington D. C. Transferred to Elmira Prison, NY May 12, 1865.	Oath of Allegiance July 11, 1865
Chilton, W. Sergeant	Unk	May 18, 1861, Lisbon, Virginia	Co. K, 42nd Virginia Infantry	May 12, 1864, Spotsylvania Court House, Virginia	Point Lookout, Maryland, transferred to Elmira Prison, NY August 2, 1864	Exchanged February 20, 1865 at Boulware's or Cox Wharf on the James River, Virginia
Chittum, James A. Private	24	June 25, 1861, Harrisonburg, Virginia	Co. C, 6th Virginia Cavalry	September 14, 1863, Near Culpepper, Virginia	Point Lookout, Maryland, transferred to Elmira Prison, NY August 12, 1864	Exchanged October 29, 1864 at Venus Point, Savannah River, GA.

Name & Rank	Age	Enlisted	Regiment and State	Where Captured	Prison	Remarks
Chitty, Harrison Benjamin Private	Unk	August 30, 1862, Southampton, North Carolina	Co. F, 25th North Carolina Infantry	June 17, 1864, Petersburg, Virginia	Point Lookout, Maryland, transferred to Elmira Prison, NY July 30, 1864	Exchanged February 25, 1865 at Boulware's or Cox Wharf on the James River, Virginia
Chitty, John T. Corporal	18	May 1, 1862, South Mills, North Carolina	Co. C, 32nd North Carolina Infantry	May 10, 1864, Spotsylvania, Virginia	Point Lookout, Maryland, transferred to Elmira Prison, NY August 6, 1864	Oath of Allegiance July 30, 1865
Choat, Calvin H. Private	Unk	April 25, 1861, Long Island, Alabama	Co. C, 6th Alabama Infantry	May 12, 1864, Spotsylvania Court House, Virginia	Point Lookout, Maryland, transferred to Elmira Prison, NY July 6, 1864	Oath of Allegiance June 16, 1865
Choate, William D. Sergeant	Unk	May 11, 1861, New Orleans, Louisiana	Co. C, 2nd Louisiana Infantry	May 12, 1864, Spotsylvania, Virginia	Point Lookout, Maryland, transferred to Elmira Prison, NY August 17, 1864	Exchanged February 25, 1865 at Boulware's or Cox Wharf on the James River, Virginia
Chrisman, James R. Private	19	May 13, 1862, Loachapoka, Tallapoosa County, Alabama	Co. F, 47th Alabama Infantry	May 24, 1864, Hanover, Virginia	Point Lookout, Maryland, transferred to Elmira Prison, NY July 11, 1864	Oath of Allegiance June 30, 1865
Chrismands, J. A. Private	Unk	Unknown	Co. E, 63rd Tennessee Infantry	June 17, 1864, Near Petersburg, Virginia	Point Lookout, Maryland, transferred to Elmira Prison, NY July 30, 1864	Oath of Allegiance July 3, 1865
Chrisp, William S. Private	25	May 1, 1862, Sparta, North Carolina	Co. F, 30th North Carolina Infantry	May 8, 1864, Wilderness, Virginia	Point Lookout, Maryland, transferred to Elmira Prison, NY August 14, 1864	Oath of Allegiance June 30, 1865
Christian, William C. Private	Unk	June 9, 1862, Richmond, Virginia	Co. F, 3rd Virginia Cavalry	August 16, 1864, Front Royal, Virginia	Old Capital Prison, Washington, DC transferred to Elmira Prison, NY August 29, 1864	Exchanged March 10, 1865 at Boulware's Wharf on the James River, Virginia

Name & Rank	Age	Enlisted	Regiment and State	Where Captured	Prison	Remarks
Christopher, Willard Sergeant	Unk	March 21, 1862, Marion, South Carolina	Co. A, 18th South Carolina Infantry	July 30, 1864, Petersburg, Virginia	New Orleans, Louisiana transferred to Elmira Prison, NY December 4, 1864.	Oath of Allegiance July 11, 1865
Christy, William L. Private	24	March 21, 1862, Marion, North Carolina	Co. B, 22nd North Carolina Infantry	July 12, 1863, Hagerstown, Pennsylvania	Point Lookout, Maryland, transferred to Elmira Prison, NY August 18, 1864	Exchanged 10/29/64. Died 11/9/64 of Empyemia and buried at sea by US Army Hospital Steamer Baltic.
Chumbley, George H. Private	22	April 17, 1861, Newbern, Virginia	Co. C, 4th Virginia Infantry	May 12, 1864, Spotsylvania Court House, Virginia	Point Lookout, Maryland, transferred to Elmira Prison, NY August 2, 1864	Oath of Allegiance June 14, 1865
Church, B. F. Private	Unk	March 10, 1863, Virginia	Co. C, Phillips Legion, Georgia	June 1, 1864, Gaines Farm, Cold Harbor, Virginia	Point Lookout, Maryland, transferred to Elmira Prison, NY July 17,1864	Exchanged October 29, 1864, at Venus Point, Savannah River, GA.
Church, Carlton Private	18	September 27, 1862, Raleigh, North Carolina	Co. G, 30th North Carolina Infantry	May 12, 1864, Near Spotsylvania, Virginia	Point Lookout, Maryland, transferred to Elmira Prison, NY August 14, 1864	Died March 22, 1865 of Pneumonia, Grave No. 1037. Name Calvin Church, 20th NC, on Headstone.
Church, James G. Private	21	April 12, 1862, Wilkes County, North Carolina	Co. K, 53rd North Carolina Infantry	July 17,1864, Near Washington, DC	Old Capital Prison, Washington, DC, transferred to Elmira Prison, NY, July 23, 1864	Died March 19, 1865 of Variola (Smallpox), Grave No. 1561, Has 5th Artillery on Headstone.
Church, Thomas A. Private	34	November 1, 1865, Williamson County, Tennessee	Co. L, Jackson's 1st Regiment, Tennessee Heavy Artillery	August 23, 1864, Fort Morgan, Alabama	New Orleans, Louisiana transferred to Elmira December 4, 1864.	Died December 23, 1864 of Pneumonia, Grave No. 1098
Church, William H. Private	17	March 14, 1862, Wilkesboro, North Carolina	Co. F, 52nd North Carolina Infantry	May 12, 1864, Spotsylvania Court House, Virginia	Point Lookout, Maryland, transferred to Elmira Prison, NY August 12, 1864	Oath of Allegiance June 12, 1865

Name & Rank	Age	Enlisted	Regiment and State	Where Captured	Prison	Remarks
Churchill, Leroy P. Private	35	July 17, 1862, Richmond County, North Carolina	Co. B, 3rd North Carolina Infantry	May 12, 1864, Near Spotsylvania, Virginia	Point Lookout, Maryland, transferred to Elmira Prison, NY August 14, 1864	Transferred for Exchange 2/20/65. Died 3/24/65 of Inflammation of Lungs at US Army Hospital, Baltimore, MD.
Clack, Robert H. L. Corporal	Unk	August 25, 1862, Richmond, Virginia	Co. G, Cobb's Legion, Georgia	August 16, 1864, Front Royal, Virginia	Old Capital Prison, Washington, DC transferred to Elmira Prison, NY August 29, 1864	Oath of Allegiance July 11, 1865
Clagett, Edward L. Private	Unk	September 18, 1862, Richmond, Virginia	Co. F, 2nd Battalion Maryland Infantry	July 5, 1863, Gettysburg, Pennsylvania	Point Lookout, Maryland, transferred to Elmira Prison, NY August 18, 1864	Exchanged February 13, 1865 at Boulware's wharf on the James River, Virginia
Clamp, Jacob B. Private	Unk	December 25, 1861, Camp Hampton, South Carolina	Co. G, 1st South Carolina Infantry	July 14, 1863, Falling Waters, Maryland	Point Lookout, Maryland, transferred to Elmira Prison, NY August 18, 1864	Exchanged March 10, 1865 at Boulware's Wharf on the James River, Virginia
Clancey, Charles S. Private	Unk	April 28, 1861, New Orleans, Louisiana	Co. D, Nelligan's 1st, Louisiana Infantry	May 12, 1864, Spotsylvania Court House, Virginia	Point Lookout Prison. Transferred to Elmira Prison, New York, July 6, 1864.	Escaped December 30, 1864.
Clancy, Arthur R. Sergeant	Unk	July 29, 1861, Columbia, South Carolina	Co. C, 1st South Carolina Infantry	May 6, 1864, Wilderness, Virginia	Old Capital Prison, Washington, DC, transferred to Elmira Prison, NY, July 23, 1864	Oath of Allegiance June 19, 1865
Clancy, Patrick Private	31	June 6, 1861, New Orleans, Louisiana	Co. C, 14th Louisiana Infantry	May 8, 1864, Wilderness, Virginia	Point Lookout, Maryland, transferred to Elmira Prison, NY July 23, 1864	Died September 26, 1864 of Asthma and Pneumonia, Grave No. 446
Clanton, Daniel C. Private	Unk	January 31, 1863, Bryan County, Georgia	Co. H, 7th Georgia Cavalry	June 11, 1864, Trevilian Station, Louisa Court House, Virginia	Point Lookout, Maryland, transferred to Elmira Prison, NY July 25, 1864	Died January 21, 1865 of Pneumonia, Grave No. 1590

Name & Rank	Age	Enlisted	Regiment and State	Where Captured	Prison	Remarks
Clanton, Francis Private	Unk	November 1, 1863, Statesville, North Carolina	Co. B, 37th North Carolina Infantry	May 12, 1864, Near Spotsylvania Court House, Virginia	Point Lookout, Maryland, transferred to Elmira Prison, NY August 14, 1864	Died May 24, 1865 of Chronic Diarrhea, Grave No. 2923
Clapp, Daniel M. Private	21	October 1, 1862, near Drury's Bluff, Virginia	Co. B, 45th North Carolina Infantry	May 10, 1864, Spotsylvania Court House, Virginia	Point Lookout, Maryland, transferred to Elmira Prison, NY July 25, 1864	Oath of Allegiance June 23, 1865
Clapp, James F. R. Corporal	24	July 8, 1862, Greensboro, North Carolina	Co. H, 1st North Carolina Infantry	May 12, 1864, Spotsylvania Court House, Virginia	Point Lookout, Maryland, transferred to Elmira Prison, NY August 6, 1864	Oath of Allegiance June 12, 1865
Clapp, John Private	Unk	February 10, 1864, Raleigh, North Carolina	Co. E, 1st North Carolina Infantry	May 12, 1864, Spotsylvania Court House, Virginia	Point Lookout, Maryland, transferred to Elmira Prison, NY August 6, 1864	Died December 5, 1864 of Pneumonia, Grave No. 1028
Clapp, Wesley Private	34	July 15, 1862, Raleigh, North Carolina	Co. E, 10th Regiment, 1st North Carolina Infantry	May 12, 1864, Spotsylvania Court House, Virginia	Point Lookout, Maryland, transferred to Elmira Prison, NY August 6, 1864	Died March 20, 1865 of Diarrhea, Grave No. 1566. Name Clamps and NC Artillery on Headstone.
Clardy, J. F. Sergeant	Unk	February 28, 1863, Wilmington, North Carolina	Co. D, 18th South Carolina Infantry	July 30, 1864, Petersburg, Virginia	Point Lookout, Maryland, transferred to Elmira Prison, NY August 12, 1864	Oath of Allegiance July 7, 1865
Clark, Angus J. Private	53	February 3, 1862, Georgetown, South Carolina	Co. F, 4th South Carolina Cavalry	May 28, 1864, Falls Church, Virginia. Gunshot Wound Left Side of Face, Severe.	Old Capital Prison, Washington, DC, transferred to Elmira Prison, NY, December 17, 1864	Exchanged February 20, 1865 at Boulware's or Cox Wharf on the James River, Virginia
Clark, Baty C. Private	17	March 11, 1863, Fort Fisher, North Carolina	Co. I, 36th Regiment, 2nd North Carolina Artillery	January 15, 1865, Fort Fisher, North Carolina. Wounded	February 1, 1865, Elmira Prison Camp, New York	Died March 8, 1865 of Chronic Diarrhea, Grave No. 2372. Headstone has 31st NC.

Name & Rank	Age	Enlisted	Regiment and State	Where Captured	Prison	Remarks
Clark, Benjamin F. Private	35	April 1, 1861, Lacy's Store, Virginia	Co. B, 44th Virginia Infantry	May 12, 1864, Spotsylvania Court House, Virginia	Point Lookout, Maryland, transferred to Elmira Prison, NY August 2, 1864	Exchanged October 29, 1864, at Venus Point, Savannah River, GA.
Clark, Benjamin W. Private	Unk	May 14, 1862, Marshall, North Carolina	Co. A, 5th Battalion North Carolina Cavalry	May 1, 1861, Ashland Station, Virginia	Point Lookout, Maryland, transferred to Elmira Prison, NY July 17,1864	Died October 8, 1864 of Typhoid Fever, Grave No. 658
Clark, Charles P. Corporal	Unk	March 5, 1861, Selma, Alabama	Co. C, 1st Battalion Alabama Artillery	August 23, 1864, Fort Morgan, Alabama	New Orleans, Louisiana transferred to Elmira December 4, 1864.	Oath of Allegiance June 21, 1865
Clark, D. Private	Unk	May 10, 1862, Franklin, Alabama	Co. K, 61st Alabama Infantry	June 10, 1864, Spotsylvania, Virginia	Point Lookout, Maryland, transferred to Elmira Prison, NY July 25, 1864	Oath of Allegiance July 11, 1865
Clark, Edward J. Sergeant	37	March 7, 1862, Floyd Court House, Virginia	Co. B, 42nd Virginia Infantry	May 12, 1864, Spotsylvania Court House, Virginia	Point Lookout, Maryland, transferred to Elmira Prison, NY August 2, 1864	Exchanged February 20, 1865 at Boulware's or Cox Wharf on the James River, Virginia
Clark, Elijah P. Corporal	21	January 14, 1862, Springfield, Missouri	Co. D, 1st Missouri Cavalry	May 17, 1863, Big Black Bridge, Mississippi	Point Lookout, Maryland, transferred to Elmira Prison, NY August 18, 1864	Exchanged February 13, 1865 at Boulware's wharf on the James River, Virginia
Clark, Henry C. Private	Unk	July 23, 1861, Mt. Airy, Wythe County, Virginia	Co. B, 29th Virginia Infantry	May 13, 1864, Near Fort Darling, Virginia	Point Lookout, Maryland, transferred to Elmira Prison, NY August 17, 1864	Died September 30, 1864 of Chronic Diarrhea, Grave No. 399. Headstone has 20th VA.
Clark, Henry R. Private	Unk	September 29, 1862, Bunkerville, Virginia	Bo. B, 40th Virginia Infantry	September 30, 1864, Weldon Railroad, Virginia. Gunshot Wound Right Foot.	Old Capital Prison, Washington, DC, transferred to Elmira Prison, NY, December 17, 1864	Oath of Allegiance June 23, 1865

Name & Rank	Age	Enlisted	Regiment and State	Where Captured	Prison	Remarks
Clark, Henry S. Private	Unk	January 1, 1863, Wilmington, North Carolina	Co. K, 10th Regiment, 1st North Carolina Artillery	January 15, 1865, Fort Fisher, North Carolina	January 30, 1865, Elmira Prison Camp, NY	Exchanged February 13, 1865 at Boulware's wharf on the James River, Virginia
Clark, Isaac N. Sergeant	Unk	May 13, 1862, Cumberland County, North Carolina	Co. E, 56th North Carolina Infantry	May 14, 1864, Near Fort Darling, Virginia	Point Lookout, Maryland, transferred to Elmira Prison, NY August 17, 1864	Oath of Allegiance May 17, 1865
Clark, J. Private	Unk	Unknown	Co. C, 4th Virginia Infantry	July 14, 1864, Falling Waters, Virginia	Point Lookout, Maryland, transferred to Elmira Prison, NY July 23, 1864	Oath of Allegiance June 14, 1865
Clark, James Private	Unk	Unknown	North Carolina Home Guards	May 2, 1864, Harper's Ferry, Virginia	Old Capital Prison, Washington, DC, transferred to Elmira Prison, NY, July 23, 1864	Oath of Allegiance May 29, 1865
Clark, James Private	19	August 11, 1861, Gates County, North Carolina	Co. E, 33rd North Carolina Infantry	May 6, 1864, Wilderness, Virginia	Old Capital Prison, Washington D. C. Transferred to Elmira Prison, NY July 12, 1864	Exchanged March 10, 1865 at Boulware's Wharf on the James River, Virginia
Clark, James Private	18	September 24, 1862, Frederick County, Virginia	Co. H, 11th Virginia Cavalry	December 8, 1864, Stony Creek, Virginia	November 11, 1864, Old Capital Prison, Washington, DC. February 4, 1865 Elmira, Prison Camp, NY	Exchanged March 14, 1865 at Boulware's Wharf on the James River, Virginia
Clark, James C. Corporal	45	March 11, 1862, Wilmington, North Carolina	Co. H, 36th Regiment, 2nd North Carolina Artillery	January 15, 1865, Fort Fisher, North Carolina. Wounded	February 1, 1865, Elmira Prison Camp, New York	Oath of Allegiance July 11, 1865
Clark, James W. Private	18	December 20, 1862, Salisbury, North Carolina	Co. K, 8th North Carolina Infantry	May 31, 1864, Cold Harbor, Virginia	Point Lookout, Maryland, transferred to Elmira Prison, NY July 11, 1864	Oath of Allegiance June 12, 1865

Name & Rank	Age	Enlisted	Regiment and State	Where Captured	Prison	Remarks
Clark, Jasper N. Private	18	May 12, 1861, Waynesboro, Georgia	Co. E, Cobb's Legion Georgia Infantry	May 5, 1864, Wilderness, Virginia	Point Lookout, Maryland, transferred to Elmira Prison, NY August 17, 1864	Died April 11, 1865 of Chronic Diarrhea, Grave No. 2693.
Clark, John A. Sergeant	20	March 31, 1862, Salisbury, North Carolina	Co. K, 8th North Carolina Infantry	June 1, 1864, Gaines Farm, Cold Harbor, Virginia	Point Lookout, Maryland, transferred to Elmira Prison, NY July 17,1864	Died April 19, 1865 of Chronic Diarrhea, Grave No. 1376
Clark, John B. Corporal	Unk	March 14, 1862, Carthage, North Carolina	Co. D, 49th North Carolina Infantry	June 2, 1864, Bermuda Hundred, Cold Harbor, Virginia	Point Lookout, Maryland, transferred to Elmira Prison, NY July 17,1864	Oath of Allegiance July 3, 1865
Clark, John D. Private	19	September 19, 1861, Red Springs, Robison County, North Carolina	Co. E, 40th Regiment, 3rd North Carolina Artillery	January 15, 1865, Fort Fisher, North Carolina	February 1, 1865, Elmira Prison Camp, New York	Oath of Allegiance July 11, 1865
Clark, John E. Private	Unk	September 30, 1861, Catawba, Virginia	Co. K, 26th Virginia Infantry	June 15, 1864, Near Petersburg, Virginia	Point Lookout, Maryland, transferred to Elmira Prison, NY July 12, 1864	Died November 7, 1864 of Pneumonia, Grave No. 776
Clark, John J. Corporal	18	April 26, 1861, City of Norfolk, Virginia	Co. J, 6th Virginia Infantry	May 12, 1864, Near Spotsylvania Court House, Virginia	Point Lookout, Maryland, transferred to Elmira Prison, NY August 6, 1864	Oath of Allegiance May 13, 1865
Clark, John W. Sergeant	22	May 6, 1862, Elizabethtown, Bladen County, North Carolina	Co. K, 40th Regiment, 3rd North Carolina Artillery	January 15, 1865, Fort Fisher, North Carolina	February 1, 1865, Elmira Prison Camp, New York	Oath of Allegiance June 12, 1865
Clark, Joseph D. Private	Unk	February 22, 1864, Camp of 52nd Regiment, Virginia	Co. E, 52nd Virginia Infantry	May 20, 1864, Spotsylvania Court House, Virginia	Point Lookout, Maryland, transferred to Elmira Prison, NY July 3, 1864	Oath of Allegiance June 19, 1865
Clark, Joseph S. Private	Unk	Unknown	Co. E, 50th Virginia Infantry	May 12, 1864, Spotsylvania Court House, Virginia	Point Lookout, Maryland, transferred to Elmira Prison, NY August 2, 1864	Exchanged February 13, 1865 at Boulware's wharf on the James River, Virginia

Name & Rank	Age	Enlisted	Regiment and State	Where Captured	Prison	Remarks
Clark, Michael Private	25	June 12, 1861, New Orleans, Louisiana	Co. K, 14th Louisiana Infantry	May 12, 1864, Spotsylvania Court House, Virginia	Point Lookout, Maryland, transferred to Elmira Prison, NY July 25, 1864	Exchanged February 20, 1865 at Boulware's or Cox Wharf on the James River, Virginia
Clark, Philip Private	Unk	August 15, 1863, Fort McAllister, Georgia	Co. E, 12th Battalion Georgia Artillery	July 8, 1864, Near Harper's Ferry, Virginia	Old Capital Prison, Washington, DC, transferred to Elmira Prison, NY, July 23, 1864	Exchanged October 29, 1864 at Venus Point, Savannah River, GA.
Clark, S. O. Private	Unk	Unknown	Engineer Corps Confederate States Army	August 24, 1863, King George County, Virginia	Point Lookout, Maryland, transferred to Elmira Prison, NY August 18, 1864	Exchanged October 29, 1864, at Venus Point, Savannah River, GA.
Clark, Samuel A. Private	18	February 24, 1863, Anson County, North Carolina	Co. B, 31st North Carolina Infantry	June 1, 1864, Cold Harbor, Virginia	Point Lookout, Maryland, transferred to Elmira Prison, NY July 17,1864	Exchanged February 13, 1865 at Boulware's wharf on the James River, Virginia
Clark, Thomas L. Private	Unk	February 26, 1862, Columbia County, Arkansas	Co. B 19th Arkansas Infantry	May 16, 1863, Big Black River, Mississippi	Point Lookout, Maryland, transferred to Elmira Prison, NY August 18, 1864	Exchanged October 29, 1864, at Venus Point, Savannah River, GA.
Clark, W. W. Private	Unk	Unknown	Co. B, Woods Regiment, C. S. A.	May 16, 1862, Champion Hill, Mississippi	Point Lookout, Maryland, transferred to Elmira Prison, NY August 18, 1864	Exchanged February 13, 1865 at Boulware's wharf on the James River, Virginia
Clark, William Private	32	Unknown	Co. J, 54th North Carolina Infantry	May 25, 1864, Hanover Junction, Virginia	Point Lookout, Maryland, transferred to Elmira Prison, NY July 11, 1864	Oath of Allegiance May 29, 1865
Clark, William Private	Unk	January 1, 1862, Camp Hampton, Columbia, South Carolina	Co. H, 18th South Carolina Infantry	July 30, 1864, Petersburg, Virginia	Point Lookout, Maryland, transferred to Elmira Prison, NY August 12, 1864	Died September 2, 1864 of Chronic Diarrhea, Grave No. 78

Name & Rank	Age	Enlisted	Regiment and State	Where Captured	Prison	Remarks
Clark, William S. Private	Unk	October 26, 1864, Fort Holmes, Brunswick County, North Carolina	Co. K, 40th Regiment, 3rd North Carolina Artillery	January 15, 1865, Fort Fisher, North Carolina	February 1, 1865, Elmira Prison Camp, New York	Oath of Allegiance June 12, 1865
Clarke, Archibald Private	18	February 22, 1864, Union County, North Carolina	Co. A, 48th North Carolina Infantry	June 2, 1864, Cold Harbor, Virginia. Gunshot Wound Left Side of Chest.	Old Capital Prison, Washington, D. C. Transferred to Elmira Prison, NY August 12, 1864	Died September 12, 1864 of Pneumonia, Grave No. 195
Clarke, Carter P. Private	19	February 13, 1863, Selma, Alabama	Co. K, 21st Alabama Infantry	August 23, 1864, Fort Morgan, Alabama	Steam Press No. 4, New Orleans, Louisiana transferred to Elmira Prison, Prison, October 8, 1864.	Exchanged February 20, 1865 at Boulware's or Cox Wharf on the James River, Virginia
Clarke, George R. Private	25	June 17, 1861, Henderson County, North Carolina	Co. D, 8th North Carolina Infantry	May 31, 1864, Gaines Farm, Cold Harbor, Virginia	Point Lookout, Maryland, transferred to Elmira Prison, NY July 17,1864	Exchanged October 29, 1864, at Venus Point, Savannah River, GA.
Clarke, Jared Corporal	Unk	June 9, 1861, Bibb County, Georgia	Co. H, 12th Georgia Infantry	May 10, 1864, Spotsylvania Court House, Virginia	Point Lookout, Maryland, transferred to Elmira Prison, NY July 25, 1864	Exchanged March 14, 1865 at Boulware's Wharf on the James River, Virginia
Clarke, John Private	Unk	February 16, 1863, Centreville, Virginia	Co. F, 26th Battalion, Virginia Infantry	June 3, 1864, Gaines Farm, Cold Harbor, Virginia	Point Lookout, Maryland, transferred to Elmira Prison, NY July 17, 1864	Exchanged February 20, 1865 at Boulware's or Cox Wharf on the James River, Virginia
Clay, David H. Private	Unk	August 1, 1861, Richmond, Virginia	Co. H, 13th Georgia Infantry	May 12, 1864, Spotsylvania Court House, Virginia	Point Lookout, Maryland, transferred to Elmira Prison, NY July 6, 1864	Exchanged March 2, 1865 at Akins Landing on the James River, Virginia
Clay, L. A. Corporal	31	July 8, 1861, Griffin, Georgia	Co. H, 13th Georgia Infantry	May 12, 1864, Spotsylvania Court House, Virginia	Point Lookout, Maryland, transferred to Elmira Prison, NY July 6, 1864	Exchanged October 29, 1864 at Venus Point, Savannah River, GA.

Name & Rank	Age	Enlisted	Regiment and State	Where Captured	Prison	Remarks
Clay, Moses Sergeant	Unk	June 15, 1861, Columbus, Georgia	Co. E, 12th Georgia Infantry	May 10, 1864, Spotsylvania Court House, Virginia	Point Lookout, Maryland, transferred to Elmira Prison, NY July 25, 1864	Oath of Allegiance June 16, 1865
Clay, Thomas R. Sergeant	Unk	March 4, 1862, Sandersville, Georgia	Co. C, 49th Georgia Infantry	May 6, 1864, Wilderness, Virginia	Point Lookout, Maryland, transferred to Elmira Prison, NY August 14, 1864	Exchanged 2/20/65. Died 3/22/65 of Chronic Diarrhea at Jackson Hospital, Richmond, VA.
Clayman, John Private	35	February 20, 1863, Zollicoffer, Sullivan County, Tennessee	Co. E, 63rd Tennessee Infantry	June 17, 1864, Petersburg, Virginia	Point Lookout, Maryland, transferred to Elmira Prison, NY July 30, 1864	Exchanged March 2, 1865 at Akins Landing on the James River, Virginia
Claymon, George W. Private	32	September 25, 1862, Zollicoffer, Tennessee	Co. C, 63rd Tennessee Infantry	June 17, 1864, Petersburg, Virginia	Point Lookout, Maryland, transferred to Elmira Prison, NY July 30, 1864	Exchanged February 25, 1865 at Boulware's or Cox Wharf on the James River, Virginia
Clayton, D. J. Private	Unk	April 11, 1862, Coles Island, South Carolina	Co. F, 25th South Carolina Infantry	January 15, 1865, Fort Fisher, North Carolina	Elmira Prison Camp January 30, 1865	Exchanged March 2, 1865 at Boulware's Wharf on the James River, Virginia
Clayton, F. R. Private	Unk	March 7, 1863, James Island, South Carolina	Co. F, 25th South Carolina Infantry	January 15, 1865, Fort Fisher, North Carolina	Elmira Prison Camp January 30, 1865	Died March 23, 1865 of Diarrhea, Grave No. 2439
Clayton, George B. Private	Unk	May 11, 1861, Richmond, Virginia	Co. C, 38th Read's Battalion, Virginia Light Artillery	June 3, 1864, Gaines Farm, Cold Harbor, Virginia	Point Lookout, Maryland, transferred to Elmira Prison, NY July 17, 1864	Oath of Allegiance June 30, 1865
Clayton, John Sergeant	Unk	September 7, 1861, Scott County, Virginia	Co. A, 48th Virginia Infantry	May 12, 1864 Spotsylvania Court House, Virginia	Point Lookout, Maryland, transferred to Elmira Prison, NY August 2, 1864	Oath of Allegiance June 23, 1865

Name & Rank	Age	Enlisted	Regiment and State	Where Captured	Prison	Remarks
Clayton, John W. Private	Unk	March 25, 1864, Pickensville, Alabama	Co. J, 7th Alabama Cavalry	July 22, 1864 at 15 Mile Station on Pensacola Railroad, Florida	Old Capital Prison, Washington, DC transferred to Elmira Prison, NY August 27, 1864	Died December 31, 1864 of Pneumonia, Grave No. 1319
Clayton, Monroe C. Private	20	August 11, 1861, Kimbrell's, North Carolina	Co. D, 8th North Carolina Infantry	June 1, 1864, Gaines Farm, Cold Harbor, Virginia	Point Lookout, Maryland, transferred to Elmira Prison, NY July 17, 1864	Died October 6, 1864 of Chronic Diarrhea, Grave No. 592
Clayton, W. H. Sergeant	23	September 25, 1861, Camp Branch, Roxboro, North Carolina	Co. E, 35th North Carolina Infantry	June 17, 1864, Petersburg, Virginia	Point Lookout, Maryland, transferred to Elmira Prison, NY July 30, 1864	Oath of Allegiance June 12, 1865
Clayton, W. W. Private	23	April 11, 1862, Coles Island, South Carolina	Co. F, 25th South Carolina Infantry	January 15, 1865, Fort Fisher, North Carolina	Elmira Prison Camp January 30, 1865	Exchanged February 20, 1865 at Boulware's or Cox Wharf on the James River, Virginia
Clayton, William T. Private	Unk	Unknown	Co. A, Captain Godwin's Home Guard Florida	September 27, 1864, Marianna, Florida	New Orleans, Louisiana transferred to Elmira November 19, 1864.	Died January 8, 1865 of Chorea Grave No. 1498
Cleaveland, William R. Private	19	October 22, 1862, Clarksville, Georgia	Co. K, 24th Georgia Infantry	June 1, 1864, Cold Harbor, Virginia	Point Lookout, Maryland, transferred to Elmira Prison, NY July 17,1864	Oath of Allegiance July 7, 1865
Cleek, Joseph D. Private	18	June 26, 1861, Scott County, Virginia	Co. H, 48th Virginia Infantry	May 12, 1864, Spotsylvania Court House, Virginia	Point Lookout, Maryland, transferred to Elmira Prison, NY August 2, 1864	Oath of Allegiance June 27, 1865
Cleek, William M. Private	23	June 26, 1861, Scott County, Virginia	Co. H, 48th Virginia Infantry	May 12, 1864, Near Spotsylvania Court House, Virginia	Point Lookout, Maryland, transferred to Elmira Prison, NY August 6, 1864	Oath of Allegiance June 19, 1865

Name & Rank	Age	Enlisted	Regiment and State	Where Captured	Prison	Remarks
Clegg, Franklin C. Private	Unk	August 8, 1863, Burton's Farm, Virginia	Co. H, 26th North Carolina Infantry	May 12, 1864, Spotsylvania Court House, Virginia	Point Lookout, Maryland, transferred to Elmira Prison, NY July 30, 1864	Died October 1, 1864 of Chronic Diarrhea, Grave No. 407
Cleghorn, J. F. Sergeant	32	May 10, 1861, Columbus, Georgia	Co. A, 10th Georgia Infantry	May 6, 1864, Wilderness, Virginia	Point Lookout, Maryland, transferred to Elmira Prison, NY August 14, 1864	Exchanged October 29, 1864 at Venus Point, Savannah River, GA.
Cleghorn, John W. A. Sergeant	Unk	August 5, 1861, Danielsville, Georgia	Co. D, 16th Georgia Infantry	August 16, 1864, Front Royal, Virginia	Old Capital Prison, Washington, DC transferred to Elmira Prison, NY August 29, 1864	Oath of Allegiance June 21, 1865
Cleghorn, W. R. Private	Unk	March 15, 1862, Danielsville, Georgia	Co. D, 16th Georgia Infantry	August 16, 1864, Front Royal, Virginia	Old Capital Prison, Washington, DC transferred to Elmira Prison, NY August 29, 1864	Died May 19, 1865 of Variola (Smallpox), Grave No. 2945
Clem, J. H. Private	Unk	Unknown	Co. H, Signal Corps, Confederate States Army	August 11, 1864, Summit Point, Virginia	Old Capital Prison, Washington, DC transferred to Elmira Prison, NY August 29, 1864	Died October 10, 1864 of Chronic Diarrhea, Grave No. 675
Clem, Roland A. Private	25	August 17, 1861, Lightwood Knot Springs, Near Columbia, South Carolina	Co. G, 14th South Carolina Infantry	July 29, 1864, Petersburg, Virginia	Point Lookout, Maryland, transferred to Elmira Prison, NY August 12, 1864	Oath of Allegiance July 3, 1865
Clem, William Private	Unk	April 18, 1864, Rudes Hill, Virginia	Co. B, 2nd Virginia Infantry	May 12, 1864, Near Spotsylvania Court House, Virginia	Point Lookout, Maryland, transferred to Elmira Prison, NY August 6, 1864	Oath of Allegiance June 27, 1865

Name & Rank	Age	Enlisted	Regiment and State	Where Captured	Prison	Remarks
Clement, Henry C. Private	22	March 20, 1862, Danville, Virginia	Co. C, 5th Virginia Cavalry	May 10, 1864, Beaver Dam Station, Virginia	Point Lookout, Maryland, transferred to Elmira Prison, NY August 17, 1864. Ward 43.	Exchanged October 29, 1864 at Venus Point, Savannah River, GA.
Clements, Bedford Booker Private	Unk	March 17, 1862, Republican Grove, Virginia	Co. F, 38th Virginia Infantry	May 10, 1864, Near Petersburg, Virginia	Point Lookout, Maryland, transferred to Elmira Prison, NY August 17, 1864	Died March 8, 1865 of Diarrhea, Grave No. 2376
Clements, Daniel G. Private	Unk	September 13, 1861, Whiteville, Georgia	Co. K, 61st Georgia Infantry	May 12, 1864, Spotsylvania Court House, Virginia	Point Lookout, Maryland, transferred to Elmira Prison, NY July 25, 1864	Exchanged March 10, 1865 at Boulware's wharf on the James River, Virginia
Clements, E. C. Private	Unk	February 16, 1864, Macon, Alabama	Co. A, Jackson's 1st Regiment, Tennessee Heavy Artillery	August 23, 1864, Fort Morgan, Alabama	New Orleans, Louisiana transferred to Elmira December 4, 1864.	No Further Information Available.
Clements, John J. Private	30	August 15, 1861, Williams Store, Amherst County, Virginia	Co. F, 58th Virginia Infantry	May 30, 1864 Mechanics-ville, Virginia	Point Lookout, Maryland, transferred to Elmira Prison, NY July 11, 1864	Oath of Allegiance June 30, 1865
Clements, Peter F. Private	Unk	May 20, 1861, Palmyra, Virginia	Co. F, 44th Virginia Infantry	May 12, 1864, Spotsylvania Court House, Virginia	Point Lookout, Maryland, transferred to Elmira Prison, NY August 2, 1864	Oath of Allegiance June 14, 1865
Clements, Thomas J. Private	Unk	October 8, 1863, Macon, Georgia	Co. K, 12th Georgia Infantry	May 12, 1864, Spotsylvania Court House, Virginia	Point Lookout, Maryland, transferred to Elmira Prison, NY July 25, 1864	Oath of Allegiance June 23, 1865
Clements, Thomas L. R. Private	21	April 20, 1861, Belle Roi., Virginia	Co. A, 26th Virginia Infantry	June 15, 1864, Near Petersburg, Virginia	Point Lookout, Maryland, transferred to Elmira Prison, NY July 12, 1864	Exchanged March 14, 1865 at Boulware's Wharf on the James River, Virginia

Name & Rank	Age	Enlisted	Regiment and State	Where Captured	Prison	Remarks
Clements, W. G. Private	Unk	December 10, 1861, Humboldt, Tennessee	Co. L, Jackson's 1st Regiment, Tennessee Heavy Artillery	August 23, 1864, Fort Morgan, Alabama	New Orleans, Louisiana transferred to Elmira December 4, 1864.	Exchanged February 25, 1865 at Boulware's or Cox Wharf on the James River, Virginia
Clements, W. H. Corporal	Unk	May 15, 1861, Clayton, Alabama	Co. A, 5th Alabama Infantry	May 5, 1864, Wilderness, Virginia	Point Lookout, Maryland, transferred to Elmira Prison, NY August 17, 1864	Oath of Allegiance July 7, 1865
Clemmons, Edward M. Private	37	February 6, 1863, Fort Caswell, North Carolina	Co. G, 36th Regiment, 2nd North Carolina Artillery	January 15, 1865, Fort Fisher, North Carolina. Wounded	February 1, 1865, Elmira Prison Camp, New York	Exchanged March 2, 1865 at Akins Landing on the James River, Virginia
Clemmons, George M. Private	25	February 6, 1863, Fort Caswell, North Carolina	Co. G, 36th Regiment, 2nd North Carolina Artillery	January 15, 1865, Fort Fisher, North Carolina. Wounded	February 1, 1865, Elmira Prison Camp, New York	Died April 24, 1865 of Pneumonia. No Grave Found in Woodlawn, Cemetery.
Clemmons, Thomas Private	21	July 15, 1862, Fort St. Philip, North Carolina	Co. G, 36th Regiment, 2nd North Carolina Artillery	January 15, 1865, Fort Fisher, North Carolina. Wounded	February 1, 1865, Elmira Prison Camp, New York	Oath of Allegiance July 11, 1865
Clemons, Samuel D. Corporal	32	May 25, 1861, Camp Howard, Brunswick County, North Carolina	Co. G, 20th North Carolina Infantry	May 12, 1864, Near Spotsylvania Court House, Virginia	Point Lookout Prison, Maryland. Transferred to Elmira Prison Camp New York August 14, 1864.	Exchanged October 29, 1864, at Venus Point, Savannah River, GA.
Cleveland, H. C. Private	Unk	April 28, 1862, Marietta, Georgia Infantry	Co. F, 3rd Battalion Georgia Sharp Shooters	August 16, 1864, Front Royal, Virginia	Old Capital Prison, Washington, DC transferred to Elmira Prison, NY August 29, 1864	Exchanged March 2, 1865 at Akins Landing on the James River, Virginia
Clifford, William G. Private	19	August 13, 1862, Camp Hill, North Carolina	Co. G, 5th North Carolina Infantry	May 12, 1864, Spotsylvania Court House, Virginia	Point Lookout, Maryland, transferred to Elmira Prison, NY August 6, 1864	Died May 12, 1865 of Chronic Diarrhea, Grave No. 2797

Name & Rank	Age	Enlisted	Regiment and State	Where Captured	Prison	Remarks
Clifton, Bedford B. Private	25	August 6, 1861, Memphis, Tennessee	Co. A, Jackson's 1st Regiment, Tennessee Heavy Artillery	August 23, 1864, Fort Morgan, Alabama	New Orleans, Louisiana transferred to Elmira December 4, 1864.	Exchanged February 25, 1865 at Boulware's or Cox Wharf on the James River, Virginia
Clifton, George Riley Private	19	June 25, 1861, Abingdon, Virginia	Co. K, 48th Virginia Infantry	May 12, 1864, Spotsylvania Court House, Virginia	Point Lookout, Maryland, transferred to Elmira Prison, NY August 2, 1864	Died March 21, 1865 of Pneumonia, Grave No. 1536
Clifton, Samuel Private	20	Unknown	Co. K, 50th Virginia Infantry	May 5, 1864, wilderness, Virginia Gunshot Wound Right Knee.	Old Capital Prison, Washington D. C. Transferred to Elmira Prison, NY August 12, 1864	Oath of Allegiance June 27, 1865
Cline, David Private	Unk	August 15, 1861, Woodville, Jackson County, Alabama	Co. G, 12th Alabama Infantry	May 12, 1864, Spotsylvania Court House, Virginia	Point Lookout, Maryland, transferred to Elmira Prison, NY July 6, 1864	Oath of Allegiance May 19, 1865
Cline, Franklin Private	Unk	October 9, 1863, Camp Holmes, North Carolina	Co. H, 28th North Carolina Infantry	July 29, 1864, Fugel's Mills, Petersburg, Virginia	Point Lookout, Maryland, transferred to Elmira Prison, NY August 12, 1864	Oath of Allegiance May 29, 1865
Cline, Henry B. Private	34	May 16, 1862, Cabarrus County, North Carolina	Co. E, 4th North Carolina Cavalry	June 13, 1864, Near City Point Railroad, Virginia	Point Lookout, Maryland, transferred to Elmira Prison, NY July 12, 1864	Died May 28, 1865 of Pneumonia, Grave No. 2913
Cline, Maxwell A. Private	19	August 13, 1861, Newton, North Carolina	Co. C, 28th North Carolina Infantry	May 12, 1864, Spotsylvania Court House, Virginia	Point Lookout, Maryland, transferred to Elmira Prison, NY August 12, 1864	Oath of Allegiance May 19, 1865
Cline, Perry R. Private	18	April 27, 1861, Newton, North Carolina	Co. F, 30th North Carolina Infantry	July 13, 1864, Near Washington, DC	Old Capital Prison, Washington, DC, transferred to Elmira Prison, NY, July 23, 1864	Exchanged March 14, 1865 at Boulware's Wharf on the James River, Virginia

Name & Rank	Age	Enlisted	Regiment and State	Where Captured	Prison	Remarks
Cline, Sylvanus Private	18	March 2, 1863, Newton, North Carolina	Co. C, 28th North Carolina Infantry	May 6, 1864, Wilderness, Virginia	Point Lookout, Maryland, transferred to Elmira Prison, NY August 14, 1864	Exchanged October 29, 1864 at Venus Point, Savannah River, GA.
Cline, Thomas Corporal	Unk	April 16, 1862, Rudes Hill, Virginia	Co. E, 2nd Virginia Infantry	May 12, 1864, Near Spotsylvania Court House, Virginia	Point Lookout, Maryland, transferred to Elmira Prison, NY August 6, 1864	Oath of Allegiance June 23, 1865
Clinebell, John T. Private	Unk	May 27, 1862, Salt Sulfur Springs, Virginia	Co. F, 26th Battalion Virginia Infantry	June 3, 1864, Gaines Farm, Cold Harbor, Virginia	Point Lookout, Maryland, transferred to Elmira Prison, NY July 17,1864	Died March 16, 1865 of Pneumonia Grave No. 1687
Clodfelter, Daniel A. Private	24	August 18, 1862, Raleigh, North Carolina	Co. I, 2nd North Carolina Infantry	October 20, 1864, Frederick County, Virginia	November 11, 1864, Old Capital Prison, Washington, DC. February 4, 1865 Elmira, Prison Camp, NY	Exchanged March 14, 1865 at Boulware's Wharf on the James River, Virginia
Clodfelter, Henry Private	Unk	February 1, 1864. Raleigh, North Carolina	Co. H, 14th North Carolina Infantry	May 20, 1864, Spotsylvania Court House, Virginia	Point Lookout, Maryland, transferred to Elmira Prison, NY July 23, 1864	Died October 24, 1864 of Pneumonia, Grave No. 713
Cloudis, Elliott Private	24	June 28, 1861, Gloucester Point, Virginia	Co. E, 5th Virginia Cavalry	May 11, 1864, Yellow Tavern, Hanover County, Virginia	Point Lookout, Maryland, transferred to Elmira Prison, NY August 17, 1864	Oath of Allegiance June 21, 1865
Clouse, Adam H. Corporal	Unk	June 29, 1861, Wytheville, Virginia	Co. B, 50th Virginia Infantry	May 12, 1864, Spotsylvania Court House, Virginia	Point Lookout, Maryland, transferred to Elmira Prison, NY August 2, 1864	Oath of Allegiance June 30, 1865
Clower, Joseph G. Private	Unk	March 1, 1863, Atlanta, Georgia	Co. E, 64th Georgia Infantry	June 17, 1864, Petersburg, Virginia	Point Lookout, Maryland, transferred to Elmira Prison, NY July 30, 1864	Died September 18, 1864 of Chronic Diarrhea, Grave No. 316

Name & Rank	Age	Enlisted	Regiment and State	Where Captured	Prison	Remarks
Clower, Noah L. Private	Unk	July 1, 1863, Coffee County, Alabama	Co. G, 61st Alabama Infantry	May 12, 1864, Spotsylvania Court House, Virginia	Point Lookout, Maryland, transferred to Elmira Prison, NY July 30, 1864	Died August 8, 1864 of Chronic Diarrhea, Grave No. 140
Coaker, William J. Private	20	December 23, 1863, Montgomery, Alabama	Co. E, 1st Battalion Alabama Artillery	August 23, 1864, Fort Morgan, Alabama	New Orleans, Louisiana transferred to Elmira December 4, 1864.	Oath of Allegiance July 7, 1865
Coates, Cornelius R. Private	25	April 23, 1861, Gloucester Point, Virginia	Co. B, 26th Virginia Infantry	June 15, 1864, Petersburg, Virginia	Point Lookout Prison Camp, Maryland. Transferred to NY, Elmira Prison, July 12, 1864	Died March 10, 1865 of Diphtheria, Grave. 1862
Coatis, Edward C. Private	Unk	March 20, 1862, Orange, Virginia	Captain Fry's Battery, Virginia Light Artillery	May 12, 1864, Spotsylvania, Virginia	Old Capital Prison, Washington, DC, transferred to Elmira Prison, NY, July 23, 1864	Exchanged March 14, 1865 at Boulware's Wharf on the James River, Virginia
Cobb, Calvin A. Private	18	December 16, 1862, Robison County, North Carolina	Co. D, 1st Battalion North Carolina Heavy Artillery	January 15, 1865, Fort Fisher, North Carolina	February 1, 1865, Elmira Prison Camp, New York	Died March 26, 1865 of Chronic Diarrhea, Grave No. 2474
Cobb, J. Y. Private	Unk	June 12, 1864, Guilford County, North Carolina	Co. A, 53rd North Carolina Infantry	June 12, 1864, Near Washington, DC	Old Capital Prison, Washington, DC transferred to Elmira Prison, NY August 27, 1864	Oath of Allegiance July 3, 1865
Cobb, James A. Private	35	February 28, 1863, Shelby, North Carolina	Co. H, 34th North Carolina Infantry	July 14, 1863, Falling Waters, Maryland	Point Lookout, Maryland, transferred to Elmira Prison, NY August 18, 1864	Exchanged October 29, 1864 at Venus Point, Savannah River, GA. Died Unknown Date and Unknown Place.
Cobb, James M. Private	Unk	July 1, 1862, Richmond, Virginia	Co. F, 6th Alabama Infantry	May 12, 1864, near Spotsylvania Court House, Virginia	Point Lookout, Maryland, transferred to Elmira Prison, NY August 17, 1864	Oath of Allegiance June 14, 1865

Name & Rank	Age	Enlisted	Regiment and State	Where Captured	Prison	Remarks
Cobb, Robert E. Sergeant	25	July 22, 1861, Selma, Alabama	Jeff Davis Alabama Artillery	May 12, 1864, Spotsylvania Court House, Virginia Gunshot Wound Right Shoulder.	Old Capital Prison, Washington D. C. Transferred to Elmira Prison, NY August 12, 1864	Exchanged October 29, 1864, at Venus Point, Savannah River, GA.
Cobb, Stephen C. Private	23	May 8, 1861, Corrine, Mississippi	Co. K, 12th Mississippi Infantry	June 23, 1864, Near Petersburg, Virginia	Point Lookout, Maryland, transferred to Elmira Prison, NY July 23, 1864	Died April 9, 1865 of Variola (Smallpox), Grave No. 2616
Coble, Augustus L. Private	20	July 15, 1862, Raleigh, North Carolina	Co. E, 1st North Carolina Infantry	May 12, 1864, Spotsylvania Court House, Virginia	Point Lookout, Maryland, transferred to Elmira Prison, NY August 6, 1864	Oath of Allegiance June 21, 1865
Coble, Daniel M. Private	24	October 1, 1862, Near Drury's Bluff, Virginia	Co. B, 45th North Carolina Infantry	May 10, 1864, Spotsylvania Court House, Virginia	Point Lookout, Maryland, transferred to Elmira Prison, NY August 6, 1864	Exchanged October 29, 1864 at Venus Point, Savannah River, GA.
Coble, Eli S. Private	26	June 4, 1861, Greensboro, North Carolina	Co. M, 21st North Carolina Infantry	May 29, 1864, Mechanics-ville, Virginia	Point Lookout, Maryland, transferred to Elmira Prison, NY July 8, 1864	Oath of Allegiance May 15, 1865
Coble, Emsley M. Private	Unk	February 26, 1864, Raleigh, North Carolina	Co. E, 1st North Carolina Infantry	May 12, 1864, Spotsylvania Court House, Virginia	Point Lookout, Maryland, transferred to Elmira Prison, NY August 6, 1864	Oath of Allegiance June 30, 1865
Coble, John A. Private	21	May 16, 1862 Guilford County, North Carolina	Co. A, 53rd North Carolina Infantry	May 15, 1864, Spotsylvania Court House, Virginia	Point Lookout, Maryland, transferred to Elmira Prison, NY July 6,1864	Exchanged March 14, 1865 at Boulware's Wharf on the James River, Virginia
Coburn Albert Private	43	July 21, 1862, Hamilton, Martin County, North Carolina	Co. F, 31st North Carolina Infantry	June 1, 1864, Gaines Farm, Cold Harbor, Virginia	Point Lookout, Maryland, transferred to Elmira Prison, NY July 17,1864	Exchanged February 13, 1865 at Boulware's wharf on the James River, Virginia

Name & Rank	Age	Enlisted	Regiment and State	Where Captured	Prison	Remarks
Cochran, A. W. Private	Unk	August 22, 1862, Manning, South Carolina	Co. J, 25th South Carolina Infantry	January 15, 1865, Fort Fisher, North Carolina	Elmira Prison Camp January 30, 1865	Died March 8, 1865 of Diarrhea, Grave No. 2373
Cochran, Elijah P. Private	20	October 9, 1861, Enfield, North Carolina	Co. F, 36th Regiment, 2nd North Carolina Artillery	January 15, 1865, Fort Fisher, North Carolina. Wounded	February 1, 1865, Elmira Prison Camp, New York	Died March 1, 1865 of Chronic Diarrhea, Grave No. 2025
Cochran, Robert J. Private	17	December 28, 1863, Mecklenburg County, North Carolina	Co. H, 35th North Carolina Infantry	June 17, 1864, Petersburg, Virginia	Point Lookout, Maryland, transferred to Elmira Prison, NY July 30, 1864	Oath of Allegiance May 15, 1865
Cochran, Robert J. Private	34	October 9, 1861, Enfield, North Carolina	Co. F, 36th Regiment, 2nd North Carolina Artillery	January 15, 1865, Fort Fisher, North Carolina. Wounded	February 1, 1865, Elmira Prison Camp, New York	Died March 1, 1865 of Pneumonia, Grave No. 2099
Cochran, William H. Private	Unk	May 27, 1861, Staunton, Virginia	Co. D, 25th Virginia Infantry	May 12, 1864, Spotsylvania Court House, Virginia	Point Lookout, Maryland, transferred to Elmira Prison, NY August 2, 1864	Exchanged March 2, 1865 at Akins Landing on the James River, Virginia
Cockerham, John Private	Unk	March 18, 1864, Dobson, North Carolina	Co. A, 28th North Carolina Infantry	May 12, 1864, Spotsylvania Court House, Virginia	Point Lookout, Maryland, transferred to Elmira Prison, NY August 12, 1864	Died 9/22/64 of Chronic Diarrhea, Grave No. 478. Name Cochran on Headstone.
Cockerham, William Private	25	May 4, 1861, Dobson, North Carolina	Co. A, 28th North Carolina Infantry	May 12, 1864, Spotsylvania Court House, Virginia	Point Lookout, Maryland, transferred to Elmira Prison, NY August 12, 1864	Exchanged March 14, 1865 at Boulware's Wharf on the James River, Virginia
Cockram, Nathan Private	Unk	Unknown	Co. H, 50th Virginia Infantry	May 12, 1864, Spotsylvania Court House, Virginia	Point Lookout, Maryland, transferred to Elmira Prison, NY August 2, 1864	Exchanged October 29, 1864 at Venus Point, Savannah River, GA.
Cockrell, B. H. Civilian	Unk	Unknown	Citizen of Prince William County, Virginia	March 23, 1864, Prince William County, Virginia	Point Lookout, Maryland, transferred to Elmira Prison, NY July 25, 1864	Oath of Allegiance June 29, 1865

Name & Rank	Age	Enlisted	Regiment and State	Where Captured	Prison	Remarks
Cockrell, Q. J. Sergeant	23	April 15, 1861, Livingston, Alabama	Co. G, 5th Alabama Infantry	April 25, 1865, Petersburg, Virginia	Old Capital Prison, Washington D. C. Transferred to Elmira Prison, NY May 2, 1865.	Oath of Allegiance July 7, 1865
Cofer, James R. Private	Unk	June 25, 1861, Wytheville, Virginia	Co. I, 50th Virginia Infantry	May 12, 1864, Spotsylvania Court House, Virginia	Point Lookout, Maryland, transferred to Elmira Prison, NY August 2, 1864	Died August 14, 1864 of Chronic Diarrhea, Grave No. 707
Cofer, James Reyburn Private	Unk	June 25, 1861, Wytheville, Virginia	Co. I, 26th Battalion, Virginia Infantry	June 3, 1864, Gaines Mill, Cold Harbor, Virginia	Point Lookout, Maryland, transferred to Elmira Prison, NY July 17, 1864	Oath of Allegiance July 11, 1865
Coffee, C. E. Private	Unk	Unknown	Co. F, 50th Virginia Infantry	May 12, 1864, Spotsylvania Court House, Virginia	Point Lookout, Maryland, transferred to Elmira Prison, NY August 2, 1864	Oath of Allegiance June 23, 1865
Coffee, Edward C. Private	40	June 6, 1861, Woodville, Mississippi	Co. E, 21st Mississippi Infantry	May 8, 1864, Wilderness, Virginia	Point Lookout, Maryland, transferred to Elmira Prison, NY July 23, 1864	Oath of Allegiance May 29, 1865
Coffee, John J. Private	Unk	Unknown	Co. F, 50th Virginia Infantry	May 12, 1864, Spotsylvania Court House, Virginia	Point Lookout, Maryland, transferred to Elmira Prison, NY August 2, 1864	Oath of Allegiance June 23, 1865
Coffey, James Private	26	June 7, 1861, Camp Moore, Louisiana	Co. C, 7th Louisiana Infantry	May 11, 1864, Spotsylvania Court House, Virginia	Point Lookout, Maryland, transferred to Elmira Prison, NY August 17, 1864	Exchanged February 25, 1865 at Boulware's or Cox Wharf on the James River, Virginia
Coffin, Cyrus C. Sergeant	19	February 28, 1862, Greensboro, North Carolina	Co. B, 45th North Carolina Infantry	July 17,1864, Near Washington, DC	Old Capital Prison, Washington, DC, transferred to Elmira Prison, NY, July 23, 1864	Oath of Allegiance May 17, 1865

Name & Rank	Age	Enlisted	Regiment and State	Where Captured	Prison	Remarks
Coffman, Benjamin F. Private	Unk	August 2, 1861, Staunton, Virginia	Co. G, 52nd Virginia Infantry	May 23, 1864, Bethel Church, Hanover Junction, Virginia	Point Lookout, Maryland, transferred to Elmira Prison, NY July 11, 1864	Oath of Allegiance May 29, 1865
Coffman, John R. Private	Unk	April 18, 1861, Harrisonburg, Virginia	Co. D, 10th Virginia Infantry	May 12, 1864, Spotsylvania Court House, Virginia	Point Lookout, Maryland, transferred to Elmira Prison, NY August 2, 1864	Transferred for Exchange 10/11/64. Exchanged 11/15/64 at Venus Point, Savannah River, GA.
Coger, J. M. Sergeant	Unk	Unknown	Co. H, 42nd Virginia Infantry	May 12, 1864, Near Spotsylvania Court House, Virginia	Point Lookout, Maryland, transferred to Elmira Prison, NY August 6, 1864	Oath of Allegiance June 19, 1865
Coggin, John J. Private	27	March 1, 1862, Nashville, North Carolina	Co. H, 32nd North Carolina Infantry	May 10, 1864, Wilderness, Virginia	Point Lookout, Maryland, transferred to Elmira Prison, NY August 6, 1864	Died July 5, 1865 of Chronic Diarrhea, Grave No. 2837
Coggin, Willie James Private	19	March 1, 1862, Nashville, North Carolina	Co. H, 32nd North Carolina Infantry	May 10, 1864, Wilderness, Virginia	Point Lookout, Maryland, transferred to Elmira Prison, NY August 6, 1864	Died January 17, 1865 of Pneumonia, Grave No. 1448
Coghill, M. T. Private	Unk	April 21, 1861, Henderson County, North Carolina	Co. D, 8th North Carolina Infantry	June 1, 1864, Gaines Farm, Cold Harbor, Virginia	Point Lookout, Maryland, transferred to Elmira Prison, NY July 17,1864	Died September 2, 1864 of Rubeola (Measles), Grave No. 83
Cohron, Nicholas Private	Unk	September 14, 1862, Henry County, Alabama	Co. L, 3rd Alabama Infantry	May 12, 1864, Spotsylvania Court House, Virginia	Point Lookout, Maryland, transferred to Elmira Prison, NY July 6, 1864	Exchanged February 15, 1865 on the James River, Virginia
Coile, William S. Private	Unk	February 29, 1864, Greenville, Tennessee	Co. B, 1st Tennessee Infantry	May 5, 1864, Wilderness, Virginia	Point Lookout, Maryland, transferred to Elmira Prison, NY August 17, 1864	Oath of Allegiance August 16, 1864 per Lincoln. Early Release per Lincoln's Proclamation, 12/8/1863.

Name & Rank	Age	Enlisted	Regiment and State	Where Captured	Prison	Remarks
Cok, Henry Private	Unk	Unknown	Co. A, Arsenal Battalion	June 11, 1864, Bottom's Bridge, Virginia	Old Capital Prison, Washington, DC, transferred to Elmira Prison, NY, July 23, 1864	Escaped April 15, 1865
Coker, Asa Private	Unk	February 7, 1862, Marietta, Georgia	Co. J, 1st South Carolina Artillery	July 10, 1863, Morris Island, South Carolina	Point Lookout, Maryland, transferred to Elmira Prison, NY August 18, 1864	Died September 25, 1864 of Chronic Diarrhea, Grave No. 375
Coker, John L. Private	Unk	April 4, 1863, Kinston, North Carolina	Co. K, 10th Regiment, 1st North Carolina Artillery	January 15, 1865, Fort Fisher, North Carolina	January 30, 1865, Elmira Prison Camp, NY	Oath of Allegiance May 15, 1865
Coker, John S. Private	Unk	May 1, 1862, Cat Island, South Carolina	Co. J, 4th South Carolina Cavalry	June 11, 1864, Trevilian Station, Louisa Court House, Virginia	Point Lookout, Maryland, transferred to Elmira Prison, NY July 25, 1864	Died December 10, 1864 of Chronic Diarrhea, Grave No. 1046
Coker, Thomas L. Private	Unk	March 12, 1861, Prattville, Alabama	Co. E, 1st Battalion Alabama Artillery	August 23, 1864, Fort Morgan, Alabama	New Orleans, Louisiana transferred to Elmira December 4, 1864.	Oath of Allegiance June 21, 1865
Coker, Thomas L. Private	16	December 20, 1861, Cheraw, South Carolina	Co. D, 21st South Carolina Infantry	January 15, 1865, Fort Fisher, North Carolina	Elmira Prison Camp January 30, 1865	Exchanged February 20, 1865 at Boulware's or Cox Wharf on the James River, Virginia
Coker, William R. Private	22	July 1, 1862, Edgecombe County, North Carolina	Co. E, 33rd North Carolina Infantry	May 6, 1864, Wilderness, Virginia	Point Lookout, Maryland, transferred to Elmira Prison, NY August 14, 1864	Died February 13, 1865 of Chronic Diarrhea, Grave No. 2064. Headstone has 31st NC.
Cole, Elijah W. Private	Unk	January 14, 1862, Camp Walsh, South Carolina	Co. J, Holcombe Legion, South Carolina Infantry	May 7, 1864, Stony Creek, Virginia	Point Lookout, Maryland, transferred to Elmira Prison, NY August 17, 1864	Died September 19, 1864 of Chronic Diarrhea, Grave No. 323

Name & Rank	Age	Enlisted	Regiment and State	Where Captured	Prison	Remarks
Cole, Perry M. Private	Unk	December 27, 1861, Camp Trousdale, Tennessee	Co. H, 44th Tennessee Infantry	May 16, 1864, Near Drury's Bluff, Virginia	Point Lookout, Maryland, transferred to Elmira Prison, NY July 23, 1864	Oath of Allegiance May 21, 1865
Cole, Voetus Private	24	February 22, 1862, Hillsboro, North Carolina	Co. D, 1st North Carolina Infantry	May 12, 1864, Spotsylvania Court House, Virginia	Point Lookout, Maryland, transferred to Elmira Prison, NY August 6, 1864	Exchanged October 29, 1864 at Venus Point, Savannah River, GA.
Cole, William Sailor	Unk	Unknown	Confederate States Navy	January 15, 1865, Fort Fisher, North Carolina. Wounded	February 1, 1865, Elmira Prison Camp, New York	Oath of Allegiance May 29, 1865
Cole, William B. Sergeant	20	July 14, 1861, Goldsboro, North Carolina	Co. F, 10th Regiment, 1st North Carolina Artillery	January 15, 1865, Fort Fisher, North Carolina	January 30, 1865, Elmira Prison Camp, NY	Oath of Allegiance May 19, 1865
Cole, William E. Private	Unk	March 20, 1863, Choctaw Bluff, Alabama	Co. A, 21st Alabama Infantry	August 23, 1864, Fort Morgan, Alabama	Steam Press No. 4, New Orleans, Louisiana transferred to Elmira Prison, Prison, October 8, 1864.	Exchanged 2/13/65. Died 3/19/65 of Variola at Howard's Grove General Hospital, Richmond, VA.
Coleman, Daniel Private	Unk	October 25, 1863, Raleigh, North Carolina	Co. C, 33rd North Carolina Infantry	May 6, 1864, Wilderness, Virginia	Point Lookout, Maryland, transferred to Elmira Prison, NY August 14, 1864	Died December 10, 1864 of Hospital Gangrene, Grave No. 1033
Coleman, Daniel J. Private	19	February 22, 1862, Fair Bluff, Cerro Gordo, Columbus County, North Carolina	Co. E, 36th Regiment, 2nd North Carolina Artillery	January 15, 1865, Fort Fisher, North Carolina. Wounded	February 1, 1865, Elmira Prison Camp, New York	Oath of Allegiance July 3, 1865
Coleman, G. W. Private	Unk	September 10, 1863, McPherson-ville South Carolina	Co. J, 4th South Carolina Cavalry	May 28, 1864, Hall's Shop, Virginia	Point Lookout, Maryland, transferred to Elmira Prison, NY July 11, 1864	Exchanged March 2, 1865 at Akins Landing on the James River, Virginia

Name & Rank	Age	Enlisted	Regiment and State	Where Captured	Prison	Remarks
Coleman, Henry Private	Unk	Unknown	Co. B, 1st Missouri Cavalry	May 16, 1863, Big Black Bridge, Champion Hill, Mississippi	Point Lookout, Maryland, transferred to Elmira Prison, NY August 18, 1864	Exchanged February 13, 1865 at Boulware's wharf on the James River, Virginia
Coleman, Isaac M. Private	Unk	April 27, 1862, Charleston, South Carolina	Co. C, 22nd South Carolina Infantry	July 30, 1864, Petersburg, Virginia	Point Lookout, Maryland, transferred to Elmira Prison, NY August 12, 1864	Died November 12, 1864 of Pneumonia, Grave No. 827
Coleman, J. A. Corporal	Unk	August 8, 1862, Statesville, North Carolina	Co. K, 5th North Carolina Infantry	May 20, 1864, Spotsylvania Court House, Virginia	Point Lookout, Maryland, transferred to Elmira Prison, NY July 6, 1864	Oath of Allegiance June 19, 1865
Coleman, Jacob Private	33	November 29, 1862, Zollicoffer, Tennessee	Co. F, 63rd Tennessee Infantry	June 17, 1864, Petersburg, Virginia	Point Lookout, Maryland, transferred to Elmira Prison, NY July 30, 1864	Died December 24, 1864 of Chronic Diarrhea, Grave No. 1102
Coleman, James Private	27	July 18, 1861, Camp Howard, North Carolina	Co. C, 30th North Carolina Infantry	May 12, 1864, Near Spotsylvania, Virginia	Point Lookout, Maryland, transferred to Elmira Prison, NY August 14, 1864	Exchanged October 29, 1864, at Venus Point, Savannah River, GA.
Coleman, James S. Private	Unk	October 4, 1863, Macon, Georgia	Co. K, 12th Georgia Infantry	May 10, 1864, Spotsylvania Court House, Virginia	Point Lookout, Maryland, transferred to Elmira Prison, NY July 30, 1864	Exchanged February 20, 1865 at Boulware's or Cox Wharf on the James River, Virginia
Coleman, John C. Sergeant	Unk	March 4, 1862, Swansboro, Georgia	Co. H, 48th Georgia Infantry	July 23, 1863, Manassas Gap, Virginia	Point Lookout, Maryland, transferred to Elmira Prison, NY August 18, 1864	Exchanged February 25, 1865 at Boulware's or Cox Wharf on the James River, Virginia
Coleman, John Q. Private	22	May 3, 1862, Fort Caswell, North Carolina	Co. E, 36th Regiment, 2nd North Carolina Artillery	January 15, 1865, Fort Fisher, North Carolina. Wounded	February 1, 1865, Elmira Prison Camp, New York	Died April 21, 1865 of Chronic Diarrhea, Grave No. 1385. Headstone has J. D. Coleman.

Name & Rank	Age	Enlisted	Regiment and State	Where Captured	Prison	Remarks
Coleman, Joseph T. Private	Unk	June 12, 1861, Farmville, Virginia	Co. G, 44th Virginia Infantry	May 12, 1864, Spotsylvania Court House, Virginia	Point Lookout, Maryland, transferred to Elmira Prison, NY August 12, 1864	Exchanged October 29, 1864 at Venus Point, Savannah River, GA.
Coleman, Marsalis August Corporal	Unk	April 23, 1861, Mobile, Alabama	Co. J, 3rd Alabama Infantry	May 23, 1864, Near Hanover Junction, Virginia	Point Lookout, Maryland, transferred to Elmira Prison, NY August 12, 1864	Exchanged February 20, 1865 at Boulware's or Cox Wharf on the James River, Virginia
Coleman, S. C. 1st Sergeant	Unk	April 26, 1861, Sumter County, Alabama	Co. E, 5th Alabama Infantry	May 12, 1864, Spotsylvania Court House, Virginia	Point Lookout, Maryland, transferred to Elmira Prison, NY July 6, 1864	Exchanged February 20, 1865 at Boulware's or Cox Wharf on the James River, Virginia
Coleman, S. H. Private	Unk	April 29, 1862, White Sulfur Springs, Virginia	Co. F, 26th Battalion, Virginia Infantry	June 3, 1864, Gaines Mill, Cold Harbor, Virginia	Point Lookout, Maryland, transferred to Elmira Prison, NY July 17, 1864	Oath of Allegiance July 3, 1865
Coleman, Samuel F. Sergeant	19	July 12, 1861, Cockletown, Virginia	Co. G, 3rd Virginia Cavalry	May 9, 1864, Spotsylvania Court House, Virginia	Point Lookout, Maryland, transferred to Elmira Prison, NY August 17, 1864	Exchanged March 2, 1865 at Akins Landing on the James River, Virginia
Coleman, Thomas Private	Unk	Unknown	Co. G, 3rd Georgia Infantry	September 18, 1864, Rapidan, Virginia	Old Capital Prison, Washington, DC transferred to Elmira Prison, NY August 27, 1864	Died January 27, 1865 of Variola (Smallpox), Grave No. 1650
Coley, George Private	Unk	February 8, 1863, Weldon, North Carolina	Co. C, 42nd North Carolina Infantry	June 1, 1864, Gaines Farm, Cold Harbor, Virginia	Point Lookout, Maryland, transferred to Elmira Prison, NY July 17, 1864	Died August 1, 1864 of Chronic Diarrhea, Grave No. 148
Coley, Isaiah Private	34	March 27, 1862, Salisbury, North Carolina	Co. C, 42nd North Carolina Infantry	June 3, 1864, Cold Harbor, Virginia	Point Lookout, Maryland, transferred to Elmira Prison, NY July 17, 1864	Exchanged October 29, 1864, at Venus Point, Savannah River, GA.

Name & Rank	Age	Enlisted	Regiment and State	Where Captured	Prison	Remarks
Coley, Isham Private	25	March 17, 1862, Salisbury, North Carolina	Co. C, 42nd North Carolina Infantry	June 3, 1864, Cold Harbor, Virginia	Point Lookout, Maryland, transferred to Elmira Prison, NY July 17,1864	Died March 13, 1865 of Pneumonia, Grave No. 1817
Coley, James M. Private	24	August 13, 1861, Alamance County, North Carolina	Co I, 8th North Carolina Infantry	June 1, 1864, Cold Harbor, Virginia	Point Lookout, Maryland, transferred to Elmira Prison, NY July 17,1864	Died April 7, 1865 of Variola (Smallpox), Grave No. 2647
Coley, Jesse M. Private	23	September 9, 1861, Albemarle, North Carolina	Co. K, 28th North Carolina Infantry	May 12, 1864, Spotsylvania Court House, Virginia	Point Lookout, Maryland, transferred to Elmira Prison, NY August 12, 1864	Oath of Allegiance May 29, 1865
Coley, John M. Private	17	Unknown	Co. K, 28th North Carolina Infantry	May 12, 1864, Spotsylvania, Virginia	Point Lookout, Maryland, transferred to Elmira Prison, NY August 12, 1864	Died April 8, 1865 of Pneumonia, Grave No. 2647
Coley, William M. Private	Unk	August 8, 1862, Camp Hill, Stanley County, North Carolina	Co. S, 5th North Carolina Infantry	May 12, 1864, Spotsylvania Court House, Virginia	Point Lookout, Maryland, transferred to Elmira Prison, NY July 6,1864	Died March 5, 1865 of Diarrhea, Grave No. 1974
Collaway, Charles W. Private	Unk	August 26, 1863, Greenbrier, Virginia	Co. C, 26th Battalion, Virginia Infantry	June 3, 1864, Gaines Farm, Cold Harbor, Virginia	Point Lookout, Maryland, transferred to Elmira Prison, NY July 17,1864	Died September 12, 1864 of Chronic Diarrhea, Grave No. 190.
Collet, Robert W. Private	25	August 13, 1862, Camp Hill, North Carolina	Co. G, 5th North Carolina Infantry	May 12, 1864, Spotsylvania Court House, Virginia	Point Lookout, Maryland, transferred to Elmira Prison, NY August 6, 1864	Died February 18, 1865 of Chronic Diarrhea, Grave No. 2205
Colley, John T. Private	24	September 2, 1861, Salisbury, North Carolina	Co. K, 8th North Carolina Infantry	May 31, 1864, Cold Harbor, Virginia	Point Lookout, Maryland, transferred to Elmira Prison, NY July 11,1864	Exchanged March 2, 1865 at Akins Landing on the James River, Virginia

Name & Rank	Age	Enlisted	Regiment and State	Where Captured	Prison	Remarks
Colley, Lorenzo W. Private	18	April 20, 1862, Athens, Georgia	Co. G, 25th North Carolina Infantry	June 17, 1864, Petersburg, Virginia	Point Lookout, Maryland, transferred to Elmira Prison, NY July 30, 1864	Transferred for Exchange 10/11/64. Died 10/24/64 of Scurvy at US Army Hospital, Baltimore, MD.
Collier, Andrew Private	Unk	April 15, 1862, New Market, Virginia	Co. L, 4th Virginia Infantry	May 12, 1864, Near Spotsylvania Court House, Virginia	Point Lookout, Maryland, transferred to Elmira Prison, NY August 2, 1864	Oath of Allegiance June 19, 1865
Collier, Thomas A. Private	Unk	July 3, 1861, Brundidge, Alabama	Co. F, 15th Alabama Infantry	May 6, 1864, Wilderness, Virginia	Point Lookout, Maryland, transferred to Elmira Prison, NY August 17, 1864	Oath of Allegiance June 14, 1865
Collins, Bernard H. Private	19	March 7, 1862, New Orleans, Louisiana	Co. H, 7th Louisiana Infantry	May 11, 1864, Spotsylvania Court House, Virginia	Point Lookout, Maryland, transferred to Elmira Prison, NY August 17, 1864	Exchanged February 25, 1865 at Boulware's or Cox Wharf on the James River, Virginia
Collins, Dallas P. Private	18	July 15, 1862, Raleigh, North Carolina	Co. G, 1st North Carolina Infantry	May 12, 1864, Near Spotsylvania Court House, Virginia	Point Lookout Prison Camp, Maryland. Transferred to Elmira Prison, August 6, 1864	Died January 20, 1865 of Pneumonia, Grave No. 1585
Collins, Gabriel Private	Unk	February 19, 1863, Union County, North Carolina	Co. J, 53rd North Carolina Infantry	May 20, 1864, Spotsylvania Court House, Virginia	Point Lookout, Maryland, transferred to Elmira Prison, NY July 6, 1864	Died August 7, 1864, of Chronic Diarrhea, Grave No. 11
Collins, George A. Private	Unk	February 27, 1862, Glouchester Point, Virginia	Co. E, 5th Virginia Cavalry	May 31, 1864, Cold Harbor, Virginia	Point Lookout, Maryland, transferred to Elmira Prison, NY July 8, 1864	Oath of Allegiance June 14, 1865
Collins, J. Benjamin Private	Unk	April 15, 1862, Marion District, South Carolina	Co. L, 21st South Carolina Infantry	July 10, 1863, Morris Island, South Carolina. Gunshot Wound.	Point Lookout, Maryland, transferred to Elmira Prison, NY August 18, 1864	Exchanged October 29, 1864, at Venus Point, Savannah River, GA.

Name & Rank	Age	Enlisted	Regiment and State	Where Captured	Prison	Remarks
Collins, James Private	Unk	March 24, 1862, Antioch, Alabama	Co. E, 5th Alabama Infantry	May 12, 1864, Spotsylvania Court House, Virginia	Point Lookout, Maryland, transferred to Elmira Prison, NY July 6, 1864	Exchanged March 10, 1865 at Boulware's Wharf on the James River, Virginia
Collins, James Private	20	May 15, 1861, Allegheny County, Virginia	Co. B, 27th Virginia Infantry	July 13, 1864, Near Washington, DC,	Old Capital Prison, Washington, DC, transferred to Elmira Prison, NY, July 23, 1864	Oath of Allegiance May 17, 1865
Collins, Jasper N. Private	32	May 3, 1862, Union County, North Carolina	Co. J, 53rd North Carolina Infantry	May 20, 1864, Spotsylvania Court House, Virginia	Point Lookout, Maryland, transferred to Elmira Prison, NY July 6, 1864	Died September 26, 1864 of Pneumonia, Grave No. 384
Collins, John Private	Unk	January 22, 1864, Bristol, Tennessee	Co. J, 14th Tennessee Infantry	May 6, 1864, Wilderness, Virginia	Point Lookout, Maryland, transferred to Elmira Prison, NY July 23, 1864	Oath of Allegiance 9/9/1864. Early Release per Lincoln's Proclamation, 12/8/1863.
Collins, John Henry Private	Unk	November 23, 1863, Camp Ransom, Virginia	Co. F, 26th Battalion, Virginia Infantry	June 3, 1864, Gaines Farm, Cold Harbor, Virginia	Point Lookout, Maryland, transferred to Elmira Prison, NY July 17, 1864	Oath of Allegiance July 3, 1865
Collins, Lewis Private	19	October 16, 1861, Yadkinville, North Carolina	Co. B, 38th North Carolina Infantry	July 14, 1863, Falling Waters, Maryland	Point Lookout, Maryland, transferred to Elmira Prison, NY August 18, 1864	Oath of Allegiance June 12, 1865
Collins, Mathew Private	46	November 25, 1862, Savannah, Georgia	Co. E, 7th Georgia Cavalry	June 11, 1864, Trevilian Station, Louisa Court House, Virginia	Point Lookout, Maryland, transferred to Elmira Prison, NY July 25, 1864	Oath of Allegiance July 14, 1865
Collins, Matthew Private	Unk	June 1, 1861, Stokes County, North Carolina	Co. H, 22nd North Carolina Infantry	May 6, 1864, Wilderness, Virginia	Point Lookout, Maryland, transferred to Elmira Prison, NY August 14, 1864	Oath of Allegiance June 19, 1865

Name & Rank	Age	Enlisted	Regiment and State	Where Captured	Prison	Remarks
Collins, P. A. Private	Unk	April 25, 1864, Columbia, South Carolina	Co. C, 4th South Carolina Cavalry	May 28, 1864, Hall's Shop, Virginia	Point Lookout, Maryland, transferred to Elmira Prison, NY July 11, 1864	Died April 11, 1865, of Remittent Fever, Grave No. 2698
Collins, R. W. Private	Unk	December 21, 1861, Nashville, Tennessee	Co. J, 44th Tennessee Infantry	June 17, 1864, Petersburg, Virginia	Point Lookout, Maryland, transferred, Elmira Prison, NY July 30, 1864	Exchanged February 25, 1865 at Boulware's or Cox Wharf on the James River, Virginia
Collins, Richard H. Private	Unk	January 30, 1862, Marion District, South Carolina	Co. L, 21st South Carolina Infantry	January 15, 1865, Fort Fisher, North Carolina	Elmira Prison Camp January 30, 1865	Died February 9, 1865 of Typhoid Fever, Grave No. 1948
Collins, Robert B. Private	Unk	December 27, 1861, Nashville, Tennessee	Co. J, 44th Tennessee Infantry	May 16, 1864, Near Drury's Bluff, Virginia	Point Lookout, Maryland, transferred to Elmira Prison, NY August 17, 1864	Exchanged March 10, 1865 at Boulware's Wharf on the James River, Virginia
Collins, Russell Private	25	May 4, 1861, Stokes County, North Carolina	Co. A, 2nd North Carolina Infantry	May 6, 1864, Wilderness, Virginia	Point Lookout, Maryland, transferred to Elmira Prison, NY August 14, 1864	Exchanged October 29, 1864 at Venus Point, Savannah River, GA.
Collins, Samuel J. Corporal	Unk	July 12, 1861, Atlanta, Georgia	Co. I, 14th Georgia Infantry	May 23, 1864, Hanover, Virginia	Point Lookout, Maryland, transferred to Elmira Prison, NY July 8, 1864	Died September 18, 1864 of Chronic Diarrhea, Grave No. 153
Collins, Thomas Private	Unk	August 24, 1861, Habersham County, Georgia	Co. H, 24th Georgia Infantry	June 3, 1864, Gaines Mill, Cold Harbor, Virginia	Point Lookout, Maryland, transferred to Elmira Prison, NY July 17,1864	Oath of Allegiance June 21, 1865
Collins, W. S. Private	22	May 14, 1862, Hempstead, Texas	Co. E, Waller's Regiment Texas Cavalry	August 18, 1864, Near Morganza, Louisiana	New Orleans, Louisiana, Transferred to Elmira November 5, 1864	Died March 22, 1865 of Pneumonia, Grave No. 1521
Collins, William H. Sergeant	Unk	April 28, 1861, Staunton, Virginia	Co. G, 5th Virginia Infantry	May 20, 1864, Spotsylvania Court House, Virginia	Point Lookout, Maryland, transferred to Elmira Prison, NY July 6,1864	Oath of Allegiance June 16, 1865

Name & Rank	Age	Enlisted	Regiment and State	Where Captured	Prison	Remarks
Collins, William T. Private	Unk	May 25, 1861, Floyd Court House, Virginia	Co. B, 42nd Virginia Infantry	May 12, 1864, Spotsylvania Court House, Virginia	Point Lookout, Maryland, transferred to Elmira Prison, NY August 2, 1864	Transferred for Exchange 10/11/1864. Died 11/4/64 of Unknown Causes at Fort Monroe, VA.
Colly, James H. Private	Unk	February 7, 1863, Little Plymouth, Virginia	Co. G, 26th Virginia Infantry	June 15, 1864, Petersburg, Virginia	Point Lookout, Maryland, transferred to Elmira Prison, NY July 30, 1864	Exchanged October 29, 1864, at Venus Point, Savannah River, GA.
Colman, J. Private	Unk	March 20, 1864, Orange County, Virginia	Co. C, 42nd Virginia Infantry	May 12, 1864, Spotsylvania Court House, Virginia	Point Lookout, Maryland, transferred to Elmira Prison, NY August 2,1864	Exchanged March 14, 1865 at Boulware's Wharf on the James River, Virginia
Colston, Edward Corporal	21	August 11, 1862, Charlottes-ville, Virginia	Co. K, 2nd Virginia Cavalry	April 6, 1865, Burksville, Virginia. Gunshot Wound Left Arm. Arm Amputated.	Old Capital Prison, Washington D. C. Transferred to Elmira Prison, NY May 12, 1865.	Oath of Allegiance May 27, 1865
Colt, William C. Sergeant	Unk	April 20, 1861, Cape Henry, Virginia	Co. C, 15th Virginia Cavalry	May 11, 1864, Near Ashland, Virginia	Point Lookout, Maryland, transferred to Elmira Prison, NY August 17, 1864	Exchanged March 2, 1865 at Akins Landing on the James River, Virginia
Coltrane, A. S. Civilian	Unk	Unknown	Citizen of Randolph County, North Carolina	April 21, 1864, Near Wilmington, North Carolina	Point Lookout, Maryland, transferred to Elmira Prison, NY July 25, 1864	Died March 31, 1865 of Diarrhea, Grave No. 2532. Name A. S. Colton on Headstone.
Colvin, John Private	Unk	April 23, 1862, Griffin, Georgia	Co. A, 53rd Georgia Infantry	June 1, 1864, Gaines Mill, Cold Harbor, Virginia	Point Lookout, Maryland, transferred to Elmira Prison, NY July 17,1864	Died January 19, 1865 of Chronic Diarrhea, Grave No. 1203
Combs, Newton P. Private	25	March 31, 1862, Alexander, North Carolina	Co. H, 56th North Carolina Infantry	May 14, 1864, Near Fort Darling, Virginia	Point Lookout, Maryland, transferred to Elmira Prison, NY August 17, 1864	Exchanged October 29, 1864. Died November 22, 1864 at Ladies General Hospital No. 3, Columbia, SC.

Name & Rank	Age	Enlisted	Regiment and State	Where Captured	Prison	Remarks
Combs, Thomas T. Corporal	30	May 16, 1861, Columbia, North Carolina	Co. F, 32nd North Carolina Infantry	May 10, 1864, Spotsylvania, Virginia	Point Lookout, Maryland, transferred to Elmira Prison, NY August 6, 1864	Oath of Allegiance June 14, 1865
Comer, James Private	Unk	June 1, 1861, Luray, Page County, Virginia	Co. H, 33rd Virginia Infantry	July 8, 1864, Near Harper's Ferry, Virginia	Old Capital Prison, Washington, DC, transferred to Elmira Prison, NY, July 23, 1864	Exchanged March 14, 1865 at Boulware's Wharf on the James River, Virginia
Commean, L. O. Private	Unk	Unknown	Co. E, General Hood's Escort	October 11, 1864, Near Bayou Manchae, Louisiana	New Orleans, Louisiana transferred to Elmira November 19, 1864.	Exchanged February 25, 1865 at Boulware's or Cox Wharf on the James River, Virginia
Compton, Elias M. Private	26	April 14, 1861, Clinton, South Carolina	Co. J, 3rd South Carolina Infantry	July 29, 1864, Malvern Hill, Virginia	Point Lookout, Maryland, transferred to Elmira Prison, NY August 12, 1864	Oath of Allegiance May 29, 1865
Comu, A. Civilian	Unk	Registered Enemy	Citizen of Louisiana	July 27, 1864, New Orleans, Louisiana	New Orleans, Louisiana transferred to Elmira November 19, 1864.	Oath of Allegiance June 20, 1865
Comu, F. Civilian	Unk	Registered Enemy	Citizen of Louisiana	July 27, 1864, New Orleans, Louisiana	New Orleans, Louisiana transferred to Elmira November 19, 1864.	Oath of Allegiance June 20, 1865
Condon, John Private	26	June 4, 1861, Camp Moore, Louisiana	Co. J, 6th Louisiana Infantry	May 5, 1864, Wilderness, Virginia	Point Lookout, Maryland, transferred to Elmira Prison, NY August 17, 1864	Exchanged February 13, 1865 at Boulware's wharf on the James River, Virginia
Condon, William Private	Unk	Unknown	Co. C, Davis' Battalion Virginia Cavalry	August 11, 1864, Summit Point, Virginia	Old Capital Prison, Washington, DC transferred to Elmira Prison, NY August 29, 1864	Oath of Allegiance May 17, 1865

Name & Rank	Age	Enlisted	Regiment and State	Where Captured	Prison	Remarks
Condry, David C. Private	18	March 6, 1862, McDowell, North Carolina	Co. A, 49th North Carolina Infantry	June 2, 1864, Bermuda Hundred, Virginia	Point Lookout, Maryland, transferred to Elmira Prison, NY July 12, 1864	Oath of Allegiance July 3, 1865
Cone, John M. Private	Unk	February 20, 1863, Albany, Georgia	Co. D, 64th Georgia Infantry	June 17, 1864, Petersburg, Virginia	Point Lookout, Maryland, transferred to Elmira Prison, NY July 30, 1864	Exchanged October 29, 1864, at Venus Point, Savannah River, GA.
Cone, John Turner Private	24	July 15, 1862, Raleigh, North Carolina	Co. C, 1st North Carolina Infantry	May 12, 1864, Spotsylvania Court House, Virginia	Point Lookout, Maryland, transferred to Elmira Prison, NY August 6, 1864	Died June 4, 1865 of Chronic Diarrhea, Grave No. 2896
Coney, Otters Private	25	April 14, 1862, Charlotte, North Carolina	Co. B, 53rd North Carolina Infantry	July 12, 1864, Near Washington, DC	Old Capital Prison, Washington DC. Transferred to Elmira Prison Camp, NY, July 25, 1864.	Died January 24, 1865 of Variola (Smallpox), Grave No. 1611
Congdon, George W. Private	Unk	August 1, 1861, Richmond, Virginia	Co. C, 38th Read's Battalion, Virginia Light Artillery	June 3, 1864, Gaines Farm, Cold Harbor, Virginia	Point Lookout, Maryland, transferred to Elmira Prison, NY July 17, 1864	Oath of Allegiance June 16, 1865
Congleton, James R. Private	18	July 13, 1861, Pitt County, North Carolina	Co. G, 8th North Carolina Infantry	June 1, 1864, Cold Harbor, Virginia	Point Lookout, Maryland, transferred to Elmira Prison, NY July 17, 1864	Exchanged February 20, 1865 at Boulware's or Cox Wharf on the James River, Virginia
Congleton, Owen Private	Unk	May 8, 1864, Wilmington, North Carolina	Co. K, 10th Regiment, 1st North Carolina Artillery	January 15, 1865, Fort Fisher, North Carolina	January 30, 1865, Elmira Prison Camp, NY	Died February 24, 1865 of Typhoid Fever, Grave No. 2271
Conley, H. E. Corporal	Unk	Unknown	Co. C, 50th Virginia Infantry	May 12, 1864 Spotsylvania Court House, Virginia	Point Lookout, Maryland, transferred to Elmira Prison, NY August 2, 1864	Oath of Allegiance June 27, 1865

Name & Rank	Age	Enlisted	Regiment and State	Where Captured	Prison	Remarks
Conlin, John P. Private	Unk	March 24, 1862, Camp Gist, South Carolina	Co. K, 27th South Carolina Infantry	June 24, 1864, Near Petersburg, Virginia	Point Lookout, Maryland, transferred to Elmira Prison, NY August 18, 1864	Died September 22, 1864 of Chronic Diarrhea, Grave No. 483.
Conn, J. M. Private	Unk	June 11, 1861, Camp McDonald, Georgia	Co. A, 3rd Battalion, Georgia Sharp Shooters	July 29, 1864, Petersburg, Virginia	Point Lookout, Maryland, transferred to Elmira Prison, NY August 12, 1864	Oath of Allegiance July 7, 1865
Connell, J. W. Private	Unk	December 15, 1862, Savannah, Georgia	Co. A, 7th Georgia Cavalry	June 11, 1864, Trevilian Station, Louisa Court House, Virginia	Point Lookout, Maryland, transferred to Elmira Prison, NY July 25, 1864	Died March 13, 1865 of Variola (Smallpox), Grave No. 2015
Connell, Jerry Private	Unk	April 1, 1861, Mobile, Alabama	Co. E, 1st Battalion Alabama Artillery	August 23, 1864, Fort Morgan, Alabama	Steam Press No. 4, New Orleans, Louisiana transferred to Elmira Prison, October 8, 1864.	Oath of Allegiance May 19, 1865
Connell, Wyatt G. Private	26	May 7, 1861, Camp Crabtree, Granville, North Carolina	Co. G, 30th North Carolina Infantry	May 12, 1864, Spotsylvania, Virginia. Gunshot Wound Right Forearm and Elbow.	Old Capital Prison, Washington, DC, transferred to Elmira Prison, NY, December 17, 1864	Exchanged February 13, 1865 at Boulware's Wharf on the James River, Virginia
Connelly, William C. Private	Unk	May 5, 1862, Goldsboro, North Carolina	Co. F, 18th North Carolina Infantry	May 6, 1864, Wilderness, Virginia	Point Lookout, Maryland, transferred to Elmira Prison, NY August 6, 1864	Died February 16, 1865 of Chronic Diarrhea, Grave No. 2180
Conner, Christopher O. Private	19	June 5, 1861, Norfolk, Virginia	Captain Moore's Co. Virginia Light Artillery	July 3, 1864, Dutch Gap, Near Richmond, Virginia	Point Lookout, Maryland, transferred to Elmira Prison, NY July 25, 1864	Oath of Allegiance November 3, 1864. Early Release by Commissary General of Prisoners.
Conniff, Daniel C. Private	Unk	August 20, 1861, Tallahassee, Florida	Co. M, 2nd Florida Infantry	July 29, 1864, Petersburg, Virginia	Point Lookout, Maryland, transferred to Elmira Prison, NY August 12, 1864	Oath of Allegiance May 12, 1865

Name & Rank	Age	Enlisted	Regiment and State	Where Captured	Prison	Remarks
Connolly, John, Private	25	June 4, 1861, Camp Moore, Louisiana	Co. F, 6th Louisiana Infantry	May 5, 1864, Wilderness, Virginia	Point Lookout, Maryland, transferred to Elmira Prison, NY August 17, 1864	Oath of Allegiance May 29, 1865
Connolly, Patrick, Sergeant	Unk	March 15, 1862, Charleston, South Carolina	Co. C, 27th South Carolina Infantry	June 24, 1864, Near Petersburg, Virginia	Point Lookout, Maryland, transferred to Elmira Prison, NY August 18, 1864	Oath of Allegiance May 17, 1865
Connor, Doctor, Private	23	February 9, 1863, Whiteville, North Carolina	Co. E, 36th Regiment, 2nd North Carolina Artillery	January 15, 1865, Fort Fisher, North Carolina. Wounded	February 1, 1865, Elmira Prison Camp, New York	Exchanged February 20, 1865 at Boulware's or Cox Wharf on the James River, Virginia
Connor, George, Private	20	May 21, 1861, Brownsburg, Virginia	Co. H, 25th Virginia Infantry	May 6, 1864, Wilderness, Virginia	Point Lookout, Maryland, transferred to Elmira Prison, NY August 14, 1864	Exchanged October 29, 1864, at Venus Point, Savannah River, GA.
Connor, Nathan F., Private	Unk	May 25, 1861, Floyd Court House, Virginia	Co. B, 42nd Virginia Infantry	May 12, 1864, Spotsylvania, Virginia	Point Lookout Prison Camp, Maryland. Transferred to Elmira Prison Camp, New York August 2, 1864	Died September 21, 1864 of Chronic Diarrhea, Grave No. 341
Connor, Pat, Private	Unk	April 5, 1863, Knoxville, Tennessee	Co. A, Jackson's 1st Regiment, Tennessee Heavy Artillery	August 23, 1864, Fort Morgan, Alabama	New Orleans, Louisiana transferred to Elmira December 4, 1864.	Exchanged February 13, 1865 at Boulware's wharf on the James River, Virginia
Connor, Phillips H., Private	18	February 27, 1864, Shelby, North Carolina	Co. E, 12th North Carolina Infantry	May 12, 1864, Near Spotsylvania County Court House, Virginia	Point Lookout, Maryland, transferred to Elmira Prison, NY August 14, 1864	Exchanged March 2, 1865 at Akins Landing on the James River, Virginia
Connor, Pinkney, Private	22	February 9, 1863, Whiteville, North Carolina	Co. E, 36th Regiment, 2nd North Carolina Artillery	January 15, 1865, Fort Fisher, North Carolina. Wounded	February 1, 1865, Elmira Prison Camp, New York	Oath of Allegiance July 11, 1865

Name & Rank	Age	Enlisted	Regiment and State	Where Captured	Prison	Remarks
Connor, William A. Private	29	May 15, 1861, Edneyville, North Carolina	Co. B, 25th North Carolina Infantry	June 17, 1864, Petersburg, Virginia	Point Lookout, Maryland, transferred to Elmira Prison, NY July 30, 1864	Oath of Allegiance July 3, 1865
Conrad, Henry R. Private	19	March 13, 1862, Forsyth County, North Carolina	Co. G, 4th North Carolina Infantry	July 13, 1864, Near Washington, DC	Old Capital Prison, Washington, DC, transferred to Elmira Prison, NY, July 23, 1864	Exchanged February 13, 1865 at Boulware's wharf on the James River, Virginia
Conway, James Private	38	July 22, 1861, Camp Moore, Louisiana	Co. A, 10th Louisiana Infantry	May 12, 1864, Spotsylvania Court House, Virginia	Point Lookout, Maryland, transferred to Elmira Prison, NY July 25, 1864	Exchanged February 25, 1865 at Boulware's or Cox Wharf on the James River, Virginia
Conyers, Ephraim G. Private	21	May 20, 1861, Louisburg, North Carolina	Co. K, 32nd North Carolina Infantry	May 10, 1864, Spotsylvania, Virginia	Point Lookout, Maryland, transferred to Elmira Prison, NY August 6, 1864	Oath of Allegiance June 16, 1865
Cook, Abraham B. Sergeant	22	July 6, 1861, Wilmington, North Carolina	Co. J, 18th North Carolina Infantry	May 12, 1864, Spotsylvania Court House, Virginia	Point Lookout, Maryland, transferred to Elmira Prison, NY August 6, 1864	Exchanged in 1865 at Boulware's Wharf on the James River, Virginia
Cook, Abram M. Private	Unk	January 20, 1864, Bluffton, South Carolina	Co. E, 11th South Carolina Infantry	June 24, 1864, Near Petersburg, Virginia	Point Lookout, Maryland, transferred to Elmira Prison, NY August 18, 1864	Exchanged February 13, 1865 at Boulware's wharf on the James River, Virginia
Cook, Alex Private	Unk	May 3, 1862, Myersville, South Carolina	Co. H, 25th South Carolina Infantry	January 15, 1865, Fort Fisher, North Carolina	Elmira Prison Camp January 30, 1865	Oath of Allegiance June 23, 1865
Cook, Augustus W. Private	Unk	May 27, 1861, Atlanta, Georgia	Co. H, 6th Georgia Infantry	August 19, 1864, Weldon Railroad, Virginia. Gunshot Wound Right Thigh and Buttocks.	Old Capital Prison, Washington, DC, transferred to Elmira Prison, NY, December 17, 1864	Oath of Allegiance June 16, 1865

Name & Rank	Age	Enlisted	Regiment and State	Where Captured	Prison	Remarks
Cook, Benjamin S. Private	Unk	September 25, 1862, Dry Creek, Lewisburg, Virginia	Co. D, 14th Virginia Cavalry	July 10, 1864, Germantown, Maryland	Old Capital Prison, Washington, DC, transferred to Elmira Prison, NY, July 23, 1864	Exchanged February 13, 1865 at Boulware's wharf on the James River, Virginia
Cook, Burton W. Private	Unk	May 1, 1862, Fayetteville, Georgia	Co. C, 53rd Georgia Infantry	June 1, 1864, Gaines Mill, Cold Harbor, Virginia	Point Lookout, Maryland, transferred to Elmira Prison, NY July 17,1864	Oath of Allegiance June 19, 1865
Cook, Doctor H. Civilian	Unk	Unknown	Citizen of North Carolina	January 15, 1865, Fort Fisher, North Carolina. Wounded	February 1, 1865, Elmira Prison Camp, New York	Oath of Allegiance June 20, 1865
Cook, Henry C. Private	23	July 15, 1862, Raleigh, North Carolina	Co. A, 5th North Carolina Infantry	May 12, 1864, Spotsylvania Court House, Virginia	Point Lookout, Maryland, transferred to Elmira Prison, NY August 6, 1864	Died April 26, 1865 of Chronic Diarrhea, Grave No. 1422
Cook, J. C. Private	18	July 18, 1861, Bay Point, South Carolina	Co. E, 11th South Carolina Infantry	June 24, 1864, Near Petersburg, Virginia	Point Lookout, Maryland, transferred to Elmira Prison, NY August 18, 1864	Oath of Allegiance July 11, 1865
Cook, Jacob H. Private	25	October 13, 1863, Mobile, Alabama	Co. C, 1st Battalion Alabama Artillery	August 23, 1864, Fort Morgan, Alabama	New Orleans, Louisiana transferred to Elmira December 4, 1864.	Oath of Allegiance May 29, 1865
Cook, James Private	Unk	August 2, 1862, Camp Watts, Alabama	Co. A, 6th Alabama Infantry	May 12, 1864, Spotsylvania Court House, Virginia	Point Lookout, Maryland, transferred to Elmira Prison, NY July 23, 1864	Oath of Allegiance July 26, 1865
Cook, James A. Private	19	August 1, 1861, Sarepta, Mississippi	Co. K, 17th Mississippi Infantry	May 24, 1864, Mott's Farm, North Anna, Virginia	Point Lookout, Maryland, transferred to Elmira Prison, NY August 17, 1864	Oath of Allegiance May 17, 1865
Cook, Jessie Private	Unk	July 25, 1863, Dawson, Georgia	Co. H, 64th Georgia Infantry	June 17, 1864, Petersburg, Virginia	Point Lookout, Maryland, transferred to Elmira Prison, NY July 30, 1864	Died November 20, 1864 of Pneumonia, Grave No. 943

Name & Rank	Age	Enlisted	Regiment and State	Where Captured	Prison	Remarks
Cook, Joel Private	24	May 2, 1862, Jonesboro, Tennessee	Co. K, 63rd Tennessee Infantry	June 17, 1864, Petersburg, Virginia	Point Lookout, Maryland, transferred to Elmira Prison, NY July 30, 1864	Died April 17, 1865 of Chronic Dysentery. No Known Grave in Woodlawn Cemetery.
Cook, Joel R. Private	Unk	April 1, 1862, Blacksburg, Virginia	Co. L, 4th Virginia Infantry	May 12, 1864, Near Spotsylvania Court House, Virginia	Point Lookout, Maryland, transferred to Elmira Prison, NY August 6, 1864	Died March 30, 1865 of Typhoid Fever, Grave No. 2527
Cook, John Private	Unk	Unknown	Henry's Battalion, Virginia Infantry	July 14, 1863, Falling Waters, Maryland	Point Lookout, Maryland, transferred to Elmira Prison, NY August 18, 1864	Exchanged March 10, 1865 at Boulware's wharf on the James River, Virginia
Cook, John W. Private	Unk	May 12, 1862, Augusta, Georgia	Co. F, 12th Battery, Georgia Light Artillery	July 14, 1864, Near Washington, DC	Old Capital Prison, Washington, DC, transferred to Elmira Prison, NY, July 23, 1864	Died January 4, 1865 of Pneumonia, Grave No. 1264
Cook, Joshua Private	16	July 1, 1863, Elizabeth City, North Carolina	Co. A, 8th North Carolina Infantry	June 1, 1864, Cold Harbor, Virginia	Point Lookout, Maryland, transferred to Elmira Prison, NY July 17,1864	Exchanged February 20, 1865 at Boulware's or Cox Wharf on the James River, Virginia
Cook, Lewis Private	32	June 5, 1861, Memphis, Tennessee	Co. B, 1st Jackson's Tennessee Heavy Artillery	August 23, 1864, Fort Morgan, Alabama.	New Orleans, Louisiana transferred to Elmira December 4, 1864.	Exchanged February 20, 1865 at Boulware's or Cox Wharf on the James River, Virginia
Cook, Samuel Private	Unk	July 14, 1864, Center Hill, Georgia	Co. B, 16th Georgia Infantry	August 16, 1864, Front Royal, Virginia	Old Capital Prison, Washington, DC transferred to Elmira Prison, NY August 29, 1864	Oath of Allegiance July 7, 1865
Cook, Thomas. J. Private	24	April 12, 1862, Battery Island, South Carolina	Co. C, 25th South Carolina Infantry	January 15, 1865, Fort Fisher, North Carolina	Elmira Prison Camp January 30, 1865	Exchanged March 2, 1865 at Boulware's Wharf on the James River, Virginia

Name & Rank	Age	Enlisted	Regiment and State	Where Captured	Prison	Remarks
Cook, Thomas W. Private	18	February 26, 1862, Franklin, North Carolina	Co. B, 47th North Carolina Infantry	May 12, 1864, Spotsylvania Court House, Virginia	Point Lookout, Maryland, transferred to Elmira Prison, NY August 12, 1864	Exchanged October 29, 1864, at Venus Point, Savannah River, GA.
Cook, William D. Private	27	April 12, 1862, Battery Island, South Carolina	Co. C, 25th South Carolina Infantry	January 15, 1865, Fort Fisher, North Carolina	Elmira Prison Camp January 30, 1865	Died March 29, 1865, Pneumonia, Grave No. 2541
Cook, W. E. Private	Unk	March 1862, Clayton, Alabama	Co. G, 5th Alabama Infantry	May 12, 1864, Spotsylvania Court House, Virginia	Point Lookout, Maryland, transferred to Elmira Prison, NY July 6, 1864	Exchanged March 2, 1865 at Akins Landing on the James River, Virginia
Cook, William Private	Unk	May 15, 1862, Camp Moore, Louisiana	Co. A, 9th Battalion Louisiana Infantry	October 9, 1864, Near Wilson's Ferry, Louisiana	New Orleans, Louisiana transferred to Elmira November 19, 1864.	Oath of Allegiance May 17, 1865
Cook, William J. Private	22	May 17, 1861, Lower Black River District, North Carolina	Co. F, 18th North Carolina Infantry	May 10, 1864, Spotsylvania Court House, Virginia	Point Lookout, Maryland, transferred to Elmira Prison, NY August 6, 1864	Exchanged March 14, 1865 at Boulware's Wharf on the James River, Virginia
Cook, William S. Sergeant	28	February 24, 1862, Coddle Creek, North Carolina	Co. J, 7th North Carolina Infantry	May 6, 1864, Wilderness, Virginia	Point Lookout, Maryland, transferred to Elmira Prison, NY August 14, 1864	Died August 30, 1864 of Remittent Fever, Grave No. 55
Cook, Young H. Private	26	July 22, 1861, Buncombe County, North Carolina	Co. J, 25th North Carolina Infantry	June 17, 1864, Petersburg, Virginia	Point Lookout Prison Camp, Maryland. Transferred to Elmira Prison Camp, New York July 30, 1864	Died August 20, 1864 of Chronic Diarrhea, Grave No. 116
Cooke, Carr Private	29	June 13, 1861, Clarkson, Virginia	Co. J, 26th North Carolina Infantry	June 17, 1864, Near Petersburg, Virginia	Point Lookout, Maryland, transferred to Elmira Prison, NY July 30, 1864	Oath of Allegiance July 3, 1865
Cooke, George Private	Unk	April 6, 1864, Camp Orange, Virginia	Co. E, 55th Virginia Infantry	May 5, 1864, Wilderness, Virginia	Point Lookout, Maryland, transferred to Elmira Prison, NY August 14, 1864	Oath of Allegiance June 23, 1865

Name & Rank	Age	Enlisted	Regiment and State	Where Captured	Prison	Remarks
Cooke, James H. Private	Unk	March 8, 1862, Fort Lowry, Virginia	Co. F, 55th Virginia Infantry	May 5, 1864, Wilderness, Virginia	Point Lookout, Maryland, transferred to Elmira Prison, NY August 14, 1864	Oath of Allegiance May 15, 1865
Cool, James L. Private	Unk	August 27, 1863, Harrisonburg, Virginia	Co. H, 12th Virginia Cavalry	May 28, 1864, Hall's Shop, Virginia	Point Lookout, Maryland, transferred to Elmira Prison, NY July 8, 1864	Oath of Allegiance June 19, 1865
Cooler, Washington Private	Unk	April 20, 1864, Bluffton, South Carolina	Co. E, 11th South Carolina Infantry	June 24, 1864, Near Petersburg, Virginia	Point Lookout, Maryland, transferred to Elmira Prison, NY August 18, 1864	Exchanged October 29, 1864, at Venus Point, Savannah River, GA.
Cooley, Stephen C. Private	23	April 2, 1861, New Orleans, Louisiana	Co. B, 1st Louisiana Infantry	May 12, 1864, Spotsylvania Court House, Virginia	Point Lookout, Maryland, transferred to Elmira Prison, NY August 17, 1864	Exchanged February 13, 1865 at Boulware's wharf on the James River, Virginia
Cooley, Wesley Private	28	May 9, 1862, Wadesboro, North Carolina	Co. I, 43rd North Carolina Infantry	May 30, 1864, Mechanics-ville, Virginia	Point Lookout, Maryland, transferred to Elmira Prison, NY July 12, 1864	Died June 10, 1865, Chronic Diarrhea, Grave No. 2888
Cooley, William C. Private	21	May 24, 1861, Raleigh, North Carolina	Co. E, 14th North Carolina Infantry	May 30, 1864, Old Church, Virginia	Point Lookout, Maryland, transferred to Elmira Prison, NY July 12, 1864	Oath of Allegiance May 29, 1865
Coolican, Thomas Private	Unk	April 8, 1863, Lewisburg, Virginia	Captain Bryan's Battery, Virginia Artillery	July 17,1864, Near Washington, DC	Old Capital Prison, Washington, DC, transferred to Elmira Prison, NY, July 23, 1864	Oath of Allegiance May 15, 1865
Coon, William W. Private	30	March 8, 1863, Williamsburg, Virginia	Co. D, 19th Virginia Cavalry	August 3, 1864, Shepherds-town, Virginia	Old Capital Prison, Washington D. C. Transferred to Elmira Prison, NY August 12, 1864	Oath of Allegiance May 17, 1865

Name & Rank	Age	Enlisted	Regiment and State	Where Captured	Prison	Remarks
Cooner, George D. Private	Unk	July 29, 1861, Satilla, Georgia	Co. D, 26th Georgia Infantry	May 20, 1864, Spotsylvania Court House, Virginia	Point Lookout, Maryland, transferred to Elmira Prison, NY July 6, 1864	Exchanged February 20, 1865 at Boulware's or Cox Wharf on the James River, Virginia
Cooney, Thomas Private	Unk	May 29, 1863, Macon County, Alabama	Co. J, 61st Alabama Infantry	May 12, 1864, Spotsylvania Court House, Virginia	Point Lookout, Maryland, transferred to Elmira Prison, NY July 25, 1864	Died September 8, 1864 of Typhoid-Pneumonia, Grave No. 212
Cooper, Charles H. Private	29	October 31, 1862, Fort Fisher, North Carolina	Co. C, 36th Regiment, 2nd North Carolina Artillery	January 15, 1865, Fort Fisher, North Carolina. Wounded	February 1, 1865, Elmira Prison Camp, New York	Died March 19, 1865 of Variola (Smallpox), Grave No. 1730
Cooper, Charles S. Private	21	April 1, 1863, Frankford, Virginia	Co. E, 19th Virginia Cavalry	July 15, 1864 Loudoun County, Virginia	Old Capital Prison, Washington, DC, transferred to Elmira Prison, NY, July 23, 1864	Exchanged March 14, 1865 at Boulware's Wharf on the James River, Virginia
Cooper, Franklin Private	18	March 25, 1862, Salisbury, North Carolina	Co. C, 42nd North Carolina Infantry	June 3, 1864, Cold Harbor, Virginia	Point Lookout, Maryland, transferred to Elmira Prison, NY July 17, 1864	Died October 28, 1864 of Unknown Disease, Grave No. 718
Cooper, George W. Corporal	21	June 15, 1861, Columbus, Georgia	Co. E, 12th Georgia Infantry	May 6, 1864, Wilderness, Virginia	Point Lookout, Maryland, transferred to Elmira Prison, NY August 14, 1864	Oath of Allegiance June 16, 1865
Cooper, Henry Private	Unk	April 7, 1862, New Orleans, Louisiana	Co. H, 7th Louisiana Infantry	July 16, 1864 Loudoun County, Virginia	Old Capital Prison, Washington, DC, transferred to Elmira Prison, NY, July 23, 1864	Exchanged March 10, 1865 at Boulware's wharf on the James River, Virginia
Cooper, Hiram B. Private	34	October 31, 1862, Fort Fisher, North Carolina	Co. D, 36th Regiment, 2nd North Carolina Artillery	January 15, 1865, Fort Fisher, North Carolina. Wounded	February 1, 1865, Elmira Prison Camp, New York	Died August 11, 1865 of Unknown Disease at US Army Hospital, Elmira, NY., Grave No. 2861

Name & Rank	Age	Enlisted	Regiment and State	Where Captured	Prison	Remarks
Cooper, Joel P. Sergeant	19	February 14, 1863, Adam's Run, South Carolina	Co. G, 7th Battalion South Carolina Infantry	August 24, 1864, Weldon Railroad, Virginia. Gunshot Wound Right Leg. Right Leg Amputated.	Old Capital Prison, Washington D. C. Transferred to Elmira Prison, NY March 26, 1865.	Oath of Allegiance June 30, 1865
Cooper, John R. Private	Unk	November 11, 1863, Cobb County, Georgia	Co. J, 7th Georgia Cavalry	June 11, 1864, Trevilian Station, Louisa Court House, Virginia	Point Lookout, Maryland, transferred to Elmira Prison, NY July 25, 1864	Died September 2, 1864 of Chronic Diarrhea, Grave No. 84
Cooper, Joseph D. Private	16	May 4, 1864, Petersburg, Virginia	Co. B, 3rd Archer's Battalion, Virginia Reserves Infantry	June 9, 1864, Plank Road, Petersburg, Virginia	Point Lookout, Maryland, transferred to Elmira Prison, NY July 12, 1864	Transferred for Exchange 10/11/64. Exchanged 11/15/64 at Venus Point, Savannah River, GA.
Cooper, M. W. Private	Unk	June 3, 1861, Decatur, Morgan County, Alabama	Co. E, 9th Alabama Infantry	May 6, 1864, Wilderness, Virginia	Point Lookout, Maryland, transferred to Elmira Prison, NY August 17, 1864	Died February 22, 1865 of Pneumonia, Grave No. 2239
Cooper, N. Columbus Private	Unk	May 8, 1862, Panola County, Mississippi	Co. K, 33rd Mississippi Infantry	May 16, 1863, Champion Hill, Mississippi	Point Lookout, Maryland, transferred to Elmira Prison, NY August 18, 1864	Exchanged October 29, 1864 at Venus Point, Savannah River, GA.
Cooper, Robert A. Private	Unk	July 1, 1861, Prince William County, Virginia	Co. A, 49th Virginia Infantry	May 30, 1864, Gaines Mill, Cold Harbor, Virginia	Point Lookout, Maryland, transferred to Elmira Prison, NY July 11, 1864	Oath of Allegiance June 30, 1865
Cooper, Robert T. Private	Unk	March 1, 1864, Vance's Depot, Tennessee	Co. G, 17th Tennessee Infantry	June 17, 1864, Petersburg, Virginia	Point Lookout, Maryland, transferred to Elmira Prison, NY July 30, 1864	Exchanged February 25, 1865 at Boulware's or Cox Wharf on the James River, Virginia
Cooper, Rueben H. W. Private	Unk	June 13, 1861, Monroe, Georgia	Co. C, 9th Georgia Infantry	May 6, 1864, Wilderness, Virginia	Point Lookout, Maryland, transferred to Elmira Prison, NY August 14, 1864	Died February 16, 1865 of Pneumonia, Grave No. 2186

Name & Rank	Age	Enlisted	Regiment and State	Where Captured	Prison	Remarks
Cooper, S. A. Corporal	Unk	April 14, 1862, Union Springs, Alabama	Co. D, 3rd Alabama Infantry	May 12, 1864, Spotsylvania Court House, Virginia	Point Lookout, Maryland, transferred to Elmira Prison, NY August 12, 1864	Oath of Allegiance June 20, 1865
Cooper, Samuel T. Sergeant	Unk	May 1, 1861, Nashville, North Carolina	Co. H, 32nd North Carolina Infantry	May 10, 1864, Spotsylvania, Virginia	Point Lookout, Maryland, transferred to Elmira Prison, NY August 6, 1864	Exchanged October 29, 1864 at Venus Point, Savannah River, GA.
Cooper, William J. Corporal	Unk	November 13, 1861, Winnsboro, South Carolina	Co. G, 7th Battalion South Carolina Infantry	May 16, 1864, Near Drury's Bluff, Virginia	Point Lookout, Maryland, transferred to Elmira Prison, NY August 17, 1864	Died November 5, 1864 of Chronic Diarrhea, Grave No. 838
Cope, Daniel Private	Unk	January 12, 1862, Bennettsville, South Carolina	Co. D, 4th South Carolina Cavalry	May 31, 1864, Cold Harbor, Virginia	Point Lookout, Maryland, transferred to Elmira Prison, NY July 11, 1864	Exchanged October 29, 1864, at Venus Point, Savannah River, GA.
Copeland, Barnabas B. Private	21	September 4, 1861, Livingston, Overton County, Tennessee	Co. D, 25th Tennessee Infantry	May 16, 1864, Near Drury's Bluff, Virginia	Point Lookout, Maryland, transferred to Elmira Prison, NY August 17, 1864	Died September 20, 1864 of Chronic Diarrhea, Grave No. 497
Copeland, William M. Private	26	April 29, 1862, White Sulfur Springs, Virginia	Co. H, 26th Battalion, Virginia Infantry	June 3, 1864, Gaines Mill, Cold Harbor, Virginia	Point Lookout, Maryland, transferred to Elmira Prison, NY July 17, 1864	Exchanged March 14, 1865 at Boulware's Wharf on the James River, Virginia
Copp, Michael Private	19	April 10, 1863, Jonesboro, Tennessee	Co. K, 63rd Tennessee Infantry	June 17, 1864, Petersburg, Virginia	Point Lookout, Maryland, transferred to Elmira Prison, NY July 30, 1864	Exchanged February 25, 1865 at Boulware's or Cox Wharf on the James River, Virginia
Coram, James T. Private	22	October 3, 1862, Drury's Bluff, Virginia	Co. G, 45th North Carolina Infantry	May 10, 1864, Spotsylvania Court House, Virginia	Point Lookout, Maryland, transferred to Elmira Prison, NY August 6, 1864	Died April 8, 1865 of Chronic Diarrhea, Grave No. 2635. Name Cornin on Headstone.

Name & Rank	Age	Enlisted	Regiment and State	Where Captured	Prison	Remarks
Coram, Robert L. Private	19	February 27, 1862, Reidsville, North Carolina	Co. G, 45th North Carolina Infantry	May 10, 1864, Spotsylvania Court House, Virginia	Point Lookout, Maryland, transferred to Elmira Prison, NY August 6, 1864	Oath of Allegiance June 27, 1865
Coram, William J. Private	29	February 27, 1862, Reidsville, North Carolina	Co. G, 45th North Carolina Infantry	May 10, 1864, Spotsylvania Court House, Virginia	Point Lookout, Maryland, transferred to Elmira Prison, NY August 6, 1864	Oath of Allegiance June 27, 1865
Corbett, John W. Sergeant	Unk	March 5, 1862, Yanceyville, North Carolina	Co. J, 45th North Carolina Infantry	May 10, 1864, Spotsylvania Court House, Virginia	Point Lookout, Maryland, transferred to Elmira Prison, NY August 6, 1864	Oath of Allegiance June 19, 1865
Corbin, Charles Private	18	July 15, 1861, Whippy Swamp, South Carolina	Co. D, 11th South Carolina Infantry	January 15, 1865, Fort Fisher, North Carolina	February 1, 1865, Elmira Prison Camp, New York	Oath of Allegiance June 23, 1865
Corbin, Edward Private	28	July 15, 1861, Whippy Swamp, South Carolina	Co. D, 11th South Carolina Infantry	January 15, 1865, Fort Fisher, North Carolina	February 1, 1865, Elmira Prison Camp, New York	Died March 23, 1865 of Variola (Smallpox), Grave No. 2926
Corbin, Philip Civilian	Unk	Unknown	Citizen of Rappahannock County, Virginia	January 31, 1864, Rappahannock County, Virginia	Point Lookout, Maryland, transferred to Elmira Prison, NY July 25, 1864	Died March 24, 1865 of Diarrhea. Grave No. 2460
Corbit, William W. Private	23	August 31, 1861, Crab Tree, North Carolina	Co. F, 30th North Carolina Infantry	May 8, 1864, Wilderness, Virginia	Point Lookout, Maryland, transferred to Elmira Prison, NY August 14, 1864	Exchanged March 14, 1865 at Boulware's Wharf on the James River, Virginia
Corcoran, Jerry Private	Unk	Unknown	Co. K, 10th Louisiana Infantry	July 13, 1864, Near Washington, DC	Old Capital Prison, Washington, DC, transferred to Elmira Prison, NY, July 23, 1864	Exchanged October 29, 1864, at Venus Point, Savannah River, GA.
Cordell, Charles Sergeant	Unk	July 8, 1861, Griffin, Georgia	Co. E, 13th Georgia Infantry	May 12, 1864, Spotsylvania Court House, Virginia	Point Lookout, Maryland, transferred to Elmira Prison, NY July 6, 1864	Exchanged March 10, 1865 at Boulware's Wharf on the James River, Virginia

Name & Rank	Age	Enlisted	Regiment and State	Where Captured	Prison	Remarks
Cordell, Ezekiel C. Private	Unk	September 19, 1861, Dalton, Georgia	Co. C, 60th Georgia Infantry	July 17,1864, Near Washington, DC	Old Capital Prison, Washington, DC, transferred to Elmira Prison, NY, July 23, 1864	Oath of Allegiance May 29, 1865
Corder, David A. Private	Unk	January 14, 1862, Camp Hampton, South Carolina	Co. D, 17th South Carolina Infantry	July 30, 1864, Petersburg, Virginia	Point Lookout, Maryland, transferred to Elmira Prison, NY August 12, 1864	Died July 4, 1865 of Chronic Diarrhea, Grave No. 2834
Corder, John A. Private	Unk	January 14, 1862, Camp Hampton, South Carolina	Co. D, 17th South Carolina Infantry	July 30, 1864, Petersburg, Virginia	Point Lookout, Maryland, transferred to Elmira Prison, NY August 12, 1864	Oath of Allegiance July 7, 1865
Cordes, George Private	Unk	January 1, 1863, Bluffton, South Carolina	Co. B, 11th South Carolina Infantry	June 24, 1864, Near Petersburg, Virginia	Point Lookout, Maryland, transferred to Elmira Prison, NY July 25, 1864	Oath of Allegiance June 30, 1865
Cordon, Sylvester Corporal	Unk	September 23, 1861, Washington, North Carolina	Co. D, 13th Battalion North Carolina Artillery	January 15, 1865, Fort Fisher, North Carolina	Elmira Prison Camp, New York, February 1, 1865	Died March 8, 1865 of Diarrhea, Grave No. 2408. Headstone has First Name Gordon and Last Name Sylvester.
Cordon, William W. Sergeant	21	April 22, 1861, Washington, North Carolina	Co. K, 10th Regiment, 1st North Carolina Artillery	January 15, 1865, Fort Fisher, North Carolina	January 30, 1865, Elmira Prison Camp, NY	Oath of Allegiance July 11, 1865
Corl, John M. Private	Unk	August 6, 1861, Mt. Pleasant, North Carolina	Co. H, 8th North Carolina Infantry	June 1, 1864, Gaines Mill, Cold Harbor, Virginia	Point Lookout, Maryland, transferred to Elmira Prison, NY July 17,1864	Oath of Allegiance Date Unknown
Corl, Joseph Private	29	May 29, 1861, Charlotte, North Carolina	Co. C, 6th North Carolina Infantry	August 22, 1864, Charlestown, Virginia	Old Capital Prison, Washington, DC transferred to Elmira Prison, NY August 29, 1864	Oath of Allegiance May 19, 1865

Name & Rank	Age	Enlisted	Regiment and State	Where Captured	Prison	Remarks
Corn, William J. Sergeant	Unk	May 20, 1862, Camp Harris, Tennessee	Co. D, 17th Tennessee Infantry	June 17, 1864, Petersburg, Virginia	Point Lookout, Maryland, transferred to Elmira Prison, NY July 30, 1864	Exchanged February 25, 1865 at Boulware's or Cox Wharf on the James River, Virginia
Cornelius, John W. Private	20	July 2, 1862, Pfafftown, North Carolina	Co. D, 33rd North Carolina Infantry	May 12, 1864, Spotsylvania Court House, Virginia	Point Lookout, Maryland, transferred to Elmira Prison, NY August 12, 1864	Died August 21, 1864 of Pneumonia, Grave No. 111
Cornelius, William P. Private	Unk	March 25, 1862, White Stone, Lancaster County, Virginia	Co. L, 55th Virginia Infantry	May 5, 1864, Wilderness, Virginia	Point Lookout, Maryland, transferred to Elmira Prison, NY July 23, 1864	Died March 22, 1865 of Variola (Smallpox), Grave No. 1522
Cornell, J. T. Private	Unk	May 8, 1862, Augusta, Georgia	Co. A, 7th Georgia Cavalry	June 11, 1864, Louisa Court House, Trevilian Station, Virginia	Point Lookout, Maryland, transferred to Elmira Prison, NY July 28, 1864	Exchanged March 2, 1865 at Boulware's Wharf on the James River, Virginia
Cornell, James C. Private	Unk	Unknown	Co. K, 50th Virginia Infantry	May 5, 1864, Wilderness, Virginia	Point Lookout, Maryland, transferred to Elmira Prison, NY August 14, 1864	Oath of Allegiance June 14, 1865
Cornwell, Nathan G. Private	Unk	Unknown	Co. E, 50th Virginia Infantry	May 12, 1864, Spotsylvania Court House, Virginia	Point Lookout, Maryland, transferred to Elmira Prison, NY August 2, 1864	Exchanged October 29, 1864 at Venus Point, Savannah River, GA.
Correll, Joseph C. Private	Unk	February 22, 1862, Martinsburg, Virginia	Co. D, 2nd Virginia Infantry	May 12, 1864, Near Spotsylvania Court House, Virginia	Point Lookout, Maryland, transferred to Elmira Prison, NY August 6, 1864	Oath of Allegiance May 15, 1865
Cortright, Jerome S. Private	21	October 13, 1861, Mobile, Alabama	Co. A, 21st Alabama Infantry	August 23, 1864, Fort Morgan, Alabama	Steam Press No. 4, New Orleans, Louisiana transferred to Elmira Prison, October 8, 1864.	Oath of Allegiance March 20, 1865. Early Release per Lincoln's Proclamation, 12/8/1863.

Name & Rank	Age	Enlisted	Regiment and State	Where Captured	Prison	Remarks
Cosby, Benjamin Private	Unk	March 31, 1862, B. A. Springs, Virginia	Co. G, 11th Virginia Cavalry	September 22, 1863, Near Madison Court House, Virginia	Point Lookout, Maryland, transferred to Elmira Prison, NY August 18, 1864	Exchanged March 10, 1865 at Boulware's wharf on the James River, Virginia
Cosdan, Daniel G. Private	Unk	July 7, 1861, Selma, Alabama	Jeff Davis Alabama Artillery	May 5, 1864, Wilderness, Virginia	Point Lookout, Maryland, transferred to Elmira Prison, NY August 17, 1864	Oath of Allegiance May 29, 1865
Costello, John Private	28	May 7, 1861, New Orleans, Louisiana	Co. K, 5th Louisiana Infantry	May 5, 1864, Wilderness, Virginia	Point Lookout, Maryland, transferred to Elmira Prison, NY August 17, 1864	Oath of Allegiance May 17, 1865
Costlow, Garrison L. Private	17	July 9, 1861, Cartersville, Georgia	Co. K, 14th Georgia Infantry	May 12, 1864, Spotsylvania, Virginia	Old Capital Prison, Washington, DC, transferred to Elmira Prison, NY, July 23, 1864	Exchanged February 13, 1865 at Boulware's wharf on the James River, Virginia
Costner, John H. Private	21	July 30, 1861, Dallas, North Carolina	Co. B, 28th North Carolina Infantry	May 12, 1864, Spotsylvania Court House, Virginia. Gunshot Wound Left Leg.	Old Capital Prison, Washington, DC transferred to Elmira Prison, NY August 29, 1864	Exchanged October 29, 1864, at Venus Point, Savannah River, GA.
Cottle, Lewis J. Private	45	January 28, 1862, Onslow County, North Carolina	Co. G, 3rd North Carolina Infantry	May 12, 1864, Near Spotsylvania Court House, Virginia	Point Lookout Prison, Maryland. Transferred to Elmira Prison Camp New York August 14, 1864.	Died February 1, 1865 of Variola (Smallpox), Grave No. 1761
Cotton, James S. Private	Unk	April 2, 1864, Bristol, Tennessee	Co. E, 3rd Battalion Georgia Sharp Shooters	August 16, 1864, Front Royal, Virginia	Old Capital Prison, Washington, DC transferred to Elmira Prison, NY August 29, 1864	Oath of Allegiance May 15, 1865

Name & Rank	Age	Enlisted	Regiment and State	Where Captured	Prison	Remarks
Cotton, William H. Private	23	July 15, 1862, Chatham County, North Carolina	Co. E, 5th North Carolina Infantry	May 12, 1864, Spotsylvania Court House, Virginia	Point Lookout, Maryland, transferred to Elmira Prison, NY August 6, 1864	Oath of Allegiance June 23, 1865
Cottrell, William Robert Private	Unk	May 10, 1861, Richmond, Virginia	Co. C, 38th Read's Battalion, Virginia Light Artillery	June 3, 1864, Gaines Farm, Cold Harbor, Virginia	Point Lookout, Maryland, transferred to Elmira Prison, NY July 17, 1864	Exchanged March 10, 1865 at Boulware's Wharf on the James River, Virginia
Couch, Jesse A. Private	Unk	December 25, 1861, Spartanburg, South Carolina	Co. E, 18th South Carolina Infantry	July 30, 1864, Petersburg, Virginia	Point Lookout, Maryland, transferred to Elmira Prison, NY August 12, 1864	Died February 12, 1865 of Chronic Diarrhea, Grave No. 2056
Couch, Tolliver R. Private	Unk	November 18, 1863, Charleston, South Carolina	Co. E, 18th South Carolina Infantry	July 30, 1864, Petersburg, Virginia	Point Lookout, Maryland, transferred to Elmira Prison, NY August 12, 1864	Oath of Allegiance May 29, 1865
Couch, William D. Private	Unk	March 1, 1862, Gainesville, Georgia	Co. C, Phillips Legion Georgia	May 12, 1864, Spotsylvania Court House, Virginia	Point Lookout, Maryland, transferred to Elmira Prison, NY August 12, 1864	Died November 16, 1864 of Pneumonia, Grave No. 956
Coulter, Benjamin M. Private	24	June 15, 1861, Columbus, Georgia	Co. E, 12th Georgia Infantry	May 10, 1864, Spotsylvania Court House, Virginia	Point Lookout, Maryland, transferred to Elmira Prison, NY July 25, 1864	Oath of Allegiance June 16, 1865
Coulter, Thomas S. Sergeant	Unk	November 1, 1862, Alvon, Virginia	Co. G, 26th Virginia Infantry	May 31, 1864, Chickahominy, Cold Harbor, Virginia	Point Lookout, Maryland, transferred to Elmira Prison, NY July 11, 1864	Oath of Allegiance May 17, 1865
Council, Thomas A. Sergeant	25	April 15, 1861, Pittsboro, North Carolina	Co. I, 32nd North Carolina Infantry	May 10, 1864, Wilderness, Virginia	Point Lookout, Maryland, transferred to Elmira Prison, NY August 6, 1864	Oath of Allegiance June 24, 1865
Councill, Jordan S. Private	20	September 4, 1861, Boone, North Carolina	Co. B, 37th North Carolina Infantry	May 12, 1864, Spotsylvania Court House, Virginia	Point Lookout, Maryland, transferred to Elmira Prison, NY August 12, 1864	Died November 17, 1864 of Pleuro-Pneumonia, Grave No. 964

Name & Rank	Age	Enlisted	Regiment and State	Where Captured	Prison	Remarks
Countis, C. I. Private	Unk	Unknown	Co. E, 50th Virginia Infantry	May 5, 1864, Wilderness, Virginia	Point Lookout, Maryland, transferred to Elmira Prison, NY August 14, 1864	Died November 11, 1864 of Erysipelas and Pneumonia, Grave No. 790
Coursey, Thomas J. Private	Unk	May 9, 1861, Reidsville, Georgia	Co. H, 61st Georgia Infantry	May 12, 1864, Spotsylvania Court House, Virginia	Point Lookout, Maryland, transferred to Elmira Prison, NY July 25, 1864	Exchanged March 10, 1865 at Boulware's wharf on the James River, Virginia
Courtney, H. E. Sergeant	Unk	March 15, 1861, Pineville, Alabama	Co. C, 5th Alabama Infantry	May 5, 1864, Wilderness, Virginia	Point Lookout, Maryland, transferred to Elmira Prison, NY August 17, 1864	Oath of Allegiance June 14, 1865
Courtney, Wilfred S. Private	Unk	December 28, 1861, Little Plymouth, Virginia	Co. G, 26th Virginia Infantry	June 15, 1864, Petersburg, Virginia	Point Lookout, Maryland, transferred to Elmira Prison, NY July 30, 1864	Oath of Allegiance July 11, 1865
Courtney, William Calvin Private	Unk	July 19, 1861, Manassas, Virginia	Co. J, 11th Virginia Infantry	November 26, 1864, Prince William County, Virginia	Old Capital Prison, Washington, DC, transferred to Elmira Prison, NY, December 17, 1864	Died February 20, 1865 of Diarrhea, Grave No. 2329. Headstone has 10th Virginia.
Courville, John Sergeant	23	July 22, 1861, Camp Moore, Louisiana	Co. K, 10th Louisiana Infantry	May 12, 1864, Spotsylvania Court House, Virginia	Point Lookout, Maryland, transferred to Elmira Prison, NY July 25, 1864	Exchanged February 25, 1865 at Boulware's or Cox Wharf on the James River, Virginia
Cousins, William M. Private	Unk	May 18, 1863, Fort Morgan, Alabama	Co. E, 1st Battalion Alabama Artillery	August 23, 1864, Fort Morgan, Alabama	New Orleans, Louisiana transferred to Elmira December 4, 1864.	Died February 20, 1865 While Being Transferred to be Exchanged. Died on the Boat, Unknown Day or Disease.
Coutre, R. Private	Unk	Unknown	Captain Norwood's Battalion Louisiana Cavalry	October 6, 1864, Clinton, Louisiana	New Orleans, Louisiana transferred to Elmira November 19, 1864.	Exchanged February 25, 1865 at Boulware's or Cox Wharf on the James River, Virginia

Name & Rank	Age	Enlisted	Regiment and State	Where Captured	Prison	Remarks
Covington, Alfred B. Private	18	July 1, 1862, Rockingham, North Carolina	Co. K, 33rd North Carolina Infantry	July 29, 1864, Petersburg, Virginia	Point Lookout, Maryland, transferred to Elmira Prison, NY August 12, 1864	Exchanged March 14, 1865 at Boulware's Wharf on the James River, Virginia
Covington, Benjamin C. Private	18	July 21, 1863, Fort Fisher, North Carolina	Co. I, 36th Regiment, 2nd North Carolina Artillery	January 15, 1865, Fort Fisher, North Carolina. Wounded	February 1, 1865, Elmira Prison Camp, New York	Oath of Allegiance June 12, 1865
Covington, John A. Corporal	Unk	June 15, 1861, Buena Vista, Georgia	Co. K, 12th Georgia Infantry	May 12, 1864, Spotsylvania Court House, Virginia	Point Lookout, Maryland, transferred to Elmira Prison, NY July 25, 1864	Oath of Allegiance June 23, 1865
Covington, John P. Private	33	May 15, 1862, Camp Holmes, North Carolina	Co. H, 43rd North Carolina Infantry	May 16, 1864, Near Drury's Bluff, Virginia	Point Lookout, Maryland, transferred to Elmira Prison, NY August 17, 1864	Oath of Allegiance July 26, 1865
Covington, Thomas B. Private	Unk	March 1, 1864, Fort Fisher, North Carolina	Co. I, 36th Regiment, 2nd North Carolina Artillery	January 15, 1865, Fort Fisher, North Carolina. Wounded	February 1, 1865, Elmira Prison Camp, New York	Oath of Allegiance June 30, 1865
Cowan, John J. Private	Unk	March 8, 1862, Camp Bartow, Georgia	Co. K, 38th Georgia Infantry	May 6, 1864, Wilderness, Virginia	Point Lookout, Maryland, transferred to Elmira Prison, NY August 14, 1864	Oath of Allegiance June 16, 1865
Cowan, John N. Private	Unk	July 10, 1861, Selma, Alabama	Jeff Davis Alabama Artillery	May 5, 1864, Wilderness, Virginia	Point Lookout, Maryland, transferred to Elmira Prison, NY August 17, 1864	Exchanged March 14, 1865 at Boulware's Wharf on the James River, Virginia
Cowan, R. A. Private	20	March 1, 1864, Blackshear, Georgia	Co. E, 20th Georgia Cavalry	May 26, 1864, Cold Harbor, Virginia	Point Lookout, Maryland, transferred to Elmira Prison, NY July 11, 1864	Exchanged October 29, 1864 at Venus Point, Savannah River, GA.

Name & Rank	Age	Enlisted	Regiment and State	Where Captured	Prison	Remarks
Cowan, Thomas J. Corporal	19	June 1, 1861, Dogwood Grove, North Carolina	Co. K, 3rd North Carolina Infantry	May 12, 1864, Near Spotsylvania Court House, Virginia	Point Lookout Prison, Maryland. Transferred to Elmira Prison Camp New York August 14, 1864.	Exchanged March 2, 1865 at Akins Landing on the James River, Virginia
Coward, James H. Private	28	June 1, 1864, Marlboro, South Carolina	Co. D, 7th Battalion South Carolina Infantry	August 31, 1864, Reims Station, Virginia. Gunshot Wound Right Hand.	Old Capital Prison, Washington, DC transferred to Elmira Prison, NY August 27, 1864	Exchanged February 13, 1865 at Boulware's Wharf on the James River, Virginia
Coweey, J. W. Private	Unk	Unable to Find Soldier's Record	Co. C, 1st Battalion Louisiana Infantry	October 6, 1864, Near Hampton's Ferry, Louisiana	New Orleans, Louisiana transferred to Elmira November 19, 1864.	Exchanged February 25, 1865 at Boulware's or Cox Wharf on the James River, Virginia
Cowles, Carter W. Corporal	Unk	January 11, 1862, Halfway House, Virginia	Co. H, 5th Virginia Cavalry	May 11, 1864, Yellow Tavern, Hanover County, Virginia	Point Lookout, Maryland, transferred to Elmira Prison, NY August 17, 1864	Died September 28, 1864 of Chronic Diarrhea, Grave No. 445. Headstone has Coles.
Cowperthwait, W. B. Corporal	25	May 9, 1862, Charleston, South Carolina	Co. A, 25th South Carolina Infantry	January 15, 1865, Fort Fisher, North Carolina	Elmira Prison Camp January 30, 1865	Oath of Allegiance June 19, 1865
Cox, D. M. Private	Unk	March 16, 1863, Camp Prichard, South Carolina	Co. B, 4th South Carolina Cavalry	June 11, 1864, Trevilian Station, Louisa Court House, Virginia	Old Capital Prison, Washington, DC, transferred to Elmira Prison, NY, July 23, 1864	Exchanged October 29, 1864, at Venus Point, Savannah River, GA.
Cox, Daniel Private	29	May 29, 1861, Christiansburg, Virginia	Co. F, 11th Virginia Infantry	June 16, 1864, Near Petersburg, Virginia	Point Lookout, Maryland, transferred to Elmira Prison, NY July 25, 1864	Exchanged October 29, 1864, at Venus Point, Savannah River, GA.
Cox, Daniel D. Private	Unk	March 10, 1862, Pittsylvania, Virginia	Co. J, 21st Virginia Infantry	May 12, 1864, Near Spotsylvania Court House, Virginia	Point Lookout, Maryland, transferred to Elmira Prison, NY August 6, 1864	Died March 7, 1865 of Diarrhea, Grave No. 2412

Name & Rank	Age	Enlisted	Regiment and State	Where Captured	Prison	Remarks
Cox, Edward A. Private	26	March 24, 1862, McDowell, North Carolina	Co. A, 49th North Carolina Infantry	May 16, 1864, Near Drury's Bluff, Virginia	Point Lookout, Maryland, transferred to Elmira Prison, NY August 18, 1864	Exchanged March 14, 1865 at Boulware's Wharf on the James River, Virginia
Cox, George Private	20	August 1, 1861, Carthage, North Carolina	Co. E, 8th North Carolina Infantry	May 31, 1864, Cold Harbor, Virginia	Point Lookout, Maryland, transferred to Elmira Prison, NY July 11, 1864	Oath of Allegiance June 19, 1865
Cox, George C. Private	Unk	Unknown	Co. E, 50th Virginia Infantry	May 5, 1864, Wilderness, Virginia	Point Lookout, Maryland, transferred to Elmira Prison, NY August 14, 1864	Oath of Allegiance May 15, 1865
Cox, George L. Private	27	April 1, 1862, Fredericks-burg, Virginia	Co. H, 50th Virginia Infantry	May 5, 1864, Wilderness, Virginia	Point Lookout, Maryland, transferred to Elmira Prison, NY August 14, 1864	Oath of Allegiance June 27, 1865
Cox, Isaac B. Private	17	November 24, 1863, Fort Pender, North Carolina	Co. B, 36th Regiment, 2nd North Carolina Artillery	January 15, 1865, Fort Fisher, North Carolina. Wounded	February 1, 1865, Elmira Prison Camp, New York	Died March 21, 1865 of Pneumonia, Grave No. 1542
Cox, J. M. Private	18	January 8, 1863, Wilmington, North Carolina	Co. B, 31st North Carolina Infantry	June 1, 1864, Cold Harbor, Virginia	Point Lookout, Maryland, transferred to Elmira Prison, NY July 17,1864	Exchanged March 10, 1865 at Boulware's wharf on the James River, Virginia
Cox, Jacob S. Private	19	July 16, 1861, Staunton, Virginia	Co. I, 52nd Virginia Infantry	May 30, 1864 Mechanics-ville, Virginia	Point Lookout, Maryland, transferred to Elmira Prison, NY July 8, 1864	Oath of Allegiance June 30, 1865
Cox, James Private	Unk	January 10, 1862, Columbia, South Carolina	Co. C, 22nd South Carolina Infantry	July 30, 1864, Petersburg, Virginia	Point Lookout, Maryland, transferred to Elmira Prison, NY August 12, 1864	Oath of Allegiance June 21, 1865
Cox, James C. Private	Unk	Unknown	Co. K, 63rd Tennessee Infantry	Unknown	Unknown	Died April 16, 1865 of Unknown Disease, Grave No. 2719

Name & Rank	Age	Enlisted	Regiment and State	Where Captured	Prison	Remarks
Cox, James W. Private	Unk	March 8, 1861, Tallapoosa, Alabama	Co. E, 1st Battalion Alabama Artillery	August 23, 1864, Fort Morgan, Alabama	New Orleans, Louisiana transferred to Elmira December 4, 1864.	Oath of Allegiance June 21, 1865
Cox, John G. Sergeant	21	December 21, 1861, Springfield, Missouri	Co. C, 1st Missouri Cavalry	May 17, 1863, Big Black Bridge, Champion Hill, Mississippi	Point Lookout, Maryland, transferred to Elmira Prison, NY August 18, 1864	Exchanged February 25, 1865 at Boulware's or Cox Wharf on the James River, Virginia
Cox, John M. Private	Unk	October 16, 1863, Camp Vance, North Carolina	Co. H, 28th North Carolina Infantry	July 29, 1864, Petersburg, Virginia	Point Lookout, Maryland, transferred to Elmira Prison, NY August 12, 1864	Died September 5, 1864 of Chronic Diarrhea, Grave No. 223.
Cox, John W. Private	30	March 11, 1862, Grogansville, North Carolina	Co. A, 45th North Carolina Infantry	May 20, 1864, Spotsylvania Court House, Virginia	Point Lookout, Maryland, transferred to Elmira Prison, NY July 6, 1864	Exchanged March 14, 1865 at Boulware's Wharf on the James River, Virginia
Cox, Maderson A. Private	Unk	Unknown	Co. E, 50th Virginia Infantry	May 12, 1864, Spotsylvania Court House, Virginia	Point Lookout, Maryland, transferred to Elmira Prison, NY August 2, 1864	Oath of Allegiance June 27, 1865
Cox, N. S. Sergeant	Unk	Unknown	Co. C, 50th Virginia Infantry	May 12, 1864 Spotsylvania Court House, Virginia	Point Lookout, Maryland, transferred to Elmira Prison, NY August 2, 1864	Exchanged March 2, 1865 at Akins Landing on the James River, Virginia
Cox, Newell G. Private	26	May 4, 1861, Francisco, Stokes County, North Carolina	Co. A, 2nd Battalion North Carolina Infantry	May 12, 1864, Near Spotsylvania County Court House, Virginia	Point Lookout, Maryland, transferred to Elmira Prison, NY August 14, 1864	Exchanged March 14, 1865 at Boulware's Wharf on the James River, Virginia
Cox, Peter B. Private	23	September 15, 1862, Raleigh, North Carolina	Co. B, 31st North Carolina Infantry	June 1, 1864, Cold Harbor, Virginia	Point Lookout, Maryland, transferred to Elmira Prison, NY July 17, 1864	Died April 16, 1865 of Chronic Diarrhea, Grave No. 2715

Name & Rank	Age	Enlisted	Regiment and State	Where Captured	Prison	Remarks
Cox, Phillip D. Sergeant	Unk	Unknown	Co. E, 50th Virginia Infantry	May 5, 1864, Wilderness, Virginia	Point Lookout, Maryland, transferred to Elmira Prison, NY August 14, 1864	Oath of Allegiance June 27, 1865
Cox, Prior J. Sergeant	Unk	Unknown	Co. D, 42nd Virginia Infantry	May 12, 1864, Near Spotsylvania Court House, Virginia	Point Lookout, Maryland, transferred to Elmira Prison, NY August 6, 1864	Transferred For Exchange October 11, 1864 to Point Lookout Prison Camp, MD. Nothing Further.
Cox, S. V. B. Private	Unk	May 11, 1861, New Orleans, Louisiana	Co. H, 2nd Louisiana Infantry	May 12, 1864, Spotsylvania Court House, Virginia	Point Lookout, Maryland, transferred to Elmira Prison, NY August 17, 1864	Exchanged February 13, 1865 at Boulware's wharf on the James River, Virginia
Cox, Solomon V. Private	Unk	March 8, 1861, Tallapoosa, Alabama	Co. K, 37th North Carolina Infantry	May 12, 1864, Spotsylvania Court House, Virginia	Point Lookout, Maryland, transferred to Elmira, New York, August 17, 1864	Exchanged February 20, 1865 at Boulware's or Cox Wharf on the James River, Virginia
Cox, Thomas E. Private	Unk	March 8, 1861, Tallapoosa, Alabama	Co. E, 1st Battalion Alabama Artillery	August 23, 1864, Fort Morgan, Alabama	New Orleans, Louisiana transferred to Elmira December 4, 1864.	Oath of Allegiance May 13, 1865
Cox, Thomas J. Private	Unk	Unknown	Co. E, 50th Virginia Infantry	May 12, 1864, Spotsylvania Court House, Virginia	Point Lookout, Maryland, transferred to Elmira Prison, NY August 2, 1864	Died January 27, 1865 of Variola (smallpox), Grave No. 1638
Cox, W. A. Ordinance Sergeant	Unk	May 20, 1861, Hamer, Georgia	Co. A, 24th Georgia Infantry	May 6, 1864, Wilderness, Virginia	Point Lookout, Maryland, transferred to Elmira Prison, NY August 14, 1864	Oath of Allegiance June 21, 1865
Cox, W. C. Corporal	Unk	May 11, 1861, New Orleans, Louisiana	Co. A, 2nd Louisiana Infantry	May 12, 1864, Spotsylvania Court House, Virginia	Point Lookout, Maryland, transferred to Elmira Prison, NY August 14, 1864	Exchanged February 13, 1865 at Boulware's on the James River, Virginia

Name & Rank	Age	Enlisted	Regiment and State	Where Captured	Prison	Remarks
Cox, William Private	30	February 1, 1862, Salisbury, North Carolina	Co. C, 42nd North Carolina Infantry	June 3, 1864, Cold Harbor, Virginia	Point Lookout, Maryland, transferred to Elmira Prison, NY July 17,1864	Oath of Allegiance June 11, 1865
Cox, William Montgomery Private	17	December 25, 1861, Springfield, Missouri	Co. K, 1st Missouri Cavalry	May 17, 1863, Big Black Bridge, Champion Hill, Mississippi	Point Lookout, Maryland, transferred to Elmira Prison, NY August 18, 1864	Exchanged February 13, 1865 at Boulware's wharf on the James River, Virginia
Cox, William Jr. Private	Unk	June 10, 1861, Athens, Alabama	Co. H, 9th Alabama Infantry	May 6, 1864, Wilderness, Virginia	Point Lookout, Maryland, transferred to Elmira Prison, NY August 17, 1864	Oath of Allegiance June 14, 1865
Coxswell, John D. Corporal	Unk	July 4, Gibson County, Georgia	Co. A, 7th Battalion Georgia Cavalry	June 11, 1864, Trevilian Station, Louisa Court House, Virginia	Point Lookout, Maryland, transferred to Elmira Prison, NY July 25, 1864	Exchanged March 10, 1865 at Boulware's Wharf on the James River, Virginia
Coyle, H. W. Private	Unk	Unknown	6th Field Battery Louisiana Light Artillery	August 8, 1864, Williamsport, Louisiana	New Orleans, Louisiana, Transferred to Fort Columbus, NY Harbor Transferred to Elmira November 5, 1864	Exchanged February 25, 1865 at Boulware's or Cox Wharf on the James River, Virginia
Cozzens, Richard W. Private	Unk	September 23, 1861, Washington, Beaufort County, North Carolina	Co. D, 13th Battalion, North Carolina Light Artillery	January 15, 1865, Fort Fisher, North Carolina	February 1, 1865, Elmira Prison Camp, New York	Died March 19, 1865 of Variola (Smallpox), Grave No. 1565
Cozzens, Richard M. Private	Unk	February 10, 1862, New Orleans, Louisiana	Co. A, Miles' Legion Louisiana	October 2, 1864, Hermitage Plantation Amite River, Louisiana	New Orleans, Louisiana transferred to Elmira November 19, 1864.	Oath of Allegiance May 17, 1865
Cozzens, Thomas F. Private	Unk	September 23, 1861, Washington, Beaufort County, North Carolina	Co. D, 13th Battalion, North Carolina Light Artillery	January 15, 1865, Fort Fisher, North Carolina	February 1, 1865, Elmira Prison Camp, New York	Died April 6, 1865 of Remittent Fever, Grave No. 2639

Name & Rank	Age	Enlisted	Regiment and State	Where Captured	Prison	Remarks
Crabtree, Albert M. Corporal	Unk	August 23, 1861, Camp Trousdale, Tennessee	Co. D, 23rd Tennessee Infantry	June 17, 1864, Petersburg, Virginia	Point Lookout, Maryland, transferred to Elmira Prison, NY July 30, 1864	Died February 21, 1865 of Pneumonia, Grave No. 2319
Crabtree, Gaston Private	30	May 15, 1862, Camp McIntosh, North Carolina	Co. D, 1st North Carolina Infantry	May 12, 1864, Spotsylvania Court House, Virginia	Point Lookout, Maryland, transferred to Elmira Prison, NY August 6, 1864	Died November 1, 1864 of Chronic Diarrhea, Grave No. 748. Headstone has 22nd NC.
Crabtree, Jerome W. Private	Unk	November 19, 1862, Estill Springs, Tennessee	Co. K, 44th Tennessee Infantry	June 17, 1864, Petersburg, Virginia	Point Lookout, Maryland, transferred to Elmira Prison, NY July 30, 1864	Exchanged February 25, 1865 at Boulware's or Cox Wharf on the James River, Virginia
Crabtree, John J. Private	Unk	December 7, 1861, Camp Trousdale, Tennessee	Co. B, 44th Tennessee Infantry	June 17, 1864, Petersburg, Virginia	Point Lookout, Maryland, transferred to Elmira Prison, NY July 30, 1864	Exchanged October 11, 1864. Nothing Further.
Crabtree, Thomas Private	38	March 1, 1862, Hillsboro, North Carolina	Co. D, 1st North Carolina Infantry	May 12, 1864, Spotsylvania Court House, Virginia	Point Lookout, Maryland, transferred to Elmira Prison, NY August 6, 1864	Oath of Allegiance June 21, 1865
Crabtree, Walter W. Private	19	July 28, 1861, Cedar Fork, North Carolina	Co. G, 7th North Carolina Infantry	May 6, 1864, Wilderness, Virginia	Point Lookout, Maryland, transferred to Elmira Prison, NY August 14, 1864	Oath of Allegiance June 23, 1865
Craddock, Ainsley W. Private	Unk	Unknown	Co. E, 66th North Carolina Infantry	August 31, 1863, Big Black, Mississippi	Point Lookout, Maryland, transferred to Elmira Prison, NY August 18, 1864	Exchanged October 29, 1864 at Venus Point, Savannah River, GA.
Cradock, Peter J. Private	Unk	June 22, 1861, Wytheville, Virginia	Co. K, 50th Virginia Infantry	May 5, 1864, Wilderness, Virginia	Point Lookout, Maryland, transferred to Elmira Prison, NY August 14, 1864	Oath of Allegiance June 23, 1865

Name & Rank	Age	Enlisted	Regiment and State	Where Captured	Prison	Remarks
Craft, Frederick Private	Unk	November 11, 1864, North Carolina	Co. A, 35th North Carolina Infantry	June 17, 1864, Petersburg, Virginia	Point Lookout Prison Camp, Maryland. Transferred to Elmira Prison Camp, NY, July 30, 1864	Died April 13, 1865 of Variola (Smallpox), Grave No. 2699
Craft, George W. Private	Unk	May 17, 1861, Montgomery, Alabama	Co. C, 6th Alabama Infantry	May 6, 1864, Wilderness, Virginia	Point Lookout, Maryland, transferred to Elmira Prison, NY August 17, 1864	Died May 19, 1865 of Chronic Diarrhea, Grave No. 2949
Craig, George Private	Unk	June 11, 1861, Pickens County, Alabama	Co. F, 11th Alabama Infantry	May 13, 1864, Spotsylvania Court House, Virginia	Point Lookout, Maryland, transferred to Elmira Prison, NY August 17, 1864	Oath of Allegiance June 19, 1865
Craig, J. T. B. Corporal	Unk	April 30, 1864, Lancaster County Court House, South Carolina	Co. I, 17th South Carolina Infantry	July 30, 1864, Near Petersburg, Virginia	Point Lookout, Maryland, transferred to Elmira Prison, NY August 12, 1864	Oath of Allegiance July 3, 1865
Craig, John S. Private	18	March 1, 1863, Camp Gregg, North Carolina	Co. C, 18th North Carolina Infantry	May 12, 1864, Spotsylvania Court House, Virginia	Point Lookout, Maryland, transferred to Elmira Prison, NY August 6, 1864	Exchanged March 2, 1865 at Akins Landing on the James River, Virginia
Craig, Joseph T. Private	20	August 28, 1861, Memphis, Tennessee	Co. B, Woods Regiment, Confederate Cavalry	May 16, 1862, Champion Hill, Mississippi	Point Lookout, Maryland, transferred to Elmira Prison, NY August 18, 1864	Exchanged March 10, 1865 at Boulware's wharf on the James River, Virginia
Craig, Leslie C. Private	Unk	June 13, 1861, Monroe, Georgia	Co. C, 9th Georgia Infantry	July 5, 1864, Rockville, Maryland	Old Capital Prison, Washington, DC. Transferred to Elmira Prison Camp July 25, 1864	Died October 6, 1864 of Typhoid-Pneumonia, Grave No. 649
Craig, Peter D. Private	Unk	March 10, 1862, Henry County, Virginia	Co. G, 42nd Virginia Infantry	May 12, 1864, Near Spotsylvania Court House, Virginia	Point Lookout, Maryland, transferred to Elmira Prison, NY August 6, 1864	Exchanged February 20, 1865 at Boulware's or Cox Wharf on the James River, Virginia

Name & Rank	Age	Enlisted	Regiment and State	Where Captured	Prison	Remarks
Craig, Thomas R. Sergeant	Unk	March 10, 1862, Henry County, Virginia	Co. G, 42nd Virginia Infantry	May 12, 1864, Near Spotsylvania Court House, Virginia	Point Lookout, Maryland, transferred to Elmira Prison, NY August 6, 1864	Oath of Allegiance June 27, 1865
Craig, William P. Private	Unk	May 18, 1861, Lisbon, Virginia	Co. C, 42nd Virginia Infantry	May 12, 1864, Spotsylvania Court House, Virginia	Point Lookout, Maryland, transferred to Elmira Prison, NY August 2,1864	Exchanged February 20, 1865 at Boulware's or Cox Wharf on the James River, Virginia
Craige, James F. Private	25	September 2, 1861, Orange County, North Carolina	Co. G, 28th North Carolina Infantry	May 12, 1864, Spotsylvania, Virginia	Point Lookout, Maryland, transferred to Elmira Prison, NY August 12, 1864	Oath of Allegiance July 3, 1865
Cranage, William H. Corporal	Unk	April 14, 1862, Fredericks-burg, Virginia	Co. C, 15th Battalion Virginia Cavalry	October 26, 1864, King George County, Virginia	Old Capital Prison, Washington, DC, transferred to Elmira Prison, NY, December 17, 1864	Exchanged February 13, 1865 at Boulware's Wharf on the James River, Virginia
Crandell, Robert C. Private	33	July 13, 1861, Pitt County, North Carolina	Co. G, 8th North Carolina Infantry	June 1, 1864, Cold Harbor, Virginia	Point Lookout, Maryland, transferred to Elmira Prison, NY July 17,1864	Oath of Allegiance July 3, 1865
Cratch, William H. Private	Unk	May 9, 1861, New Orleans, Louisiana	Co. H, 2nd Louisiana Infantry	May 12, 1864, Wilderness, Virginia	Point Lookout, Maryland, transferred to Elmira Prison, NY August 15, 1864	Oath of Allegiance June 24, 1865
Crauford, John J. Private	Unk	March 24, 1862, Covington, Louisiana	Co. C, Miles Legion Louisiana	October 7, 1864, Osyka, Mississippi	New Orleans, Louisiana transferred to Elmira November 19, 1864.	Exchanged February 13, 1865 at Boulware's Wharf on the James River, Virginia
Craven, Benjamin Private	25	July 17, 1862, Randolph County, North Carolina	Co. H, 3rd North Carolina Infantry	May 12, 1864, Near Spotsylvania Court House, Virginia	Point Lookout, Maryland, transferred to Elmira Prison, NY August 14, 1864	Died February 17, 1865 of Pneumonia, Grave No. 2356

Name & Rank	Age	Enlisted	Regiment and State	Where Captured	Prison	Remarks
Craven, Thomas Private	Unk	March 19, 1862, Walterboro, South Carolina	Co. J, 11th South Carolina Infantry	June 24, 1864, Near Petersburg, Virginia	Point Lookout, Maryland, transferred to Elmira Prison, NY August 18, 1864	Died December 2, 1864 of Chronic Diarrhea, Grave No. 1010
Crawford, Charles R. Private	20	February 19, 1862, Centreville, Virginia	Co. F, 26th Battalion, Virginia Infantry	June 3, 1864, Gaines Farm, Cold Harbor, Virginia	Point Lookout, Maryland, transferred to Elmira Prison, NY July 17, 1864	Exchanged March 14, 1865 at Boulware's Wharf on the James River, Virginia
Crawford, Emmett Private	Unk	February 10, 1863, Port Royal, Virginia	Co. F, 31st Virginia Infantry	May 30, 1864, Old Church, Virginia	Point Lookout, Maryland, transferred to Elmira Prison, NY July 11, 1864	Oath of Allegiance June 14, 1865
Crawford, Franklin M. Sergeant	Unk	June 1, 1861, Buena Vista, Georgia	Co. G, 59th Georgia Infantry	May 6, 1864, Wilderness, Virginia	Point Lookout, Maryland, transferred to Elmira Prison, NY August 14, 1864	Oath of Allegiance June 14, 1865
Crawford, Henry C. Corporal	18	December 20, 1861, Orange County, North Carolina	Co. G, 28th North Carolina Infantry	May 12, 1864, Spotsylvania Court House, Virginia	Point Lookout, Maryland, transferred to Elmira Prison, NY August 12, 1864	Oath of Allegiance June 30, 1865
Crawford, James M. Private	32	March 21, 1862, Charleston, South Carolina	Co. B, 18th South Carolina Infantry	July 30, 1864, Petersburg, Virginia	Point Lookout, Maryland, transferred to Elmira Prison, NY August 12, 1864	Exchanged October 29, 1864 at Venus Point, Savannah River, GA.
Crawford, James W. Private	Unk	September 1, 1862, Gainesville, Virginia	Co. B, 6th Virginia Cavalry	June 4, 1864, White Oak Swamp, Virginia	Point Lookout, Maryland, transferred to Elmira Prison, NY July 8, 1864	Escaped October 7, 1864 by Tunneling Under Fence.
Crawford, Jasper H. Private	Unk	July 15, 1862, Hendersonville, North Carolina	Co. D, 6th North Carolina Cavalry	June 22, 1864, Jackson's Mills, Near Kinston, North Carolina	Point Lookout, Maryland, transferred to Elmira Prison, NY July 25, 1864	Oath of Allegiance July 3, 1865
Crawford, John Private	27	May 14, 1862, Sullivan County, Tennessee	Co. F, 63rd Tennessee Infantry	June 17, 1864, Petersburg, Virginia	Point Lookout, Maryland, transferred to Elmira Prison, NY July 25, 1864	Oath of Allegiance May 29, 1865

Name & Rank	Age	Enlisted	Regiment and State	Where Captured	Prison	Remarks
Crawford, John A. Private	18	April 11, 1863, Centreville, Virginia	Co. F, 26th Battalion, Virginia Infantry	June 3, 1864, Gaines Farm, Cold Harbor, Virginia	Point Lookout, Maryland, transferred to Elmira Prison, NY July 17, 1864	Exchanged March 14, 1865 at Boulware's Wharf on the James River, Virginia
Crawford, Joseph H. Private	21	August 10, 1863, Camp Sam Jones, Virginia	Co. F, 26th Battalion, Virginia Infantry	June 3, 1864, Gaines Farm, Cold Harbor, Virginia	Point Lookout, Maryland, transferred to Elmira Prison, NY July 17, 1864	Died September 7, 1864 of Chronic Diarrhea, Grave No. 216
Crawford, Mathias Private	Unk	September 25, 1863, Goldsboro, North Carolina	Co. F, 10th Regiment, 1st North Carolina Artillery	January 15, 1865, Fort Fisher, North Carolina	January 30, 1865, Elmira Prison Camp, NY	Died March 12, 1865 of Pneumonia, Grave No. 1818
Crawford, Thomas C. Private	Unk	January 12, 1864, Columbus, South Carolina	Co. E, 1st South Carolina Infantry	April 2, 1865, Petersburg, Virginia. Gunshot Wounds Left Hip and Chest.	Old Capital Prison, Washington D. C. Transferred to Elmira Prison, NY May 2, 1865.	Oath of Allegiance July 7, 1865
Crawford, W. H. Sergeant	Unk	June 21, 1862, Savannah, Georgia	Co. E, 7th Georgia Cavalry	June 11, 1864, Trevilian Station, Louisa Court House, Virginia	Point Lookout, Maryland, transferred to Elmira Prison, NY July 25, 1864	Exchanged October 29, 1864, at Venus Point, Savannah River, GA.
Crawford, William Private	Unk	May 1, 1863, Calhoun County, Georgia	Co. E, 51st Georgia Infantry	June 3, 1864, Gaines Farm, Cold Harbor, Virginia	Point Lookout, Maryland, transferred to Elmira Prison, NY July 17,1864	Exchanged March 10, 1865 at Boulware's wharf on the James River, Virginia
Crawford, William E. Private	Unk	April 11, 1862, Coles Island, South Carolina	Co. G, 25th South Carolina Infantry	January 15, 1865, Fort Fisher, North Carolina	Elmira Prison Camp January 30, 1865	Died March 7, 1865 of Pneumonia, Grave No. 2406
Crawford, William H. Corporal	24	April 18, 1862, Pitt County, North Carolina	Co. C, 44th North Carolina Infantry	June 1, 1864, Hanover Junction, Virginia	Point Lookout, Maryland, transferred to Elmira Prison, NY July 17,1864	Exchanged October 29, 1864, at Venus Point, Savannah River, GA.
Crawley, Hider D. Private	18	February 18, 1862, Newbern, North Carolina	Co. F, 36th Regiment, 2nd North Carolina Artillery	January 15, 1865, Fort Fisher, North Carolina. Wounded	February 1, 1865, Elmira Prison Camp, New York	Died on Route to be Exchanged February 20, 1865.

Name & Rank	Age	Enlisted	Regiment and State	Where Captured	Prison	Remarks
Crayton, Lemuel R. Corporal	Unk	June 1, 1863, Tallapoosa County, Alabama	Co. C, 61st Alabama Infantry	May 12, 1864, Spotsylvania Court House, Virginia	Point Lookout, Maryland, transferred to Elmira Prison, NY July 30, 1864	Oath of Allegiance June 19, 1865
Creech, Doctor L. Private	Unk	February 7, 1862, Bennettsville, South Carolina	Co. F, 21st South Carolina Infantry	January 15, 1865, Fort Fisher, North Carolina	Elmira Prison Camp January 30, 1865	Died June 3, 1865, Chronic Diarrhea, Grave No. 2900
Creekmore, Alexander O. Private	Unk	July 11, 1862, Norfolk County, Virginia	Co. F, 15th Virginia Cavalry	September 14, 1863, Near Culpepper, Virginia	Point Lookout, Maryland, transferred to Elmira Prison, NY August 18, 1864	Died September 26, 1864 of Chronic Diarrhea, Grave No. 452
Creekmore, Malachi Private	Unk	January 1, 1864, Orange County, Virginia	Co. F, 15th Virginia Cavalry	May 12, 1864, Mechanics-ville, Virginia	Point Lookout, Maryland, transferred to Elmira Prison, NY August 17, 1864	Died September 22, 1864 of Typhoid-Pneumonia, Grave No. 490
Creekmore, R. M. Private	Unk	Unknown	Co. C, Virginia Legion Infantry	June 4, 1864, Gaines Farm, Cold Harbor, Virginia	Point Lookout, Maryland, transferred to Elmira Prison, NY July 17,1864	Oath of Allegiance July 3, 1865
Creel, Jam J. Private	32	July 15, 1862, Raleigh, North Carolina	Co. E, 3rd North Carolina Infantry	May 12, 1864, Near Spotsylvania, Virginia	Point Lookout, Maryland, transferred to Elmira Prison, NY August 14, 1864	Oath of Allegiance June 23, 1865
Creese, R. J. Sergeant	Unk	Unknown	Co. K, 8th North Carolina Infantry	Unknown	Unknown	Died April 28, 1865 of Unknown Disease, Grave No. 2732
Cremer, Adam Private	Unk	June 11, 1861, Hevener's Store, Virginia	Co. F, 25th Virginia Infantry	May 5, 1864, Wilderness, Virginia	Point Lookout, Maryland, transferred to Elmira Prison, NY August 14, 1864	Died May 18, 1865 of Dysentery, Grave No. 2950. Name Cremer on Headstone.
Crenshaw, John T. Private	24	May 24, 1861, Appomattox Court House, Virginia	Co. H, 2nd Virginia Cavalry	May 28, 1864, Hall's Shop, Virginia	Point Lookout, Maryland, transferred to Elmira Prison, NY July 8, 1864	Exchanged October 29, 1864, at Venus Point, Savannah River, GA.

Name & Rank	Age	Enlisted	Regiment and State	Where Captured	Prison	Remarks
Crenshaw, Samuel Private	26	July 20, 1861, Camp Pickens, Anderson District, South Carolina	Co. C, 1st South Carolina Infantry	July 14, 1863, Falling Waters, Maryland	Point Lookout, Maryland, transferred to Elmira Prison, NY August 18, 1864	Exchanged March 10, 1865 at Boulware's Wharf on the James River, Virginia
Crenshaw, William W. Corporal	Unk	May 31, 1861, Yellow Branch, Virginia	Co. D, 42nd Virginia Infantry	May 12, 1864, Near Spotsylvania Court House, Virginia	Point Lookout, Maryland, transferred to Elmira Prison, NY August 6, 1864	Oath of Allegiance July 3, 1865
Crepps, Monroe Private	41	August 8, 1862, Camp Hill, Stanley County, North Carolina	Co. F, 5th North Carolina Infantry	May 20, 1864, Near Spotsylvania Court House, Virginia	Point Lookout Prison Camp, Maryland. Transferred to Elmira Prison, NY, July 6, 1864	Died February 27, 1865 of Variola (Smallpox), Grave No. 2128
Cress, John A. Private	20	August 20, 1862, Raleigh, North Carolina	Co. G, 7th North Carolina Infantry	May 6, 1864, Wilderness, Virginia	Point Lookout, Maryland, transferred to Elmira Prison, NY July 23, 1864	Died September 16, 1864 of Chronic Diarrhea, Grave No. 298
Creswell, John W. Private	27	May 7, 1861, New Prospect, Virginia	Co. C, 26th Virginia Infantry	June 16, 1864, Webb's Farm, Near Petersburg, Virginia	Point Lookout, Maryland, transferred to Elmira Prison, NY July 23, 1864	Oath of Allegiance May 29, 1865
Crew, Thomas A. Private	20	May 16, 1861, Gloucester Point, Virginia	Co. A, 26th Virginia Infantry	June 15, 1864, Near Petersburg, Virginia	Point Lookout, Maryland, transferred to Elmira Prison, NY July 30, 1864	Oath of Allegiance July 3, 1865
Crewes, M. L. Private	Unk	September 22, 1862, Waynesville, Georgia	Co. G, 7th Georgia Cavalry	June 11, 1864, Trevilian Station, Louisa Court House, Virginia	Point Lookout, Maryland, transferred to Elmira Prison, NY July 25, 1864	Died October 9, 1864 of Chronic Diarrhea, Grave No. 655
Crews, David P. Private	Unk	February 20, 1864, Campbell County, Virginia	Co. I, 42nd Virginia Infantry	May 12, 1864 Spotsylvania Court House, Virginia	Point Lookout, Maryland, transferred to Elmira Prison, NY August 2, 1864	Oath of Allegiance June 27, 1865

Name & Rank	Age	Enlisted	Regiment and State	Where Captured	Prison	Remarks
Crews, Richard R. Private	Unk	February 24, 1864, Camp Pisgah, Virginia	Co. I, 42nd Virginia Infantry	May 12, 1864 Spotsylvania Court House, Virginia	Point Lookout, Maryland, transferred to Elmira Prison, NY August 2, 1864	Exchanged October 29, 1864 at Venus Point, Savannah River, GA.
Crews, Thomas W. Private	17	August 15, 1861, Carrollton, Georgia	Co. F, Cobb's Legion Georgia	August 16, 1864, Front Royal, Virginia	Old Capital Prison, Washington, DC transferred to Elmira Prison, NY August 29, 1864	Exchanged March 10, 1865 at Boulware's Wharf on the James River, Virginia
Cribb, A. J. Private	Unk	January 1, 1862, Camp Harlee, Georgetown, South Carolina	Co. A, 21st South Carolina Infantry	January 15, 1865, Fort Fisher, North Carolina	Elmira Prison Camp January 30, 1865	Oath of Allegiance July 7, 1865
Cribb, Isham G. Private	17	March 20, 1862, Whiteville, North Carolina	Co. H, 51st North Carolina Infantry	June 1, 1864, Cold Harbor, Virginia	Point Lookout, Maryland, transferred to Elmira Prison, NY July 17,1864	Exchanged March 2, 1865 at Akins Landing on the James River, Virginia
Crickenberger, Daniel D. Sergeant	Unk	April 18, 1861, Harrisonburg, Virginia	Co. G, 10th Virginia Infantry	May 12, 1864, Spotsylvania Court House, Virginia	Point Lookout, Maryland, transferred to Elmira Prison, NY August 2, 1864	Oath of Allegiance June 21, 1865
Crickman, Josiah G. Private	17	September 10, 1861, Nash County, North Carolina	Co. J, 30th, North Carolina Infantry	May 12, 1864, Spotsylvania Court House, Virginia	Point Lookout, Maryland, transferred to Elmira Prison, NY July 6, 1864	Oath of Allegiance June 27, 1865
Crickman, Solomon Private	19	January 27, 1862, Newbern, North Carolina	Co. F, 36th Regiment, 2nd North Carolina Artillery	January 15, 1865, Fort Fisher, North Carolina. Wounded	February 1, 1865, Elmira Prison Camp, New York	Oath of Allegiance July 11, 1865
Criswell, Jacob D. Private	28	July 4, 1862, Salisbury, North Carolina	Co. C, 57th North Carolina Infantry	July 8, 1864, Near Harper's Ferry, Virginia	Old Capital Prison, Washington, DC, transferred to Elmira Prison, NY, July 23, 1864	Died August 22, 1864 of Scorbutus (Scurvy), Grave No. 30

Name & Rank	Age	Enlisted	Regiment and State	Where Captured	Prison	Remarks
Crites, Elam T. Sergeant	Unk	May 27, 1861, Buckhannon, Virginia	Co. B, 25th Virginia Infantry	May 12, 1864, Spotsylvania Court House, Virginia	Point Lookout, Maryland, transferred to Elmira Prison, NY August 12, 1864	Oath of Allegiance June 16, 1865
Croak, John Private	27	June 9, 1861, Camp Moore, Louisiana	Co. J, 15th Louisiana Infantry	May 12, 1864, Spotsylvania, Virginia	Old Capital Prison, Washington, DC, transferred to Elmira Prison, NY, July 23, 1864	Exchanged October 29, 1864, at Venus Point, Savannah River, GA.
Crocker, William D. Landsman	Unk	Unknown	Confederate States Navy	May 5, 1864, Albemarle Sound on Steamer CSS Bombshell	Point Lookout, Maryland, transferred to Elmira Prison, NY August 17, 1864	Died March 25, 1865 of Rheumatism, Grave No. 2455
Crocker, William J. Private	30	August 15, 1862, Iredell County, North Carolina	Co. J, 37th North Carolina Infantry	May 12, 1864, Spotsylvania Court House, Virginia	Point Lookout, Maryland, transferred to Elmira Prison, NY August 12, 1864	Transferred for Exchange 10/11/64. Died 11/3/64 of Chronic Diarrhea at Point Lookout, MD.
Croft, Jacob Corporal	Unk	July 15, 1861, Staunton, Virginia	Co. A, 52nd Virginia Infantry	May 30, 1864, Mechanics-ville, Virginia	Point Lookout, Maryland, transferred to Elmira Prison, NY July 8, 1864	Oath of Allegiance June 30, 1865
Croft, Jacob S. Private	Unk	July 16, 1861, Staunton, Virginia	Co. A, 52nd Virginia Infantry	May 30, 1864, Mechanics-ville, Virginia	Point Lookout, Maryland, transferred to Elmira Prison, NY July 8, 1864	Oath of Allegiance June 30, 1865
Croft, William Y. Private	Unk	December 4, 1861, Mountain Spring, Anderson District, South Carolina	Co. D, 18th South Carolina Infantry	July 30, 1864, Petersburg, Virginia	Point Lookout, Maryland, transferred to Elmira Prison, NY August 12, 1864	Oath of Allegiance July 3, 1865
Croley, Thomas A. Private	Unk	August 14, 1862, Tallapoosa County, Alabama	Co. C, 5th Alabama Infantry	May 8, 1864, Wilderness, Virginia	Point Lookout, Maryland, transferred to Elmira Prison, NY August 17, 1864	Exchanged October 29, 1864 at Venus Point, Savannah River, GA.

Name & Rank	Age	Enlisted	Regiment and State	Where Captured	Prison	Remarks
Cromell, J. M. Civilian Telegraph Operator	Unk	Unknown	Louisiana Citizen	August 23, 1864, Fort Morgan, Alabama	Steam Press No. 4, New Orleans, Louisiana transferred to Elmira Prison, October 8, 1864.	Oath of Allegiance March 6, 1865. Early Release per Lincoln's Proclamation, 12/8/1863.
Cromwell, Lewis Private	Unk	June 8, 1861, New Orleans, Louisiana	Co. K, 15th Louisiana Infantry	May 12, 1864, Spotsylvania Court House, Virginia	Point Lookout, Maryland, transferred to Elmira Prison, NY July 6, 1864	Exchanged February 20, 1865 at Boulware's or Cox Wharf on the James River, Virginia
Crone, James Private	Unk	June 23, 1863, Lewisburg, Virginia	Co. B, 26th Battalion, Virginia Infantry	June 3, 1864, Gaines Mill, Cold Harbor, Virginia	Point Lookout, Maryland, transferred to Elmira Prison, NY July 17, 1864	Died September 5, 1864 of Chronic Diarrhea, Grave No. 236
Croom, John A. Private	31	April 18, 1862, Wilmington, North Carolina	Co. D, 10th Regiment, 1st Battalion North Carolina Heavy Artillery	January 15, 1865, Fort Fisher, North Carolina	February 1, 1865, Elmira Prison Camp, New York	Exchanged March 2, 1865 at Boulware's Wharf on the James River, Virginia
Croom, John F. Sergeant	20	May 17, 1861, Lower Black River District, North Carolina	Co. E, 18th North Carolina Infantry	May 12, 1864, Spotsylvania Court House, Virginia	Point Lookout, Maryland, transferred to Elmira Prison, NY August 6, 1864	Exchanged March 14, 1865 at Boulware's Wharf on the James River, Virginia
Croom, Judson W. Sergeant		February 8, 1862, Piney Woods, North Carolina	Co. A, 51st North Carolina Infantry	February 3, 1864, New Berne, North Carolina	Point Lookout, Maryland, transferred to Elmira Prison, NY July 17,1864	Oath of Allegiance May 25, 1865
Crooms, Isaac Private	Unk	May 23, 1863, Wilmington, North Carolina	Co. F, 10th Regiment, 1st North Carolina Artillery	January 15, 1865, Fort Fisher, North Carolina	January 30, 1865, Elmira Prison Camp, NY	Oath of Allegiance May 29, 1865
Crosby, Abraham Private	Unk	June 17, 1861, Waterboro, South Carolina	Co. J, 11th South Carolina Infantry	June 24, 1864, Near Petersburg, Virginia	Point Lookout, Maryland, transferred to Elmira Prison, NY August 18, 1864	Exchanged October 29, 1864, at Venus Point, Savannah River, GA.

Name & Rank	Age	Enlisted	Regiment and State	Where Captured	Prison	Remarks
Crosby, Alexander W. Sergeant	27	July 18, 1861, Bay Point, South Carolina	Co. E, 11th South Carolina Infantry	June 16, 1864, Petersburg, Virginia	Point Lookout, Maryland, transferred to Elmira Prison, NY July 25, 1864	Exchanged March 10, 1865 at Boulware's Wharf on the James River, Virginia
Crosby, J. N. Private	Unk	September 5, 1863, Calhoun, Mississippi	Co. B, 48th Mississippi Infantry	July 6, 1864, Rockville, Maryland	Old Capital Prison, Washington, DC, transferred to Elmira Prison, NY, July 23, 1864	Died September 26, 1864 of Chronic Diarrhea, Grave No. 455
Crosby, James D. Private	Unk	August 28, 1861, Walterboro, South Carolina	Co. J, 11th South Carolina Infantry	May 16, 1864, Drury's Bluff, Near Richmond, Virginia	Old Capital Prison, Washington, DC, transferred to Elmira Prison, NY, December 17, 1864	Exchanged March 14, 1865 at Boulware's Wharf on the James River, Virginia
Cross, Isaac Private	Unk	June 26, 1861, Scott County, Virginia	Co. H, 48th Virginia Infantry	May 12, 1864, Near Spotsylvania Court House, Virginia	Point Lookout, Maryland, transferred to Elmira Prison, NY August 6, 1864	Transferred for Exchange 10/11/64. Died 10/20/64 of Unknown Causes at Point Lookout, MD.
Cross, John A. Private	Unk	July 2, 1861, Bethel Am., Virginia	Co. F, 50th Virginia Infantry	May 12, 1864, Spotsylvania Court House, Virginia	Point Lookout, Maryland, transferred to Elmira Prison, NY August 2, 1864	Oath of Allegiance July 7, 1865
Cross, Sampson T. Private	38	February 20, 1863, Zollicoffer, Tennessee	Co. F, 63rd Tennessee Infantry	June 17, 1864, Petersburg, Virginia. Gunshot Wound Left Chest, Penetrating Lung.	Old Capital Prison, Washington, DC, transferred to Elmira Prison, NY, December 17, 1864	Exchanged February 20, 1865 at Boulware's or Cox Wharf on the James River, Virginia
Cross, William F. Private	35	November 28, 1862, Knoxville, Tennessee	Co. F, 63rd Tennessee Infantry	June 17, 1864, Petersburg, Virginia	Point Lookout, Maryland, transferred to Elmira Prison, NY July 30, 1864	Exchanged February 25, 1865 at Boulware's or Cox Wharf on the James River, Virginia

Name & Rank	Age	Enlisted	Regiment and State	Where Captured	Prison	Remarks
Crossland, William Private	Unk	December 9, 1861, Camp Trousdale, Tennessee	Co. D, 44th Tennessee Infantry	June 17, 1864, Petersburg, Virginia	Point Lookout, Maryland, transferred to Elmira Prison, NY July 30, 1864	Oath of Allegiance May 29, 1865
Crotty, Robert S. Private	Unk	April 29, 1863, White Sulfur Springs, Virginia	Co. B, 26th Battalion, Virginia Infantry	June 3, 1864, Gaines Mill, Cold Harbor, Virginia	Point Lookout, Maryland, transferred to Elmira Prison, NY July 17, 1864	Oath of Allegiance July 7, 1865
Crouch, John R. Private	21	August 18, 1862, Raleigh, North Carolina	Co. I, 2nd North Carolina Infantry	May 31, 1864, Mechanics-ville, Virginia	Point Lookout, Maryland, transferred to Elmira Prison, NY July 8, 1864	Died October 26, 1864 of Typhoid-Pneumonia, Grave No. 853
Crouch, John Y. Private	Unk	March 7, 1864, Camp Vance, North Carolina	Co. H, 13th North Carolina Infantry	May 6, 1864, Wilderness, Virginia	Point Lookout, Maryland, transferred to Elmira Prison, NY July 25, 1864	Oath of Allegiance May 29, 1865
Crouch, Thomas B. Private	Unk	August 24, 1862, Calhoun, Georgia	Co. D, 8th Georgia Infantry	May 31, 1864, Gaines Mill, Cold Harbor, Virginia	Point Lookout, Maryland, transferred to Elmira Prison, NY July 17, 1864	Died May 8, 1865 of Pneumonia, Grave No. 2775
Crouch, Thomas D. Private	Unk	February 4, 1862, Camp Winder, Goochland, Virginia	Co. H, 22nd Battalion Virginia Infantry	July 14, 1863, Falling Waters, Maryland	Point Lookout, Maryland, transferred to Elmira Prison, NY August 18, 1864	Exchanged March 10, 1865 at Boulware's Wharf on the James River, Virginia
Crough, Timothy Private	Unk	July 17, 1861, Camp Pulaski, Louisiana	Co. H, 14th Louisiana Infantry	May 5, 1864, Wilderness, Virginia	Point Lookout, Maryland, transferred to Elmira Prison, NY July 25, 1864	Exchanged February 18, 1865 at Akins Landing on the James River, Virginia
Croushon, David C. Private	23	April 13, 1863, Tazewell, Tennessee	Co. A, 63rd Tennessee Infantry	May 16, 1864, Near Drury's Bluff, Virginia	Point Lookout, Maryland, transferred to Elmira Prison, NY August 17, 1864	Exchanged February 25, 1865 at Boulware's or Cox Wharf on the James River, Virginia

Elmira Prison Camp Roster Volume I

Name & Rank	Age	Enlisted	Regiment and State	Where Captured	Prison	Remarks
Crow, F. I. Sergeant	Unk	May 4, 1862, Clarksville, Georgia	Co. K, 24th Georgia Infantry	August 16, 1864, Front Royal, Virginia	Old Capital Prison, Washington, DC transferred to Elmira Prison, NY August 29, 1864	Exchanged March 10, 1865 at Boulware's Wharf on the James River, Virginia
Crowder, Lucanus Private	20	October 13, 1861, Camp Mangum, Raleigh, North Carolina	Co. H, 31st North Carolina Infantry	June 1, 1864, Gaines Mill, Cold Harbor, Virginia	Point Lookout, Maryland, transferred to Elmira Prison, NY July 17,1864	Died October 4, 1864 Chronic Diarrhea, Grave No. 636
Crowell, Alfred N. Corporal	17	April 17, 1861, Newbern, Virginia	Co. C, 4th Virginia Infantry	May 12, 1864, Spotsylvania Court House, Virginia	Point Lookout, Maryland, transferred to Elmira Prison, NY August 2, 1864	Oath of Allegiance June 27, 1865
Crowell, James Private	36	March 15, 1862, Albemarle, North Carolina	Co. D, 28th North Carolina Infantry	May 12, 1864, Spotsylvania Court House, Virginia	Point Lookout, Maryland, transferred to Elmira Prison, NY August 12, 1864	Oath of Allegiance May 29, 1865
Crowell, Robert N. Private	19	June 18, 1861, Washington County, Virginia	Co. J, 48th Virginia Infantry	May 12, 1864, Near Spotsylvania Court House, Virginia	Point Lookout, Maryland, transferred to Elmira Prison, NY August 6, 1864	Oath of Allegiance June 21, 1865
Crowley, Daniel Corporal	Unk	October 13, 1861, Mobile, Alabama	Co. A, 21st Alabama Infantry	August 23, 1864, Fort Morgan, Alabama	Steam Press No. 4, New Orleans, Louisiana transferred to Elmira Prison, October 8, 1864.	Exchanged March 2, 1865 at Akins Landing on the James River, Virginia
Crowley, Timothy Civilian	Unk	Unknown	Citizen of Chester, Virginia	May 12, 1864, Chester, Virginia	Point Lookout, Maryland, transferred to Elmira Prison, NY July 25, 1864	Oath of Allegiance 11/12/64. Early Release per Lincoln's Proclamation, 12/8/1863.
Crownover, Joseph Private	Unk	March 5, 1861, Selma, Alabama	Co. C, 1st Battalion Alabama Artillery	August 23, 1864, Fort Morgan, Alabama	New Orleans, Louisiana transferred to Elmira December 4, 1864.	Died December 29, 1864 of Variola (Smallpox), Grave No. 1311

356

Name & Rank	Age	Enlisted	Regiment and State	Where Captured	Prison	Remarks
Crozier, Frederick W. Private	18	February 24, 1862, New Orleans, Louisiana	Co. C, 5th Louisiana Infantry	May 5, 1864, Wilderness, Virginia Gunshot Wound Right Thigh, Severe. Amputation Right Leg.	Old Capital Prison, Washington D. C. Transferred to Elmira Prison, NY August 12, 1864	Exchanged March 10, 1865 at Boulware's Wharf on the James River, Virginia
Crum, Jacob Private	Unk	July 16, 1861, Staunton, Virginia	Co. D, 52nd Virginia Infantry	May 5, 1864, Wilderness, Virginia	Point Lookout, Maryland, transferred to Elmira Prison, NY August 14, 1864	Exchanged March 14, 1865 at Boulware's Wharf on the James River, Virginia
Crump, Christopher C. Private	37	April 20, 1861, Belle Roi., Virginia	Co. A, 26th Virginia Infantry	June 15, 1864, Near Petersburg, Virginia	Point Lookout, Maryland, transferred to Elmira Prison, NY July 30, 1864	Oath of Allegiance June 23, 1865
Crump, Daniel Private	32	July 18, 1862, Camp Hill, Statesville, North Carolina	Co. C, 18th North Carolina Infantry	May 12, 1864, Spotsylvania Court House, Virginia	Point Lookout, Maryland, transferred to Elmira Prison, NY August 6, 1864	Exchanged February 20, 1865 at Boulware's or Cox Wharf on the James River, Virginia
Crumpler, Micajah H. Private	42	July 23, 1863, New Hanover County, North Carolina	Co. G, 40th Regiment, 3rd North Carolina Artillery	January 15, 1865, Fort Fisher, North Carolina	February 1, 1865, Elmira Prison Camp, New York	Transferred for Exchange February 20, 1865. Died February 21, 1865 of Unknown Disease on Route to be Exchanged.
Crumps, William L. Private	Unk	August 13, 1861, Camp Moore, Louisiana	Co. C, 12th Louisiana Infantry	May 16, 1863, Baker's Creek, Champion Hill, Mississippi	Point Lookout, Maryland, transferred to Elmira Prison, NY August 18, 1864	Exchanged February 25, 1865 at Boulware's wharf on the James River, Virginia
Cruse, Asa C. Private	Unk	July 3, 1861, Lynchburg, Virginia	Co. G, 42nd Virginia Infantry	May 12, 1864, Near Spotsylvania Court House, Virginia	Point Lookout, Maryland, transferred to Elmira Prison, NY August 6, 1864	Died September 21, 1864 of Typhoid Fever, Grave No. 339

Name & Rank	Age	Enlisted	Regiment and State	Where Captured	Prison	Remarks
Cruse, Moses Private	26	May 24, 1861, Charlotte, North Carolina	Co. E, 1st North Carolina Cavalry	May 12, 1864, Spotsylvania Court House, Virginia	Point Lookout, Maryland, transferred to Elmira Prison, NY August 12, 1864	Exchanged March 14, 1864 at Boulware's Wharf on the James River, Virginia
Cruse, Rufus J. Sergeant	20	July 13, 1861, Salisbury, North Carolina	Co. K, 8th North Carolina Infantry	June 1, 1864, Gaines Farm, Cold Harbor, Virginia	Point Lookout, Maryland, transferred to Elmira Prison, NY July 17,1864	Died April 29, 1865 of Chronic Diarrhea. No Grave Found in Woodlawn, Cemetery.
Crussell, Michael Private	38	May 14, 1862, Zollicoffer, Sullivan County, Tennessee	Co. F, 63rd Tennessee Infantry	June 17, 1864, Petersburg, Virginia	Point Lookout, Maryland, transferred to Elmira Prison, NY July 30, 1864	Died February 20, 1865 of Pneumonia, Grave No. 2350. Name M. Cressel on Headstone.
Crutchfield, Joseph F. Private	19	July 8, 1862, Pittsboro, North Carolina	Co. G, 5th North Carolina Cavalry	June 1, 1864, Ashland Station, Cold Harbor, Virginia	Point Lookout, Maryland, transferred to Elmira Prison, NY July 17,1864	Oath of Allegiance July 11, 1865
Crutchfield, Rob F. Private	Unk	June 21, 1862, Savannah, Georgia	Co. E, 7th Georgia Cavalry	June 11, 1864, Trevilian Station, Louisa Court House, Virginia	Point Lookout, Maryland, transferred to Elmira Prison, NY July 25, 1864	Died January 30, 1865 of Variola (Smallpox), Grave No. 1793
Cudworth, Alfred Private	20	February 24, 1862, Charleston, South Carolina	Co. B, 25th South Carolina Infantry	January 15, 1865, Fort Fisher, North Carolina	Elmira Prison Camp January 30, 1865	Oath of Allegiance June 16, 1865
Culbreth, Daniel M. Private	44	September 13, 1863, Sampson County, North Carolina	Co. B, 36th Regiment, 2nd North Carolina Artillery	January 15, 1865, Fort Fisher, North Carolina. Wounded	February 1, 1865, Elmira Prison Camp, New York	Died February 21, 1865 of Diarrhea, Grave No. 2265
Culbreth, Duncan J. Private	24	March 31, 1862, Cumberland County, North Carolina	Co. J, 51st North Carolina Infantry	June 16, 1864, Near Petersburg, Virginia	Point Lookout, Maryland, transferred to Elmira Prison, NY July 9, 1864	Oath of Allegiance May 13, 1865
Culbreth, William Private	18	April 10, 1863, Sampson County, North Carolina	Co. B, 36th Regiment, 2nd North Carolina Artillery	January 15, 1865, Fort Fisher, North Carolina. Wounded	February 1, 1865, Elmira Prison Camp, New York	Oath of Allegiance July 26, 1865

Name & Rank	Age	Enlisted	Regiment and State	Where Captured	Prison	Remarks
Cullam, W. E. Private	Unk	Unknown	Co. G, 3rd North Carolina Infantry	May 12, 1864, Spotsylvania County Court House, Virginia	Point Lookout, Maryland, transferred to Elmira Prison, NY August 14, 1864	Oath of Allegiance June 30, 1865
Cullin, James Private	Unk	June 1, 1863, Montgomery, Alabama	Co. C, 61st Alabama Infantry	July 17,1864, Frederick, Maryland	Old Capital Prison, Washington, DC, transferred to Elmira Prison, NY, July 23, 1864	Died October 23, 1864 of Chronic Diarrhea, Grave No. 860
Cullum, James R. Private	Unk	July 15, 1862, Raleigh, North Carolina	Co. K, 1st North Carolina Infantry	May 12, 1864, Spotsylvania Court House, Virginia	Point Lookout, Maryland, transferred to Elmira Prison, NY August 6, 1864	Exchanged March 10, 1865 at Boulware's Wharf on the James River, Virginia
Culp, D. F. Private	21	September 7, 1861, Mount Pleasant, North Carolina	Co. H, 8th North Carolina Infantry	June 1, 1864, Gaines Mill, Cold Harbor, Virginia	Point Lookout, Maryland, transferred to Elmira Prison, NY July 17, 1864	Exchanged March 2, 1865 at Akins Landing on the James River, Virginia
Culp, Robert N. Corporal	28	January 20, 1862, Camp Hampton, Grahamville, South Carolina	Co. B, 4th South Carolina Cavalry	May 28, 1864, Cold Harbor, Virginia	Old Capital Prison, Washington, DC, transferred to Elmira Prison, NY, July 25, 1864	Exchanged October 29, 1864, at Venus Point, Savannah River, GA.
Cumbee, Benjamin Private	19	February 12, 1862, Wilmington, North Carolina	Co. D, 36th Regiment, 2nd North Carolina Artillery	January 15, 1865, Fort Fisher, North Carolina. Wounded	February 1, 1865, Elmira Prison Camp, New York	Died March 18, 1865 of Diarrhea, Grave No. 1557
Cumbee, John T. Private	20	May 25, 1861, Camp Howard, Brunswick County, North Carolina	Co. G, 20th North Carolina Infantry	May 12, 1864, Near Spotsylvania Court House, Virginia	Point Lookout Prison, Maryland. Transferred to Elmira Prison Camp New York August 14, 1864.	Exchanged March 2, 1865 at Akins Landing on the James River, Virginia
Cumbee, Solomon Private	45	February 12, 1862, Wilmington, North Carolina	Co. D, 36th Regiment, 2nd North Carolina Artillery	January 15, 1865, Fort Fisher, North Carolina. Wounded.	February 1, 1865, Elmira Prison Camp, New York	Died April 12, 1865, Variola (Smallpox), Grave No. 2684

Name & Rank	Age	Enlisted	Regiment and State	Where Captured	Prison	Remarks
Cumber, J. T Corporal	Unk	May 25, 1861, Camp Howard, Brunswick County, North Carolina	Co. G, 20th North Carolina Infantry	May 12, 1864, Near Spotsylvania Court House, Virginia	Point Lookout Prison, Maryland. Transferred to Elmira Prison Camp New York August 14, 1864.	Exchanged March 2, 1865 at Akins Landing on the James River, Virginia
Cummings, Albert L. Private	19	March 5, 1862, Reidsville, North Carolina	Co. G, 45th North Carolina Infantry	May 10, 1864, Spotsylvania Court House, Virginia	Point Lookout, Maryland, transferred to Elmira Prison, NY August 6, 1864	Exchanged March 2, 1865 at Akins Landing on the James River, Virginia
Cummings, W. J. Private	Unk	Unknown	Co. K, 41st Alabama Infantry	May 15, 1864, Near Drury's Bluff, Virginia	Point Lookout, Maryland, transferred to Elmira Prison, NY August 17, 1864	Oath of Allegiance June 16, 1865
Cummings, William Private	Unk	February 26, 1862, Columbia County, Arkansas	Co. B, 19th Arkansas Infantry	May 16, 1863, Big Black River, Mississippi	Point Lookout, Maryland, transferred to Elmira Prison, NY August 18, 1864	Exchanged February 13, 1865 at Boulware's or Cox Wharf on the James River, Virginia
Cummons, Daniel Private	47	May 12, 1862, Pittsboro, North Carolina	Co. D, 61st North Carolina Infantry	August 27, 1863, Battery Wagner, Morris Island, South Carolina	Point Lookout, Maryland, transferred to Elmira Prison, NY August 18, 1864	Exchanged October 29, 1864, at Venus Point, Savannah River, GA.
Cumpton, James F. Private	Unk	March 27, 1864, Henry County, Virginia	Co. F, 42nd Virginia Infantry	May 12, 1864, Near Spotsylvania Court House, Virginia	Point Lookout, Maryland, transferred to Elmira Prison, NY August 6, 1864	Exchanged October 29, 1864 at Venus Point, Savannah River, GA.
Cundiff, Giles Private	Unk	July 24, 1861, John Pasley's, Franklin County, Virginia	Co. A, 58th Virginia Infantry	May 20, 1864, Spotsylvania Court House, Virginia	Point Lookout, Maryland, transferred to Elmira Prison, NY July 6, 1864	Oath of Allegiance June 30, 1865
Cunningham, Adam Private	Unk	May 13, 1862, Blacksburg, Virginia	Co. E, 4th Virginia Infantry	May 12, 1864, Near Spotsylvania Court House, Virginia	Point Lookout, Maryland, transferred to Elmira Prison, NY August 2, 1864	Died September 18, 1864 of Secondary Syphilis from Vaccination. Grave No. 154

Name & Rank	Age	Enlisted	Regiment and State	Where Captured	Prison	Remarks
Cunningham, Edward Private	28	May 29, 1861, Corinth, Mississippi	Co. B, 18th Mississippi Infantry	May 8, 1864, Wilderness, Virginia	Point Lookout, Maryland, transferred to Elmira Prison, NY July 25, 1864	Oath of Allegiance 3/6/65. Early Release per Lincoln's Proclamation, 12/8/1863.
Cunningham, G. E. Private	Unk	Unknown	Co. K, 1st North Carolina Infantry	June 1, 1864, Addington, Virginia	Point Lookout, Maryland, transferred to Elmira Prison, NY August 6, 1864	Oath of Allegiance July 3, 1865
Cunningham, George F. Sergeant	Unk	July 21, 1862, Washington County, Virginia	Co. L, 26th Battalion, Virginia Infantry	June 3, 1864, Gaines Farm, Cold Harbor, Virginia	Point Lookout, Maryland, transferred to Elmira Prison, NY July 17,1864	Exchanged March 2, 1865 at Akins Landing on the James River, Virginia
Cunningham, John E. Private	Unk	August 18, 1862, Louisa Court House, Virginia	Co. I, 3rd Virginia Cavalry	July 15, 1864, Prince George County, Virginia	Old Capital Prison, Washington, DC, transferred to Elmira Prison, NY, July 23, 1864	Oath of Allegiance May 13, 1865
Cunningham, Patrick Private	20	March 1, 1863, Liberty Church, Virginia	Co. H, 5th Louisiana Infantry	May 5, 1864, Wilderness, Virginia	Old Capital Prison, Washington, DC, transferred to Elmira Prison, NY, July 23, 1864	Exchanged October 29, 1864, at Venus Point, Savannah River, GA.
Cunningham, Shadrach M. Private	18	May 4, 1861, Dobson, North Carolina	Co. A, 28th North Carolina Infantry	May 12, 1864, Spotsylvania Court House, Virginia	Point Lookout, Maryland, transferred to Elmira Prison, NY August 12, 1864	Exchanged March 14, 1865 at Boulware's Wharf on the James River, Virginia
Cunningham, Thomas N. Private	Unk	June 8, 1861, New Orleans, Louisiana	Co. K, 15th Louisiana Infantry	July 17,1864, Near Washington, DC	Old Capital Prison, Washington, DC, transferred to Elmira Prison, NY, July 23, 1864	Oath of Allegiance June 3, 1865
Cunningham, William Sergeant	32	July 22, 1861, Camp Moore, Louisiana	Co. H, 10th Louisiana Infantry	May 12, 1864, Spotsylvania Court House, Virginia	Point Lookout, Maryland, transferred to Elmira Prison, NY July 25, 1864	Exchanged February 13, 1865 at Boulware's wharf on the James River, Virginia

Name & Rank	Age	Enlisted	Regiment and State	Where Captured	Prison	Remarks
Cunningham, William J. Private	33	July 13, 1861, Camp Boone, Tennessee	Co. E, 2nd Kentucky Infantry	May 26, 1864, Port Royal, Virginia	Point Lookout, Maryland, transferred to Elmira Prison, NY July 25, 1864	Died March 26, 1865 of Pneumonia, Grave No. 2476
Cupp, James O. Private	22	May 12, 1863, Rogersville, Tennessee	Co. C, 63rd Tennessee Infantry	June 17, 1864, Petersburg, Virginia	Point Lookout, Maryland, transferred to Elmira Prison, NY July 30, 1864	Exchanged February 25, 1865 at Boulware's or Cox Wharf on the James River, Virginia
Cupp, Jesse Private	24	June 10, 1861, Romney, Virginia	Co. F, 7th Virginia Cavalry	September 14, 1863, Near Culpepper, Virginia	Point Lookout, Maryland, transferred to Elmira Prison, NY August 18, 1864	Died September 18, 1864 of Typhoid Fever, Grave No. 522
Curlee, Churchwell N. Private	21	March 20, 1862, Union County, North Carolina	Co. J, 53rd North Carolina Infantry	May 20, 1864, Spotsylvania Court House, Virginia	Point Lookout Prison. Transferred to Elmira Prison, New York, July 6, 1864.	Exchanged October 29, 1864, at Venus Point, Savannah River, GA.
Curlee, William Private	19	March 9, 1862, Wadesboro, North Carolina	Co. J, 43rd North Carolina Infantry	May 25, 1864, Hanover, Virginia	Point Lookout, Maryland, transferred to Elmira Prison, NY July 8, 1864	Exchanged March 14, 1865 at Boulware's Wharf on the James River, Virginia
Currie, David Private	Unk	May 13, 1862, Montgomery County, Georgia	Co. E, 61st Georgia Infantry	May 12, 1864, Spotsylvania Court House, Virginia	Point Lookout, Maryland, transferred to Elmira Prison, NY July 25, 1864	Oath of Allegiance June 23, 1865
Currie, Nicholas R. Private	Unk	February 1, 1863, Bennettsville, South Carolina	Co. F, 21st South Carolina Infantry	January 15, 1865, Fort Fisher, North Carolina	Elmira Prison Camp January 30, 1865	Died May 14, 1865 of Pneumonia, Grave No. 2802
Currin, Wyatt Private	37	November 28, 1863, Camp Holmes, North Carolina	Co. F, 23rd North Carolina Infantry	May 12, 1864, Near Spotsylvania Court House, Virginia	Point Lookout, Maryland, transferred to Elmira Prison, NY August 14, 1864	Died February 15, 1865 of Variola (Smallpox), Grave No. 2195

Name & Rank	Age	Enlisted	Regiment and State	Where Captured	Prison	Remarks
Curry, George W. Private	Unk	March 4, 1862, Montgomery County, Georgia	Co. F, 48th Georgia Infantry	August 16, 1864, New Market, Virginia	Old Capital Prison, Washington, DC transferred to Elmira Prison, NY August 29, 1864	Died November 7, 1864 of Chronic Diarrhea, Grave No. 778
Curry, George W. Private	Unk	March 29, 1862, Lewisburg, Virginia	Co. D, 26th Battalion Virginia Infantry	May 31, 1864, Cold Harbor, Virginia	Point Lookout, Maryland, transferred to Elmira Prison, NY July 17, 1864	Oath of Allegiance May 12, 1865
Curry, Green R. Corporal	Unk	June 9, 1861, Jones County, Georgia	Co. B, 12th Georgia Infantry	May 10, 1864, Spotsylvania Court House, Virginia	Point Lookout, Maryland, transferred to Elmira Prison, NY July 25, 1864	Oath of Allegiance June 19, 1865
Curry, James M. Private	Unk	Unknown	Co. C, 12th Virginia Cavalry	October 26, 1864, Fauquier County, Virginia	Old Capital Prison, Washington, DC, transferred to Elmira Prison, NY, December 17, 1864	Exchanged March 10, 1865 at Boulware's Wharf on the James River, Virginia
Curry, Joseph H. Private	Unk	April 21, 1862, Camp Pillow, South Carolina	Co. D, 17th South Carolina Infantry	July 30, 1864, Petersburg, Virginia	Point Lookout, Maryland, transferred to Elmira Prison, NY August 12, 1864	Oath of Allegiance June 19, 1865
Curry, Samuel Private	42	August 1, 1861, Bronson, Florida	Co. G, 9th Florida Infantry	July 29, 1864, Petersburg, Virginia	Point Lookout, Maryland, transferred to Elmira Prison, NY August 12, 1864	Died November 14, 1864 of Chronic Diarrhea, Grave No. 808
Curry, William H. Private	Unk	July 2, 1861, Bethel Am., Virginia	Co. F, 50th Virginia Infantry	May 12, 1864, Spotsylvania Court House, Virginia	Point Lookout, Maryland, transferred to Elmira Prison, NY August 2, 1864	Died February 23, 1865 of Remittent Fever, Grave No. 2256
Curt, C. Private	Unk	Unknown	Co. A, Captain Godwin's Home Guard Florida	September 27, 1864, Marianna, Florida	New Orleans, Louisiana transferred to Elmira November 19, 1864.	Exchanged February 13, 1865 at Boulware's Wharf on the James River, Virginia

Name & Rank	Age	Enlisted	Regiment and State	Where Captured	Prison	Remarks
Curtis, B. R. Private	Unk	January 29, 1864, Wilcox, Alabama	Co. F, 1st Battalion Alabama Artillery	August 23, 1864, Fort Morgan, Alabama	Steam Press No. 4, New Orleans, Louisiana transferred to Elmira Prison, October 8, 1864.	Oath of Allegiance June 21, 1865
Curtis, Hiram L. Private	Unk	Unknown	Co. G, 3rd Louisiana Infantry	May 18, 1863, Snyder's Mills, Mississippi	Point Lookout, Maryland, transferred to Elmira Prison, NY July 23, 1864	Died November 21, 1864 of Chronic Diarrhea, Grave No. 931.
Curtis, John F. Private	Unk	August 1, 1861, Aquia Creek, Virginia	Co. J, 47th Virginia Infantry	May 5, 1864, Wilderness, Virginia	Point Lookout, Maryland, transferred to Elmira Prison, NY August 14, 1864	Exchanged March 10, 1865 at Boulware's Wharf on the James River, Virginia
Curtis, Samuel Private	Unk	October 19, 1863, Caldwell County, North Carolina	Co. K, 38th North Carolina Infantry	June 22, 1864, Petersburg, Virginia	Point Lookout, Maryland, transferred to Elmira Prison, NY July 23, 1864	Died February 23, 1865 of Chronic Diarrhea, Grave No. 2246
Cuser, G. W. Private	Unk	Unknown	Co. D, 26th Virginia Infantry	May 31, 1864, Cold Harbor, Virginia	Point Lookout, Maryland, transferred to Elmira Prison, NY July 17, 1864	Oath of Allegiance May 12, 1865
Cusler, C. N. Private	Unk	Unknown	Co. J, 53rd, North Carolina Infantry	May 20, 1864, Spotsylvania Court House, Virginia	Point Lookout, Maryland, transferred to Elmira Prison, NY July 6, 1864	Exchanged October 11, 1864. Nothing Further.
Custer, Ephraim G. Private	30	April 18, 1861, Martinsburg, Virginia	Co. D, 2nd Virginia Infantry	May 12, 1864, Near Spotsylvania Court House, Virginia	Point Lookout, Maryland, transferred to Elmira Prison, NY August 6, 1864	Exchanged March 2, 1865 at Akins Landing on the James River, Virginia
Cutchen, W. T. Private	Unk	Unknown	Co. F, 36th Regiment, 2nd North Carolina Artillery	January 15, 1865, Fort Fisher, North Carolina. Wounded	February 1, 1865, Elmira Prison Camp, New York	Died March 11, 1865 of Pneumonia, Grave No. 1837. Headstone has Cutchin.

Name & Rank	Age	Enlisted	Regiment and State	Where Captured	Prison	Remarks
Cutlip, F. Leonard Private	Unk	May 18, 1861, Sutton, Virginia	Co. C, 25th Virginia Infantry	May 5, 1864, Wilderness, Virginia	Point Lookout, Maryland, transferred to Elmira Prison, NY August 14, 1864	Oath of Allegiance June 23, 1865
Cutlip, James F. Private	27	June 13, 1861, Conrad's, Hacks Valley, Virginia	Co. G, 25th Virginia Infantry	May 6, 1864, Wilderness, Virginia	Point Lookout, Maryland, transferred to Elmira Prison, NY August 14, 1864	Exchanged October 29, 1864, at Venus Point, Savannah River, GA.
Cutlip, Sinnett J. Private	Unk	May 18, 1861, Sutton, Virginia	Co. C, 25th Virginia Infantry	May 5, 1864, Wilderness, Virginia	Point Lookout, Maryland, transferred to Elmira Prison, NY August 14, 1864	Oath of Allegiance June 27, 1865
Cyphers, Aaron Private	Unk	Unknown	Co. E, 50th Virginia Infantry	May 12, 1864, Spotsylvania Court House, Virginia	Point Lookout, Maryland, transferred to Elmira Prison, NY August 2, 1864	Died September 25, 1864 of Chronic Diarrhea, Grave No. 358
Cyrus, Richard R. Corporal	Unk	July 11, 1861, Lynchburg, Virginia	Co. I, 42nd Virginia Infantry	May 12, 1864, Spotsylvania Court House, Virginia	Point Lookout, Maryland, transferred to Elmira Prison, NY August 2, 1864	Exchanged October 29, 1864, at Venus Point, Savannah River, GA.

Name & Rank	Age	Enlisted	Regiment and State	Where Captured	Prison	Remarks
Daffin, George W. Private	32	June 23, 1861, Camp Moore, Louisiana	Co. G, 8th Louisiana Infantry	May 12, 1864, Spotsylvania Court House, Virginia	Point Lookout, Maryland, transferred to Elmira Prison, NY July 17,1864	Exchanged October 29, 1864, at Venus Point, Savannah River, GA.
Dahmer, Sampson C. Private	Unk	May 18, 1861, Franklin, Virginia	Co. K, 25th Virginia Infantry	May 6, 1864, Wilderness, Virginia	Old Capital Prison, Washington D. C. Transferred to Elmira Prison, NY July 14, 1864	Oath of Allegiance June 27, 1865
Daigle, Aristide Private	Unk	April 21, 1862, Assumption Parish, Louisiana	Co. H, Thomas' 28th Louisiana Infantry	August 20, 1864, Bayou Goula, Louisiana	New Orleans, Louisiana transferred to Elmira November 19, 1864.	Exchanged February 25, 1865 at Boulware's or Cox Wharf on the James River, Virginia

Name & Rank	Age	Enlisted	Regiment and State	Where Captured	Prison	Remarks
Daigre, Omer P. Private	37	September 1, 1862, New Road, Louisiana	Co. J, 2nd Louisiana Cavalry	August 10, 1864, Bayou Grosstette, Louisiana	New Orleans, Louisianna Transferred to Elmira Prison, New York, November 19, 1864	Exchanged February 25, 1865 at Boulware's or Cox Wharf on the James River, Virginia
Dail, Stephen B. Private	22	February 1, 1862, Duplin County, North Carolina	Co. A, 43rd North Carolina Infantry	June 1, 1864, Cold Harbor, Virginia	Point Lookout, Maryland, transferred to Elmira Prison, NY July 17,1864	Oath of Allegiance May 29, 1865
Dailey, Benjamin F. Private	18	April 14, 1863, Wayne County, North Carolina	Co. G, 40th Regiment, 3rd North Carolina Artillery	January 15, 1865, Fort Fisher, North Carolina	Elmira Prison Camp January 30, 1865	Died March 4, 1865 of Diarrhea, Grave No. 1984
Dailey, Daniel Private	24	July 22, 1861, Camp Moore, Louisiana	Co. A, 10th Louisiana Infantry	May 12, 1864, Spotsylvania Court House, Virginia	Point Lookout, Maryland, transferred to Elmira Prison, NY July 25, 1864	Exchanged February 20, 1865 at Boulware's or Cox Wharf on the James River, Virginia
Daily, John J. Private	30	August 22, 1861, Cleveland County, North Carolina	Co. H, 28th North Carolina Infantry	May 12, 1864, Spotsylvania Virginia	Point Lookout, Maryland, transferred to Elmira Prison, NY August 12, 1864	Exchanged February 13, 1865 at Boulware's Wharf on the James River, Virginia
Dakin, William Ordinance Sergeant	33	February 27, 1861, Mobile, Alabama	Field and Staff, 1st Alabama Artillery	August 23, 1864, Fort Morgan, Alabama.	New Orleans, Louisiana transferred to Elmira December 4, 1864.	Oath of Allegiance May 13, 1865
Dale, James C. Private	18	October 21, 1861, Wilmington, New Hanover County, North Carolina	Co. D, 36th Regiment 2nd North Carolina Artillery	January 15, 1865, Fort Fisher, North Carolina	February 1, 1865, Elmira Prison Camp, New York	Died March 27, 1865 of Pneumonia, Grave No. 2528
Dale, William L. Private	Unk	July 3, 1861, Atlanta, Georgia	Co. D, 11th Georgia Infantry	May 6, 1864, Wilderness, Virginia	Point Lookout, Maryland, transferred to Elmira Prison, NY August 14, 1864	Oath of Allegiance June 19, 1865

Name & Rank	Age	Enlisted	Regiment and State	Where Captured	Prison	Remarks
Daley, James T. Private	Unk	July 30, 1863, Richmond, Virginia	Co. C, 41st Battalion Virginia Cavalry	July 29, 1864, Leesburg, Virginia	Old Capital Prison, Washington D. C. Transferred to Elmira Prison, NY August 12, 1864	Oath of Allegiance June 14, 1865
Daley, Mathias Private	Unk	June 21, 1861, New Orleans, Louisiana	Co. F, 15th Louisiana Infantry	May 12, 1864, Spotsylvania Court House, Virginia	Point Lookout, Maryland, transferred to Elmira Prison, NY July 25, 1864	Exchanged October 29, 1864, at Venus Point, Savannah River, GA.
Daley, Robert T. Private	22	May 6, 1861, Mobile, Alabama	Co. J, 8th Alabama Infantry	May 6, 1864, Wilderness, Virginia	Point Lookout, Maryland, transferred to Elmira Prison, NY August 17, 1864	Exchanged March 14, 1865 at Boulware's Wharf on the James River, Virginia
Dalton, Joseph L. Private	32	December 31, 1861, Charlotte, Virginia	Co. B, 22nd Virginia Infantry	May 6, 1864, Wilderness, Virginia	Point Lookout, Maryland, transferred to Elmira Prison, NY August 14, 1864	Oath of Allegiance June 19, 1865
Dalton, Nicholas Private	39	March 18, 1862, Pervis' Store, Virginia	Co. H, 42nd Virginia Infantry	May 12, 1864, Near Spotsylvania Court House, Virginia	Point Lookout, Maryland, transferred to Elmira Prison, NY August 6, 1864	Died January 13, 1865 of Chronic Diarrhea, Grave No. 1473
Daly, Marion M. Private	Unk	May 17, 1861, Atlanta, Georgia	Co. F, 8th Georgia Infantry	May 6, 1864, Wilderness, Virginia	Point Lookout, Maryland, transferred to Elmira Prison, NY August 14, 1864	Exchanged February 13, 1865 at Boulware's wharf on the James River, Virginia
Dame, John M. Private	Unk	March 19, 1864, Macon, Georgia	Co. B, 12th Georgia Infantry	May 10, 1864, Spotsylvania, Virginia	Old Capital Prison, Washington, DC, transferred to Elmira Prison, NY, July 23, 1864	Died September 22, 1864 of Pneumonia, Grave No. 482
Dameron, C. M. Private	Unk	September 14, 1861, Smyth County, Virginia	Co. E, 23rd Battalion Virginia Infantry	June 2, 1864, Chickahominy, Cold Harbor, Virginia	Point Lookout, Maryland, transferred to Elmira Prison, NY July 11,1864	Oath of Allegiance May 29, 1865

Name & Rank	Age	Enlisted	Regiment and State	Where Captured	Prison	Remarks
Dameron, Lorenzo L. Private	Unk	July 15, 1863, Raleigh, North Carolina	Co. K, 24th North Carolina Infantry	June 17, 1864, Near Petersburg, Virginia	Point Lookout, Maryland, transferred to Elmira Prison, NY July 30, 1864	Exchanged February 13, 1865 at Boulware's wharf on the James River, Virginia
Dampier, H. J. Private	Unk	Unknown	Co. H, 26th Georgia Infantry	May 5, 1864, Wilderness, Virginia	Point Lookout, Maryland, transferred to Elmira Prison, NY August 17, 1864	Exchanged February 20, 1865 at Boulware's or Cox Wharf on the James River, Virginia
Dampier, John H. Private	Unk	June 14, 1861, Valdosta, Georgia	Co. J, 12th Georgia Infantry	May 10, 1864, Spotsylvania Court House, Virginia	Point Lookout, Maryland, transferred to Elmira Prison, NY July 25, 1864	Oath of Allegiance June 16, 1865
Dance, Robert M. Private	36	April 7, 1862, Petersburg, Virginia	Co. K, 5th Virginia Cavalry	June 11, 1864, Trevilian Station, Louisa Court House, Virginia	Point Lookout, Maryland, transferred to Elmira Prison, NY July 25, 1864	Exchanged March 2, 1865 at Akins Landing on the James River, Virginia
Dancey, John M. Private	30	September 8, 1862, Statesville, North Carolina	Co. G, 18th North Carolina Infantry	May 10, 1864, Spotsylvania Court House, Virginia	Point Lookout, Maryland, transferred to Elmira Prison, NY August 6, 1864	Died January 3, 1865 of Chronic Diarrhea, Grave No. 1507. Woodlawn Death Register has Name Dancy.
Dangerfield, Owen Private	Unk	April 29, 1863, White Sulfur Springs, Virginia	Co. C, 26th Battalion, Virginia Infantry	June 3, 1864, Gaines Farm, Cold Harbor, Virginia	Point Lookout, Maryland, transferred to Elmira Prison, NY July 17, 1864	Oath of Allegiance June 21, 1865
Daniel, Alfred B. Private	18	March 26, 1862, Danville, Virginia	Co. C, 5th Virginia Cavalry	June 11, 1864, Louisa Court House, Trevilian Station, Virginia	Point Lookout, Maryland, transferred to Elmira Prison, NY July 30, 1864	Oath of Allegiance May 29, 1865

Name & Rank	Age	Enlisted	Regiment and State	Where Captured	Prison	Remarks
Daniel, D. P. Private	Unk	July 20, 1861, Jefferson, Georgia	Co. G, 16th Georgia Infantry	August 16, 1864, Front Royal, Virginia	Old Capital Prison, Washington, DC transferred to Elmira Prison, NY August 29, 1864	Oath of Allegiance July 7, 1865
Daniel, Elisha Private	Unk	June 14, 1861, Valdosta, Georgia	Co. J, 12th Georgia Infantry	May 10, 1864, Spotsylvania Court House, Virginia	Point Lookout, Maryland, transferred to Elmira Prison, NY July 25, 1864	Died January 25, 1865 of Chronic Diarrhea, Grave No. 1615
Daniel, Ello K. Private	Unk	September 1, 1862, Prince George Court House, Virginia	Co. E, 12th Virginia Infantry	May 8, 1864, Wilderness, Virginia	Point Lookout, Maryland, transferred to Elmira Prison, NY July 12, 1864	Exchanged October 29, 1864, at Venus Point, Savannah River, GA.
Daniel, Henry Private	22	July 9, 1861, Goldsboro, North Carolina	Co. F, 10th Regiment, 1st North Carolina Artillery	January 15, 1865, Fort Fisher, North Carolina	January 30, 1865, Elmira Prison Camp, NY	Died April 18, 1865 of Acute Inflammation of Liver, Grave No. 1363
Daniel, James W. Private	Unk	December 7, 1861, Camp Trousdale, Tennessee	Co. E, 44th Tennessee Infantry	June 17, 1864, Petersburg, Virginia	Point Lookout, Maryland, transferred to Elmira Prison, NY July 30, 1864	Oath of Allegiance July 25, 1865
Daniel, John Private	Unk	Unknown	Co. A, Mosby's Virginia Cavalry	August 19, 1863, Loudoun County, Virginia	Point Lookout, Maryland, transferred to Elmira Prison, NY August 18, 1864	Exchanged March 2, 1865 at Boulware's Wharf on the James River, Virginia
Daniel, Joseph H. Private	38	June 15, 1863, Pitt County, North Carolina	Co. G, 8th North Carolina Infantry	June 1, 1864, Cold Harbor, Virginia	Point Lookout, Maryland, transferred to Elmira Prison, NY July 17, 1864. Ward 17	Died August 12, 1864 of Remittent Fever, Grave No. 129
Daniel, R. H. Private	Unk	Unknown	Petersburg Militia, Virginia Infantry	June 9, 1864, Petersburg, Virginia	Unknown	Exchanged October 11, 1864. Nothing Further.

Name & Rank	Age	Enlisted	Regiment and State	Where Captured	Prison	Remarks
Daniel, Robert M. Private	24	February 26, 1862, Chapel Hill, North Carolina	Co. G, 11th North Carolina Infantry	July 14, 1863, Falling Waters, Maryland	Point Lookout, Maryland, transferred to Elmira Prison, NY August 18, 1864	Exchanged February 20, 1865 at Boulware's or Cox Wharf on the James River, Virginia
Daniel, William C. Private	Unk	May 11, 1862, Jonesboro, Georgia	Co. D, 44th Georgia Infantry	May 30, 1864 Mechanics-ville, Virginia	Point Lookout, Maryland, transferred to Elmira Prison, NY July 11,1864	Exchanged October 29, 1864, at Venus Point, Savannah River, GA.
Daniel, William E. Private	17	January 2, 1864, Fort Campbell, Brunswick County, North Carolina	Co. G, 36th Regiment North Carolina, 2nd Artillery	January 15, 1865, Fort Fisher, North Carolina	February 1, 1865, Elmira Prison Camp, New York	Died of Variola (Smallpox), March 28, 1865. Grave No. 1670. Headstone has M. E. Daniel.
Daniel, William H. Private	20	June 23, 1861, Fair Bluff, Columbus County, North Carolina	Co. C, 20th North Carolina Infantry	May 12, 1864, Near Spotsylvania Court House, Virginia	Point Lookout Prison, Maryland. Transferred to Elmira Prison Camp New York August 14, 1864.	Exchanged March 10, 1865 at Boulware's Wharf on the James River, Virginia
Daniel, William S. Corporal	Unk	March 24, 1861, Gainesville, Florida	Co. H, 1st Florida Infantry	September 26, 1864, Mariana, Florida	Fort Columbus, New York Harbor. Transferred to Elmira November 7, 1864	Died December 25, 1864 of Chronic Diarrhea, Grave No. 1112
Daniel, William W. Private	20	February 25, 1862, Lew's Store, North Carolina	Co. J, 12th North Carolina Infantry	May 12, 1864, Near Spotsylvania, Virginia	Point Lookout, Maryland, transferred to Elmira Prison, NY August 14, 1864	Died September 5, 1864 of Chronic Diarrhea, Grave No. 238
Daniels, A. P. Private	Unk	April 26, 1861, Sumpter County, Alabama	Co. E, 5th Alabama Infantry	May 20, 1864, Spotsylvania Court House, Virginia	Point Lookout, Maryland, transferred to Elmira Prison, NY July 6,1864	Oath of Allegiance June 14, 1865
Daniels, James W. Private	27	September 15, 1861, Tampa, Florida	Co. K, 8th Florida Infantry	May 25, 1864, North Anna, Near Hanover Junction, Virginia	Point Lookout, Maryland, transferred to Elmira Prison, NY July 11,1864	Died October 17, 1864 of Typhoid Fever, Grave No. 549

Elmira Prison Camp Roster Volume I

Name & Rank	Age	Enlisted	Regiment and State	Where Captured	Prison	Remarks
Daniels, John D. Corporal	Unk	May 7, 1862, Hyde County, North Carolina	Co. H, 33rd North Carolina Infantry	July 29, 1864, Petersburg, Virginia	Point Lookout, Maryland, transferred to Elmira Prison, NY August 12, 1864	Oath of Allegiance July 3, 1865
Daniels, John E. Sergeant	Unk	March 26, 1861, Union Springs, Alabama	Co. E, 1st Battalion Alabama Artillery	August 23, 1864, Fort Morgan, Alabama	New Orleans, Louisiana transferred to Elmira December 4, 1864.	Exchanged March 14, 1865 at Boulware's Wharf on the James River, Virginia
Daniels, Lawson Private	Unk	March 14, 1862, Marianna, Florida	Co. B, 15th Confederate Cavalry	September 22, 1864, Shoe River, Florida	New Orleans, Louisiana transferred to Elmira November 19, 1864.	Died April 14, 1865 of General Debility, Grave No. 2704
Daniels, Leroy R. Corporal	Unk	May 1, 1862, Nichol's Depot, South Carolina	Co. F, 51st North Carolina Infantry	June 1, 1864, Cold Harbor, Virginia	Point Lookout, Maryland, transferred to Elmira Prison, NY July 17,1864	Exchanged March 10, 1865 at Boulware's Wharf on the James River, Virginia
Daniels, Lott M. Private	Unk	December 19, 1862, Macon, Georgia	Co. H, 14th Georgia Infantry	May 12, 1864, Spotsylvania Court House, Virginia	Point Lookout, Maryland, transferred to Elmira Prison, NY July 30, 1864	Transferred for Exchange 10/11/64. Died 10/13/64. Buried at Port Royal, South Carolina.
Daniels, Perry J. Private	23	April 26, 1861, Sumpter County, Alabama	Co. G, 5th Alabama Infantry	May 6, 1864, Wilderness, Virginia	Point Lookout, Maryland, transferred to Elmira, New York, August 17, 1864	Oath of Allegiance June 14, 1865
Daniels, Samuel H. Private	23	May 10, 1861, Washington, North Carolina	Co. J, 3rd North Carolina Infantry	May 12, 1864, Near Spotsylvania Court House, Virginia	Point Lookout Prison, Maryland. Transferred to Elmira Prison Camp New York August 14, 1864.	Oath of Allegiance June 30, 1865
Danneley, James W. Private	Unk	June 25, 1862, Calhoun, Georgia	Co. G, 12th Georgia Infantry	May 20, 1864, Spotsylvania Court House, Virginia	Point Lookout, Maryland, transferred to Elmira Prison, NY July 6, 1864	Died February 14, 1865, of Smallpox, Grave No. 2029

Name & Rank	Age	Enlisted	Regiment and State	Where Captured	Prison	Remarks
Dantin, Henry Sergeant	23	July 22, 1861, Camp Moore, Louisiana	Co. G, 10th Louisiana Infantry	May 12, 1864, Spotsylvania Court House, Virginia	Point Lookout, Maryland, transferred to Elmira Prison, NY July 25, 1864	Exchanged February 25, 1865 at Boulware's or Cox Wharf on the James River, Virginia
Dantzler, Allen P. Private	Unk	April 11, 1862, Coles Island, South Carolina	Co. F, 25th South Carolina Infantry	January 15, 1865, Fort Fisher, North Carolina	Elmira Prison Camp January 30, 1865	Exchanged March 2, 1865 at Boulware's Wharf on the James River, Virginia
Dantzler, David W. Sergeant	Unk	April 11, 1862, Coles Island, South Carolina	Co. G, 25th South Carolina Infantry	January 15, 1865, Fort Fisher, North Carolina	Elmira Prison Camp January 30, 1865	Died April 1, 1865 of Pneumonia, Grave No. 2588
Dantzler, F. W. Private	16	April 11, 1862, Coles Island, South Carolina	Co. F, 25th South Carolina Infantry	January 15, 1865, Fort Fisher, North Carolina	Elmira Prison Camp January 30, 1865	Oath of Allegiance July 26, 1865
Dantzler, Henry F. Sergeant	Unk	April 11, 1862, Coles Island, South Carolina	Co. F, 25th South Carolina Infantry	January 15, 1865, Fort Fisher, North Carolina	Elmira Prison Camp January 30, 1865	Oath of Allegiance July 17, 1865
Daougherty, William T. Sergeant	Unk	June 1, 1862, Richmond, Virginia	Co. B, 3rd Virginia Cavalry	August 16, 1864, Front Royal, Virginia	Old Capital Prison, Washington, DC transferred to Elmira Prison, NY August 29, 1864	Exchanged March 10, 1865 at Boulware's Wharf on the James River, Virginia
Darby, Benjamin F. Private	Unk	March 1, 1861, Union Springs, Alabama	Co. E, 1st Battalion Alabama Artillery	August 23, 1864, Fort Morgan, Alabama	New Orleans, Louisiana transferred to Elmira December 4, 1864.	Oath of Allegiance June 21, 1865
Darcy, Michael Private	Unk	June 20, 1861, Clarksville, Tennessee	Co. B, Jackson's 1st Regiment, Tennessee Heavy Artillery	August 23, 1864, Fort Morgan, Alabama	New Orleans, Louisiana transferred to Elmira December 4, 1864.	Oath of Allegiance May 17, 1865
Darden, Calvin Private Musician	Unk	February 26, 1863, Goldsboro, North Carolina	Co. F, 10th Regiment, 1st North Carolina Artillery	January 15, 1865, Fort Fisher, North Carolina	January 30, 1865, Elmira Prison Camp, NY	Oath of Allegiance May 29, 1865

Name & Rank	Age	Enlisted	Regiment and State	Where Captured	Prison	Remarks
Darden, Daniel Private	Unk	Unknown	Co. C, 3rd Battalion North Carolina Artillery	January 15, 1865, Fort Fisher, North Carolina	February 1, 1865, Elmira Prison Camp, New York	Died April 2, 1865 of Unknown Disease Grave No. 2571
Darden, George T. Private	24	June 12, 1863, Murphysboro, Hertford County, North Carolina	Co. C, 3rd Battalion, North Carolina Light Artillery	January 15, 1865, Fort Fisher, North Carolina	February 1, 1865, Elmira Prison Camp, New York	Exchanged March 14, 1865 at Boulware's Wharf on the James River, Virginia
Darden, Paul Private	Unk	September 1, 1864, Murfreesboro, Hertford County, North Carolina	Co. C, 3rd Battalion, North Carolina Light Artillery	January 15, 1865, Fort Fisher, North Carolina	February 1, 1865, Elmira Prison Camp, New York	Died of Pneumonia April 2, 1865. No Grave in Woodlawn National Cemetery.
Daring, James T. Private	27	June 24, 1862, Coosawhatchie, South Carolina	Co. E, 11th South Carolina Infantry	June 18, 1864, Petersburg, Virginia	Point Lookout, Maryland, transferred to Elmira Prison, NY July 30, 1864	Died May 20, 1865 of Chronic Diarrhea, Grave No. 2940
Dark, H. E. Private	Unk	August 15, 1861, Camp Harris, Cumberland Gap, Tennessee	Co. F, 17th Tennessee Infantry	June 17, 1864, Petersburg, Virginia	Point Lookout, Maryland, transferred to Elmira Prison, NY July 23, 1864	Oath of Allegiance May 19, 1865
Darley, H. C. Sergeant	Unk	September 12, 1862, Lowndes, Alabama	Co. E, 1st Battalion Alabama Artillery	August 23, 1864, Fort Morgan, Alabama	Steam Press No. 4, New Orleans, Louisiana transferred to Elmira Prison, October 8, 1864.	Oath of Allegiance June 19, 1865
Darley, William Private	Unk	April 17, 1861, Alexandria, Virginia	Co. E, 17th Virginia Infantry	July 21, 1863, Manassas Gap, Virginia	Point Lookout, Maryland, transferred to Elmira Prison, NY August 18, 1864	Exchanged March 10, 1865 at Boulware's Wharf on the James River, Virginia
Darnall, Andrew M. Private	Unk	May 10, 1864, Rocky Mount, Virginia	Captain Archibald Graham's Battery, Virginia Light Artillery	July 27, 1864, Petersburg, Virginia	Point Lookout, Maryland, transferred to Elmira Prison, NY August 12, 1864	Exchanged March 14, 1865 at Boulware's Wharf on the James River, Virginia

Name & Rank	Age	Enlisted	Regiment and State	Where Captured	Prison	Remarks
Darnel, Morgan Van Buron Sergeant	20	June 19, 1861, Encampment at Abingdon, Virginia	Co. C, 48th Virginia Infantry	May 12, 1864, Spotsylvania Court House, Virginia	Point Lookout, Maryland, transferred to Elmira Prison, NY August 12, 1864	Died March 28, 1865 of Diarrhea, Grave No. 2518
Darwin, William H. Corporal	21	February 13, 1862, Livingston, Tennessee	Co. G, 25th Tennessee Infantry	June 17, 1864, Petersburg, Virginia	Point Lookout, Maryland, transferred to Elmira Prison, NY July 23, 1864	Oath of Allegiance May 15, 1865
Daughtrey, William T. Sergeant	28	August 30, 1861, Beaver Dam, Isle of Wight County, Virginia	Co. F, 61st Virginia Infantry	June 1, 1864, Cold Harbor, Virginia	Point Lookout, Maryland, transferred to Elmira Prison, NY July 17,1864	Died January 18, 1865 of Variola (Smallpox), Grave No. 1432
Dauthit, Edward J. Private	22	June 4, 1861, Mocksville, North Carolina	Co. G, 4th, North Carolina Infantry	May 20, 1864, Spotsylvania Court House, Virginia	Point Lookout, Maryland, transferred to Elmira Prison, NY July 6, 1864	Oath of Allegiance June 30, 1865
Dautridge, Willie Private	47	March 1, 1863, Kinston, North Carolina	Co. H, 32nd North Carolina Infantry	May 10, 1864, Near Mine Run, Spotsylvania, Virginia	Point Lookout, Maryland, transferred to Elmira Prison, NY August 6, 1864	Died April 17, 1865 of Pneumonia, Grave No. 1358. Name Doddridge on Headstone.
Davault, Jacob W. Sergeant	Unk	June 29, 1861, Wytheville, Virginia	Co. B, 50th Virginia Infantry	May 12, 1864, Spotsylvania, Virginia	Point Lookout, Maryland, transferred to Elmira Prison, NY July 23, 1864	Oath of Allegiance May 19, 1865
Davenport, Bedford K. Private	32	March 7, 1861, Milton, North Carolina	Co. I, 45th North Carolina Infantry	June 1, 1864, Gaines Farm, Cold Harbor, Virginia	Point Lookout, Maryland, transferred to Elmira Prison, NY July 17,1864	Oath of Allegiance May 13, 1865
Davenport, Benjamin W. Private	21	May 16, 1861, Columbia, North Carolina	Co. F, 32nd North Carolina Infantry	May 10, 1864, Near Mine Run, Spotsylvania, Virginia	Point Lookout, Maryland, transferred to Elmira Prison, NY August 6, 1864	Exchanged October 29, 1864, at Venus Point, Savannah River, GA.

Name & Rank	Age	Enlisted	Regiment and State	Where Captured	Prison	Remarks
Davenport, E. B. Private	Unk	May 8, 1861, Kanawha Court House, Virginia	Co. H, 22nd Virginia Infantry	June 3, 1864, Gaines Mill, Cold Harbor, Virginia	Point Lookout, Maryland, transferred to Elmira Prison, NY July 17,1864	Exchanged February 25, 1865 at Boulware's or Cox Wharf on the James River, Virginia
Davenport, Henry F. Private	Unk	June 15, 1861, Americus, Sumter County, Georgia	Co. A, 12th Georgia Infantry	May 10, 1864, Spotsylvania Court House, Virginia	Point Lookout, Maryland, transferred to Elmira Prison, NY July 25, 1864	Exchanged March 10, 1865 at Boulware's Wharf on the James River, Virginia
Davenport, Phineas Private	Unk	January 28, 1862, Lenoir Court House, North Carolina	Co. E, 66th North Carolina Infantry	June 3, 1864, Gaines Mill, Cold Harbor, Virginia	Point Lookout, Maryland, transferred to Elmira Prison, NY July 17,1864	Oath of Allegiance July 3, 1865
Davenport, S. B. Ordinance Seaman	Unk	Unknown	Confederate States Navy	May 5, 1864, Albemarle Sound on Steamer CSS Bombshell	Point Lookout, Maryland, transferred to Elmira Prison, NY August 17, 1864	Transferred For Exchange October 11, 1864 to Point Lookout Prison Camp, MD. Nothing Further.
David, James H. S. Private	Unk	April 20, 1862, Suffolk, Virginia	Co. B, 53rd Virginia Infantry	May 24, 1864, Hanover Junction, Virginia	Point Lookout, Maryland, transferred to Elmira Prison, NY July 11,1864	Oath of Allegiance June 30, 1865
David, John Private	33	December 29, 1861, Williamsburg, South Carolina	Co. K, 25th South Carolina Infantry	January 15, 1865, Fort Fisher, North Carolina	Elmira Prison Camp January 30, 1865	Exchanged March 2, 1865 at Boulware's Wharf on the James River, Virginia
David, John W. Private	23	August 15, 1861, Athens, Clark County, Georgia	Co. C, Cobb's Legion Georgia	May 31, 1864, Hanover Court House, Virginia	Point Lookout, Maryland, transferred to Elmira Prison, NY July 17,1864	Died February 15, 1865 of Typhoid Fever, Grave No. 2184
Davidson, Frank L. Private	Unk	Unknown	Co. A, 9th Alabama Cavalry	August 29, 1864, Milton, Florida	New Orleans, Louisianna Transferred to Elmira Prison, New York, November 19, 1864	Died December 29, 1864 of Pneumonia, Grave No. 1061

Name & Rank	Age	Enlisted	Regiment and State	Where Captured	Prison	Remarks
Davidson, James Private	Unk	Unknown	Co. J, Hood's Battalion Virginia Reserves	June 16, 1864, Petersburg, Virginia	Point Lookout, Maryland, transferred to Elmira Prison, NY July 25, 1864	Died September 15, 1864 of Chronic Diarrhea, Grave No. 295
Davidson, John Private	Unk	May 4, 1864, Petersburg, Virginia	Co. C, Archer's Battalion, Virginia Reserves	June 9, 1864, Petersburg, Virginia	Point Lookout, Maryland, transferred to Elmira Prison, NY July 12, 1864	Exchanged October 29, 1864, at Venus Point, Savannah River, GA.
Davidson, Joseph F, Private	Unk	May 19, 1862, Wilkinson, Georgia	Co. A, 49th Georgia Infantry	May 6, 1864, Wilderness, Virginia	Old Capital Prison, Washington, DC, transferred to Elmira Prison, NY, July 23, 1864	Exchanged October 29, 1864, at Venus Point, Savannah River, GA.
Davidson, O. L. Private	Unk	April 27, 1864, Nacogoches, Texas	Co. G, 37th Texas Cavalry	August 17, 1864, Near Morganza, Louisiana	New Orleans, Louisiana, Transferred to Elmira Prison, New York, November 19, 1864	Died December 12, 1864 of Variola (Smallpox), Grave No. 1145
Davidson, Robert A. Sergeant	Unk	July 7, 1862, Charlotte, North Carolina	Co. F, 5th North Carolina Cavalry	September 22, 1863, Near Madison Court House, Virginia	Point Lookout, Maryland, transferred to Elmira Prison, NY August 18, 1864	Exchanged February 20, 1865 at Boulware's or Cox Wharf on the James River, Virginia
Davidson, Thomas Private	28	September 1, 1864, Duplin County, North Carolina	Co. D, 1st Battalion North Carolina Heavy Artillery	January 15, 1865, Fort Fisher, North Carolina. Wounded.	February 1, 1865, Elmira Prison Camp, New York	Died May 10, 1865 of Variola (Smallpox), Grave No. 2786
Davidson, Thomas D. Private	Unk	May 4, 1864, Petersburg, Virginia	Co. C, Archer Battalion, Virginia Reserves	June 9, 1864, Petersburg, Virginia	Point Lookout, Maryland, transferred to Elmira Prison, NY July 12, 1864	Exchanged October 29, 1864, at Venus Point, Savannah River, GA.
Davidson, W. H. Civilian	Unk	King William County, Virginia	Citizen of Virginia	June 14, 1864, Came into Lines at White House, Virginia	Point Lookout, Maryland, transferred to Elmira Prison, NY July 23, 1864	Oath of Allegiance June 20, 1865

Name & Rank	Age	Enlisted	Regiment and State	Where Captured	Prison	Remarks
Davidson, William, Private	Unk	June 18, 1863, Fairfield, Tennessee	Co. D, 23rd Tennessee Infantry	June 17, 1864, Petersburg, Virginia	Point Lookout, Maryland, transferred to Elmira Prison, NY July 30, 1864	Exchanged February 25, 1865 at Boulware's or Cox Wharf on the James River, Virginia
Davidson, William D., Private	Unk	April 4, 1861, Bibb County, Georgia	Co. H, 12th Georgia Infantry	May 10, 1864, Spotsylvania Court House, Virginia	Point Lookout, Maryland, transferred to Elmira Prison, NY July 25, 1864	Exchanged October 29, 1864, at Venus Point, Savannah River, GA.
Davidson, William N., Private	22	July 18, 1862, Camp Hill, North Carolina	Co. E, 18th North Carolina Infantry	July 29, 1864, Gravel Hill, Petersburg, Virginia	Point Lookout, Maryland, transferred to Elmira Prison, NY August 12, 1864	Died September 25, 1864 of Chronic Diarrhea, Grave No. 456
Davidson, William R. D., Private	Unk	July 8, 1861, Bristol, Tennessee	Co. F, 37th North Carolina Infantry	May 12, 1864, Spotsylvania, Virginia, Gunshot Wound Left Thigh	Old Capital Prison, Washington, DC, transferred to Elmira Prison, NY, July 23, 1864	Transferred for Exchange 10/11/64. Died 10/27/64 of Typhoid Fever at Point Lookout Prison Camp, MD.
Davis, A. B., Private	Unk	Unknown	Co. C, 17th Tennessee Infantry	June 17, 1864, Petersburg, Virginia	Point Lookout, Maryland, transferred to Elmira Prison, NY July 30, 1864	Exchanged February 25, 1865 at Boulware's or Cox Wharf on the James River, Virginia
Davis, Albert F., Private	Unk	October 12, 1862, Berryville, Virginia	Co. D, 6th Virginia Cavalry	January 13, 1865, Jefferson County, Virginia	Old Capital Prison, Washington, DC. February 4, 1865 Elmira, Prison Camp, NY	Oath of Allegiance June 27, 1865
Davis, Alexander Smith, Private	33	May 5, 1862, Elizabethtown, Bladen County, North Carolina	Co. H, 36th Regiment, 2nd North Carolina Artillery	January 15, 1865, Fort Fisher, North Carolina	Elmira Prison Camp, New York, February 1, 1865	Died February 18, 1865 of Chronic Diarrhea, Grave No. 2346
Davis, Alpheus L., Private	18	September 19, 1861, Teague Town, Forsythe County, North Carolina	Co. G, 2nd Battalion North Carolina Infantry	July 10, 1864, Near Harper's Ferry, Virginia	Old Capital Prison, Washington, DC, transferred to Elmira Prison, NY, July 23, 1864	Died November 26, 1864 of Chronic Diarrhea, Grave No. 978

Name & Rank	Age	Enlisted	Regiment and State	Where Captured	Prison	Remarks
Davis, Amos L. Private	18	April 16, 1862, Fort Fisher, North Carolina	Co. I, 36th Regiment 2nd North Carolina Artillery	January 15, 1865, Fort Fisher, North Carolina. Wounded	February 1, 1865, Elmira Prison Camp, New York	Died March 28, 1865 of Variola (Smallpox), Grave No. 2486
Davis, Bartlett Private	22	September 15, 1862, Statesville, North Carolina	Co. B, 37th North Carolina Infantry	May 6, 1864, Wilderness, Virginia	Point Lookout, Maryland, transferred to Elmira Prison, NY August 14, 1864	Oath of Allegiance June 30, 1865
Davis, Benthall Private	Unk	April 1, 1862, Norfolk, Virginia	Co. B, 6th Virginia Infantry	June 6, 1864, Cold Harbor, Virginia	Point Lookout, Maryland, transferred to Elmira Prison, NY July 23, 1864	Died January 24, 1865 of Variola (Smallpox), Grave No. 1622. Name Benjamin Davis on headstone.
Davis, Burrell Sergeant	Unk	June 21, 1862, Goldsboro, North Carolina	Co. C, 66th North Carolina Infantry	January 15, 1865, Fort Fisher, North Carolina	Elmira Prison Camp January 30, 1865	Died February 9, 1865 of Chronic Diarrhea, Grave No. 1941
Davis, Calvin C. Private	23	August 15, 1862, Statesville, North Carolina	Co. C, 37th North Carolina Infantry	May 24, 1864, Hanover Junction, Virginia	Point Lookout, Maryland, transferred to Elmira Prison, NY July 11, 1864	Exchanged March 10, 1865 at Boulware's Wharf on the James River, Virginia
Davis, Charles H. Private	23	August 22, 1862, Wilkes County, North Carolina	Co. D, 18th North Carolina Infantry	May 12, 1864, Spotsylvania Court House, Virginia	Point Lookout, Maryland, transferred to Elmira Prison, NY August 12, 1864	Oath of Allegiance June 12, 1865
Davis, Charles L. Private	25	August 23, 1861, Camp Trousdale, Tennessee	Co. D, 23rd Tennessee Infantry	June 17, 1864, Petersburg, Virginia	Point Lookout, Maryland, transferred to Elmira Prison, NY July 30, 1864	Exchanged February 25, 1865 at Boulware's or Cox Wharf on the James River, Virginia
Davis, Charles S. Private	Unk	July 1, 1861, Prince William County, Virginia	Co. A, 49th Virginia Infantry	May 30, 1864, Gaines Mill, Cold Harbor, Virginia	Point Lookout, Maryland, transferred to Elmira Prison, NY July 11, 1864	Exchanged October 29, 1864, at Venus Point, Savannah River, GA.

Name & Rank	Age	Enlisted	Regiment and State	Where Captured	Prison	Remarks
Davis, D. D. Private	25	March 18, 1862, Shelby, North Carolina	Co. G, 49th North Carolina Infantry	July 17, 1864, Petersburg, Virginia	Old Capital Prison, Washington, DC, transferred to Elmira Prison, NY, July 23, 1864	Died February 9, 1865 of Variola (Smallpox), Grave No. 1923
Davis, Drewey T. Private	23	May 7, 1862, Camp McIntosh, North Carolina	Co. F, 1st North Carolina Infantry	May 12, 1864, Spotsylvania Court House, Virginia	Point Lookout Prison Camp, Maryland. Transferred to Elmira Prison, August 6, 1864	Died March 27, 1865 of Chronic Diarrhea, Grave No. 2501
Davis, Edmund Private	Unk	March 8, 1862, Mansfield, Louisiana	Co. F, 9th Louisiana Infantry	May 12, 1864, Spotsylvania Court House, Virginia	Point Lookout, Maryland, transferred to Elmira Prison, NY August 17, 1864	Exchanged October 29, 1864, at Venus Point, Savannah River, GA.
Davis, Edward Private	Unk	March 7, 1863, King and Queen County Court House, Virginia	Co. E, 24th Virginia Cavalry	June 13, 1864, Turkey Hill, Virginia	Point Lookout, Maryland, transferred to Elmira Prison, NY July 30, 1864	Exchanged October 29, 1864, at Venus Point, Savannah River, GA.
Davis, Edward W. Private	23	Fort St. Philip, Brunswick County, NC, 7/7/1862,	2nd Co. K, 40th Regiment, 3rd North Carolina Light Artillery	January 15, 1865, Fort Fisher, North Carolina	January 30, 1865, Elmira Prison Camp, New York	Exchanged 3/2/1865, Died of Consumption 5/17/1865, Richmond, Jackson Hospital, VA. Buried Hollywood Cemetery, VA
Davis, Ellis H. Private	Unk	Unknown	Co. A, Captain Norwood's Home Guard Florida	September 27, 1864, Marianna, Florida	New Orleans, Louisiana transferred to Elmira November 19, 1864.	No further Information Available
Davis, Ephraim P. Private	Unk	September 12, 1862, Lowndes, Alabama	Co. F, 1st Battalion Alabama Artillery	August 23, 1864, Fort Morgan, Alabama	Steam Press No. 4, New Orleans, Louisiana transferred to Elmira Prison, October 8, 1864.	Oath of Allegiance May 19, 1865

Name & Rank	Age	Enlisted	Regiment and State	Where Captured	Prison	Remarks
Davis, Ervin Q. Private	Unk	April 26, 1862, Crossroads, North Carolina	Co. D, 51st North Carolina Infantry	June 1, 1864, Cold Harbor, Virginia	Point Lookout, Maryland, transferred to Elmira Prison, NY July 17, 1864	Died February 1, 1865 of Remittent Fever, Grave No. 1757
Davis, Eugene Sergeant Major	Unk	August 15, 1863, Culpepper County, Virginia	Field & Staff, 6th Virginia Cavalry	May 11, 1864, Henrico County, Virginia	Point Lookout, Maryland, transferred to Elmira Prison, NY August 17, 1864	Exchanged February 25, 1865 at Boulware's or Cox Wharf on the James River, Virginia
Davis, F. W. Private	21	October 26, 1861, Cleveland, Tennessee	Co. H, 63rd Tennessee Infantry	June 17, 1864, Petersburg, Virginia	Point Lookout, Maryland, transferred to Elmira Prison, NY July 30, 1864	Died November 7, 1864 of Pleuro Pneumonia, Grave No. 774
Davis, G. R. 1st Sergeant	Unk	Unknown	Co. C, 20th North Carolina Infantry	May 20, 1864, Spotsylvania Court House, Virginia	Point Lookout, Maryland, transferred to Elmira Prison, NY July 6, 1864	Oath of Allegiance June 30, 1865
Davis, Garrison P. Sergeant	Unk	December 7, 1861, Spring Hill, Sumter District, South Carolina	Co G, 20th South Carolina Infantry	June 1, 1864, Cold Harbor, Virginia	Point Lookout, Maryland, transferred to Elmira Prison, NY July 17, 1864	Exchanged March 2, 1865 at Akins Landing on the James River, Virginia
Davis, George Private	Unk	Unknown	Co. D, 18th Georgia Infantry	June 1, 1864, Cold Harbor, Virginia	Point Lookout, Maryland, transferred to Elmira Prison, NY July 17, 1864	Oath of Allegiance June 30, 1865
Davis, George S. Private	Unk	July 18, 1861, Urbana, Virginia	Co. D, 24th Virginia Cavalry	July 29, 1864, Petersburg, Virginia	Point Lookout, Maryland, transferred to Elmira Prison, NY August 12, 1864	Exchanged March 2, 1865 at Akins Landing on the James River, Virginia
Davis, George W. Civilian	Unk	Unknown	Citizen of Prince William County, Virginia	March 3, 1863, Prince William County, Virginia	Point Lookout, Maryland, transferred to Elmira Prison, NY July 25, 1864	Exchanged March 10, 1865 at Boulware's Wharf on the James River, Virginia

Name & Rank	Age	Enlisted	Regiment and State	Where Captured	Prison	Remarks
Davis, George W. Sergeant	25	April 18, 1861, Warrenton, North Carolina	Co. F, 12th North Carolina Infantry	May 12, 1864, Near Spotsylvania, Virginia	Point Lookout, Maryland, transferred to Elmira Prison, NY August 14, 1864	Oath of Allegiance June 19, 1865
Davis, George W. Private	20	July 29, 1861, Albemarle, North Carolina	Co. D, 28th North Carolina Infantry	May 12, 1864, Spotsylvania Court House, Virginia	Point Lookout, Maryland, transferred to Elmira Prison, NY August 12, 1864	Exchanged October 29, 1864, at Venus Point, Savannah River, GA.
Davis, H. Private	Unk	January 14, 1864, Greenville, Alabama	Co. F, 1st Battalion Alabama Artillery	August 23, 1864, Fort Morgan, Alabama	Steam Press No. 4, New Orleans, Louisiana transferred to Elmira Prison, October 8, 1864.	Oath of Allegiance May 15, 1865
Davis, Hendren H. Private	Unk	May 14, 1861, Franklin, Virginia	Co. E, 25th Virginia Infantry	May 12, 1864, Spotsylvania Court House, Virginia	Point Lookout, Maryland, transferred to Elmira Prison, NY August 12, 1864	Oath of Allegiance June 16, 1865
Davis, Hiram Private	18	October 19, 1861, Elizabethtown, Bladen County, North Carolina	Co. J, 36th Regiment 2nd North Carolina Artillery	January 15, 1865, Fort Fisher, North Carolina	February 1, 1865, Elmira Prison Camp, New York	Died May 21, 1865 of Unknown Disease, Grave No. 2920. Headstone has 25th North Carolina
Davis, Horatio E. Private	Unk	March 27, 1862, Lynnhaven Beach, Virginia	Co. K, 15th Virginia Cavalry	September 14, 1863, Near Culpepper, Virginia	Point Lookout, Maryland, transferred to Elmira Prison, NY August 18, 1864	Died October 31, 1864 of Chronic Diarrhea, Grave No. 735. Headstone has Henry E. Davis.
Davis, Hugh Private	Unk	Unknown	Co. A, 6th Georgia Infantry	Deserted from Richmond. Surrendered April 28, 1864 at Eastville, Virginia	Point Lookout, Maryland, transferred to Elmira Prison, NY August 18, 1864	Oath of Allegiance May 17, 1865
Davis, J. B. Sergeant	Unk	Unknown	Co. H, 50th Virginia Infantry	May 12, 1864 Spotsylvania Court House, Virginia	Point Lookout, Maryland, transferred to Elmira Prison, NY August 2, 1864	Oath of Allegiance June 23, 1865

Name & Rank	Age	Enlisted	Regiment and State	Where Captured	Prison	Remarks
Davis, J. M. Corporal	Unk	August 7, 1861, Pickensville, Alabama	Co. H, 5th Alabama Infantry	May 5, 1864, Wilderness, Virginia	Point Lookout, Maryland, transferred to Elmira Prison, NY August 17, 1864	Oath of Allegiance June 14, 1865
Davis, James E. Private	Unk	June 11, 1861, Camp McDonald, Georgia	Co. G, 18th Georgia Infantry	June 1, 1864, Cold Harbor, Virginia	Point Lookout, Maryland, transferred to Elmira Prison, NY July 17, 1864	Oath of Allegiance June 21, 1865
Davis, James F. Sergeant	20	Unknown	Co. C, 50th Virginia Infantry	May 12, 1864, Spotsylvania, Virginia	Old Capital Prison, Washington, DC, transferred to Elmira Prison, NY, July 23, 1864	Oath of Allegiance June 27, 1865
Davis, James L. Private	26	June 4, 1861, Camp Moore, Louisiana	Co. A, 6th Louisiana Infantry	May 5, 1864, Wilderness, Virginia	Point Lookout, Maryland, transferred to Elmira Prison, NY August 17, 1864	Exchanged March 10, 1865 at Boulware's Wharf on the James River, Virginia
Davis, James W. Private	Unk	March 16, 1862, Grove Hill, Alabama	Co. I, 5th Alabama Infantry	May 5, 1864, Wilderness, Virginia	Point Lookout, Maryland, transferred to Elmira Prison, NY August 17, 1864	Oath of Allegiance June 19, 1865
Davis, John D. Private	18	March 27, 1862, Cumberland County, North Carolina	Co. J, 51st North Carolina Infantry	June 1, 1864, Cold Harbor, Virginia	Transferred From Point Lookout Prison, MD, July 12, 1864. Train Never Arrived at Elmira Prison Camp, NY.	Died July 15, 1864 in Train Wreck at Shohola, Pennsylvania.
Davis, John P. Corporal	33	October 26, 1861, Charleston, Tennessee	Co. H, 63rd Tennessee Infantry	June 17, 1864, Petersburg, Virginia	Point Lookout, Maryland, transferred to Elmira Prison, NY July 30, 1864	Died November 30, 1864 of Pneumonia, Grave No. 996
Davis, John R. Private	18	March 16, 1862, Fort Fisher, North Carolina	Co. J, 36th Regiment 2nd North Carolina Artillery	January 15, 1865, Fort Fisher, North Carolina	February 1, 1865, Elmira Prison Camp, New York	Oath of Allegiance June 15, 1865

Name & Rank	Age	Enlisted	Regiment and State	Where Captured	Prison	Remarks
Davis, John W. Sergeant	24	October 10, 1861, Carteret County, North Carolina	Co. G, 40th Regiment, 3rd North Carolina Artillery	January 15, 1865, Fort Fisher, North Carolina	February 1, 1865, Elmira Prison Camp, New York	Oath of Allegiance May 19, 1865
Davis, Jordan D. Corporal	Unk	May 14, 1862, Fort St. Philips, North Carolina	Co. J, 36th Regiment 2nd North Carolina Artillery	January 15, 1865, Fort Fisher, North Carolina	February 1, 1865, Elmira Prison Camp, New York	Exchanged March 2, 1865 at Boulware's Wharf on the James River, Virginia
Davis, Joseph Private	Unk	June 15, 1861, Columbus, Georgia	Co. E, 12th Georgia Infantry	July 17,1864, Near Washington, DC,	Old Capital Prison, Washington, DC, transferred to Elmira Prison, NY, July 23, 1864	Exchanged March 14, 1865 at Boulware's Wharf on the James River, Virginia
Davis, Joseph B. Private	22	May 10, 1861, Washington, North Carolina	Co. G, 3rd North Carolina Infantry	May 12, 1864, Near Spotsylvania Court House, Virginia	Point Lookout Prison, Maryland. Transferred to Elmira Prison Camp New York August 14, 1864.	Exchanged March 14, 1865 at Boulware's Wharf on the James River, Virginia
Davis, Josiah Private	23	July 29, 1862, Camp Leon, Florida	Co. E, 10th Florida Infantry	July 1, 1864, Near Petersburg, Virginia	Point Lookout, Maryland, transferred to Elmira Prison, NY July 23, 1864	Oath of Allegiance May 29, 1865
Davis, L. C. Private	Unk	August 12, 1863, Perry County, Alabama	Co. A, 21st Alabama Infantry	August 23, 1864, Fort Morgan, Alabama	Steam Press No. 4, New Orleans, Louisiana transferred to Elmira Prison, October 8, 1864.	Exchanged March 14, 1865 at Boulware's Wharf on the James River, Virginia
Davis, L. D. Private	Unk	March 27, 1864, Scott's Hill, Virginia	Captain Young's Battery Virginia Artillery	June 15, 1864, Petersburg, Virginia	Point Lookout, Maryland, transferred to Elmira Prison, NY July 25, 1864	Exchanged March 10, 1865 at Boulware's Wharf on the James River, Virginia
Davis, Laban C. Private	18	April 5, 1862, Camp Shenandoah, Virginia	Co. E, 25th Virginia Infantry	May 12, 1864, Spotsylvania Court House, Virginia	Point Lookout, Maryland, transferred to Elmira Prison, NY August 12, 1864	Oath of Allegiance June 23, 1865

Name & Rank	Age	Enlisted	Regiment and State	Where Captured	Prison	Remarks
Davis, Leander Alfred Private	20	August 6, 1861, Camp Pulaski, Louisiana	Co. G, 15th Louisiana Infantry	May 12, 1864, Spotsylvania Court House, Virginia	Point Lookout, Maryland, transferred to Elmira Prison, NY July 25, 1864	Died April 10, 1865 of Acute Dysentery, Grave No. 2669
Davis, M. G. Corporal	Unk	April 15, 1861, Livingston, Alabama	Co. E, 5th Alabama Infantry	May 20, 1864, Spotsylvania Court House, Virginia	Point Lookout, Maryland, transferred to Elmira Prison, NY August 17, 1864	Oath of Allegiance June 14, 1865
Davis, Marion C. Private	24	September 9, 1861, Camp Myers, Tennessee	Co. A, 25th Tennessee Infantry	May 16, 1864, Near Drury's Bluff, Virginia	Point Lookout, Maryland, transferred to Elmira Prison, NY August 18, 1864	Exchanged February 25, 1865 at Boulware's or Cox Wharf on the James River, Virginia
Davis, Marshall T. Private	22	March 1, 1863, Spartanburg, South Carolina	Co. F, 6th South Carolina Cavalry	July 30, 1864, Lee's Mill, Petersburg, Virginia	Point Lookout, Maryland, transferred to Elmira Prison, NY August 12, 1864	Oath of Allegiance June 19, 1865
Davis, Matthew H. Private	Unk	December 20, 1863, Greenville, South Carolina	Co. H, 22nd South Carolina Infantry	July 30, 1864, Petersburg, Virginia	Point Lookout, Maryland, transferred to Elmira Prison, NY August 12, 1864	Oath of Allegiance July 3, 1865
Davis, Michael Private	22	July 15, 1862, Guilford County, North Carolina	Co. A, 1st North Carolina Infantry	May 12, 1864, Spotsylvania Court House, Virginia	Point Lookout Prison Camp, Maryland. Transferred to Elmira Prison, August 6, 1864	Died December 20, 1864 of Pneumonia, Grave No. 1076
Davis, Morgan A. Private	Unk	February 10, 1864, Columbia, South Carolina	Co. F, 25th South Carolina Infantry	June 16, 1864, Petersburg, Virginia	Point Lookout, Maryland, transferred to Elmira Prison, NY July 30, 1864	Oath of Allegiance July 3, 1865
Davis, Nathanial S. Private	Unk	June 22, 1861, Camp McDonald, Georgia	Co. J, 18th Georgia Infantry	June 1, 1864, Cold Harbor, Virginia	Point Lookout, Maryland, transferred to Elmira Prison, NY July 17, 1864	Died October 13, 1864 of Chronic Diarrhea, Grave No. 702

Name & Rank	Age	Enlisted	Regiment and State	Where Captured	Prison	Remarks
Davis, Robert Private	46	November 1, 1862, Elizabeth City, North Carolina	Co. A, 8th North Carolina Infantry	June 1, 1864, Cold Harbor, Virginia	Point Lookout, Maryland, transferred to Elmira Prison, NY July 17,1864	Died February 12, 1865 of Typhoid Fever, Grave No. 2055
Davis, Robert N. Private	Unk	June 22, 1861, Camp Trousdale, Tennessee	Co. H, 17th Tennessee Infantry	June 17, 1864, Petersburg, Virginia	Point Lookout, Maryland, transferred to Elmira Prison, NY July 30, 1864	Exchanged February 13, 1865 at Boulware's wharf on the James River, Virginia
Davis, Sampson Private	22	August 19, 1862, Coffee County, , Alabama	Co. E, 1st Battalion Alabama Artillery	August 23, 1864, Fort Morgan, Alabama	New Orleans, Louisiana transferred to Elmira December 4, 1864.	Orders for Elmira, NY. Died in Transit February 10, 1865 of Variola at US Army Hospital Fort Columbus, NY Harbor.
Davis, Samuel J. Color Corporal	Unk	June 15, 1861, Lynchburg, Virginia	Co. A, 42nd Virginia Infantry	May 12, 1864, Spotsylvania Court House, Virginia	Point Lookout, Maryland, transferred to Elmira Prison, NY August 2, 1864	Died December 14, 1864 of Pneumonia, Grave No. 1127. Headstone has 24th Virginia.
Davis, Samuel W. D. Private	Unk	May 16, 1862, Montgomery, Alabama	Co. E, 23rd Battalion Alabama Sharp Shooters	June 15, 1864, Drury's Bluff, Petersburg, Virginia	Point Lookout, Maryland, transferred to Elmira Prison, NY July 25, 1864	Oath of Allegiance June 16, 1865
Davis, T. F. Private	20	December 20, 1861, Chesterfield District, South Carolina	Co. J, 21st South Carolina Infantry	June 24, 1864, Petersburg, Virginia	Point Lookout, Maryland, transferred to Elmira Prison, NY August 18, 1864	Exchanged March 2, 1865 at Akins Landing on the James River, Virginia
Davis, Thaddeus C. Sergeant	19	October 16, 1861, Carteret County, North Carolina	Co. G, 40th Regiment, 3rd North Carolina Artillery	January 15, 1865, Fort Fisher, North Carolina	February 1, 1865, Elmira Prison Camp, New York	Oath of Allegiance May 19, 1865
Davis, Thomas Private	Unk	January 14, 1864, Greenville, Alabama	Co. F, 1st Battalion Alabama Artillery	August 23, 1864, Fort Morgan, Alabama	Steam Press No. 4, New Orleans, Louisiana transferred to Elmira Prison, October 8, 1864.	Oath of Allegiance May 17, 1865

Name & Rank	Age	Enlisted	Regiment and State	Where Captured	Prison	Remarks
Davis, Thomas Private	23	January 1, 1861, Wilmington, New Hanover County, North Carolina	Co. B, 36th Regiment North Carolina, 2nd Artillery	January 15, 1865, Fort Fisher, North Carolina	February 1, 1865, Elmira Prison Camp, New York	Exchanged March 2, 1865 at Boulware's Wharf on the James River, Virginia
Davis, Thomas H. Private	20	March 21, 1862, Williamston, North Carolina	Co. A, 17th North Carolina Infantry	August 31, 1863, Big Black, Mississippi	Point Lookout, Maryland, transferred to Elmira Prison, NY August 18, 1864	Exchanged March 10, 1865 at Boulware's wharf on the James River, Virginia
Davis, Thomas J. Private	17	June 9, 1861, Quitman, Georgia	Co. H, 9th Georgia Infantry	May 6, 1864, Wilderness, Virginia	Point Lookout, Maryland, transferred to Elmira Prison, NY August 14, 1864	Died October 8, 1864 of Chronic Diarrhea, Grave No. 659
Davis, Wiley Private	38	July 29, 1861, Warrenton, North Carolina	Co. D, 1st North Carolina Infantry	May 12, 1864, Spotsylvania Court House, Virginia	Point Lookout, Maryland, transferred to Elmira Prison, NY August 6, 1864	Oath of Allegiance June 30, 1865
Davis, William Sergeant	Unk	April 15, 1862, Louisiana	Co. C, Gober's Battalion Louisiana Cavalry	October 15, 1864, East Baton Rouge, Louisiana	New Orleans, Louisiana transferred to Elmira November 19, 1864.	Oath of Allegiance May 19, 1865
Davis, William Private	23	March 14, 1861, Mobile, Alabama	Co. F, 1st Battalion Alabama Artillery	August 23, 1864, Fort Morgan, Alabama	Steam Press No. 4, New Orleans, Louisiana transferred to Elmira Prison, October 8, 1864.	Exchanged February 20, 1865. Died on the Route of Unknown Causes.
Davis, William Private	23	June 8, 1861, Duplin County, North Carolina	Co. B, 3rd North Carolina Infantry	May 12, 1864, Near Spotsylvania, Virginia	Point Lookout, Maryland, transferred to Elmira Prison, NY August 14, 1864	Oath of Allegiance June 27, 1865
Davis, William Private	Unk	February 20, 1863, Buckingham, Virginia	Co. H, 4th Virginia Cavalry	July 14, 1863, Germania Ford, Virginia	Point Lookout, Maryland, transferred to Elmira Prison, NY August 18, 1864	Exchanged March 10, 1865 at Boulware's Wharf on the James River, Virginia

Name & Rank	Age	Enlisted	Regiment and State	Where Captured	Prison	Remarks
Davis, William A. Private	20	October 19, 1861, Elizabethtown, Bladen County, North Carolina	Co. J, 36th Regiment 2nd North Carolina Artillery	January 15, 1865, Fort Fisher, North Carolina	February 1, 1865, Elmira Prison Camp, New York	Exchanged March 2, 1865 at Boulware's Wharf on the James River, Virginia
Davis, William A. Private	Unk	March 29, 1862, Lewisburg, Virginia	Co. B, 26th Virginia Infantry	May 31, 1864, Chickahominy, Cold Harbor, Virginia	Point Lookout, Maryland, transferred to Elmira Prison, NY July 11, 1864	Exchanged March 10, 1865 at Boulware's Wharf on the James River, Virginia
Davis, William C. Private	Unk	October 24, 1863, Raleigh, North Carolina	Co. F, 18th North Carolina Infantry	May 12, 1864, Spotsylvania Court House, Virginia	Point Lookout, Maryland, transferred to Elmira Prison, NY August 6, 1864	Exchanged October 29, 1864, at Venus Point, Savannah River, GA.
Davis, William Daniel Private	23	February 27, 1862, Greensboro, North Carolina	Co. B, 45th North Carolina Infantry	May 10, 1864, Spotsylvania Court House, Virginia	Point Lookout, Maryland, transferred to Elmira Prison, NY August 6, 1864	Died August 16, 1864 of Remittent Fever, Grave No. 123
Davis, William G. Private	22	July 1, 1861, Staunton, Virginia	Co. E, 6th Cavalry, Virginia	June 1, 1864, Cold Harbor, Virginia	Point Lookout, Maryland, transferred to Elmira Prison, NY July 17, 1864	Oath of Allegiance June 27, 1865
Davis, William H. Private	18	May 1, 1862, Fort Fisher, New Hanover County, North Carolina	Co. C, 36th Regiment 2nd North Carolina Artillery	January 15, 1865, Fort Fisher, North Carolina	February 1, 1865, Elmira Prison Camp, New York	Died April 27, 1865 of Pneumonia, Grave No. 1428
Davis, William J. Private	Unk	October 1, 1861, Augusta, Georgia	Co. C, 38th Georgia Infantry	May 6, 1864, Wilderness, Virginia	Point Lookout, Maryland, transferred to Elmira Prison, NY August 17, 1864	Exchanged March 14, 1865 at Boulware's Wharf on the James River, Virginia
Davis, William W. Private	Unk	July 31, 1863, Bryan County, Georgia	Co. K, 7th Georgia Cavalry	June 11, 1864, Trevilian Station, Louisa Court House, Virginia	Point Lookout, Maryland, transferred to Elmira Prison, NY July 25, 1864	Exchanged October 29, 1864, at Venus Point, Savannah River, GA.
Davis, William W. Sergeant	18	April 5, 1862, Camp Shenandoah, Virginia	Co. E, 25th Virginia Infantry	May 12, 1864, Spotsylvania Court House, Virginia	Point Lookout, Maryland, transferred to Elmira Prison, NY August 12, 1864	Oath of Allegiance June 27, 1865

Name & Rank	Age	Enlisted	Regiment and State	Where Captured	Prison	Remarks
Davis, Willis D. M. Private	Unk	March 22, 1861, Selma, Alabama	Co. C, 1st Battalion Alabama Artillery	August 23, 1864, Fort Morgan, Alabama	New Orleans, Louisiana transferred to Elmira December 4, 1864.	Died June 4, 1865 of Chronic Diarrhea, Grave No. 2898
Davison, S. T. Private	Unk	January 1, 1862, Camp Hampton, Columbia, South Carolina	Co. H, 18th South Carolina Infantry	July 30, 1864, Petersburg, Virginia	Point Lookout, Maryland, transferred to Elmira Prison, NY August 12, 1864	Exchanged March 14, 1865 at Boulware's Wharf on the James River, Virginia
Dawes, William C. Private	Unk	Unknown	Co. J, 12th Virginia Cavalry	August 15, 1864, Milldale, Virginia	Old Capital Prison, Washington, DC transferred to Elmira Prison, NY August 29, 1864	Exchanged October 29, 1864, at Venus Point, Savannah River, GA.
Dawkins, John M. Private	Unk	March 17, 1864, Green Pond, South Carolina	Co. D, 17th South Carolina Infantry	July 30, 1864, Petersburg, Virginia	Point Lookout, Maryland, transferred to Elmira Prison, NY August 12, 1864	Died September 23, 1864 of Acute Diarrhea, Grave No. 35
Dawkins, William C. Private	Unk	March 30, 1862, Camp Pillow, South Carolina	Co. D, 17th South Carolina Infantry	July 30, 1864, Near Petersburg, Virginia	Point Lookout, Maryland, transferred to Elmira Prison, NY August 12, 1864	Died September 4, 1864 of Diarrhea, Grave No. 229. Dorkins on Headstone.
Dawson, Dory W. Corporal	24	June 1, 1861, Romney, Virginia	Co. F, 7th Virginia Cavalry	September 14, 1863, Near Culpepper, Virginia	Point Lookout, Maryland, transferred to Elmira Prison, NY August 18, 1864	Exchanged March 10, 1865 at Boulware's Wharf on the James River, Virginia
Dawson, James D. Private	Unk	May 27, 1861, Buckhannon, Virginia	Co. B, 25th Virginia Infantry	May 12, 1864, Spotsylvania Court House, Virginia	Point Lookout, Maryland, transferred to Elmira Prison, NY August 12, 1864	Oath of Allegiance July 11, 1865
Dawson, James H. Sergeant	Unk	June 15, 1861, Columbus, Georgia	Co. E, 12th Georgia Infantry	May 10, 1864, Spotsylvania Court House, Virginia	Point Lookout, Maryland, transferred to Elmira Prison, NY July 25, 1864	Exchanged March 10, 1865 at Boulware's Wharf on the James River, Virginia

Name & Rank	Age	Enlisted	Regiment and State	Where Captured	Prison	Remarks
Dawson, John B. Private	29	August 17, 1862, Raleigh, North Carolina	Co. I, 18th North Carolina Infantry	May 12, 1864, Spotsylvania Court House, Virginia	Point Lookout, Maryland, transferred to Elmira Prison, NY August 6, 1864	Died April 24, 1865 of Chronic Diarrhea, Grave No. 1407
Dawson, John D. Private	Unk	September 18, 1862, Sharpsburg, Maryland	Co. B, 25th Virginia Infantry	May 12, 1864, Spotsylvania Court House, Virginia	Point Lookout, Maryland, transferred to Elmira Prison, NY August 12, 1864	Oath of Allegiance July 11, 1865
Dawson, W. W. Private	Unk	Unknown	Co. F, 50th Virginia Infantry	May 12, 1864, Spotsylvania Court House, Virginia	Point Lookout, Maryland, transferred to Elmira Prison, NY August 2, 1864	Died October 10, 1864 of Chronic Diarrhea, Grave No. 689
Dawson, William F. Private	24	September 1, 1863, Drury's Bluff, Virginia	Co. H, 45th, North Carolina Infantry	May 20, 1864, Spotsylvania Court House, Virginia	Point Lookout, Maryland, transferred to Elmira Prison, NY July 6, 1864	Died December 6, 1864 of Diarrhea, Grave No. 1691
Day, Benjamin S. Private	26	April 15, 1861, Sheveport, Louisiana	Co. F, 1st Louisiana Infantry	May 20, 1864, Spotsylvania Court House, Virginia	Point Lookout, Maryland, transferred to Elmira Prison, NY July 6, 1864	Died December 6, 1864 of Pneumonia, Grave No. 1024
Day, Eli Private	24	February 28, 1862, Iredell County, North Carolina	Co. A, 4th, North Carolina Infantry	May 20, 1864, Spotsylvania Court House, Virginia	Point Lookout, Maryland, transferred to Elmira Prison, NY July 6, 1864	Died April 21, 1865, of Chronic Diarrhea, Grave No. 1390
Day, James M. Private	Unk	July 11, 1862, Lynchburg, Virginia	Co. I, 42nd Virginia Infantry	May 12, 1864, Near Spotsylvania Court House, Virginia	Point Lookout, Maryland, transferred to Elmira Prison, NY August 6, 1864	Oath of Allegiance June 21, 1865
Day. John T. Private	32	May 6, 1862, Grahamville, South Carolina	Co. C, 4th South Carolina Cavalry	May 28, 1864, Hanover Town, VA. Gunshot Wound Right Chest and Left Wrist and Hip.	Old Capital Prison, Washington, DC transferred to Elmira Prison, NY August 27, 1864	Exchanged February 13, 1865 at Boulware's Wharf on the James River, Virginia

Name & Rank	Age	Enlisted	Regiment and State	Where Captured	Prison	Remarks
Day, John W. Sergeant	23	May 10, 1861, Washington, North Carolina	Co. J, 3rd North Carolina Infantry	May 12, 1864, Near Spotsylvania Court House, Virginia	Point Lookout Prison, Maryland. Transferred to Elmira Prison Camp New York August 14, 1864.	Exchanged February 13, 1865 at Boulware's wharf on the James River, Virginia
Day, Marion F. Private	Unk	June 15, 1864, Chafin's Bluff, North Carolina	Co. A, 24th North Carolina Infantry	June 17, 1864, Petersburg, Virginia	Point Lookout, Maryland, transferred to Elmira Prison, NY July 30, 1864	Died August 28, 1864 of Chronic Diarrhea, Grave No. 47
Deal, Abel D. Private	23	September 5, 1861, Newton, North Carolina	Co. E, 32nd North Carolina Infantry	May 10, 1864, Wilderness, Virginia	Point Lookout, Maryland, transferred to Elmira Prison, NY August 6, 1864	Oath of Allegiance June 30, 1865
Deal, David L. Sergeant	28	August 8, 1862, Statesville, North Carolina	Co. G, 37th North Carolina Infantry	July 29, 1864, Petersburg, Virginia	Point Lookout, Maryland, transferred to Elmira Prison, NY August 12, 1864	Died April 10, 1865 of Chronic Bronchitis, Grave No. 2673
Deal, E. D. Private	Unk	April 1, 1862, Newton, North Carolina	Co. A, 12th North Carolina Infantry	May 12, 1864, Near Spotsylvania, Virginia	Point Lookout, Maryland, transferred to Elmira Prison, NY August 14, 1864	Oath of Allegiance June 30, 1865
Deal, James M. Private	35	February 1, 1862, Bannerman's, Dogwood Grove, North Carolina	Co. K, 3rd North Carolina Infantry	May 12, 1864, Near Spotsylvania Court House, Virginia	Point Lookout Prison, Maryland. Transferred to Elmira Prison Camp New York August 14, 1864.	Exchanged October 29, 1864, at Venus Point, Savannah River, GA.
Deal, John Private	Unk	August 8, 1863, Macon, Georgia	Co. H, 7th Georgia Cavalry	June 11, 1864, Trevilian Station, Louisa Court House, Virginia	Point Lookout, Maryland, transferred to Elmira Prison, NY July 25, 1864	Oath of Allegiance July 11, 1865
Deal, John A. Corporal	16	August 20, 1861, Fayetteville, North Carolina	Co. B, 8th North Carolina Infantry	May 31, 1864, Cold Harbor, Virginia	Point Lookout, Maryland, transferred to Elmira Prison, NY July 11, 1864	Exchanged October 29, 1864, at Venus Point, Savannah River, GA.

Name & Rank	Age	Enlisted	Regiment and State	Where Captured	Prison	Remarks
Deal, Linton W. Private	37	February 2, 1863, Wilmington, New Hanover, North Carolina	Co. D, 1st Battalion North Carolina Heavy Artillery	January 15, 1865, Fort Fisher, North Carolina. Wounded.	February 1, 1865, Elmira Prison Camp, New York	Exchanged March 2, 1865 at Boulware's Wharf on the James River, Virginia
Deal, M. M. Private	Unk	November 1, 1863, Newton, North Carolina	Co. A, 12th North Carolina Infantry	May 12, 1864, Near Spotsylvania, Virginia	Point Lookout, Maryland, transferred to Elmira Prison, NY August 14, 1864	Died April 20, 1865 of Pneumonia, Grave No. 1380
Deal, Peter Private	Unk	April 24, 1864, C. Gawley, Virginia	Co. C, 22nd Virginia Infantry	July 15, 1864, Near Washington, DC,	Old Capital Prison, Washington, DC, transferred to Elmira Prison, NY, July 23, 1864	Died February 15, 1865 of Typhoid Fever, Grave No. 2168
Deal, Richard L. Private	Unk	May 1, 1862, White Sulfur Springs, Virginia	Co. C, 22nd Virginia Infantry	July 13, 1864, Hagerstown, Maryland	Old Capital Prison, Washington, DC, transferred to Elmira Prison, NY, July 23, 1864	Oath of Allegiance November 18, 1864
Deal, Thaidus H. Private	Unk	September 26, 1862, Camp Charleston, Virginia	Co. C, 22nd Virginia Infantry	July 15, 1864, Near Washington, DC,	Old Capital Prison, Washington, DC, transferred to Elmira Prison, NY, July 23, 1864	Oath of Allegiance May 29, 1865
Deal, William Private	Unk	October 1, 1863, Greenville, North Carolina	Co. J, 67th North Carolina Infantry	October 12, 1863, Sift Creek Bridge, Currituck County, North Carolina	Point Lookout, Maryland, transferred to Elmira Prison, NY July 12, 1864	Exchanged February 20, 1865 at Boulware's or Cox Wharf on the James River, Virginia
Dean, Elisha W. Private	Unk	May 22, 1861, Alisona, Tennessee	Co. A, 17th Tennessee Infantry	June 17, 1864, Petersburg, Virginia	Point Lookout, Maryland, transferred to Elmira Prison, NY July 30, 1864	Exchanged October 29, 1864, at Venus Point, Savannah River, GA.

Name & Rank	Age	Enlisted	Regiment and State	Where Captured	Prison	Remarks
Dean, Frank A. Private	Unk	Unknown	Co. B, Confederate States Marines	January 15, 1865, Fort Fisher, North Carolina	February 1, 1865, Elmira Prison Camp, New York	Died of Chronic Diarrhea July 18, 1865. No Grave in Woodlawn National Cemetery.
Dean, G. A. Private	Unk	February 5, 1863, Camden, South Carolina	Co. G, 7th Battalion, South Carolina Infantry	July 10, 1863, Morris Island, South Carolina	Point Lookout, Maryland, transferred to Elmira Prison, NY August 18, 1864	Exchanged October 29, 1864, at Venus Point, Savannah River, GA.
Dean, John Private	Unk	September 2, 1862, Butler County, Alabama	Co. A, 1st Alabama Artillery	August 23, 1864, Fort Morgan, Alabama	New Orleans, Louisiana transferred to Elmira December 4, 1864.	Died January 27, 1865 of Variola (Smallpox), Grave No. 1642
Dean, John L. Private	Unk	September 2, 1862, Butler County, Alabama	Co. E, 1st Battalion Alabama Artillery	August 23, 1864, Fort Morgan, Alabama	New Orleans, Louisiana transferred to Elmira December 4, 1864.	Oath of Allegiance July 11, 1865
Dean, John R. Corporal	Unk	May 22, 1861, Alisona, Tennessee	Co. A, 17th Tennessee Infantry	June 17, 1864, Petersburg, Virginia	Point Lookout, Maryland, transferred to Elmira Prison, NY July 30, 1864	Exchanged October 29, 1864, at Venus Point, Savannah River, GA.
Dean, Lorenzo D. Private	Unk	March 9, 1863, Conecuh, Alabama	Co. A, 1st Alabama Artillery	August 23, 1864, Fort Morgan, Alabama	New Orleans, Louisiana transferred to Elmira December 4, 1864.	Died May 15, 1865 of Chronic Diarrhea, Grave No. 2805. Headstone has L. D. Lee.
Dean, Rowan Private	Unk	March 9, 1863, Conecuh, Alabama	Co. A, 1st Alabama Artillery	August 23, 1864, Fort Morgan, Alabama	New Orleans, Louisiana transferred to Elmira December 4, 1864.	Oath of Allegiance July 11, 1865
Dean, Simpson Sergeant	21	September 7, 1861, Camp Crabtree, Granville County, North Carolina	Co. G, 30th North Carolina Infantry	May 12, 1864, Near Spotsylvania, Virginia	Point Lookout, Maryland, transferred to Elmira Prison, NY August 14, 1864	Oath of Allegiance June 21, 1865
Dean, William Edward Sergeant	Unk	April 23, 1861, Mobile, Alabama	Co. E, 3rd Alabama Infantry	May 12, 1864, Spotsylvania Court House, Virginia	Point Lookout, Maryland, transferred to Elmira Prison, NY August 12, 1864	Oath of Allegiance June 19, 1865

Name & Rank	Age	Enlisted	Regiment and State	Where Captured	Prison	Remarks
Deans, Daniel O. Civilian	Unk	Unknown	Citizen of Guilford County, North Carolina	April 21, 1864, Wilmington, North Carolina	Point Lookout, Maryland, transferred to Elmira Prison, NY July 25, 1864	Died August 23, 1864 of Chronic Diarrhea. Grave No. 36
Deans, Dempsey Private	25	May 25, 1861, Wilson, North Carolina	Co. E, 7th North Carolina Infantry	May 5, 1864, Wilderness, Virginia	Point Lookout, Maryland, transferred to Elmira Prison, NY July 23, 1864	Died January 13, 1865 of Variola (Smallpox), Grave No. 1485
Deans, Jesse W. Private	Unk	September 6, 1862, Cumberland County, North Carolina	Co. E, 8th, North Carolina Infantry	May 31, 1864, Cold Harbor, Virginia	Point Lookout, Maryland, transferred to Elmira Prison, NY July 11, 1864	Exchanged February 20, 1865 at Boulware's or Cox Wharf on the James River, Virginia
Dearman, James F. Private	20	June 19, 1861, Statesville, North Carolina	Co. A, 33rd North Carolina Infantry	July 14, 1863, Falling Waters, Maryland	Point Lookout, Maryland, transferred to Elmira Prison, NY August 18, 1864	Exchanged March 10, 1865 at Boulware's Wharf on the James River, Virginia
Dearmond, George Private	Unk	May 19, 1861, Guntersville, Marshall County, Alabama	Co. K, 9th Alabama Infantry	May 6, 1864, Wilderness, Virginia	Point Lookout, Maryland, transferred to Elmira Prison, NY August 17, 1864	Oath of Allegiance June 14, 1865
Dearring, John Private	32	May 14, 1862, Saltills, Mississippi	Co. K, 42nd Mississippi Infantry	May 5, 1864, Wilderness, Virginia	Point Lookout, Maryland, transferred to Elmira Prison, NY July 23, 1864	Died December 13, 1864 of Chronic Diarrhea, Grave No. 1135. Name John Derring on Headstone.
Deatherage, L. H. Private	Unk	Unknown	Co. K, 50th Virginia Infantry	May 6, 1864, Wilderness, Virginia	Point Lookout, Maryland, transferred to Elmira Prison, NY August 14, 1864	Oath of Allegiance June 3, 1865
Deaton, Elijah Sergeant	Unk	August 3, 1861, Cartersville, Georgia	Co. K, 18th Georgia Infantry	June 1, 1864, Cold Harbor, Virginia	Point Lookout, Maryland, transferred to Elmira Prison, NY July 17, 1864	Exchanged March 14, 1865 at Boulware's Wharf on the James River, Virginia

Name & Rank	Age	Enlisted	Regiment and State	Where Captured	Prison	Remarks
Deaton, McDonald Private	Unk	August 24, 1861, Lawrenceville, Gwinnett County, Georgia	Co. F, 24th Georgia Infantry	August 16, 1864, Front Royal, Virginia	Old Capital Prison, Washington, DC transferred to Elmira Prison, NY August 29, 1864	Oath of Allegiance May 29, 1865
Deaton, Pinckney T. Corporal	Unk	August 24, 1861, Clarksville, Georgia	Co. K, 24th Georgia Infantry	June 1, 1864, Cold Harbor, Virginia	Point Lookout, Maryland, transferred to Elmira Prison, NY July 17,1864	Exchanged March 10, 1865 at Boulware's wharf on the James River, Virginia
Deaton, William Thomas	18	August 19, 1861, Luka, Mississippi	Co. A, 26th Mississippi Infantry	May 16, 1863, Baker's Creek, Champion Hill, Mississippi	Point Lookout, Maryland, transferred to Elmira Prison, NY August 18, 1864	Exchanged March 10, 1865 at Boulware's wharf on the James River, Virginia
Deau, William Private	Unk	Unknown	Co. A, Battery, Louisiana Artillery	July 16, 1864, Loudoun County, Virginia	Old Capital Prison, Washington, DC, transferred to Elmira Prison, NY, July 23, 1864	Oath of Allegiance May 29, 1865
Deaver, John R. Private	27	July 14, 1863, Richmond, Virginia	Co. F, 1st Maryland Cavalry	July 30, 1864, Potomac Run, Virginia	Old Capital Prison, Washington D. C. Transferred to Elmira Prison, NY August 12, 1864	Exchanged October 29, 1864, at Venus Point, Savannah River, GA.
Deaver, Nathan H. Private	Unk	April 11, 1862, Cumberland County, North Carolina	Co. I, 51st North Carolina Infantry	June 1, 1864, Cold Harbor, Virginia	Transferred From Point Lookout Prison, MD, July 12, 1864. Train Never Arrived at Elmira Prison Camp, NY.	Died July 15, 1864 in Train Wreck at Shohola, Pennsylvania.
De Berry, David D. Private	Unk	February 22, 1864, Liberty Mills, Virginia	Co. E, 28th, North Carolina Infantry	May 24, 1864, Spotsylvania Court House, Virginia	Point Lookout, Maryland, transferred to Elmira Prison, NY July 11,1864	Exchanged October 29, 1864, at Venus Point, Savannah River, GA.

Name & Rank	Age	Enlisted	Regiment and State	Where Captured	Prison	Remarks
Deck, George W. Private	20	February 20, 1863, Zollicotter, Tennessee	Co. F, 63rd Tennessee Infantry	June 17, 1864, Near Petersburg, Virginia	Point Lookout, Maryland, transferred to Elmira Prison, NY July 23, 1864	Died September 16, 1864 of Chronic Diarrhea and Scurvy, Grave No. 171
Decker, Samuel H. Corporal	Unk	August 1, 1861, Staunton, Virginia	Co. H, 25th Virginia Infantry	May 6, 1864, Wilderness, Virginia	Old Capital Prison, Washington D. C. Transferred to Elmira Prison, NY July 14, 1864	Oath of Allegiance June 23, 1865
Decker, William H. C. Corporal	Unk	August 1, 1861, Staunton, Virginia	Co. H, 25th Virginia Infantry	May 6, 1864, Wilderness, Virginia	Old Capital Prison, Washington D. C. Transferred to Elmira Prison, NY July 14, 1864	Oath of Allegiance June 30, 1865
Deegan, John Private	30	June 19, 1861, Camp Moore, Tagipho, Louisiana	Co. C, 8th Louisiana Infantry	May 20, 1864, Spotsylvania Court House, Virginia	Point Lookout, Maryland, transferred to Elmira Prison, NY July 6,1864	Exchanged February 25, 1865 at Boulware's or Cox Wharf on the James River, Virginia
Deering, J. Private	Unk	March 17, 1861, Union County, North Carolina	Co. F, 1st Missouri Cavalry	May 17, 1863, Big Black Bridge, Champion Hill, Mississippi	Point Lookout, Maryland, transferred to Elmira Prison, NY August 18, 1864	Exchanged February 13, 1865 at Boulwares wharf on the James River, Virginia
Dees, Briant W. Private	36	March 17, 1861, Union County, North Carolina	Co. A, 48th North Carolina Infantry	June 3, 1864, Talapatomoy Creek, Brown's Farm, Cold Harbor, Virginia	Point Lookout, Maryland, transferred to Elmira Prison, NY July 17,1864	Exchanged March 14, 1865 at Boulware's Wharf on the James River, Virginia
Dees, Frank Private	Unk	August 2, 1863, Lancaster County Court House, South Carolina	Co. I, 17th South Carolina Infantry	July 30, 1864, Petersburg, Virginia	Point Lookout, Maryland, transferred to Elmira Prison, NY August 12, 1864	Exchanged October 29, 1864, at Venus Point, Savannah River, GA.
Dees, John A. W. Private	19	April 29, 1863, Richmond County, North Carolina	Co. B, 36th Regiment 2nd North Carolina Artillery	January 15, 1865, Fort Fisher, North Carolina	February 1, 1865, Elmira Prison Camp, New York	Died February 27, 1865 of Chronic Diarrhea and Variola (Smallpox), Grave No. 2140

Name & Rank	Age	Enlisted	Regiment and State	Where Captured	Prison	Remarks
Dees, Robert Private	24	March 10, 1862, Lumberton, North Carolina	Co. F, 51st North Carolina Infantry	June 1, 1864, Cold Harbor, Virginia	Point Lookout, Maryland, transferred to Elmira Prison, NY July 17,1864	Exchanged March 14, 1865 at Boulware's Wharf on the James River, Virginia
Deese, Henry Private	42	September 8, 1863, Charleston, South Carolina	Co. B, 31st North Carolina Infantry	June 1, 1864, Cold Harbor, Virginia	Point Lookout, Maryland, transferred to Elmira Prison, NY July 17,1864	Exchanged March 14, 1865 at Boulware's Wharf on the James River, Virginia
Deese, Joel Private	Unk	March 8, 1862, Abbeville, Alabama	Co. B, 6th Alabama Infantry	May 5, 1864, Wilderness, Virginia	Point Lookout, Maryland, transferred to Elmira Prison, NY August 17, 1864	Oath of Allegiance June 14, 1865
Deets, Mathew J. Private	22	September 5, 1861, Newton, North Carolina	Co. E, 32nd North Carolina Infantry	May 10, 1864, Wilderness, Virginia	Point Lookout, Maryland, transferred to Elmira Prison, NY August 6, 1864	Oath of Allegiance July 11, 1865
Defoor, James D. Private	Unk	March 4, 1862, Macon, Georgia	Co. B, 45th Georgia Infantry	July 14, 1863, Falling Waters, Maryland	Point Lookout, Maryland, transferred to Elmira Prison, NY August 18, 1864	Exchanged March 10, 1865 at Boulware's Wharf on the James River, Virginia
Defreese, Joseph Private	Unk	August 20, 1863, Calhoun, Alabama	Jeff Davis Alabama Artillery	May 5, 1864, Wilderness, Virginia	Point Lookout, Maryland, transferred to Elmira Prison, NY August 17, 1864	Transferred For Exchange October 11, 1864 to Point Lookout Prison, MD. Died November 4, 1864 of Unknown Causes at Fort Monroe, VA.
Degoux, G. Civilian	Unk	Louisiana	Citizen of Louisiana	May 25, 1864, Lake Ponchatrain, Louisiana	New Orleans, Louisiana transferred to Elmira November 19, 1864	Oath of Allegiance February 10, 1865 per Orders Commissary General Prisoners.

Name & Rank	Age	Enlisted	Regiment and State	Where Captured	Prison	Remarks
DeHard, Henry C. Private	Unk	March 20, 1862, North Carolina	Co. H, 51st North Carolina Infantry	July 10, 1864, Frederick, Maryland	Old Capital Prison, Washington, DC, transferred to Elmira Prison, NY, July 23, 1864	Exchanged March 2, 1865 at Akins Landing on the James River, Virginia
DeLichtenstein Charles William 1st Sergeant	Unk	March 4, 1861, Selma, Alabama	Co. C, 1st Battalion Alabama Artillery	August 23, 1864, Fort Morgan, Alabama	New Orleans, Louisiana transferred to Elmira December 4, 1864.	Oath of Allegiance May 13, 1865
Dellahanty, James Sergeant	25	July 22, 1861, Camp Moore, Louisiana	Co. A, 10th Louisiana Infantry	May 12, 1864, Spotsylvania Court House, Virginia	Point Lookout, Maryland, transferred to Elmira Prison, NY July 25, 1864	Oath of Allegiance May 17, 1865
Dellinger, Monroe Private	24	July 6, 1863, Lincoln County, North Carolina	Co. H, 52nd North Carolina Infantry	July 14, 1863, Falling Waters, Maryland	Point Lookout, Maryland, transferred to Elmira Prison, NY August 18, 1864	Exchanged March 10, 1865 at Boulware's Wharf on the James River, Virginia
Dellinger, Samuel Private	22	October 1, 1861, Shelby, North Carolina	Co. H, 34th North Carolina Infantry	April 2, 1865, Petersburg, Virginia. Gunshot Wound Right Thigh, Severe.	Old Capital Prison, Washington D. C. Transferred to Elmira Prison, NY May 2, 1865.	Oath of Allegiance July 19, 1865
DeLoach, Nelson Private	37	January 1, 1862, Camp Harlee, Georgetown, South Carolina	Co. J, 25th South Carolina Infantry	January 15, 1865, Fort Fisher, North Carolina	Elmira Prison Camp January 30, 1865	Died March 4, 1865 of Chronic Diarrhea, Grave No. 1980
DeLoach, Wiley Private	Unk	March 29, 1864, Dorchester, Georgia	Co. B, 7th Georgia Cavalry	June 11, 1864, Trevilian Station, Louisa Court House, Virginia	Point Lookout, Maryland, transferred to Elmira Prison, NY July 25, 1864	Exchanged February 20, 1865 at Boulware's or Cox Wharf on the James River, Virginia
Demeneti, J. Civilian	Unk	Registered Enemy	Citizen of Louisiana	July 27, 1864, New Orleans, Louisiana	New Orleans, Louisiana transferred to Elmira November 19, 1864.	Oath of Allegiance June 30, 1865

Name & Rank	Age	Enlisted	Regiment and State	Where Captured	Prison	Remarks
Deming, A. J. Private	Unk	June 11, 1863, Fayetteville, Pennsylvania	Co. A, 2nd Florida Infantry	May 12, 1864, Spotsylvania Court House, Virginia	Point Lookout, Maryland, transferred to Elmira Prison, NY August 12, 1864	Oath of Allegiance July 7, 1865
Dempsey, John A. Private	21	May 18, 1861, Seven Mile Ford, Virginia	Co. D, 48th Virginia Infantry	May 12, 1864, Spotsylvania Court House, Virginia	Point Lookout, Maryland, transferred to Elmira Prison, NY August 2, 1864	Oath of Allegiance, May 15, 1865
Dempsey, Thomas G. 1st Sergeant	20	August 15, 1861, Millner's Store, Amherst County, Virginia	Co. F, 58th Virginia Infantry	May 20, 1864, Spotsylvania Court House, Virginia	Point Lookout, Maryland, transferred to Elmira Prison, NY July 6, 1864	Exchanged October 29, 1864, at Venus Point, Savannah River, GA.
Dendy, Daniel Sergeant	Unk	December 3, 1861, Camp Hampton, South Carolina	Co. C, 7th South Carolina Cavalry	June 13, 1864, Malvern Hill, Virginia	Point Lookout, Maryland, transferred to Elmira Prison, NY July 30, 1864	Transferred For Exchange October 11, 1864 to Point Lookout Prison Camp, MD. Nothing Further.
Dendy, James H. Private	Unk	May 20, 1864, Montgomery, Alabama	Co. G, 59th Alabama Infantry	June 17, 1864, Near Petersburg, Virginia	Point Lookout, Maryland, transferred to Elmira Prison, NY July 30, 1864	Oath of Allegiance June 21, 1865
Denmark, Malachi Private	Unk	August 29, 1863, Bryan County, Georgia	Co. H, 7th Georgia Cavalry	June 11, 1864, Trevilian Station, Louisa Court House, Virginia	Point Lookout, Maryland, transferred to Elmira Prison, NY July 25, 1864	Exchanged 11/15/64 at Venus Point, Savannah River, GA.
Dennis, John S. Private	Unk	August 5, 1861, Livingston, Overton County, Tennessee	Co. H, 25th Tennessee Infantry	May 16, 1864, Near Drury's Bluff, Virginia	Point Lookout, Maryland, transferred to Elmira Prison, NY August 17, 1864	Exchanged February 25, 1865 at Boulware's or Cox Wharf on the James River, Virginia
Dennis, Joseph A. Private	Unk	July 24, 1861, Union, Virginia	Co. F, 6th Virginia Cavalry	June 11, 1864, Trevilian Station, Louisa Court House, Virginia	Point Lookout, Maryland, transferred to Elmira Prison, NY July 25, 1864	Died March 29, 1865 of Pneumonia, Grave No. 2519

Name & Rank	Age	Enlisted	Regiment and State	Where Captured	Prison	Remarks
Dennis, Moses L. Private	20	August 5, 1861, Livingston, Overton County, Tennessee	Co. H, 25th Tennessee Infantry	June 17, 1864, Near Petersburg, Virginia	Point Lookout, Maryland, transferred to Elmira Prison, NY July 30, 1864	Exchanged February 25, 1865 at Boulware's or Cox Wharf on the James River, Virginia
Dennis, W. L. Private	Unk	May 8, 1862, Macon, Georgia	Co. G, 59th Georgia Infantry	May 9, 1864, Spotsylvania Court House, Virginia	Point Lookout, Maryland, transferred to Elmira Prison, NY July 30, 1864	Oath of Allegiance June 16, 1865
Denson, L. John Private	Unk	August 4, 1863, Moundsville, Louisiana	Co. A, 2nd Louisiana Infantry	September 19, 1864, Tensan Parish, Louisiana	New Orleans, Louisianna, Transferred to Elmira Prison, New York, November 19, 1864	Exchanged February 25, 1865 at Boulware's or Cox Wharf on the James River, Virginia
Denton, C. C. Private	44	August 1, 1863, Cleveland, Tennessee	Co. H, 63rd Tennessee Infantry	June 17, 1864, Petersburg, Virginia	Point Lookout, Maryland, transferred to Elmira Prison, NY July 30, 1864	Exchanged February 25, 1865 at Boulware's or Cox Wharf on the James River, Virginia
Denton, John G. Sergeant	20	July 8, 1861, Knoxville, Tennessee	Co. F, 63rd Tennessee Infantry	June 17, 1864, Petersburg, Virginia	Point Lookout, Maryland, transferred to Elmira Prison, NY July 30, 1864	Exchanged February 25, 1865 at Boulware's or Cox Wharf on the James River, Virginia
Denton, John S. Corporal	Unk	August 24, 1861, Hiawassee, Georgia	Co. D, 24th Georgia Infantry	June 1, 1864, Cold Harbor, Virginia	Point Lookout, Maryland, transferred to Elmira Prison, NY July 17,1864	Oath of Allegiance July 11, 1865
Denton, Samuel J. Private	25	May 14, 1862, Zollicoffer, Tennessee	Co. F, 63rd Tennessee Infantry	June 17, 1864, Petersburg, Virginia	Point Lookout, Maryland, transferred to Elmira Prison, NY July 30, 1864	Died February 3, 1865 of Pneumonia, Grave No. 1745
Derieux, Alfred Sergeant	Unk	May 21, 1861, Tappahannock, Virginia	Co. F, 55th Virginia Infantry	May 6, 1864, Wilderness, Virginia	Point Lookout, Maryland, transferred to Elmira Prison, NY August 14, 1864	Exchanged March 10, 1865 at Boulware's Wharf on the James River, Virginia

Name & Rank	Age	Enlisted	Regiment and State	Where Captured	Prison	Remarks
Deriso, George H. Private	Unk	June 21, 1861, Camp Donald, Georgia	Co. D, 18th Georgia Infantry	June 1, 1864, Cold Harbor, Virginia	Point Lookout, Maryland, transferred to Elmira Prison, NY July 17,1864	Oath of Allegiance June 30, 1865
Derman, H. Private	Unk	Unknown	Co. J, 5th Virginia Infantry	Unknown	Unknown	Died February 27, 1865 of Unknown Disease, Grave No. 2111
Derr, Charles H. Private	19	May 10, 1861, Lynchburg, Virginia	Captain Shoemaker's Company Virginia Horse Artillery	September 14, 1863, Near Culpepper, Virginia	Point Lookout, Maryland, transferred to Elmira Prison, NY August 18, 1864	Exchanged March 2, 1865 at Boulware's Wharf on the James River, Virginia
Derr, John C. Private	19	February 2, 1863, Fort Strong, New Hanover County, North Carolina	Co. D, 1st Battalion North Carolina Heavy Artillery	January 15, 1865, Fort Fisher, North Carolina	February 1, 1865, Elmira Prison Camp, New York	Oath of Allegiance July 11, 1865
Desel, John B. Private	22	March 25, 1862, Grahamville, South Carolina	Co. K, 4th South Carolina Cavalry	May 30, 1864, Church, Virginia. Gunshot Wound Right of Median Line.	Old Capital Prison, Washington D. C. Transferred to Elmira Prison, NY August 12, 1864	Exchanged October 29, 1864, at Venus Point, Savannah River, GA.
Deshazo, George W. Private	Unk	June 4, 1861, Montevallo, Alabama	Co. C, 10th Alabama Infantry	May 6, 1864, Wilderness, Virginia	Point Lookout, Maryland, transferred to Elmira Prison, NY August 17, 1864	Died March 18, 1865 of Diarrhea, Grave No. 1559. James M. Deshozo, 16th Ala on Headstone.
Desmond, Jerry S. Private	Unk	May 19, 1861, New Orleans, Louisiana	Co. A, 59th Virginia Infantry	June 18, 1864, Petersburg, Virginia	Point Lookout, Maryland, transferred to Elmira Prison, NY July 30, 1864	Oath of Allegiance June 27, 1865
Devall, John W. Private	Unk	August 1, 1861, Montgomery, Alabama	Jeff Davis Alabama Artillery	May 5, 1864, Wilderness, Virginia	Point Lookout, Maryland, transferred to Elmira Prison, NY August 17, 1864	Oath of Allegiance June 19, 1865

Name & Rank	Age	Enlisted	Regiment and State	Where Captured	Prison	Remarks
DeVane Robert Harvey Private	18	August 5, 1863, Fort Fisher, North Carolina	Co. I, 36th Regiment 2nd North Carolina Artillery	January 15, 1865, Fort Fisher, North Carolina	February 1, 1865, Elmira Prison Camp, New York	Oath of Allegiance June 12, 1865
Deveaux, William P. Corporal	Unk	March 24, 1862, Camp Gist, South Carolina	Co. B, 27th South Carolina Infantry	June 24, 1864, Near Petersburg, Virginia	Point Lookout, Maryland, transferred to Elmira Prison, NY August 18, 1864	Oath of Allegiance June 21, 1865
Devine, John Corporal	Unk	June 15, 1861, Camp Moore near Tangiahoa, Louisiana	Co. G, 7th Louisiana Infantry	May 12, 1864, Near Spotsylvania Court House, Virginia	Point Lookout, Maryland, transferred to Elmira Prison, NY August 17, 1864	Exchanged February 25, 1865 at Boulware's or Cox Wharf on the James River, Virginia
Devine, Thomas Private	Unk	April 28, 1861, New Orleans, Louisiana	Co. D, 1st Louisiana Infantry	May 20, 1864, Near Spotsylvania, Virginia	Point Lookout, Maryland, transferred to Elmira Prison, NY July 23, 1864	Oath of Allegiance May 17, 1865
Devine, William T. Private	33	August 15, 1862, Iredell County, North Carolina	Co. J, 37th North Carolina Infantry	May 12, 1864, Spotsylvania Court House, Virginia	Point Lookout, Maryland, transferred to Elmira Prison, NY August 12, 1864	Exchanged October 29, 1864, at Venus Point, Savannah River, GA.
Deviney, James L. Private	Unk	December 24, 1861, Springfield, Missouri	Co. F, 3rd Battalion Missouri Cavalry	May 17, 1863, Big Black Bridge, Champion Hill, Mississippi	Point Lookout, Maryland, transferred to Elmira Prison, NY August 18, 1864	Exchanged February 13, 1865 at Boulware's wharf on the James River, Virginia
DeVo, James H. Private	25	April 16, 1862, Charleston, South Carolina	Co. B, 25th South Carolina Infantry	January 15, 1865, Fort Fisher, North Carolina	Elmira Prison Camp January 30, 1865	Oath of Allegiance March 22, 1865. Per Orders of Commissary General Prisoners.
DeWitt, R. R. Private	Unk	February 15, 1864, James Island, South Carolina	Co. G, 11th South Carolina Infantry	June 15, 1864, Petersburg, Virginia	Point Lookout, Maryland, transferred to Elmira Prison, NY July 25, 1864	Oath of Allegiance June 21, 1865

Name & Rank	Age	Enlisted	Regiment and State	Where Captured	Prison	Remarks
Dews, Zachariah Private	Unk	January 14, 1863, King and Queen Court House, Virginia	Co. D, 24th Virginia Cavalry	July 28, 1864, Petersburg, Virginia	Point Lookout, Maryland, transferred to Elmira Prison, NY August 12, 1864	Oath of Allegiance July 3, 1865
Dial, Jacob Private	27	December 25, 1861, Bennettsville, South Carolina	Co. F, 21st South Carolina Infantry	January 15, 1865, Fort Fisher, North Carolina	Elmira Prison Camp January 30, 1865	Died March 19, 1865 of Pneumonia, Grave No. 1583
Dial, Matthew Private	Unk	June 19, 1861, Camp Moore, Louisiana	Co. H, 8th Louisiana Infantry	May 12, 1864, Spotsylvania Court House, Virginia	Point Lookout, Maryland, transferred to Elmira Prison, NY August 17, 1864	Exchanged February 13, 1865 at Boulware's wharf on the James River, Virginia
Diamond, George W. Private	21	September 1, 1862, Rockingham County, North Carolina	Co. F, 45th North Carolina Infantry	July 12, 1864, Near Washington, DC	Old Capital Prison, Washington, DC transferred to Elmira Prison, NY August 27, 1864	Died December 11, 1864 of Chronic Diarrhea, Grave No. 1042
Diamond, William R. Private	Unk	June 22, 1861, Raleigh Court House, Virginia	Co. F, 30th Virginia Sharp Shooters	May 30, 1864, Cold Harbor, Virginia	Point Lookout, Maryland, transferred to Elmira Prison, NY July 17, 1864	Oath of Allegiance May 17, 1865
Dibble, M. W. Private	Unk	Unknown	Co. B, 25th South Carolina Infantry	January 15, 1865, Fort Fisher, North Carolina	Elmira Prison Camp January 30, 1865	Oath of Allegiance June 15, 1865
Dice, Thomas M. Private	Unk	August 12, 1862, Harrisonburg, Virginia	Co. G, 10th Virginia Infantry	May 12, 1864, Spotsylvania Court House, Virginia	Point Lookout, Maryland, transferred to Elmira Prison, NY August 2, 1864	Oath of Allegiance June 27, 1865
Dickens, B. L. Private	Unk	August 10, 1861, Albany, Georgia	Co. D, Cobb's Legion, Georgia	May 31, 1864, Hanover Court House, Cold Harbor, Virginia	Point Lookout, Maryland, transferred to Elmira Prison, NY July 17, 1864	Exchanged October 29, 1864, at Venus Point, Savannah River, GA.
Dickens, Charles Augustus Sergeant	20	July 5, 1861, Weldon, North Carolina	Co. K, 1st North Carolina Infantry	May 12, 1864, Spotsylvania Court House, Virginia	Point Lookout, Maryland, transferred to Elmira Prison, NY August 6, 1864	Oath of Allegiance June 12, 1865

Name & Rank	Age	Enlisted	Regiment and State	Where Captured	Prison	Remarks
Dickens, Henry B. Corporal	27	February 25, 1862, Lew's Store, North Carolina	Co. I, 12th North Carolina Infantry	May 12, 1864, Near Spotsylvania, Virginia	Point Lookout, Maryland, transferred to Elmira Prison, NY August 14, 1864	Exchanged October 29, 1864, at Venus Point, Savannah River, GA.
Dickens, Hider C. Private	24	February 11, 1862, Weldon, North Carolina	Co. K, 1st North Carolina Infantry	May 12, 1864, Spotsylvania Court House, Virginia	Point Lookout, Maryland, transferred to Elmira Prison, NY August 6, 1864	Exchanged February 20, 1865 at Boulware's or Cox Wharf on the James River, Virginia
Dickens, Hiram Private	34	October 9, 1861, Enfield, Halifax County, North Carolina	Co. F, 36th Regiment 2nd North Carolina Artillery	January 15, 1865, Fort Fisher, North Carolina	February 1, 1865, Elmira Prison Camp, New York	Died March 14, 1865 of Variola (Smallpox), Grave No. 1692.
Dickens, Rovan Sergeant	18	August 7, 1863, Fort Caswell, Brunswick County, North Carolina	Co. F, 36th Regiment 2nd North Carolina Artillery	January 15, 1865, Fort Fisher, North Carolina	February 1, 1865, Elmira Prison Camp, New York	Died March 18, 1865 of Variola (Smallpox), Grave No. 1692. Headstone has J. Dickens.
Dickens, William Private	Unk	July 15, 1862, Raleigh, North Carolina	Co. K, 1st North Carolina Infantry	May 12, 1864, Spotsylvania Court House, Virginia	Point Lookout, Maryland, transferred to Elmira Prison, NY August 6, 1864	Died March 23, 1865 of Diarrhea, Grave No. 1516
Dickenson, Samuel H. Private	Unk	June 9, 1861, Hevener's Store, Highland County, Virginia	Co. E, 25th Virginia Infantry	May 12, 1864, Spotsylvania Court House, Virginia	Point Lookout, Maryland, transferred to Elmira Prison, NY August 12, 1864	Died January 3, 1865 of Pneumonia, Grave No. 1336
Dickerson, Dozier D. Private	Unk	August 24, 1861, Hartwell, Hart County, Georgia	Co. B, 24th Georgia Infantry	August 16, 1864, Front Royal, Virginia	Old Capital Prison, Washington, DC transferred to Elmira Prison, NY August 29, 1864	Oath of Allegiance June 30, 1865
Dickerson, Ethelbert F. Private	Unk	October 10, 1863, Richmond, Virginia	Co. E, 25th Battalion Virginia Infantry	July 12, 1864, Cox's Farm, Virginia	Point Lookout, Maryland, transferred to Elmira Prison, NY August 6, 1864	Exchanged 3/14/65. Died 3/20/65 of Unknown Causes at Unknown Location.

Name & Rank	Age	Enlisted	Regiment and State	Where Captured	Prison	Remarks
Dickerson, Maston Private	48	August 26, 1863, Granville County, North Carolina	Co. G, 30th North Carolina Infantry	May 12, 1864, Near Spotsylvania, Virginia	Point Lookout, Maryland, transferred to Elmira Prison, NY August 14, 1864	Exchanged 3/14/65. Died of Acute Gastritis from Over Draught of Water.
Dickerson, Samuel T. Private	Unk	March 15, 1862, Kittrell's, North Carolina	Co. G, 23rd North Carolina Infantry	May 20, 1864, Spotsylvania Court House, Virginia	Point Lookout, Maryland, transferred to Elmira Prison, NY July 6, 1864	Oath of Allegiance July 3, 1865
Dickerson, William M. Private	22	December 4, 1861, Mountain Spring, Anderson District, South Carolina	Co. D, 18th South Carolina Infantry	July 30, 1864, Petersburg, Virginia	Point Lookout, Maryland, transferred to Elmira Prison, NY August 12, 1864	Died December 18, 1864 of Pneumonia, Grave No. 1066
Dickey, James H. Sergeant	Unk	June 22, 1861, Dranesville, Virginia	Co. G, 8th Virginia Infantry	April 20, 1865, Fairfax County, Virginia	Old Capital Prison, Washington D. C. Transferred to Elmira Prison, NY May 12, 1865.	Oath of Allegiance July 11, 1865
Dickinson, James H. Sergeant	20	February 24, 1862, Charleston, South Carolina	Co. A, 25th South Carolina Infantry	January 15, 1865, Fort Fisher, North Carolina	Elmira Prison Camp January 30, 1865	Exchanged March 2, 1865 at Boulware's Wharf on the James River, Virginia
Dickson, A. J. Corporal	Unk	April 28, 1862, Griffin, Georgia	Co. A, 53rd Georgia Infantry	June 1, 1864, Gaines Mill, Cold Harbor, Virginia	Point Lookout, Maryland, transferred to Elmira Prison, NY July 17,1864	Oath of Allegiance June 16, 1865
Dickson, George W. Private	Unk	July 25, 1863, Manning, South Carolina	Co. J, 25th South Carolina Infantry	January 15, 1865, Fort Fisher, North Carolina	Elmira Prison Camp January 30, 1865	Exchanged March 14, 1865 at Boulware's Wharf on the James River, Virginia
Dickson, Major E. Private	Unk	January 11, 1862, Goldsboro, North Carolina	Co. A, 51st North Carolina Infantry	June 15, 1864, Petersburg, Virginia	Point Lookout, Maryland, transferred to Elmira Prison, NY July 30, 1864	Exchanged October 29, 1864, at Venus Point, Savannah River, GA.

Name & Rank	Age	Enlisted	Regiment and State	Where Captured	Prison	Remarks
Diggs, David Private	31	September 1, 1861, Matthews Court House, Virginia	Co. F, 5th Virginia Cavalry	May 11, 1864, Yellow Tavern, Hanover County, Virginia	Point Lookout, Maryland, transferred to Elmira Prison, NY August 17, 1864	Oath of Allegiance June 19, 1865
Diggs, Thomas E. Sergeant	28	September 15, 1862, Camp Mangum, Raleigh, North Carolina	Co. B, 31st North Carolina Infantry	May 31, 1864, Cold Harbor, Virginia	Point Lookout, Maryland, transferred to Elmira Prison, NY July 17,1864	Exchanged March 10, 1865 at Boulware's wharf on the James River, Virginia
Diggs, William J. Private	28	Unknown	Captain Carpenter's Virginia Light Artillery	May 20, 1864, Spotsylvania Court House, Virginia	Point Lookout, Maryland, transferred to Elmira Prison, NY July 6, 1864	Transferred for Exchange 10/11/64. Admitted 1/31/1865 to US Army Hospital at Point Lookout, MD. Nothing Further.
Diggs, William Riley Private	21	September 15, 1862, Camp Mangum, Raleigh, North Carolina	Co. B, 31st North Carolina Infantry	May 31, 1864, Cold Harbor, Virginia	Point Lookout, Maryland, transferred to Elmira Prison, NY July 17,1864	Died November 26, 1864 of Chronic Diarrhea Grave No. 980
Diggs, William S. Private	33	December 19, 1862, Wilmington, North Carolina	Co. B, 31st North Carolina Infantry	June 1, 1864, Cold Harbor, Virginia	Point Lookout, Maryland, transferred to Elmira Prison, NY July 17,1864	Exchanged October 29, 1864, at Venus Point, Savannah River, GA.
Dildy, James R. Private	Unk	January 25, 1862, Gates County, North Carolina	Co. E, 33rd North Carolina Infantry	July 29, 1864, Petersburg, Virginia	Point Lookout, Maryland, transferred to Elmira Prison, NY August 12, 1864	Died April 5, 1865 of Chronic Diarrhea, Grave No. 2545. Diddy and 53rd NC on Headstone.
Dildy, William J. Private	Unk	April 26, 1862, Gates County, North Carolina	Co. E, 33rd North Carolina Infantry	May 6, 1864, Wilderness, Virginia	Point Lookout, Maryland, transferred to Elmira Prison, NY August 14, 1864	Oath of Allegiance June 21, 1865
Dill, Isaac N. Private	Unk	August 24, 1861, Homer, Georgia	Co. A, 24th Georgia Infantry	August 16, 1864, Front Royal, Virginia	Old Capital Prison, Washington, DC transferred to Elmira Prison, NY August 29, 1864	Oath of Allegiance May 29, 1865

Name & Rank	Age	Enlisted	Regiment and State	Where Captured	Prison	Remarks
Dill, Samuel L. Private	Unk	July 1, 1863, Wilmington, North Carolina	Co. K, 10th Regiment, 1st North Carolina Artillery	January 15, 1865, Fort Fisher, North Carolina	January 30, 1865, Elmira Prison Camp, NY	Exchanged March 14, 1865 at Boulware's Wharf on the James River, Virginia
Dillard, H. P. Corporal	Unk	March 18, 1862, Salem, Virginia	Co. E, 42nd Virginia Infantry	May 12, 1864, Near Spotsylvania Court House, Virginia	Point Lookout, Maryland, transferred to Elmira Prison, NY August 2, 1864	Oath of Allegiance June 27, 1865
Dillard, James Park Private	Unk	March 15, 1862, Laurens District, South Carolina	Co. K, 14th South Carolina Infantry	July 29, 1864, Petersburg, Virginia	Point Lookout, Maryland, transferred to Elmira Prison, NY August 12, 1864	Exchanged March 14, 1865 at Boulware's Wharf on the James River, Virginia
Dillard, R. H. Private	Unk	March 6, 1863, Franklin County, Virginia	Co. F, 21st Virginia Infantry	May 20, 1864, Spotsylvania Court House, Virginia	Point Lookout, Maryland, transferred to Elmira Prison, NY July 6, 1864	Exchanged March 14, 1865 at Boulware's Wharf on the James River, Virginia
Dillard, S. H. Private	Unk	September 1, 1864, Sampson County, North Carolina	Co. D, 1st Battalion North Carolina Heavy Artillery	January 15, 1865, Fort Fisher, North Carolina. Wounded.	February 1, 1865, Elmira Prison Camp, New York	Exchanged February 20, 1865. Died March 8, 1865 of Typhoid Fever at CSA Hospital, Richmond, VA.
Dillehay, John F. Private	35	March 9, 1862, Roxboro, North Carolina	Co. A, 24th North Carolina Infantry	June 17, 1864, Petersburg, Virginia	Point Lookout, Maryland, transferred to Elmira Prison, NY July 30, 1864	Died December 10, 1864 of Chronic Diarrhea, Grave No. 1155
Dillion, Henry H. Corporal	Unk	June 15, 1861, Lynchburg, Virginia	Co. A, 42nd Virginia Infantry	May 12, 1864, Spotsylvania Court House, Virginia	Point Lookout, Maryland, transferred to Elmira Prison, NY July 30, 1864	Exchanged October 29, 1864, at Venus Point, Savannah River, GA.
Dillion, Samuel H. Private	Unk	January 20, 1864, Orange County, Virginia	Co. E, 58th Virginia Infantry	May 20, 1864, Spotsylvania Court House, Virginia	Point Lookout, Maryland, transferred to Elmira Prison, NY July 6, 1864	Died August 15, 1864 of Chronic Diarrhea, Grave No. 125

Name & Rank	Age	Enlisted	Regiment and State	Where Captured	Prison	Remarks
Dillon, Eaton B. Sergeant	Unk	July 24, 1861, Delps Muster Ground, Carroll County, Virginia	Co. C, 29th, Virginia Infantry	June 1, 1864, Gaines Mill, Cold Harbor, Virginia	Point Lookout, Maryland, transferred to Elmira Prison, NY July 12, 1864	Oath of Allegiance July 3, 1865
Dillon, Henry A. Private	18	November 14, 1862, Drury's Bluff, Virginia	Co. E, 45th North Carolina Infantry	May 10, 1864, Spotsylvania Court House, Virginia	Point Lookout, Maryland, transferred to Elmira Prison, NY August 6, 1864	Oath of Allegiance June 27, 1865
Dillon, James Private	Unk	June 19, 1861, Camp Moore, Louisiana	Co. J, 8th Louisiana Infantry	May 12, 1864, Spotsylvania Court House, Virginia	Point Lookout, Maryland, transferred to Elmira Prison, NY August 17, 1864	Exchanged February 13, 1865 at Boulware's wharf on the James River, Virginia
Dillon, John H. Private	Unk	January 1, 1864, Camp Holmes, Raleigh, North Carolina	Co. L, 21st North Carolina Infantry	May 22, 1864, Near Spotsylvania Court House, Virginia	Point Lookout, Maryland, transferred to Elmira Prison, NY July 23, 1864	Died December 11, 1864 of Pneumonia, Grave No. 1051
Dillon, Johnathan A. Private	21	July 26, 1861, Greensboro, North Carolina	Co. G, 2nd North Carolina Infantry	May 31, 1864, Mechanics-ville, Virginia	Point Lookout, Maryland, transferred to Elmira Prison, NY July 12, 1864	Oath of Allegiance May 17, 1865
Dillon, Joseph L. Private	Unk	September 1, 1862, Charlestown, Virginia	Co. A, 12th Virginia Cavalry	March 30, 1865, Jefferson County, Virginia	Old Capital Prison, Washington D. C. Transferred to Elmira Prison, NY May 12, 1865.	Oath of Allegiance June 16, 1865
Dillon, Lee W. Private	Unk	March 10, 1862, Washington Point, Norfolk County, Virginia	Co. K, 61st Virginia Infantry	September 22, 1863, Rapidan Station, Virginia	Point Lookout, Maryland, transferred to Elmira Prison, NY August 18, 1864	Oath of Allegiance June 19, 1865
Dillon, Nelson Private	Unk	August 25, 1861, Bethel, Tennessee	Co. A, Jackson's 1st Regiment, Tennessee Heavy Artillery	August 23, 1864, Fort Morgan, Alabama	New Orleans, Louisiana transferred to Elmira December 4, 1864.	Exchanged March 10, 1865 at Boulware's Wharf on the James River, Virginia

Name & Rank	Age	Enlisted	Regiment and State	Where Captured	Prison	Remarks
Dillon, Robert Private	Unk	December 6, 1862, Port Royal, Alabama	Co. G, 6th Alabama Infantry	May 20, 1864, Spotsylvania Court House, Virginia	Point Lookout, Maryland, transferred to Elmira Prison, NY July 6, 1864	Died September 7, 1864, Chronic Diarrhea, Grave No. 222
Dillon, Samuel H. Private	Unk	January 20, 1864, Orange County, Virginia	Co. E, 58th Virginia Infantry	May 20, 1864, Spotsylvania Court House, Virginia	Point Lookout, Maryland, transferred to Elmira New York, July 6, 1864	Died August 15, 1864 of Chronic Diarrhea, Grave No. 125
Dillon, William J. Corporal	30	May 16, 1861, Columbia, North Carolina	Co. F, 32nd North Carolina Infantry	May 10, 1864, Spotsylvania, Virginia	Old Capital Prison, Washington, DC, transferred to Elmira Prison, NY, July 23, 1864	Exchanged February 13, 1865 at Boulware's wharf on the James River, Virginia
Dimitry, Theodore J. Private	Unk	April 26, 1861, New Orleans, Louisiana	Captain Green's Co., Louisiana Artillery	October 7, 1864, Osyka, Mississippi	New Orleans, Louisiana transferred to Elmira November 19, 1864.	Exchanged February 13, 1865 at Boulware's Wharf on the James River, Virginia
Dinan, Cornelius Private	Unk	January 1, 1863, Charleston, South Carolina	Co. H, 27th South Carolina Infantry	June 24, 1864, Petersburg, Virginia	Point Lookout, Maryland, transferred to Elmira Prison, NY July 23, 1864	Died August 14, 1864 of Chronic Diarrhea, Grave No. 22
Dingler, Jeremiah P. Private	Unk	July 19, 1861, Montgomery, Alabama	Co. D, 13th Alabama Infantry	May 5, 1864, Spotsylvania Court House, Virginia	Point Lookout, Maryland, transferred to Elmira Prison, NY July 30, 1864	Oath of Allegiance June 23, 1865
Dingus, Jasper N. Sergeant	Unk	July 27, 1861, Wytheville, Virginia	Co. A, 50th Virginia Infantry	May 12, 1864 Spotsylvania Court House, Virginia	Point Lookout, Maryland, transferred to Elmira Prison, NY August 2, 1864	Died January 14, 1865 of Phthis Pulmonalis, Grave No. 1465
Dinkins, William Private	31	June 15, 1861, Washington, Virginia	Co. F, 48th Virginia Infantry	May 12, 1864, Spotsylvania Court House, Virginia	Point Lookout, Maryland, transferred to Elmira Prison, NY August 12, 1864	Oath of Allegiance July 11, 1865

Name & Rank	Age	Enlisted	Regiment and State	Where Captured	Prison	Remarks
Dirickson, John M. Private	Unk	July 26, 1861, Gallatin, Tennessee	Co. A, 23rd Tennessee Infantry	June 17, 1864, Petersburg, Virginia	Point Lookout, Maryland, transferred to Elmira Prison, NY July 30, 1864	Exchanged February 25, 1865 at Boulware's or Cox Wharf on the James River, Virginia
Dismukes, D. J. Private	Unk	January 11, 1864, Mobile, Alabama	Co. A, Jackson's 1st Regiment, Tennessee Heavy Artillery	August 23, 1864, Fort Morgan, Alabama	New Orleans, Louisiana transferred to Elmira December 4, 1864.	No Further Information Available.
Ditto, Thomas B. Private	Unk	May 19, 1861, Guntersville, Marshall County, Alabama	Co. K, 9th Alabama Infantry	May 6, 1864, Wilderness, Virginia	Point Lookout, Maryland, transferred to Elmira Prison, NY August 17, 1864	Oath of Allegiance June 14, 1865
Diviney, Robert Private	28	February 26, 1863, Raleigh, North Carolina	Co. D, 12th North Carolina Infantry	May 12, 1864, Near Spotsylvania, Virginia	Point Lookout, Maryland, transferred to Elmira Prison, NY August 14, 1864	Died December 4, 1864 of Pneumonia, Grave No. 885. Name Devinney on Headstone.
Dix, James R. Private	Unk	July 15, 1861, Rawlinsburg, North Carolina	Co. G, 14th North Carolina Infantry	May 30, 1864, Mechanics-ville, Virginia	Point Lookout, Maryland, transferred to Elmira Prison, NY July 12, 1864	Oath of Allegiance May 17, 1865
Dix, W. R. Private	Unk	Unknown	Co. A, 38th Louisiana Infantry	May 20, 1864, Spotsylvania Court House, Virginia	Point Lookout, Maryland, transferred to Elmira Prison, NY July 6, 1864	Oath of Allegiance June 14, 1865
Dixon, Benjamin F. Private	23	April 27, 1861, Snow Hill, North Carolina	Co. A, 3rd North Carolina Infantry	May 12, 1864, Near Spotsylvania, Virginia	Point Lookout, Maryland, transferred to Elmira Prison, NY August 14, 1864	Exchanged March 10, 1865 at Boulware's Wharf on the James River, Virginia
Dixon, Charles E. Private	21	December 31, 1861, Charlotte, Virginia	Co. B, 22nd Virginia Infantry	August 11, 1864, Winchester, Virginia	Old Capital Prison, Washington, DC transferred to Elmira Prison, NY August 27, 1864	Oath of Allegiance May 17, 1865

Name & Rank	Age	Enlisted	Regiment and State	Where Captured	Prison	Remarks
Dixon, James Private	Unk	January 27, 1864, George Town, South Carolina	Co. E, 7th Georgia Cavalry	June 11, 1864, Trevilian Station, Louisa Court House, Virginia	Point Lookout, Maryland, transferred to Elmira Prison, NY July 25, 1864	Died September 25, 1864 of Typhoid Fever, Grave No. 369
Dixon, James D. Private	21	June 3, 1861, Jefferson, North Carolina	Co. A, 1st North Carolina Cavalry	September 13, 1863, Near Culpepper, Virginia	Point Lookout, Maryland, transferred to Elmira Prison, NY August 18, 1864	Died March 28, 1865 of Chronic Diarrhea, Grave No. 2489
Dixon, James William Sergeant	Unk	August 1, 1861, Staunton, Virginia	Co. H, 25th Virginia Infantry	May 5, 1864, Wilderness, Virginia	Point Lookout, Maryland, transferred to Elmira Prison, NY August 14, 1864	Oath of Allegiance May 17, 1865
Dixon, John Private	23	October 17, 1862, Camp Holmes, North Carolina	Co. H, 26th North Carolina Infantry	May 12, 1864, Spotsylvania Court House, Virginia	Point Lookout, Maryland, transferred to Elmira Prison, NY August 12, 1864	Exchanged February 13, 1865 at Boulware's Wharf on the James River, Virginia
Dixon, John J. Private	Unk	August 7, 1861, Lynchburg, Virginia	Co. C, 34th Virginia Infantry	June 15, 1864, Petersburg, Virginia	Point Lookout, Maryland, transferred to Elmira Prison, NY July 12, 1864	Oath of Allegiance July 11, 1865
Dixon, John S. Private	Unk	February 27, 1862, Camp Bartow, Savannah, Georgia	Co. H, 30th Georgia Infantry	July 8, 1864, Near Harper's Ferry, Virginia	Old Capital Prison, Washington, DC, transferred to Elmira Prison, NY, July 23, 1864	Exchanged March 10, 1865 at Boulware's wharf on the James River, Virginia
Dixon, Kirvin Private	Unk	May 15, 1862, Savannah, Georgia	Co. B, 7th Georgia Cavalry	June 11, 1864, Trevilian Station, Louisa Court House, Virginia	Point Lookout, Maryland, transferred to Elmira Prison, NY July 25, 1864	Died February 24, 1865 of Chronic Diarrhea, Grave No. 2259. Name K. Dickson on Headstone.
Dixon, L. W. Private	Unk	January 22, 1863, Petersburg, Virginia	Captain Young's Battery Virginia Artillery	June 15, 1864, Petersburg, Virginia	Point Lookout, Maryland, transferred to Elmira Prison, NY July 25, 1864	Exchanged October 29, 1864, at Venus Point, Savannah River, GA.

Name & Rank	Age	Enlisted	Regiment and State	Where Captured	Prison	Remarks
Dixon, William Private	Unk	Unknown	Co. I, 18th North Carolina Infantry	July 29, 1864, Petersburg, Virginia	Point Lookout, Maryland, transferred to Elmira Prison, NY August 12, 1864	Died March 17, 1865 of Unknown Causes, Grave No. 1707
Doares, James D. Private	16	April 16, 1862, Old Brunswick Town, North Carolina	Co. G, 36th Regiment 2nd North Carolina Artillery	January 15, 1865, Fort Fisher, North Carolina	February 1, 1865, Elmira Prison Camp, New York	Oath of Allegiance August 7, 1865
Dobbs, Clayton Private	26	June 16, 1862, Carrollton, Georgia	Co. B, 7th Confederate States Cavalry	May 7, 1864, Littleton, Virginia	Point Lookout, Maryland, transferred to Elmira Prison, NY August 14, 1864	Exchanged October 29, 1864 at Venus Point, Savannah River, GA.
Dobbs, William U. Private	Unk	February 1, 1863, Choctaw Bluff, Alabama	Co. A, 21st Alabama Infantry	August 23, 1864, Fort Morgan, Alabama	Steam Press No. 4, New Orleans, Louisiana transferred to Elmira Prison, October 8, 1864.	Died November 8, 1864 of Chronic Diarrhea, Grave No. 785
Dobson, Charles R. Private	Unk	January 4, 1862, Hardeeville, South Carolina	Co. E, 11th South Carolina Infantry	June 18, 1864, Petersburg, Virginia	Point Lookout, Maryland, transferred to Elmira Prison, NY July 30, 1864	Died January 3, 1865 of Pneumonia, Grave No. 1343
Dobson, J. S. Private	25	June 24, 1861, Coosawhatchie, South Carolina	Co. E, 11th South Carolina Infantry	June 24, 1864, Near Petersburg, Virginia	Point Lookout, Maryland, transferred to Elmira Prison, NY August 18, 1864	Transferred For Exchange October 11, 1864 to Point Lookout Prison Camp, MD. Died November 1, 1864 of Unknown Causes at Fort Monroe, VA.
Doby, J. P. Private	28	July 16, 1862, Raleigh, North Carolina	Co. D, 14th North Carolina Infantry	May 20, 1864, Spotsylvania Court House, Virginia	Point Lookout, Maryland, transferred to Elmira Prison, NY July 6, 1864	Oath of Allegiance June 30, 1865
Dock, John C. Private	Unk	Unknown	Co. F, Unknown Battalion Georgia Artillery	Unknown	Unknown	Died January 4, 1865 of Unknown Disease, Grave No. 1264

Name & Rank	Age	Enlisted	Regiment and State	Where Captured	Prison	Remarks
Dockery, James R. Sergeant	Unk	July 1, 1862, Rockingham, North Carolina	Co. K, 33rd North Carolina Infantry	July 29, 1864, Petersburg, Virginia	Point Lookout, Maryland, transferred to Elmira Prison, NY August 12, 1864	Oath of Allegiance June 12, 1865
Dodd, Thomas A. Private	Unk	August 24, 1861, Homer, Georgia	Co. A, 24th Georgia Infantry	August 16, 1864, Front Royal, Virginia	Old Capital Prison, Washington, DC transferred to Elmira Prison, NY August 29, 1864	Died March 12, 1865 of Pneumonia, Grave No. 1838
Dodson, Isaac P. Private	Unk	May 1, 1862, Tyler, Texas	Co. H, 15th Texas Infantry	September 19, 1864, Tensan the Parish, Louisiana	New Orleans, Louisiana. Transferred to Elmira Prison Camp, New York November 19, 1864.	Oath of Allegiance June 23, 1865
Dodson, Samuel Private	Unk	July 8, 1861, Griffin, Georgia	Co. F, 13th Georgia Infantry	May 20, 1864, Spotsylvania Court House, Virginia	Point Lookout, Maryland, transferred to Elmira Prison, NY July 6, 1864	Oath of Allegiance June 16, 1865
Doggett, John W. Private	Unk	May 23, 1861, Columbus, Georgia	Co. B, 20th Georgia Infantry	July 14, 1863, Falling Waters, Maryland	Point Lookout, Maryland, transferred to Elmira Prison, NY August 18, 1864	Exchanged February 25, 1865 at Boulware's or Cox Wharf on the James River, Virginia
Doil, Jacob C. Private	Unk	March 29, 1862, Allegheny, Virginia	Co. B, 31st Virginia Infantry	May 5, 1864, Wilderness, Virginia	Point Lookout, Maryland, transferred to Elmira Prison, NY August 2, 1864	Died September 18, 1864 of Pneumonia, Grave No. 512
Dolan, Patrick Private	Unk	April 30, 1861, New Orleans, Louisiana	Co. H, 5th Louisiana Infantry	May 5, 1864, Wilderness, Virginia	Point Lookout, Maryland, transferred to Elmira Prison, NY August 17, 1864	Exchanged February 13, 1865 at Boulware's Wharf on the James River, Virginia

Name & Rank	Age	Enlisted	Regiment and State	Where Captured	Prison	Remarks
Dolan, Richard Private	Unk	Unknown	Co. B, 18th Virginia Cavalry	October 28, 1864, Newmaine Furnace, Hampshire County, Virginia	Old Capital Prison, Washington, DC, transferred to Elmira Prison, NY, December 17, 1864	Oath of Allegiance June 23, 1865
Dolands, C. W. Private	Unk	Unknown	Co. J, 22nd Virginia Infantry	May 29, 1864, King and Queen County, Virginia	Point Lookout, Maryland, transferred to Elmira Prison, NY July 11, 1864	Oath of Allegiance May 29, 1865
Dolen, Darius Private	Unk	August 5, 1861, Knoxville, Tennessee	Co. D, 1st Tennessee Cavalry	July 24, 1864, Winchester, Virginia	Old Capital Prison, Washington D. C. Transferred to Elmira Prison, NY August 12, 1864	Exchanged October 29, 1864, at Venus Point, Savannah River, GA.
Doll, John Private	Unk	March 3, 1862, Richmond, Virginia	Captain Lyneman's Co., Virginia Infantry	May 27, 1864, Chancellors-ville, Virginia	Point Lookout, Maryland, transferred to Elmira Prison, NY July 11, 1864	Oath of Allegiance May 29, 1865
Dominy, Daniel J. Private	Unk	February 24, 1862, Abbeville, Alabama	Co. B, 6th Alabama Infantry	May 8, 1864, Ely's Ford, Wilderness, Virginia	Point Lookout, Maryland, transferred to Elmira Prison, NY August 17, 1864	Oath of Allegiance June 14, 1865
Donahoe, Edward Private	Unk	September 27, 1862, Richmond, Virginia	Co. G, 24th Virginia Cavalry	December 13, 1863, Charles City Court House, Virginia	Point Lookout, Maryland, transferred to Elmira Prison, NY July 25, 1864	Oath of Allegiance May 14, 1865
Donald, Hugh M. Corporal	20	September 12, 1861, Carthage, North Carolina	Co. C, 35th North Carolina Infantry	June 17, 1864, Petersburg, Virginia	Point Lookout, Maryland, transferred to Elmira Prison, NY July 30, 1864	Oath of Allegiance June 12, 1865
Donald, Robert A. Private	Unk	Unknown	Co. H, 4th Virginia Infantry	May 12, 1864, Spotsylvania Court House, Virginia	Point Lookout, Maryland, transferred to Elmira Prison, NY August 2, 1864	Died October 27, 1864 of Chronic Diarrhea, Grave No. 720

Name & Rank	Age	Enlisted	Regiment and State	Where Captured	Prison	Remarks
Donald, Watson A. Private	17	May 31, 1861, Corinth, Mississippi	Co. F, 16th Mississippi Infantry	May 12, 1864, Spotsylvania Court House, Virginia. Gunshot Wound Head.	Old Capital Prison, Washington, DC transfered to Elmira Prison, NY August 27, 1864	Oath of Allegiance May 29, 1865
Donaldson, Armistead Private	Unk	May 25, 1861, Centreville, Virginia	Co. F, 6th Virginia Cavalry	June 11, 1864, Louisa Court House, Trevilian Station, Virginia	Point Lookout, Maryland, transferred to Elmira Prison, NY August 12, 1864	Oath of Allegiance June 19, 1865
Donaldson, John J. Private	Unk	Unknown	Co. B, 44th Tennessee Infantry	June 17, 1864, Petersburg, Virginia	Point Lookout, Maryland, transferred to Elmira Prison, NY July 30, 1864	Oath of Allegiance May 29, 1865
Donaldson, William Private	Unk	May 13, 1862, Savannah, Georgia	Co. E, 7th Georgia Cavalry	June 11, 1864, Louisa Court House, Trevilian Station, Virginia	Point Lookout, Maryland, transferred to Elmira Prison, NY July 30, 1864	Oath of Allegiance July 7, 1865
Donnally, Andrew V. Private	Unk	June 1, 1861, Kanawha Court House, Virginia	Co. H, 22nd Virginia Infantry	June 3, 1864, Gaines Farm, Cold Harbor, Virginia	Point Lookout, Maryland, transferred to Elmira Prison, NY July 17,1864	Exchanged March 10, 1865 at Boulware's Wharf on the James River, Virginia
Donnelly, John Private	Unk	June 22, 1862, Camp Pulaski, New Orleans, Louisiana	Co. F, 15th Louisiana Infantry	August 12, 1864, Perryville, Virginia	Old Capital Prison, Washington, DC transferred to Elmira Prison, NY August 29, 1864	Oath of Allegiance May 29, 1865
Donnelly, John Brake Private	Unk	July 1, 1861, New Orleans, Louisiana	Co. H, 14th Louisiana Infantry	May 12, 1864, Spotsylvania Court House, Virginia	Point Lookout, Maryland, transferred to Elmira Prison, NY July 25, 1864	Exchanged March 2, 1865 at Akins Landing on the James River, Virginia
Donner, C. C. Civilian	Unk	Louisiana	Citizen of Louisiana	September 19, 1864, Tenan Parish, Louisiana	New Orleans, Louisiana transferred to Elmira November 19, 1864.	Oath of Allegiance June 20, 1865

Name & Rank	Age	Enlisted	Regiment and State	Where Captured	Prison	Remarks
Donnigan, Ashley G. Private	Unk	Unknown	Co. F, 3rd North Carolina Infantry	May 12, 1864, Spotsylvania Court House, Virginia	Point Lookout, Maryland, transferred to Elmira Prison, NY July 25, 1864	Died February 28, 1865 of Variola (Smallpox), Grave No. 2125.
Donovan, James Private	24	May 9, 1861, Chesterfield Depot, Virginia	Co. E, 30th Virginia Infantry	May 24, 1864, Millford Station, Virginia	Point Lookout, Maryland, transferred to Elmira Prison, NY July 23, 1864	Oath of Allegiance 3/22/1865. Early Release per Lincoln's Proclamation, 12/8/1863.
Doolittle, Benjamin Private	Unk	February 1, 1864, Charleston, South Carolina	Co. K, 1st South Carolina Infantry	July 29, 1864, Petersburg, Virginia	Point Lookout, Maryland, transferred to Elmira Prison, NY August 12, 1864	Died October 30, 1864 of Disease of Heart, Grave No. 746
Dooly, Jackson H. Private	27	June 22, 1863, Sharpsburg, Virginia	Co. B, 25th Virginia Infantry	May 12, 1864, Spotsylvania, Virginia	Point Lookout, Maryland, transferred to Elmira Prison, NY July 23, 1864	Died September 9, 1864 of Typhoid-Pneumonia, Grave No. 203
Dorman, John J. Private	Unk	May 1, 1864, Petersburg, Virginia	Co. E, 8th North Carolina Infantry	June 1, 1864, Gaines Mill, Cold Harbor, Virginia	Point Lookout, Maryland, transferred to Elmira Prison, NY July 17,1864	Died September 9, 1864, Chronic Diarrhea, Grave No. 205
Dorman, Shannon Private	Unk	April 30, 1864, Monroe Draft, Virginia	Co. A, 26th Battalion Virginia Infantry	May 31, 1864, Chickahom-iny, Cold Harbor, Virginia	Point Lookout, Maryland, transferred to Elmira Prison, NY July 11, 1864	Oath of Allegiance May 29, 1865
Dough, John C. Private	26	August 6, 1861, Currituck Court House, North Carolina	Co. B, 8th North Carolina Infantry	June 1, 1864, Cold Harbor, Virginia	Point Lookout, Maryland, transferred to Elmira Prison, NY July 17,1864	Died April 2, 1865 of Chronic Diarrhea, Grave No. 928
Dough, Thomas T. Private	27	August 6, 1861, Currituck Court House, North Carolina	Co. B, 8th North Carolina Infantry	June 1, 1864, Cold Harbor, Virginia	Point Lookout, Maryland, transferred to Elmira Prison, NY July 17,1864	Died November 22, 1864 of Pneumonia, Grave No. 2572

Name & Rank	Age	Enlisted	Regiment and State	Where Captured	Prison	Remarks
Dougherty, C. Sergeant	Unk	Unknown	Co. J, 3rd Louisiana Cavalry	September 14, 1864, Tunica, Louisiana	New Orleans, Louisiana transferred to Elmira November 19, 1864.	Oath of Allegiance June 16, 1865
Dougherty, Charles L. Private	Unk	May 15, 1862, Decatur, Georgia	3rd Battalion Georgia Sharp shooters	August 16, 1864, Front Royal, Virginia	Old Capital Prison, Washington, DC transferred to Elmira Prison, NY August 29, 1864	Died January 31, 1865 of Variola (Smallpox), Grave No. 1780
Dougherty, P. Private	Unk	Unknown	Co. J, 3rd Louisiana Cavalry	September 14, 1864, Tunica, Louisiana	New Orleans, Louisiana transferred to Elmira November 19, 1864.	Oath of Allegiance May 29, 1865
Dougherty, William T. Sergeant See Listing for Daougherty, William T.						
Doughtie, Alpheus P. Private	17	April 30, 1862, Hertford County, North Carolina	Co. C, 3rd Battalion North Carolina Artillery	January 15, 1865, Fort Fisher, North Carolina	February 1, 1865, Elmira Prison Camp, New York	Died February 24, 1865 of Variola (Smallpox), Grave No. 2261
Doughtie, Thomas Private	18	September 15, 1862, Camp Mangum, Raleigh, North Carolina	Co. B, 31st North Carolina Infantry	May 31, 1864, Cold Harbor, Virginia	Point Lookout, Maryland, transferred to Elmira Prison, NY July 17,1864	Exchanged October 11, 1864. Died October 20, 1864 of Chronic Diarrhea at Point Lookout, MD.
Doughtie, William E. Private	18	September 15, 1862, Petersburg, Virginia	Co. B, 31st North Carolina Infantry	June 1, 1864, Cold Harbor, Virginia	Point Lookout, Maryland, transferred to Elmira Prison, NY July 17,1864	Died March 12, 1865 of Chronic Diarrhea, Grave No. 1830
Doughton, Flemin S. Private	35	May 17, 1861, Jefferson, North Carolina	Co. A, 26th North Carolina Infantry	July 14, 1863, Falling Waters, Maryland	Point Lookout, Maryland, transferred to Elmira Prison, NY August 18, 1864	Exchanged March 10, 1865 at Boulware's Wharf on the James River, Virginia

Name & Rank	Age	Enlisted	Regiment and State	Where Captured	Prison	Remarks
Douglas, George Private	18	May 26, 1861, Raleigh, North Carolina	Co. A, 5th North Carolina Infantry	May 12, 1864, Spotsylvania Court House, Virginia	Point Lookout, Maryland, transferred to Elmira Prison, NY August 6, 1864	Oath of Allegiance June 21, 1865
Douglas, James W. Private	Unk	January 29, 1864, Bristol, Tennessee	Co. J, 14th Tennessee Infantry	May 6, 1864, Wilderness, Virginia	Point Lookout, Maryland, transferred to Elmira Prison, NY July 23, 1864	Died, October 13, 1864 of Chronic Diarrhea, Grave No. 574
Douglas, William Private	23	January 31, 1864, Wetumpka, Alabama	Co. E, 1st Battalion Alabama Artillery	August 23, 1864, Fort Morgan, Alabama	New Orleans, Louisiana transferred to Elmira December 4, 1864.	Exchanged March 14, 1865 at Boulware's Wharf on the James River, Virginia
Douglass, D. E. Sergeant	Unk	June 21, 1862, Savannah, Georgia	Co. E, 7th Georgia Cavalry	June 11, 1864, Trevilian Station, Louisa Court House, Virginia	Point Lookout, Maryland, transferred to Elmira Prison, NY July 25, 1864	Died September 25, 1864 of Remittent Fever, Grave No. 376
Douglass, Henry A. Private	Unk	May 1, 1863, Chesterfield, South Carolina	Co. D, 21st South Carolina Infantry	January 15, 1865, Fort Fisher, North Carolina	Elmira Prison Camp January 30, 1865	Died April 2, 1865 of Epilepsy, Grave No. 1699
Douglass, James E. Private	18	March 10, 1862, Lumberton, North Carolina	Co. F, 51st North Carolina Infantry	June 1, 1864, Cold Harbor, Virginia	Point Lookout, Maryland, transferred to Elmira Prison, NY July 17, 1864	Oath of Allegiance July 3, 1865
Douglass, John F. Private	Unk	Unknown	Co. G, 2nd Texas Infantry	April 23, 1864, Cane River, Louisiana	New Orleans, Louisianna Transferred to Elmira Prison, New York, November 19, 1864	Died December 11, 1864 of Typhoid-Pneumonia, Grave No. 1149
Douglass, William W. Private	26	July 20, 1861, Camp Pickens, Anderson District, South Carolina	Co. B, 1st South Carolina Infantry	July 14, 1863, Falling Waters, Maryland	Point Lookout, Maryland, transferred to Elmira Prison, NY August 18, 1864	Died February 7, 1865 of Remittent Fever, Grave No. 1915
Douthat, F. L. Civilian	Unk	Unknown	Citizen of Chesterfield County, Virginia	May 8, 1864, Chesterfield County, Virginia	Point Lookout, Maryland, transferred to Elmira Prison, NY July 17,1864	No Additional Information.

Name & Rank	Age	Enlisted	Regiment and State	Where Captured	Prison	Remarks
Douthat, Robert Civilian	Unk	Unknown	Citizen of Chesterfield County, Virginia	May 8, 1864, Chesterfield County, Virginia	Point Lookout, Maryland, transferred to Elmira Prison, NY July 17,1864	No Additional Information.
Dove, George Private	21	June 20, 1861, Rockingham County, Virginia	Co. C, 11th Virginia Cavalry	September 14, 1863, Near Culpepper, Virginia	Point Lookout, Maryland, transferred to Elmira Prison, NY August 18, 1864	Oath of Allegiance June 30, 1865
Dove, George W. Corporal	Unk	June 17, 1861, Rocky Mount, Virginia	Co. K, 42nd Virginia Infantry	May 12, 1864, Spotsylvania Court House, Virginia	Point Lookout, Maryland, transferred to Elmira Prison, NY August 2, 1864	Oath of Allegiance July 11, 1865
Dove, Harrison Private	Unk	June 20, 1861, Rockingham County, Virginia	Co. C, 11th Virginia Cavalry	September 14, 1863, Near Culpepper, Virginia	Point Lookout, Maryland, transferred to Elmira Prison, NY August 18, 1864	Exchanged March 14, 1865 at Boulware's Wharf on the James River, Virginia
Dove, Rueben Private	19	June 20, 1861, Rockingham County, Virginia	Co. C, 11th Virginia Cavalry	September 14, 1863, Near Culpepper, Virginia	Point Lookout, Maryland, transferred to Elmira Prison, NY August 18, 1864	Exchanged October 29, 1864, at Venus Point, Savannah River, GA.
Dover, John A. Private	19	May 25, 1863, Randolph, Alabama	Co. A, 7th Alabama Cavalry	April 2, 1864, Near Brownsville, Near Barrancas, Florida	New Orleans, Louisianna Transferred to Elmira Prison, New York, November 19, 1864	Oath of Allegiance June 14, 1865
Dover, T. C. Corporal	Unk	July 19, 1861, Camp McDonald, Georgia	Co. E, 18th Georgia Infantry	June 1, 1864, Cold Harbor, Virginia	Point Lookout, Maryland, transferred to Elmira Prison, NY July 17, 1864	Exchanged March 2, 1865 at Akins Landing on the James River, Virginia
Dover, Winston H. Private	Unk	February 11, 1862, Scottsville, Alabama	Co. C, 1st Battalion Alabama Artillery	August 23, 1864, Fort Morgan, Alabama	New Orleans, Louisiana transferred to Elmira December 4, 1864.	Died April 25, 1865 of Chronic Diarrhea, Grave No. 1415

Name & Rank	Age	Enlisted	Regiment and State	Where Captured	Prison	Remarks
Dowd, Patrick Private	Unk	June 21, 1861, New Orleans, Louisiana	Co, F, 15th Louisiana Infantry	August 12, 1864, Winchester, Virginia	Old Capital Prison, Washington, DC transferred to Elmira Prison, NY August 29, 1864	Oath of Allegiance May 13, 1865
Dowdy, Robert C. Private	17	July 1, 1863, Chatham County, North Carolina	Co. D, 61st North Carolina Infantry	August 27, 1863, Battery Wagner, Morris Island, South Carolina	Point Lookout, Maryland, transferred to Elmira Prison, NY August 18, 1864	Died September 24, 1864 of Typhoid-Pneumonia, Grave No. 465
Dowdy, William A. Private	21	July 25, 1761, Bunker Hill, Virginia	Co. A, 58th Virginia Infantry	May 30, 1864 Mechanics-ville, Virginia	Point Lookout, Maryland, transferred to Elmira Prison, NY July 12, 1864	Died October 10, 1864 of Pneumonia, Grave No. 688
Dowdy, William B. Private	22	June 8, 1861, Lynchburg, Virginia	Co. J, 2nd Virginia Cavalry	July 18, 1861, Hamilton, Virginia	Point Lookout, Maryland, transferred to Elmira Prison, NY August 18, 1864	Exchanged March 10, 1865 at Boulware's Wharf on the James River, Virginia
Dowdy, William H. Private	Unk	March 21, 1862, Young's Mills, Virginia	Co. G, 3rd Virginia Cavalry	August 16, 1864, Front Royal, Virginia	Old Capital Prison, Washington, DC transferred to Elmira Prison, NY August 29, 1864	Died October 19, 1864 of Acute Diarrhea, Grave No. 535
Dowling, David T. Private	18	June 15, 1861, Camp Carolina, Virginia	Co. C, 12th, North Carolina Infantry	May 20, 1864, Spotsylvania Court House, Virginia	Point Lookout, Maryland, transferred to Elmira Prison, NY July 6, 1864	Exchanged March 2, 1865 at Akins Landing on the James River, Virginia
Downey, E. J. Sergeant	Unk	November 27, 1861, Columbia, South Carolina	Co. F, 17th South Carolina Infantry	July 30, 1864, Petersburg, Virginia	Point Lookout, Maryland, transferred to Elmira Prison, NY August 12, 1864	Oath of Allegiance June 14, 1865
Downing, George A. Private	23	June 1, 1861, Cedar Creek, North Carolina	Co. F, 24th North Carolina Infantry	June 18, 1864, Near Petersburg, Virginia	Point Lookout, Maryland, transferred to Elmira Prison, NY July 25, 1864	Oath of Allegiance May 16, 1865

Name & Rank	Age	Enlisted	Regiment and State	Where Captured	Prison	Remarks
Downing, Hays B. Private	16	October 10, 1864, Cumberland County, North Carolina	Co. G, 36th Regiment 2nd North Carolina Artillery	January 15, 1865, Fort Fisher, North Carolina	February 1, 1865, Elmira Prison Camp, New York	Oath of Allegiance May 13, 1865
Downing, John B. Sergeant	Unk	January 24, 1863, Lock's Creek, Cumberland County, North Carolina	Co. J, 36th Regiment 2nd North Carolina Artillery	January 15, 1865, Fort Fisher, North Carolina	February 1, 1865, Elmira Prison Camp, New York	Oath of Allegiance June 17, 1865
Downing, Timothy Private	25	June 7, 1861, Camp Moore, Louisiana	Co. C, 7th Louisiana Infantry	May 11, 1864, Spotsylvania Court House, Virginia	Point Lookout, Maryland, transferred to Elmira Prison, NY August 17, 1864	Oath of Allegiance March 2, 1865. Early Release per Lincoln's Proclamation, 12/8/1863.
Downing, Valentine Private	18	March 31, 1864, New Hanover County, North Carolina	Co. H, 36th Regiment 2nd North Carolina Artillery	January 15, 1865, Fort Fisher, North Carolina	February 1, 1865, Elmira Prison Camp, New York	Died April 5, 1865 of Chronic Diarrhea, Grave No. 2552
Downs, Benjamin F. Private	Unk	April 30, 1864, Monroe Draft, Virginia	Co. G, 26th Battalion Virginia Infantry	July 10, 1864, Frederick, Maryland	Old Capital Prison, Washington, DC, transferred to Elmira Prison, NY, July 23, 1864	Released from Confinement August 11, 1864. Early Release per Lincoln's Proclamation, 12/8/1863.
Downs, James T. Private	19	August 20, 1861, Woodville, Mississippi	Co. D, 21st Mississippi Infantry	May 3, 1863, Fredericksburg, Virginia. Gunshot Wound Right Thigh. Right Leg Amputated.	Old Capital Prison, Washington, DC, transferred to Elmira Prison, July 6, 1864	Exchanged October 29, 1864, at Venus Point, Savannah River, GA.
Downs, Jerry Private	Unk	April 20, 1863, Fort Morgan, Alabama	Co. F, 1st Battalion Alabama Artillery	August 23, 1864, Fort Morgan, Alabama	Steam Press No. 4, New Orleans, Louisiana transferred to Elmira Prison, October 8, 1864.	Died October 21, 1864 of Typhoid Fever, Grave No. 877. Headstone has Downes.

Name & Rank	Age	Enlisted	Regiment and State	Where Captured	Prison	Remarks
Downs, John B. Private	22	August 4, 1862, Brookhaven, Mississippi	Co. D, 17th Mississippi Infantry	May 8, 1864, Spotsylvania Court House, Virginia	Point Lookout, Maryland, transferred to Elmira Prison, NY August 17, 1864	Transferred For Exchange October 11, 1864 to Point Lookout Prison Camp, MD. Died November 1, 1864 at US Army Hospital, Baltimore, MD.
Doxy, John V. Private	Unk	March 5, 1864, Petersburg, Virginia	Co. B, 8th, North Carolina Infantry	May 31, 1864, Cold Harbor, Virginia	Point Lookout, Maryland, transferred to Elmira Prison, NY July 11, 1864	Died November 13, 1864 of Pneumonia, Grave No. 818
Doyle, Garrett Corporal	30	April 20, 1861, Harper's Ferry, Virginia	Co. K, 2nd Virginia Infantry	May 12, 1864, Near Spotsylvania Court House, Virginia	Point Lookout, Maryland, transferred to Elmira Prison, NY August 2, 1864	Transferred to Elmira Prison Hospital July 13, 1865. No Further Information.
Doyle, John Private	Unk	March 17, 1862, Allegheny, Virginia	Co. G, 31st Virginia Infantry	May 5, 1864, Wilderness, Virginia	Point Lookout, Maryland, transferred to Elmira Prison, NY August 2, 1864	Died March 3, 1865 of Diarrhea, Grave No. 2012
Doyle, Joseph M. Private	Unk	May 18, 1864, Henry Court House, Virginia	Co. A, 42nd Virginia Infantry	July 9, 1864, Near Harper's Ferry, Virginia	Old Capital Prison, Washington, DC, transferred to Elmira Prison, NY, July 23, 1864	Died September 28, 1864 of Chronic Diarrhea, Grave No. 393
Doyle, Thomas Private	43	July 22, 1861, Camp Moore, Louisiana	Co. A, 10th Louisiana Infantry	May 12, 1864, Spotsylvania Court House, Virginia	Point Lookout, Maryland, transferred to Elmira Prison, NY July 25, 1864	Oath of Allegiance May 17, 1865
Dozier, Fred J. Private	52	Unknown	Co. E, 36th Regiment 2nd North Carolina Artillery	January 15, 1865, Fort Fisher, North Carolina	February 1, 1865, Elmira Prison Camp, New York	Died March 9, 1865 of Chronic Diarrhea, Grave No. 1877
Dozier, S. Private	Unk	Unknown	Co. B, 8th North Carolina Infantry	June 1, 1864, Cold Harbor, Virginia	Point Lookout, Maryland, transferred to Elmira Prison, NY July 17,1864	Oath of Allegiance July 3, 1865

Name & Rank	Age	Enlisted	Regiment and State	Where Captured	Prison	Remarks
Drake, Benjamin F. Sergeant	20	March 1, 1861, Nashville, North Carolina	Co. H, 32nd North Carolina Infantry	May 10, 1864, Near Mine Run, Spotsylvania, Virginia	Point Lookout, Maryland, transferred to Elmira Prison, NY August 6, 1864	Exchanged March 14, 1865 at Boulware's Wharf on the James River, Virginia
Drake, H. J. Private	Unk	Unknown	Co. B, 57th North Carolina Infantry	July 13, 1864, Near Washington, DC,	Old Capital Prison, Washington, DC, transferred to Elmira Prison, NY, July 23, 1864	Died February 15, 1865 of Variola (Smallpox), Grave No. 2194
Drake, James Private	Unk	August 26, 1862, Camp Randolph, Georgia	Co. K, 8th Georgia Infantry	May 6, 1864, Wilderness, Virginia	Point Lookout, Maryland, transferred to Elmira Prison, NY August 14, 1864	Oath of Allegiance May 19, 1865
Drake, John R. Private	16	May 1, 1861, Nashville, North Carolina	Co. H, 32nd North Carolina Infantry	May 10, 1864, Near Spotsylvania County Court House, Virginia	Point Lookout, Maryland, transferred to Elmira Prison, NY August 14, 1864	Oath of Allegiance June 19, 1865
Dreyfus, Samuel Private	Unk	March 19, 1864, Montgomery, Alabama	Co. F, 1st Battalion Alabama Artillery	August 23, 1864, Fort Morgan, Alabama	Steam Press No. 4, New Orleans, Louisiana transferred to Elmira Prison, October 8, 1864.	Oath of Allegiance February 27, 1865. Early Release per Lincoln's Proclamation, 12/8/1863.
Drew, James F. Marine	23	March 1, 1861. Transferred from Co. A, 1st Georgia Infantry	Confederate States Navy, assigned to CSS Tallahassee	January 15, 1865, Fort Fisher, North Carolina	February 1, 1865, Elmira Prison Camp, New York	Died February 27, 1865 of Pneumonia, Grave No. 2121
Drew, William Private	Unk	April 26, 1862, Camp Leon, Madison, Florida	Co. D, 5th Florida Infantry	May 12, 1864, Spotsylvania Court House, Virginia	Point Lookout, Maryland, transferred to Elmira Prison, NY July 30, 1864	Oath of Allegiance June 16, 1865
Drewry, R. W. Private	Unk	March 31, 1864, Richmond, Virginia	Co. B, 3rd Virginia Cavalry	August 16, 1864, Front Royal, Virginia	Old Capital Prison, Washington, DC transferred to Elmira Prison, NY August 29, 1864	Exchanged October 29, 1864, at Venus Point, Savannah River, GA.

Name & Rank	Age	Enlisted	Regiment and State	Where Captured	Prison	Remarks
Driskel, Lunsford Private	Unk	March 31, 1862, Haynesville, Alabama	Co. K, 5th Alabama Infantry	August 10, 1864, Winchester, Virginia	Old Capital Prison, Washington, DC transferred to Elmira Prison, NY August 29, 1864	Exchanged February 20, 1865 at Boulware's or Cox Wharf on the James River, Virginia
Driver, John E. Private	21	May 26, 1861, Raleigh, North Carolina	Co. K, 14th, North Carolina Infantry	May 31, 1864, Old Church, Cold Harbor, Virginia	Point Lookout, Maryland, transferred to Elmira Prison, NY July 17, 1864	Oath of Allegiance May 17, 1865
Drum, Martin V. Private	26	October 18, 1862, Newton, North Carolina	Co. F, 32nd North Carolina Infantry	May 10, 1864, Wilderness, Virginia	Point Lookout, Maryland, transferred to Elmira Prison, NY August 6, 1864	Transferred for Exchange 10/11/64. Died 11/6/64 of Unknown Causes at Fort Monroe, VA
Drummond, J. W. C. Private	Unk	December 28, 1861, Camp Hampton, South Carolina	Co. F, Holcombe Legion, South Carolina	May 8, 1864, Jarrett's Depot, Virginia	Point Lookout, Maryland, transferred to Elmira Prison, NY August 17, 1864	Oath of Allegiance June 21, 1865
Drummond, William H. Private	Unk	September 1862, Calhoun, Georgia	Co. F, 18th Georgia Infantry	June 1, 1864, Cold Harbor, Virginia	Point Lookout, Maryland, transferred to Elmira Prison, NY July 17, 1864	Died September 9, 1864 of Chronic Diarrhea, Grave No. 499
Drumwright, James. E. Private	Unk	May 1, 1862, Richmond, Virginia	Sturdivant's Co. A, Virginia Light Artillery	June 15, 1864, Petersburg, Virginia	Point Lookout, Maryland, transferred to Elmira Prison, NY July 30, 1864	Oath of Allegiance June 28, 1865
Drury, Patrick Private	26	March 15, 1862, New Orleans, Louisiana	Co. C, 5th Louisiana Infantry	June 11, 1864, Wilderness, Virginia	Old Capital Prison, Washington, DC, transferred to Elmira Prison, NY, July 23, 1864	Exchanged March 10, 1865 at Boulware's wharf on the James River, Virginia
Dry, Tobias A. Private	39	August 6, 1861, Mount Pleasant, North Carolina	Co. H, 8th North Carolina Infantry	June 1, 1864, Gaines Mill, Cold Harbor, Virginia	Point Lookout, Maryland, transferred to Elmira Prison, NY July 17, 1864	Died March 4, 1865 of Chronic Diarrhea, Grave No. 1995. Name J. A. Dry on Headstone.

Name & Rank	Age	Enlisted	Regiment and State	Where Captured	Prison	Remarks
Dubois, B. Private	Unk	February 26, 1862, Tallapoosa, Alabama	Co. E, 1st Battalion Alabama Artillery	August 23, 1864, Fort Morgan, Alabama	New Orleans, Louisiana transferred to Elmira December 4, 1864.	Oath of Allegiance June 21, 1865
Dubois, Samuel Private	Unk	March 8, 1861, Tallapoosa, Alabama	Co. E, 1st Battalion Alabama Artillery	August 23, 1864, Fort Morgan, Alabama	New Orleans, Louisiana transferred to Elmira December 4, 1864.	Oath of Allegiance June 21, 1865
DuBose, H. K. Private	Unk	December 1, 1863, Darlington District, South Carolina	Co. B, 21st South Carolina Infantry	June 24, 1864, Near Petersburg, Virginia	Point Lookout, Maryland, transferred to Elmira Prison, NY August 18, 1864	Oath of Allegiance June 30, 1865
Dudley, John R. Private	Unk	September 29, 1863, Sampson County, North Carolina	Co. A, 36th Regiment 2nd North Carolina Artillery	January 15, 1865, Fort Fisher, North Carolina	February 1, 1865, Elmira Prison Camp, New York	Oath of Allegiance July 11, 1865
Dudley, Sampson Private	Unk	November 12, 1861, Sampson County, North Carolina	Co. A, 36th Regiment 2nd North Carolina Artillery	January 15, 1865, Fort Fisher, North Carolina	February 1, 1865, Elmira Prison Camp, New York	Died May 26, 1865 of Bronchitis, Grave No. 2918
Dudley, Samuel A. Cororal	24	August 31, 1861, Pitt County, North Carolina	Co. G, 8th, North Carolina Infantry	May 31, 1864, Cold Harbor, Virginia	Point Lookout, Maryland, transferred to Elmira Prison, NY July 11, 1864	Exchanged March 14, 1865 at Boulware's Wharf on the James River, Virginia
Dudley, W. Thomas Private	Unk	May 31, 1861, Yellow Branch, Virginia	Co. D, 42nd Virginia Infantry	May 12, 1864, Near Spotsylvania Court House, Virginia	Point Lookout, Maryland, transferred to Elmira Prison, NY August 2, 1864	Exchanged February 20, 1865 at Boulware's or Cox Wharf on the James River, Virginia
Duff, Richard H. Sergeant	Unk	May 28, 1861, Lowery's Point, Virginia	Co. D, 55th Virginia Infantry	May 23, 1864, Hanover Junction, Virginia	Point Lookout, Maryland, transferred to Elmira Prison, NY August 14, 1864	Exchanged October 29, 1864, at Venus Point, Savannah River, GA.
Dugger, David C. Private	21	September 8, 1861, Boone, North Carolina	Co. E, 37th North Carolina	May 6, 1864, Wilderness, Virginia	Point Lookout, Maryland, transferred to Elmira Prison, NY August 17, 1864	Exchanged October 29, 1864, at Venus Point, Savannah River, GA.

Name & Rank	Age	Enlisted	Regiment and State	Where Captured	Prison	Remarks
Duke, Elisha Private	Unk	May 15, 1862, Savannah, Georgia	Co. A, 13th Georgia Infantry	May 20, 1864, Spotsylvania Court House, Virginia	Point Lookout, Maryland, transferred to Elmira Prison, NY July 6, 1864	Exchanged March 2, 1865 at Akins Landing on the James River, Virginia
Duke, G. L. Civilian	Unk	Unknown	Citizen of Louisiana	September 19, 1864, Tensan Parish, Louisiana	New Orleans, Louisianna Transferred to Elmira Prison, New York, November 19, 1864	Died November 26, 1864 of Pneumonia, Grave No. 977
Duke, Henry M. Private	21	July 26, 1861, Gallatin, Tennessee	Co. A, 23rd Tennessee Infantry	June 17, 1864, Petersburg, Virginia	Point Lookout, Maryland, transferred to Elmira Prison, NY July 30, 1864	Died April 30, 1865 of Variola (Smallpox), Grave No. 2734
Duke, Hiram Private	Unk	July 26, 1861, Auburn, Macon County, Georgia	Co. D, 14th Alabama Infantry	May 6, 1864, Wilderness, Virginia	Point Lookout, Maryland, transferred to Elmira Prison, NY August 18, 1864	Oath of Allegiance June 14, 1865
Duke, James B. Private	20	May 16, 1861, Franklinton, North Carolina	Co. E, 15th North Carolina Infantry	May 12, 1864, Spotsylvania Court House, Virginia	Point Lookout, Maryland, transferred to Elmira Prison, NY August 12, 1864	Oath of Allegiance June 19, 1865
Duke, John Private	Unk	August 24, 1861, Lawrenceville, Gwinnett County, Georgia	Co. F, 24th Georgia Infantry	August 16, 1864, Front Royal, Virginia	Old Capital Prison, Washington, DC transferred to Elmira Prison, NY August 29, 1864	Oath of Allegiance June 16, 1865
Duke, John W. Sergeant	Unk	September 7, 1861, Quitman County, Georgia	Co. C, 61st Georgia Infantry	May 12, 1864, Spotsylvania Court House, Virginia	Point Lookout, Maryland, transferred to Elmira Prison, NY July 30, 1864	Exchanged February 20, 1865 at Boulware's or Cox Wharf on the James River, Virginia
Duke, Leonidas Private	Unk	June 10, 1861, Morgan, Georgia	Co. D, 12th Georgia Infantry	May 10, 1864, Spotsylvania Court House, Virginia	Point Lookout, Maryland, transferred to Elmira Prison, NY July 25, 1864	Oath of Allegiance June 14, 1865

Name & Rank	Age	Enlisted	Regiment and State	Where Captured	Prison	Remarks
Duke, Martin V. Private	Unk	September 5, 1862, Randolph, Alabama	Co. C, 3rd Alabama Infantry	May 12, 1864, Spotsylvania Court House, Virginia	Point Lookout, Maryland, transferred to Elmira Prison, NY August 12, 1864	Died June 23, 1865 of Chronic Diarrhea, Grave No. 2816
Duke, R. E. Private	20	April 12, 1862, Battery Island, South Carolina	Co. C, 25th South Carolina Infantry	May 14, 1864, Near Fort Darling, Virginia	Point Lookout, Maryland, transferred to Elmira Prison, NY August 17, 1864	Oath of Allegiance June 19, 1865
Duke, Thomas J. Private	18	April 12, 1862, Battery Island, South Carolina	Co. C, 25th South Carolina Infantry	May 14, 1864, Near Fort Darling, Virginia	Point Lookout, Maryland, transferred to Elmira Prison, NY August 17, 1864	Oath of Allegiance June 19, 1865
Duke, Wiley Private	22	May 30, 1861, Camden County, North Carolina	Co. B, 32nd North Carolina Infantry	May 10, 1864, Near Mine Run, Spotsylvania, Virginia	Point Lookout, Maryland, transferred to Elmira Prison, NY August 6, 1864	Exchanged March 2, 1865 at Akins Landing on the James River, Virginia
Duke, William P. Private	Unk	Unknown	Co. A, 1st Battalion Alabama Artillery	August 23, 1864, Fort Morgan, Alabama	Steam Press No. 4, New Orleans, Louisiana transferred to Elmira Prison, October 8, 1864.	Died January 28, 1865 of Typhoid-Pneumonia, Grave No. 1657
Dula, Simpson J. Private	Unk	April 1, 1864, Lenore County, North Carolina	Co. J, 26th North Carolina Infantry	May 12, 1864, Spotsylvania Court House, Virginia	Point Lookout, Maryland, transferred to Elmira Prison, NY August 12, 1864	Exchanged October 29, 1864, at Venus Point, Savannah River, GA.
Dulin, Charles H. Private	Unk	June 16, 1861, Flint Hill, Virginia	Co. E, 49th Virginia Infantry	May 30, 1864, Gaines Mill, Virginia	Point Lookout, Maryland, transferred to Elmira Prison, NY July 11, 1864	Oath of Allegiance June 23, 1865
Dulin, Daniel H. Sergeant	33	September 3, 1861, Mecklenburg County, North Carolina	Co. H, 35th North Carolina Infantry	June 17, 1864, Petersburg, Virginia	Point Lookout, Maryland, transferred to Elmira Prison, NY July 30, 1864	Exchanged February 13, 1865 at Boulware's wharf on the James River, Virginia

Name & Rank	Age	Enlisted	Regiment and State	Where Captured	Prison	Remarks
Dumond, Eugene Sergeant	24	June 12, 1861, New Orleans, Louisiana	Co. K, 14th Louisiana Infantry	May 5, 1864, Wilderness, Virginia	Point Lookout, Maryland, transferred to Elmira Prison, NY July 25, 1864	Exchanged February 25, 1865 at Boulware's or Cox Wharf on the James River, Virginia
Dumoulin, Augustin Private	Unk	September 1, 1862, New Road, Louisiana	Co. K, 2nd Louisiana Cavalry	October 20, 1864, False River, Pointe Coupee Parish, Louisiana	New Orleans, Louisiana transferred to Elmira November 19, 1864.	Exchanged February 25, 1865 at Boulware's or Cox Wharf on the James River, Virginia
Dunaway, William Private	Unk	July 19, 1861, Montgomery, Alabama	Co. D, 13th Alabama Infantry	May 5, 1864, Spotsylvania Court House, Virginia	Point Lookout, Maryland, transferred to Elmira Prison, NY July 30, 1864	Exchanged October 29, 1864, at Venus Point, Savannah River, GA.
Duncan, Charles Private	35	February 27, 1862, Reidsville, North Carolina	Co. G, 45th North Carolina Infantry	May 10, 1864, Spotsylvania Court House, Virginia	Point Lookout, Maryland, transferred to Elmira Prison, NY August 6, 1864	Exchanged March 14, 1865 at Boulware's Wharf on the James River, Virginia
Duncan, G. W. Private	Unk	May 20, 1862, Camp Harris, Tennessee	Co. D, 17th Tennessee Infantry	June 17, 1864, Petersburg, Virginia	Point Lookout, Maryland, transferred to Elmira Prison, NY July 30, 1864	Exchanged February 25, 1865 at Boulware's or Cox Wharf on the James River, Virginia
Duncan, George W. Private	21	September 15, 1861, Allegheny County, North Carolina	Co. K, 37th North Carolina Infantry	August 16, 1864, New Market, Virginia	Old Capital Prison, Washington, DC transferred to Elmira Prison, NY August 27, 1864	Oath of Allegiance May 29, 1865
Duncan, George W. Corporal	28	December 28, 1861, Camp Hampton Legion, South Carolina	Co. F, Holcombe Legion, South Carolina	May 8, 1864, Jarrett's Depot, Virginia	Point Lookout, Maryland, transferred to Elmira Prison, NY August 17, 1864	Died January 14, 1865 of Disease of the Heart, Grave No. 1461
Duncan, J. S. Private	Unk	August 2, 1861, New Orleans, Louisiana	Co. B, 1st Louisiana Infantry	May 12, 1864, Spotsylvania Court House, Virginia	Point Lookout, Maryland, transferred to Elmira Prison, NY August 17, 1864	Exchanged February 25, 1865 at Boulware's or Cox Wharf on the James River, Virginia

Name & Rank	Age	Enlisted	Regiment and State	Where Captured	Prison	Remarks
Duncan, James Private	21	June 10, 1861, Meadow Bluff, Virginia	Co. C, 46th Virginia Infantry	June 16, 1864, Petersburg, Virginia	Point Lookout, Maryland, transferred to Elmira Prison, NY July 23, 1864	Died September 29, 1864 of Chronic Diarrhea, Grave No. 432
Duncan, James H. Private	Unk	April 28, 1861, New Orleans, Louisiana	Co. A, 1st Louisiana Infantry	May 12, 1864, Spotsylvania Court House, Virginia	Point Lookout, Maryland, transferred to Elmira Prison, NY August 17, 1864	Exchanged February 25, 1865 at Boulware's or Cox Wharf on the James River, Virginia
Duncan, James K. Private	39	July 8, 1862, Oxford, North Carolina	Co. J, 23rd North Carolina Infantry	May 12, 1864, Near Spotsylvania Court House, Virginia	Point Lookout, Maryland, transferred to Elmira Prison, NY August 14, 1864	Exchanged February 20, 1865 at Boulware's or Cox Wharf on the James River, Virginia
Duncan, James P. Private	Unk	August 9. 1861, Cumberland Gap, Tennessee	Co. D, 17th Tennessee Infantry	June 17, 1864, Petersburg, Virginia	Point Lookout, Maryland, transferred to Elmira Prison, NY July 30, 1864	Exchanged February 25, 1865 at Boulware's or Cox Wharf on the James River, Virginia
Duncan, James W. Corporal	Unk	July 30, 1861, Marion, Virginia	Co. D, 4th Virginia Infantry	May 12, 1864 Spotsylvania Court House, Virginia	Point Lookout, Maryland, transferred to Elmira Prison, NY August 2, 1864	Exchanged March 2, 1865 at Akins Landing on the James River, Virginia
Duncan, John Sergeant	Unk	August 24, 1861, Clayton, Georgia	Co. E, 24th Georgia Infantry	August 16, 1864, Front Royal, Virginia	Old Capital Prison, Washington, DC. Transferred to Elmira August 29, 1864	Died November 14, 1864 of Typhoid-Pneumonia, Grave No. 813
Duncan, John Private	Unk	Unknown	Co. D, 50th Virginia Infantry	May 12, 1864, Spotsylvania Court House, Virginia	Point Lookout, Maryland, transferred to Elmira Prison, NY August 2, 1864	Oath of Allegiance June 19, 1865
Duncan, John F. Private	Unk	May 20, 1862, Camp Harris, Tennessee	Co. D, 17th Tennessee Infantry	June 17, 1864, Petersburg, Virginia	Point Lookout, Maryland, transferred to Elmira Prison, NY July 30, 1864	Exchanged February 25, 1865 at Boulware's or Cox Wharf on the James River, Virginia

Name & Rank	Age	Enlisted	Regiment and State	Where Captured	Prison	Remarks
Duncan, John J. Private	38	December 15, 1863, Fort Caswell, Brunswick County, North Carolina	Co. F, 36th Regiment 2nd North Carolina Artillery	January 15, 1865, Fort Fisher, North Carolina	February 1, 1865, Elmira Prison Camp, New York	Died March 30, 1865 of Diarrhea, Grave No. 2600
Duncan, Noah Private	Unk	Unknown	Co. C, 50th Virginia Infantry	May 12, 1864, Spotsylvania Court House, Virginia	Point Lookout, Maryland, transferred to Elmira Prison, NY August 2, 1864	Died January 13, 1865 of Chronic Diarrhea, Grave No. 1487
Duncan, Robert Private	30	February 27, 1862, Reidsville, North Carolina	Co. G, 45th North Carolina Infantry	May 10, 1864, Spotsylvania Court House, Virginia	Point Lookout, Maryland, transferred to Elmira Prison, NY August 6, 1864	Died December 12, 1864 of Chronic Diarrhea, Grave No. 1056
Duncan, Thomas Private	38	April 29, 1862, Camp Mangum, North Carolina	Co. G, 45th North Carolina Infantry	May 10, 1864, Spotsylvania Court House, Virginia	Point Lookout, Maryland, transferred to Elmira Prison, NY August 6, 1864	Exchanged February 13, 1865 at Boulware's wharf on the James River, Virginia
Duncan, Tilman C. Private	25	July 25, 1861, Tullahoma, Tennessee	Co. E, 25th Tennessee Infantry	June 17, 1864, Near Petersburg, Virginia	Point Lookout, Maryland, transferred to Elmira Prison, NY July 30, 1864	Exchanged February 20, 1865 at Boulware's or Cox Wharf on the James River, Virginia
Duncan, William H. Private	40	October 8, 1863, Richmond, Virginia	Co. G, 45th North Carolina Infantry	May 10, 1864, Spotsylvania Court House, Virginia	Point Lookout, Maryland, transferred to Elmira Prison, NY August 6, 1864	Exchanged October 29, 1864, at Venus Point, Savannah River, GA.
Dunegan, E. J. Private	Unk	June 12, 1862, Hall County, Georgia	Co. B, 7th Georgia Cavalry	June 11, 1864, Trevilian Station, Louisa Court House, Virginia	Point Lookout, Maryland, transferred to Elmira Prison, NY July 25, 1864	Oath of Allegiance June 14, 1865
Dunham, Joseph W. Private	25	May 1, 1861, Elizabethtown, North Carolina	Co. K, 18th North Carolina Infantry	July 29, 1864, Petersburg, Virginia	Point Lookout, Maryland, transferred to Elmira Prison, NY August 12, 1864	Exchanged 3/2/65. Died 4/3/65 of General Debility at Jackson Hospital, Richmond, VA.

Name & Rank	Age	Enlisted	Regiment and State	Where Captured	Prison	Remarks
Dunken, Seabron H. Private	Unk	July 19, 1861, Montgomery, Alabama	Co. D, 13th Alabama Infantry	May 12, 1864, Spotsylvania Court House, Virginia	Point Lookout, Maryland, transferred to Elmira Prison, NY August 2, 1864	Oath of Allegiance June 21, 1865
Dunker, J. Private	Unk	Unknown	Co. I, 50th Virginia Infantry	May 12, 1864, Spotsylvania Court House, Virginia	Point Lookout, Maryland, transferred to Elmira Prison, NY August 2, 1864	Transferred for Exchange 10/11/64. Nothing Further.
Dunkley, Samuel H. Sergeant	Unk	June 22, 1861, Wytheville, Virginia	Co. J, 50th Virginia Infantry	May 6, 1864, Wilderness, Virginia	Point Lookout, Maryland, transferred to Elmira Prison, NY August 14, 1864	Oath of Allegiance June 23, 1865
Dunlap, George Private	Unk	Unknown	Co. C, 14th Battalion North Carolina Cavalry	July 16, 1864, Loudoun County, Virginia	Old Capital Prison, Washington, DC, transferred to Elmira Prison, NY, July 23, 1864	Exchanged March 10, 1865 at Boulware's Wharf on the James River, Virginia
Dunlap, Robert B. Private	22	July 16, 1861, Staunton, Virginia	Co. A, 52nd Virginia Infantry	May 30, 1864, Old Church, Cold Harbor, Virginia. Gunshot Wound Right Shoulder.	Old Capital Prison, Washington, DC transferred to Elmira Prison, NY August 29, 1864	Exchanged October 29, 1864, at Venus Point, Savannah River, GA.
Dunlap, Rueben A. Private	Unk	May 28, 1864, Columbia, South Carolina	Co. A, 17th South Carolina Infantry	July 30, 1864, Petersburg, Virginia	Point Lookout, Maryland, transferred to Elmira Prison, NY August 12, 1864	Exchanged October 29, 1864, at Venus Point, Savannah River, GA.
Dunlop, William Marine Corporal	34	November 3, 1862, Mobile, Alabama	Co. E, Confederate States Marine Corps	June 17, 1863, CSS Atlanta, Savannah, Georgia	Point Lookout, Maryland, transferred to Elmira Prison, NY July 12, 1864	Exchanged October 29, 1864, at Venus Point, Savannah River, GA.
Dunn, Franklin Private	26	April 1, 1864, Edgecombe County, North Carolina	Co. D, 40th Regiment, 3rd North Carolina Artillery	January 15, 1865, Fort Fisher, North Carolina	February 1, 1865, Elmira Prison Camp, New York	Died April 9, 1865 of Variola (Smallpox), Grave No. 2618

Name & Rank	Age	Enlisted	Regiment and State	Where Captured	Prison	Remarks
Dunn, George Private	43	July 1, 1863, Raleigh, North Carolina	Co. K, 30th North Carolina Infantry	May 8, 1864, Wilderness, Virginia	Point Lookout, Maryland, transferred to Elmira Prison, NY August 14, 1864	Died December 1, 1864 of Pneumonia, Grave No. 1008
Dunn, James W. Private	Unk	March 3, 1862, Fort Lowry, Virginia	Co. G, 55th Virginia Infantry	May 6, 1864, Wilderness, Virginia	Point Lookout, Maryland, transferred to Elmira Prison, NY August 14, 1864	Transferred for Exchange 10/11/64. Died 10/22/64 of Unknown Causes at Point Lookout, MD.
Dunn, John F. Marine	Unk	February 27, 1863, Place Unknown	Confederate States Navy, assigned to CSS Atlanta	January 15, 1865, Fort Fisher, North Carolina	February 1, 1865, Elmira Prison Camp, New York	Oath of Allegiance July 11, 1865
Dunn, John A. Private	Unk	June 12, 1861, Red Sulfur Springs, Virginia	Co. F, 26th Battalion, Virginia Infantry	June 3, 1864, Gaines Farm, Cold Harbor, Virginia	Point Lookout, Maryland, transferred to Elmira Prison, NY July 17, 1864	Oath of Allegiance July 3, 1865
Dunn, Lewis A. Private	26	April 29, 1863, White Sulfur Springs, Virginia	Co. F, 26th Battalion, Virginia Infantry	June 3, 1864, Gaines Farm, Cold Harbor, Virginia	Point Lookout, Maryland, transferred to Elmira Prison, NY July 17, 1864	Exchanged March 14, 1865 at Boulware's Wharf on the James River, Virginia
Dunn, Muscoe R. Private	Unk	March 1, 1862, Fort Lowry, Virginia	Co. A, 55th Virginia Infantry	May 6, 1864, Wilderness, Virginia	Point Lookout, Maryland, transferred to Elmira Prison, NY August 14, 1864	Exchanged March 10, 1865 at Boulware's Wharf on the James River, Virginia
Dunn, R. W. Private	Unk	April 24, 1861, Richmond, Virginia	Captain Young's Battery Virginia Artillery	June 15, 1864, Petersburg, Virginia	Point Lookout, Maryland, transferred to Elmira Prison, NY July 25, 1864	Transferred to Elmira Post Hospital July 13, 1865. Nothing Further.
Dunn, Thomas J. Private	Unk	April 24, 1861, Richmond, Virginia	Captain Young's Battery Virginia Artillery	June 15, 1864, Petersburg, Virginia	Point Lookout, Maryland, transferred to Elmira Prison, NY July 25, 1864	Died September 11, 1864 of Pneumonia, Grave No. 196
Dunn, W. L. Sergeant	Unk	Unknown	Co. A, 2nd Louisiana Cavalry	August 25, 1864, Near Clinton, Louisiana	New Orleans, Louisianna Transferred to Elmira Prison, New York, November 19, 1864	Exchanged February 25, 1865 at Boulware's or Cox Wharf on the James River, Virginia

Name & Rank	Age	Enlisted	Regiment and State	Where Captured	Prison	Remarks
Dunnaway, William T. Private	Unk	March 13, 1862, Fredericksburg, Virginia	Co. M, 55th Virginia Infantry	May 5, 1864, Wilderness, Virginia	Point Lookout, Maryland, transferred to Elmira Prison, NY August 14, 1864	Exchanged October 29, 1864 at Venus Point, Savannah River, GA.
Dunnevant, William B. Corporal	22	July 29, 1861, Madison, Georgia	Co. G, Cobb's Legion Georgia	August 16, 1864, Front Royal, Virginia	Old Capital Prison, Washington, DC transferred to Elmira Prison, NY August 29, 1864	Oath of Allegiance July 7, 1865
Dunning, Francis H. Private	Unk	Unknown	Co. A, 10th Mississippi Cavalry	September 15, 1865, Natchez, Mississippi	New Orleans, Louisianna, Transferred to Elmira Prison, New York, November 19, 1864	Died December 15, 1864 of Pneumonia, Grave No. 1117. Headstone has Francis Derming.
Dunsmore, William H. Private	Unk	March 28, 1862, Lewisburg, Virginia	Co. D, 26th Battalion Virginia Infantry	June 3, 1864, Cold Harbor, Virginia	Point Lookout, Maryland, transferred to Elmira Prison, NY July 17,1864	Oath of Allegiance May 17, 1865
Dunstan, James Richard Private	20	June 2, 1861, Gloucester Point, Virginia	Co. B, 26th Virginia Infantry	June 15, 1864, Near Petersburg, Virginia	Point Lookout, Maryland, transferred to Elmira Prison, NY July 12,1864	Oath of Allegiance July 11, 1865
Dunston, Howell C. Corporal	32	April 24, 1861, Arbacoochee, Alabama	Co. J, 44th Alabama Infantry	May 6, 1864, Wilderness, Virginia	Point Lookout, Maryland, transferred to Elmira Prison, NY August 17, 1864	Oath of Allegiance June 14, 1865
Duplantier, Joseph Private	Unk	Unknown	Co. A, Ogden's Louisiana Cavalry	October 6, 1864, Clinton, Louisiana	New Orleans, Louisiana transferred to Elmira November 19, 1864.	Exchanged February 13, 1865 at Boulware's wharf on the James River, Virginia
Dupratter, Marianna Private	Unk	January 6, 1862, Monticello, Florida	Co. A, 5th Florida Infantry	May 12, 1864, Spotsylvania Court House, Virginia	Point Lookout, Maryland, transferred to Elmira Prison, NY August 12, 1864	Oath of Allegiance June 14, 1865

Name & Rank	Age	Enlisted	Regiment and State	Where Captured	Prison	Remarks
Dupree, Peter C. Sergeant	Unk	July 22, 1861, Weldon, North Carolina	Co. K, 1st North Carolina Infantry	May 12, 1864, Spotsylvania Court House, Virginia	Point Lookout, Maryland, transferred to Elmira Prison, NY August 6, 1864	Oath of Allegiance June 12, 1865
Dupriest, James L. Private	Unk	August 21, 1861, Irwinton, Georgia	Co. J, 3rd Georgia Infantry	July 23, 1863, Manassas Gap, Virginia	Point Lookout, Maryland, transferred to Elmira Prison, NY August 18, 1864	Exchanged October 29, 1864 at Venus Point, Savannah River, GA.
Dupuis, Cesaire Private	24	June 19, 1861, Camp Moore, Louisiana	Co. C, 8th Louisiana Infantry	May 12, 1864, Spotsylvania Court House, Virginia	Point Lookout, Maryland, transferred to Elmira Prison, NY August 17, 1864	Exchanged February 25, 1865 at Boulware's or Cox Wharf on the James River, Virginia
Dupuy, P. O. Private	Unk	September 1, 1862, New Road, Louisiana	Co. J, 2nd Louisiana Cavalry	August 10, 1864, Bayou Grosstette, Louisiana	New Orleans, Louisianna Transferred to Elmira Prison, New York, November 19, 1864	Oath of Allegiance May 17, 1865
Durance, James H. Private	Unk	November 6, 1863, Byran County, Georgia	Co. H, 7th Georgia Cavalry	June 11, 1864, Trevilian Station, Louisa Court House, Virginia	Point Lookout, Maryland, transferred to Elmira Prison, NY July 25, 1864	Oath of Allegiance July 7, 1865
Durand, G. Civilian	Unk	Registered Enemy	Citizen of Louisiana	July 27, 1864, New Orleans, Louisiana	New Orleans, Louisiana transferred to Elmira November 19, 1864.	Oath of Allegiance June 20, 1865
Duren, William A. Private	Unk	October 23, 1863, Tallapoosa County, Alabama	Co. J, 61st Alabama Infantry	May 8, 1864, Wilderness, Virginia	Point Lookout, Maryland, transferred to Elmira Prison, NY July 30, 1864	Oath of Allegiance June 19, 1865
Durfees, J. K. Private	Unk	Unknown	Co. H, 5th North Carolina Infantry	May 31, 1864, Hanover Court House, Virginia	Point Lookout, Maryland, transferred to Elmira Prison, NY July 17, 1864	Exchanged March 10, 1865 at Boulware's wharf on the James River, Virginia

Name & Rank	Age	Enlisted	Regiment and State	Where Captured	Prison	Remarks
Durham, Henry Private	18	January 20, 1862, Petersburg, Virginia	Co. J, 24th North Carolina Infantry	May 16, 1864, Near Drury's Bluff, Virginia	Point Lookout, Maryland, transferred to Elmira Prison, NY August 18, 1864	Oath of Allegiance June 14, 1865
Durham, James A. Private	Unk	March 23, 1862, Fort Lowry, Virginia	Co. D, 55th Virginia Infantry	July 14, 1863, Falling Waters, Maryland	Point Lookout, Maryland, transferred to Elmira Prison, NY August 18, 1864	Exchanged March 10, 1865 at Boulware's Wharf on the James River, Virginia
Durham, John S. Private	Unk	May 14, 1862, Orange County Court House, North Carolina	Co. G, 28th North Carolina Infantry	May 6, 1864, Wilderness, Virginia	Point Lookout, Maryland, transferred to Elmira Prison, NY August 14, 1864	Oath of Allegiance June 23, 1865
Durham, Lewis G. M. Private	Unk	June 11, 1861, Bledsoe's Store, Virginia	Co. K, 44th Virginia Infantry	May 12, 1864, Spotsylvania Court House, Virginia	Point Lookout, Maryland, transferred to Elmira Prison, NY August 2, 1864	Oath of Allegiance June 27, 1865
Durham, Robert A. Corporal	19	December 20, 1861, Orange County, North Carolina	Co. K, 28th North Carolina Infantry	May 10, 1864, Spotsylvania, Virginia	Point Lookout, Maryland, transferred to Elmira Prison, NY August 12, 1864	Oath of Allegiance June 19, 1865
Durham, Thomas H. Private	23	May 9, 1861, Osberne Ford, Scott County, Virginia	Co. B, 48th Virginia Infantry	May 12, 1864, Spotsylvania Court House, Virginia	Point Lookout, Maryland, transferred to Elmira Prison, NY August 2, 1864	Oath of Allegiance, June 27, 1865
Durham, Thomas M. Private	22	September 2, 1861, Orange County, North Carolina	Co. G, 28th North Carolina Infantry	May 10, 1864, Spotsylvania, Virginia	Point Lookout, Maryland, transferred to Elmira Prison, NY August 12, 1864	Oath of Allegiance June 27, 1865
Durham, William Private	19	May 30, 1861, Garysburg, North Carolina	Co. C, 5th North Carolina Infantry	May 12, 1864, Spotsylvania Court House, Virginia	Point Lookout, Maryland, transferred to Elmira Prison, NY August 6, 1864	Oath of Allegiance June 21, 1865
Durmire, N. W. Private	Unk	September 3, 1862, Statesville, North Carolina	Co. F, 23rd North Carolina Infantry	May 12, 1864, Near Spotsylvania Court House, Virginia	Point Lookout, Maryland, transferred to Elmira Prison, NY August 14, 1864	Exchanged October 29, 1864, at Venus Point, Savannah River, GA.

Name & Rank	Age	Enlisted	Regiment and State	Where Captured	Prison	Remarks
Dusenberry, John A. Private	Unk	Unknown	Co. J, 50th Virginia Infantry	May 12, 1864, Spotsylvania Court House, Virginia	Point Lookout, Maryland, transferred to Elmira Prison, NY August 2, 1864	Exchanged February 20, 1865 at Boulware's or Cox Wharf on the James River, Virginia
Dutraunois, William J. Private	Unk	June 19, 1861, Camp Moore, Louisiana	Co. J, 8th Louisiana Infantry	May 10, 1864, Spotsylvania, Virginia	Point Lookout, Maryland, transferred to Elmira Prison, NY August 17, 1864	Exchanged February 25, 1865 at Boulware's or Cox Wharf on the James River, Virginia
Dutton, Albert C. Private	25	April 23, 1861, Gloucester Court House, Virginia	Co. B, 26th Virginia Infantry	June 15, 1864, Near Petersburg, Virginia	Point Lookout, Maryland, transferred to Elmira Prison, NY July 12, 1864	Exchanged March 2, 1865 at Akins Landing on the James River, Virginia
Duval, Franklin C. Sergeant	Unk	May 8, 1861, Gloucester Court House, Virginia	Co. B, 26th Virginia Infantry	June 15, 1864, Near Petersburg, Virginia	Point Lookout, Maryland, transferred to Elmira Prison, NY July 12, 1864	Exchanged March 10, 1865 at Boulware's Wharf on the James River, Virginia
Duval, William A. Private	Unk	July 1, 1861, Gloucester Point, Virginia	Co. B, 26th Virginia Infantry	June 15, 1864, Near Petersburg, Virginia	Point Lookout, Maryland, transferred to Elmira Prison, NY July 12, 1864	Exchanged March 10, 1865 at Boulware's Wharf on the James River, Virginia
Duvall, Melville J. Private	Unk	May 11, 1861, Richmond, Virginia	Co. C, 38th Read's Battalion, Virginia Light Artillery	June 3, 1864, Gaines Farm, Cold Harbor, Virginia	Point Lookout, Maryland, transferred to Elmira Prison, NY July 17, 1864	Exchanged March 2, 1865 at Akins Landing on the James River, Virginia
DuVall, William E. Private	Unk	June 19, 1861, Camp Moore, New Orleans, Louisiana	Co. H, 8th Louisiana Infantry	May 12, 1864, Spotsylvania Court House, Virginia	Point Lookout, Maryland, transferred to Elmira Prison, NY August 17, 1864	Exchanged October 29, 1864, at Venus Point, Savannah River, GA.
Duvall, William G. Private	Unk	March 21, 1862, Richmond, Virginia	2nd Battery Maryland Artillery	July 17,1864, Beltville, Maryland	Old Capital Prison, Washington, DC, transferred to Elmira Prison, NY, July 23, 1864	Exchanged March 10, 1865 at Boulware's wharf on the James River, Virginia

Name & Rank	Age	Enlisted	Regiment and State	Where Captured	Prison	Remarks
Duvell, William B. Private	19	January 20, 1862, Springfield, Missouri	Co. H, 1st Missouri Cavalry	May 17, 1863, Big Black Bridge, Champion Hill, Mississippi	Point Lookout, Maryland, transferred to Elmira Prison, NY August 18, 1864	Exchanged February 13, 1865 at Boulware's wharf on the James River, Virginia
Dwyer, Daniel Private	Unk	September 4, 1861, Nashville, Tennessee	Co. L, 1st Jackson's Tennessee Heavy Artillery	August 23, 1864, Fort Morgan, Alabama.	New Orleans, Louisiana transferred to Elmira December 4, 1864.	Oath of Allegiance May 17, 1865
Dwyle, Mathew Private	51	May 29, 1861, Corinth, Mississippi	Co. B, 18th Mississippi Infantry	July 22, 1864, Falls Church, Virginia	Old Capital Prison, Washington D. C. Transferred to Elmira Prison, NY August 12, 1864	Oath of Allegiance May 17, 1865
Dye, William David Private	20	March 23, 1862, Bowdon, Georgia	Co. B, Cobb's Legion Georgia	August 16, 1864, Front Royal, Virginia	Old Capital Prison, Washington, DC transferred to Elmira Prison, NY August 29, 1864	Oath of Allegiance May 29, 1865
Dyer, Frank Sergeant	Unk	May 25, 1861, Centreville, Virginia	Co. F, 6th Virginia Cavalry	June 11, 1864, Louisa Court House, Trevilian Station, Virginia	Point Lookout, Maryland, transferred to Elmira Prison, NY August 12, 1864	Oath of Allegiance June 14, 1865
Dyer, James Private	24	February 16, 1862, Camp Allegheny, Virginia	Co. B, 6th Virginia Cavalry	May 11, 1864, Henrico County, Virginia	Point Lookout, Maryland, transferred to Elmira Prison, NY August 17, 1864	Died January 16, 1865 of Chronic Diarrhea, Grave No. 1452
Dyer, Thomas O. Private	30	September 7, 1863, Orange Court House, Virginia	2nd Co. Washington Artillery, Louisiana	April 25, 1865, Briantown, Virginia	Old Capital Prison, Washington D. C. Transferred to Elmira Prison, NY May 12, 1865.	Oath of Allegiance June 21, 1865

Name & Rank	Age	Enlisted	Regiment and State	Where Captured	Prison	Remarks
Dyson, W. B. Private	Unk	April 15, 1864, Ashland, Virginia	Co. K, 5th Virginia Cavalry	May 11, 1864, Yellow Tavern, Hanover County, Virginia	Point Lookout, Maryland, transferred to Elmira Prison, NY August 17, 1864	Exchanged March 10, 1865 at Boulware's Wharf on the James River, Virginia

Name & Rank	Age	Enlisted	Regiment and State	Where Captured	Prison	Remarks
Eader, Charles W. Private	Unk	Unknown	Co. B, 35th Battalion Virginia Cavalry	July 30, 1864, Potomac River, Maryland	Old Capital Prison, Washington D. C. Transferred to Elmira Prison, NY August 12, 1864	Exchanged March 14, 1865 at Boulware's Wharf on the James River, Virginia
Eads, Robert H. Private	Unk	April 20, 1861, Lexington, Virginia	Co. H, 4th Virginia Infantry	May 12, 1864, Spotsylvania Court House, Virginia	Point Lookout, Maryland, transferred to Elmira Prison, NY August 2, 1864	Oath of Allegiance June 30, 1865
Eagle, Robert A. Private	26	July 11, 1862, Lynchburg, Virginia	Co. I, 42nd Virginia Infantry	May 12, 1864, Near Spotsylvania Court House, Virginia	Point Lookout, Maryland, transferred to Elmira Prison, NY August 6, 1864	Oath of Allegiance June 30, 1865
Eakin, Joseph D. Private	Unk	January 16, 1863, Hodges, South Carolina	Co. F, Holcombe Legion, South Carolina	May 8, 1864, Jarrett's Depot, Virginia	Point Lookout, Maryland, transferred to Elmira Prison, NY August 17, 1864	Exchanged February 13, 1865. Died March 25, 1865 of Chronic Diarrhea at Jackson Hospital, Richmond, VA
Eans, William J. Private	Unk	March 10, 1862, Henry County, Virginia	Co. G, 42nd Virginia Infantry	May 12, 1864, Near Spotsylvania Court House, Virginia	Point Lookout, Maryland, transferred to Elmira Prison, NY August 6, 1864	Exchanged 2/13/65. Died 3/29/65 of Chronic Laryngitis at Richmond Hospital no. 9, Richmond, VA
Earley, Moses C. Private	17	September 12, 1864, Hertford County, North Carolina	Co. C, 3rd Battalion North Carolina Light Artillery	January 15, 1865, Fort Fisher, North Carolina	February 1, 1865, Elmira Prison Camp, New York	Died February 10, 1865 of Pneumonia and Typhoid Fever, Grave No. 2047

Name & Rank	Age	Enlisted	Regiment and State	Where Captured	Prison	Remarks
Earley, Thomas J. Private	18	April 1, 1862, Windsor, North Carolina	Co. G, 32nd North Carolina Infantry	May 10, 1864, Wilderness, Virginia	Point Lookout, Maryland, transferred to Elmira Prison, NY August 6, 1864	Died September 20, 1864 of Pneumonia, Grave No. 517
Earley, William J. Sergeant	25	April 1, 1862, Windsor, North Carolina	Co. G, 32nd North Carolina Infantry	May 10, 1864, Wilderness, Virginia	Point Lookout, Maryland, transferred to Elmira Prison, NY August 6, 1864	Oath of Allegiance June 16, 1865
Earls, Daniel Private	Unk	February 26, 1863, Cleveland County, North Carolina	Co. K, 1st North Carolina Artillery	January 15, 1865, Fort Fisher, North Carolina	Elmira Prison Camp, New York, January 30, 1865	Died April 1, 1865 of Ulcer Around the Neck, Grave No. 2594
Early, Moses Citizen	Unk	Unknown	North Carolina Citizen	January 15, 1865, Fort Fisher, North Carolina	Elmira Prison Camp, New York, January 30, 1865	Died of Chronic Diarrhea February 12, 1865. Grave Not Found at Woodlawn Cemtery.
Earnest, Elisha W. Private	Unk	April 1, 1864, Randolph County, Alabama	Co. J, 12th Alabama Infantry	May 20, 1864, Spotsylvania Court House, Virginia	Point Lookout, Maryland, transferred to Elmira Prison, NY July 6, 1864	Oath of Allegiance May 19, 1865
Earnhardt, Crusoe Private	Unk	September 1, 1861, Mount Pleasant, North Carolina	Co. G, 8th North Carolina Infantry	June 1, 1864, Gaines Mill, Cold Harbor, Virginia	Point Lookout, Maryland, transferred to Elmira Prison, NY July 17,1864	Oath of Allegiance May 29, 1865
Earnhart, Jacob C. Corporal	Unk	August 8, 1862, Statesville, North Carolina	Co. K, 5th North Carolina Infantry	May 20, 1864, Spotsylvania Court House, Virginia	Point Lookout, Maryland, transferred to Elmira Prison, NY July 6, 1864	Exchanged October 29, 1864, at Venus Point, Savannah River, GA.
Easily, Edward W. Private	Unk	January 1, 1863, Osyka, Mississippi	Co. F, 14th Confederate States Cavalry	October 7, 1864, Camp Moore, Louisiana	New Orleans, Louisiana transferred to Elmira November 19, 1864.	Oath of Allegiance May 29, 1865

Name & Rank	Age	Enlisted	Regiment and State	Where Captured	Prison	Remarks
Easley, Samuel Private	Unk	November 9, 1863, Mobile, Alabama	Co. E, 1st Battalion Alabama Artillery	August 23, 1864, Fort Morgan, Alabama	Steam Press No. 4 New Orleans, Louisiana transferred to Elmira October 8, 1864.	Exchanged March 2, 1865 at Akins Landing on the James River, Virginia
Easly, John L. Private	24	March 12, 1862, Mecklenburg County, North Carolina	Co. J, 48th North Carolina Infantry	June 2, 1864, Talapatomoy Creek, Brown's Farm Cold Harbor, Virginia	Point Lookout, Maryland, transferred to Elmira Prison, NY July 17,1864	Oath of Allegiance July 3, 1865
Eason, Abner Private	24	May 29, 1861, Goldsboro, North Carolina	Co. D, 2nd North Carolina Infantry	May 12, 1864, Near Spotsylvania, Virginia	Point Lookout, Maryland, transferred to Elmira Prison, NY August 14, 1864	Oath of Allegiance June 14, 1865
Eason, John T. Private	19	May 14, 1861, Rome, Georgia	Co. E, 8th Georgia Infantry	August 1, 1864, Turkey Bend, Virginia	Point Lookout, Maryland, transferred to Elmira Prison, NY August 18, 1864	Oath of Allegiance June 10, 1865
Eason, William Private	Unk	August 1, 1861 Bowdon, Georgia	Co. D, Cobb's Legion Georgia	August 16, 1864, Front Royal, Virginia	Old Capital Prison, Washington, DC transferred to Elmira Prison, NY August 29, 1864	Exchanged October 29, 1864, at Venus Point, Savannah River, GA.
East, James W. Private	Unk	July 15, 1861, Lexington, Virginia	Co. H, 27th Virginia Infantry	August 10, 1864, Berryville, Virginia	Old Capital Prison, Washington, DC transferred to Elmira Prison, NY August 29, 1864	Exchanged March 14, 1865 at Boulware's Wharf on the James River, Virginia
East, John W. Private	17	February 18, 1864, Henry County, Virginia	Co. H, 42nd Virginia Infantry	May 12, 1864, Near Spotsylvania Court House, Virginia	Point Lookout, Maryland, transferred to Elmira Prison, NY August 6, 1864	Oath of Allegiance June 21, 1865
Easterling, Andrew Jackson Private	Unk	May 12, 1862, Bennettsville, South Carolina	Co. F, 21st South Carolina Infantry	January 15, 1865, Fort Fisher, North Carolina	January 30, 1865, Elmira Prison Camp, NY	Died May 26, 1865 of Intermittent Fever, Grave No. 2917

Name & Rank	Age	Enlisted	Regiment and State	Where Captured	Prison	Remarks
Easterling, Thomas J. Sergeant	Unk	April 13, 1861, Florence, South Carolina	Co. B, 8th South Carolina Infantry	July 9, 1863, Gettysburg, Pennsylvania	Point Lookout, Maryland, transferred to Elmira Prison, NY August 18, 1864	Exchanged October 29, 1864 at Venus Point, Savannah River, GA.
Easterling, William T. Private	Unk	January 1, 1864, Bennettsville, South Carolina	Co. F, 21st South Carolina Infantry	January 15, 1865, Fort Fisher, North Carolina	January 30, 1865, Elmira Prison Camp, NY	Oath of Allegiance July 11, 1865
Eastridge, John W. Private	Unk	January 9, 1862, Columbia, South Carolina	Co. E, 22nd South Carolina Infantry	July 29, 1864, Petersburg, Virginia	Point Lookout, Maryland, transferred to Elmira Prison, NY August 12, 1864	Exchanged March 2, 1865 at Akins Landing on the James River, Virginia
Eastridge, John W. Private	38	June 20, 1861, Abingdon, Virginia	Co. B, 48th Virginia Infantry	May 12, 1864, Spotsylvania Court House, Virginia	Point Lookout, Maryland, transferred to Elmira Prison, NY August 2, 1864	Oath of Allegiance August 7, 1865
Eastridge, Jonas N. Private	Unk	February 25, 1862, Wilmington, North Carolina	Co. E, 22nd South Carolina Infantry	July 30, 1864, Petersburg, Virginia	Point Lookout, Maryland, transferred to Elmira Prison, NY August 12, 1864	Died February 3, 1865 of Chronic Diarrhea, Grave No. 1890. Name John and 27th Regiment on Headstone.
Eastridge, William M. Private	Unk	January 9, 1862, Columbia, South Carolina	Co. E, 22nd South Carolina Infantry	July 30, 1864, Petersburg, Virginia	Point Lookout, Maryland, transferred to Elmira Prison, NY August 12, 1864	Oath of Allegiance July 11, 1865
Eastwood, Alexander Private	Unk	Unknown	Co. B, Hood's Battalion Virginia Reserve Infantry	June 15, 1864, Near Petersburg, Virginia	Point Lookout, Maryland, transferred to Elmira Prison, NY July 30, 1864	Oath of Allegiance July 3, 1865
Ebberhart, Jacob W. Private	Unk	October 24, 1863, Hall County, Georgia	Co. D, 7th Georgia Cavalry	June 11, 1864, Trevilian Station, Louisa Court House, Virginia	Point Lookout, Maryland, transferred to Elmira Prison, NY July 25, 1864	Died October 3, 1864 of Chronic Diarrhea, Grave No. 614

Name & Rank	Age	Enlisted	Regiment and State	Where Captured	Prison	Remarks
Eberhart, E. B. Private	Unk	Unknown	Co. H, 38th Georgia Infantry	May 20, 1864, Spotsylvania Court House, Virginia	Point Lookout, Maryland, transferred to Elmira Prison, NY July 25, 1864	Oath of Allegiance July 7, 1865
Eccles, John C. Private	Unk	February 20, 1864 Camp Holmes, North Carolina	Co. H, 34th North Carolina Infantry	May 6, 1864, Wilderness, Virginia	Point Lookout, Maryland, transferred to Elmira Prison, NY July 25, 1864	Died March 13, 1865 of Inflammation of Lungs, Grave No. 1819. First Name James on Headstone.
Echols, A. H. Private		August 12, 1861, Richmond, Virginia	Co. H, 13th Georgia Infantry	May 20, 1864, Spotsylvania Court House, Virginia	Point Lookout, Maryland, transferred to Elmira Prison, NY July 6, 1864	Oath of Allegiance June 30, 1865
Echols, William E. Corporal	Unk	March 10, 1862, Pittsylvania, Virginia	Co. G, 6th Virginia Cavalry	May 11, 1864, Yellow Tavern, Hanover County, Virginia	Point Lookout, Maryland, transferred to Elmira Prison, NY August 17, 1864	Died March 23, 1865 of Pneumonia, Grave No. 1512
Eck, Henry Private	Unk	January 7, 1863, Richmond, Virginia	Co. A, 5th Battalion Virginia, Local Defense	June 11, 1864, Bottoms Bridge, Virginia	Point Lookout, Maryland, transferred to Elmira Prison, NY July 17, 1864	Escaped April 15, 1865
Edds, George W. Private	Unk	February 23, 1863, Carroll County, Virginia	Co. C, 29th Virginia Infantry	June 1, 1864, Gaines Mill, Cold Harbor, Virginia	Point Lookout, Maryland, transferred to Elmira Prison, NY July 26, 1864	Died December 21, 1864 of Phthisis Pulmonalis, Grave No. 1084.
Edds, Lindsey Private	41	August 2, 1863, Dublin, Virginia	Co. F, 4th Virginia Infantry	May 12, 1864, Spotsylvania Court House, Virginia	Point Lookout, Maryland, transferred to Elmira Prison, NY July 25, 1864	Oath of Allegiance May 11, 1865
Edell, H. J. Private	Unk	August 15, 1861, Richmond, Virginia	2nd Battalion Maryland Artillery	May 11, 1864, Yellow Tavern, Hanover County, Virginia	Point Lookout, Maryland, transferred to Elmira Prison, NY August 17, 1864	Exchanged March 10, 1865 at Boulware's Wharf on the James River, Virginia

Name & Rank	Age	Enlisted	Regiment and State	Where Captured	Prison	Remarks
Edens, Allen R. Corporal	Unk	April 15, 1862, Charleston, South Carolina	Co. F, 22nd South Carolina Infantry	June 17, 1864, Petersburg, Virginia	Point Lookout, Maryland, transferred to Elmira Prison, NY July 30, 1864	Exchanged March 14, 1865 at Boulware's Wharf on the James River, Virginia
Edey, Arthur H. Private	25	July 19, 1861, Houston, Texas	Co. A, 5th Texas Infantry	July 5, 1863, Gettysburg, Pennsylvania. Gunshot Wound Right Thigh.	Point Lookout, Maryland, transferred to Elmira Prison, NY July 30, 1864	Exchanged February 25, 1865 at Boulware's or Cox Wharf on the James River, Virginia
Edge, Kelly Private	39	October 19, 1861, Elizabethtown, New Hanover County, North Carolina	Co. I, 36th Regiment 2nd North Carolina Artillery	January 15, 1865, Fort Fisher, North Carolina	February 1, 1865, Elmira Prison Camp, New York	Exchanged February 20, 1865 at Boulware's Wharf on the James River, Virginia
Edge, Hugh P. Private	24	May 10, 1863, Fort Fisher, North Carolina	Co. J, 36th Regiment 2nd North Carolina Artillery	January 15, 1865, Fort Fisher, North Carolina	February 1, 1865, Elmira Prison Camp, New York	Exchanged March 14, 1865 at Boulware's Wharf on the James River, Virginia
Edge, Marshall Private	19	November 13, 1861, Petersburg, Virginia	Co. F, 24th North Carolina Infantry	June 17, 1864, Near Petersburg, Virginia	Point Lookout, Maryland, transferred to Elmira Prison, NY July 30, 1864	Oath of Allegiance June 19, 1865
Edge, Robert D. Private	30	March 16, 1862, New Hanover County, North Carolina	Co. J, 36th Regiment 2nd North Carolina Artillery	January 15, 1865, Fort Fisher, North Carolina	February 1, 1865, Elmira Prison Camp, New York	Died March 17, 1865 of Pneumonia, Grave No. 1718
Edington, James P. Private	Unk	May 26, 1864, Salem, Virginia	Co. E, 42nd Virginia Infantry	May 12, 1864, Near Spotsylvania Court House, Virginia	Point Lookout, Maryland, transferred to Elmira Prison, NY August 2, 1864	Died January 15, 1865 of Typhoid Pneumonia, grave No. 1463
Edmandson, John Private	Unk	Unknown	Co. A, 33rd Virginia Infantry	July 10, 1864, Frederick, Maryland	Old Capital Prison, Washington, DC, transferred to Elmira Prison, NY, July 23, 1864	Exchanged October 29, 1864, at Venus Point, Savannah River, GA.

Name & Rank	Age	Enlisted	Regiment and State	Where Captured	Prison	Remarks
Edmonds, Henry F. Private	Unk	March 4, 1862, G. Navy Yard, Virginia	Co. F, 41st Virginia Infantry	July 20, 1864, Petersburg, Virginia. Deserted to Union Lines.	Old Capital Prison, Washington D. C. Transferred to Elmira Prison, NY August 12, 1864	Oath of Allegiance October 21, 1864. Early Release per Lincoln's Proclamation, 12/8/1863.
Edmonds, T. T. Private	Unk	Unknown	Co. A, 26th Virginia Infantry	May 22, 1864, North Anna, Virginia	Point Lookout, Maryland, transferred to Elmira Prison, NY July 12, 1864	Oath of Allegiance August 16, 1864
Edmondson, George Sergeant	Unk	Unknown	Co. H, 4th Virginia Cavalry	October 17, 1864, Warrington, Virginia	November 11, 1864, Old Capital Prison, Washington, DC. February 4, 1865 Elmira, Prison Camp, NY	Exchanged March 2, 1865 at Akins Landing on the James River, Virginia
Edmunds, George R. Sergeant	27	December 5, 1861, Sac River, St. Clair County, Missouri	Co. K, 1st Missouri Cavalry	May 17, 1863, Big Black Bridge, Champion Hill, Mississippi	Point Lookout, Maryland, transferred to Elmira Prison, NY August 18, 1864	Exchanged February 25, 1865 at Boulware's wharf on the James River, Virginia
Edmunds, John R. Private	Unk	Unknown	Co. B, 44th Virginia Infantry	June 15, 1864, Near Petersburg, Virginia	Point Lookout, Maryland, transferred to Elmira Prison, NY July 12, 1864	Exchanged October 29, 1864, at Venus Point, Savannah River, GA.
Edmunds, Turner T. Private	Unk	April 20, 1861, Columbus, Georgia	Co. A, 2nd Battalion Georgia Infantry	May 22, 1864, North Anna, Virginia	Point Lookout, Maryland, transferred to Elmira Prison, NY August 17, 1864	Oath of Allegiance August 9, 1864 per Lincoln. Early Release per Lincoln's Proclamation, 12/8/1863.
Edney, Alexander Private	19	May 30, 1861, Camden County, North Carolina	Co. B, 32nd North Carolina Infantry	May 10, 1864, Near Mine Run, Spotsylvania, Virginia	Point Lookout, Maryland, transferred to Elmira Prison, NY August 6, 1864	Died October 4, 1864 of Chronic Diarrhea, Grave No. 611.

Name & Rank	Age	Enlisted	Regiment and State	Where Captured	Prison	Remarks
Edney, Lewis M. Sergeant	18	May 15, 1861, Edneyville, North Carolina	Co. A, 25th North Carolina Infantry	June 4, 1864, Bottoms Bridge, Chickahominy River, Cold Harbor, Virginia	Point Lookout, Maryland, transferred to Elmira Prison, NY July 23, 1864	Oath of Allegiance July 26, 1865
Edwards, A. N. V. Sergeant	Unk	June 11, 1861, Georgia	Co. F, 3rd Battalion Georgia Sharp Shooters	August 16, 1864, Front Royal, Virginia	Old Capital Prison, Washington, DC transferred to Elmira Prison, NY August 29, 1864	Oath of Allegiance June 21, 1865
Edwards, A. O. Private	Unk	March 27, 1864, Dorchester, Georgia	Co. B, 7th Georgia Cavalry	June 11, 1864, Trevilian Station, Louisa Court House, Virginia	Point Lookout, Maryland, transferred to Elmira Prison, NY July 25, 1864	Exchanged March 2, 1865 at Akins Landing on the James River, Virginia
Edwards, Alexander Private	19	January 1, 1862, Chesterfield, South Carolina	Co. B, 21st South Carolina Infantry	July 10, 1863, Morris Island, South Carolina. Gunshot Wound Right Side of Head.	Point Lookout, Maryland, transferred to Elmira Prison, NY August 18, 1864	Exchanged March 14, 1865 at Boulware's Wharf on the James River, Virginia
Edwards, Benjamin E. Private	19	April 23, 1861, Danville, Virginia	Co. A, 18th Virginia Infantry	July 3, 1863, Gettysburg, Pennsylvania	Point Lookout, Maryland, transferred to Elmira Prison, NY July 23, 1864	Oath of Allegiance May 17, 1865
Edwards, Calvin Private	17	September 13, 1863, Garysburg, North Carolina	Co. A, 24th North Carolina Infantry	June 17, 1864, Petersburg, Virginia	Point Lookout, Maryland, transferred to Elmira Prison, NY July 30, 1864	Died November 14, 1864 of Typhoid Fever, Grave No. 811
Edwards, Edward F. Private	16	April 1, 1862, Elizabethtown, Bladen County, North Carolina	Co. J, 36th Regiment 2nd North Carolina Artillery	January 15, 1865, Fort Fisher, North Carolina	February 1, 1865, Elmira Prison Camp, New York	Died March 11, 1865 of Variola (Smallpox), Grave No. 1849

Name & Rank	Age	Enlisted	Regiment and State	Where Captured	Prison	Remarks
Edwards, Fern D. Private	Unk	September 4, 1861, Columbus, Georgia	Co. A, 31st Georgia Infantry	May 12, 1864, Spotsylvania, Virginia	Old Capital Prison, Washington D. C. Transferred to Elmira Prison, NY August 28, 1864	Exchanged 3/14/65. Died 3/27/65 of Pneumonia at Wayside General Hospital No. 9, Richmond, VA.
Edwards, George W. Private	24	March 1, 1864, Liberty Mills, Virginia	Co. B, 18th North Carolina Infantry	May 6, 1864, Wilderness, Virginia	Point Lookout, Maryland, transferred to Elmira Prison, NY August 14, 1864	Oath of Allegiance May 29, 1865
Edwards, Ira Private	Unk	July 13, 1861, Hartwell, Georgia	Co. C, 16th Georgia Infantry	August 16, 1864, Front Royal, Virginia	Old Capital Prison, Washington, DC transferred to Elmira Prison, NY August 29, 1864	Oath of Allegiance June 16, 1865
Edwards, Isaac N. Private	34	August 28, 1861, Teachey's, North Carolina	Co. E, 30th North Carolina Infantry	May 12, 1864, Near Spotsylvania Court House, Virginia	Point Lookout, Maryland, transferred to Elmira Prison, NY August 14, 1864	Oath of Allegiance June 23, 1865
Edwards, John Private	Unk	July 8, 1862, Hillsboro, North Carolina	Co. F, 33rd North Carolina Infantry	July 30, 1864, Petersburg, Virginia	Point Lookout, Maryland, transferred to Elmira Prison, NY August 12, 1864	Died March 28, 1865 of Diarrhea, Grave No. 2483
Edwards, John L. Private	Unk	March 28, 1861, Madison, Florida	Co. A, 1st Florida Infantry	September 29, 1864, Near Vernon, Florida	New Orleans, Louisiana transferred to Elmira November 19, 1864	Died February 10, 1865 of Pneumonia, Grave No. 1957. Headstone has 5th Florida Cavalry.
Edwards, John W. Private	Unk	February 7, 1862, Gloucester Point, Virginia	Co. B, 26th Virginia Infantry	June 15, 1864, Near Petersburg, Virginia	Point Lookout, Maryland, transferred to Elmira Prison, NY July 30, 1864	Died December 29, 1864 of Pneumonia, Grave No. 1318

Name & Rank	Age	Enlisted	Regiment and State	Where Captured	Prison	Remarks
Edwards, Leroy S. Sergeant	21	April 19, 1861, Petersburg, Virginia	Co. E, 12th Virginia Infantry	May 12, 1864, Spotsylvania Court House, Virginia	Point Lookout, Maryland, transferred to Elmira Prison, NY August 12, 1864	Exchanged February 25, 1865 at Boulware's or Cox Wharf on the James River, Virginia
Edwards, M. A. Private	Unk	February 6, 1862, Center Hill, Georgia	Co. B, 16th Georgia Infantry	August 16, 1864, Front Royal, Virginia	Old Capital Prison, Washington, DC transferred to Elmira Prison, NY August 29, 1864	Oath of Allegiance June 16, 1865
Edwards, Oliver P. Private	Unk	October 15, 1863, Camp Vance, North Carolina	Co. K, 16th North Carolina Infantry	May 6, 1864, Wilderness, Virginia	Point Lookout, Maryland, transferred to Elmira Prison, NY August 14, 1864	Died September 10, 1864 of Chronic Diarrhea, Grave No. 254
Edwards, Ralsey Private	19	May 6, 1862, Elizabethtown, Bladen County, North Carolina	Co. K, 40th Regiment, 3rd North Carolina Artillery	January 15, 1865, Fort Fisher, North Carolina	February 1, 1865, Elmira Prison Camp, New York	Oath of Allegiance July 19, 1865
Edwards, Richard T. Private	18	February 13, 1862, Winton, North Carolina	Co. F, 1st North Carolina Infantry	May 12, 1864, Wilderness, Spotsylvania Court House, Virginia	Point Lookout, Maryland, transferred to Elmira Prison, NY August 6, 1864	Oath of Allegiance June 16, 1865
Edwards, Samuel A. Private	22	March 5, 1862, Orange County, North Carolina	Co. G, 30th North Carolina Infantry	May 12, 1864, Spotsylvania Court House, Virginia	Point Lookout, Maryland, transferred to Elmira Prison, NY August 14, 1864	Died September 25, 1864 of Chronic Diarrhea, Grave No. 373
Edwards, T. B. Private	Unk	Unknown	Co. G, 2nd Louisiana Cavalry	October 27, 1864, Bayou Grosstete, Point Coupee Parish, Louisiana	New Orleans, Louisiana transferred to Elmira November 19, 1864.	Exchanged February 25, 1865 at Boulware's or Cox Wharf on the James River, Virginia
Edwards, Thomas Private	Unk	February 1, 1864, Liberty Mills, North Carolina	Co. C, 7th North Carolina Infantry	July 29, 1864, Petersburg, Virginia	Point Lookout, Maryland, transferred to Elmira Prison, NY August 12, 1864	Died January 7, 1865 of Chronic Diarrhea, Grave No. 1233. Headstone has 37th NC.

Name & Rank	Age	Enlisted	Regiment and State	Where Captured	Prison	Remarks
Edwards, Walker A. Private	18	July 5, 1863, Orange County, North Carolina	Co. D, 30th North Carolina Infantry	May 12, 1864, Near Spotsylvania Court House, Virginia	Point Lookout, Maryland, transferred to Elmira Prison, NY August 14, 1864	Died October 14, 1864 of Chronic Diarrhea, Grave No. 708. Name Walter Edwards on Headstone.
Edwards, Wesley F. Private	Unk	April 3, 1862, Saltville, Virginia	Co. F, 29th, Virginia Infantry	June 1, 1864, Gaines Mill, Cold Harbor, Virginia	Point Lookout, Maryland, transferred to Elmira Prison, NY July 17, 1864	Oath of Allegiance July 3, 1865
Edwards, William Private	29	March 10, 1863, Bladen County, North Carolina	Co. B, 36th Regiment 2nd North Carolina Artillery	January 15, 1865, Fort Fisher, North Carolina	February 1, 1865, Elmira Prison Camp, New York	Oath of Allegiance July 11, 1865
Edwards, William E. Private	Unk	May 6, 1861, Montgomery, Alabama	Co. H, 6th Alabama Infantry	June 11, 1864, Spotsylvania, Virginia	Point Lookout, Maryland, transferred to Elmira Prison, NY July 25, 1864	Oath of Allegiance June 14, 1865
Egerton, W. B. Private	Unk	Unknown	Co. B, Hood's Battalion, Virginia Reserve Infantry	June 15, 1864, Near Petersburg, Virginia	Point Lookout, Maryland, transferred to Elmira Prison, NY July 30, 1864	Died August 1, 1864 of Typhoid Fever, Grave No. 38
Eggleton, George K. Private	Unk	June 22, 1861, Henry County, Virginia	Co. F, 42nd Virginia Infantry	May 12, 1864, Near Spotsylvania Court House, Virginia	Point Lookout, Maryland, transferred to Elmira Prison, NY August 6, 1864	Exchanged October 29, 1864, at Venus Point, Savannah River, GA.
Eggleton, Joseph L. Private	Unk	March 12, 1864, Henry County, Virginia	Co. F, 42nd Virginia Infantry	May 12, 1864, Near Spotsylvania Court House, Virginia	Point Lookout, Maryland, transferred to Elmira Prison, NY August 6, 1864	Died September 16, 1864 of Chronic Diarrhea, Grave No. 169.
Eggleton, Newsom T. Private	Unk	June 22, 1861, Henry County, Virginia	Co. F, 42nd Virginia Infantry	May 12, 1864, Near Spotsylvania Court House, Virginia	Point Lookout, Maryland, transferred to Elmira Prison, NY August 6, 1864	Oath of Allegiance July 3, 1865

Name & Rank	Age	Enlisted	Regiment and State	Where Captured	Prison	Remarks
Eichbaum, Joseph Private	Unk	June 15, 1861, Macon County, Georgia	Co. C, 12th Georgia Infantry	May 12, 1864, Spotsylvania Court House, Virginia	Point Lookout, Maryland, transferred to Elmira Prison, NY July 25, 1864	Oath of Allegiance May 17, 1865
Eichelberger, Danielle G. Private	Unk	Unknown	Co. B, 1st Maryland Cavalry	October 27, 1864, Fauquier County, Virginia	Old Capital Prison, Washington, DC, transferred to Elmira Prison, NY, December 17, 1864	Oath of Allegiance June 14, 1865
Eidson, James E. Private	Unk	April 26, 1862, Maxey's, Georgia	Co. K, 8th Georgia Infantry	May 6, 1864, Wilderness, Virginia	Point Lookout, Maryland, transferred to Elmira Prison, NY August 14, 1864	Exchanged March 10, 1865 at Boulware's Wharf on the James River, Virginia
Eidson, John Private	Unk	May 25, 1863, Randolph, Alabama	Co. A, 7th Alabama Cavalry	April 2, 1864, Near Barrancas, Florida	New Orleans, Louisianna Transferred to Elmira Prison, New York, November 19, 1864	Exchanged February 20, 1865 at Boulware's or Cox Wharf on the James River, Virginia
Eison, A. J. Sergeant	Unk	September 26, 1861, Camp Kirkpatrick, County,	Co. A, 38th Georgia Infantry	May 20, 1864, Spotsylvania Court House, Virginia	Point Lookout, Maryland, transferred to Elmira Prison, NY July 6, 1864	Exchanged March 10, 1865 at Boulware's Wharf on the James River, Virginia
Elam, John F. Private	Unk	Unknown	6th Field Battery Louisiana Light Artillery	October 4, 1864, Bayou Satauches, Louisiana	New Orleans, Louisiana transferred to Elmira November 19, 1864.	Exchanged February 20, 1865 at Boulware's wharf on the James River, Virginia
Elam, Samuel S. Private	19	April 26, 1862, Trinity, Louisiana	Co. J, 15th Louisiana Infantry	May 20, 1864, Spotsylvania Court House, Virginia	Point Lookout, Maryland, transferred to Elmira Prison, NY July 6, 1864	Exchanged February 13, 1865 at Boulware's wharf on the James River, Virginia

Name & Rank	Age	Enlisted	Regiment and State	Where Captured	Prison	Remarks
Elarbee, Nathanial Private	Unk	April 3, 1862, Bryan County, Georgia	Co. K, 7th Georgia Cavalry	June 11, 1864, Trevilian Station, Louisa Court House, Virginia	Point Lookout, Maryland, transferred to Elmira Prison, NY July 25, 1864	Died October 30, 1864 of Chronic Diarrhea, Grave No. 739
Elder, James Private	Unk	March 5, 1862, Lynchburg, Virginia	Co. I, 42nd Virginia Infantry	May 12, 1864, Near Spotsylvania Court House, Virginia	Point Lookout, Maryland, transferred to Elmira Prison, NY August 6, 1864	Exchanged October 29, 1864, at Venus Point, Savannah River, GA.
Elder, Philip Lawrence Private	Unk	February 23, 1863, Colston District, South Carolina	Co. C, 1st Maryland Cavalry	July 14, 1864, Near Washington, DC,	Old Capital Prison, Washington, DC, transferred to Elmira Prison, NY, July 23, 1864	Exchanged October 29, 1864, at Venus Point, Savannah River, GA.
Elder, Robert S. Sergeant	Unk	March 5, 1862, Lynchburg, Virginia	Co. I, 42nd Virginia Infantry	May 12, 1864, Spotsylvania Court House, Virginia	Point Lookout, Maryland, transferred to Elmira Prison, NY August 2, 1864	Oath of Allegiance June 19, 1865
Elder, William C. Private	25	August 9, 1862, Statesville, North Carolina	Co. K, 7th North Carolina Infantry	May 6, 1864, Wilderness, Virginia	Point Lookout, Maryland, transferred to Elmira Prison, NY August 14, 1864	Died November 25, 1864 of Pneumonia, Grave No. 917
Eldridge, Samuel Private	21	July 16, 1862, Raleigh, North Carolina	Co. D, 5th North Carolina Infantry	May 20, 1864, Spotsylvania Court House, Virginia	Point Lookout, Maryland, transferred to Elmira Prison, NY July 6,1864	Oath of Allegiance June 30, 1865
Elfer, Eugene Private	Unk	September 1, 1862, Baton Rouge, Louisiana	Co. A, Miles Legion Louisiana Cavalry	April 29, 1864, Yellow Bayou, Near Baton Rouge, Louisiana	New Orleans, Louisianna Transferred to Elmira Prison, New York, November 19, 1864	Died December 22, 1864 of Pneumonia, Grave No. 1090
Elington, Gustavus B. Private	Unk	November 7, 1862, Lewisburg, Tennessee	Co. H, 17th Tennessee Infantry	June 17, 1864, Petersburg, Virginia	Point Lookout, Maryland, transferred to Elmira Prison, NY July 30, 1864	Exchanged February 25, 1865 at Boulware's or Cox Wharf on the James River, Virginia

Name & Rank	Age	Enlisted	Regiment and State	Where Captured	Prison	Remarks
Elkers, Augustus Private	Unk	June 4, 1861, Camp Moore, Louisiana	Co. G, 6th Louisiana Infantry	November 7, 1863, Rappahannock Station, Virginia	Point Lookout, Maryland, transferred to Elmira Prison, NY July 23, 1864	Oath of Allegiance May 17, 1865
Elkins, Willis M. Private	Unk	September 4, 1862, Covington, Alabama	Co. C, 1st Battalion Alabama Artillery	August 23, 1864, Fort Morgan, Alabama	New Orleans, Louisiana transferred to Elmira December 4, 1864.	Oath of Allegiance June 19, 1865
Ellender, Benjamin Private	23	February 28, 1862, Louisiana	Co. K, 10th Louisiana Infantry	May 12, 1864, Spotsylvania Court House, Virginia	Point Lookout, Maryland, transferred to Elmira Prison, NY July 25, 1864	Oath of Allegiance June 16, 1865
Eller, Caleb Private	Unk	August 20, 1862, Statesville, North Carolina	Co. F, 7th North Carolina Infantry	July 12, 1864, Rickets' Farm, Virginia	Point Lookout, Maryland, transferred to Elmira Prison, NY August 6, 1864	Oath of Allegiance June 12, 1865
Eller, David Private	28	March 24, 1862, Salisbury, North Carolina	Co. D, 42nd North Carolina Infantry	June 2, 1864, Cold Harbor, Virginia	Point Lookout, Maryland, transferred to Elmira Prison, NY July 17, 1864	Died March 10, 1865 of Variola (Smallpox), Grave No. 1855
Eller, Jacob F. Private	Unk	August 24, 1861, Hiwassee, Town County, Georgia	Co. D, 24th Georgia Infantry	August 16, 1864, Front Royal, Virginia	Old Capital Prison, Washington, DC transferred to Elmira Prison, NY August 29, 1864	Died February 9, 1865 of Variola (Smallpox), Grave No. 1953
Eller, Rufus R. Private	18	March 1, 1862, Wilkesboro, North Carolina	Co. B, 1st North Carolina Infantry	May 12, 1864, Spotsylvania Court House, Virginia	Point Lookout, Maryland, transferred to Elmira Prison, NY August 6, 1864	Oath of Allegiance June 27, 1865
Eller, Samuel F. Private	25	July 15, 1862, Raleigh, North Carolina	Co. B, 49th North Carolina Infantry	May 16, 1864, Near Drury's Bluff, Virginia	Point Lookout, Maryland, transferred to Elmira Prison, NY August 18, 1864	Oath of Allegiance June 16, 1865

Name & Rank	Age	Enlisted	Regiment and State	Where Captured	Prison	Remarks
Eller, W. W. Private	Unk	February 11, 1862, Hiawassee, Georgia	Co. C, 24th Georgia Infantry	June 1, 1864, Cold Harbor, Virginia	Point Lookout, Maryland, transferred to Elmira Prison, NY July 17,1864	Oath of Allegiance January 7, 1865
Ellett, B. H. Private	Unk	Unknown	Co. C, 3rd Virginia Infantry	July 30, 1864, Petersburg, Virginia	Point Lookout, Maryland, transferred to Elmira Prison, NY August 12, 1864	Oath of Allegiance July 30, 1865
Ellington, Byrd Private	24	July 1, 1861, Camp Carolina, North Carolina	Co. B, 12th North Carolina Infantry	May 20, 1864, Spotsylvania Court House, Virginia	Point Lookout, Maryland, transferred to Elmira Prison, NY July 6,1864	Oath of Allegiance June 30, 1865
Ellington, Elisha Alfred Sergeant	20	February 28, 1862, Wentworth, North Carolina	Co. G, 45th North Carolina Infantry	May 10, 1864, Spotsylvania Court House, Virginia	Point Lookout, Maryland, transferred to Elmira Prison, NY August 6, 1864	Exchanged March 10, 1865 at Boulware's Wharf on the James River, Virginia
Ellington, Horace H. Private	32	May 3, 1862, Henderson, Granville County, North Carolina	Co. K, 54th North Carolina Infantry	March 25, 1865, Fort Steadman, Petersburg, Virginia. Gunshot Wound Left Jaw.	Old Capital Prison, Washington D. C. Transferred to Elmira Prison, NY May 2, 1865.	Oath of Allegiance July 7, 1865
Elliot, Benjamin F. Private	21	April 4, 1862, Stanardsville, Virginia	Co. D, 34th, Virginia Infantry	June 15, 1864, Near Petersburg, Virginia	Point Lookout, Maryland, transferred to Elmira Prison, NY July 17,1864	Oath of Allegiance June 16, 1865
Elliot, J. W. Corporal	Unk	June 11, 1861, Georgia	Co. F, 3rd Battalion Georgia Sharp Shooters	August 16, 1864, Front Royal, Virginia	Old Capital Prison, Washington, DC transferred to Elmira Prison, NY August 29, 1864	Died September 8, 1864 of Typhoid Fever, Grave No. 214
Elliot, Julius A. Private	23	March 19, 1862, Rowan County, North Carolina	Co. C, 49th North Carolina Infantry	May 14, 1864, Near Fort Darling, Virginia	Point Lookout, Maryland, transferred to Elmira Prison, NY August 17, 1864	Exchanged February 13, 1865 at Boulware's Wharf on the James River, Virginia

Name & Rank	Age	Enlisted	Regiment and State	Where Captured	Prison	Remarks
Elliot, R. H. Private	29	July 16, 1862, Raleigh, North Carolina	Co. H, 14th North Carolina Infantry	August 10, 1864, Berryville, Virginia	Old Capital Prison, Washington, DC transferred to Elmira Prison, NY August 29, 1864	Oath of Allegiance June 27, 1865
Elliot, W. F. Private	18	January 1, 1862, Georgetown, South Carolina	Co. A, 21st South Carolina Infantry	June 24, 1864, Near Petersburg, Virginia	Point Lookout, Maryland, transferred to Elmira Prison, NY August 18, 1864	Oath of Allegiance July 3, 1865
Ellis, A. B. Sergeant	Unk	October 13, 1861, Hall's Mill, Alabama	Co. B, 21st Alabama Infantry	August 23, 1864, Fort Morgan, Alabama	Steam Press No. 4 New Orleans, Louisiana transferred to Elmira October 8, 1864.	Exchanged March 14, 1865 at Boulware's Wharf on the James River, Virginia
Ellis, Anderson Private	30	September 22, 1862, Camp Holmes, North Carolina	Co. D, 26th North Carolina Infantry	May 12, 1864, Spotsylvania Court House, Virginia	Point Lookout, Maryland, transferred to Elmira Prison, NY August 12, 1864	Exchanged March 14, 1865 at Boulware's Wharf on the James River, Virginia
Ellis, Benjamin F. Private	Unk	April 10, 1863, Columbia, South Carolina	Hart's Battalion, South Carolina, Horse Artillery	May 9, 1864, Spotsylvania Court House, Virginia	Point Lookout, Maryland, transferred to Elmira Prison, NY August 17, 1864	Oath of Allegiance June 21, 1865
Ellis, Charles T. Private	Unk	May 17, 1864, Wilmington, North Carolina	Co. K, 10th Regiment, 1st North Carolina Artillery	January 15, 1865, Fort Fisher, North Carolina	January 30, 1865, Elmira Prison Camp, NY	Died March 28, 1865 of Diarrhea, Grave No. 2502
Ellis, Durell Private	34	July 15, 1862, Durham's Department, North Carolina	Co. F, 1st North Carolina Infantry	May 12, 1864, Wilderness, Spotsylvania Court House, Virginia	Point Lookout, Maryland, transferred to Elmira Prison, NY August 6, 1864	Died October 10, 1864 of Pneumonia, Grave No. 674. Name Duville, 9th Regiment on Headstone.
Ellis, E. S. Private	Unk	April 12, 1862, Battery Island, South Carolina	Co. C, 25th South Carolina Infantry	January 15, 1865, Fort Fisher, North Carolina	Elmira Prison Camp January 30, 1865	Died May 17, 1865 of Chronic Diarrhea, Grave No. 2953

Name & Rank	Age	Enlisted	Regiment and State	Where Captured	Prison	Remarks
Ellis, Ezekiel P Private	32	September 3, 1862, Mocksville, North Carolina	Co. M, 7th Confederate Cavalry	May 6, 1864, Buck Island, Virginia	Point Lookout, Maryland, transferred to Elmira Prison, NY August 17, 1864	Exchanged February 20, 1865 at Boulware's or Cox Wharf on the James River, Virginia
Ellis, G. R. Private	Unk	July 26, 1863, Fort Morgan, Alabama	Co. J, 21st Alabama Infantry	August 23, 1864, Fort Morgan, Alabama	Steam Press No. 4 New Orleans, Louisiana transferred to Elmira October 8, 1864.	Oath of Allegiance June 30, 1865
Ellis, George W. Private	24	July 15, 1862, Camp Holmes, Raleigh, North Carolina	Co. D, 24th North Carolina Infantry	June 17, 1864, Petersburg, Virginia	Point Lookout, Maryland, transferred to Elmira Prison, NY July 30, 1864	Oath of Allegiance July 7, 1865
Ellis, Harrison G. Private	Unk	April 29, 1862, White Sulfur Springs, Virginia	Co. F, 26th Battalion, Virginia Infantry	June 3, 1864, Gaines Mill, Virginia	Point Lookout, Maryland, transferred to Elmira Prison, NY July 17, 1864	Died December 6, 1864 of Chronic Valvular Disease of Heart, Grave No. 1187
Ellis, James G. Private	Unk	February 20, 1863, Darlington District, South Carolina	Co. B, 21st South Carolina Infantry	June 24, 1864, Near Petersburg, Virginia	Point Lookout, Maryland, transferred to Elmira Prison, NY August 18, 1864	Exchanged October 29, 1864, at Venus Point, Savannah River, GA.
Ellis, R. D. Private	Unk	Unknown	Co. F, 50th Virginia Infantry	May 12, 1864, Spotsylvania Court House, Virginia	Point Lookout, Maryland, transferred to Elmira Prison, NY July 30, 1864	Transferred For Exchange October 11, 1864 to Point Lookout Prison Camp, MD. Nothing Further.
Ellis, Samuel Private	48	November 8, 1861, Loan Island, South Carolina	Co. B, 23rd South Carolina Infantry	June 17, 1864, Near Petersburg, Virginia	Point Lookout, Maryland, transferred to Elmira Prison, NY July 30, 1864	Died January 24, 1865 of Chronic Diarrhea, Grave No. 1619

Name & Rank	Age	Enlisted	Regiment and State	Where Captured	Prison	Remarks
Ellis, Solomon J. Private	Unk	June 8, 1861, Mobile County, Alabama	Co. I, 12th Alabama Infantry	May 8, 1864, wilderness, Virginia	Point Lookout, Maryland, transferred to Elmira Prison, NY August 17, 1864	Exchanged October 29, 1864, at Venus Point, Savannah River, GA.
Ellis, Thomas C. Sergeant	20	September 14, 1861, Raleigh, North Carolina	Co. C, 2nd North Carolina Infantry	May 12, 1864, Spotsylvania Court House, Virginia	Point Lookout, Maryland, transferred to Elmira Prison, NY August 14, 1864	Oath of Allegiance June 14, 1865
Ellis, W. W. Private	Unk	February 20, 1863, Darlington District, South Carolina	Co. B, 21st South Carolina Infantry	January 15, 1865, Fort Fisher, North Carolina	January 30, 1865, Elmira Prison Camp, NY	Died March 6, 1865 of Chronic Diarrhea, Grave No. 1961
Ellis, Wiley J. Private	Unk	Unknown	Co. G, 7th North Carolina Cavalry	August 18, 1864, Petersburg, Virginia	Old Capital Prison, Washington, DC transferred to Elmira Prison, NY August 29, 1864	Died December 30, 1864 of Pneumonia Grave No. 1315
Ellis, William B. Private	Unk	May 12, 1862, Cumberland County, North Carolina	Co. J, 51st North Carolina Infantry	June 1, 1864, Cold Harbor, Virginia	Point Lookout, Maryland, transferred to Elmira Prison, NY July 17,1864	Exchanged October 29, 1864, at Venus Point, Savannah River, GA.
Ellis, William H. Private	27	July 15, 1862, Raleigh, North Carolina	Co. B, 49th North Carolina Infantry	May 16, 1864, Near Drury's Bluff, Virginia	Point Lookout, Maryland, transferred to Elmira Prison, NY August 18, 1864	Oath of Allegiance June 16, 1865
Ellison, James J. Private	28	April 1, 1862, Mercer County, Virginia	Co. E, 17th Virginia Infantry	July 10, 1864, Frederick, Maryland	Old Capital Prison, Washington, DC, transferred to Elmira Prison, NY, July 23, 1864	Exchanged October 29, 1864, at Venus Point, Savannah River, GA.
Elmer, Jacob Private	20	June 4, 1861, Corinth, Mississippi	Co. H, 18th Mississippi Infantry	April 15, 1864, Opposite Pascagoula, Louisiana	New Orleans, Louisianna Transferred to Elmira Prison, New York, November 19, 1864	Oath of Allegiance June 23, 1865

Name & Rank	Age	Enlisted	Regiment and State	Where Captured	Prison	Remarks
Elmore, John Private	Unk	Unknown	Co. K, 46th Virginia Infantry	June 17, 1864, Petersburg, Virginia	Point Lookout, Maryland, transferred to Elmira Prison, NY July 30, 1864	Died February 28, 1865 of Chronic Diarrhea, Grave No. 2149
Elmore, M. G. Corporal	23	July 7, 1862, Pittsboro, North Carolina	Co. D, 61st North Carolina Infantry	August 27, 1863, Battery Wagner, Morris Island, South Carolina	Point Lookout, Maryland, transferred to Elmira Prison, NY August 18, 1864	Exchanged March 10, 1865 at Boulware's Wharf on the James River, Virginia
Elmore, Mark Private	Unk	Unknown	Co. A, Captain Parson's Home Guard Florida	September 27, 1864, Marianna, Florida	New Orleans, Louisiana transferred to Elmira November 19, 1864.	Died December 12, 1864 of Pneumonia, Grave No. 1137
Elrod, Everet Private	37	April 1, 1862, Charleston, South Carolina	Co. D, 18th South Carolina Infantry	July 30, 1864, Petersburg, Virginia	Point Lookout, Maryland, transferred to Elmira Prison, NY August 12, 1864	Oath of Allegiance July 3, 1865
Elter, Albert Private	Unk	May 17, 1861, New Orleans, Louisiana	Co. K, 3rd Louisiana Infantry	May 20, 1863, Near Vicksburg, Mississippi	Point Lookout, Maryland, transferred to Elmira Prison, NY August 18, 1864	Exchanged March 10, 1865 at Boulware's wharf on the James River, Virginia
Elvington, Nathan T. Private	Unk	August 1, 1861, Marion Court House, South Carolina	Co. E, 1st South Carolina Infantry	July 29, 1864, Petersburg, Virginia	Point Lookout, Maryland, transferred to Elmira Prison, NY August 12, 1864	Exchanged February 13, 1865 at Boulware's wharf on the James River, Virginia
Elwood, Elmer Private	Unk	Unknown	Co. K, 40th Virginia Infantry	June 14, 1864, Edwards' Ferry, Muddy Creek, Virginia	Old Capital Prison, Washington, DC, transferred to Elmira Prison, NY, July 23, 1864	Died April 17, 1865 of Chronic Diarrhea, Grave No. 1355
Elyard, Josiah Private	22	April 5, 1862, Camp Shenandoah, Virginia	Co. E, 25th Virginia Infantry	May 12, 1864, Spotsylvania Court House, Virginia	Point Lookout, Maryland, transferred to Elmira Prison, NY August 12, 1864	Oath of Allegiance June 27, 1865

Name & Rank	Age	Enlisted	Regiment and State	Where Captured	Prison	Remarks
Emerson, C. Private	Unk	Unknown	Co. J, 61st Georgia Infantry	May 12, 1864, Spotsylvania Court House, Virginia	Point Lookout, Maryland, transferred to Elmira Prison, NY July 25, 1864	Oath of Allegiance June 30, 1865
Emerson, N. R. Private	23	January 15, 1862, Martinsburg, Virginia	Co. G, 7th Virginia Cavalry	July 25, 1863, Shepardstown, Virginia	Point Lookout, Maryland, transferred to Elmira Prison, NY August 18, 1864	Exchanged October 29, 1864 at Venus Point, Savannah River, GA.
Emerson, R. W. Private	Unk	December 15, 1862, Lewisburg, Tennessee	Co. C, 17th Tennessee Infantry	June 17, 1864, Petersburg, Virginia	Point Lookout, Maryland, transferred to Elmira Prison, NY July 30, 1864	Exchanged February 25, 1865 at Boulware's or Cox Wharf on the James River, Virginia
Emerson, Thomas Private	Unk	Unknown	Co. E, 3rd Arkansas Infantry	May 12, 1864, Spotsylvania Court House, Virginia	Point Lookout, Maryland, transferred to Elmira Prison, NY July 30, 1864	Exchanged February 13, 1865 at Boulware's wharf on the James River, Virginia
Emil, Jacob Sergeant	Unk	February 20, 1862, Atlanta, Georgia	Co. F, 8th Georgia Infantry	May 6, 1864, Wilderness, Virginia	Point Lookout, Maryland, transferred to Elmira Prison, NY August 14, 1864	Oath of Allegiance May 17, 1865
Endy, John F. Private	23	August 8, 1862, Camp Hill, Stanley County, North Carolina	Co. F, 5th North Carolina Infantry	May 20, 1864, Spotsylvania Court House, Virginia	Point Lookout Prison Camp, Maryland. Transferred to Elmira Prison, New York, July 6, 1864	Died March 11, 1865 Of Variola (Smallpox), Grave No. 1857
Engel, Jones Private	21	March 14, 1862, Charlotte, North Carolina	Co. B, 53rd North Carolina Infantry	May 6, 1864, Wilderness, Virginia	Point Lookout, Maryland, transferred to Elmira Prison, NY July 25, 1864	Oath of Allegiance May 11, 1865
England, J. S. Private	Unk	September 25, 1862, Danville, Kentucky	Co. K, 25th Tennessee Infantry	May 16, 1864, Near Drury's Bluff, Virginia	Point Lookout, Maryland, transferred to Elmira Prison, NY August 17, 1864	Exchanged February 25, 1865 at Boulware's or Cox Wharf on the James River, Virginia

Name & Rank	Age	Enlisted	Regiment and State	Where Captured	Prison	Remarks
England, Robert E. Private	Unk	August 2, 1861, Bowling Green, Virginia	Co. G, 47th Virginia Infantry	June 5, 1864, Gaines Mill, Cold Harbor, Virginia	Point Lookout, Maryland, transferred to Elmira Prison, NY July 17,1864	Oath of Allegiance July 11, 1865
England, William C. Private	Unk	June 21, 1861, Port Royal, Virginia	Co. E, 47th Virginia Infantry	May 6, 1864, Wilderness, Virginia	Point Lookout, Maryland, transferred to Elmira Prison, NY August 14, 1864	Oath of Allegiance June 16, 1865
Engle, Benjamin D. Private	27	September 25, 1862, Charlestown, Virginia	Co. A, 12th Virginia Cavalry	April 4, 1865, Shepherdstown, Virginia	Old Capital Prison, Washington D. C. Transferred to Elmira Prison, NY May 12, 1865.	Oath of Allegiance July 3, 1865
Engle, Theophile Lieutenant	30	June 23, 1861, Camp Moore, Louisiana	Co. H, 8th Louisiana Infantry	May 20, 1864, Spotsylvania Court House, Virginia	Point Lookout, Maryland, transferred to Elmira Prison, NY July 6,1864	Exchanged February 25, 1865 at Boulware's or Cox Wharf on the James River, Virginia
Englert, John W. Private	23	March 25, 1862, Charleston, South Carolina	Co. E, 25th South Carolina Infantry	January 15, 1865, Fort Fisher, North Carolina	Elmira Prison Camp January 30, 1865	Oath of Allegiance May 15, 1865
English, Charles D. Private	Unk	March 1, 1862, Wilmington, North Carolina	Co. D, 3rd North Carolina Infantry	May 12, 1864, Near Spotsylvania, Virginia	Point Lookout, Maryland, transferred to Elmira Prison, NY August 14, 1864	Oath of Allegiance June 27, 1865
English, George W. Private	22	May 28, 1861, Wilmington, North Carolina	Co. D, 3rd North Carolina Infantry	May 12, 1864, Near Spotsylvania Court House, Virginia	Point Lookout, Maryland, transferred to Elmira Prison, NY August 14, 1864	Exchanged March 14, 1865 at Boulware's Wharf on the James River, Virginia
English, James C. Private	29	April 15, 1863, Bedford County, Virginia	Co. F, 21st Virginia Infantry	April 1, 1865, Petersburg, Virginia. Gunshot Wound Right Thigh.	Old Capital Prison, Washington D. C. Transferred to Elmira Prison, NY May 2, 1865.	Oath of Allegiance July 7, 1865

Name & Rank	Age	Enlisted	Regiment and State	Where Captured	Prison	Remarks
English, Jesse Private	Unk	March 16, 1862, Bell's Landing, Alabama	Co. C, 5th Alabama Infantry	May 5, 1864, Wilderness, Virginia	Point Lookout, Maryland, transferred to Elmira Prison, NY August 17, 1864	Oath of Allegiance May 15, 1865
English, John W. Private	Unk	March 1, 1863, Liberty, Virginia	Co. C, 42nd Virginia Infantry	May 12, 1864, Spotsylvania Court House, Virginia	Point Lookout, Maryland, transferred to Elmira Prison, NY August 2,1864	Exchanged February 20, 1865 at Boulware's or Cox Wharf on the James River, Virginia
English, T. J. Private	Unk	Unknown	Co. A, 21st Alabama Infantry	August 23, 1864, Fort Morgan, Alabama	Steam Press No. 4 New Orleans, Louisiana transferred to Elmira October 8, 1864.	Oath of Allegiance July 11, 1865
Engton, J. S. Private	Unk	June 11, 1861, Camp McDonald, Georgia	Co. G, 18th Georgia Infantry	June 1, 1864, Cold Harbor, Virginia	Point Lookout, Maryland, transferred to Elmira Prison, NY July 17, 1864	Exchanged March 14, 1865 at Boulware's Wharf on the James River, Virginia
Ennis, James Private	32	July 15, 1862, Raleigh, North Carolina	Co. G, 1st North Carolina Infantry	May 12, 1864, Wilderness, Spotsylvania Court House, Virginia	Point Lookout, Maryland, transferred to Elmira Prison, NY August 6, 1864	Oath of Allegiance June 16, 1865
Ennis, Raymond Sergeant	22	June 12, 1861, Smithfield, North Carolina	Co. J, 24th North Carolina Infantry	May 16, 1864, Near Drury's Bluff, Virginia	Point Lookout, Maryland, transferred to Elmira Prison, NY August 18, 1864	Oath of Allegiance June 21, 1865
Ennis, William B. Private	19	July 17, 1862, Kenansville, North Carolina	Co. G, 61st North Carolina Infantry	August 27, 1863, Battery Wagner, Morris Island, South Carolina	Point Lookout, Maryland, transferred to Elmira Prison, NY August 18, 1864	Exchanged March 10, 1865 at Boulware's Wharf on the James River, Virginia
Epler, Rufus Hammond Sergeant	23	November 13, 1863, Fort Smith, Arkansas	Co. C, 11th and 17th Consolidated Arkansas Cavalry	June 20, 1863, Near Port Hudson, Louisiana. Gunshot Wound Unknown Thigh.	New Orleans, Louisiana transferred to Elmira November 19, 1864.	Exchanged February 13, 1865 at Boulware's wharf on the James River, Virginia

Name & Rank	Age	Enlisted	Regiment and State	Where Captured	Prison	Remarks
Epps, Caswell Green Private	33	March 15, 1862, Albemarle, North Carolina	Co. F, 28th North Carolina Infantry	July 29, 1864, Petersburg, Virginia	Point Lookout, Maryland, transferred to Elmira Prison, NY August 12, 1864	Oath of Allegiance July 3, 1865
Epps, E. Private	29	July 6, 1862, Raleigh, North Carolina	Co. D, 14th North Carolina Infantry	May 20, 1864, Spotsylvania Court House, Virginia	Point Lookout, Maryland, transferred to Elmira Prison, NY July 6, 1864	Died August 16, 1864 of Remittent Fever, Grave No. 26
Epps, J. H. Private	20	April 12, 1862, Battery Island, South Carolina	Co. C, 25th South Carolina Infantry	January 15, 1865, Fort Fisher, North Carolina	Elmira Prison Camp January 30, 1865	Oath of Allegiance July 7, 1865
Ervin, Lawrence N. Private	Unk	October 17, 1863, James Island, South Carolina	Co. J, 25th South Carolina Infantry	January 15, 1865, Fort Fisher, North Carolina	January 30, 1865, Elmira Prison Camp, NY	Oath of Allegiance July 11, 1865
Erwin, Adolphus S. Private	Unk	May 1, 1862, Adams Run, South Carolina	Co. K, Holcombe Legion, South Carolina Infantry	May 7, 1864, Stony Creek, Virginia	Point Lookout, Maryland, transferred to Elmira Prison, NY August 17, 1864	Died October 29, 1864 of Pneumonia, Grave No. 731
Erwin, Freeman B. Private	Unk	Unknown	Co. A, Captain Jones' Home Guard Florida	September 27, 1864, Marianna, Florida	New Orleans, Louisiana transferred to Elmira November 19, 1864.	Died February 7, 1865 of General Debility, Grave No. 1930
Erwin, George Private	Unk	April 13, 1863, Brevard, North Carolina	Co. D, 6th North Carolina Cavalry	June 21, 1864, Jackson's Mills, Near Kinston, North Carolina	Point Lookout, Maryland, transferred to Elmira Prison, NY July 25, 1864	Transferred for Exchange 10/11/64. Died 10/21/64 of Unknown Disease at Point Lookout Prison, MD.
Erwin, William L. Private	20	July 25, 1861, Tullahoma, Tennessee	Co. E, 25th Tennessee Infantry	May 16, 1864, Near Drury's Bluff, Virginia	Point Lookout, Maryland, transferred to Elmira Prison, NY August 17, 1864	Exchanged February 20, 1865 at Boulware's or Cox Wharf on the James River, Virginia

Name & Rank	Age	Enlisted	Regiment and State	Where Captured	Prison	Remarks
Escew, Azmaveth Corporal	33	December 17, 1861, Camp Trousdale, Tennessee	Co. H, 44th Tennessee Infantry	May 16, 1864, Near Drury's Bluff, Virginia	Point Lookout, Maryland, transferred to Elmira Prison, NY August 17, 1864	Oath of Allegiance March 10, 1865 Early Release per Lincoln's Proclamation, 12/8/1863.
Escew, William T. Private	Unk	December 27, 1861, Camp Trousdale, Tennessee	Co. H, 44th Tennessee Infantry	June 17, 1864, Petersburg, Virginia	Point Lookout, Maryland, transferred to Elmira Prison, NY July 23, 1864	Oath of Allegiance May 17, 1865
Eskew, Casey B. Corporal	26	May 13, 1862, Buffalo, Virginia	Co. A, 36th Virginia Infantry	July 16, 1864, Loudoun County, Virginia	Old Capital Prison, Washington, DC, transferred to Elmira Prison, NY, July 23, 1864	Died March 17, 1865 of Diarrhea, Grave No. 1572
Eskridge, John M. Sergeant	31	March 16, 1863, Camp Bona Bella, Georgia	Co. E, 20th Georgia Cavalry	May 28, 1864, Hawes Shop, Old Church, Virginia, Gunshot Wound Right Thigh.	Old Capital Prison, Washington, DC transferred to Elmira Prison, NY August 29, 1864	Died November 9, 1864 of Pneumonia Grave No. 835
Estep, Harrison Private	Unk	April 14, 1862, Rudes Hill, Virginia	Co. K, 2nd Virginia Infantry	May 12, 1864, Near Spotsylvania Court House, Virginia	Point Lookout, Maryland, transferred to Elmira Prison, NY August 2, 1864	Oath of Allegiance June 14, 1865
Estep, James M. Private	Unk	January 15, 1864, Bunker Hill, Virginia	Co. B, 10th Virginia Infantry	May 12, 1864, Spotsylvania Court House, Virginia	Point Lookout, Maryland, transferred to Elmira Prison, NY August 2, 1864	Oath of Allegiance May 29, 1865
Estes, Edmund A. Corporal	28	June 12, 1861, Center Cross, Virginia	Co. K, 55th Virginia Infantry	November 27, 1863, Mine Run, Virginia	Old Capital Prison, Washington, DC, transferred to Elmira Prison, NY, July 23, 1864	Exchanged October 29, 1864, at Venus Point, Savannah River, GA.

Elmira Prison Camp Roster Volume I

Name & Rank	Age	Enlisted	Regiment and State	Where Captured	Prison	Remarks
Estes, Lindsay A Private	Unk	August 7, 1863, Stanardsville, Virginia	Co. D, 34th, Virginia Infantry	June 15, 1864, Near Petersburg, Virginia	Point Lookout, Maryland, transferred to Elmira Prison, NY July 17,1864	Died December 28, 1864 of Chronic Bronchitis, Grave No. 1094
Estis, William F. Private	24	June 2, 1861, Little Plymouth, Virginia	Co. G, 26th Virginia Infantry	June 15, 1864, Petersburg, Virginia	Point Lookout, Maryland, transferred to Elmira Prison, NY July 30, 1864	Died December 9, 1864 of Pleuro Pneumonia, Grave No. 1166
Etheridge, Abednago Private	Unk	May 11, 1861, Abbeville, Alabama	Co. B, 6th Alabama Infantry	May 20, 1864, Spotsylvania Court House, Virginia	Point Lookout, Maryland, transferred to Elmira Prison, NY July 6, 1864	Oath of Allegiance June 30, 1865
Etheridge, James William Corporal	22	May 30, 1861, Camden County, North Carolina	Co. B, 32nd North Carolina Infantry	May 10, 1864, Near Mine Run, Spotsylvania, Virginia	Point Lookout, Maryland, transferred to Elmira Prison, NY August 6, 1864	Transferred for Exchange February 13, 1865. Died Enroute from Elmira February 18, 1865.
Ethridge, David E. Private	30	May 1, 1861, Nashville, North Carolina	Co. H, 32nd North Carolina Infantry	May 10, 1864, Near Spotsylvania County Court House, Virginia	Point Lookout, Maryland, transferred to Elmira Prison, NY August 14, 1864	Oath of Allegiance June 21, 1865
Ethridge, Moses A. Private	29	September 4, 1862, Camp Mangum, Raleigh, North Carolina	Co. H, 31st North Carolina Infantry	June 1, 1864, Gaines Mill, Virginia	Point Lookout, Maryland, transferred to Elmira Prison, NY July 17,1864	Died March 13, 1865 of Pneumonia, Grave No. 1825
Ethridge, Ransom Private	42	August 19, 1863, Brunswick County, North Carolina	Co. F, 36th Regiment 2nd North Carolina Artillery	January 15, 1865, Fort Fisher, North Carolina	February 1, 1865, Elmira Prison Camp, New York	Exchanged February 20, 1865. Died April 6, 1865 of Chronic Diarrhea, at Jackson Hospital, Richmond, VA
Ethridge, William H. Private	27	October 14, 1861, Camp Mangum, Raleigh, North Carolina	Co. H, 31st North Carolina Infantry	June 1, 1864, Gaines Mill, Virginia	Point Lookout, Maryland, transferred to Elmira Prison, NY July 17,1864	Exchanged October 29, 1864, at Venus Point, Savannah River, GA.

Name & Rank	Age	Enlisted	Regiment and State	Where Captured	Prison	Remarks
Eubank, Archibald H. Private	21	June 2, 1861, Little Plymouth, Virginia	Co. G, 26th Virginia Infantry	June 15, 1864, Petersburg, Virginia	Point Lookout, Maryland, transferred to Elmira Prison, NY July 30, 1864	Oath of Allegiance June 19, 1865
Eubank, George W. Private	Unk	May 13, 1861, Richmond, Virginia	Captain Young's Battery Virginia Artillery	June 15, 1864, Petersburg, Virginia	Point Lookout, Maryland, transferred to Elmira Prison, NY July 25, 1864	Oath of Allegiance June 21, 1865
Eubanks, Aaron Private	23	July 1, 1861, Jacksonville, Onslow County, North Carolina	Co. J, 3rd North Carolina Infantry	May 12, 1864, Near Spotsylvania Court House, Virginia	Point Lookout Prison, Maryland. Transferred to Elmira Prison Camp New York August 14, 1864.	Exchanged October 29, 1864, at Venus Point, Savannah River, GA.
Eubanks, Ambrose Private	18	April 15, 1861, Pittsboro, North Carolina	Co. J, 32nd North Carolina Infantry	May 10, 1864, Wilderness, Virginia	Point Lookout, Maryland, transferred to Elmira Prison, NY August 6, 1864	Oath of Allegiance June 11, 1865
Eubanks, Isaac Private	Unk	January 14, 1862, Camp Walsh, South Carolina	Co. J, Holcombe Legion, South Carolina Infantry	May 7, 1864, Stony Creek, Virginia	Point Lookout, Maryland, transferred to Elmira Prison, NY August 17, 1864	Transferred For Exchange October 11, 1864 to Point Lookout Prison Camp, MD. Nothing Further.
Eubanks, J. Private	Unk	Unknown	Co. K, 11th Georgia Infantry	May 6, 1864, Wilderness, Virginia	Point Lookout, Maryland, transferred to Elmira Prison, NY August 14, 1864	Oath of Allegiance June 27, 1865
Eubanks, John Private	22	May 6, 1861, Jacksonville, North Carolina	Co. B, 24th North Carolina Infantry	June 17, 1864, Petersburg, Virginia	Point Lookout, Maryland, transferred to Elmira Prison, NY July 30, 1864	Transferred for Exchange 10/11/64. Died 11/2/64 of Unknown Disease at Fort Monroe, VA.
Eure, Elisha H. Private	26	November 5, 1863, Gates County, North Carolina	Co. E, 33rd North Carolina Infantry	May 6, 1864, Wilderness, Virginia	Point Lookout, Maryland, transferred to Elmira Prison, NY August 14, 1864	Died January 9, 1865 of Typhoid-Pneumonia, Grave No. 1228

Name & Rank	Age	Enlisted	Regiment and State	Where Captured	Prison	Remarks
Eure, Elisha W. Private	22	June 20, 1861, Camp Advance, North Carolina	Co. E, 7th North Carolina Infantry	May 12, 1864, Spotsylvania Court House, Virginia	Point Lookout, Maryland, transferred to Elmira Prison, NY August 6, 1864	Died February 2, 1865 of Pneumonia, Grave No. 1768
Eure, William W. Sergeant	21	October 9, 1861, Halifax County, North Carolina	Co. F, 36th Regiment 2nd North Carolina Artillery	January 15, 1865, Fort Fisher, North Carolina	February 1, 1865, Elmira Prison Camp, New York	Died March 29, 1865 of Chronic Diarrhea, Grave No. 2525
Eury, J. F. Private	Unk	Unknown	Co. F, 5th North Carolina Infantry	May 20, 1864, Spotsylvania Court House, Virginia	Point Lookout, Maryland, transferred to Elmira Prison, NY July 6, 1864	Died March 1, 1865 of Variola (Smallpox),
Evans, Alan J. Private	50	June 19, 1861, Camp Moore, Louisiana	Co. H, 8th Louisiana Infantry	May 10, 1864, Spotsylvania, Virginia	Point Lookout, Maryland, transferred to Elmira Prison, NY August 17, 1864	Exchanged October 29, 1864, at Venus Point, Savannah River, GA.
Evans, Angus J. Private	18	February 24, 1864, Fort Holmes, Brunswick County, North Carolina	Co. K, 40th Regiment, 3rd North Carolina Artillery	January 15, 1865, Fort Fisher, North Carolina	February 1, 1865, Elmira Prison Camp, New York	Exchanged March 14, 1865 at Boulware's Wharf on the James River, Virginia
Evans, C. T. C. Private	17	March 19, 1864, Adams Run, South Carolina	Co. K, 6th South Carolina Cavalry	June 11, 1864, Trevilian Station, Louisa Court House, Virginia	Point Lookout, Maryland, transferred to Elmira Prison, NY July 25, 1864	Exchanged October 11, 1864. Nothing Further.
Evans, Daniel Private	21	October 19, 1861, Elizabethtown, Bladen County, North Carolina	Co. J, 36th Regiment 2nd North Carolina Artillery	January 15, 1865, Fort Fisher, North Carolina	February 1, 1865, Elmira Prison Camp, New York	Died February 9, 1865 of Pneumonia, Grave No. 1942
Evans, E. M. Private	Unk	May 13, 1862, Savannah, Georgia	Co. F, 7th Georgia Cavalry	June 11, 1864, Trevilian Station, Louisa Court House, Virginia	Point Lookout, Maryland, transferred to Elmira Prison, NY July 25, 1864	Oath of Allegiance June 3, 1865

Name & Rank	Age	Enlisted	Regiment and State	Where Captured	Prison	Remarks
Evans, George W. Private	52	March 8, 1862, Milton, North Carolina	Co. J, 45th North Carolina Infantry	May 10, 1864, Spotsylvania Court House, Virginia	Point Lookout, Maryland, transferred to Elmira Prison, NY August 6, 1864	Oath of Allegiance June 19, 1865
Evans, Green C. Private	Unk	January 2, 1863, Roanoke County, Virginia	Co. L, 26th Battalion Virginia Infantry	June 3, 1864, Gaines Farm Cold Harbor, Virginia	Point Lookout, Maryland, transferred to Elmira Prison, NY July 17,1864	Oath of Allegiance June 21, 1865
Evans, H. R. Corporal	Unk	March 1, 1862, Camp Walton, Florida	Co. E, 1st Florida Infantry	September 28, 1864, Near Vernon, Florida	New Orleans, Louisiana transferred to Elmira November 19, 1864.	Oath of Allegiance July 7, 1865
Evans, Hinton Private	34	August 24, 1861, Raleigh, North Carolina	Co. K, 1st North Carolina Infantry	May 12, 1864, Spotsylvania Court House, Virginia	Point Lookout, Maryland, transferred to Elmira Prison, NY August 6, 1864	Oath of Allegiance June 16, 1865
Evans, Iredell Private	32	July 2, 1862, Pfafftown, North Carolina	Co. C, 33rd North Carolina Infantry	May 12, 1864, Spotsylvania Court House, Virginia	Point Lookout, Maryland, transferred to Elmira Prison, NY July 25, 1864	Oath of Allegiance May 19, 1865
Evans, J. C. Private	Unk	Unknown	Co. F, 28th North Carolina Infantry	July 30, 1864, Petersburg, Virginia	Point Lookout, Maryland, transferred to Elmira Prison, NY August 12, 1864	Oath of Allegiance May 19, 1865
Evans, J. H. Private	24	May 16, 1862, Charleston, South Carolina	Co. C, 25th South Carolina Infantry	January 15, 1865, Fort Fisher, North Carolina	Elmira Prison Camp January 30, 1865	Died July 21, 1865 of Unknown Disease, Grave No. 2866
Evans, J. L. Private	Unk	May 4, 1864, Petersburg, Virginia	Co. A, 3rd Archer's Battalion, Virginia Reserves Infantry	June 9, 1864, Petersburg, Virginia	Point Lookout, Maryland, transferred to Elmira Prison, NY July 12, 1864	Exchanged February 20, 1865 at Boulware's or Cox Wharf on the James River, Virginia

Name & Rank	Age	Enlisted	Regiment and State	Where Captured	Prison	Remarks
Evans, J. R. Private	Unk	July 9, 1863, Decatur, Georgia	Co. C, 7th Georgia Infantry	June 1, 1864, Gaines Mill, Cold Harbor, Virginia	Point Lookout, Maryland, transferred to Elmira Prison, NY July 17,1864	Oath of Allegiance June 14, 1865
Evans, J. V. Private	Unk	Unknown	Co. H, 12th North Carolina Infantry	May 12, 1864, Near Spotsylvania, Virginia	Point Lookout, Maryland, transferred to Elmira Prison, NY August 14, 1864	Oath of Allegiance July 7, 1865
Evans, James Private	24	March 7, 1862, Fort Fisher, North Carolina	Co. J, 36th Regiment 2nd North Carolina Artillery	January 15, 1865, Fort Fisher, North Carolina	February 1, 1865, Elmira Prison Camp, New York	Exchanged March 2, 1865 at Boulware's Wharf on the James River, Virginia
Evans, James A. Private	20	October 9, 1861, Fort Fisher, North Carolina	Co. D, 18th North Carolina Infantry	May 12, 1864, Spotsylvania Court House, Virginia	Point Lookout, Maryland, transferred to Elmira Prison, NY August 6, 1864	Died December 28, 1864 of Pneumonia, Grave No. 1295
Evans, James M. Private	18	June 15, 1861, Harrison's Church, Caswell County, North Carolina	Co. I, 5th North Carolina Infantry	July 15, 1864, Rockville, Maryland	Old Capital Prison, Washington, DC, transferred to Elmira Prison, NY, July 23, 1864	Oath of Allegiance May 15, 1865
Evans, John Private	30	May 8, 1862, Robeson, County, North Carolina	Co. C, 40th Regiment, 3rd North Carolina Artillery	January 15, 1865, Fort Fisher, North Carolina	February 1, 1865, Elmira Prison Camp, New York	Oath of Allegiance June 20, 1865
Evans, John A. Private	Unk	March 10, 1862, Jump Hollow, Virginia	Co. A, 9th Virginia Cavalry	September 14, 1863, Near Culpepper, Virginia	Point Lookout, Maryland, transferred to Elmira Prison, NY August 18, 1864	Exchanged March 10, 1865 at Boulware's Wharf on the James River, Virginia
Evans, Nathan J. Private	19	March 20, 1864, Marion, South Carolina	Co. L, 21st South Carolina Infantry	January 15, 1865, Fort Fisher, North Carolina	Elmira Prison Camp January 30, 1865	Oath of Allegiance July 11, 1865
Evans, R. M. Corporal	Unk	April 11, 1862, Coles Island, South Carolina	Co. F, 25th South Carolina Infantry	January 15, 1865, Fort Fisher, North Carolina	Elmira Prison Camp January 30, 1865	Died June 2, 1865 of Pneumonia, Grave No. 2903

Name & Rank	Age	Enlisted	Regiment and State	Where Captured	Prison	Remarks
Evans, S. W. Private	Unk	February 24, 1862, McClellansville, South Carolina	Co. H, 26th South Carolina Infantry	July 30, 1864, Petersburg, Virginia	Point Lookout, Maryland, transferred to Elmira Prison, NY August 12, 1864	Exchanged March 2, 1865 at Akins Landing on the James River, Virginia
Evans, Samuel Private	Unk	January 1, 1862, Richmond, Virginia	Co. E, 59th Virginia Infantry	June 17, 1864, Petersburg, Virginia	Point Lookout, Maryland, transferred to Elmira Prison, NY July 30, 1864	Exchanged October 29, 1864, at Venus Point, Savannah River, GA.
Evans, Samuel A. Private	21	March 5, 1862, Yanceyville, North Carolina	Co. I, 45th North Carolina Infantry	May 10, 1864, Spotsylvania Court House, Virginia	Point Lookout, Maryland, transferred to Elmira Prison, NY August 6, 1864	Oath of Allegiance June 27, 1865
Evans, T. R. Private	21	May 16, 1862, Charleston, South Carolina	Co. J, 25th South Carolina Infantry	January 15, 1865, Fort Fisher, North Carolina	Elmira Prison Camp January 30, 1865	Oath of Allegiance June 23, 1865
Evans, William B. Private	46	July 1, 1863, Richmond, Virginia	Co. G, 41st Battalion Virginia Cavalry	July 15, 1864, Rockville, Maryland	Old Capital Prison, Washington, DC, transferred to Elmira Prison, NY, July 23, 1864	Exchanged February 25, 1865 at Boulware's or Cox Wharf on the James River, Virginia
Everett, Hayes B. Private	18	May 18, 1861, Bladen County, North Carolina	Co. H, 3rd North Carolina Infantry	May 12, 1864, Near Spotsylvania Court House, Virginia	Point Lookout, Maryland, transferred to Elmira Prison, NY August 14, 1864	Oath of Allegiance June 30, 1865
Everett, Myles Private	Unk	Unknown	Co. A, 1st Florida Reserves Infantry	September 27, 1864, Marianna, Florida	New Orleans, Louisiana transferred to Elmira November 19, 1864.	Exchanged March 2, 1865 at Akins Landing on the James River, Virginia
Everett, Nance Private	28	March 3, 1862, Cerogordo, North Carolina	Co. E, 36th Regiment 2nd North Carolina Artillery	January 15, 1865, Fort Fisher, North Carolina	February 1, 1865, Elmira Prison Camp, New York	Oath of Allegiance July 3, 1865
Everett, Neill Private	Unk	Date Unknown, Cumberland County, North Carolina	Co. C, 36th Regiment 2nd North Carolina Artillery	January 15, 1865, Fort Fisher, North Carolina	February 1, 1865, Elmira Prison Camp, New York	Oath of Allegiance June 12, 1865

Name & Rank	Age	Enlisted	Regiment and State	Where Captured	Prison	Remarks
Everitt, Elias W. Private	Unk	Unknown	Co. F, 50th Virginia Infantry	May 12, 1864, Spotsylvania Court House, Virginia	Point Lookout, Maryland, transferred to Elmira Prison, NY August 2, 1864	Oath of Allegiance June 19, 1865
Everly, George W. Sergeant	24	March 1, 1862, Strasburg, Virginia	Captain J. W. Carter's Virginia Horse Artillery	September 14, 1863, Near Culpepper, Virginia	Point Lookout, Maryland, transferred to Elmira Prison, NY August 18, 1864	Exchanged March 10, 1865 at Boulware's Wharf on the James River, Virginia
Evers, Dennis Private	18	October 23, 1863, Elizabethtown, Bladen County, North Carolina	Co. K, 40th Regiment, 3rd North Carolina Artillery	January 15, 1865, Fort Fisher, North Carolina	February 1, 1865, Elmira Prison Camp, New York	Died March 29, 1865 of Variola (Smallpox), Grave No. 2512
Evers, Ephraim Private	22	May 7, 1863, Fort Fisher, North Carolina	Co. K, 40th Regiment, 3rd North Carolina Artillery	January 15, 1865, Fort Fisher, North Carolina	February 1, 1865, Elmira Prison Camp, New York	Died March 14, 1865 of Pneumonia, Grave No. 1675
Evers, Philip Sergeant	29	May 3, 1861, Elizabethtown, North Carolina	Co. B, 18th North Carolina Infantry	May 6, 1864, Wilderness, Virginia	Point Lookout, Maryland, transferred to Elmira Prison, NY August 14, 1864	Died April 14, 1865 of Variola (Smallpox), Grave No. 2710
Evers, William H. Private	23	October 27, 1862, New Hanover County, North Carolina	Co. K, 40th Regiment, 3rd North Carolina Artillery	January 15, 1865, Fort Fisher, North Carolina	February 1, 1865, Elmira Prison Camp, New York	Died March 27, 1865 of Variola (Smallpox), Grave No. 2478
Eversole, Charles H. Corporal	Unk	March 10, 1862, Wytheville, Virginia	Co. A, 4th Virginia Infantry	May 12, 1864, Spotsylvania Court House, Virginia	Point Lookout, Maryland, transferred to Elmira Prison, NY August 2, 1864	Oath of Allegiance June 19, 1865
Ewing, Miles E. Sergeant	Unk	August 24, 1861, Lawrenceville, Gwinnett County, Georgia	Co. F, 24th Georgia Infantry	June 1, 1864, Cold Harbor, Virginia	Point Lookout, Maryland, transferred to Elmira Prison, NY July 17, 1864	Oath of Allegiance June 21, 1865
Ewing, Robert B. Private	22	April 18, 1861, Harrisonburg, Virginia	Co. B, 10th Virginia Infantry	May 12, 1864, Spotsylvania Court House, Virginia	Point Lookout, Maryland, transferred to Elmira Prison, NY August 2, 1864	Exchanged March 2, 1865 at Akins Landing on the James River, Virginia

Name & Rank	Age	Enlisted	Regiment and State	Where Captured	Prison	Remarks
Exley, Francis A. Private	Unk	May 13, 1863, Savannah, Georgia	Co. E, 7th Georgia Cavalry	June 11, 1864, Trevilian Station, Louisa Court House, Virginia	Point Lookout, Maryland, transferred to Elmira Prison, NY July 25, 1864	Oath of Allegiance July 7, 1865
Exum, Benjamin Private	Unk	February 26, 1863, Cleveland, South Carolina	Co. K, 25th South Carolina Infantry	January 15, 1865, Fort Fisher, North Carolina	Elmira Prison Camp January 30, 1865	Died of Variola (smallpox), 3/10/1865, Buried Woodlawn Cemetery, Elmira, NY, Grave No. 2361
Exum, James I. Private	Unk	May 14, 1862, Starkville, Georgia	Co. B, 11th Georgia Infantry	May 6, 1864, Wilderness, Virginia	Point Lookout, Maryland, transferred to Elmira Prison, NY August 14, 1864	Oath of Allegiance June 16, 1865
Eye, Ammi Private	Unk	May 14, 1861, Franklin, Virginia	Co. E, 25th Virginia Infantry	May 12, 1864, Spotsylvania Court House, Virginia	Point Lookout, Maryland, transferred to Elmira Prison, NY August 12, 1864	Oath of Allegiance June 27, 1865
Ezelle, Edward P. Private	Unk	June 4, 1861, Athens, Alabama	Co. F, 9th Alabama Infantry	May 13, 1864, Spotsylvania Court House, Virginia	Point Lookout, Maryland, transferred to Elmira Prison, NY August 17, 1864	Oath of Allegiance May 17, 1865
Ezzel, Alexander H. Private	27	July 23, 1862, North Carolina	Co. G, 3rd North Carolina Infantry	May 12, 1864, Near Spotsylvania, Virginia	Point Lookout, Maryland, transferred to Elmira Prison, NY August 14, 1864	Died May 23, 1865 of Chronic Diarrhea. No Grave Found in Woodlawn Cemetery.
Ezzell, John K. Private	20	May 9, 1861, Clinton, North Carolina	Co. D, 20th North Carolina Infantry	May 12, 1864, Near Spotsylvania Court House, Virginia	Point Lookout Prison, Maryland. Transferred to Elmira Prison Camp New York August 14, 1864.	Exchanged March 2, 1865 at Akins Landing on the James River, Virginia

Name & Rank	Age	Enlisted	Regiment and State	Where Captured	Prison	Remarks
Fagan, Thomas Private	Unk	Unknown	Co. J, 21st Alabama Infantry	August 23, 1864, Fort Morgan, Alabama	Steam Press No. 4 New Orleans, Louisiana transferred to Elmira October 8, 1864.	Exchanged February 13, 1865 at Boulware's wharf on the James River, Virginia
Fagg, John R. D. Private	Unk	May 20, 1862, Camp Harris, Tennessee	Co. D, 17th Tennessee Infantry	June 17, 1864, Petersburg, Virginia	Point Lookout, Maryland, transferred to Elmira Prison, NY July 30, 1864	Exchanged February 25, 1865 at Boulware's or Cox Wharf on the James River, Virginia
Faggot, Paul A. Private	20	May 6, 1862, Concord, North Carolina	Co A, 20th North Carolina Infantry	May 12, 1864, Near Spotsylvania Court House, Virginia	Point Lookout, Maryland, transferred to Elmira Prison, NY August 14, 1864	Oath of Allegiance June 30, 1865
Fain, Abram Private	Unk	June 22, 1861, Wytheville, Virginia	Co. K, 50th Virginia Infantry	May 12, 1864, Near Spotsylvania Court House, Virginia	Point Lookout, Maryland, transferred to Elmira Prison, NY August 2, 1864	Died September 7, 1864 of Chronic Diarrhea, Grave No. 218.
Fain, Ebenezer Private	Unk	June 10, 1861, Morgan, Georgia	Co. D, 12th Georgia Infantry	May 10, 1864, Spotsylvania Court House, Virginia	Point Lookout, Maryland, transferred to Elmira Prison, NY July 25, 1864	Exchanged March 2, 1865 at Akins Landing on the James River, Virginia
Fairburn, James A. Private	Unk	April 16, 1862, Rudes Hill, Virginia	Co. C, 2nd Virginia Infantry	May 12, 1864, Near Spotsylvania Court House, Virginia	Point Lookout, Maryland, transferred to Elmira Prison, NY August 6, 1864	Died February 21, 1865 of Diarrhea, Grave No. 2299
Fairchild, J. F. Private	Unk	Unknown	Co. F, Wingfield's Regiment 3rd Louisiana Cavalry	September 16, 1864, Greenville Springs, Near East Baton Rouge, Louisiana	New Orleans, Louisiana transferred to Elmira November 19, 1864.	Exchanged February 13, 1865 at Boulware's wharf on the James River, Virginia
Faircloth, Archer Private	Unk	May 19, 1864, Sampson County, North Carolina	Co. E, 2nd North Carolina Infantry	July 17, 1864, Beltsville, Maryland	Old Capital Prison, Washington, DC, transferred to Elmira Prison, NY, July 23, 1864	Exchanged October 29, 1864, at Venus Point, Savannah River, GA.

Name & Rank	Age	Enlisted	Regiment and State	Where Captured	Prison	Remarks
Faircloth, Daniel J. Private	33	August 1, 1861, Fayetteville, North Carolina	Co. E, 8th North Carolina Infantry	June 1, 1864, Gaines Mill, Cold Harbor, Virginia	Point Lookout, Maryland, transferred to Elmira Prison, NY July 17, 1864	Died December 29, 1864, Chronic Diarrhea, Grave No. 1316
Faircloth, Reason Private	30	August 5, 1861, Fayetteville, North Carolina	Co. E, 8th North Carolina Infantry	May 31, 1864, Cold Harbor, Virginia	Point Lookout, Maryland, transferred to Elmira Prison, NY July 12, 1864	Died November 14, 1864, Chronic Diarrhea, Grave No. 804
Faircloth, Sampson Private	23	July 20, 1861, Fayetteville, North Carolina	Co. E, 8th North Carolina Infantry	June 1, 1864, Gaines Mill, Cold Harbor, Virginia	Point Lookout, Maryland, transferred to Elmira Prison, NY July 17, 1864	Oath of Allegiance May 29, 1865
Faircloth, T. Private	Unk	Unknown	Co. E, 36th Regiment, 2nd North Carolina Artillery	January 15, 1865, Fort Fisher, North Carolina	February 1, 1865, Elmira Prison Camp, New York	Died March 17, 1865 of Rheumatism, Grave No. 1703
Faircloth, Thomas H. Private	20	February 20, 1862, Terribinth, Cumberland County, North Carolina	Co. C, 36th Regiment, 2nd North Carolina Artillery	January 15, 1865, Fort Fisher, North Carolina	February 1, 1865, Elmira Prison Camp, New York	Died March 14, 1865 of Chronic Diarrhea, Grave No. 2430
Fairey, Philip W. Private	29	May 6, 1862, Grahamville, Virginia	Co. G, 4th South Carolina Cavalry	May 28, 1864, Cold Harbor, Virginia. Gunshot Wound fracture Left Leg and Left Forearm. Leg Amputated.	Old Capital Prison, Washington, DC, transferred to Elmira Prison, NY, December 17, 1864	Exchanged March 14, 1865 at Boulware's Wharf on the James River, Virginia
Fairfax, Addison S. Private	17	July 1, 1861, Prince William County, Virginia	Co. B, 49th Virginia Infantry	October 1, 1864, Prince William County, Virginia	Old Capital Prison, Washington, DC transferred to Elmira Prison, NY August 27, 1864	Oath of Allegiance May 29, 1865
Faland, Patrick Private	Unk	August 20, 1861, Tallahassee, Florida	Co. M, 2nd Florida Infantry	May 12, 1864, Spotsylvania Court House, Virginia	Point Lookout, Maryland, transferred to Elmira Prison, NY August 12, 1864	Oath of Allegiance June 19, 1865

Name & Rank	Age	Enlisted	Regiment and State	Where Captured	Prison	Remarks
Falkner, Benjamin Private	Unk	July 16, 1862, Raleigh, North Carolina	Co. B, 14th North Carolina Infantry	May 6, 1864, Wilderness, Virginia	Point Lookout, Maryland, transferred to Elmira Prison, NY August 14, 1864	Died December 6, 1864 of Chronic Diarrhea, Grave No. 1032
Falkner, Edward T. Private	21	June 20, 1862, Henderson, North Carolina	Co. E, 1st North Carolina Cavalry	September 22, 1863, Jack's Shop, Near Madison Court House, Virginia	Point Lookout, Maryland, transferred to Elmira Prison, NY August 18, 1864	Exchanged October 29, 1864, at Venus Point, Savannah River, GA.
Falkner, Larken L. Private	19	December 29, 1861, Port Royal Ferry, South Carolina	Co. B, 14th South Carolina Infantry	July 29, 1864, Petersburg, Virginia	Point Lookout, Maryland, transferred to Elmira Prison, NY August 12, 1864	Exchanged October 29, 1864, at Venus Point, Savannah River, GA.
Falkner, William Private	21	June 11, 1862, Henderson, North Carolina	Co. C, 23rd North Carolina Infantry	May 12, 1864, Near Spotsylvania Court House, Virginia	Point Lookout, Maryland, transferred to Elmira Prison, NY August 14, 1864	Oath of Allegiance June 30, 1865
Fallen, Michael Corporal	Unk	May 27, 1861, New Orleans, Louisiana	Co. E, 15th Louisiana Infantry	May 12, 1864, Spotsylvania Court House, Virginia	Point Lookout, Maryland, transferred to Elmira Prison, NY July 25, 1864	Exchanged February 13, 1865 at Boulware's Wharf on the James River, Virginia
Fallen, William Private	23	August 16, 1862, Mobile, Alabama	Co. D, 6th Alabama Infantry	May 12, 1864, Spotsylvania, Virginia	Point Lookout, Maryland, transferred to Elmira Prison, NY July 23, 1864	Oath of Allegiance May 2, 1865
Fallis, William R. Sergeant	Unk	Unknown	Co. A, 1st Maryland Cavalry	July 10, 1864, Frederick, Maryland	Old Capital Prison, Washington, DC, transferred to Elmira Prison, NY, July 23, 1864	Exchanged February 25, 1865 at Boulware's or Cox Wharf on the James River, Virginia
Falls, Jeremiah Private	Unk	May 27, 1861, Staunton, Virginia	Co. D, 25th Virginia Infantry	May 12, 1864, Spotsylvania Court House, Virginia	Point Lookout, Maryland, transferred to Elmira Prison, NY August 2, 1864	Exchanged October 29, 1864, at Venus Point, Savannah River, GA.

Name & Rank	Age	Enlisted	Regiment and State	Where Captured	Prison	Remarks
Falls, William W. Private	Unk	February 18, 1864, Harrisonburg, Virginia	Co. C, 10th Virginia Infantry	May 12, 1864, Spotsylvania Court House, Virginia	Point Lookout, Maryland, transferred to Elmira Prison, NY August 2, 1864	Died March 8, 1865 Chronic Diarrhea Grave No. 2370
Fann, James A. Private	20	April 15, 1861, Pittsboro, North Carolina	Co. I, 32nd North Carolina Infantry	May 10, 1864, Wilderness, Virginia	Point Lookout, Maryland, transferred to Elmira Prison, NY August 6, 1864	Oath of Allegiance May 19, 1865
Fann, William E. Private	Unk	May 10, 1863, Raleigh, North Carolina	Co. K, 32nd North Carolina Infantry	May 10, 1864, Wilderness, Virginia	Point Lookout, Maryland, transferred to Elmira Prison, NY August 6, 1864	Oath of Allegiance May 19, 1865
Fanning, Charles Private	Unk	July 18, 1861, New Orleans, Louisiana	Co. D, 15th Louisiana Infantry	May 12, 1864, Spotsylvania Court House, Virginia	Point Lookout, Maryland, transferred to Elmira Prison, NY July 25, 1864	Oath of Allegiance May 15, 1865
Fanning, Joshua Soule Sergeant Major	18	July 2, 1861, Nickelsville, Scott County, Virginia	Co. E, 48th Virginia Infantry	May 12, 1864, Near Spotsylvania Court House, Virginia	Point Lookout, Maryland, transferred to Elmira Prison, NY August 6, 1864	Exchanged March 2, 1865 at Akins Landing on the James River, Virginia
Fanshaw, John Private	21	May 6, 1862, Currituck County, North Carolina	Co. A, 56th North Carolina Infantry	July 28, 1864, Camden County, North Carolina	Point Lookout, Maryland, transferred to Elmira Prison, NY August 18, 1864	Oath of Allegiance July 3, 1865
Fant, C. M. Private	Unk	May 6, 1862, Camp Pickens, Grahamville, South Carolina	Co. C, 4th South Carolina Cavalry	May 28, 1864, Hall's Shop, Virginia	Point Lookout, Maryland, transferred to Elmira Prison, NY July 12, 1864	Died March 20, 1865 of Pneumonia, Grave No. 1574
Farinholt, David A. Private	Unk	August 8, 1863, Hanover Junction, Virginia	Co. C, 24th Virginia Cavalry	July 28, 1864, Petersburg, Virginia	Point Lookout, Maryland, transferred to Elmira Prison, NY August 12, 1864	Exchanged October 29, 1864, at Venus Point, Savannah River, GA.
Faris, William A. Private	33	May 18, 1861, Seven Mile Ford, Virginia	Co. D, 48th Virginia Infantry	May 12, 1864, Spotsylvania Court House, Virginia	Point Lookout, Maryland, transferred to Elmira Prison, NY August 2, 1864	Died January 26, 1865 of Chronic Diarrhea, Grave No. 1632

Name & Rank	Age	Enlisted	Regiment and State	Where Captured	Prison	Remarks
Farley, John E. Private	17	March 23, 1862, Milton, North Carolina	Co. I, 45th North Carolina Infantry	July 13, 1864, Near Washington DC,	Old Capital Prison, Washington, DC, transferred to Elmira Prison, NY, July 23, 1864	Oath of Allegiance June 21, 1865
Farley, Thomas A. Sergeant	Unk	September 5, 1861, Patrick Court House, Virginia	Co. H, 58th Virginia Infantry	May 30, 1864, Mechanics-ville, Virginia	Point Lookout, Maryland, transferred to Elmira Prison, NY July 11, 1864	Oath of Allegiance June 19, 1865
Farmer, Asa Private	Unk	April 25, 1861, Long Island, Alabama	Co. D, 6th Alabama Infantry	May 15, 1864, Spotsylvania Court House, Virginia	Point Lookout, Maryland, transferred to Elmira Prison, NY July 6, 1864	Oath of Allegiance June 19, 1865
Farmer, J. Private	Unk	Unknown	Co. H, 36th Regiment, 2nd North Carolina Artillery	January 15, 1865, Fort Fisher, North Carolina	February 1, 1865, Elmira Prison Camp, New York	Died March 8, 1865 of Pneumonia. No Grave at Woodlawn Cemetery.
Farmer, Joel A. Private	Unk	June 10, 1863, Greenville, South Carolina	Co. H, 6th South Carolina Cavalry	June 11, 1864, Trevilian Station, Louisa Court House, Virginia	Point Lookout, Maryland, transferred to Elmira Prison, NY July 25, 1864	Oath of Allegiance July 3, 1865
Farmer, John Private	42	July 20, 1863, Wayne County, North Carolina	Co. G, 40th Regiment, 3rd North Carolina Artillery	January 15, 1865, Fort Fisher, North Carolina	February 1, 1865, Elmira Prison Camp, New York	Exchanged March 14, 1865 at Boulware's Wharf on the James River, Virginia
Farmer, Samuel B. Private	Unk	Unnown	Co. B, 1st Virginia Artillery	July 4, 1864, Major Allen's Farm, Virginia	Point Lookout, Maryland, transferred to Elmira Prison, NY August 6, 1864	Oath of Allegiance May 29, 1865
Farmer, Samuel J. Private	Unk	April 17, 1863, Charleston, South Carolina	Co. A, 7th Georgia Cavalry	June 11, 1864, Trevilian Station, Louisa Court House, Virginia	Point Lookout, Maryland, transferred to Elmira Prison, NY July 25, 1864	Exchanged March 10, 1865 at Boulware's wharf on the James River, Virginia

Name & Rank	Age	Enlisted	Regiment and State	Where Captured	Prison	Remarks
Farmer, W. R. Private	Unk	Unknown	Co. C, 2nd South Carolina Infantry	June 1, 1864, Cold Harbor, Virginia	Point Lookout, Maryland, transferred to Elmira Prison, NY July 17,1864	Oath of Allegiance May 29, 1865
Farmer, William A. Private	18	October 1, 1862, Drury's Bluff, Virginia	Co. B, 45th North Carolina Infantry	May 10, 1864, Spotsylvania Court House, Virginia	Point Lookout, Maryland, transferred to Elmira Prison, NY July 23, 1864	Oath of Allegiance May 29, 1865
Farr, Christopher C. Private	Unk	July 15, 1861, Columbus, Georgia	Co. G, 20th Georgia Infantry	May 6, 1864, Wilderness, Virginia	Point Lookout, Maryland, transferred to Elmira Prison, NY August 14, 1864	Exchanged October 29, 1864, at Venus Point, Savannah River, GA.
Farrar, Samuel H. Private	38	September 25, 1863, Richmond, Virginia	Co. G, 45th North Carolina Infantry	May 10, 1864, Spotsylvania Court House, Virginia	Point Lookout, Maryland, transferred to Elmira Prison, NY August 6, 1864	Died September 14, 1864 of Chronic Diarrhea, Grave No. 272
Farrell, John Private	Unk	March 27, 1861, Selma, Alabama	Co. A, 1st Alabama Artillery	August 23, 1864, Fort Morgan, Alabama	New Orleans, Louisiana transferred to Elmira December 4, 1864.	Oath of Allegiance May 13, 1865
Farrell, O. Private	Unk	Unknown	Co. A, 30th Virginia Infantry	July 16, 1864, Loudoun County, Virginia	Old Capital Prison, Washington, DC, transferred to Elmira Prison, NY, July 23, 1864	Exchanged March 14, 1865 at Boulware's Wharf on the James River, Virginia
Farrill, B. H. Private	Unk	April 10, 1862, Fort Pillow, Tennessee	Co. B, Jackson's 1st Regiment, Tennessee Heavy Artillery	August 23, 1864, Fort Morgan, Alabama	New Orleans, Louisiana transferred to Elmira December 4, 1864.	Exchanged February 25, 1865 at Boulware's or Cox Wharf on the James River, Virginia
Farris, Lewis A. Private	Unk	March 19, 1861, Montgomery, Alabama	Co. A, 1st Battalion Alabama Artillery	August 23, 1864, Fort Morgan, Alabama	Steam Press No. 4 New Orleans, Louisiana transferred to Elmira October 8, 1864.	Oath of Allegiance May 19, 1865

Name & Rank	Age	Enlisted	Regiment and State	Where Captured	Prison	Remarks
Farris, Preston T. Private	18	September 8, 1863, Liberty Mills, Virginia	Co. C, 28th North Carolina Infantry	May 12, 1864, Spotsylvania Court House, Virginia	Point Lookout, Maryland, transferred to Elmira Prison, NY August 14, 1864	Oath of Allegiance July 11, 1865
Farron, Joel Private	Unk	September 1, 1862, Calhoun, Georgia	Co. H, 24th Georgia Infantry	June 3, 1864, Gaines Mill, Cold Harbor, Virginia	Point Lookout, Maryland, transferred to Elmira Prison, NY July 17, 1864	Died November 11, 1864 of Chronic Diarrhea Grave No. 823
Farrow, J. Private	Unk	Unknown	Co. F, 5th Alabama Infantry	May 5, 1864, Wilderness, Virginia	Point Lookout, Maryland, transferred to Elmira Prison, NY August 17, 1864	Oath of Allegiance June 16, 1865
Fary, James T. Corporal	29	April 23, 1861, Gloucester Court House, Virginia	Co. B, 26th Virginia Infantry	June 15, 1864, Near Petersburg, Virginia	Point Lookout, Maryland, transferred to Elmira Prison, NY July 17, 1864	Oath of Allegiance July 3, 1865
Fath, Michael Private	26	June 4, 1861, Camp Moore, Louisiana	Co. G, 5th Louisiana Infantry	May 5, 1864, Wilderness, Virginia	Point Lookout, Maryland, transferred to Elmira Prison, NY July 23, 1864	Oath of Allegiance May 21, 1865
Faucett, Robert J. Private	34	July 15, 1862, Raleigh, North Carolina	Co. E, 1st North Carolina Infantry	May 12, 1864, Spotsylvania Court House, Virginia	Point Lookout, Maryland, transferred to Elmira Prison, NY August 6, 1864	Died April 8, 1865 of Chronic Diarrhea, Grave No. 2634.
Faucett, William J. Private	26	July 15, 1862, Raleigh, North Carolina	Co. E, 1st North Carolina Infantry	May 12, 1864, Spotsylvania Court House, Virginia	Point Lookout, Maryland, transferred to Elmira Prison, NY August 6, 1864	Oath of Allegiance July 3, 1865
Faulk, Jonathan G. Private	33	April 24, 1861, Bug Hill, North Carolina	Co. C, 18th North Carolina Infantry	July 29, 1864, Petersburg, Virginia	Point Lookout, Maryland, transferred to Elmira Prison, NY August 12, 1864	Oath of Allegiance June 12, 1865
Faulk, Thomas D. Private	Unk	February 14, 1864, Camp Near Liberty Mills, Virginia	Co. C, 18th North Carolina Infantry	May 12, 1864, Spotsylvania Court House, Virginia	Point Lookout, Maryland, transferred to Elmira Prison, NY August 6, 1864	Died October 3, 1864 of Chronic Diarrhea, Grave No. 629

Name & Rank	Age	Enlisted	Regiment and State	Where Captured	Prison	Remarks
Faulk, William H. Private	15	May 5, 1862, Fort St. Philips, Brunswick County, North Carolina	Co. E, 36th Regiment 2nd North Carolina Artillery	January 15, 1865, Fort Fisher, North Carolina	February 1, 1865, Elmira Prison Camp, New York	Exchanged March 2, 1865 at Boulware's Wharf on the James River, Virginia
Faulk, William R. Private	42	April 24, 1861, Bug Hill, North Carolina	Co. C, 18th North Carolina Infantry	May 12, 1864, Spotsylvania Court House, Virginia	Point Lookout, Maryland, transferred to Elmira Prison, NY August 6, 1864	Died January 28, 1865 of Erysipelas, Grave No. 1658
Faulkner, S. Jack V. Private	Unk	April 28, 1862, Camp Pillow, South Carolina	Co. J, 17th South Carolina Infantry	July 30, 1864, Petersburg, Virginia	Point Lookout, Maryland, transferred to Elmira Prison, NY August 12, 1864	Oath of Allegiance June 21, 1865
Faulkner, W. L. Private	Unk	February 15, 1863, Landcaster County Court House, South Carolina	Co. J, 17th South Carolina Infantry	July 30, 1864, Petersburg, Virginia	Point Lookout, Maryland, transferred to Elmira Prison, NY August 12, 1864	Died September 17, 1864 of Typhoid Fever, Grave No. 309
Faust, John C. Private	Unk	Unknown	Co. A, Jackson's 1st Regiment, Tennessee Heavy Artillery	August 23, 1864, Fort Morgan, Alabama	New Orleans, Louisiana transferred to Elmira December 4, 1864.	Died January 27, 1865 of Chronic Diarrhea, Grave No. 1636. Headstone has Frank Faust.
Fawcett, Burke H. Private	Unk	Unknown	Co. B, 1st Jackson's Tennessee Heavy Artillery	August 23, 1864, Fort Morgan, Alabama.	New Orleans, Louisiana transferred to Elmira December 4, 1864.	Oath of Allegiance May 29, 1865
Fay, James Private	22	June 19, 1861, Camp Moore, Louisiana	Co. A, 8th Louisiana Infantry	July 16, 1864, Loudoun County, Virginia	Old Capital Prison, Washington, DC, transferred to Elmira Prison, NY, July 23, 1864	Exchanged February 13, 1865 at Boulware's wharf on the James River, Virginia
Feagans, George W. Private	Unk	July 2, 1861, Bethel, Virginia	Co. F, 50th Virginia Infantry	May 12, 1864, Spotsylvania Court House, Virginia	Point Lookout, Maryland, transferred to Elmira Prison, NY July 30, 1864	Oath of Allegiance June 15, 1865

Name & Rank	Age	Enlisted	Regiment and State	Where Captured	Prison	Remarks
Feagles, Drayton Private	29	August 2, 1862, Lake City, Florida	Co. H, 10th Florida Infantry	September 10, 1864, Petersburg, Virginia. Gunshot Wound Left Arm.	Old Capital Prison, Washington, DC transferred to Elmira Prison, NY August 27, 1864	Exchanged February 13, 1865 at Boulware's Wharf on the James River, Virginia
Feasel, James N. Private	23	March 31, 1862, Lynchburg, Virginia	Captain Shoemaker's Company Virginia Horse Artillery	September 14, 1863, Near Culpepper, Virginia	Point Lookout, Maryland, transferred to Elmira Prison, NY August 18, 1864	Exchanged March 10, 1865 at Boulware's Wharf on the James River, Virginia
Feaster, W. J. Private	Unk	May 15, 1861, Savannah, Georgia	Co. B, 20th Battalion Georgia Cavalry	May 30, 1864, Old Church, Cold Harbor, Virginia	Point Lookout, Maryland, transferred to Elmira Prison, NY July 6, 1864	Exchanged October 29, 1864 at Venus Point, Savannah River, GA.
Featherston, Calvin R. Private	21	May 15, 1861, Edneyville, North Carolina	Co. A, 25th North Carolina Infantry	June 4, 1864, Cold Harbor, Virginia	Point Lookout, Maryland, transferred to Elmira Prison, NY July 25, 1864	Oath of Allegiance May 29, 1865
Felder, C. E. Private	Unk	April 11, 1862, Coles Island, South Carolina	Co. F, 25th South Carolina Infantry	January 15, 1865, Fort Fisher, North Carolina	January 30, 1865, Elmira Prison Camp, NY	Oath of Allegiance July 11, 1865
Felder, David B. Private	Unk	January 4, 1862, Walterboro, South Carolina	Co. J, 11th South Carolina Infantry	May 16, 1864, Near Drury's Bluff, Virginia	Point Lookout, Maryland, transferred to Elmira Prison, NY August 17, 1864	Exchanged February 13, 1865 at Boulware's wharf on the James River, Virginia
Felkel, Wesley R. Private	25	February 26, 1862, Centerville, Florida	Co. K, 5th Florida Infantry	May 12, 1864, Spotsylvania Court House, Virginia	Point Lookout, Maryland, transferred to Elmira Prison, NY July 30, 1864	Died June 2, 1865 of Chronic Diarrhea, Grave No. 2901
Fellows, Henry Private	18	July 15, 1862, Guilford County, North Carolina	Co. A, 1st North Carolina Infantry	May 12, 1864, Wilderness, Spotsylvania Court House, Virginia	Point Lookout, Maryland, transferred to Elmira Prison, NY August 6, 1864	Died February 21, 1865 of Pneumonia, Grave No. 2323

Name & Rank	Age	Enlisted	Regiment and State	Where Captured	Prison	Remarks
Felthouse, Henry Private	Unk	September 28, 1862, Benton, Tennessee	Co. B, 62nd Tennessee Mounted Infantry	May 16, 1863, Big Black, Mississippi	Point Lookout, Maryland, transferred to Elmira Prison, NY July 25, 1864	Oath of Allegiance May 29, 1865
Felton, James L. Corporal	Unk	April 17, 1863, Tyler, Texas	Co. H, 37th Texas Cavalry	August 25, 1864, Near Morganza, Louisiana	New Orleans, Louisianna Transferred to Elmira Prison, New York, November 19, 1864	Died April 20, 1865 of Pneumonia, Grave No. 1395. Headstone has 35th Virginia.
Felts, Aaron W. Corporal	21	July 26, 1861, Lenior County, North Carolina	Co. J, 26th North Carolina Infantry	May 12, 1864, Spotsylvania Court House, Virginia	Point Lookout, Maryland, transferred to Elmira Prison, NY July 30, 1864	Oath of Allegiance May 13, 1865
Felts, Nathanial G. Private	26	May 4, 1861, Warrenton, North Carolina	Co. C, 12th North Carolina Infantry	May 12, 1864, Near Spotsylvania, Virginia	Point Lookout, Maryland, transferred to Elmira Prison, NY August 14, 1864	Died September 9, 1864 of Diphtheria, Grave No. 198. Name Felt on Headstone.
Fendor, Ransom Private	Unk	March 20, 1862, Colleton, South Carolina	Co. K, 11th South Carolina Infantry	June 16, 1864, Petersburg, Virginia	Point Lookout, Maryland, transferred to Elmira Prison, NY July 25, 1864	Exchanged March 14, 1865 at Boulware's Wharf on the James River, Virginia
Fennell, James R. Private	39	March 14, 1862, Jasper, Florida	Co. B, 5th Florida Infantry	May 12, 1864, Spotsylvania Court House, Virginia	Point Lookout, Maryland, transferred to Elmira Prison, NY July 30, 1864	Died October 9, 1864 of Chronic Diarrhea, Grave No. 660
Fennell, William M. Private	Unk	January 17, 1862, Columbia, South Carolina	Co. G, 22nd South Carolina Infantry	July 30, 1864, Petersburg, Virginia	Point Lookout, Maryland, transferred to Elmira Prison, NY August 12, 1864	Died September 6, 1864 of Chronic Diarrhea, Grave No. 221
Fenters, T. J. Private	Unk	May 2, 1862, Georgetown, South Carolina	Co. A, 21st South Carolina Infantry	June 24, 1864, Near Petersburg, Virginia	Point Lookout, Maryland, transferred to Elmira Prison, NY August 18, 1864	Oath of Allegiance July 11, 1865

Name & Rank	Age	Enlisted	Regiment and State	Where Captured	Prison	Remarks
Ferebee, Grandy Private	29	March 7, 1862, Washington Point, Virginia	Co. E, 61st Virginia Infantry	August 19, 1864, Weldon Railroad, Near Petersburg, Virginia. Gunshot Wound Left Foot.	DeCamp General Hospital, David's Island New York Harbor.	Died February 12, 1865 of Variola (Smallpox), Grave No. 2078
Ferebee, W. H. Corporal	27	July 12, 1862, Mocksville, North Carolina	Co. E, 5th North Carolina Cavalry	September 22, 1863, Near Madison Court House, Virginia	Point Lookout, Maryland, transferred to Elmira Prison, NY August 18, 1864	Exchanged March 10, 1865 at Boulware's Wharf on the James River, Virginia
Ferguson, Allen Private	Unk	August 28, 1863, Camp Vance, North Carolina	Co. C, 13th North Carolina Infantry	May 6, 1864, Wilderness, Virginia	Point Lookout, Maryland, transferred to Elmira Prison, NY August 14, 1864	Died August 22, 1864 of Chronic Diarrhea, Grave No. 33. Name Furgerson and 3rd NC on Headstone.
Ferguson, Angus Private	31	March 7, 1863, Wilmington, North Carolina	Co. E, 35th North Carolina Infantry	June 17, 1864, Petersburg, Virginia	Point Lookout, Maryland, transferred to Elmira Prison, NY July 30, 1864	Died February 22, 1865 of Diarrhea, Grave No. 2302. Name Allen Fergerson on Headstone.
Ferguson, Dorris Private	Unk	May 11, 1863, Camp Holmes, Near Raleigh, North Carolina	Co. C, 3rd Battalion North Carolina Light Artillery	January 15, 1865, Fort Fisher, North Carolina and	Elmira Prison Camp, New York, February 1, 1865	Died March 10, 1865 of Convulsions, Grave No. 1868
Ferguson, George S. Sergeant	Unk	November 18, 1861, College Green, Columbia, South Carolina	Co. A, 17th South Carolina Infantry	July 30, 1864, Petersburg, Virginia	Point Lookout, Maryland, transferred to Elmira Prison, NY August 12, 1864	Died January 5, 1865 of Chronic Diarrhea, Grave No. 1257. Furguson on Headstone.
Ferguson, James R. Private	26	May 1, 1862, Richmond, Virginia	Sturdivant's Co. A, Virginia Light Artillery	June 15, 1864, Petersburg, Virginia	Point Lookout, Maryland, transferred to Elmira Prison, NY July 17,1864	U. S. Army General Hospital, Baltimore, Maryland, Released June 7, 1865

Name & Rank	Age	Enlisted	Regiment and State	Where Captured	Prison	Remarks
Ferguson, John Sergeant	Unk	May 9, 1864, Columbia, South Carolina	Co. A, 17th South Carolina Infantry	July 30, 1864, Petersburg, Virginia	Point Lookout, Maryland, transferred to Elmira Prison, NY August 12, 1864	Oath of Allegiance July 3, 1865
Ferguson, Thomas B. Private	Unk	July 2, 1861, Bethel Am., Virginia	Co. C, 50th Virginia Infantry	May 12, 1864, Spotsylvania Court House, Virginia	Point Lookout, Maryland, transferred to Elmira Prison, NY August 2, 1864	Died December 18, 1864 of Chronic Diarrhea, Grave No. 1277
Ferguson, William H. Private	23	April 24, 1861, Philadelphia, Mississippi	Co. D, 11th Mississippi Infantry	May 5, 1864, wilderness, Virginia	Old Capital Prison, Washington, DC, transferred to Elmira Prison, NY, July 23, 1864	Exchanged October 29, 1864, at Venus Point, Savannah River, GA.
Fernandez, J. Civilian	Unk	Registered Enemy	Citizen of Louisiana	July 26, 1864, New Orleans, Louisiana	New Orleans, Louisiana transferred to Elmira November 19, 1864.	Exchanged February 13, 1865 at Boulware's Wharf on the James River, Virginia
Ferrel, Aaron Private	Unk	April 22, 1862, Wilson, North Carolina	Co. H, 7th Confederate Cavalry	May 7, 1864, Lyttleton, Virginia	Point Lookout, Maryland, transferred to Elmira Prison, NY August 17, 1864	Exchanged February 13, 1865 at Boulware's wharf on the James River, Virginia
Ferrell, A. S. Private	Unk	November 25, 1864, New Hanover County, North Carolina	Co. D, 13th Battalion North Carolina Light Artillery	January 15, 1865, Fort Fisher, North Carolina	February 1, 1865, Elmira Prison Camp, New York	Exchanged March 14, 1865 at Boulware's Wharf on the James River, Virginia
Ferrell, J. G. Private	Unk	April 5, 1864, Camp Holmes, North Carolina	Co. H, 38th North Carolina Infantry	May 23, 1864, North Anna, Virginia	Point Lookout, Maryland, transferred to Elmira Prison, NY July 25, 1864	Oath of Allegiance May 29, 1865
Ferrell, James R. Private	30	May 10, 1863, Raleigh, North Carolina	Co. F, 32nd North Carolina Infantry	May 10, 1864, Wilderness, Virginia	Point Lookout, Maryland, transferred to Elmira Prison, NY August 6, 1864	Exchanged February 20, 1865 at Boulware's or Cox Wharf on the James River, Virginia

Name & Rank	Age	Enlisted	Regiment and State	Where Captured	Prison	Remarks
Ferrell, John A. Private	Unk	Unknown	Co. I, 10th Virginia Infantry	May 12, 1864, Spotsylvania Court House, Virginia	Point Lookout, Maryland, transferred to Elmira Prison, NY August 2, 1864	Oath of Allegiance May 13, 1865
Ferrell, John C. Sergeant	18	August 10, 1861, Wake County, North Carolina	Co. D, 30th North Carolina Infantry	May 12, 1864, Near Spotsylvania Court House, Virginia	Point Lookout, Maryland, transferred to Elmira Prison, NY August 14, 1864	Exchanged February 20, 1865 at Boulware's or Cox Wharf on the James River, Virginia
Ferrell, John G. Sergeant	20	June 20, 1861, Oxford, North Carolina	Co. E, 23th North Carolina Infantry	May 15, 1864, Spotsylvania Court House, Virginia	Point Lookout, Maryland, transferred to Elmira Prison, NY July 6, 1864	Exchanged March 2, 1865 at Akins Landing on the James River, Virginia
Ferrell, William B. Private	23	July 15, 1862, Raleigh, North Carolina	Co. J, 3rd North Carolina Infantry	May 12, 1864, Near Spotsylvania Court House, Virginia	Point Lookout Prison, Maryland. Transferred to Elmira Prison Camp New York August 14, 1864.	Oath of Allegiance June 14, 1865
Ferrell, William F. Private	24	April 29, 1861, Yanceyville, North Carolina	Co. A, 13th North Carolina Infantry	June 12, 1864, Cold Harbor, Virginia	Point Lookout, Maryland, transferred to Elmira Prison, NY July 30, 1864	Oath of Allegiance June 16, 1865
Ferrill, John H. Private	18	February 24, 1862, Morganton, North Carolina	Co. D, 6th North Carolina Infantry	May 29, 1864, Mechanicsville, Virginia	Point Lookout, Maryland, transferred to Elmira Prison, NY July 11,1864	Oath of Allegiance May 29, 1865
Fersner, W. F. Ordinance Sergeant	Unk	April 11, 1862, Coles Island, South Carolina	Field & Staff, 25th South Carolina Infantry	January 15, 1865, Fort Fisher, North Carolina	January 30, 1865, Elmira Prison Camp, NY	Oath of Allegiance July 7, 1865
Fertic, John Private	Unk	April 11, 1862, Coles Island, South Carolina	Co. F, 25th South Carolina Infantry	January 15, 1865, Fort Fisher, North Carolina	January 30, 1865, Elmira Prison Camp, NY	Oath of Allegiance July 7, 1865
Fewell, L. N. Private	Unk	April 6, 1862, Orange County Court House, Virginia	Co. H, 17th Virginia Infantry	July 29, 1864, Petersburg, Virginia	Point Lookout, Maryland, transferred to Elmira Prison, NY August 12, 1864	Oath of Allegiance June 19, 1865

Name & Rank	Age	Enlisted	Regiment and State	Where Captured	Prison	Remarks
Fibbs, R. J. Private	Unk	Unknown	Co. A, 1st North Carolina Artillery	Unknown	Unknown	Died February 3, 1865 of Unknown Disease, Grave No. 1751
Fickling, Mortimer C. Private	Unk	March 4, 1862, Burke County, Georgia	Co. D, 48th Georgia Infantry	May 24, 1864, Hanover Junction, Virginia	Point Lookout, Maryland, transferred to Elmira Prison, NY July 11, 1864	Oath of Allegiance May 29, 1865
Fiddle, William G. Private	30	January 8, 1862, Greensboro, North Carolina	Co. H, 1st North Carolina Infantry	May 12, 1864, Spotsylvania, Virginia	Point Lookout Prison Camp, Maryland. Transferred to Elmira Prison, August 6, 1864	Died August 29, 1864 of Typhoid Fever, Grave No. 51
Fiddler, Milton H. Private	22	July 1, 1862, Pfafftown, North Carolina	Co. C, 33rd North Carolina Infantry	May 6, 1864, Wilderness, Virginia	Point Lookout, Maryland, transferred to Elmira Prison, NY August 14, 1864	Exchanged October 29, 1864, at Venus Point, Savannah River, GA.
Fielder, Robert D. Private	Unk	May 22, 1861, Rose Hill, Virginia	Co. E, 37th Virginia Infantry	May 12, 1864, Spotsylvania Court House, Virginia	Point Lookout, Maryland, transferred to Elmira Prison, NY August 2, 1864	Oath of Allegiance June 19, 1865
Fields, A. M. Private	Unk	July 20, 1862, Moore County, North Carolina	Co. C, 3rd North Carolina Infantry	May 12, 1864, Near Spotsylvania Court House, Virginia	Point Lookout Prison, Maryland. Transferred to Elmira Prison Camp New York August 14, 1864.	Died February 13, 1865 of Variola (Smallpox), Grave No. 2041
Fields, D. G. Private	Unk	Unknown	Co. K, 18th North Carolina Infantry	May 12, 1864, Spotsylvania Court House, Virginia	Point Lookout, Maryland, transferred to Elmira Prison, NY August 6, 1864	Exchanged February 20, 1865 at Boulware's or Cox Wharf on the James River, Virginia
Fields, F. J. Corporal	Unk	Unknown	Co. E, Cobb's Legion Georgia	August 16, 1864, Front Royal, Virginia	Old Capital Prison, Washington, DC transferred to Elmira Prison, NY August 29, 1864	Oath of Allegiance June 16, 1865

Name & Rank	Age	Enlisted	Regiment and State	Where Captured	Prison	Remarks
Fields, Frank Private	31	May 10, 1861, New Orleans, Louisiana	Co. B, 5th Louisiana Infantry	May 10, 1864, Spotsylvania, Virginia	Point Lookout, Maryland, transferred to Elmira Prison, NY August 17, 1864	Oath of Allegiance May 29, 1865
Fields, James H. Private	32	May 3, 1861, Elizabethtown, North Carolina	Co. B, 18th North Carolina Infantry	May 12, 1864, Spotsylvania Court House, Virginia	Point Lookout, Maryland, transferred to Elmira Prison, NY August 6, 1864	Oath of Allegiance June 16, 1865
Fields, James K. Private	Unk	March 15, 1862, Wilmington, North Carolina	Co. H, 51st North Carolina Infantry	June 1, 1864, Cold Harbor, Virginia	Point Lookout, Maryland, transferred to Elmira Prison, NY July 17,1864	Exchanged March 14, 1865 at Boulware's Wharf on the James River, Virginia
Fields, John Private	Unk	April 19, 1862, Lake City, Florida	Co. B, 5th Florida Infantry	May 12, 1864, Spotsylvania Court House, Virginia	Point Lookout, Maryland, transferred to Elmira Prison, NY August 12, 1864	Died April 24, 1865 of General Debility, Grave No. 1405
Fields, John Private	19	August 24, 1861, Kingsbury, North Carolina	Co. E, 8th North Carolina Infantry	May 31, 1864, Cold Harbor, Virginia	Point Lookout, Maryland, transferred to Elmira Prison, NY July 17,1864	Died November 15, 1864 of Chronic Diarrhea, Grave No. 953
Fields, John Private	Unk	March 15, 1862, Wilmington, North Carolina	Co. H, 51st North Carolina Infantry	June 1, 1864, Cold Harbor, Virginia	Point Lookout, Maryland, transferred to Elmira Prison, New York, July 17, 1864	Exchanged March 14, 1865 at Boulware's Wharf on the James River, Virginia
Fields, John B. Private	Unk	September 16, 1861, Walton County, Georgia	Co. G, 35th Georgia Infantry	May 6, 1864, Wilderness, Virginia	Point Lookout, Maryland, transferred to Elmira Prison, NY August 14, 1864	Died September 16, 1864 of Remittent Fever, Grave No. 165
Fields, Lindsey Private	18	July 8, 1862, Greensboro, North Carolina	Co. H, 1st North Carolina Infantry	May 12, 1864, Spotsylvania Court House, Virginia	Point Lookout, Maryland, transferred to Elmira Prison, NY July 25, 1864	Oath of Allegiance May 21, 1865

Name & Rank	Age	Enlisted	Regiment and State	Where Captured	Prison	Remarks
Fields, R. J. Private	19	July 9, 1861, Camp McDonald, Cobb County, Georgia	Co. E, Phillips Legion, Georgia	June 2, 1864, Gaines Farm, Virginia	Point Lookout, Maryland, transferred to Elmira Prison, NY July 17,1864	Died March 5, 1865 of Variola (Smallpox), Grave No. 1969
Fields, Tobias Private	19	July 24, 1863, Fort Branch, Martin County, North Carolina	Co. G, 40th Regiment, 3rd North Carolina Artillery	January 15, 1865, Fort Fisher, North Carolina	Elmira Prison Camp January 30, 1865	Died March 4, 1865 of Pneumonia, Grave No. 2002
Fields, Wesley Private	17	January 1, 1862, Darlington District, South Carolina	Co. B, 21st South Carolina Infantry	June 24, 1864, Near Petersburg, Virginia	Point Lookout, Maryland, transferred to Elmira Prison, NY August 18, 1864	Oath of Allegiance July 3, 1865
Files, James M. Private	20	September 20, 1863, Hampshire County, Virginia	Co. K, 18th Virginia Cavalry	July 22, 1864, Cold Spring, Frederick, Maryland	Old Capital Prison, Washington D. C. Transferred to Elmira Prison, NY August 12, 1864	Exchanged March 10, 1865 at Boulware's Wharf on the James River, Virginia
Fincannon, James M. Private	23	March 12, 1862, Lenore County, North Carolina	Co. D, 1st North Carolina Infantry	July 17,1864, Beltsville, Maryland	Old Capital Prison, Washington, DC, transferred to Elmira Prison, NY, July 23, 1864	Oath of Allegiance May 29, 1865
Finch, C. W. Sergeant	Unk	July 20, 1861, Jefferson, Georgia	Co. G, 16th Georgia Infantry	July 5, 1863, Gettysburg, Pennsylvania	Point Lookout, Maryland, transferred to Elmira Prison, NY July 17,1864	Oath of Allegiance June 14, 1865
Finch, Ira J. Private	36	July 16, 1863, Raleigh, North Carolina	Co. B, 30th North Carolina Infantry	August 10, 1864, Winchester, Virginia	Old Capital Prison, Washington, DC transferred to Elmira Prison, NY August 29, 1864	Exchanged February 20, 1865 at Boulware's or Cox Wharf on the James River, Virginia
Finch, John B. Private	Unk	May 31, 1861, Yellow Branch, Virginia	Co. D, 42nd Virginia Infantry	May 12, 1864, Near Spotsylvania Court House, Virginia	Point Lookout, Maryland, transferred to Elmira Prison, NY August 6, 1864	Exchanged October 29, 1864, at Venus Point, Savannah River, GA.

Name & Rank	Age	Enlisted	Regiment and State	Where Captured	Prison	Remarks
Findley, Charles L. Private	Unk	January 1, 1864, Orange Court House, Virginia	Co. F, 6th Virginia Cavalry	August 3, 1864, Burke's Station, Virginia	Old Capital Prison, Washington D. C. Transferred to Elmira Prison, NY August 12, 1864	Died July 3, 1865 of Chronic Diarrhea, Grave No. 2833
Findley, George W. Corporal	Unk	December 15, 1863, Butler County, Alabama	Co. D, 61st Alabama Infantry	May 12, 1864, Spotsylvania Court House, Virginia	Point Lookout, Maryland, transferred to Elmira Prison, NY July 30, 1864	Exchanged March 14, 1865 at Boulware's Wharf on the James River, Virginia
Fine, Elisha Private	44	August 15, 1862, Jonesboro, Tennessee	Co. K, 63rd Tennessee Infantry	June 17, 1864, Petersburg, Virginia	Point Lookout, Maryland, transferred to Elmira Prison, NY July 30, 1864	Exchanged October 29, 1864, at Venus Point, Savannah River, GA.
Fine, Gabriel Private	37	August 8, 1862, Davidson County, North Carolina	Co. D, 48th North Carolina Infantry	May 5, 1864, Wilderness, Virginia. Gunshot Left Abdominal Cavity.	Old Capital Prison, Washington D. C. Transferred to Elmira Prison, NY August 12, 1864	Exchanged October 29, 1864, at Venus Point, Savannah River, GA.
Fink, Rueben Sergeant	31	August 6, 1861, Mount Pleasant, North Carolina	Co. H, 8th North Carolina Infantry	May 31, 1864, Cold Harbor, Virginia	Point Lookout, Maryland, transferred to Elmira Prison, NY July 17,1864	Oath of Allegiance June 12, 1865
Finley, R. J. Private	Unk	July 26, 1861, Auburn, Alabama	Co. A, 14th Alabama Infantry	May 24, 1864, Hanover Junction, Virginia	Point Lookout, Maryland, transferred to Elmira Prison, NY July 11, 1864	Oath of Allegiance June 19, 1865
Finley, Rufus A. Private	19	August 1, 1861, Livingston, Overton County, Tennessee	Co. D, 25th Tennessee Infantry	May 16, 1864, Near Drury's Bluff, Virginia	Point Lookout, Maryland, transferred to Elmira Prison, NY August 17, 1864	Exchanged October 29, 1864, at Venus Point, Savannah River, GA.
Finley, William M. Private	21	August 13, 1861, Yorkville, South Carolina	Co. B, 12th South Carolina Infantry	July 28, 1864, Malvern Hill, Virginia	Point Lookout, Maryland, transferred to Elmira Prison, NY August 12, 1864	Exchanged March 14, 1865 at Boulware's Wharf on the James River, Virginia

Name & Rank	Age	Enlisted	Regiment and State	Where Captured	Prison	Remarks
Finn, Henry Private	36	June 18, 1861, Wilmington, North Carolina	Co. E, 1st North Carolina Infantry	May 12, 1864, Spotsylvania Court House, Virginia	Point Lookout, Maryland, transferred to Elmira Prison, NY August 6, 1864	Oath of Allegiance June 27, 1865
Finnegan, Thomas J. Private	25	May 4, 1861, New Orleans Barracks, Louisiana	Co. K, 1st Louisiana Infantry	May 20, 1864, Spotsylvania Court House, Virginia	Point Lookout, Maryland, transferred to Elmira Prison, NY July 3, 1864	Exchanged February 13, 1865 at Boulware's wharf on the James River, Virginia
Firnon, John Private	Unk	Unknown	Co. E, 45th North Carolina Infantry	May 15, 1864, Spotsylvania Court House, Virginia	Point Lookout, Maryland, transferred to Elmira Prison, NY July 6, 1864	Oath of Allegiance May 29, 1865
Fisher, Alfred E. Private	25	April 26, 1861, Columbus County, North Carolina	Co. K, 20th North Carolina Infantry	May 20, 1864, Spotsylvania Court House, Virginia	Point Lookout, Maryland, transferred to Elmira Prison, NY July 6, 1864	Exchanged February 13, 1865 at Boulware's wharf on the James River, Virginia
Fisher, Benjamin F. Private	Unk	April 16, 1862, Rudes Hill, Virginia	Co. D, 2nd Virginia Infantry	May 12, 1864, Near Spotsylvania Court House, Virginia	Point Lookout, Maryland, transferred to Elmira Prison, NY August 6, 1864	Oath of Allegiance June 30, 1865
Fisher, Bryant Private	29	April 23, 1863, Whiteville, North Carolina	Co. H, 18th North Carolina Infantry	May 12, 1864, Spotsylvania Court House, Virginia	Point Lookout, Maryland, transferred to Elmira Prison, NY August 6, 1864	Exchanged October 29, 1864, at Venus Point, Savannah River, GA.
Fisher, C. A. Private	Unk	April 15, 1863, Cabarrus County, North Carolina	Co. E, 4th North Carolina Cavalry	May 16, 1864, City Point Railroad, Virginia	Point Lookout, Maryland, transferred to Elmira Prison, NY July 12, 1864	Oath of Allegiance June 12, 1865
Fisher, George C. Private	Unk	October 6, 1862, Cumberland County, North Carolina	Co. I, 51st North Carolina Infantry	June 1, 1864, Gaines Farm, Virginia	Point Lookout, Maryland, transferred to Elmira Prison, NY July 17,1864	Exchanged October 29, 1864, at Venus Point, Savannah River, GA.
Fisher, Henry C. Private	19	March 19, 1862, Lenoir County, North Carolina	Co. A, 22nd North Carolina Infantry	June 2, 1864, Old Church, Virginia	Point Lookout, Maryland, transferred to Elmira Prison, NY July 17,1864	Oath of Allegiance July 3, 1865

Name & Rank	Age	Enlisted	Regiment and State	Where Captured	Prison	Remarks
Fisher, James W. Private	Unk	Unknown	2nd Class Virginia Militia	June 15, 1864, Petersburg, Virginia	Point Lookout, Maryland, transferred to Elmira Prison, NY July 25, 1864	Transferred for Exchange 10/11/64. Died 10/17/64 of Unknown Disease at Point Lookout, MD.
Fisher, James W. Private	19	April 18, 1861, Martinsburg, Virginia	Co. D, 2nd Virginia Infantry	May 12, 1864, Near Spotsylvania Court House, Virginia	Point Lookout, Maryland, transferred to Elmira Prison, NY August 6, 1864	Exchanged March 14, 1865 at Boulware's Wharf on the James River, Virginia
Fisher, John W. Private	32	July 7, 1862, Concord, North Carolina	Co. F, 57th North Carolina Infantry	August 7, 1864, Hagerstown, Maryland	Old Capital Prison, Washington, DC transferred to Elmira Prison, NY August 29, 1864	Oath of Allegiance May 29, 1865
Fisher, Johnston L. Private	Unk	April 1, 1862, Ocean View, Virginia	Co. C, 15th Virginia Infantry	May 11, 1864, Near Mechanicsville, Virginia	Point Lookout, Maryland, transferred to Elmira Prison, NY August 17, 1864	Oath of Allegiance June 19, 1865
Fisher, Marshall Private	35	March 15, 1863, Fort Fisher, New Hanover, North Carolina	Co. C, 36th Regiment, 2nd North Carolina Artillery	January 15, 1865, Fort Fisher, North Carolina	February 1, 1865, Elmira Prison Camp, New York	Died May 2, 1865 of Chronic Diarrhea, Grave No. 2747
Fisher, Samuel W. Private	Unk	February 26, 1863, Charleston, South Carolina	Co. D, 27th South Carolina Infantry	June 24, 1864, Near Petersburg, Virginia	Point Lookout, Maryland, transferred to Elmira Prison, NY August 18, 1864	Exchanged October 29, 1864, at Venus Point, Savannah River, GA.
Fisher, Samuel W. Private	21	April 18, 1861, Blacksburg, Virginia	Co. E, 4th Virginia Infantry	May 12, 1864, Near Spotsylvania Court House, Virginia	Point Lookout, Maryland, transferred to Elmira Prison, NY August 2, 1864	Exchanged February 20, 1865 at Boulware's or Cox Wharf on the James River, Virginia
Fisher, Solomon C. Private	Unk	September 1, 1863, Camp Vance, North Carolina	Co. A, 34th North Carolina Infantry	May 23, 1864, Spotsylvania Court House, Virginia	Point Lookout, Maryland, transferred to Elmira Prison, NY August 8, 1864	Died October 17, 1864 of Chronic Diarrhea, Grave No. 547

Name & Rank	Age	Enlisted	Regiment and State	Where Captured	Prison	Remarks
Fisher, Thomas H. Private	23	April 23, 1861, Manchester, Virginia	Co. B, 4th Virginia Cavalry	September 19, 1863, Germania Ford, Virginia	Point Lookout, Maryland, transferred to Elmira Prison, NY August 18, 1864	Exchanged March 10, 1865 at Boulware's Wharf on the James River, Virginia
Fisher, William A. Private	22	July 20, 1861, Camp Pickens, Anderson District, South Carolina	Co. G, 1st South Carolina Infantry	July 14, 1863, Falling Waters, Maryland	Point Lookout, Maryland, transferred to Elmira Prison, NY August 18, 1864	Exchanged March 10, 1865 at Boulware's Wharf on the James River, Virginia
Fisher, William D. Private	Unk	February 1, 1863, Tazewell County, Virginia	Co. J, 16th Virginia Cavalry	July 16, 1864, Loudoun County, Virginia	Old Capital Prison, Washington, DC, transferred to Elmira Prison, NY, July 23, 1864	Died December 18, 1864 of Pneumonia, Grave No. 1281
Fisher, William G. Private	27	August 14, 1861, Newton, North Carolina	Co. E, 32nd North Carolina Infantry	May 10, 1864, Wilderness, Virginia	Point Lookout, Maryland, transferred to Elmira Prison, NY August 6, 1864	Oath of Allegiance June 23, 1865
Fisher, William T. Private	39	March 15, 1863, Fort Fisher, New Hanover, North Carolina	Co. C, 36th Regiment, 2nd North Carolina Artillery	January 15, 1865, Fort Fisher, North Carolina	February 1, 1865, Elmira Prison Camp, New York	Oath of Allegiance June 12, 1865
Fisk, Richard B. Private	Unk	March 12, 1862, Norfolk County, Virginia	Co. F, 15th Virginia Cavalry	May 12, 1864, Mechanicsville, Virginia	Point Lookout, Maryland, transferred to Elmira Prison, NY August 17, 1864	Exchanged March 2, 1865 at Akins Landing on the James River, Virginia
Fiske, James W. Private	33	March 12, 1862, Norfolk County, Virginia	Co. F, 15th Virginia Cavalry	June 11, 1864, Louisa Court House, Virginia	Point Lookout, Maryland, transferred to Elmira Prison, NY July 23, 1864	Oath of Allegiance May 17, 1865
Fitchett, William P. Private	Unk	March 4, 1862, G. Navy Yard, Virginia	Co. F, 41st Virginia Infantry	July 20, 1864, Petersburg, Virginia. Deserted to Union Lines.	Old Capital Prison, Washington D. C. Transferred to Elmira Prison, NY August 12, 1864	Oath of Allegiance October 21, 1864. Early Release per Lincoln's Proclamation, 12/8/1863.

Name & Rank	Age	Enlisted	Regiment and State	Where Captured	Prison	Remarks
Fite, F. C. Sergeant	Unk	November 1, 1862, Lebanon, Tennessee	Co. A, Jackson's 1st Regiment, Tennessee Heavy Artillery	August 23, 1864, Fort Morgan, Alabama	New Orleans, Louisiana transferred to Elmira December 4, 1864.	Exchanged February 25, 1865 at Boulware's or Cox Wharf on the James River, Virginia
Fite, William F. Private	17	June 12, 1861, Gaston County, North Carolina	Co. H, 23rd North Carolina Infantry	May 12, 1864, Near Spotsylvania Court House, Virginia	Point Lookout Prison, Maryland. Transferred to Elmira Prison Camp New York August 14, 1864.	Oath of Allegiance May 19, 1865
Fittington, John Private	Unk	Unknown	General's Escort State Unknown	August 16, 1864, Waterproof, State Unknown	New Orleans, Louisiana transferred to Elmira November 19, 1864.	Died March 11, 1865 of Pneumonia, Grave No. 1853
Fitzgerald, John W. Corporal	23	May 27, 1861, Nottaway Court House, Virginia	Co. E, 3rd Virginia Cavalry	May 8, 1864, Spotsylvania, Virginia	Old Capital Prison, Washington, DC, transferred to Elmira Prison, NY, July 23, 1864	Oath of Allegiance June 16, 1865
Fitzgerald, Morris Private	Unk	February 16, 1863, Atlanta, Georgia	Co. A, 64th Georgia Infantry	June 17, 1864, Near Petersburg, Virginia	Point Lookout, Maryland, transferred to Elmira Prison, NY July 23, 1864	Oath of Allegiance May 29, 1865
Fitzgerald, Rufus Corporal	Unk	June 7, 1861, New Market, Virginia	Co. H, 49th Virginia Infantry	May 30, 1864, Gaines Mill, Virginia	Point Lookout, Maryland, transferred to Elmira Prison, NY July 23, 1864	Oath of Allegiance May 17, 1865
Fitzgerald, Samuel M. Private	18	March 4, 1862, Aberdeen, Alabama	Co. J, 11th Mississippi Infantry	June 6, 1864, Cold Harbor, Virginia	Point Lookout, Maryland, transferred to Elmira Prison, NY July 25, 1864	Oath of Allegiance May 29, 1865
Fitzgerald, Thomas Seaman	Unk	Unknown	Confederate States Steamer Bomb Shell	May 5, 1864, Albemarle Sound, North Carolina	Point Lookout, Maryland, transferred to Elmira Prison, NY July 23, 1864	Oath of Allegiance October 10, 1864

Name & Rank	Age	Enlisted	Regiment and State	Where Captured	Prison	Remarks
Fitzgerald, Thomas Private	Unk	April 30, 1861, New Orleans, Louisiana	Co. H, 5th Louisiana Infantry	May 5, 1864, Wilderness, Virginia	Point Lookout, Maryland, transferred to Elmira Prison, NY August 17, 1864	Exchanged February 13, 1865 at Boulware's Wharf on the James River, Virginia
Fitzhugh, Richard Allen Sergeant	18	April 23, 1861, Gloucester Court House, Virginia	Co. B, 26th Virginia Infantry	June 15, 1864, Near Petersburg, Virginia	Point Lookout, Maryland, transferred to Elmira Prison, NY July 17,1864	Exchanged March 10, 1865 at Boulware's Wharf on the James River, Virginia
Fitzpatrick, John Private	Unk	January 17, 1863, Pulaski, Virginia	Co. E, 30th Battalion Virginia Sharp Shooters	July 15, 1864, Leesburg, Virginia	Old Capital Prison, Washington D. C. Transferred to Elmira Prison, NY August 12, 1864	Oath of Allegiance May 29, 1865
Fitzpatrick, Thomas Corporal	Unk	April 15, 1861, Livingston, Alabama	Co. G, 5th Alabama Infantry	May 5, 1864, Wilderness, Virginia	Point Lookout, Maryland, transferred to Elmira Prison, NY August 17, 1864	Oath of Allegiance June 19, 1865
Fitzsimmons, Michael Private	Unk	Unknown	Co. B, 35th Battalion Virginia Cavalry	August 2, 1864, Potomac Run, Maryland	Old Capital Prison, Washington D. C. Transferred to Elmira Prison, NY August 12, 1864	Exchanged March 14, 1865 at Boulware's Wharf on the James River, Virginia
Fix, James Private	25	April 23, 1861, Brownsburg, Virginia	Co. H, 25th Virginia Infantry	May 5, 1864, Wilderness, Virginia	Point Lookout, Maryland, transferred to Elmira Prison, NY August 2, 1864	Exchanged March 2, 1865 at Akins Landing on the James River, Virginia
Fix, William J. Private	28	July 16, 1861, Staunton, Virginia	Co. C, 52nd Virginia Infantry	May 30, 1864 Mechanicsville, Virginia	Point Lookout, Maryland, transferred to Elmira Prison, NY July 11, 1864	Oath of Allegiance May 13, 1865

Name & Rank	Age	Enlisted	Regiment and State	Where Captured	Prison	Remarks
Fizer, David Private	26	March 20, 1864, Orange, Virginia	Co. C, 42nd Virginia Infantry	May 12, 1864, Spotsylvania, Virginia	Old Capital Prison, Washington, DC, transferred to Elmira Prison, NY, July 23, 1864	Oath of Allegiance June 27, 1865
Fizer, Robert A. Private	Unk	May 18, 1861, Lisbon, Virginia	Co. C, 42nd Virginia Infantry	May 12, 1864, Spotsylvania Court House, Virginia	Point Lookout, Maryland, transferred to Elmira Prison, NY August 2,1864	Oath of Allegiance June 30, 1865
Flanagan, George P. Private	Unk	March 29, 1862, Lewisburg, Virginia	Co. D, 26th Virginia Infantry	June 1, 1864, Gaines Mill, Virginia	Point Lookout, Maryland, transferred to Elmira Prison, NY July 17,1864	Oath of Allegiance May 17, 1865
Flanagan, George W. Private	18	July 30, 1861, Livingston, Tennessee	Co. B, 25th Tennessee Infantry	May 16, 1864, Drury's Bluff, Virginia	Point Lookout, Maryland, transferred to Elmira Prison, NY July 23, 1864	Oath of Allegiance May 29, 1865
Flanagan, W. B. Private	Unk	Unknown	Co. E, 12th Battalion North Carolina Cavalry	October 13, 1863, Near Weldon, Pasquotank County, North Carolina	Point Lookout, Maryland, transferred to Elmira Prison, NY July 23, 1864	Oath of Allegiance May 17, 1865
Flanders, W. T. Private	Unk	Unknown	Co. K, 8th Georgia Infantry	May 6, 1864, Wilderness, Virginia	Point Lookout, Maryland, transferred to Elmira Prison, NY August 14, 1864	Exchanged October 29, 1864, at Venus Point, Savannah River, GA.
Flanegan, Barney Private	Unk	December 31, 1862, Mobile, Alabama	Co. A, 1st Battalion Alabama Artillery	August 23, 1864, Fort Morgan, Alabama	Fort Columbus, NY Harbor. Transferred to Elmira Prison Camp, NY, December 5, 1864	Died April 5, 1865 of Pneumonia, Grave No. 2660. Headstone has Flanagan.
Flanigan, Alfred Private	Unk	August 22, 1863, Fort Caswell, Brunswick County, North Carolina	Co. D, 36th Regiment, 2nd North Carolina Artillery	January 15, 1865, Fort Fisher, North Carolina	February 1, 1865, Elmira Prison Camp, New York	Exchanged March 14, 1865 at Boulware's Wharf on the James River, Virginia

Name & Rank	Age	Enlisted	Regiment and State	Where Captured	Prison	Remarks
Flapps, W. Private	Unk	Unknown	Co. B, 1st Louisiana Infantry	May 15, 1864, Spotsylvania Court House, Virginia	Point Lookout, Maryland, transferred to Elmira Prison, NY July 11, 1864	Exchanged February 25, 1865 at Boulware's or Cox Wharf on the James River, Virginia
Fleenor, Adam B. Private	Unk	July 25, 1862, Warrington County, Virginia	Co. F, 30th Battalion Virginia Sharp Shooters	July 8, 1864, Harper's Ferry, Virginia	Old Capital Prison, Washington, DC, transferred to Elmira Prison, NY, July 23, 1864	Oath of Allegiance May 17, 1865
Fleenor, Harvey G. Private	Unk	April 5, 1863, Washington County, Virginia	Co. I, 48th Virginia Infantry	May 12, 1864, Spotsylvania Court House, Virginia	Point Lookout Prison Camp, Maryland. Transferred to Elmira Prison, August 6, 1864	Died January 13, 1865 of Pneumonia, Grave No. 1467
Fleenor, William H. Private	21	June 26, 1861, Scott County, Virginia	Co. H, 48th Virginia Infantry	May 12, 1864, Near Spotsylvania Court House, Virginia	Point Lookout, Maryland, transferred to Elmira Prison, NY August 6, 1864	Died August 29, 1864 of Typhoid Fever, Grave No. 1467
Fleenor, William W. Private	18	June 16, 1861, Washington County, Virginia	Co. J, 48th Virginia Infantry	May 12, 1864, Near Spotsylvania Court House, Virginia	Point Lookout, Maryland, transferred to Elmira Prison, NY August 6, 1864	Oath of Allegiance June 14, 1865
Fleming, Abraham Private	Unk	April 16, 1862, Rudes Hill, Virginia	Co. F, 2nd Virginia Infantry	May 12, 1864, Near Spotsylvania Court House, Virginia	Point Lookout, Maryland, transferred to Elmira Prison, NY August 6, 1864	Oath of Allegiance May 29, 1865
Fleming, George W. Private	Unk	June 9, 1862, Louisa, Virginia	Co. F, 4th Virginia Cavalry	June 11, 1864, Trevilian Station, Louisa Court House, Virginia	Point Lookout, Maryland, transferred to Elmira Prison, NY July 25, 1864	Exchanged February 25, 1865 at Boulware's Wharf on the James River, Virginia
Fleming, James H. Private	Unk	March 1, 1863, E. H. Rowe's Store, Virginia	Co. F, 26th North Carolina Infantry	June 17, 1864, Near Petersburg, Virginia	Point Lookout, Maryland, transferred to Elmira Prison, NY July 30, 1864	Oath of Allegiance July 11, 1865

Name & Rank	Age	Enlisted	Regiment and State	Where Captured	Prison	Remarks
Fleming, John W. Private	17	February 22, 1864, Gloucester, Virginia	Co. F, 26th Virginia Infantry	June 24, 1864, Near Petersburg, Virginia	Point Lookout Prison Camp, Maryland. Transferred to Elmira Prison Camp, New York July 30, 1864	Died August 21, 1864 of Chronic Diarrhea, Grave No. 31
Fleming, R. H. Private	18	July 8, 1862, Raleigh, North Carolina	Co. E, 23rd North Carolina Infantry	May 20, 1864, Spotsylvania Court House, Virginia	Point Lookout, Maryland, transferred to Elmira Prison, NY July 3, 1864	Oath of Allegiance June 30, 1865
Fleming, S. W. Private	Unk	July 20, 1863, James Island, South Carolina	Co. J, 25th South Carolina Infantry	January 15, 1865, Fort Fisher, North Carolina	January 30, 1865, Elmira Prison Camp, NY	Oath of Allegiance July 11, 1865
Fleming, W. D. Private	19	January 1, 1862, Camp Harley, Georgetown South Carolina	Co. J, 25th South Carolina Infantry	January 15, 1865, Fort Fisher, North Carolina	January 30, 1865, Elmira Prison Camp, NY	Died April 26,1865 of Pneumonia, Grave No. 1637
Flemming, Isaac Private	Unk	November 1, 1862, Raleigh, North Carolina	Co. H, 21st North Carolina Infantry	May 16, 1864, Near Drury's Bluff, Virginia	Point Lookout Prison Camp, Maryland. Transferred to Elmira Prison, NY, August 17, 1864	Died February 9, 1865 of Chronic Diarrhea, Grave No. 1946. Headstone has Fleming, 54th NC.
Flemming, John W. Sergeant	30	May 11, 1862, Charleston, South Carolina	Co. J, 25th South Carolina Infantry	August 21, 1864, Weldon Railroad, Virginia. Gunshot Wound Face and Head.	Old Capital Prison, Washington, DC, transferred to Elmira Prison, NY, December 17, 1864	Exchanged March 2, 1865 at Boulware's Wharf on the James River, Virginia
Flemming, Samuel W. Private	Unk	July 20, 1863, Secessionsville, James Island, South Carolina	Co. I, 25th South Carolina Infantry	January 15, 1865, Fort Fisher, North Carolina	Elmira Prison Camp, New York, January 30, 1865	Died April 26, 1865 of Pneumonia, Grave No. 1423
Fletcher, Garrett H. Sergeant	Unk	June 29, 1861, Wytheville, Virginia	Co. B, 50th Virginia Infantry	May 12, 1864, Spotsylvania Court House, Virginia	Point Lookout, Maryland, transferred to Elmira Prison, NY August 2, 1864	Exchanged March 10, 1865 at Boulware's wharf on the James River, Virginia

Name & Rank	Age	Enlisted	Regiment and State	Where Captured	Prison	Remarks
Fletcher, J. B. Private	Unk	June 29, 1861, Wytheville, Virginia	Co. B, 50th Virginia Infantry	May 12, 1864, Spotsylvania Court House, Virginia	Point Lookout, Maryland, transferred to Elmira Prison, NY August 2, 1864	Oath of Allegiance June 30, 1865
Fletcher, James Private	Unk	April 1, 1863, Lacation Unknown	Co. B, 50th Virginia Infantry	May 12, 1864, Spotsylvania, Virginia	Point Lookout, Maryland, transferred to Elmira Prison, NY July 23, 1864	Oath of Allegiance May 29, 1865
Fletcher, John C. Sergeant	Unk	September 22, 1862, Waynesville, Georgia	Co. G, 7th Georgia Cavalry	June 11, 1864, Trevilian Station, Louisa Court House, Virginia	Point Lookout, Maryland, transferred to Elmira Prison, NY July 25, 1864	Exchanged 10/11/64. Died 10/20/64 of Unknown Disease at Point Lookout Prison, MD.
Fletcher, Richard Private	24	June 19, 1861, Camp Moore, Louisiana	Co. K, 8th Louisiana Infantry	May 5, 1864, Wilderness, Virginia	Point Lookout, Maryland, transferred to Elmira Prison, NY August 17, 1864	Exchanged February 13, 1865 at Boulware's wharf on the James River, Virginia
Fletcher, William A. Private	20	October 20, 1862, Petersburg, Virginia	Co. D, 42nd North Carolina Infantry	June 3, 1864, Gaines Mill, Cold Harbor, Virginia	Point Lookout Prison Camp, Maryland. Transferred to Elmira Prison, NY, July 17, 1864	Died January 27, 1865 of Variola (Smallpox), Grave No. 1637. Headstone has 24th NC.
Flick, Francis M. Private	Unk	April 18, 1861, Harrisonburg, Virginia	Co. B, 10th Virginia Infantry	May 12, 1864, Spotsylvania Court House, Virginia	Point Lookout, Maryland, transferred to Elmira Prison, NY August 2, 1864	Exchanged February 13, 1865 at Boulware's wharf on the James River, Virginia
Flint, Ezekiel Private	Unk	June 1, 1863, Handlie's Hill, Virginia	Co. A, 26th Battalion, Virginia Infantry	June 3, 1864, Gaines Mill, Cold Harbor, Virginia	Point Lookout, Maryland, transferred to Elmira Prison, NY July 17, 1864	Died September 12, 1864 of Chronic Diarrhea, Grave No. 182
Flint, J. E. Private	Unk	May 7, 1862, Augusta, Georgia	Co. C, 20th Battalion Georgia Cavalry	May 30, 1864, Cold Harbor, Virginia	Point Lookout, Maryland, transferred to Elmira Prison, NY July 12, 1864	Exchanged October 29, 1864 at Venus Point, Savannah River, GA.

Name & Rank	Age	Enlisted	Regiment and State	Where Captured	Prison	Remarks
Flippen, Henry W., Private	Unk	June 6, 1861, New Canton, Virginia	Co. C, 44th Virginia Infantry	May 12, 1864, Spotsylvania Court House, Virginia	Point Lookout Prison, Maryland, transferred to Elmira Prison, NY August 2, 1864	Died April 15, 1865 of Chronic Diarrhea, Grave No. 2712
Florrell, Patrick, Private	Unk	December 10, 1861, Farmville, Tennessee	Co. A, Jackson's 1st Regiment, Tennessee Heavy Artillery	August 23, 1864, Fort Morgan, Alabama	New Orleans, Louisiana transferred to Elmira December 4, 1864.	Exchanged February 25, 1865 at Boulware's or Cox Wharf on the James River, Virginia
Flottwell, Richard, Private	27	March 19, 1862, Charleston, South Carolina	Co. E, 25th South Carolina Infantry	January 15, 1865, Fort Fisher, North Carolina	Elmira Prison Camp January 30, 1865	Oath of Allegiance May 29, 1865
Flournoy, D. A., Corporal	Unk	July 29, 1862, Columbus, Tennessee	Co. A, Jackson's 1st Regiment, Tennessee Heavy Artillery	August 23, 1864, Fort Morgan, Alabama	New Orleans, Louisiana transferred to Elmira December 4, 1864.	Exchanged February 13, 1865 at Boulware's wharf on the James River, Virginia
Flournoy, George William, Private	Unk	August 29, 1861, Pensacola, Florida	Co. A, 2nd Florida Infantry	May 12, 1864, Spotsylvania Court House, Virginia	Point Lookout, Maryland, transferred to Elmira Prison, NY August 12, 1864	Oath of Allegiance June 16, 1865
Flowers, Andrew, Private	28	January 1, 1864, Darlington District, South Carolina	Co. B, 21st South Carolina Infantry	June 17, 1864, Petersburg, Virginia	Point Lookout, Maryland, transferred to Elmira Prison, NY July 30, 1864	Died March 29, 1865 of Diarrhea, Grave No. 2498
Flowers, B. Franklin, Private	Unk	Unknown	Co. A, Jackson's 1st Regiment, Tennessee Heavy Artillery	August 23, 1864, Fort Morgan, Alabama	New Orleans, Louisiana transferred to Elmira December 4, 1864.	Had orders for Elmira, New York. Died 12/2/64 of Chronic Diarrhea at Fort Columbus NY Harbor.
Flowers, Henry, Private	Unk	June 28, 1862, Georgetown, South Carolina	Co. F, 4th South Carolina Cavalry	June 11, 1864, Trevilian Station, Louisa Court House, Virginia	Point Lookout Prison Camp, Maryland. Transferred to Elmira Prison Camp, New York July 28, 1864	Died September 22, 1864, of Remittent Fever, Grave No. 479

Name & Rank	Age	Enlisted	Regiment and State	Where Captured	Prison	Remarks
Flowers, James Private	23	May 5, 1862, Fort St. Philips, Brunswick County, North Carolina	Co. G, 36th Regiment 2nd North Carolina Artillery	January 15, 1865, Fort Fisher, North Carolina	February 1, 1865, Elmira Prison Camp, New York	Exchanged February 20, 1865 at Boulware's or Cox Wharf on the James River, Virginia
Flowers, Joel A. Private	Unk	February 3, 1862, Georgetown, South Carolina	Co. F, 4th South Carolina Cavalry	May 28, 1864, Hall's Shop, Virginia	Point Lookout, Maryland, transferred to Elmira Prison, NY July 12, 1864	Died March 15, 1865 of Chronic Diarrhea, Grave No. 1660
Flowers, Thomas D. Private	Unk	February 20, 1863, Darlington District, South Carolina	Co. G, 21st South Carolina Infantry	January 15, 1865, Fort Fisher, North Carolina	January 30, 1865, Elmira Prison Camp, NY	Oath of Allegiance July 11, 1865
Flowers, William T. Private	21	July 10, 1861, Luka, Mississippi	Co. A, 20th Mississippi Infantry	May 16, 1863, Baker's Creek, Champion Hill, Mississippi	Point Lookout, Maryland, transferred to Elmira Prison, NY August 18, 1864	Exchanged February 20, 1865 at Boulware's or Cox Wharf on the James River, Virginia
Floyd, David S. Private	Unk	February 11, 1862, Charleston, South Carolina	Co. G, 27th South Carolina Infantry	June 24, 1864, Near Petersburg, Virginia	Point Lookout, Maryland, transferred to Elmira Prison, NY August 18, 1864	Exchanged February 20, 1865 at Boulware's or Cox Wharf on the James River, Virginia
Floyd, G. W. Private	Unk	November 15, 1862, Shelbyville, Tennessee	Co. A, 17th Tennessee Infantry	June 17, 1864, Petersburg, Virginia	Point Lookout, Maryland, transferred to Elmira Prison, NY July 30, 1864	Exchanged February 25, 1865 at Boulware's or Cox Wharf on the James River, Virginia
Floyd, John F. Corporal	Unk	March 4, 1862, Albany, Georgia	Co. E, 51st Georgia Infantry	June 3, 1864, Gaines Farm Cold Harbor, Virginia	Point Lookout, Maryland, transferred to Elmira Prison, NY July 17, 1864	Oath of Allegiance June 30, 1865
Floyd, John W. Private	Unk	August 4, 1862, Choctaw County, Alabama	Co. E, 1st Battalion Alabama Artillery	August 23, 1864, Fort Morgan, Alabama	Fort Columbus, NY Harbor. Transferred to Elmira Prison Camp, NY, December 5, 1864.	Died February 25, 1865 of Chronic Diarrhea, Grave No. 2273

Name & Rank	Age	Enlisted	Regiment and State	Where Captured	Prison	Remarks
Flynn, Barnard Private	22	February 26, 1862, New Orleans, Louisiana	Co. G, 7th Louisiana Infantry	May 12, 1864, Near Spotsylvania Court House, Virginia	Point Lookout, Maryland, transferred to Elmira Prison, NY August 17, 1864	Exchanged February 25, 1865 at Boulware's or Cox Wharf on the James River, Virginia
Flynn, John Private	Unk	March 15, 1862, Charleston, South Carolina	Co. C, 27th South Carolina Infantry	June 24, 1864, Near Petersburg, Virginia	Point Lookout, Maryland, transferred to Elmira Prison, NY July 25, 1864	Died August 15, 1864 of Chronic Diarrhea, Grave No. 20
Flynn, John Private	Unk	Unknown	Co. G, 12th Virginia Infantry	May 23, 1864, South Anna, Virginia	Point Lookout, Maryland, transferred to Elmira Prison, NY July 25, 1864	Oath of Allegiance May 13, 1865
Flynn, John Private	38	April 30, 1861, Manassas Junction, Virginia	Co. F, 17th Virginia Infantry	April 1, 1865, Petersburg, Virginia. Shell Contusion of Right Leg.	Old Capital Prison, Washington D. C. Transferred to Elmira Prison, NY May 2, 1865.	Oath of Allegiance July 7, 1865
Flynn, M. Civilian	Unk	Unknown	Citizen of Louisiana	September 19, 1864, Tensan Parish, Louisiana	New Orleans, Louisianna Transferred to Elmira Prison, New York, November 19, 1864	Oath of Allegiance June 20, 1865
Flynn, Thomas Private	20	June 4, 1861, Camp Moore, Louisiana	Co. A, 6th Louisiana Infantry	May 5, 1864, Wilderness, Virginia	Point Lookout, Maryland, transferred to Elmira Prison, NY August 17, 1864	Exchanged March 10, 1865 at Boulware's Wharf on the James River, Virginia
Flythe, Henry T. Private	19	May 1, 1862, South Mills, North Carolina	Co. D, 32nd North Carolina Infantry	May 10, 1864, Near Mine Run, Spotsylvania, Virginia	Point Lookout, Maryland, transferred to Elmira Prison, NY August 6, 1864	Died January 7, 1865 of Pneumonia, Grave No. 1502
Flythe, James F. A. Sergeant	Unk	May 13, 1861, Fetterman, Virginia	Co. A, 25th Virginia Infantry	May 12, 1864, Spotsylvania Court House, Virginia	Point Lookout, Maryland, transferred to Elmira Prison, NY August 2, 1864	Died November 27, 1864 of Chronic Diarrhea, Grave No. 902

Name & Rank	Age	Enlisted	Regiment and State	Where Captured	Prison	Remarks
Foard, John J. Private	32	April 29, 1862, White Sulfur Springs, Virginia	Co. F, 26th Virginia Infantry	May 31, 1864, Cold Harbor, Virginia	Point Lookout, Maryland, transferred to Elmira Prison, NY July 17, 1864	Died February 26, 1865 of Chronic Diarrhea, Grave No. 2162
Fogle, W. J. Private	Unk	April 19, 1862, Orangeburg, South Carolina	Co. F, 25th South Carolina Infantry	January 15, 1865, Fort Fisher, North Carolina	January 30, 1865, Elmira Prison Camp, NY	Died March 16, 1865 of Chronic Diarrhea, Grave No. 1679
Folds, George W. Private	Unk	March 1, 1863, Atlanta, Georgia	Co. E, 64th Georgia Infantry	August 16, 1864, New Market, Virginia	Old Capital Prison, Washington, DC. Transferred to Elmira October 27, 1864	Died December 14, 1864 of Pneumonia, Grave No. 1121
Folds, Flannagan Corporal	Unk	August 18, 1862, Orange Court House, Virginia	Co. B, 39th Battalion Virginia	August 16, 1864, Falls Church, Virginia	Old Capital Prison, Washington, DC transferred to Elmira Prison, NY August 27, 1864	Oath of Allegiance May 17, 1865
Foley, Coleman Private	Unk	December 25, 1861, Camp Allegheny, Virginia	Co. G, 25th Virginia Infantry	May 6, 1864, Wilderness, Virginia	Old Capital Prison, Washington D. C. Transferred to Elmira Prison, NY July 14, 1864	Died November 18, 1864 of Pneumonia, Grave No. 967
Folker, Albert Private	22	April 12, 1862, Savannah, Georgia	Co. B, 18th Battalion Georgia Infantry	April 6, 1865, Sailor's Creek, Virginia. Gunshot Wound Face and Right Cheek.	Old Capital Prison, Washington D. C. Transferred to Elmira Prison, NY May 12, 1865.	Oath of Allegiance July 11, 1865
Folks, John A. Private	20	October 21, 1861, Fort Caswell, Brunswick County, North Carolina	Co. A, 36th Regiment, 2nd North Carolina Artillery	January 15, 1865, Fort Fisher, North Carolina	February 1, 1865, Elmira Prison Camp, New York	Died March 14, 1865 of Gangrene of Feet, Grave No. 1672
Folmar, John N. Sergeant	Unk	Unknown	Co. G, 59th Alabama Infantry	May 16, 1864, Bermuda Hundred, Virginia	Point Lookout, Maryland, transferred to Elmira Prison, NY July 6, 1864	Oath of Allegiance June 21, 1865

Name & Rank	Age	Enlisted	Regiment and State	Where Captured	Prison	Remarks
Fontenot, Benjamin Private	Unk	June 4, 1861, Camp Moore, Louisiana	Co. C, 6th Louisiana Infantry	May 5, 1864, Wilderness, Virginia	Point Lookout, Maryland, transferred to Elmira Prison, NY August 17, 1864	Exchanged February 25, 1865 at Boulware's or Cox Wharf on the James River, Virginia
Fontenot, Denis Private	28	March 30, 1862, Opalousas, Louisiana	Co. F, 8th Louisiana Infantry	May 15, 1864, Spotsylvania Court House, Virginia	Point Lookout, Maryland, transferred to Elmira Prison, NY July 6, 1864	Exchanged February 25, 1865 at Boulware's or Cox Wharf on the James River, Virginia
Fontenot, Paul H. Private	Unk	March 3, 1862, St. Landry, Louisiana	Co. C, 6th Louisiana Infantry	May 5, 1864, Wilderness, Virginia	Point Lookout, Maryland, transferred to Elmira Prison, NY August 17, 1864	Exchanged February 25, 1865 at Boulware's or Cox Wharf on the James River, Virginia
Forbes, William T. Private	Unk	June 17, 1861, Rocky Mount, Virginia	Co. K, 42nd Virginia Infantry	May 12, 1864, Spotsylvania Court House, Virginia	Point Lookout, Maryland, transferred to Elmira Prison, NY August 2, 1864	Oath of Allegiance June 27, 1865
Force, George H. Private	20	February 24, 1862, Charleston, South Carolina	Co. B, 25th South Carolina Infantry	January 15, 1865, Fort Fisher, North Carolina	Elmira Prison Camp January 30, 1865	Oath of Allegiance August 7, 1865
Force, L. L. Sergeant	Unk	May 8, 1862, Augusta, Georgia	Co. A, 7th Georgia Cavalry	June 11, 1864, Trevilian Station, Louisa Court House, Virginia	Point Lookout, Maryland, transferred to Elmira Prison, NY July 25, 1864	Oath of Allegiance June 29, 1865
Ford, Charles A. H. Private	34	May 15, 1862, Mecklenburg County, North Carolina	Co. H, 35th North Carolina Infantry	June 17, 1864, Petersburg, Virginia	Point Lookout, Maryland, transferred to Elmira Prison, NY July 30, 1864	Oath of Allegiance July 7, 1865
Ford, Darly D. Private	Unk	June 19, 1861, Camp McDonald, Georgia	Co. K, 18th Georgia Infantry	June 1, 1864, Cold Harbor, Virginia	Point Lookout, Maryland, transferred to Elmira Prison, NY July 17, 1864	Oath of Allegiance June 27, 1865

Name & Rank	Age	Enlisted	Regiment and State	Where Captured	Prison	Remarks
Ford, David C. Private	30	March 8, 1862, Franklinton, Louisiana	Co. J, 9th Louisiana Infantry	May 12, 1864, Spotsylvania Court House, Virginia	Point Lookout, Maryland, transferred to Elmira Prison, NY August 17, 1864	Oath of Allegiance May 29, 1865
Ford, David R. Private	Unk	March 1, 1863, Atlanta, Georgia	Co. E, 64th Georgia Infantry	August 16, 1864, New Market, Virginia	Old Capital Prison, Washington, DC transferred to Elmira Prison, NY August 27, 1864	Died April 19, 1865 of Pneumonia, Grave No. 1375
Ford, Isaac M. Sergeant	Unk	July 25, 1863, Tuskegee, Alabama	Co. H, 61st Alabama Infantry	May 12, 1864, Spotsylvania Court House, Virginia	Point Lookout, Maryland, transferred to Elmira Prison, NY July 30, 1864	Exchanged March 2, 1865 at Akins Landing on the James River, Virginia
Ford, J. L. Private	Unk	November 25, 1862, Camp Prichard, South Carolina	Co. B, 4th South Carolina Cavalry	June 11, 1864, Trevilian Station, Louisa Court House, Virginia	Point Lookout, Maryland, transferred to Elmira Prison, NY July 25, 1864	Exchanged October 29, 1864, at Venus Point, Savannah River, GA.
Ford, J. R. Private	18	July 15, 1862, Raleigh, North Carolina	Co. E, 3rd North Carolina Infantry	May 12, 1864, Near Spotsylvania Court House, Virginia	Point Lookout, Maryland, transferred to Elmira Prison, NY August 14, 1864	Exchanged October 29, 1864, at Venus Point, Savannah River, GA.
Ford, James Private	Unk	Unknown	Co. B, Davis' Battalion, Virginia Infantry	July 16, 1864, Loudoun County, Virginia	Old Capital Prison, Washington, DC, transferred to Elmira Prison, NY, July 23, 1864	Exchanged March 10, 1865 at Boulware's wharf on the James River, Virginia
Ford, James C. Private	Unk	May 27, 1861, Camp Doles, Georgia	Co. K, 4th Georgia Infantry	July 13, 1864, Near Washington DC,	Old Capital Prison, Washington, DC, transferred to Elmira Prison, NY, July 23, 1864	Oath of Allegiance May 13, 1865
Ford, John Private	Unk	May 23, 1861, Guntersville, Marshall County, Alabama	Co. B, 9th Alabama Infantry	May 6, 1864, Wilderness, Virginia	Point Lookout, Maryland, transferred to Elmira Prison, NY August 17, 1864	Oath of Allegiance May 17, 1865

Name & Rank	Age	Enlisted	Regiment and State	Where Captured	Prison	Remarks
Ford, John H. Private	27	March 15, 1864, Fort Fisher, New Hanover, North Carolina	Co. G, 36th Regiment, 2nd North Carolina Artillery	January 15, 1865, Fort Fisher, North Carolina	February 1, 1865, Elmira Prison Camp, New York	Exchanged March 2, 1865. Died May 2, 1865 of Typhoid Fever at Jackson Hospital Richmond, VA
Ford, John T. Private	20	June 6, 1861, Person County, North Carolina	Co. H, 24th North Carolina Infantry	June 17, 1864, Petersburg, Virginia	Point Lookout, Maryland, transferred to Elmira Prison, NY July 30, 1864	Exchanged March 14, 1865 at Boulware's Wharf on the James River, Virginia
Ford, John W. Private	Unk	June 9, 1863, Richmond, Virginia	Co. D, 57th Virginia Infantry	May 30, 1864, Hanover Junction, Virginia	Point Lookout, Maryland, transferred to Elmira Prison, NY July 11,1864	Exchanged October 29, 1864, at Venus Point, Savannah River, GA.
Ford, Joshua Corporal	Unk	March 25, 1862, Scott County, Virginia	Co. A, 48th Virginia Infantry	May 12, 1864, Near Spotsylvania Court House, Virginia	Point Lookout, Maryland, transferred to Elmira Prison, NY August 6, 1864	Died January 1, 1865 of Variola (Smallpox), Grave No. 1139
Ford, Nelson T. Private	Unk	January 14, 1862, Camp Hampton, South Carolina	Co. D, 17th South Carolina Infantry	July 30, 1864, Petersburg, Virginia	Point Lookout, Maryland, transferred to Elmira Prison, NY August 12, 1864	Oath of Allegiance July 7, 1865
Ford, W. Laugley Private	Unk	January 14, 1862, Camp Hampton, South Carolina	Co. D, 17th South Carolina Infantry	July 30, 1864, Petersburg, Virginia	Point Lookout, Maryland, transferred to Elmira Prison, NY August 12, 1864	Oath of Allegiance July 3, 1865
Ford, Z. M. Private	23	October 1, 1863, Raleigh, North Carolina	Co. B, 52nd North Carolina Infantry	May 6, 1864, Wilderness, Virginia	Point Lookout, Maryland, transferred to Elmira Prison, NY July 11, 1864	Exchanged March 2, 1865 at Akins Landing on the James River, Virginia
Fordham, B. J. Private	Unk	Unknown	Co. A, 4th Florida Infantry	September 27, 1864, Marianna, Florida	New Orleans, Louisiana transferred to Elmira November 19, 1864.	Oath of Allegiance June 23, 1865

501

Name & Rank	Age	Enlisted	Regiment and State	Where Captured	Prison	Remarks
Fore, T. R. Private	19	April 13, 1862, South Carolina	Co. L, 8th South Carolina Infantry	July 29, 1864, Petersburg, Virginia	Point Lookout, Maryland, transferred to Elmira Prison, NY August 12, 1864	Oath of Allegiance July 3, 1865
Forelarger, James H. Private	Unk	Unknown	1st Battalion Maryland Artillery	July 12, 1863, Hagerstown, Maryland	Point Lookout, Maryland, transferred to Elmira Prison, NY August 18, 1864	Exchanged October 29, 1864 at Venus Point, Savannah River, GA.
Foreman, Columbus W. Sergeant	23	August 13, 1861, Craney Island, Virginia	Co. F, 15th Virginia Cavalry	September 14, 1863, Near Culpepper, Virginia	Point Lookout, Maryland, transferred to Elmira Prison, NY August 18, 1864	Exchanged February 25, 1865 at Boulware's or Cox Wharf on the James River, Virginia
Foreman, Jacob K. Sergeant	Unk	September 22, 1862, Waynesville, Georgia	Co. G, 7th Georgia Cavalry	June 11, 1864, Trevilian Station, Louisa Court House, Virginia	Point Lookout, Maryland, transferred to Elmira Prison, NY July 25, 1864	Died August 27, 1864 of Typhoid Fever, Grave No. 98
Foreman, John W. Private	39	August 8, 1861, Oak Grove, Norfolk County, Virginia	Co. G, 61st Virginia Infantry	August 18, 1864, Weldon Railroad Near Petersburg, Virginia. Gunshot Wound Right Hand and Left Side.	Old Capital Prison, Washington, DC transferred to Elmira Prison, NY August 27, 1864	Died February 12, 1865 of Chronic Diarrhea, Grave No. 2053
Foreman, Joshua B. Private	Unk	Unknown Date, Albemarle Sound, North Carolina	Co. H, 17th North Carolina Infantry	June 17, 1864, Beaufort County, North Carolina	Point Lookout, Maryland, transferred to Elmira Prison, NY July 23, 1864	Died December 6, 1864 of Pneumonia, Grave No. 1025
Forest, Calvin Private	17	August 20, 1861, Pitt County, North Carolina	Co. G, 8th North Carolina Infantry	June 1, 1864, Cold Harbor, Virginia. Gunshot Wound Left Temple, Destroying Both Eyes.	Old Capital Prison, Washington, DC transferred to Elmira Prison, NY August 27, 1864	Exchanged February 13, 1865 at Boulware's Wharf on the James River, Virginia
Forester, Thomas A. Private	Unk	July 19, 1861, Monroe, Georgia	Co. F, 16th Georgia Infantry	June 1, 1864, Gaines Farm, Virginia	Point Lookout, Maryland, transferred to Elmira Prison, NY July 17, 1864	Oath of Allegiance July 7, 1865

Name & Rank	Age	Enlisted	Regiment and State	Where Captured	Prison	Remarks
Formyduval, Coval L. Private	17	March 7, 1862, Wilmington, North Carolina	Co. H, 51st North Carolina Infantry	May 16, 1864, Near Drury's Bluff, Virginia	Point Lookout, Maryland, transferred to Elmira Prison, NY August 18, 1864	Exchanged February 13, 1865 at Boulware's wharf on the James River, Virginia
Forrest, John J. Private	Unk	March 23, 1864, Quitman, Georgia	Co. F, 61st Georgia Infantry	May 12, 1864, Spotsylvania Court House, Virginia	Point Lookout, Maryland, transferred to Elmira Prison, NY July 25, 1864	Oath of Allegiance July 11, 1865
Forster, W. P. Civilian	Unk	Unknown	Citizen of Prince William County, Virginia	October 28, 1863, Prince William County, Virginia	Point Lookout, Maryland, transferred to Elmira Prison, NY July 25, 1864	Exchanged October 11, 1864. Nothing Further.
Fort, John H. Private	24	June 1, 1861, Lock's Creek, Fayetteville, North Carolina	Co. F, 24th North Carolina Infantry	June 17, 1864, Petersburg, Virginia	Point Lookout, Maryland, transferred to Elmira Prison, NY July 30, 1864	Died May 10, 1865 of Chronic Diarrhea, Grave No. 2791
Fort, William H. Private	21	February 24, 1862, Wadesboro, North Carolina	Co. H, 43rd North Carolina Infantry	July 14, 1864, Near Washington DC,	Old Capital Prison, Washington, DC, transferred to Elmira Prison, NY, July 23, 1864	Died December 18, 1864 of Pneumonia, Grave No. 1276
Fortlouis, Michael Private	Unk	June 29, 1861, New Orleans, Louisiana	Co. A, Point Coupee Artillery Louisiana	June 18, 1864, Near Morganza, Louisiana	New Orleans, Louisianna Transferred to Elmira Prison, New York, November 19, 1864	Died November 29, 1864 of Pneumonia, Grave No. 995. Headstone has Lewis Forthewis.
Fortner, Benjamin F. Private	Unk	Unknown	Co. C, 50th Virginia Infantry	May 12, 1864, Spotsylvania Court House, Virginia	Point Lookout, Maryland, transferred to Elmira Prison, NY August 2, 1864	Died August 15, 1864 of Chronic Diarrhea, Grave No. 21. Headstone has 5th Virginia.
Fortner, Benjamin G. Private	Unk	February 22, 1862, Wrightsville, Georgia	Co. F, 14th Georgia Infantry	May 12, 1864, Spotsylvania Court House, Virginia	Point Lookout, Maryland, transferred to Elmira Prison, NY July 17, 1864	Oath of Allegiance June 21, 1865

Name & Rank	Age	Enlisted	Regiment and State	Where Captured	Prison	Remarks
Fortner, Julian Private	22	July 15, 1862, Raleigh, North Carolina	Co. E, 1st North Carolina Infantry	May 12, 1864, Spotsylvania Court House, Virginia	Point Lookout, Maryland, transferred to Elmira Prison, NY August 6, 1864	Oath of Allegiance June 14, 1865
Foster, Alva B. Private	Unk	February 26, 1863, Atlanta, Georgia	Co. K, 64th Georgia Infantry	August 17, 1864, Deep Bottom, New Market, Georgia	Old Capital Prison, Washington, DC transferred to Elmira Prison, NY August 29, 1864	Transferred For Exchange 10/11/64 to Point Lookout Prison, MD. Died 10/18/64 of Unknown Causes at US Army Hospital, Baltimore, MD.
Foster, Dean Private	Unk	January 25, 1862, Columbia, South Carolina	Co. H, 22nd South Carolina Infantry	July 29, 1864, Petersburg, Virginia	Point Lookout, Maryland, transferred to Elmira Prison, NY August 12, 1864	Died March 4, 1865 of Diarrhea, Grave No. 2420
Foster, Durrant H. Private	37	March 28, 1863, Magnolia, North Carolina	Co. B, 24th North Carolina Infantry	June 17, 1864, Petersburg, Virginia	Point Lookout, Maryland, transferred to Elmira Prison, NY July 30, 1864	Died October 2, 1864 of Chronic Diarrhea, Grave No. 632. Name Burt H. Foster on Headstone.
Foster, Elisha P. Private	Unk	August 26, 1862, Calhoun, Georgia	Co. A, 21st Georgia Infantry	July 16, 1864, Loudoun County, Virginia	Old Capital Prison, Washington, DC, transferred to Elmira Prison, NY, July 23, 1864	Oath of Allegiance June 16, 1865
Foster, Estly M. Private	Unk	February 21, 1863, Camp Centerville, Virginia	Co. H, 26th, Virginia Infantry	June 3, 1864, Gaines Mill, Cold Harbor, Virginia	Point Lookout, Maryland, transferred to Elmira Prison, NY July 17, 1864	Died September 4, 1864 of Chronic Diarrhea, Grave No. 226
Foster, J. H. Sergeant	Unk	May 18, 1861, Lisbon, Virginia	Co. K, 42nd Virginia Infantry	May 12, 1864, Spotsylvania Court House, Virginia	Point Lookout, Maryland, transferred to Elmira Prison, NY August 2, 1864	Oath of Allegiance June 27, 1865

Name & Rank	Age	Enlisted	Regiment and State	Where Captured	Prison	Remarks
Foster, James B. Sergeant	Unk	August 28, 1861, Summerville, Georgia	Co. K, 21st Georgia Infantry	July 16, 1864, Loudoun County, Virginia	Old Capital Prison, Washington, DC, transferred to Elmira Prison, NY, July 23, 1864	Died December 7, 1864 of Pneumonia, Grave No. 1183
Foster, Jesse M. Private	Unk	Unknown	Co. D, Gober's Regiment Louisiana Cavalry	August 25, 1864, Near Clinton, Louisiana	New Orleans, Louisianna Transferred to Elmira Prison, New York, November 19, 1864	Exchanged February 25, 1865 at Boulware's or Cox Wharf on the James River, Virginia
Foster, John B. Private	Unk	February 7, 862, Gloucester Point, Virginia	Co. B, 26th Virginia Infantry	June 15, 1864, Near Petersburg, Virginia	Point Lookout, Maryland, transferred to Elmira Prison, NY July 12, 1864	Died 12/7/64 of Pneumonia at Elmira, NY. No Grave Found in Woodlawn Cemetery.
Foster, Joseph K. Corporal	21	August 31, 1861, Camp McDonald, Georgia	Co. B, 23rd Georgia Infantry	June 18, 1864, Petersburg, Virginia. Gunshot Wound Right Side Chest.	Old Capital Prison, Washington, DC transferred to Elmira Prison, NY August 29, 1864	Oath of Allegiance June 30, 1865
Foster, Kinard Private	Unk	December 25, 1863, Spartanburg, South Carolina	Co. H, 6th South Carolina Cavalry	July 30, 1864, Lee's Mill, Petersburg, Virginia	Point Lookout, Maryland, transferred to Elmira Prison, NY August 12, 1864	Exchanged February 13, 1865 at Boulware's Wharf on the James River, Virginia
Foster, N. H. Private	Unk	June 20, 1864, Waterproof, Louisiana	Co. A, Harrison's 3rd Louisiana Cavalry	September 30, 1864, Tensan Parish, Louisiana	New Orleans, Louisiana transferred to Elmira November 19, 1864.	Exchanged February 13, 1865 at Boulware's wharf on the James River, Virginia
Foster, Oliver H. Corporal	35	June 2, 1862, Salt Sulfur Springs, Virginia	Co. H, 26th Battalion, Virginia Infantry	June 3, 1864, Gaines Mill, Cold Harbor, Virginia	Point Lookout, Maryland, transferred to Elmira Prison, NY July 17, 1864	Exchanged October 29, 1864, at Venus Point, Savannah River, GA.

Name & Rank	Age	Enlisted	Regiment and State	Where Captured	Prison	Remarks
Foster, Ransom Private	Unk	December 4, 1861, Mountain Spring, Anderson District, South Carolina	Co. J, 18th South Carolina Infantry	July 30, 1864, Petersburg, Virginia	Point Lookout, Maryland, transferred to Elmira Prison, NY August 12, 1864	Exchanged October 29, 1864, at Venus Point, Savannah River, GA.
Foster, Robert Private	35	July 27, 1861, Camp Moore, Louisiana	Co. G, 10th Louisiana Infantry	May 13, 1864, Spotsylvania Court House, Virginia	Old Capital Prison, Washington, DC, transferred to Elmira Prison, NY, July 23, 1864	Exchanged February 13, 1865 at Boulware's wharf on the James River, Virginia
Foster, T. A. Private	Unk	February 1, 1863, Choctaw Bluff, Alabama	Co. A, 21st Alabama Infantry	August 23, 1864, Fort Morgan, Alabama	Steam Press No. 4 New Orleans, Louisiana transferred to Elmira October 8, 1864.	Exchanged March 2, 1865 at Akins Landing on the James River, Virginia
Foster, Thomas Private	25	March 18, 1862, Mocksville, Davie County, North Carolina	Co. E, 42nd North Carolina Infantry	June 1, 1864, Gaines Farm, Virginia	Point Lookout, Maryland, transferred to Elmira Prison, NY July 17, 1864	Died June 12, 1865 of Chronic Diarrhea, Grave No. 2884
Foster, Thomas R. Private	Unk	Unknown	Co. A, 21st Alabama Infantry	August 23, 1864, Fort Morgan, Alabama	Steam Press No. 4 New Orleans, Louisiana transferred to Elmira October 8, 1864.	Exchanged March 2, 1865 at Akins Landing on the James River, Virginia
Fountain, William Private	Unk	February 26, 1863, Thunderbolt, Georgia	Co. G, 7th Georgia Cavalry	June 11, 1864, Trevilian Station, Louisa Court House, Virginia	Point Lookout, Maryland, transferred to Elmira Prison, NY July 23, 1864	Died February 21, 1865 of Variola (Smallpox), Grave No. 2234
Foust, John F. Private	Unk	March 1, 1864, Raleigh, North Carolina	Co. M, 21st North Carolina Infantry	July 8, 1864, Harper's Ferry, Virginia	Old Capital Prison, Washington, DC, transferred to Elmira Prison, NY, July 23, 1864	Oath of Allegiance June 23, 1865
Fowler, Farrington Private	20	April 1, 1861, Pittsboro, North Carolina	Co. I, 32nd North Carolina Infantry	May 10, 1864, Wilderness, Virginia	Point Lookout, Maryland, transferred to Elmira Prison, NY August 6, 1864	Oath of Allegiance May 29, 1865

Name & Rank	Age	Enlisted	Regiment and State	Where Captured	Prison	Remarks
Fowler, Henry Private	30	April 27, 1861, Winchester, Tennessee	Co. B, 1st Tennessee Infantry	May 2, 1864, Ely's Ford, Wilderness, Virginia	Point Lookout, Maryland, transferred to Elmira Prison, NY August 17, 1864	Exchanged February 25, 1865 at Boulware's or Cox Wharf on the James River, Virginia
Fowler, Hosea Private	Unk	February 17, 1863, Charleston, South Carolina	Co. K, 27th South Carolina Infantry	June 24, 1864, Near Petersburg, Virginia	Point Lookout, Maryland, transferred to Elmira Prison, NY August 18, 1864	Died February 3, 1865 of Typhoid Fever, Grave No. 1750
Fowler, J. S. Private	Unk	Unknown	Co. H, Collins' Regiment Texas Cavalry	September 5, 1864, Near Alchafalaya Bayou, Louisiana	New Orleans, Louisianna Transferred to Elmira Prison, New York, November 19, 1864	Died January 28, 1865 of Typhoid Fever, Grave No. 1654
Fowler, Newton F. Private	Unk	January 28, 1864, Charleston, South Carolina	Co. F, 18th South Carolina Infantry	July 30, 1864, Petersburg, Virginia	Point Lookout, Maryland, transferred to Elmira Prison, NY August 12, 1864	Died August 31, 1864 of Typhoid Fever, Grave No. 93
Fowler, W. Private	20	15th 1861, Brevard, North Carolina	Co. E, 25th North Carolina Infantry	June 17, 1864, Petersburg, Virginia	Point Lookout, Maryland, transferred to Elmira Prison, NY July 30, 1864	Oath of Allegiance July 3, 1865
Fowler, W. H. Private	Unk	February's 1st 1861, Hall County, Georgia	Co. G, 24th Georgia Infantry	August 16, 1864, Front Royal, Virginia	Old Capital Prison, Washington, DC transferred to Elmira Prison, NY August 29, 1864	Oath of Allegiance July 7, 1865
Fowler, William Private	Unk	September 17, 1862, Hot Springs, Arkansas	Co. K, 3rd Arkansas Infantry	May 12, 1864, Spotsylvania Court House, Virginia	Point Lookout, Maryland, transferred to Elmira Prison, NY July 30, 1864	Oath of Allegiance June 19, 1865
Fowler, William B. Private	Unk	January 29, 1863, Choctaw Bluff, Alabama	Co. A, 21st Alabama Infantry	August 23, 1864, Fort Morgan, Alabama	Steam Press No. 4 New Orleans, Louisiana transferred to Elmira October 8, 1864.	Died January 3, 1865 of Chronic Diarrhea, Grave No. 1337

Name & Rank	Age	Enlisted	Regiment and State	Where Captured	Prison	Remarks
Fowler, Young A. Private	Unk	December 28, 1861, Camp Walsh, Adam's Run, South Carolina	Co. E, Holcombe Legion, South Carolina	May 8, 1864, Jarrett's Depot, Virginia	Point Lookout, Maryland, transferred to Elmira Prison, NY August 17, 1864	Exchanged October 29, 1864, at Venus Point, Savannah River, GA.
Fox, Anderson H. Private	25	June 11, 1861, Hevener's Store, Virginia	Co. H, 25th Virginia Infantry	May 6, 1864, Wilderness, Virginia	Old Capital Prison, Washington D. C. Transferred to Elmira Prison, NY July 14, 1864	Exchanged March 10, 1865 at Boulware's Wharf on the James River, Virginia
Fox, Andrew J. Private	23	April 1, 1861, Pittsboro, North Carolina	Co. I, 32nd North Carolina Infantry	May 10, 1864, Wilderness, Virginia	Point Lookout, Maryland, transferred to Elmira Prison, NY August 6, 1864	Oath of Allegiance June 23, 1865
Fox, Gabriel C. Sergeant	Unk	July 2, 1861, Wytheville, Virginia	Co. C, 50th Virginia Infantry	May 12, 1864 Spotsylvania Court House, Virginia	Point Lookout, Maryland, transferred to Elmira Prison, NY August 2, 1864	Oath of Allegiance June 23, 1865
Fox, George Private	25	June 7, 1861, Camp Moore, Louisiana	Co. B, 7th Louisiana Infantry	May 11, 1864, Near Spotsylvania Court House, Virginia	Point Lookout, Maryland, transferred to Elmira Prison, NY August 17, 1864	Exchanged February 25, 1865 at Boulware's or Cox Wharf on the James River, Virginia
Fox, Henry C. Private	Unk	June 18, 1863, Augusta, Virginia	Co. F, 21st Virginia Infantry	July 15, 1864, Loudoun County, Virginia	Old Capital Prison, Washington, DC, transferred to Elmira Prison, NY, July 23, 1864	Exchanged October 29, 1864, at Venus Point, Savannah River, GA.
Fox, Isaiah Private	37	March 26, 1863, Chatham County, North Carolina	Co. G, 40th Regiment, 3rd North Carolina Artillery	January 15, 1865, Fort Fisher, North Carolina	Elmira Prison Camp January 30, 1865	Died April 4, 1865 of Chronic Rheumatism, Grave No. 2561
Fox, J. Private	Unk	Unknown	Co. A, 30th Virginia Infantry	June 1, 1864, Ashland, Virginia	Point Lookout, Maryland, transferred to Elmira Prison, NY July 17,1864	Oath of Allegiance June 16, 1865

Name & Rank	Age	Enlisted	Regiment and State	Where Captured	Prison	Remarks
Fox, James L. Private	Unk	August 19, 1863, Morganton, North Carolina	Co. L, 16th North Carolina Infantry	May 6, 1864, Wilderness, Virginia	Point Lookout, Maryland, transferred to Elmira Prison, NY August 14, 1864	Exchanged October 29, 1864, at Venus Point, Savannah River, GA.
Fox, James M. Private	Unk	March 25, 1864, Lick's Creek, Tennessee	Co. H, 23rd Tennessee Infantry	June 17, 1864, Petersburg, Virginia	Point Lookout, Maryland, transferred to Elmira Prison, NY July 30, 1864	Oath of Allegiance May 17, 1865
Fox, James R. Private	Unk	May 31, 1861, Yellow Branch, Virginia	Co. I, 42nd Virginia Infantry	May 12, 1864, Spotsylvania Court House, Virginia	Point Lookout, Maryland, transferred to Elmira Prison, NY August 12, 1864	Oath of Allegiance June 23, 1865
Fox, John M. Corporal	19	July 15, 1862, Raleigh, North Carolina	Co. A, 5th North Carolina Infantry	May 12, 1864, Spotsylvania Court House, Virginia	Point Lookout, Maryland, transferred to Elmira Prison, NY August 6, 1864	Oath of Allegiance June 12, 1865
Fox, John M. Private	22	April 15, 1861, Pittsboro, North Carolina	Co. J, 32nd North Carolina Infantry	July 14, 1864, Near Washington DC,	Old Capital Prison, Washington, DC, transferred to Elmira Prison, NY, July 23, 1864	Oath of Allegiance May 29, 1865
Fox, Wesley Private	Unk	August 8, 1862, Statesville, North Carolina	Co. G, 37th North Carolina Infantry	June 15, 1864, Petersburg, Virginia	Point Lookout, Maryland, transferred to Elmira Prison, NY July 30, 1864	Died January 30, 1865 of Variola (Smallpox), Grave No. 1794
Foxwell, George W. Sergeant	32	May 28, 1861, E. H. Rowe's Store, Virginia	Co. E, 26th North Carolina Infantry	June 17, 1864, Near Petersburg, Virginia	Point Lookout, Maryland, transferred to Elmira Prison, NY July 30, 1864	Oath of Allegiance July 7, 1865
Foxworth, Samuel W. Private	Unk	April 1, 1864, Green Pond, South Carolina	Co. F, 4th South Carolina Cavalry	May 28, 1864, Hall's Shop, Virginia	Point Lookout, Maryland, transferred to Elmira Prison, NY July 12, 1864	Exchanged October 29, 1864, at Venus Point, Savannah River, GA.

Name & Rank	Age	Enlisted	Regiment and State	Where Captured	Prison	Remarks
Foy, George W. Private	21	May 13, 1861, Golden Place, Onslow County, North Carolina	Co. E, 3rd North Carolina Infantry	May 12, 1864, Near Spotsylvania Court House, Virginia	Point Lookout Prison, Maryland. Transferred to Elmira Prison Camp New York August 14, 1864.	Oath of Allegiance June 30, 1865
Fraley, Nelson H. Private	Unk	August 19, 1863, Russell County, Virginia	Co. A, 22nd Virginia Cavalry	July 8, 1864, Harper's Ferry, Virginia	Old Capital Prison, Washington, DC, transferred to Elmira Prison, NY, July 23, 1864	Oath of Allegiance June 27, 1865
France, Robert L. Private	Unk	Unknown	Co. H, 1st Maryland Cavalry	November 28, 1864, Loudoun County, Virginia	Old Capital Prison, Washington, DC, transferred to Elmira Prison, NY, December 17, 1864	Exchanged March 14, 1865 at Boulware's Wharf on the James River, Virginia
Frances, William Private	18	June 10, 1864, Fort Caswell, North Carolina	Co. F, 25th North Carolina Infantry	March 25, 1865, Fort Steadman, Virginia. Gunshot Wound Right Chest.	Old Capital Prison, Washington D. C. Transferred to Elmira Prison, NY May 12, 1865.	Oath of Allegiance July 7, 1865
Francis, Presley Private	22	May 4, 1861, Stokes County, North Carolina	Co. A, 2nd Battalion North Carolina Infantry	July 17, 1864, Beltsville, Maryland	Old Capital Prison, Washington, DC, transferred to Elmira Prison, NY, July 23, 1864	Died September 27, 1864 of Chronic Diarrhea, Grave No. 392
Francis, Samuel Private	24	June 27, 1861, Halifax County, North Carolina	Co. K, 1st North Carolina Infantry	May 12, 1864, Spotsylvania Court House, Virginia	Point Lookout, Maryland, transferred to Elmira Prison, NY August 6, 1864	Oath of Allegiance June 12, 1865
Franklin, Charles R. Private	Unk	May 18, 1861, Lisbon, Virginia	Co. C, 42nd Virginia Infantry	May 12, 1864, Spotsylvania Court House, Virginia	Point Lookout, Maryland, transferred to Elmira Prison, NY August 2, 1864	Exchanged March 14, 1865 at Boulware's Wharf on the James River, Virginia

Name & Rank	Age	Enlisted	Regiment and State	Where Captured	Prison	Remarks
Franklin, D. B. Private	Unk	June 14, 1861, Camp McDonald, Georgia	Co. C, 18th Georgia Infantry	June 1, 1864, Cold Harbor, Virginia	Point Lookout, Maryland, transferred to Elmira Prison, NY July 17, 1864	Oath of Allegiance July 11, 1865
Franklin, Ennis Private	Unk	Unknown	Co. A, 1st Battalion Alabama Artillery	August 23, 1864, Fort Morgan, Alabama	New Orleans, Louisiana transferred to Elmira December 4, 1864.	Died March 6, 1865 of Variola (Smallpox), Grave No. 2387
Franklin, George T. Sergeant	Unk	June 15, 1861, Lynchburg, Virginia	Co. A, 42nd Virginia Infantry	May 12, 1864, Spotsylvania Court House, Virginia	Point Lookout, Maryland, transferred to Elmira Prison, NY August 2, 1864	Oath of Allegiance June 19, 1865
Franklin, L. L. Sergeant	Unk	July 11, 1861, Lynchburg, Virginia	Co. I, 42nd Virginia Infantry	May 12, 1864, Spotsylvania Court House, Virginia	Point Lookout, Maryland, transferred to Elmira Prison, NY August 2, 1864	Exchanged October 29, 1864, at Venus Point, Savannah River, GA.
Franklin, William H. Private	Unk	July 15, 1861, Salem, Virginia	Co. D, 5th Virginia Cavalry	May 31, 1864, Cold Harbor, Virginia	Point Lookout, Maryland, transferred to Elmira Prison, NY July 11,1864	Died March 28, 1865 of Variola (Smallpox), Grave No. 2479
Franklin, William W. Private	Unk	July 19, 1861, Richmond, Virginia	Co. D, 25th North Carolina Infantry	June 17, 1864, Petersburg, Virginia	Point Lookout, Maryland, transferred to Elmira Prison, NY July 30, 1864	Died November 2, 1864 of Chronic Diarrhea, Grave No. 755
Franks, Francis M. Private	Unk	June 9, 1861, Jones County, Georgia	Co. B, 12th Georgia Infantry	May 10, 1864, Spotsylvania Court House, Virginia	Point Lookout, Maryland, transferred to Elmira Prison, NY July 25, 1864	Oath of Allegiance July 11, 1865
Franks, N. Private	Unk	Unknown	Co. J, 20th North Carolina Infantry	May 20, 1864, Spotsylvania Court House, Virginia	Point Lookout, Maryland, transferred to Elmira Prison, NY July 12,1864	Exchanged February 20, 1865 at Boulware's or Cox Wharf on the James River, Virginia

Name & Rank	Age	Enlisted	Regiment and State	Where Captured	Prison	Remarks
Frasier, H. J. Private	Unk	May 11, 1861, New Orleans, Louisiana	Co. K, 2nd Louisiana Infantry	May 10, 1864, Spotsylvania, Virginia	Point Lookout, Maryland, transferred to Elmira Prison, NY August 17, 1864	Exchanged February 25, 1865 at Boulware's or Cox Wharf on the James River, Virginia
Frazel, Vulcan Private	21	May 6, 1861, Jacksonville, North Carolina	Co. B, 24th North Carolina Infantry	June 17, 1864, Petersburg, Virginia	Point Lookout, Maryland, transferred to Elmira Prison, NY July 30, 1864	Oath of Allegiance June 19, 1865
Frazier, Hugh Private	40	May 17, 1861, Montgomery, Alabama	Co. H, 6th Alabama Infantry	July 28, 1864, Near Washington, DC. Gunshot Wound Right Leg.	Old Capital Prison, Washington, DC, transferred to Elmira Prison, NY, December 17, 1864	Exchanged February 13, 1865. Sent to Fort McHenry, MD, Where he Died May 10, 1865 from Infection.
Frazier, Jacob Private	17	March 8, 1862, Rolesville, North Carolina	Co. J, 1st North Carolina Infantry	May 12, 1864, Spotsylvania Court House, Virginia	Point Lookout, Maryland, transferred to Elmira Prison, NY August 6, 1864	Oath of Allegiance June 12, 1865
Frazier, Tison W. Private	19	March 1, 1862, Stokes County, North Carolina	Co. H, 22nd North Carolina Infantry	May 31, 1864, Mechanicsville, Virginia	Point Lookout, Maryland, transferred to Elmira Prison, NY July 11, 1864	Oath of Allegiance June 30, 1865
Frazier, William O. Private	Unk	March 15, 1862, Lynchburg, Virginia	Co. D, 42nd Virginia Infantry	May 12, 1864, Near Spotsylvania Court House, Virginia	Point Lookout, Maryland, transferred to Elmira Prison, NY August 2, 1864	Exchanged February 20, 1865 at Boulware's or Cox Wharf on the James River, Virginia
Frazor, William Private	Unk	December 17, 1861, Camp Trousdale, Tennessee	Co. H, 44th Tennessee Infantry	June 17, 1864, Petersburg, Virginia	Point Lookout, Maryland, transferred to Elmira Prison, NY July 30, 1864	Exchanged February 25, 1865 at Boulware's or Cox Wharf on the James River, Virginia
Frederick, Alfred E. Private	Unk	February 15, 1862, Kenansville, Duplin County, North Carolina	Co. B, 3rd North Carolina Infantry	May 12, 1864, Near Spotsylvania, Virginia	Point Lookout, Maryland, transferred to Elmira Prison, NY August 14, 1864	Died December 4, 1864 of Pneumonia, Grave No. 886

Name & Rank	Age	Enlisted	Regiment and State	Where Captured	Prison	Remarks
Frederick, Elihu Private	24	May 27, 1861, Wilmington, North Carolina	Co. D, 3rd North Carolina Infantry	May 12, 1864, Near Spotsylvania, Virginia	Point Lookout, Maryland, transferred to Elmira Prison, NY August 14, 1864	Died January 22, 1865 of Variola (Smallpox), Grave No. 1592. Elisha on Headstone.
Frederick, Patrick Private	21	May 27, 1861, Wilmington, North Carolina	Co. D, 3rd North Carolina Infantry	May 12, 1864, Near Spotsylvania, Virginia	Point Lookout, Maryland, transferred to Elmira Prison, NY August 14, 1864	Oath of Allegiance June 21, 1865
Free, R. M. Civilian	Unk	Randolph County, North Carolina	Citizen of North Carolina	April 21, 1864, Wilmington, North Carolina	Point Lookout, Maryland, transferred to Elmira Prison, NY July 23, 1864	Oath of Allegiance May 11, 1865
Freeman, Ansel H. Private	27	May 5, 1861, Roxboro, North Carolina	Co. A, 24th North Carolina Infantry	June 17, 1864, Petersburg, Virginia	Point Lookout, Maryland, transferred to Elmira Prison, NY July 30, 1864	Oath of Allegiance May 13, 1865
Freeman, Chapman Private	15	December 20, 1861, Cheraw, South Carolina	Co. D, 21st South Carolina Infantry	January 15, 1865, Fort Fisher, North Carolina	January 30, 1865, Elmira Prison Camp, NY	Oath of Allegiance July 11, 1865
Freeman, George Private	28	April 1, 1862, Windsor, North Carolina	Co. G, 32nd North Carolina Infantry	July 4, 1864, Harper's Ferry, Virginia	Old Capital Prison, Washington, DC, transferred to Elmira Prison, NY, July 23, 1864	Exchanged March 10, 1865 at Boulware's wharf on the James River, Virginia
Freeman, George Private	24	April 22, 1862, Guilford County, North Carolina	Co. A, 53rd North Carolina Infantry	May 15, 1864, Spotsylvania Court House, Virginia	Point Lookout, Maryland, transferred to Elmira Prison, NY July 6, 1864	Oath of Allegiance June 14, 1865
Freeman, George Private	Unk	Unknown	Co. D, 25th South Carolina Infantry	January 15, 1865, Fort Fisher, North Carolina	Elmira Prison Camp January 30, 1865	Died February 25, 1865 of Pneumonia, Grave No. 2270
Freeman, George W. Private	30	February 1, 1862, Jamesville, North Carolina	Co. H, 1st North Carolina Infantry	May 12, 1864, Spotsylvania Court House, Virginia	Point Lookout, Maryland, transferred to Elmira Prison, NY August 6, 1864	Died September 20, 1864 of chronic Diarrhea, Grave No. 329

Name & Rank	Age	Enlisted	Regiment and State	Where Captured	Prison	Remarks
Freeman, Isaac P. Private	24	May 7, 1862, Goldsboro, North Carolina	Co. G, 45th North Carolina Infantry	May 10, 1864, Spotsylvania Court House, Virginia	Point Lookout, Maryland, transferred to Elmira Prison, NY August 6, 1864	Oath of Allegiance June 16, 1865
Freeman, John H. Private	28	May 6, 1862, Coffeyville, Texas	Co. H, 18th Texas Infantry	March 14, 1864, Fort DeRussy, Louisiana	New Orleans, Louisianna Transferred to Elmira Prison, New York, November 19, 1864	Oath of Allegiance May 29, 1865
Freeman, Lewis L. Private	30	December 20, 1861, Chesterfield District, South Carolina	Co. E, 21st South Carolina Infantry	June 24, 1864, Petersburg, Virginia	Point Lookout, Maryland, transferred to Elmira Prison, NY August 18, 1864	Exchanged October 29, 1864, at Venus Point, Savannah River, GA.
Freeman, Samuel J. B. Private	Unk	May 3, 1862, Covington, Georgia	Co. E, 53rd Georgia Infantry	June 1, 1864, Gaines Mill, Cold Harbor, Virginia	Point Lookout, Maryland, transferred to Elmira Prison, NY July 17,1864	Oath of Allegiance June 19, 1865
Freeman, William Private	23	December 20, 1861, Chesterfield District, South Carolina	Co. E, 21st South Carolina Infantry	June 24, 1864, Petersburg, Virginia	Point Lookout, Maryland, transferred to Elmira Prison, NY August 18, 1864	Exchanged October 29, 1864, at Venus Point, Savannah River, GA.
Freeman, William Private	43	August 17, 1863, Fort Branch, Martin County, North Carolina	Co. G, 40th Regiment, 3rd North Carolina Artillery	January 15, 1865, Fort Fisher, North Carolina	Elmira Prison Camp January 30, 1865	Died February 9, 1865 of Pneumonia, Grave No. 1939
Freez, John M. Private	19	August 14, 1864, Mount Pleasant, North Carolina	Co. H, 8th North Carolina Infantry	June 1, 1864, Gaines Mill, Cold Harbor, Virginia	Point Lookout, Maryland, transferred to Elmira Prison, NY July 17,1864	Oath of Allegiance June 16, 1865
French, Ellis Private	21	June 15, 1861, Buena Vista, Georgia	Co. K, 12th Georgia Infantry	May 10, 1864, Spotsylvania Court House, Virginia	Old Capital Prison, Washington, DC transferred to Elmira Prison, NY August 27, 1864	Exchanged February 20, 1865 at Boulware's or Cox Wharf on the James River, Virginia

Name & Rank	Age	Enlisted	Regiment and State	Where Captured	Prison	Remarks
French, James H. Private	Unk	October 15, 1864, New Market, Virginia	Co. I, 60th Virginia Infantry	August 22, 1863, Woodstock, Virginia	Point Lookout, Maryland, transferred to Elmira Prison, NY August 18, 1864	Exchanged March 10, 1865 at Boulware's Wharf on the James River, Virginia
French, John J. Private	Unk	April 25, 1861, Powhatan Court House, Virginia	Co. E, 4th Virginia Cavalry	August 16, 1864, Front Royal, Virginia	Old Capital Prison, Washington, DC transferred to Elmira Prison, NY August 29, 1864	Exchanged October 29, 1864, at Venus Point, Savannah River, GA.
French, John W. Private	Unk	June 25, 1861, Wyhteville, Virginia	Co. I, 50th Virginia Infantry	May 12, 1864, Spotsylvania Court House, Virginia	Point Lookout, Maryland, transferred to Elmira Prison, NY August 2, 1864	Exchanged February 13, 1865 at Boulware's wharf on the James River, Virginia
French, William Thomas Private	Unk	March 8, 1862, Clarksburg, Virginia	Co. M, 55th Virginia Infantry	May 5, 1864, Wilderness, Virginia	Point Lookout, Maryland, transferred to Elmira Prison, NY August 14, 1864	Exchanged October 29, 1864 at Venus Point, Savannah River, GA.
Friar, William Private	Unk	June 6, 1861, Greenville, Alabama	Co. G, 9th Alabama Infantry	May 10, 1864, Spotsylvania Court House, Virginia	Point Lookout, Maryland, transferred to Elmira Prison, NY August 17, 1864	Died January 25, 1865 of Chronic Diarrhea, Grave No. 1618
Friary, John Private	27	June 7, 1861, Camp Moore, Louisiana	Co. C, 7th Louisiana Infantry	May 11, 1864, Spotsylvania Court House, Virginia	Point Lookout, Maryland, transferred to Elmira Prison, NY August 17, 1864	Exchanged February 25, 1865 at Boulware's or Cox Wharf on the James River, Virginia
Frick, Daniel Private	31	August 8, 1862, Statesville, North Carolina	Co. I, 5th North Carolina Infantry	May 12, 1864, Spotsylvania Court House, Virginia	Point Lookout, Maryland, transferred to Elmira Prison, NY August 6, 1864	Died January 29, 1865 of Chronic Diarrhea, Grave No. 1805
Fricks, Joseph Private	20	April 9, 1862, Walhalla, South Carolina	Co. C, 1st Orr's South Carolina Infantry	May 24, 1864, Charlesburg, Virginia	Point Lookout, Maryland, transferred to Elmira Prison, NY July 17,1864	Oath of Allegiance June 30, 1865

Name & Rank	Age	Enlisted	Regiment and State	Where Captured	Prison	Remarks
Friday, James G. Private	Unk	August 10, 1861, Richmond, Virginia	McCreary's Co. C, 1st South Carolina Infantry	May 24, 1864, Hanover Junction, Virginia	Point Lookout, Maryland, transferred to Elmira Prison, NY July 12,1864	Exchanged March 10, 1865 at Boulware's Wharf on the James River, Virginia
Friddle, Lewis Private	34	July 8, 1862, Greensboro, North Carolina	Co. A, 1st North Carolina Infantry	May 12, 1864, Wilderness, Spotsylvania Court House, Virginia	Point Lookout, Maryland, transferred to Elmira Prison, NY August 6, 1864	Exchanged October 29, 1864, at Venus Point, Savannah River, GA.
Fridell, John W. Private	Unk	May 1, 1862, Marietta, Georgia	Co. L, Phillips Legion, Georgia	June 2, 1864, Gaines Farm, Virginia	Point Lookout, Maryland, transferred to Elmira Prison, NY July 17,1864	Oath of Allegiance May 14, 1865
Friend, E. B. Private	Unk	March 1, 1863, Tullahoma, Tennessee	Co. A, 17th Tennessee Infantry	June 17, 1864, Petersburg, Virginia	Point Lookout, Maryland, transferred to Elmira Prison, NY July 30, 1864	Exchanged February 25, 1865 at Boulware's or Cox Wharf on the James River, Virginia
Frierson, J. M. Private	Unk	May 9, 1862, Morris Island, South Carolina	Co. K, 23rd South Carolina Infantry	June 15, 1864, Petersburg, Virginia	Point Lookout, Maryland, transferred to Elmira Prison, NY July 25, 1864	Oath of Allegiance June 16, 1865
Fripp, M. S. Private	Unk	May 6, 1862, Camp Gregg, South Carolina	Co. B, 4th South Carolina Cavalry	June 11, 1864, Trevilian Station, Louisa Court House, Virginia	Point Lookout, Maryland, transferred to Elmira Prison, NY July 25, 1864	Exchanged March 14, 1865 at Boulware's Wharf on the James River, Virginia
Fritts, Henry Private	28	July 15, 1862, Raleigh, North Carolina	Co. C, 49th North Carolina Infantry	May 16, 1864, Near Drury's Bluff, Virginia	Point Lookout, Maryland, transferred to Elmira Prison, NY August 18, 1864	Oath of Allegiance January 30, 1865. Early Release per Lincoln's Proclamation, 12/8/1863.
Frizle, John J. Private	27	May 13, 1862, Green County, North Carolina	Co. E, 61st North Carolina Infantry	August 27, 1863, Battery Wagner, Morris Island, South Carolina	Point Lookout, Maryland, transferred to Elmira Prison, NY August 18, 1864	Exchanged March 10, 1865 at Boulware's Wharf on the James River, Virginia

Name & Rank	Age	Enlisted	Regiment and State	Where Captured	Prison	Remarks
Frizzle, Henry H. Sergeant	21	May 13, 1862, Green County, North Carolina	Co. E, 61st North Carolina Infantry	August 27, 1863, Battery Wagner, Morris Island, South Carolina	Point Lookout, Maryland, transferred to Elmira Prison, NY August 18, 1864	Exchanged March 10, 1865 at Boulware's Wharf on the James River, Virginia
Frost, W. T. Private	Unk	March 4, 1862, Hartwell, Georgia	Co. C, 16th Georgia Infantry	June 1, 1864, Gaines Farm, Virginia	Point Lookout, Maryland, transferred to Elmira Prison, NY July 17,1864	Oath of Allegiance June 21, 1865
Fry, Allen H. Sergeant	Unk	Unknown	Co. A, 42nd Virginia Infantry	May 12, 1864, Spotsylvania Court House, Virginia	Point Lookout, Maryland, transferred to Elmira Prison, NY August 2, 1864	Died September 23, 1864 of Remittent Fever, Grave No. 475
Fry, Degraftin Reidt Private	18	March 15, 1862, Carthage, North Carolina	Co. D, 49th North Carolina Infantry	June 2, 1864, Bermuda 100, Cold Harbor, Virginia	Point Lookout, Maryland, transferred to Elmira Prison, NY July 12,1864	Exchanged March 14, 1865 at Boulware's Wharf on the James River, Virginia
Fry, J. S. Private	Unk	February 25, 1863, Catawba Station, North Carolina	Co. F, 32nd North Carolina Infantry	May 10, 1864, Wilderness, Virginia	Point Lookout, Maryland, transferred to Elmira Prison, NY August 6, 1864	Oath of Allegiance July 26, 1865
Fugate, Henry C. Sergeant	23	July 15, 1861, Lee County, Virginia	Co. G, 48th Virginia Infantry	May 12, 1864, Spotsylvania Court House, Virginia	Point Lookout, Maryland, transferred to Elmira Prison, NY August 12, 1864	Oath of Allegiance June 30, 1865
Fuget, R. Private	Unk	Unknown	Co. K, 50th Virginia Infantry	May 6, 1864, Wilderness, Virginia	Point Lookout, Maryland, transferred to Elmira Prison, NY August 14, 1864	Died April 1, 1865 of Diarrhea, Grave No. 2593
Fulcher, Spencer Corporal	Unk	September 5, 1861, Patrick Court House, Virginia	Co. H, 58th Virginia Infantry	May 30, 1864, Mechanicsville, Virginia	Point Lookout, Maryland, transferred to Elmira Prison, NY July 11, 1864	Died April 1, 1865 of Pneumonia, Grave No. 2597

Name & Rank	Age	Enlisted	Regiment and State	Where Captured	Prison	Remarks
Fulenwider, John A Private	Unk	March 20, 1863, Camden, Arkansas	Co. I, 3rd Arkansas Infantry	May 12, 1864, Spotsylvania Court House, Virginia	Point Lookout, Maryland, transferred to Elmira Prison, NY August 12, 1864	Died February 17, 1865 of Pneumonia, Grave No. 2228. Name John A. Thomas on Headstone.
Fulford, Arthur Sergeant	25	March 12, 1862, Norfolk County, Virginia	Co. F, 15th Virginia Cavalry	September 14, 1863, Near Culpepper, Virginia	Point Lookout, Maryland, transferred to Elmira Prison, NY August 18, 1864	Exchanged February 13, 1865 at Boulware's or Cox Wharf on the James River, Virginia
Fulk, William R. M. Private	31	May 30, 1861, Germanton, North Carolina	Co. G, 21st North Carolina Infantry	July 8, 1864, Harper's Ferry, Virginia	Old Capital Prison, Washington, DC, transferred to Elmira Prison, NY, July 23, 1864	Died March 20, 1865 of Diarrhea, Grave No. 1550
Fulkner, A. A. Private	Unk	April 29, 1863, White Sulfur Springs, Virginia	Co. C, 26th Battalion, Virginia Infantry	June 3, 1864, Gaines Farm, Cold Harbor, Virginia	Point Lookout, Maryland, transferred to Elmira Prison, NY July 17, 1864	Oath of Allegiance July 3, 1865
Fuller, Barney Private	Unk	March 9, 1861, Selma, Alabama	Co. C, 1st Battalion Alabama Artillery	August 23, 1864, Fort Morgan, Alabama	New Orleans, Louisiana transferred to Elmira December 4, 1864.	Oath of Allegiance July 11, 1865
Fuller, Byam Private	Unk	March 1, 1862, Franklin County, Georgia	Co. H, 24th Georgia Infantry	June 3, 1864, Gaines Mill, Cold Harbor, Virginia	Transferred From Point Lookout Prison, MD, July 12, 1864. Train Never Arrived at Elmira Prison Camp, NY.	Died July 15, 1864 in Train Wreck at Shohola, Pennsylvania.
Fuller, James R. Private	22	May 5, 1861, Roxboro, North Carolina	Co. A, 24th North Carolina Infantry	June 17, 1864, Petersburg, Virginia	Point Lookout, Maryland, transferred to Elmira Prison, NY July 30, 1864	Oath of Allegiance May 29, 1865

Name & Rank	Age	Enlisted	Regiment and State	Where Captured	Prison	Remarks
Fuller, Robert B. Private	Unk	April 28, 1862, Wilson, North Carolina	Co. H, 7th Confederate Cavalry	May 7, 1864, Lyttleton, Virginia	Point Lookout, Maryland, transferred to Elmira Prison, NY August 17, 1864	Died October 19, 1864 of Chronic Diarrhea, Grave No. 533. Headstone has SC as State.
Fuller, William L. Private	Unk	January 1, 1862, Daviston, Alabama	Co. D, 14th Alabama Infantry	May 6, 1864, Wilderness, Virginia	Point Lookout, Maryland, transferred to Elmira Prison, NY August 17, 1864	Oath of Allegiance June 14, 1865
Fullerton, Henry Private	20	October 28, 1861, Hempstead, Texas	Co. F, 12th Texas Cavalry	August 26, 1864, Concordia Parish, Louisiana	New Orleans, Louisianna Transferred to Elmira Prison, New York, November 19, 1864	Oath of Allegiance June 21, 1865
Fulp, John W. Private	Unk	March 19, 1863, High Point, North Carolina	Co. I, 57th North Carolina Infantry	July 17, 1864, Beltsville, Maryland	Old Capital Prison, Washington, DC, transferred to Elmira Prison, NY, July 23, 1864	Exchanged March 14, 1865 at Boulware's Wharf on the James River, Virginia
Fulton, E. A. Sergeant	Unk	December 18, 1862, Bryan County, Georgia	Co. H, 7th Georgia Cavalry	June 11, 1864, Trevilian Station, Louisa Court House, Virginia	Point Lookout, Maryland, transferred to Elmira Prison, NY July 25, 1864	Oath of Allegiance June 21, 1865
Fulton, Henry H. Private	18	August 6, 1862, Winston, North Carolina	Co. D, 57th North Carolina Infantry	July 8, 1864, Harper's Ferry, Virginia	Old Capital Prison, Washington, DC, transferred to Elmira Prison, NY, July 23, 1864	Oath of Allegiance July 3, 1865
Fulton, R. J. Private	Unk	January 25, 1864, Pocotaligo, South Carolina	Co. J, 4th South Carolina Cavalry	June 11, 1864, Trevilian Station, Louisa Court House, Virginia	Point Lookout, Maryland, transferred to Elmira Prison, NY July 25, 1864	Oath of Allegiance June 19, 1865
Fulton, William T. Private	Unk	May 10, 1862, Americus, Georgia	Co. K, 4th Georgia Infantry	May 15, 1864, wilderness, Virginia	Old Capital Prison, Washington, DC, transferred to Elmira Prison, NY, July 23, 1864	Died August 18, 1864 of Chronic Diarrhea, Grave No. 122

Name & Rank	Age	Enlisted	Regiment and State	Where Captured	Prison	Remarks
Fultz, James B. Sergeant	Unk	May 13, 1861, Harrisonburg, Virginia	Co. B, 10th Virginia Infantry	May 12, 1864, Spotsylvania Court House, Virginia	Point Lookout, Maryland, transferred to Elmira Prison, NY August 2, 1864	Exchanged February 20, 1865 at Boulware's or Cox Wharf on the James River, Virginia
Funck, Charles Private	20	October 5, 1861, Indianola, Texas	Co. B, 8th Texas Infantry	May 4, 1864, Indianola, Texas	New Orleans, Louisianna Transferred to Elmira Prison, New York, November 19, 1864	Oath of Allegiance May 29, 1865
Funderburg, William M. Private	Unk	April 10, 1864, Talladega, Alabama	Co. D, 12th Alabama Infantry	July 10, 1864, Frederick, Maryland	Old Capital Prison, Washington, DC. Transferred to Elmira July 25, 1864	Died November 1, 1864 of Typhoid Fever, Grave No. 747
Funderburk, Laney Nathan Private	Unk	January 9, 1862, Columbia, South Carolina	Co. E, 22nd South Carolina Infantry	July 30, 1864, Petersburg, Virginia	Point Lookout, Maryland, transferred to Elmira Prison, NY August 12, 1864	Died May 26, 1865 of Chronic Diarrhea, Grave No. 2921
Funderburk, William A. Private	27	May 10, 1862, Morgan, Georgia	Co. B, 12th Georgia Infantry	May 10, 1864, Spotsylvania Court House, Virginia	Point Lookout, Maryland, transferred to Elmira Prison, NY July 25, 1864	Oath of Allegiance June 14, 1865
Funk, Andrew J. Private	24	April 24, 1862, Elk Creek, Virginia	Co. F, 4th Virginia Infantry	May 12, 1864 Spotsylvania Court House, Virginia	Point Lookout, Maryland, transferred to Elmira Prison, NY August 2, 1864	Transferred for Exchange 10/11/64. Died 10/18/64 of Unknown Causes at Point Lookout, MD.
Fuqua, W. H. Private	Unk	April 10, 1863, Fincastle, Virginia	Co. L, 26th Battalion, Virginia Infantry	June 3, 1864, Gaines Farm Cold Harbor, Virginia	Point Lookout, Maryland, transferred to Elmira Prison, NY July 17, 1864	Oath of Allegiance July 3, 1865
Fuqua, William F. Private	26	March 5, 1862, Rockingham, North Carolina	Co. G, 45th North Carolina Infantry	May 10, 1864, Spotsylvania Court House, Virginia	Old Capital Prison, Washington, DC transferred to Elmira Prison, NY August 27, 1864	Exchanged February 20, 1865 at Boulware's or Cox Wharf on the James River, Virginia

Name & Rank	Age	Enlisted	Regiment and State	Where Captured	Prison	Remarks
Furgason, Daniel Private	21	August 1, 1861, Confederate Point, Fort Fisher, North Carolina	Co. K, 18th North Carolina Infantry	May 12, 1864, Spotsylvania Court House, Virginia	Point Lookout, Maryland, transferred to Elmira Prison, NY August 6, 1864	Oath of Allegiance June 16, 1865
Furr, Crittenton Sergeant	21	September 7, 1861, Albemarle, North Carolina	Co. K, 28th North Carolina Infantry	May 12, 1864, Spotsylvania Court House, Virginia	Point Lookout, Maryland, transferred to Elmira Prison, NY August 14, 1864	Oath of Allegiance May 29, 1865
Furr, John B. Private	Unk	March 24, 1864, Wilmington, North Carolina	Co. K, 10th Regiment, 1st North Carolina Artillery	January 15, 1865, Fort Fisher, North Carolina	January 30, 1865, Elmira Prison Camp, NY	Died March 3, 1865 of Variola (Smallpox), No Grave Found at Woodlawn National Cemetery.
Furr, Lauson A. Sergeant	28	March 15, 1862, Albemarle, North Carolina	Co. K, 28th North Carolina Infantry	May 12, 1864, Spotsylvania Court House, Virginia	Point Lookout, Maryland, transferred to Elmira Prison, NY August 14, 1864	Died December 6, 1864 of Pneumonia, Grave No. 1191
Furr, Martin Private	20	April 8, 1863, Camp Holmes, Near Raleigh, Wake County, North Carolina	Co. C, 3rd Battalion North Carolina Light Artillery	January 15, 1865, Fort Fisher, North Carolina	February 1, 1865, Elmira Prison Camp, New York	Died February 22, 1865 of Typhoid Fever, Grave No. 2242
Furr, Pinkney Private	Unk	April 27, 1864, Mount Pleasant, North Carolina	Co. H, 8th North Carolina Infantry	June 3, 1864, Gaines Mill, Cold Harbor, Virginia	Point Lookout, Maryland, transferred to Elmira Prison, NY July 17, 1864	Oath of Allegiance June 12, 1865
Furren, Hezekiah P. Private	Unk	October 21, 1863, Dublin Depot, Virginia	Co. L, 26th Battalion, Virginia Infantry	June 3, 1864, Gaines Farm Cold Harbor, Virginia	Point Lookout, Maryland, transferred to Elmira Prison, NY July 17,1864	Exchanged February 13, 1865 at Boulware's wharf on the James River, Virginia
Futch, James I. Private	Unk	April 3, 1862, Bryan County, Georgia	Co. H, 7th Georgia Cavalry	June 11, 1864, Trevilian Station, Louisa Court House, Virginia	Point Lookout, Maryland, transferred to Elmira Prison, NY July 25, 1864. Ward No. 7	Died August 11, 1864 of Chronic Diarrhea, Grave No. 136

Name & Rank	Age	Enlisted	Regiment and State	Where Captured	Prison	Remarks
Futch, Stephen Private	Unk	May 14, 1862, Camp McCarthy, Putnam County, Florida	Co. B, 9th Florida Infantry	August 16, 1864, Petersburg, Virginia	Old Capital Prison, Washington, DC. Transferred to Elmira Prison Camp, NY, October 27, 1864.	Died February 23, 1865 Pneumonia, Grave No. 2268
Futrell, Littleberry Private	30	July 17, 1862, North Hampton, Wake County, North Carolina	Co. E, 56th North Carolina Infantry	June 18, 1864, Petersburg, Virginia	Point Lookout, Maryland, transferred to Elmira Prison, NY July 30, 1864	Died August 25, 1864 of Chronic Diarrhea, Grave No. 44
Futrell, Noah Private	37	February 9, 1863, Wheelersville, North Carolina	Co. D, 32nd North Carolina Infantry	May 10, 1864, Near Mine Run, Spotsylvania, Virginia	Point Lookout, Maryland, transferred to Elmira Prison, NY August 6, 1864	Died December 10, 1864 of Chronic Diarrhea, Grave No. 1047

Notes

Elmira Prison Camp Roster, Volume I

Introduction:

1. To see a copy of the "Elmira Prison Camp Monthly Returns" go to page 478 of volume III of this series or go to the War of the Rebellion Offical Records Series II, Volume 8, Prisoners of War, pages 997-1003.

Why Make a Roster of Confederate Soldiers at Elmira Prison Camp?
Pages 9-10

1. Clay Holmes, *The Elmira Prison Camp,* Page 380.
2. Official Records: Series II, Volume VII, page 891-992.

Elmira Prisoner of War Camp
Pages 11-16

1. Official Records, Series II, Volume VII, pages 62-63;
2. Official Records, Series II, Volume IV, page 68-70;
3. Official Records, Series II, Volume IV, page 70-73;
4. Official Records, Series II, Volume IV, page 67-69;
5. Official Records, Series II, Volume IV, page 72-75;
6. Official Records, Series II, Volume VII, page 146;
7. Official Records, Series II, Volume VII, page 152;
8. Official Records, Series II, Volume VII, page 156-157;
9. Official records, Series II, Volume VII, page 152;
10. Official records, Series II, Volume VII, page 157;
11. Official Records, Series II, Volume VII, page 394;
12. Official Records, Series II, Volume VII, page 152;
13. Official Records, Series II, Volume VII, pages 603-604;
14. Official Records, Series II, Volume VII, pages 604-605;
15. Official Records, Series II, Volume VII, page 1093;
16. Official Records, Series II, Volume VII, page 424;
17. Official Records, Series II, Volume VII, pages 450-451, 465-466;
18. Official Records, Series II, Volume VII, page 502;
19. Official Records, Series I, Volume XXXVI, 36, Part I, pages 133, 149, 164, 180, 188;
20. Official Records, Series II, Volume VII, page 424;
21. Addison Walter D., Southern Historical Collection of the University of North Carolina Library, Chapel Hill, North Carolina;
22. Keiley, Anthony M., *In Vinculis Or, The Prisoner Of War: Being The Experience Of A Rebel In Two Federal Pens,* page 117-120;
23. Benson, Berry, B*erry Benson's Civil War Book, Memoirs of a Confederate Scout and Sharpshooter,* page 126-127; Byrne, Thomas E., *"Elmira's Civil War Prison Camp: 1864-1865," Chemung Historical Journal, volume 10, No. 1, (September 1964)*: page 1287;

The Shohola Train Wreck
Pages 17-19

1. Official Records, Series II, Volume VII, page 488-489;
2. *Elmira Daily Advertiser,* July 18, 1864, *The Train Accident at Shohola,* page 2;
3. Holmes, Clay W., *The Elmira Prison Camp, A History of the Military Prison at Elmira,*

N. Y., July 6, 1864 to July 10, 1865, pages 30-34;

4. New York Tribune, July 18, 1864;

Elmira's Observatories
Pages 19-21

1. *New York Evening Post*, August 24, 1864;
2. *Rochester Daily Union and Advertiser*, New York, reprinted in *Elmira Daily Advertiser*, August13, 1864;
3. Huffman, James, *Ups and Down of a Confederate Soldier*, page 105;
4. Towner, Ashburn. *A History of the Chemung County, New York*, pages 269-270;
5. *Elmira Daily Advertiser*, August 30, 1864;
6. Rochester, New York, *Union Dailey and Advertiser*, September 13, 1864;
7. Porter, G. W. D, page 159, *Nine Months in a Northern Prison, Annals of the Army of Tennessee and Early Western History*, July, 1878;
8. Huffman, James, *Ups and Down of a Confederate Soldier*, page 105;
9. Towner, Ashburn, *A History of the Chemung County, New York*, page 270;
10. *Elmira Dailey Gazette*, September 3, 1864;
11. Keiley, Anthony, M., In Vinculis; Or the Prisoner of War, page 158;

Ration Reduction
Pages 21-25

1. Official Records, Series II, Vol. VII, page 72-75; Speers, Lonnie, *War of Vengeance, Acts of Retaliation Against Civil War POWs*, page 117;
2. Official Records, Series II, Vol. VI, page 503-504;
3. Official Records, Series II, Vol. VI, page 489;
4. Official Records, Series II, Volume VII, pages 150-151, 183-184;
5. Crocker, James F., *Prison Reminiscences*, pages 43-44;
6. *Diagnostic and Statistical Manual of Mental Disorders*, 5th Edition, *Arlington: American Psychiatric Publishing, pages 160–168; Richards, C. Steven, PhD, and O'Hara, Michael W., PhD, The Oxford Handbook of Depression and Comorbidity, pages 160-168,*
7. King, John R., *My Experience in the Confederate Army and In Northern Prisons*, page 40;
8. Neese, George M., *Three Years in the Confederate Horse Artillery*, pages 344-345;
9. Holmes, Clay, *Elmira Prison Camp*, page 336;
10. Wilkeson, Frank, *Recollections of a Private Soldier in the Army of the Potomac*, page 226;
11. Keiley, Anthony M., *In Vinculis Or, The Prisoner of War: Being the Experience of a Rebel in Two Federal Pens*, 154-155;
12. Wyeth, John Allen, *Cold Cheer at Camp Morton, Century Magazine*, volume 41 no. 6, April 1891, page 848;
13. Huffman, James, *Ups and Downs of a Confederate Soldier*, page 100;
14. King, John R., *My Experience in the Confederate Army and in Northern Prisons*, page 40;
15. National Archives, *General and Special Orders*, Volume 3, page 287;
16. *Elmira Daily Advertiser*, December 14, 1878;
17. Keiley, Anthony M. *In Vinculis, or The Prisoner of War*, page 145-146;
18. Keiley, Anthony M. *In Vinculis, or The Prisoner of War*, page 141;
19. Benson, Berry, *Civil War Book*, page 134;

20. Benson, Berry, *Civil War Book,* page 134;
21. Toney, Marcus, *Privations of a Private*, pages 100-101;
22. Toney, Marcus, *Privations of a Private*, pages 143;
23. Addison, Walter D., *Recollections of a Confederate Soldier*, page 9;
24. Stamp, James B., *Ten Months Experience in Northern Prisons,* page 496;
25. Ewan, R. B., *Prison Life*, page 14; Holmes, Clay, *Elmira Prison Camp*, page 305;

Disease Becomes Epidemic
Pages 25-28
1. Official Records, Series II, Volume VI, pages 523-524;
2. Official Records, Series II, Volume VII, pages 113-114, Official Records, Series II, Volume VII, pages 150-151;
3. *The Medical and Surgical History of the War of the Rebellion, (1861-65),* Volume I, Part 3, page 46; there is a later publication entitled *The Medical and Surgical History of the Civil War,* the same information can be found in Volume 5, page 46; Broadfoot Publishing Company, Wilmington, North Carolina, 1991;
4. Eugene F. Sanger Papers, Records of the Office of the Adjutant General, Regimental Correspondence, 1861-1865, Maine State Archives;
5. Keiley, Anthony M., *In Vinculis Or, The Prisoner of War: Being the Experience Of A Rebel in Two Federal Pens*, pages144-145;

Introduction of Smallpox at Elmira Prison Camp
Pages 28-30
1. Official Records, Series II, volume 7, pages 1272-1273;
2. Official Records, Series II, volume 8, page 25;
3. *The medical and Surgical History of the War of the Rebellion,* volume I, part III, page
4. Smart, Major and Surgeon Charles, *The medical and Surgical History of the War of the Rebellion,* volume I, part III, page 625;
5. Addison, Walter D., *Recollections of a Confederate Soldier of the Prison-Pens of Point Lookout, Maryland, and Elmira, New York,* pages 4-5;
6. Smart, Major and Surgeon Charles, *The medical and Surgical History of the War of the Rebellion,* volume I, part III, pages 647-648;
7. Toney, Marcus B., *The Privations of a Private*, Nashville, Tennessee, 1905, pages 110-112.

Trades Flourished in Elmira Prison Camp
Pages 30-31
1. Holt, David, *A Mississippi Rebel in the Army of Northern Virginia*, pages 323-324;
2. Berry, Berry, *Berry Benson's Civil War Book,* page 94;
3. King, John R., *My Experience in the Confederate Army and in Northern Prisons,* page 42;

Prison Letters and Packages
Pages 31-34
1. Kieley, Anthony M., *In Vinculis Or, The Prisoner of War: Being the Experience Of a Rebel In Two Federal Pens,* pages 90-91;
2. Official Records, Series II, Volume VIII, pages 52-53;
3. Official Records, Series II, Volume VIII, pages 76-77;
4. Wilkeson, Frank, *Turned Inside Out: Recollection of a Private Soldier in the Army of*

the Potomac, page 225;

5. Toney, Marcus B., *The Privations of a Private,* page 98;
6. Official Records, Series II, Volume VIII, pages 767-768;
7. Official Records, Series II, Volume VII, pages 1134-1136, Inspector Surgeon William Sloan's November 14, 1864, report to Medical Director's Office, Department of the East, Green Lumber mentioned on page 1,136;

Escapes From Elmira Prison Camp:
Pages 34-41

1. Lieber Code of 1863, section III, article number 77;
2. Holmes, Clay, page 161;
3. Holmes, Clay, page 162;
4. Holmes, Clay, page 162;
5. Holmes, Clay, *The Elmira Prison Camp,* page 151;
6. Holmes, Clay, *The Elmira Prison Camp,* page 171-172;
7. Holmes, Clay, *The Elmira Prison Camp,* page 172;
8. *Montgomery, Alabama, Advertiser,* June 22, 1902;
9. Maull, John F., *The Elmira Prison Camp,* page 172-173;
10. Benson, Berry, *Berry Benson's Civil War Book,* page 137; Holmes, Clay, *The Elmira Prison Camp,* page 174;
11. Benson Papers, page 445-446;
12. Maull, John F., Holmes, Clay, *The Elmira Prison Camp,* page 174;
13. Benson, Berry, *Berry Benson's Civil War Book,* page 139;
14. Benson, Berry, *Berry Benson's Civil War Book,* page 138;
15. Benson, Berry, *Berry Benson's Civil War Book,* page 140;
16. Benson, Berry, *Berry Benson's Civil War Book,* page 140;
17. Maull, John F., Holmes, Clay, *The Elmira Prison Camp,* page 175;
18. Maull, John F., Holmes, Clay, *The Elmira Prison Camp,* page 173; Benson, Berry, *Berry Benson's Civil War Book,* page 138;
19. Maull, John F., Holmes, Clay, *The Elmira Prison Camp,* page 108;
20. Benson, Berry, *Berry Benson's Civil War Book,* page 142;
21. Benson, Berry, *Berry Benson's Civil War Book,* page 143;
22. Benson, Berry, *Berry Benson's Civil War Book,* page 143;
23. Holmes, Clay, *The Elmira Prison Camp,* page 195;
24. Benson, Berry, *Berry Benson's Civil War Book,* page 144
25. Benson, Berry, *Berry Benson's Civil War Book,* page 145;
26. Benson, Berry, page 115;
27. Benson, Berry, page 148;
28. Wade, F. S., *Getting Out of Prison* The Confederate Veteran Magazine, October 1926; Holmes, Clay, *Elmira Prison Camp,* page 160; Gray, Michael P., *The Business of Captivity, Elmira and Its Civil War Prison,* page 115;
29. Wade, F. S., *Getting Out of Prison,* The Confederate Veteran Magazine, October 1926; Horigan, Michael, *Elmira: Death Camp of the North,* page 114;

The Fort Fisher Prisoners
Pages 41-42

1. Lamb, William, *Colonel Lamb's Story of Fort Fisher,* pages 14-16, 18, 22-23;
2. *The Medical and Surgical History of the War of the Rebellion, (1861-65),* Volume III, Part I, page 56-57, 63;
3. Triebe, Richard H., *Fort Fisher to Elmira,* page viii;
4. *The Medical and Surgical History of the War of the Rebellion, (1861-65),* Volume III,

Part I, page 57;

Elmira Prison Camp Flood:
Pages 43-45
1. Holmes, Clay W., *Elmira Prison Camp*, pages 89-91, 96-97;
2. National Archives, "General and Special Orders", Volume 3, page 287;
3. Holmes, Clay W., *Elmira Prison Camp*, pages 68-69;
4. Keiley, Anthony M., *In Vinculis; or, The Prisoner of War*, page 130; Ottman, Walter H., *A History of the City of Elmira, New York*, page 170; *Elmira Daily Advertiser*, February 11, 1865; Holmes, Clay W., *Elmira Prison Camp*, pages 68-69;
5. Official Records, Volume 8, pages 419-420;
6. Holmes, Clay W., *Elmira Prison Camp*, page 124;
7. King, John A., *My Experience in the Confederate Army and in Northern Prisons*, page 47;
8. Holmes, Clay W., *Elmira Prison Camp*, page 124;
9. King, John A., *My Experience in the Confederate Army and in Northern Prisons*, page 47;
10. Elmira (N.Y.) Daily Advertiser, March 17, 1865;
11. Official Records, Volume 8, pages 419-420;
12. King, John A., *My Experience in the Confederate Army and in Northern Prisons*, page 47;
13. Huffman, James, *Ups and Downs*, page 103;
14. Inspection Reports 3/20/1865;
15. Holmes, Clay W., *Elmira Prison Camp*, page 295;
16. Official records, Volume 8, page 1001;

Prisoner Exchanges Resume
Pages 45-46
1. Official records, Series II, Volume 8, pages 122-123;
2. Official records, Series II, Volume 8, page 182;
3. Official records, Series II, Volume 8, page 182
4. *Elmira Daily Advertiser* February 14, 1865
5. Official records, series II, Volume 8, page 232

Woodlawn Cemetery Sexton John W. Jones
Page 47
1. *New York Sun*, August 13, 1880;
2. Holmes, Clay, *Elmira Prison Camp*, pages 145-150;

Bibliography

Articles and Periodicals:

Bowden, the Reverend Malachi, *My Life as a Yankee Captive.* Published in the Atlanta Journal and
     Constitution Magazine.
Byrne, Thomas E., *"Elmira's Civil War Prison Camp: 1864-1865," Chemung Historical
     Journal, volume 10, No. 1, (September1964)*: page 1287,
Davis, Thaddeus C., *Confederate Veteran* Magazine, February 1899, page 65;
Ewan, R.B., *Reminiscences of Prison Life at Elmira, N.Y.,* January 1908;
Huffman, James, *Prisoner of War, Atlantic Magazine* 163, no. 4, April 1939;
Jones, James P., *A Rebel's Diary of Elmira Prison Camp, Chemung Historical Journal* 20, no. 3,
     March 1975;
Sherrill, Miles, *A Soldier's Story: Prison Life and Other Incidents,* University of North Carolina at
     Chapel Hill, 1998;
Stamp, James B., *Ten Months Experience in Northern Prisons, Alabama Historical Quarterly 18,*
     pages 486-498;
Taylor, G.T., *Prison Experience in Elmira, N.Y., Confederate Veteran* Magazine 20, no. 7, July 1912;
The Treatment of Prisoners during the War Between the States, Southern Historical Society Papers
     1, no. 3, March 1876;
The Treatment of Prisoners during the War, Southern Historical Society Papers 1, no. 4, April 1876;
Turner, Henry M. *Civil War Times Illustrated,* 31 (October/November, 1980);
Wade, F.S., *Getting Out of Prison, Confederate Veteran* magazine 34, no. 10, October 1926;
Ward, John Shirley, *Responsibility for the Death of Prisoners, Confederate Veteran* magazine 4, no.
     1, January 1896;
Wyeth, John Allan, *Cold Cheer at Camp Morton, Century Magazine* 41 no. 6 (April 1891) 848;

Books:

Benson, Berry, Susan W. Benson, ed., *Berry Benson's Civil War Book: Memoirs of a Confederate Scout
     and Sharpshooter,* Athens, Ga.: University of Georgia Press, 1962;
Diagnostic and Statistical Manual of Mental Disorders, 5th Edition, *Arlington:
     American Psychiatric Publishing, pages 160–168,* American Psychiatric Publishing,
     May 27, 2013;
Gray, Michael P., *The Business of Captivity: Elmira and It's Civil War Prison,* The Kent State
     University Press, 2001;
Hampson, Helen (Wyeth), My Great-Great Grandfather Was a Prisoner of War . . . Libby Prison, 2002;
Heartsill, W. W., *Fourteen Hundred and 91 Days in the Confederate Army,* Edited by Bell Irvin Wiley,
     Broadfoot Publishing Co., Wilmington North Carolina, 1987.
Holmes, Clay W., *The Elmira Prison Camp: A History of the Military Prison at Elmira, N.Y. July 6,
     1864, to July 10, 1865.* New York: Knickerbocker Press, 1912;
Hopkins, Luther, *Prison life at Point Lookout.*
Horigan, Michael, *Elmira: Death Camp of the North,* Stackpole Books, 2002;
Huffman, James, *Ups and Downs of a Confederate Soldier,* New York: William E. Rudge's Sons, 1940;
Keiley, Anthony M., *In Vinculis; or, The Prisoner of War: Being The Experience Of A
     Rebel In Two Federal Pens,* Blelock & Co., No. 19 Beekman Street, New York, 1866;
King, John A., *My Experience in the Confederate Army, and in Northern Prisons,* Roanoke, West
     Virginia, Stonewall Jackson Chapter No. 1333, United Daughters of the Confederacy, Clarksburg,
     West Virginia, 1917;

Leon, Louis, *Diary of a Tarheel Confederate Prisoner,* Charlotte, N.C.: Stone, 1913;

Malone,Whatley Pierson Jr., *The Diary of Bartlett Yancy Malone,* Published by the University of Chapel Hill, 1919.

Manarin, Louis H. and Weymouth T. Jordan, eds., *North Carolina Troops1861-1865: A Roster,* 13 volumes, Raleigh, North Carolina: Division of Archives and History, 1966-1993;

Miller-Keane, *Encyclopedia & Dictionary of Medicine, Nursing, & Allied Heath, Fifth Edition,* W. B. Saunders Company, Philadelphia.

Opie, John N., *A Rebel Cavalryman with Lee, Stuart, and Jackson,* Morningside Press, Chicago: W.B. Conkey, 1899.

Ottman, Walter H., *A History of the City of Elmira, New York;*

Pickenpaugh, Roger, *Captives In Gray,* The University of Alabama Press, 2009;

Speer, Lonnie R., *Portals To Hell: Military Prisons of the Civil War,* Stackpole Books, 1997;

Speer, Lonnie R., *War of Vengeance: Acts of Retaliation against Civil War POWs,* Stackpole Books, 2002;

Toney, Marcus B., *The Privations of a Private,* Nashville and Dallas: M.E. Church, South, Smith and Lamar, 1907;

Towner, Ausburn, *Our County and Its People - A History of the Valley and County of Chemung From the Closing years of the Eighteenth Century,* D. Mason & Publishers, 1892;

Watkins, Sam R., *Co. Aytch, Maury Grays, First Tennessee Regiment or, A Side Show to the Big Show,* Chattanooga, Tennessee, Times Printing Company, 1900;

Wilkeson, Frank, *Turned Inside Out: Recollections of a Private Soldier in the Army of the Potomac,* New York and London: G.P. Putnam's Sons, 1887;

Williamson, James J., *Prison Life in the Old Capital and Reminiscences of the Civil War,* West Orange, New Jersey, 1911.

Manuscripts:

Greer, William R. Papers, *Recollections of a Private Soldier of the Army of the Confederate States,* Manuscript Department, William R. Perkins Library, Duke University, North Carolina

Papers:

Sanger, Eugene F., *Eugene F. Sanger Papers, Records of the Office of the Adjutant General, Regimental Correspondence, 1861-1865,* Maine State Archives. College of William and Mary, William Lamb Collection;

Official Publications:

Confederate States of America, Congress, *Joint Select Committee to Investigate the Condition and Treatment of Prisoners of War,* March, 1865;

The Medical and Surgical History of the War of the Rebellion, (1861-65), Prepared in Accordance Acts of Congress, Under the Direction of Surgeon General Joseph K. Barnes, United States Army, Washington Government Printing Office, 1870, Volumes I, III, VI.

North Carolina Troops 1861-1865, 22 Volumes, Broadfoot Publishing, edited by Louis H. Marin, and Numerous authors.

War of the Rebellion Official Records of the Union and Confederate Armies, Series II, Volumes IV,

VII, XXVI. Washington, D.C., Government Printing Office, 1870.

Confederate States of America, Congress, *Joint Select Committee to Investigate the Condition and Treatment of Prisoners of War,* March, 1865;

Newspapers:

Daily National Intelligencer, Washington, D. C.,
Elmira Daily Advertiser,
Elmira Daily Gazette,
New York Times,
New York Tribune,

Index

2

A

B

C

D

www.ingramcontent.com/pod-product-compliance
Lightning Source LLC
Chambersburg PA
CBHW062019090426
42811CB00005B/898